P9-DBM-918

HERMAN O'NEIL, Inauguration of the Statue of Liberty, New York, 1886.

A PATRIOT'S
HANDBOOK

A PATRIOT'S HANDBOOK

SONGS, POEMS, STORIES,
AND SPEECHES CELEBRATING
THE LAND WE LOVE

Selected and Introduced by

Caroline Kennedy

NEW YORK

Copyright © 2003 Caroline Kennedy
All rights reserved. No part of this book may be used or reproduced in any
manner whatsoever without the written permisssion of the Publisher.
Printed in the United States of America. For information address:
Hyperion, 77 West 66th Street, New York, New York 10023-6298.

The permissions and credits section, beginning p. 649,
constitutes a continuation of this copyright page.

Library of Congress Cataloging-in-Publication Data has been applied for.

ISBN 0-7868-6918-6

Hyperion books are available for special promotions and premiums. For
details contact Hyperion Special Markets, 77 West 66th Street, 11th floor,
New York, New York 10023, or call 212-456-0133.

FIRST EDITION

10 9 8 7 6 5 4 3 2 1

CONTENTS

THE FLAG

VISIONS OF AMERICA

PORTRAITS OF AMERICANS

RULE OF LAW

FREEDOM

FREEDOM OF SPEECH AND OF THE PRESS

FREEDOM OF RELIGION

THE RIGHT TO BE LET ALONE

EQUALITY

THE INDIVIDUAL

WAR AND PEACE

WORK, OPPORTUNITY, AND INVENTION

OUR LAND

ILLUSTRATIONS

ACKNOWLEDGMENTS

I WOULD LIKE TO thank my family for all they taught me during this project, especially my daughter Tatiana, who inherited her grandfather's love of American history and contributed the best title for this book out of the many that were suggested. I would like to thank my son, Jack, for his curiosity and spirit, and his understanding of the relationship between Little League and patriotism. I would like to thank my daughter Rose for her thoughtful observations and probing questions about our country's future, as well as our past. As always, talking to my husband, Ed, made the whole project worth doing.

This book involved a tremendous amount of research and coordination in a short period of time. I was fortunate to have the help of an outstanding group of people to help gather and check the information in the headnotes, led by researcher extraordinaire Mike Hill, Claudia Slavin, whose illustrious legal career we eagerly await, the talented and creative Joanna Shea, and the dynamic Megan Kultgen. One of the highlights of the project was renewing an old friendship with my own high school U.S. history teacher, Bill Bailey, who provided inspiration to a generation of students and sent us forth with a love of our nation's past. Thanks to my valued and special friend Janet Elder, I was fortunate to work with Jeff Roth, who contributed his discerning eye and encyclopedic knowledge of the images of American history. As always, backup support was provided by the indefatigable veterans Marta Sgubin and Elsa DeMelo and the indispensable newcomer Diane Saltzman.

This is the third book I have worked on with the publishing team at Hyperion. I am grateful to Bob Miller for his support on the truly important matters; my editor, Gretchen Young, who has the soul of a research historian; Natalie Kaire, who kept track of towers of paper; David Lott, for performing a production tour de force; and Katie Long and Karin Maake, who make book tours what they should be. I would also like to thank my agent, Esther Newberg, whose belief that her authors are always right is right, and who is always willing to go the distance from Bergdorf Goodman to Ethan Allen.

INTRODUCTION

THIS BOOK IS my collage of America. It is for my children and others growing up in a world where being an American brings responsibilities as well as opportunities. As parents, we are part of a continuum between generations and must decide what important values we want to pass on. As we gather with family and friends over Thanksgiving or the Fourth of July, we have a chance to reflect on the continuity of ideas and principles that have inspired Americans for the past 225 years. That process must be ongoing, for now it is our turn to reinterpret these values for our children, to strengthen their belief in America, and in the spirit of limitless possibilities that will determine their future.

In the days before mass media, the stories of our Founding Fathers were passed down orally from generation to generation. My grandmother, who was born in 1890, carried on this tradition in our family, and gatherings at her house almost always included a recitation of Longfellow's poem "Paul Revere's Ride." The poem combined Grandma's patriotism and love of history with her belief that one person could change the course of history. Reciting it together became a powerful way of reinforcing those values in our family.

In our own time, books and photographs, plays, movies, and television play a similar role. War movies like *Gone With the Wind*, *All Quiet on the Western Front*, *The Longest Day*, *Patton*, *Apocalypse Now*, and *The Deer Hunter* have shaped our national mythology; *The Civil War* series on PBS deepened our national understanding of that conflict. When I was a child, my mother took my brother, John, and me to the Broadway musical *1776*, which brought the Founding Fathers to life. We memorized the songs, disagreed fiercely over the relative superiority of John Adams and Thomas Jefferson, and wondered why New York abstained from all the important votes. A recent revival cast the same spell over my own children and prompted a curiosity about American history that extended throughout the process of researching this book. When I asked for their help, my daughter Tatiana responded with the best title, *A Patriot's Handbook*.

The story of the American Revolution has a special appeal for children, who identify with the triumph of the ragtag colonists over the mighty King George. It appeals to their love of the underdog, their sense of fairness, and a desire for a happy ending. But more important, children have an immense capacity for faith and for patriotism. If their introduction to the story of our country is captivating, they can develop a lifelong interest in history and a willingness to engage in civic life. As we grow older, that interest becomes more informed, and more critical. I have tried to include selections in this book that reflect different views of America—what is best, and what could be better—because patriotism requires understanding our limitations as well as our strengths.

Understanding and renewing our commitment to our fundamental civic values is a process of turning and returning to the words that defined the challenges of the past, inspired generations before us, and offer renewed insight for our own time. The words and images in this book are for sharing, as a conversation helps make the ideals our own. As I researched the selections, I was struck by the fact that we often talk with friends about movies, sports, or TV, but less often about patriotism, although being an American is one of the most profound experiences that we share. I hope that making these documents more accessible will make it easier for these conversations to occur. Of course, there are many varied realities within our society, but as a nation, there is more that unites than divides us. One of the ways we come to understand something is to compose our own narrative. Each person's story may be different, but in the process of assembling it, we can discover themes that connect us. As this book is intended for families, I have tried to include selections for all ages, songs and poems that appeal to children, speeches that helped turn the tide of history, judicial opinions that transformed our society, images that capture America's sense of self at a particular time, and expressions of personal yet universal truths.

Ultimately, this is a personal selection, but one that I hope will encourage others to create similar collections of their own. The best part of putting it together was researching the myriad possibilities; the difficult part was deciding what to leave out. I read new works, as well as old favorites. I thought it important that the documents be long enough to give a sense of the whole, and decided not to use quotations or short excerpts, even though it meant there could be fewer entries. I wanted the selections to go beyond politics yet remain focused on the ideal of America.

In the process I rediscovered how many gifts we are given as Americans. Among the most precious are the freedoms we cherish yet sometimes take for granted, the diversity of heritage and experience that strengthens us, a society that celebrates tolerance and community, and a belief in the power of words to change the world. This country was founded on ideas—freedom, equality, the pursuit of happiness—and the fact that we have the oldest written Constitution in the world is proof of the enduring power of those principles. Those words and ideas have drawn millions to this country in search of the American dream. In order for our democracy to thrive, each of us must give something back. We must make a commitment not just to vote, but to be engaged, to understand the sources of our rights and freedoms and the struggles of those who fought and died to preserve them. Our nation celebrates the individual, and just as it provides for us, so it expects of us. America has given us her best. Now it is our turn.

THE FLAG

DAN McELLENEY, Boy Scout troop marching in Army Day parade, New York, 1949.

WHEN THE STARS and Stripes is raised in celebration, or lowered to half-mast, as Americans we feel a surge of emotion that connects us to each other and to a larger sense of belonging. Our flag is the enduring symbol of our country, changing and evolving as our nation has grown. On June 14, 1777, later celebrated as Flag Day, Congress passed a resolution specifying that the flag of the United States be "thirteen stripes alternating red and white" to symbolize the thirteen original states, and thirteen stars representing "a new constellation." Two hundred twenty-five years later that new constellation has grown to fill the skies, just as the flag fills our hearts in times of war and peace, in protest, on parade, and in song.

As we learn in school, Francis Scott Key wrote our national anthem to honor the flag that flew throughout the night of the British bombardment of Fort McHenry during the War of 1812. Ever since, we have believed in its power to inspire and protect us. Many of the popular songs about our flag were written in wartime. "The Battle Cry of Freedom" has been passed down since the Civil War. In our own time, John McCain's story of Vietnam War POW Mike Christian shows the importance of the flag to those who risk their lives for our country. Through countless acts of bravery and of patriotism, the flag has become a symbol of their sacrifice and our faith.

There is another dimension to the symbolism of the flag. Just as it represents our shared love of country, it also represents our fundamental freedoms, among them the right to dissent. The power of the flag to embrace the spectrum of patriotism from jingoism to protest is one of its signal characteristics.

There are few more eloquent statements of our freedom to dissent, yet to love our country, than Justice Jackson's eloquent opinion in *West Virginia v. Barnette*. Written during World War II, when patriotic feeling was running high, the Supreme Court held that Jehovah's Witnesses could not be forced to participate in a compulsory flag salute. "The case is made difficult not because the principles of its decision are obscure, but because the flag involved is our own. . . . Freedom to differ is not limited to things that do not matter much. That would be a mere shadow of freedom. The test of its substance is the right to differ as to things that touch the heart of the existing order."

Nearly fifty years later in 1989, settling an argument that divided our country, the Supreme Court reaffirmed this principle in the flag-burning case with the words, "We can imagine no more appropriate response to burning a flag than waving one's own, no better way to counter a flag burner's message than by saluting the flag that burns. . . . We do not consecrate the flag by punishing its desecration, for in doing so we dilute the freedom that this cherished emblem represents."

The flag also has the power to unite Americans of all ages. As children, we celebrate the flag with summertime and family on the glorious Fourth of July. The intertwining of nation and family is a powerful lesson, one that stays with us throughout our lives. "You're a Grand Old Flag" by George M. Cohan best captures this sense of joy for me. Our family sang it in Hyannis Port on July 4, and on my grandfather's birthday around Labor Day. It bookended my summers, and hearing it today unlocks all the memories in between.

Perhaps Edward Everett Hale spoke for all of us when he wrote in 1863, "And for that flag, . . . never dream a dream but of serving her as she bids you, though the service carry you through a thousand hells. No matter what happens to you, no matter who flatters or abuses you, never look at another flag, never let a night pass but you pray to God to bless that flag."

FRANCIS SCOTT KEY AND JOHN STAFFORD SMITH

THE STAR-SPANGLED BANNER

1814

Three weeks after the British forces had captured and burned Washington, D.C., during the War of 1812, Maryland attorney Francis Scott Key (1779–1843) watched the horrific nighttime bombardment of Baltimore's Fort McHenry. When he peered through the next morning's haze and saw an enormous American flag still flying, Key wrote a poem titled "Defense of Fort McHenry." Later set to the tune "To Anacreon in Heaven," it became a popular patriotic song, and in 1931, Congress adopted it as the national anthem. A 30 × 34 foot fragment of the giant flag is now on display at the Smithsonian's National Museum of American History.

O say, can you see, by the dawn's early light.
What so proudly we hailed at the twilight's last gleaming?
Whose broad stripes and bright stars, through the perilous fight,
O'er the ramparts we watched, were so gallantly streaming!
And the rockets' red glare, the bombs bursting in air,
Gave proof through the night that our flag was still there:
O say, does that star-spangled banner yet wave
O'er the land of the free and the home of the brave?

On the shore, dimly seen through the mists of the deep.
Where the foe's haughty host in dread silence reposes,
What is that which the breeze, o'er the towering steep,
As it fitfully blows, half conceals, half discloses?
Now it catches the gleam of the morning's first beam,
In full glory reflected now shines on the stream:
'Tis the star-spangled banner! O long may it wave
O'er the land of the free and the home of the brave!

And where is that band who so vauntingly swore
That the havoc of war and the battle's confusion
A home and a country should leave us no more?
Their blood has washed out their foul footsteps' pollution.
No refuge could save the hireling and slave
From the terror of flight, or the gloom of the grave:
And the star-spangled banner in triumph doth wave
O'er the land of the free and the home of the brave.

O thus be it ever when freemen shall stand
Between their loved homes and the war's desolation!
Blest with victory and peace, may the heaven-rescued land
Praise the Power that hath made and preserved us a nation.
Then conquer we must when our cause it is just
And this be our motto: "In God is our trust."
And the star-spangled banner in triumph shall wave
O'er the land of the free and the home of the brave!

THE PLEDGE OF ALLEGIANCE

1892

Originally written by socialist minister Francis Bellamy and published in the magazine *The Youth's Companion* in 1892 in honor of the four hundredth anniversary of the arrival of Christopher Columbus, the Pledge of Allegiance has long been recited in public schools across America as a daily patriotic ritual. In 1954, Congress amended the Pledge, adding the words "under God." In 2002, a federal judge declared those words an unconstitutional violation of the separation of church and state, placing the Pledge of Allegiance at the center of national attention, as it has been so many times before.

I pledge allegiance to the flag of the United States of America and to the Republic for which it stands, one nation under God, indivisible, with liberty and justice for all.

JACOB A. RIIS, Flag salute, Mott Street Industrial School, New York, c. 1892.

THE BATTLE CRY OF FREEDOM

C. 1861

After the outbreak of the Civil War in 1861, George Frederick Root (1820–1895) was one of the first to respond with music to President Lincoln's call to arms. A music educator and composer, Root wrote "The Battle Cry of Freedom" in July 1862 in the Chicago office of his music publishing business. By composing the song, he hoped "that if I could not shoulder a musket in defense of my country I could serve her in this way." Its effect on the morale of the troops was immediate.

1.

Yes, we'll rally round the flag, boys, we'll rally once again,

Shouting the battle cry of Freedom;

We will rally from the hillside, we'll gather from the plain,

Shouting the battle cry of Freedom!

2.

We are springing to the call of our brothers gone before,

Shouting the battle cry of Freedom;

And we'll fill the vacant ranks with a million free men more,

Shouting the battle cry of Freedom!

CHORUS:

It's Freedom forever, Hurrah boys, Hurrah!

Down with the shackle and up with the star!

While we rally round the flag, boys, we'll rally once again,

Shouting the battle cry of Freedom!

THE FLAG GOES BY

C. 1900

Author and poet Henry Holcomb Bennett (1863–1924) wrote this poem, "Hats Off—the Flag Goes By."

Hats off!
Along the street there comes
A blare of bugles, a ruffle of drums,
A flash of color beneath the sky:
Hats off!
The flag is passing by!

Blue and crimson and white it shines,
Over the steel-tipped, ordered lines.
Hats off!
The colors before us fly;
But more than the flag is passing by:
Sea-fights and land-fights, grim and great,
Fought to make and to save the State;
Weary marches and sinking ships;
Cheers of victory on dying lips;

Days of plenty and years of peace;
March of a strong land's swift increase;
Equal justice, right and law,
Stately honor and reverend awe;
Sign of a nation great and strong
To ward her people from foreign wrong;
Pride and glory and honor—all
Live in the colors to stand or fall.

Hats off!
Along the street there comes
A blare of bugles, a ruffle of drums;
And loyal hearts are beating high:
Hats off!
The flag is passing by!

GEORGE M. COHAN

YOU'RE A GRAND OLD FLAG

1906

Born in Rhode Island, George M. Cohan (1878–1942) had formal schooling only for a six-month period, after which he and his family went on the vaudeville circuit. Cohan became a leading figure in American theater in the early 1900s, and wrote some forty plays and over five hundred songs. In 1905, while attending a funeral, he witnessed a Civil War veteran patting a folded American flag, and commenting, "You're a grand old rag." The moment inspired Cohan to write "You're a Grand Old Flag," which was first performed on Broadway in the 1906 musical *George Washington, Jr.* (Cohan changed the last word of the title at the request of veterans' groups.) The movie *Yankee Doodle Dandy*, starring James Cagney, was based on Cohan's life and career.

You're a grand old flag,
You're a high flying flag
And forever in peace may you wave.
You're the emblem of
The land I love.
The home of the free and the brave.

Ev'ry heart beats true
'neath the Red, White and Blue,
Where there's never a boast or brag.
Should auld acquaintance be forgot,
Keep your eye on the grand old flag.

ARTHUR J. TELFER, Orphanage pageant, Cooperstown, New York, 1918.

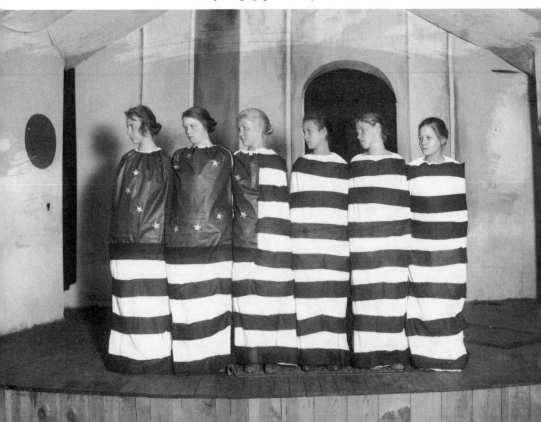

West Virginia State Board of
Education v. Barnette
319 U.S. 624

1943

In the midst of World War II, when patriotic sentiment was running high, the Supreme Court was faced with the question of whether schoolchildren could be required to salute the flag and recite the Pledge of Allegiance. The case was brought by a group of parents—Jehovah's Witnesses—whose children had been expelled for refusing to salute the flag, claiming it violated their religious beliefs. The Court overruled an earlier decision to hold that a compulsory flag salute was unconstitutional. The ruling was handed down on Flag Day, 1943. Justice Robert Jackson (1892–1954), who served as attorney general before his nomination to the Supreme Court in 1941, and later as chief prosecutor for the United States at the Nuremberg trials of Nazi war criminals, wrote the opinion celebrating freedom and the Bill of Rights.

. . . MR. JUSTICE JACKSON delivered the opinion of the Court.

The Board of Education on January 9, 1942, adopted a resolution . . . ordering that the salute to the flag become "a regular part of the program of activities in the public schools," that all teachers and pupils "shall be required to participate in the salute honoring the Nation represented by the Flag; provided, however, that refusal to salute the Flag be regarded as an act of insubordination, and shall be dealt with accordingly." . . .

The resolution originally required the "commonly accepted salute to the Flag" which it defined. Objections to the salute as "being too much like Hitler's" were raised by the Parent and Teachers Association, the Boy and Girl Scouts, the Red Cross, and the Federation of Women's Clubs. Some modification appears to have been made in deference to these objections, but no concession was made to Jehovah's Witnesses. What is now required is the "stiff-arm" salute, the saluter to keep the right hand raised with palm turned up while the following is repeated: "I pledge allegiance to the Flag of the United States of America and to the Republic for which it stands; one Nation, indivisible, with liberty and justice for all." . . .

Failure to conform is "insubordination" dealt with by expulsion. Readmission is denied by statute until compliance. Meanwhile the expelled child is "unlawfully absent" and may be proceeded against as a delinquent. His parents or guardians are liable to prosecution, and if convicted are subject to fine not exceeding $50 and jail term not exceeding thirty days. . . .

[Some families] brought suit in the United States District Court . . . asking to restrain enforcement of these laws against Jehovah's Witnesses. . . . Their religious beliefs include a literal version of Exodus, Chapter 20, verses 4 and 5, which says: "Thou shalt not make unto thee any graven image, or any likeness of anything that is in heaven above, or that is in the earth beneath, or that is in the water under the earth; thou shalt not bow down thyself to them nor serve them." They consider that the flag is an "image" within this command. For this reason they refuse to salute it.

Children of this faith have been expelled from school and are threatened with exclusion for no other cause. Officials threaten to send them to reformatories maintained for criminally inclined juveniles. Parents of such children have been prosecuted and are threatened with prosecutions for causing delinquency. . . .

The freedom asserted by these appellees does not bring them into collision with rights asserted by any other individual. It is such conflicts which most frequently require intervention of the State to determine where the rights of one end and those of another begin. But the refusal of these persons to participate in the ceremony does not interfere with or deny rights of others to do so. Nor is there any question in this case that their behavior is peaceable and orderly. The sole conflict is between authority and rights of the individual. . . .

There is no doubt that, in connection with the pledges, the flag salute is a form of utterance. Symbolism is a primitive but effective way of communicating ideas. The use of an emblem or flag to symbolize some system, idea, institution, or personality, is a short cut from mind to mind. Causes and nations, political parties, lodges and ecclesiastical groups seek to knit the loyalty of their followings to a flag or banner, a color or design. The State announces rank, function, and authority through crowns and maces, uniforms and black robes; the church speaks through the Cross, the Crucifix, the altar and shrine, and clerical raiment. Symbols of State often convey political ideas just as religious symbols come to convey theological ones. Associated with many of these symbols are appropriate gestures of acceptance or respect: a salute, a bowed or bared head, a bended knee. A person gets from a symbol the meaning he puts into it, and what is one man's comfort and inspiration is another's jest and scorn. . . .

It is also to be noted that the compulsory flag salute and pledge requires affirmation of a belief and an attitude of mind. It is not clear whether the regulation contemplates that pupils forego any contrary convictions of their own and become unwilling converts to the prescribed ceremony or whether it will be acceptable if they simulate assent by words without belief and by a gesture barren of meaning. It is now a commonplace that censorship or suppression of expression of opinion is tolerated by our Constitution only when the expression presents a clear and present danger of action of a kind the State is empowered to prevent and punish. It would seem that involuntary affirmation could be commanded only on even more immediate and urgent grounds than silence. But here the power of compulsion is invoked without any allegation that remaining passive during a flag salute ritual creates a clear and present danger that would justify an effort even to muffle expression. To sustain the compulsory flag salute we are required to say that a Bill of Rights which guards the individual's right to speak his own mind, left it open to public authorities to compel him to utter what is not in his mind. . . .

Government of limited power need not be anemic government. Assurance that rights are secure tends to diminish fear and jealousy of strong government, and by making us feel safe to live under it makes for its better support. Without promise of a limiting Bill of Rights it is doubtful if our Constitution could have mustered enough strength to enable its ratification. To enforce those rights today is not to choose weak government over strong government. It is only to adhere as a means of strength to individual freedom of mind in preference to officially disciplined uniformity for which history indicates a disappointing and disastrous end. . . .

The very purpose of a Bill of Rights was to withdraw certain subjects from the vicissitudes of political controversy, to place them beyond the reach of majorities and officials and to establish them as legal principles to be applied by the courts. One's right to life, liberty, and property, to free speech, a free press, freedom of worship and assembly, and other fundamental rights may not be submitted to vote; they depend on the outcome of no elections. . . .

Struggles to coerce uniformity of sentiment in support of some end thought essential to their time and country have been waged by many good as well as by evil men. Nationalism is a relatively recent phenomenon but at other times and places the ends have been racial or territorial security, support of a dynasty or regime, and particular plans for saving souls. As first and moderate methods to attain unity have failed, those bent on its accomplishment must resort to an ever-increasing severity. As governmental pressure toward unity becomes greater, so strife becomes more bitter as to whose unity it shall be. Probably no deeper division of our people could proceed from any provocation than from finding it necessary to choose what doctrine and whose program public educational officials shall compel youth to unite in embracing. Ultimate futility of such attempts to compel coherence is the lesson of every such effort from the Roman drive to stamp out Christianity as a disturber of its pagan unity, the Inquisition, as a means to religious and dynastic unity, the Siberian exiles as a means to Russian unity, down to the fast failing efforts of our present totalitarian enemies. Those who begin coercive elimination of dissent soon find themselves exterminating dissenters. Compulsory unification of opinion achieves only the unanimity of the graveyard.

It seems trite but necessary to say that the First Amendment to our Constitution was designed to avoid these ends by avoiding these beginnings. There is no mysticism in the American concept of the State or of the nature or origin of its authority. We set up government by consent of the governed, and the Bill of Rights denies those in power any legal opportunity to coerce that consent. Authority here is to be controlled by public opinion, not public opinion by authority.

The case is made difficult not because the principles of its decision are obscure but because the flag involved is our own. Nevertheless, we apply the limitations of the Constitution with no fear that freedom to be intellectually and spiritually diverse or even contrary will disintegrate the social organization. To believe that patriotism will not flourish if patriotic ceremonies are voluntary and spontaneous instead of a compulsory routine is to make an unflattering estimate of the appeal of our institutions to free minds. We can have intellectual individualism and the rich cultural diversities that we owe to exceptional minds only at the price of occasional eccentricity and abnormal attitudes. When they are so harmless to others or to the State as those we deal with here, the price is not too great. But freedom to differ is not limited to things that do not matter much. That would be a mere shadow of freedom. The test of its substance is the right to differ as to things that touch the heart of the existing order.

If there is any fixed star in our constitutional constellation, it is that no official, high or petty, can prescribe what shall be orthodox in politics, nationalism, religion, or other matters of opinion or force citizens to confess by word or act their faith therein. If there are any circumstances which permit an exception, they do not now occur to us. . . .

We think the action of the local authorities in compelling the flag salute and pledge transcends constitutional limitations on their power and invades the sphere of intellect and spirit which it is the purpose of the First Amendment to our Constitution to reserve from all official control. . . .

GWENDOLYN BROOKS

FLAGS

1944

Gwendolyn Brooks (1917–2000) was born in Topeka, Kansas, but spent most of her life and career on the South Side of Chicago. Her interest in poetry developed as a teenager when she would fill notebooks with "careful rhymes" and "lofty meditations." Upon publication of *Annie Allen* in 1949, she became the first African American poet to receive the Pulitzer Prize. "Flags" is one of a series of poems that Brooks based on letters home from African American soldiers during World War II expressing the frustration they felt serving in the armed forces of a country that treated them as second-class citizens.

Still, it is dear defiance now to carry
Fair flags of you above my indignation,
Top, with a pretty glory and a merry
Softness, the scattered pound of my cold passion.
I pull you down my foxhole. Do you mind?
You burn in bits of saucy color then.
I let you flutter out against the pained
Volleys. Against my power crumpled and wan.
You, and the yellow pert exuberance
Of dandelion days, unmocking sun;
The blowing of clear wind in your gay hair;
Love changeful in you (like a music, or
Like a sweet mournfulness, or like a dance,
Or like the tender struggle of a fan).

THE MIKE CHRISTIAN STORY

1971

In 1967, decorated naval aviator John McCain (1936–), the son and grandson of prominent Navy admirals and descendant of a Revolutionary War commander, was shot down over Vietnam. With fellow POWs, he was tortured, held in solitary confinement, and imprisoned for five and a half years. After the war, McCain was elected to the U.S. House of Representatives from Arizona in 1982, and in 1986 he was elected to the Senate. His autobiography, *Faith of My Fathers* (1999), tells the story of his wartime and political experiences, including the story below. After release in 1973, bombardier navigator Mike Christian (1940–1983) continued to serve in the U.S. Navy and retired as a highly decorated lieutenant commander in 1978.

Let me tell you what I think about our Pledge of Allegiance, our flag, and our country. I want to tell you a story about when I was a prisoner of war. I spent five years in the Hanoi Hilton. In the early years of our imprisonment, the North Vietnamese kept us in solitary confinement or two or three to a cell.

In 1971, the North Vietnamese moved us from these conditions of isolation into large rooms with as many as 30 to 40 men to a room. This was, as you can imagine, a wonderful change. And was a direct result of the efforts of millions of Americans, led by people like Nancy and Ronald Reagan, on behalf of a few hundred POWs, 10,000 miles from home.

One of the men moved into my cell was Mike Christian. Mike came from a small town near Selma, Alabama. He didn't wear a pair of shoes until he was thirteen years old. At seventeen, he enlisted in the U.S. Navy. He later earned a commission. He became a Naval flying officer, and was shot down and captured in 1967. Mike had a keen and deep appreciation for the opportunities this country—and our military—provide for people who want to work and want to succeed.

The uniforms we wore in prison consisted of a blue short-sleeved shirt, trousers that looked like pajama trousers and rubber sandals that were made out of automobile tires. I recommend them highly; one pair lasted my entire stay.

As part of the change in treatment, the Vietnamese allowed some prisoners to receive packages from home. In some of these packages were handkerchiefs, scarves and other items of clothing. Mike got himself a piece of white cloth and a piece of red cloth and fashioned himself a bamboo needle. Over a period of a couple of months, he sewed the American flag on the inside of his shirt.

Every afternoon, before we had a bowl of soup, we would hang Mike's shirt on the wall of our cell, and say the Pledge of Allegiance. I know that saying the Pledge of Allegiance may not seem the most important or meaningful part of our day now, but I can assure you that—for those men in that stark prison cell—it was indeed the most important and meaningful event of our day.

One day, the Vietnamese searched our cell and discovered Mike's shirt with the flag sewn inside, and removed it. That evening they returned, opened the door of the cell, called for Mike Christian to come out, closed the door of the cell, and for the benefit of all of us, beat Mike Christian severely for the next couple of hours. Then they opened the door of the cell and threw him back inside. He was not in good shape. We tried to comfort and take care of him as well as we could. The cell in which we lived had a concrete slab in the middle on which we slept. Four naked light bulbs in each corner of the room.

After things quieted down, I went to lie down to go to sleep. As I did, I happened to look in the corner of the room. Sitting there beneath that dim light bulb, with a piece of white cloth, a piece of red cloth, another shirt and his bamboo needle, was my friend, Mike Christian. Sitting there, with his eyes almost shut from his beating, making another American flag. He was not making the flag because it made Mike Christian feel better. He was making that flag because he knew how important it was for us to be able to pledge our allegiance to our flag and country.

Duty, Honor, Country. We must never forget those thousands of Americans who, with their courage, with their sacrifice, and with their lives, made those words live for all of us.

Texas v. Johnson
491 U.S. 397

1989

In a 5–4 decision, the Supreme Court held that flag-burning as a means of political protest is protected by the First Amendment's guarantee of free speech. The opinion was written by Justice William J. Brennan (1906–1997), a member of the Court from 1956 until 1990. Justice Brennan authored many landmark opinions, particularly in the areas of civil liberties, the First Amendment, and criminal justice. In *Texas v. Johnson* his majority opinion drew on a line of decisions in which the Supreme Court had rejected government attempts to suppress the expression of unpopular beliefs. This decision sparked a national outcry and an effort—ultimately unsuccessful—to amend the Bill of Rights to prohibit flag-burning. Congress also passed the Flag Protection Act, which was declared unconstitutional by the Supreme Court. The public debate over this issue illuminates the power of the flag as our national symbol as well as the deep reverence Americans have for the Bill of Rights.

. . . MR. JUSTICE BRENNAN delivered the opinion of the Court.

After publicly burning an American flag as a means of political protest, Gregory Lee Johnson was convicted of desecrating a flag in violation of Texas law. This case presents the question whether his conviction is consistent with the First Amendment. We hold that it is not.

While the Republican National Convention was taking place in Dallas in 1984, respondent Johnson participated in a political demonstration dubbed the "Republican War Chest Tour." As explained in literature distributed by the demonstrators and in speeches made by them, the purpose of this event was to protest the policies of the Reagan administration and of certain Dallas-based corporations. The demonstrators marched through the Dallas streets, chanting political slogans and stopping at several corporate locations to stage "die-ins" intended to dramatize the consequences of nuclear war. On several occasions they spray-painted the walls of buildings and overturned potted plants, but Johnson himself took no part in such activities. He did, however, accept an American flag handed to him by a fellow protestor who had taken it from a flagpole outside one of the targeted buildings.

The demonstration ended in front of Dallas City Hall, where Johnson unfurled the American flag, doused it with kerosene, and set it on fire. While the flag burned, the protestors chanted: "America, the red, white, and blue, we spit on you." After the demonstrators dispersed, a witness to the flag burning collected the flag's remains and buried them in his backyard. No one was physically injured or threatened with injury, though several witnesses testified that they had been seriously offended by the flag burning.

Of the approximately 100 demonstrators, Johnson alone was charged with a crime. . . . After a trial, he was convicted, sentenced to one year in prison, and fined $2,000. . . .

Johnson was convicted of flag desecration for burning the flag rather than for uttering insulting words. This fact somewhat complicates our consideration of his conviction under the First Amendment. We must first determine whether Johnson's burning of the flag constituted expressive conduct, permitting him to invoke the First Amendment in challenging his conviction. . . .

The First Amendment literally forbids the abridgment only of "speech," but we have long recognized that its protection does not end at the spoken or written word. . . .

Especially pertinent to this case are our decisions recognizing the communicative nature of conduct relating to flags. . . .

That we have had little difficulty identifying an expressive element in conduct relating to flags should not be surprising. The very purpose of a national flag is to serve as a symbol of our country; it is, one might say, "the one visible manifestation of two hundred years of nationhood." . . .

We have not automatically concluded, however, that any action taken with respect to our flag is expressive. Instead, in characterizing such action for First Amendment purposes, we have considered the context in which it occurred. . . .

Johnson burned an American flag as part—indeed, as the culmination—of a political demonstration that coincided with the convening of the Republican Party and its renomination of Ronald Reagan for President. The expressive, overtly political nature of this conduct was both intentional and overwhelmingly apparent. At his trial, Johnson explained his reasons for burning the flag as follows: "The American flag was burned as Ronald Reagan was being renominated as President. And a more powerful statement of symbolic speech, whether you agree with it or not, couldn't have been made at that time. It's quite a just position [juxtaposition]. We had new patriotism and no patriotism." In these circumstances, Johnson's burning of the flag was conduct "sufficiently imbued with elements of communication" to implicate the First Amendment.

The government generally has a freer hand in restricting expressive conduct than it has in restricting the written or spoken word. It may not, however, proscribe particular conduct *because* it has expressive elements. . . .

Thus, we have not permitted the government to assume that every expression of a provocative idea will incite a riot, but have instead required careful consideration of the actual circumstances surrounding such expression, asking whether the expression "is directed to inciting or producing imminent lawless action and is likely to incite or produce such action." . . .

Johnson was not prosecuted for the expression of just any idea; he was prosecuted for his expression of dissatisfaction with the policies of this country, expression situated at the core of our First Amendment values. . . .

Moreover, Johnson was prosecuted because he knew that his politically charged expression would cause "serious offense." If he had burned the flag as a means of disposing of it because it was dirty or torn, he would not have been convicted of flag desecration under this Texas law: federal law designates burning as the preferred means of disposing of a flag "when it is in such condition that it is no longer a fitting emblem for display," and Texas has no quarrel with this means of disposal. The Texas law is thus not aimed at protecting the physical integrity of the flag in all circumstances, but is designed instead to protect it only against impairments that would cause serious offense to others. . . .

If there is a bedrock principle underlying the First Amendment, it is that the government may not prohibit the expression of an idea simply because society finds the idea itself offensive or disagreeable. . . .

We have not recognized an exception to this principle even where our flag has been involved. . . .

Texas' focus on the precise nature of Johnson's expression, moreover, misses the point of our prior decisions: their enduring lesson, that the government may not prohibit expression simply because it disagrees with its message, is not dependent on the particular mode in which one chooses to express an idea. . . .

We are tempted to say, in fact, that the flag's deservedly cherished place in our community will be strengthened, not weakened, by our holding today. Our decision is a reaffirmation of the principles of freedom and inclusiveness that the flag best reflects, and of the conviction that our toleration of criticism such as Johnson's is a sign and source of our strength. Indeed, one of the proudest images of our flag, the one immortalized in our own national anthem, is of the bombardment it survived at Fort McHenry. It is the Nation's resilience, not its rigidity, that Texas sees reflected in the flag—and it is that resilience that we reassert today. . . .

We can imagine no more appropriate response to burning a flag than waving one's own, no better way to counter a flag burner's message than by saluting the flag that burns, no surer means of preserving the dignity even of the flag that burned than by—as one witness here did—according its remains a respectful burial. We do not consecrate the flag by punishing its desecration, for in doing so we dilute the freedom that this cherished emblem represents.

Johnson was convicted for engaging in expressive conduct. The State's interest in preventing breaches of the peace does not support his conviction because Johnson's conduct did not threaten to disturb the peace. Nor does the State's interest in preserving the flag as a symbol of nationhood and national unity justify his criminal conviction for engaging in political expression. . . .

GRATEFUL DEAD

U.S. BLUES

1973

The Grateful Dead was formed in the San Francisco Bay Area in 1965. Over the next thirty years, the Dead became one of the most popular touring bands in America. Its inspirational lead guitarist, Jerry Garcia (1942–1995), once said, "To the kids today, the Grateful Dead represents America: the spirit of being able to go out and have an adventure."

Red and white, blue suede shoes, I'm Uncle Sam, how do you do?
Gimme five, I'm still alive, ain't no luck, I learned to duck.
Check my pulse, it don't change. Stay seventy-two come shine or rain.
Wave the flag, pop the bag, rock the boat, skin the goat.
Wave that flag, wave it wide and high.
Summertime done, come and gone, my, oh, my.

I'm Uncle Sam, that's who I am; Been hidin' out in a rock and roll band.
Shake the hand that shook the hand of P.T. Barnum and Charlie Chan.
Shine your shoes, light your fuse. Can you use them ol' U.S. Blues?
I'll drink your health, share your wealth, run your life, steal your wife.
Wave that flag, wave it wide and high.
Summertime done, come and gone, my, oh, my.

Back to back chicken shack. Son of a gun, better change your act.
We're all confused, what's to lose?
Wave that flag, wave it wide and high.
Summertime done, come and gone, my, oh, my.

GOD BLESS THE U.S.A.

1984

After years of playing the Las Vegas circuit and working as a casino blackjack dealer, California musician Lee Greenwood (1942–) broke into country music with his 1982 hit "It Turns Me Inside Out." In 1984, he wrote the stirring patriotic song "God Bless the U.S.A.," which became an unofficial anthem of Operation Desert Storm in 1991.

If tomorrow all the things were gone
I'd worked for all my life,
And I had to start again
with just my children and my wife,
I'd thank my lucky stars
to be living here today,
'Cause the flag still stands for freedom
and they can't take that away.

I'm proud to be an American
where at least I know I'm free,
And I won't forget the men who died
who gave that right to me,
And I gladly stand up next to you
and defend her still today,
'Cause there ain't no doubt I love this land
God Bless the U.S.A.

From the lakes of Minnesota
to the hills of Tennessee,
Across the plains of Texas
from sea to shining sea.
From Detroit down to Houston
and New York to L.A.,
There's pride in every American heart
and it's time we stand and say:

I'm proud to be an American
where at least I know I'm free,
And I won't forget the men who died
who gave that right to me,
And I gladly stand up next to you
and defend her still today,
'Cause there ain't no doubt I love this land
God Bless the U.S.A.

HARLAN A. MARSHALL, Flag woven by mill-workers, Manchester, New Hampshire, 1914.

VISIONS OF AMERICA

VIC DELUCIA, Ronald Reagan,
Liberty State Park, New Jersey, 1980.

SETTLED IN PURSUIT of freedom, founded on the idea of equality, America has always had a special sense of destiny. Visions of that destiny have been articulated at various critical moments in our history both by statesmen and by poets. Presidents have used the Inaugural Address or the Farewell Address to define America's goals and to challenge our society, while poets inspire us through reflection. This section contains examples of both public and personal visions of America.

George Washington took office as the leader of an emerging nation in a world dominated by the rival powers of Europe. As the commanding hero of the Revolution, he was the one man with the stature to be our first president. Some feared he would usurp power like the tyrant-king from whom America had recently become liberated. However, Washington's decision to retire after two terms proved that power could be transferred peacefully, and the presidential transition process could be an orderly one. Against the backdrop of the French Revolution, in an age of hereditary monarchies, the importance of this transition cannot be overestimated. Washington described his Farewell Address with characteristic humility as "the disinterested warnings of a parting friend." He advised America to avoid alliances that could lead to war with more powerful European states, and cautioned Americans not to become involved in regional conflicts, nor partisan political battles that could destroy the young country. "The name American which belongs to you, in your national capacity, must always exalt the just pride of Patriotism, more than any appellation which derives from local discriminations. . . . You have in common cause fought and triumphed together, the Independence and liberty you possess are the work of joint counsels and joint efforts—of common dangers, sufferings and successes."

Thomas Jefferson's First Inaugural is an equally extraordinary speech. After a bitter and highly partisan election, Jefferson sought to unite the country with the words, "Every difference of opinion is not a difference of principle. We are all Republicans. We are all Federalists." He renewed Washington's commitment to our constitutional form of government, which provides within it the means of peaceful change, and reiterated his belief in freedom of speech and thought. "If there be any among us who would wish to dissolve this Union, or to change its republican form, let them stand undisturbed as monuments of safety with which error of opinion may be tolerated where reason is left free to combat it." He then set forth his "essential principles" of government, beginning with "equal and exact justice to all men," an ideal we are still struggling to reach today.

It is interesting to compare these early speeches with Franklin D. Roosevelt's Second Inaugural Address and Ronald Reagan's Farewell Address. Roosevelt redefined the role of government during the Great Depression and World War II. "We are determined to make every American the object of his country's interest and concern. . . . The test of our progress is not whether we add more to the abundance of those who have much; it is whether we provide enough for those who have too little." He echoed both Washington and Jefferson when he reiterated the importance of national unity, and reinforced American faith in the ability of our democratic government to meet the enormous challenges of the Great Depression and then World War II. "In our personal ambitions we are individualists. But in our seeking for economic and political progress as a nation, we all go up, or else we all go down, as one people. . . ."

In his Farewell Address, Ronald Reagan also spoke of economic recovery and freedom. He emphasized the need for an "informed patriotism" that requires all Americans to take on the responsibility of learning about our country. "We've got to do a better job of getting across that America is freedom—freedom of speech, freedom of religion, freedom of enterprise. . . . Let's start with some basics: more attention to American history, and a greater emphasis on civic ritual." Reagan closed his speech with one of the most enduring metaphors for our national experiment: John Winthrop's "City on a Hill."

In 1629, John Winthrop, later governor of the Massachusetts Bay Colony, sailed to New England on board his flagship *Arbella*, in search of a new and better world. The creation of a New Jerusalem, God's Kingdom here on Earth, had inspired Europeans since the Crusades, and the early Puritan settlers in the New World were animated by that spirit. "For we must consider that we shall be as a City on a Hill. The eyes of all people are upon us," Winthrop wrote. One hundred and forty years later, the leaders of the American Revolution believed that they too were part of a transforming moment in history. The sense that the world is watching to see if America can live up to those expectations is as strong today as in those times.

Soon after my father was elected president, he addressed the Massachusetts legislature and quoted John Winthrop. "Today the eyes of all people are truly upon us—and our government, in every branch, at every level, . . . we must be as a city on a hill—constructed and inhabited by men aware of their grave trust and great responsibilities." He went on to outline the qualities by which history would judge our leaders: courage, judgment, integrity, and dedication. He believed that our country was once again facing a critical historic moment, and that in the age of television, the world was truly watching. Two weeks later, in his Inaugural Address, he laid out a vision that redefined America's role in the world. "Let every nation know, whether it wishes us well or ill, that we shall pay any price, bear any burden, meet any hardship, support any friend, oppose any foe, to assure the survival and success of liberty." The speech concluded with the words that inspired a generation to public service: "And so, my fellow Americans: ask not what your country can do for you—ask what you can do for your country. My fellow citizens of the world: ask not what America will do for you, but what together we can do for the freedom of man."

The voyage that perhaps best evokes Winthrop's *Arbella* is that of *Apollo 11*. Both were hazardous, both journeys led to new worlds, and both changed history. In 1961, President Kennedy had committed America to "landing a man on the moon and returning him safely to the earth," recognizing that it would require sacrifice and effort, but realizing that it could bring new hope for knowledge and peace. This section includes the first words spoken by a man on the moon, the defining moment of an event that truly mesmerized the world.

JOHN WINTHROP

A MODEL OF CHRISTIAN CHARITY

1630

John Winthrop (1588–1649) was the governor of the Massachusetts Bay Colony for most of the period from 1630 to 1649. In this speech, Winthrop, who fled England in pursuit of religious freedom, set forth the moral vision for the society he and his fellow Puritan colonists sought to establish in the New World.

God Almighty in His most holy and wise providence hath so disposed of the condition of mankind, as in all times: some must be rich, some poor; some high and eminent in power and dignity, others mean and in subjection. . . .

From hence we may frame these Conclusions.

First, all true Christians are of one body in Christ. (1 Corinthians: 12.12-27) *Ye are the body of Christ and members of their part.* . . .

Second, the ligaments of this body which knit together are love.

Third, no body can be perfect which wants its proper ligaments.

Fourth, all the parts of this body being thus united are made so contiguous in a special relation as they must partake of each other's strength and infirmity, joy, and sorrow, weal and woe. (1 Corinthians: 12.26) *If one member suffers, all suffer with it; if one be in honor, all rejoice in it.*

Fifth, this sensibleness and Sympathy of each other's Conditions will necessarily infuse into each part a native desire and endeavor, to strengthen, defend, preserve, and comfort the other.

To insist a little on this Conclusion being the product of all the former, the truth hereof will appear both by precept and pattern (1 John: 3.10) *Ye ought to lay down your lives for the brethren.* (Galatians: 6.2) *Bear ye one another's burdens and so fulfill the law of Christ.* . . .

Thus stands the cause between God and us. We are entered into covenant with Him for this work. We have taken out a commission. The Lord hath given us leave to draw our own articles. We have professed to enterprise these actions upon these. And these ends we have hereupon besought Him of favor and blessing. Now if the Lord shall please to hear us and bring us in peace to the place we desire, then hath He ratified this covenant and sealed our commission, and will expect a strict performance of the articles contained in it. But if we shall neglect the observation of these articles which are the ends we have propounded and, dissembling with our

God, shall fall to embrace this present world and prosecute our carnal intentions, seeking great things for our selves and our posterity, the Lord will surely break out in wrath against us to be revenged of such a perjured people and make us know the price of the breach of such a covenant.

Now the only way to avoid this shipwreck and to provide for our posterity is to follow the counsel of Micah: *to do Justly, to love mercy, to walk humbly with our God.* For this end, we must be knit together in this work as one man. We must entertain each other in brotherly affection. We must be willing to abridge our selves of our superfluities, for the supply of others' necessities. We must uphold a familiar commerce together in all meekness, gentleness, patience, and liberality. We must delight in each other, make others' conditions our own—rejoice together, mourn together, labor and suffer together, always having before our eyes our commission and community in the work, our community as members of the same body. So shall we *keep the unity of the spirit in the bond of peace.* The Lord will be our God and delight to dwell among us, as His own people and will command a blessing upon us in all our ways, so that we shall see much more of His wisdom, power, goodness, and truth than formerly we have been acquainted with. We shall find that the God of Israel is among us, when ten of us shall be able to resist a thousand of our enemies, when He shall make us a praise and glory, that men shall say of succeeding plantations: "The Lord make it like that of NEW ENGLAND." For we must consider that we shall be as a City upon a Hill. The eyes of all people are upon us; so that if we shall deal falsely with our God in this work we have undertaken and so cause Him to withdraw His present help from us, we shall be made a story and a byword through the world. We shall open the mouths of enemies to speak evil of the ways of God and all professors for God's sake. We shall shame the faces of many of God's worthy servants, and cause their prayers to be turned into curses upon us till we be consumed out of the good land whither we are going. . . .

Therefore let us choose life,
that we and our seed
may live; by obeying His
voice, and cleaving to Him,
for He is our life, and
our prosperity.

GEORGE WASHINGTON

FAREWELL ADDRESS

SEPTEMBER 19, 1796

After serving two terms as president, George Washington (1732–1799) set a precedent for the peaceful transition of power by stepping down as chief executive. In his Farewell Address, he urged Americans to set aside divisive party disputes and political partisanship and, in foreign relations, to avoid becoming entangled in the rivalries of Europe. The address first appeared on page two of the *American Daily Advertiser* on September 19, 1796, as Washington departed Philadelphia for his home at Mount Vernon.

Friends and Fellow-Citizens:

The period for a new election of a Citizen, to administer the Executive Government of the United States, being not far distant, and the time actually arrived, when your thoughts must be employed in designating the person, who is to be clothed with that important trust, it appears to me proper, especially as it may conduce to a more distinct expression of the public voice, that I should now apprize you of the resolution I have formed, to decline being considered among the number of those, out of whom a choice is to be made. . . .

The impressions, with which I first undertook the arduous trust, were explained on the proper occasion. In the discharge of this trust, I will only say, that I have, with good intentions, contributed towards the organization and administration of the government, the best exertions of which a very fallible judgment was capable.—Not unconscious, in the outset, of the inferiority of my qualifications, experience in my own eyes, perhaps still more in the eyes of others, has strengthened the motives to diffidence of myself; and every day the increasing weight of years admonishes me more and more, that the shade of retirement is as necessary to me as it will be welcome.—Satisfied, that, if any circumstances have given peculiar value to my services, they were temporary, I have the consolation to believe, that, while choice and prudence invite me to quit the political scene, patriotism does not forbid it.

In looking forward to the moment, which is intended to terminate the career of my public life, my feelings do not permit me to suspend the deep acknowledgment of that debt of gratitude, which I owe to my beloved country,—for the many honors it has conferred upon me; still more for the steadfast confidence with which it has supported me; and for the opportunities I have thence enjoyed of manifesting my inviolable attachment, by services faithful and persevering, though in usefulness unequal to my zeal. . . .

Here, perhaps, I ought to stop.—But a solicitude for your welfare, which cannot end but with my life, and the apprehension of danger, natural to that solicitude, urge me on an occasion like the present, to offer to your solemn contemplation, and to recommend to your frequent review, some sentiments; which are the result of much reflection, of no inconsiderable observation and which appear to me all important to the permanency of your felicity as a People. These will be offered to you with the more freedom, as you can only see in them the disinterested warnings of a parting friend, who can possibly have no personal motive to bias his counsel.—Nor can I forget, as an encouragement to it, your indulgent reception of my sentiments on a former and not dissimilar occasion.

Interwoven as is the love of liberty with every ligament of your hearts, no recommendation of mine is necessary to fortify or confirm the attachment.—

The Unity of Government, which constitutes you one people, is also now dear to you.—It is justly so; for it is a main Pillar in the Edifice of your real independence; the support of your tranquillity at home; your peace abroad; of your safety; of your prosperity in every shape; of that very Liberty, which you so highly prize.—But as it is easy to foresee, that, from different causes, and from different quarters, much pains will be taken, many artifices employed, to weaken in your minds the conviction of this truth;—as this is the point in your political fortress against which the batteries of internal and external enemies will be most constantly and actively (though often covertly and insidiously) directed it is of infinite moment, that you should properly estimate the immense value of your national Union to your collective and individual happiness;—that you should cherish a cordial, habitual, and immoveable attachment to it; accustoming yourselves to think and speak of it as of the Palladium of your political safety and prosperity; watching for its preservation with jealous anxiety; discountenancing whatever may suggest even a suspicion, that it can in any event be abandoned, and indignantly frowning upon the first dawning of every attempt to alienate any portion of our Country from the rest, or to enfeeble the sacred ties which now link together the various parts.

For this you have every inducement of sympathy and interest.—Citizens by birth or choice of a common country, that country has a right to concentrate your affections.—The name of AMERICAN, which belongs to you, in your national capacity, must always exalt the just pride of Patriotism, more than any appellation derived from local discriminations. With slight shades of difference, you have the same Religion, Manners, Habits, and Political Principles. You have in a common cause fought and triumphed together; the Independence and Liberty you possess are the work of joint counsels, and joint efforts—of common dangers, sufferings, and successes.—

But these considerations, however powerfully they address themselves to your sensibility, are greatly outweighed by those which apply more immediately to your Interest. Here every portion of our country finds the most commanding motives for carefully guarding and preserving the Union of the whole. . . .

In contemplating the causes which may disturb our Union, it occurs as matter of serious concern, that any ground should have been furnished for characterizing parties by *geographical* discriminations—*Northern* and *Southern, Atlantic* and *Western;* whence designing men may endeavour to excite a belief, that there is a real difference of local interests and views. One of the expedients of Party to acquire influence, within particular districts, is to misrepresent the opinions and aims of other districts.—You cannot shield yourselves too much against the jealousies and heart burnings, which spring from these misrepresentations;—they tend to render alien to each other those, who ought to be bound together by fraternal affection. . . .

To the efficacy and permanency of your Union, a Government for the whole is indispensable.—No alliances, however strict between the parts can be an adequate substitute.—They must inevitably experience the infractions and interruptions which all alliances in all times have experienced. Sensible of this momentous truth, you have improved upon your first essay, by the adoption of a Constitution of Government, better calculated than your former for an intimate Union, and for the efficacious management of your common concerns. . . . The basis of our political systems is the right of the people to make and to alter their Constitutions of Government.—But the Constitution which at any time exists, till changed by an explicit and authentic act of the whole People, is sacredly obligatory upon all.—The very idea of the power and the right of the People to establish Government presupposes the duty of every individual to obey the established Government. . . .

Towards the preservation of your Government, and the permanency of your present happy state, it is requisite, not only that you steadily discountenance irregular oppositions to its acknowledged authority, but also that you resist with care the spirit of innovation upon its principles, however specious the pretexts.—One method of assault may be to effect, in the forms of the Constitution, alterations which will impair the energy of the system, and thus to undermine what cannot be directly overthrown.—In all the changes to which you may be invited, remember that time and habit are at least as necessary to fix the true character of Governments, as of other human institutions—that experience is the surest standard, by which to test the real tendency of the existing Constitution of a Country—that facility in changes upon the credit of mere hypothesis and opinion exposes to perpetual change, from the endless variety of hypothesis and opinion:—and remember, especially, that, for the efficient management of your common interests, in a country so extensive as ours, a Government of as much vigor as is consistent with the perfect security of Liberty is indispensible.—Liberty itself will find in such a government, with powers properly distributed and adjusted, its surest Guardian.—It is, indeed, little else than a name, where the Government is too feeble to withstand the enterprise of faction, to confine each member of the society within the limits prescribed by the laws, and to maintain all in the secure and tranquil enjoyment of the rights of person and property.

I have already intimated to you the danger of parties in the State, with particular reference to the founding of them on Geographical discriminations.—Let me now take a more comprehensive view, and warn you in the most solemn manner against the baneful effects of the Spirit of Party, generally.

This Spirit, unfortunately, is inseparable from our nature, having its root in the strongest passions of the human mind.—It exists under different shapes in all Governments, more or less stifled, controuled, or repressed; but, in those of the popular form, it is seen in its greatest rankness, and is truly their worst enemy.—

The alternate domination of one faction over another, sharpened by the spirit of revenge, natural to party dissension, which in different ages and countries has perpetrated the most horrid enormities, is itself a frightful despotism.—But this leads at length to a more formal and permanent despotism.—The disorders and miseries, which result, gradually incline the minds of men to seek security and repose in the absolute power of an Individual; and sooner or later the chief of some prevailing faction, more able or more fortunate than his competitors, turns this disposition to the purposes of his own elevation, on the ruins of Public Liberty. . . .

There is an opinion, that parties in free countries are useful checks upon the Administration of the Government, and serve to keep alive the spirit of Liberty.— This within certain limits is probably true—and in Governments of a Monarchical cast, Patriotism may look with indulgence, if not with favor, upon the spirit of party.—But in those of the popular character, in Governments purely elective, it is a spirit not to be encouraged.—From their natural tendency, it is certain there will always be enough of that spirit for every salutary purpose,—and there being constant danger of excess, the effort ought to be, by force of public opinion, to mitigate and assuage it.—A fire not to be quenched; it demands a uniform vigilance to prevent its bursting into a flame, lest, instead of warming, it should consume.

It is important, likewise, that the habits of thinking in a free country should inspire caution in those intrusted with its administration, to confine themselves within their respective constitutional spheres; avoiding in the exercise of the powers of one department to encroach upon another. The spirit of encroachment tends to consolidate the powers of all the departments in one, and thus to create, whatever the form of government, a real despotism.—A just estimate of that love of power, and proneness to abuse it, which predominates in the human heart, is sufficient to satisfy us of the truth of this position.—The necessity of reciprocal checks in the exercise of political power, by dividing and distributing it into different depositories, and constituting each the Guardian of the Public Weal against invasions by the others, has been evinced by experiments ancient and modern; some of them in our country and under our own eyes.—To preserve them must be as necessary as to institute them. If, in the opinion of the People, the distribution or modification of the Constitutional powers be in any particular wrong, let it be corrected by an amendment in the way which the Constitution designates.—But let there be no change by usurpation; for though this, in one instance, may be the instrument of good, it is the customary weapon by which free governments are destroyed. . . .

Of all the dispositions and habits, which lead to political prosperity, Religion, and Morality are indispensable supports.—In vain would that man claim the tribute of Patriotism, who should labor to subvert these great pillars of human happiness, these firmest props of the duties of Men and Citizens.—The mere Politician, equally with the pious man, ought to respect and to cherish them.—A volume could not trace all their connexions with private and public felicity.—Let it simply be asked where is the security for property, for reputation, for life, if the sense of religious obligation *desert* the oaths, which are the instruments of investigation in Courts of Justice? And let us with caution indulge the supposition, that morality can be maintained without religion.—Whatever may be conceded to the influence of refined education on minds of peculiar structure—reason and experience both forbid us to expect, that national morality can prevail in exclusion of religious principle. . . .

Promote, then, as an object of primary importance, institutions for the general diffusion of knowledge. In proportion as the structure of a government gives force to public opinion, it is essential that public opinion should be enlightened.

As a very important source of strength and security, cherish public credit.—One method of preserving it is, to use it as sparingly as possible: —avoiding occasions of expense by cultivating peace, but remembering also that timely disbursements to prepare for danger frequently prevent much greater disbursements to repel it— avoiding likewise the accumulation of debt, not only by shunning occasions of expense, but by vigorous exertions in time of Peace to discharge the debts which unavoidable wars may have occasioned, not ungenerously throwing upon posterity the burthen which we ourselves ought to bear. The execution of these maxims belongs to your Representatives, but it is necessary that public opinion should coöperate.—To facilitate to them the performance of their duty, it is essential that you should practically bear in mind, that towards the payment of debts there must be Revenue—that to have Revenue there must be taxes—that no taxes can be devised, which are not more or less inconvenient and unpleasant—that the intrinsic embarrassment, inseparable from the selection of the proper objects (which is always a choice of difficulties) ought to be a decisive motive for a candid construction of the conduct of the Government in making it, and for a spirit of acquiescence in the measures for obtaining Revenue, which the public exigencies may at any time dictate.—

Observe good faith and justice towards all Nations. Cultivate peace and harmony with all.—Religion and Morality enjoin this conduct; and can it be, that good policy does not equally enjoin it?—It will be worthy of a free, enlightened, and, at no distant period, a great nation, to give to mankind the magnanimous and too novel example of a People always guided by an exalted justice and benevolence. . . .

In the execution of such a plan nothing is more essential than that permanent, inveterate antipathies against particular nations and passionate attachments for others, should be excluded; and that, in place of them, just and amicable feelings towards all should be cultivated.—The Nation, which indulges towards another an habitual hatred or an habitual fondness, is in some degree a slave. It is a slave to its animosity or to its affection, either of which is sufficient to lead it astray from its duty and its interest. . . .

So likewise a passionate attachment of one Nation for another produces a variety of evils.—Sympathy for the favorite nation, facilitating the illusion of an imaginary common interest in cases where no real common interest exists, and infusing into one the enmities of the other, betrays the former into a participation in the quarrels and wars of the latter, without adequate inducement or justification. . . .

Our detached and distant situation invites and enables us to pursue a different course.—If we remain one People, under an efficient government, the period is not far off, when we may defy material injury from external annoyance; when we may take such an attitude as will cause the neutrality we may at any time resolve upon to be scrupulously respected. When belligerent nations, under the impossibility of making acquisitions upon us, will not lightly hazard the giving us provocation when we may choose peace or war, as our interest, guided by our justice, shall counsel.

Why forego the advantages of so peculiar a situation?—Why quit our own to stand upon foreign ground?—Why, by interweaving our destiny with that of any part of Europe, entangle our peace and prosperity in the toils of European ambition, rivalship, interest, humor, or caprice?—

'Tis our true policy to steer clear of permanent alliances, with any portion of the foreign world;—so far, I mean, as we are now at liberty to do it;—for let me not be understood as capable of patronizing infidelity to existing engagements. (I hold the maxim no less applicable to public than to private affairs, that honesty is always the best policy.)—I repeat it therefore let those engagements be observed in their genuine sense.—But in my opinion it is unnecessary and would be unwise to extend them. . . .

In offering to you, my Countrymen, these counsels of an old and affectionate friend, I dare not hope they will make the strong and lasting impression, I could wish,—that they will controul the usual current of the passions, or prevent our Nation from running the course which has hitherto marked the destiny of Nations. But if I may even flatter myself, that they may be productive of some partial benefit; some occasional good; that they may now and then recur to moderate the fury of party spirit, to warn against the mischiefs of foreign intrigue, to guard against the impostures of pretended patriotism, this hope will be a full recompense for the solicitude for your welfare, by which they have been dictated. . . .

Though, in reviewing the incidents of my Administration, I am unconscious of intentional error—I am nevertheless too sensible of my defects not to think it probable that I may have committed many errors.—Whatever they may be, I fervently beseech the Almighty to avert or mitigate the evils to which they may tend.—I shall also carry with me the hope that my country will never cease to view them with indulgence; and that, after forty-five years of my life dedicated to its service with an upright zeal, the faults of incompetent abilities will be consigned to oblivion, as myself must soon be to the mansions of rest.

Relying on its kindness in this as in other things, and actuated by that fervent love towards it, which is so natural to a man, who views in it the native soil of himself and his progenitors for several generations;—I anticipate with pleasing expectation that retreat, in which I promise myself to realize, without alloy, the sweet enjoyment of partaking, in the midst of my fellow-citizens, the benign influence of good Laws under a free Government, the ever favorite object of my heart, and the happy reward, as I trust, of our mutual cares, labors, and dangers.

THOMAS JEFFERSON

FIRST INAUGURAL ADDRESS

MARCH 4, 1801

The Declaration of Independence is only one of the legendary accomplishments of Thomas Jefferson (1743–1826). An apostle of liberty throughout his life, though he himself was a slave owner, Jefferson also authored "A Bill for Establishing Religious Freedom in Virginia," the precursor to the First Amendment's guarantee of freedom of religion. His interest in the natural world led him to help organize Lewis and Clark's westward expedition and push through the Louisiana Purchase, which doubled the size of the United States and banished feuding European powers from American shores. He founded and designed the University of Virginia and was the architect for his own estate, Monticello. Jefferson also served as governor of Virginia (1779–1781) and minister to Paris (1785–1789). Jefferson was elected to the presidency in the hotly contested election of 1800, in which he and Aaron Burr received an equal number of electoral votes. The deadlocked election was resolved in the House of Representatives only after thirty-six ballots had been cast. Jefferson's election marked the first transition of presidential power from one political party to another, and his Inaugural Address was the first to be given in Washington, D.C., a city he helped to plan. But the speech is primarily remembered for the tone and spirit of Jefferson's remarks, in which he called for an end to partisanship and urged all Americans to unite for the good of the Republic.

Called upon to undertake the duties of the first executive office of our country, I avail myself of the presence of that portion of my fellow-citizens which is here assembled to express my grateful thanks for the favor with which they have been pleased to look toward me, to declare a sincere consciousness that the task is above my talents, and that I approach it with those anxious and awful presentiments which the greatness of the charge and the weakness of my powers so justly inspire. A rising nation, spread over a wide and fruitful land, traversing all the seas with the rich productions of their industry, engaged in commerce with nations who feel power and forget right, advancing rapidly to destinies beyond the reach of mortal eye—when I contemplate these transcendent objects, and see the honor, the happiness, and the hopes of this beloved country committed to the issue, and the auspices of this day, I shrink from the contemplation, and humble myself before the magnitude of the undertaking. Utterly, indeed, should I despair did not the presence of many whom I here see remind me that in the other high authorities provided by our Constitution I shall find resources of wisdom, of virtue, and of zeal on which to rely under all difficulties. To you, then, gentlemen, who are charged with the sovereign functions of legislation, and to those associated with you, I look with encouragement for that guidance and support which may enable us to steer with safety the vessel in which we are all embarked amidst the conflicting elements of a troubled world.

During the contest of opinion through which we have passed the animation of discussions and of exertions has sometimes worn an aspect which might impose on strangers unused to think freely and to speak and to write what they think; but this being now decided by the voice of the nation, announced according to the rules of the Constitution, all will of course arrange themselves under the will of the law, and unite in common efforts for the common good. All, too, will bear in mind this sacred principle, that though the will of the majority is in all cases to prevail, that will to be rightful must be reasonable; that the minority possesses their equal rights, which equal law must protect, and to violate would be oppression. Let us, then, fellow-citizens, unite with one heart and one mind. Let us restore to social intercourse that harmony and affection without which liberty and even life itself are but dreary things. And let us reflect that, having banished from our land that religious intolerance under which mankind so long bled and suffered, we have yet gained little if we countenance a political intolerance as despotic, as wicked, and capable of as bitter and bloody persecutions. During the throes and convulsions of the ancient world, during the agonizing spasms of infuriated man, seeking through blood and slaughter his long-lost liberty, it was not wonderful that the agitation of the billows should reach even this distant and peaceful shore; that this should be more felt and feared by some and less by others, and should divide opinions as to measures of safety. But every difference of opinion is not a difference of principle. We have called by different names brethren of the same principle. . . . We are all republicans, we are all federalists. If there be any among us who would wish to dissolve this Union or to change its republican form, let them stand undisturbed as monuments of the safety with which error of opinion may be tolerated where reason is left free to combat it. I know, indeed, that some honest men fear that a republican government can not be strong, that this Government is not strong enough; but would the honest patriot, in the full tide of successful experiment, abandon a government which has so far kept us free and firm on the theoretic and visionary fear that this Government, the world's best hope, may by possibility want energy to preserve itself? I trust not. I believe this, on the contrary, the strongest Government on earth. I believe it the only one where every man, at the call of the law, would fly to the standard of the law, and would meet invasions of the public order as his own personal concern. Sometimes it is said that man can not be trusted with the government of himself. Can he, then, be trusted with the government of others? Or have we found angels in the forms of kings to govern him? Let history answer this question.

Let us, then, with courage and confidence pursue our own Federal and Republican principles, our attachment to union and representative government. Kindly separated by nature and a wide ocean from the exterminating havoc of one quarter of the globe; too high-minded to endure the degradations of the others; possessing a chosen country, with room enough for our descendants to the thousandth and thousandth generation; entertaining a due sense of our equal right to the use of our own faculties, to the acquisitions of our own industry, to honor and confidence from our fellow-citizens, resulting not from birth, but from our actions and their sense of them; enlightened by a benign religion, professed, indeed, and practiced in various forms, yet all of them inculcating honesty, truth, temperance, gratitude, and the love of man; acknowledging and adoring an overruling Providence, which by all its dispensations proves that it delights in the happiness of man here and his greater happiness hereafter—with all these blessings, what more is necessary to make us a happy and a prosperous people? Still one thing more, fellow-citizens—a wise and frugal Government, which shall restrain men from injuring one another, shall leave them otherwise free to regulate their own pursuits of industry and improvement, and shall not take from the mouth of labor the bread it has earned. This is the sum of good government, and this is necessary to close the circle of our felicities.

About to enter, fellow-citizens, on the exercise of duties which comprehend everything dear and valuable to you, it is proper you should understand what I deem the essential principles of our Government, and consequently those which ought to shape its Administration. I will compress them within the narrowest compass they will bear, stating the general principle, but not all its limitations. Equal and exact justice to all men, of whatever state or persuasion, religious or political; peace, commerce, and honest friendship with all nations, entangling alliances with none; the support of the State governments in all their rights, as the most competent administrations for our domestic concerns and the surest bulwarks against antirepublican tendencies; the preservation of the General Government in its whole constitutional vigor, as the sheet anchor of our peace at home and safety abroad; a jealous care of the right of election by the people—a mild and safe corrective of abuses which are lopped by the sword of revolution where peaceable remedies are unprovided; absolute acquiescence in the decisions of the majority, the vital principle of republics, from which is no appeal but to force, the vital principle and immediate parent of despotism; a well-disciplined militia, our best reliance in peace and for the first moments of war, till regulars may relieve them; the supremacy of the civil over the military authority; economy in the public expense, that labor may be lightly burthened; the honest payment of our debts and sacred preservation of the public faith; encouragement of agriculture, and of commerce as its handmaid; the diffusion of information and arraignment of all abuses at the bar of the public reason; freedom of religion; freedom of the press, and freedom of person under the protection of the habeas corpus, and trial by juries impartially selected. These principles form the bright constellation which has gone before us and guided our steps through an age of revolution and reformation. The wisdom of our sages and blood of our heroes have been devoted to their attainment. They should be the creed of our political faith, the text of civic instruction, the touchstone by which to try the services of those we trust; and should we wander from them in moments of error or of alarm, let us hasten to retrace our steps and to regain the road which alone leads to peace, liberty, and safety.

I repair, then, fellow-citizens, to the post you have assigned me. With experience enough in subordinate offices to have seen the difficulties of this the greatest of all, I have learnt to expect that it will rarely fall to the lot of imperfect man to retire from this station with the reputation and the favor which bring him into it. Without pretentions to that high confidence you reposed in our first and greatest revolutionary character, whose preeminent services had entitled him to the first place in his country's love and destined for him the fairest page in the volume of faithful history, I ask so much confidence only as may give firmness and effect to the legal administration of your affairs. I shall often go wrong through defect of judgment. When right, I shall often be thought wrong by those whose positions will not command a view of the whole ground. I ask your indulgence for my own errors, which will never be intentional, and your support against the errors of others, who may condemn what they would not if seen in all its parts. The approbation implied by your suffrage is a great consolation to me for the past, and my future solicitude will be to retain the good opinion of those who have bestowed it in advance, to conciliate that of others by doing them all the good in my power, and to be instrumental to the happiness and freedom of all.

Relying, then, on the patronage of your good will, I advance with obedience to the work, ready to retire from it whenever you become sensible how much better choice it is in your power to make. And may that Infinite Power which rules the destinies of the universe lead our councils to what is best, and give them a favorable issue for your peace and prosperity.

DEDICATION OF THE BUNKER HILL MONUMENT

JUNE 17, 1825

Renowned orator Daniel Webster (1782–1852) delivered this speech to commemorate the fiftieth anniversary of the Revolutionary War Battle of Bunker Hill, in which the outnumbered colonists inflicted heavy losses on the mighty British forces attempting to invade Boston. Webster served as a U.S. senator from Massachusetts from 1827 to 1841 and 1845 to 1850, and also as U.S. secretary of state (1841–1843; 1850–1852). He argued many important cases before the U.S. Supreme Court and became famous for his eloquent defense of the Union against the threat of secession in the years preceding the Civil War.

We are among the sepulchers of our fathers. We are on ground distinguished by their valor, their constancy, and the shedding of their blood. We are here, not to fix an uncertain date in our annals, nor to draw into notice an obscure and unknown spot. If our humble purpose had never been conceived, if we ourselves had never been born, the seventeenth of June, 1775, would have been a day on which all subsequent history would have poured its light, and the eminence where we stand, a point of attraction to the eyes of successive generations. But we are Americans. We live in what may be called the early age of this great continent; and we know that our posterity, through all time, are here to suffer and enjoy the allotments of humanity. We see before us a probable train of great events; we know that our own fortunes have been happily cast; and it is natural, therefore, that we should be moved by the contemplation of occurrences which have guided our destiny before many of us were born, and settled the condition in which we should pass that portion of our existence which God allows to men on earth. . . .

The great event, in the history of the continent, which we are now met here to commemorate—that prodigy of modern times, at once the wonder and the blessing of the world—is the American Revolution. In a day of extraordinary prosperity and happiness, of high national honor, distinction, and power, we are brought together, in this place, by our love of country, by our admiration of exalted character, by our gratitude for signal services and patriotic devotion. . . .

The great wheel of political revolution began to move in America. Here its rotation was guarded, regular, and safe. Transferred to the other continent, from unfortunate but natural causes, it received an irregular and violent impulse; it whirled along with a fearful celerity, till at length, like the chariot wheels in the races of antiquity, it took fire from the rapidity of its own motion and blazed onward, spreading conflagration and terror around. . . .

When Louis XIV said, "I am the state," he expressed the essence of the doctrine of unlimited power. By the rules of that system, the people are disconnected from the state; they are its subjects; it is their lord. These ideas, founded in the love of power, and long supported by the excess and the abuse of it, are yielding in our age to other opinions; and the civilized world seems at last to be proceeding to the conviction of that fundamental and manifest truth, that the powers of government are but a trust, and that they cannot be lawfully exercised but for the good of the community. . . .

We may hope that the growing influence of enlightened sentiments will promote the permanent peace of the world. Wars, to maintain family alliances, to uphold or to cast down dynasties, to regulate successions to thrones, which have occupied so much room in the history of modern times, if not less likely to happen at all, will be less likely to become general and involve many nations, as the great principle shall be more and more established, that the interest of the world is peace, and its first great statute, that every nation possesses the power of establishing a government for itself. But public opinion has attained also an influence over government which do not admit the popular principle into their organization. A necessary respect for the judgment of the world operates, in some measure, as a control over the most unlimited forms of authority. . . . Let us thank God that we live in an age when something has influence besides the bayonet, and when the sternest authority does not venture to encounter the scorching power of public reproach. . . .

And now let us indulge an honest exultation in the conviction of the benefit which the example of our country has produced and is likely to produce on human freedom and human happiness. And let us endeavor to comprehend in all its magnitude and to feel in all its importance the part assigned to us in the great drama of human affairs. We are placed at the head of the system of representative and popular governments. Thus far our example shows that such governments are compatible, not only with respectability and power, but with repose, with peace, with security of personal rights, with good laws and a just administration.

We are not propagandists. Wherever other systems are preferred, either as being thought better in themselves or as better suited to existing conditions, we leave the preference to be enjoyed. Our history hitherto proves, however, that the popular form is practicable and that, with wisdom and knowledge, men may govern themselves; and the duty incumbent on us is to preserve the consistency of this cheering example and take care that nothing may weaken its authority with the world. If in our case the representative system ultimately fail, popular governments must be pronounced impossible. No combination of circumstances more favorable to the experiment can ever be expected to occur. The last hopes of mankind, therefore, rest with us; and if it should be proclaimed that our example had become an argument against the experiment, the knell of popular liberty would be sounded throughout the earth.

These are incitements to duty; but they are not suggestions of doubt. Our history and our condition, all that is gone before us and all that surrounds us, authorize the belief that popular governments, though subject to occasional variations, perhaps not always for the better in form, may yet in their general character be as durable and permanent as other systems. We know, indeed, that in our country any other is impossible. The principle of free governments adheres to the American soil. It is bedded in it—immovable as its mountains.

And let the sacred obligations which have devolved on this generation and on us sink deep into our hearts. Those are daily dropping from among us who established our liberty and our government. The great trust now descends to new hands. Let us apply ourselves to that which is presented to us as our appropriate object. We can win no laurels in a war for independence. Earlier and worthier hands have gathered them all. Nor are there places for us by the side of Solon, and Alfred, and other founders of states. Our fathers have filled them. But there remains to us a great duty of defense and preservation; and there is opened to us also a noble pursuit to which the spirit of the times strongly invites us.

Our proper business is improvement. Let our age be the age of improvement. In a day of peace let us advance the arts of peace and the works of peace. Let us develop the resources of our land, call forth its powers, build up its institutions, promote all its great interests, and see whether we also, in our day and generation, may not perform something worthy to be remembered. Let us cultivate a true spirit of union and harmony. In pursuing the great objects which our condition points out to us, let us act under a settled conviction, and a habitual feeling that these twenty-four states are one country. Let our conceptions be enlarged to the circle of our duties. Let us extend our ideas over the whole of the vast field in which we are called to act. Let our object be our country, our whole country, and nothing but our country. And by the blessing of God may that country itself become a vast and splendid monument, not of oppression and terror, but of wisdom, of peace, and of liberty, upon which the world may gaze with admiration forever.

HENRY WADSWORTH LONGFELLOW

THE SHIP OF STATE

1849

Born in Portland, Maine (then part of Massachusetts), Henry Wadsworth Longfellow (1807–1882) became one of America's most celebrated poets. A professor of modern languages at his alma mater, Bowdoin College, as well as at Harvard, Longfellow's most famous poems, such as "The Wreck of the Hesperus," "The Children's Hour," "The Song of Hiawatha," and "Paul Revere's Ride," played a prominent role in the creation of American patriotic folklore. Longfellow was the first American to be honored with a bust in the Poet's Corner in London's Westminster Abbey.

Thou, too, sail on, O Ship of State!
Sail on, O UNION, strong and great!
Humanity with all its fears,
With all the hopes of future years,
Is hanging breathless on thy fate!
We know what Master laid thy keel,
What Workmen wrought thy ribs of steel,
Who made each mast, and sail, and rope,
What anvils rang, what hammers beat,
In what a forge and what a heat
Were shaped the anchors of thy hope!
Fear not each sudden sound and shock,
'T is of the wave and not the rock;
'T is but the flapping of the sail,
And not a rent made by the gale!
In spite of rock and tempest's roar,
In spite of false lights on the shore,
Sail on, nor fear to breast the sea!
Our hearts, our hopes, are all with thee,
Our hearts, our hopes, our prayers, our tears,
Our faith triumphant o'er our fears,
Are all with thee,—are all with thee!

THEODORE ROOSEVELT

THE STRENUOUS LIFE

APRIL 10, 1899

A larger-than-life character, Teddy Roosevelt (1858–1919) dominated the American political scene around the turn of the century. As assistant secretary of the Navy under McKinley, he became an outspoken supporter of U.S. military expansion. During the Spanish-American War he resigned to organize a volunteer regiment, the Rough Riders, then returned to New York and was elected governor in 1898. He was the vice-presidential candidate with McKinley in 1900, and became the youngest president a few months later when McKinley was assassinated. As president, he was known for his "trust busting" suits against the powerful business interests of the Robber Baron era. He favored government regulation of railroads, and of workplace health and safety. He believed passionately in conservation of our natural resources and added millions of acres to public lands. He pursued an imperialist foreign policy, which added the Roosevelt corollary to the Monroe Doctrine (declaring American hegemony over Latin America) and culminated in the building of the Panama Canal. He was awarded the 1906 Nobel Peace Prize for mediating an end to the Russo-Japanese War. Succeeded as president by William Howard Taft, Roosevelt then founded the Progressive Party and ran an unsuccessful third-party campaign against Woodrow Wilson in 1912. After his retirement from politics, he led expeditions to the Amazon and continued his prolific career as an author. He is also the person for whom the teddy bear is named.

. . . I wish to preach, not the doctrine of ignoble ease, but the doctrine of the strenuous life. The life of toil and effort, of labor gold strife; to preach that highest form of success which comes, not to the man who desires mere easy peace, but to the man who does not shrink from danger, from hardship or from bitter toil, and who out of these wins the splendid ultimate triumph.

A life of slothful ease, a life of that peace which springs merely from lack either of desire or of power to strive after great things, is as little worthy of a nation as of an individual. I ask only that what every self-respecting American demands from himself and from his sons shall be demanded of the American nation as a whole. Who among you would teach your boys that ease, that peace, is to be the first Consideration in their eyes—to be the ultimate goal after which they strive? . . . If you are rich and are worth your salt, you will teach your sons that though they may have leisure, it is not to be spent in idleness; for wisely used leisure merely means that those who possess it, being free from the necessity of working for their livelihood, are all the more bound to carry on some kind of non-remunerative work in science, in letters, in art, in exploration, in historical research—work of the type we most need in this country, the successful carrying out of which reflects most honor upon the nation. We do not admire the man of timid peace. We admire the man who embodies victorious effort;

the man who never wrongs his neighbor, who is prompt to help a friend, but who has those virile qualities necessary to win in the stern strife of actual life. It is hard to fail, but it is worse never to have tried to succeed. In this life we get nothing save by effort. Freedom from effort in the present merely means that there has been stored up effort in the past. A man can be freed from the necessity of work only by the fact that he or his fathers before him have worked to good purpose. If the freedom thus purchased is used aright, and the man still does actual work, though of a different kind, whether as a writer or a general, whether in the field of politics or in the field of exploration and adventure, he shows he deserves his good fortune. But if he treats this period of freedom from the need of actual labor as a period, not of preparation, but of mere enjoyment, even though perhaps not of vicious enjoyment, he shows that he is simply a cumberer of the earth's surface, and he surely unfits himself to hold his own with his fellows if the need to do so should again arise. A mere life of ease is not in the end a very satisfactory life, and, above all, it is a life which ultimately unfits those who follow it for serious work in the world. . . .

As it is with the individual, so it is with the nation. It is a base untruth to say that happy is the nation that has no history. Thrice happy is the nation that has a glorious history. Far better it is to dare mighty things, to win glorious triumphs, even though checkered by failure, than to take rank with those poor spirits who neither enjoy much nor suffer much, because they live in the gray twilight that knows not victory nor defeat. . . .

If we are to be a really great people, we must strive in good faith to play a great part in the world. We cannot avoid meeting great issues. All that we can determine for ourselves is whether we shall meet them well or ill. In 1898 we could not help being brought face to face with the problem of war with Spain. All we could decide was whether we should shrink like cowards from the contest, or enter into it as beseemed a brave and highspirited people; and, once in, whether failure or success should crown our banners. So it is now. We cannot avoid the responsibilities that confront us in Hawaii, Cuba, Porto Rico, and the Philippines. All we can decide is whether we shall meet them in a way that will redound to the national credit, or whether we shall make of our dealings with these new problems a dark and shameful page in our history. To refuse to deal with them at all merely amounts to dealing with them badly. We have a given problem to solve. If we undertake the solution, there is, of course, always danger that we may not solve it aright; but to refuse to undertake the solution simply renders it certain that we cannot possibly solve it aright. The timid man, the lazy man, the man who distrusts his country, the over-civilized man, who has lost the great fighting, masterful virtues, the ignorant man, and the man of dull mind, whose soul is incapable of feeling the mighty lift that thrills "stern men with empires in their brains"—all these, of course, shrink from seeing the nation undertake its new duties; shrink from seeing us build a navy and an army adequate to our needs; shrink from seeing us do our share of the world's work, by bringing order out of chaos in the great, fair tropic islands from which the valor of our soldiers and sailors has driven the Spanish flag. These are the men who fear the strenuous life, who fear the only national life which is really worth leading. They believe in that cloistered life which saps the hardy virtues in a nation, as it saps them in the individual; or else they were wedded to that base spirit of gain and greed which recognizes in commercialism the be-all and end-all of national life, instead of realizing that, though an indispensable element, it is, after all, but one of the many elements that go to make up true national greatness. No country can long endure if its foundations are not laid deep in the material prosperity which comes from thrift, from business energy and enterprise, from hard, unsparing effort in the fields of industrial activity; but neither was any nation ever yet truly great if it relied upon material prosperity alone. All honor must lie paid to the architects of our material prosperity, to the great captains of industry who have built our factories and our rail-

Theodore Roosevelt, New York, 1904.

roads, to the strong men who toil for wealth with brain or hand; for great is the debt of the nation to these and their kind. But our debt is yet greater to the men whose highest type is to be found in a statesman like Lincoln, a soldier like Grant. They showed by their lives that they recognized the law of work, the law of strife; they toiled to win a competence for themselves and those dependent upon them; but they recognized that there were yet other and even loftier duties—duties to the nation and duties to the race.

We cannot sit huddled within our own borders and avow ourselves merely an assemblage of well-to-do hucksters who care nothing for what happens beyond. Such a policy would defeat even its own end; for as the nations grow to have ever wider and wider interests, and are brought into closer and closer contact, if we are to hold our own in the struggle for naval and commercial supremacy, we must build up our Dower without our own borders. We must build the isthmian canal, and we must Rasp the points of vantage which will enable us to have our say in deciding the destiny of the oceans of the East and the West. . . .

Now, apply all this to our public men of to-day. Our army has never been built up as it should be built up. I shall not discuss with an audience like this the puerile suggestion that a nation of seventy millions of freemen is in danger of losing its liberties from the existence of an army of one hundred thousand men, three fourths of whom will be employed in certain foreign islands, in certain coast fortresses, and on Indian reservations. No man of good sense and stout heart can take such a proposition seriously. If we are such weaklings as the proposition implies, then we are unworthy of freedom in any event. To no body of men in the United States is the country so much indebted as to the splendid officers and enlisted men of the regular army and navy. There is no body from which the country has less to fear, and none of which it should be prouder, none which it should be more anxious to upbuild. . . .

Yet, incredible to relate, Congress has shown a queer inability to learn some of the lessons of the war. There were large bodies of men in both branches who opposed the declaration of war, who opposed the ratification of peace, who opposed the upbuilding of the army, and who even opposed the purchase of armour at a reasonable price for the battle-ships and cruisers, thereby putting an absolute stop to the building of any new fighting-ships for the navy. If, during the years to come, any disaster should befall our arms, afloat or ashore, and thereby any shame come to the United States, remember that the blame will lie upon the men whose names appear upon the roll-calls of Congress on the wrong side of these great questions. On them will lie the burden of any loss of our soldiers and sailors, of any dishonor to the flag; and upon you and the people of this country will lie the blame if you do not repudiate, in no unmistakable way, what these men have done. The blame will not rest upon the untrained commander of untried troops, upon the civil officers of a department the organization of which has been left utterly inadequate, or upon the admiral with an insufficient number of ships; but upon the public men who have so lamentably failed in forethought as to refuse to remedy these evils long in advance, and upon the nation that stands behind those public men. . . .

I preach to you, then, my countrymen, that our country calls not for the life of ease but for the life of strenuous endeavor. The twentieth century looms before us big with the fate of many nations. If we stand idly by, if we seek merely swollen, slothful ease and ignoble peace, if we shrink from the hard contests where men must win at hazard of their lives and at the risk of all they hold dear, then the bolder and stronger peoples will pass us by, and will win for themselves the domination of the world. Let us therefore boldly face the life of strife, resolute to do our duty well and manfully; resolute to uphold righteousness by deed and by word; resolute to be both honest and brave, to serve high ideals, yet to use practical methods. Above all, let us shrink from no strife, moral or physical, within or without the nation, provided we are certain that the strife is justified, for it is only through strife, through hard and dangerous endeavor, that we shall ultimately win the goal of true national greatness.

LET AMERICA BE AMERICA AGAIN

JULY 1936

After growing up in the Midwest, Langston Hughes (1902–1967) attended Columbia University. While writing poetry, he traveled the world as a sailor on a freighter and lived in Paris working as a nightclub doorman and cook. Returning to the United States in the 1920s, he became one of the leading figures of the prewar literary and artistic movement known as the Harlem Renaissance. His work showed an astonishing versatility; he wrote essays, plays, and poetry and worked as a journalist. His poetry explored the black experience, incorporating blues, dialect, and jazz rhythms into a powerful artistic vision, through which he condemned the segregated American society of his time.

Let America be America again.
Let it be the dream it used to be.
Let it be the pioneer on the plain
Seeking a home where he himself is free.

(America never was America to me.)

Let America be the dream the dreamers dreamed—
Let it be that great strong land of love
Where never kings connive nor tyrants scheme
That any man be crushed by one above.

(It never was America to me.)

O, let my land be a land where Liberty
Is crowned with no false patriotic wreath,
But opportunity is real, and life is free,
Equality is in the air we breathe.

(There's never been equality for me,
Nor freedom in this "homeland of the free.")

Say who are you that mumbles in the dark?
And who are you that draws your veil across the stars?

I am the poor white, fooled and pushed apart,
I am the Negro bearing slavery's scars.
I am the red man driven from the land,
I am the immigrant clutching the hope I seek—
And finding only the same old stupid plan
Of dog eat dog, of mighty crush the weak.

I am the young man, full of strength and hope,
Tangled in that ancient endless chain
Of profit, power, gain, of grab the land!
Of grab the gold! Of grab the ways of satisfying need!
Of work the men! Of take the play!
Of owning everything for one's own greed!

I am the farmer, bondsman to the soil.
I am the worker sold to the machine.
I am the Negro, servant to you all.
I am the people, worried, hungry, mean—
Hungry yet today despite the dream.
Beaten yet today—O, Pioneers!
I am the man who never got ahead,
The poorest worker bartered through the years.

Yet I'm the one who dreamt our basic dream
In that Old World while still a serf of kings,
Who dreamt a dream so strong, so brave, so true,
That even yet its mighty daring sings
In every brick and stone, in every furrow turned
That's made America the land it has become.
O, I'm the man who sailed those early seas
In search of what I meant to be my home—
For I'm the one who left dark Ireland's shore,
And Poland's plain, and England's grassy lea,
And torn from Black Africa's strand I came
To build a "homeland of the free."
The free?

A dream—
Still beckoning to me!

O, let America be America again—
The land that never has been yet—
And yet must be—
The land where *every* man is free.
The land that's mine—
The poor man's, Indian's, Negro's, ME—
Who made America,
Whose sweat and blood, whose faith and pain,
Whose hand at the foundry, whose plow in the rain,
Must bring back our mighty dream again.

Sure, call me any ugly name you choose—
The steel of freedom does not stain.
From those who live like leeches on the people's lives,
We must take back our land again,
America!

O, yes,
I say it plain,
America never was America to me,
And yet I swear this oath—
America will be!
An ever-living seed,
Its dream
Lies deep in the heart of me.

We, the people, must redeem
Our land, the mines, the plants, the rivers,
The mountains and the endless plain—
All, all the stretch of these great green states—
And make America again!

FRANKLIN DELANO ROOSEVELT

SECOND INAUGURAL ADDRESS

JANUARY 20, 1937

Franklin Delano Roosevelt (1882–1945) is the only person to have been elected to the presidency four times, serving from 1933 until his death in office in 1945. Prior to the presidency, in 1921 Roosevelt was stricken with polio, which left him in a wheelchair for the rest of his life. After serving as assistant secretary of the Navy during World War I, he was elected governor of New York in 1928 and reelected in 1930, and during the depths of the Great Depression defeated Herbert Hoover in the presidential election of 1932. Under Roosevelt's transformative New Deal economic recovery program, the federal government assumed responsibility for the economic security of Americans through programs and agencies such as the Securities and Exchange Commission, the Social Security Administration, and the Tennessee Valley Authority. Roosevelt's landslide victory in 1936 showed public approval for his policies.

When four years ago we met to inaugurate a President, the Republic, single-minded in anxiety, stood in spirit here. We dedicated ourselves to the fulfillment of a vision—to speed the time when there would be for all the people that security and peace essential to the pursuit of happiness. We of the Republic pledged ourselves to

Franklin Delano Roosevelt's Inauguration, Washington, D.C., 1933.

drive from the temple of our ancient faith those who had profaned it; to end by action, tireless and unafraid, the stagnation and despair of that day. We did those first things first.

Our covenant with ourselves did not stop there. Instinctively we recognized a deeper need—the need to find through government the instrument of our united purpose to solve for the individual the ever-rising problems of a complex civilization. Repeated attempts at their solution without the aid of government had left us baffled and bewildered. For, without that aid, we had been unable to create those moral controls over the services of science which are necessary to make science a useful servant instead of a ruthless master of mankind. To do this we knew that we must find practical controls over blind economic forces and blindly selfish men.

We of the Republic sensed the truth that democratic government has innate capacity to protect its people against disasters once considered inevitable, to solve problems once considered unsolvable. We would not admit that we could not find a way to master economic epidemics just as, after centuries of fatalistic suffering, we had found a way to master epidemics of disease. We refused to leave the problems of our common welfare to be solved by the winds of chance and the hurricanes of disaster.

In this we Americans were discovering no wholly new truth; we were writing a new chapter in our book of self-government.

This year marks the one hundred and fiftieth anniversary of the Constitutional Convention which made us a nation. At that Convention our forefathers found the way out of the chaos which followed the Revolutionary War; they created a strong government with powers of united action sufficient then and now to solve problems utterly beyond individual or local solution. A century and a half ago they established the Federal Government in order to promote the general welfare and secure the blessings of liberty to the American people.

Today we invoke those same powers of government to achieve the same objectives.

Four years of new experience have not belied our historic instinct. They hold out the clear hope that government within communities, government within the separate States, and government of the United States can do the things the times require, without yielding its democracy. Our tasks in the last four years did not force democracy to take a holiday.

Nearly all of us recognize that as intricacies of human relationships increase, so power to govern them also must increase power to stop evil; power to do good. The essential democracy of our Nation and the safety of our people depend not upon the absence of power, but upon lodging it with those whom the people can change or continue at stated intervals through an honest and free system of elections. The Constitution of 1787 did not make our democracy impotent.

To hold to progress today, however, is more difficult. Dulled conscience, irresponsibility, and ruthless self-interest already reappear. Such symptoms of prosperity may become portents of disaster! Prosperity already tests the persistence of our progressive purpose.

Let us ask again: Have we reached the goal of our vision of that fourth day of March, 1933? Have we found our happy valley?

I see a great nation, upon a great continent, blessed with a great wealth of natural resources. Its hundred and thirty million people are at peace among themselves; they are making their country a good neighbor among the nations. I see a United States which can demonstrate that, under democratic methods of government, national wealth can be translated into a spreading volume of human comforts hitherto unknown, and the lowest standard of living can be raised far above the level of mere subsistence.

But here is the challenge to our democracy: In this nation I see tens of millions of its citizens—a substantial part of its whole population—who at this very moment are denied the greater part of what the very lowest standards of today call the necessities of life.

I see millions of families trying to live on incomes so meager that the pall of family disaster hangs over them day by day.

I see millions whose daily lives in city and on farm continue under conditions labeled indecent by a so-called polite society half a century ago.

I see millions denied education, recreation, and the opportunity to better their lot and the lot of their children.

I see millions lacking the means to buy the products of farm and factory and by their poverty denying work and productiveness to many other millions.

I see one-third of a nation ill-housed, ill-clad, ill-nourished.

It is not in despair that I paint you that picture. I paint it for you in hope—because the Nation, seeing and understanding the injustice in it, proposes to paint it out. We are determined to make every American citizen the subject of his country's interest and concern; and we will never regard any faithful, law-abiding group within our borders as superfluous. The test of our progress is not whether we add more to the abundance of those who have much; it is whether we provide enough for those who have too little.

If I know aught of the spirit and purpose of our Nation, we will not listen to Comfort, Opportunism, and Timidity. We will carry on.

Overwhelmingly, we of the Republic are men and women of good will; men and women who have more than warm hearts of dedication; men and women who have cool heads and willing hands of practical purpose as well. They will insist that every agency of popular government use effective instruments to carry out their will.

Government is competent when all who compose it work as trustees for the whole people. It can make constant progress when it keeps abreast of all the facts. It can obtain justified support and legitimate criticism when the people receive true information of all that government does.

If I know aught of the will of our people, they will demand that these conditions of effective government shall be created and maintained. They will demand a nation uncorrupted by cancers of injustice and, therefore, strong among the nations in its example of the will to peace.

Today we reconsecrate our country to long-cherished ideals in a suddenly changed civilization. In every land there are always at work forces that drive men apart and forces that draw men together. In our personal ambitions we are individualists. But in our seeking for economic and political progress as a nation, we all go up, or else we all go down, as one people.

To maintain a democracy of effort requires a vast amount of patience in dealing with differing methods, a vast amount of humility. But out of the confusion of many voices rises an understanding of dominant public need. Then political leadership can voice common ideals, and aid in their realization.

In taking again the oath of office as President of the United States, I assume the solemn obligation of leading the American people forward along the road over which they have chosen to advance.

While this duty rests upon me I shall do my utmost to speak their purpose and to do their will, seeking Divine guidance to help us each and every one to give light to them that sit in darkness and to guide our feet into the way of peace.

JOHN F. KENNEDY

INAUGURAL ADDRESS

JANUARY 20, 1961

John F. Kennedy (1917–1963) was the youngest man and the first Catholic elected to the presidency when he won a narrow victory over Richard M. Nixon in 1960. After attending Harvard, Kennedy served in World War II, earning the Navy and Marine Corps Medal for rescuing his crew after a Japanese destroyer rammed his PT boat. He was first elected to Congress in 1946 and then served as U.S. senator from Massachusetts from 1953 to 1960. He was awarded the Pulitzer Prize in 1957 for *Profiles in Courage*, which chronicled the careers of courageous senators. In his Inaugural Address, he addressed the challenging global politics of the cold war era. His eloquent defense of freedom and his call to public service inspired a generation of Americans and offered hope to people around the world.

We observe today not a victory of party but a celebration of freedom—symbolizing an end as well as a beginning—signifying renewal as well as change. For I have sworn before you and Almighty God the same solemn oath our forebears prescribed nearly a century and three quarters ago.

The world is very different now. For man holds in his mortal hands the power to abolish all forms of human poverty and all forms of human life. And yet the same revolutionary beliefs for which our forebears fought are still at issue around the globe—the belief that the rights of man come not from the generosity of the state but from the hand of God.

We dare not forget today that we are the heirs of that first revolution. Let the word go forth from this time and place, to friend and foe alike, that the torch has been passed to a new generation of Americans—born in this century, tempered by war, disciplined by a hard and bitter peace, proud of our ancient heritage—and unwilling to witness or permit the slow undoing of those human rights to which this nation has always been committed, and to which we are committed today at home and around the world.

Let every nation know, whether it wishes us well or ill, that we shall pay any price, bear any burden, meet any hardship, support any friend, oppose any foe, to assure the survival and the success of liberty.

This much we pledge—and more.

To those old allies whose cultural and spiritual origins we share, we pledge the loyalty of faithful friends. United, there is little we cannot do in a host of cooperative ventures. Divided, there is little we can do—for we dare not meet a powerful challenge at odds and split asunder.

To those new states whom we welcome to the ranks of the free, we pledge our word that one form of colonial control shall not have passed away merely to be replaced by a far more iron tyranny. We shall not always expect to find them supporting our view. But we shall always hope to find them strongly supporting their own freedom—and to remember that in the past, those who foolishly sought power by riding the back of the tiger ended up inside.

To those peoples in the huts and villages of half the globe struggling to break the bonds of mass misery, we pledge our best efforts to help them help themselves, for whatever period is required—not because the Communists may be doing it, not because we seek their votes, but because it is right. If a free society cannot help the many who are poor, it cannot save the few who are rich.

To our sister republics south of our border, we offer a special pledge—to convert our good words into good deeds—in a new alliance for progress—to assist free men and free governments in casting off the chains of poverty. But this peaceful revolution of hope cannot become the prey of hostile powers. Let all our neighbors know that we shall join with them to oppose aggression or subversion anywhere in the Americas. And let every other power know that this hemisphere intends to remain the master of its own house.

To that world assembly of sovereign states, the United Nations, our last best hope in an age where the instruments of war have far outpaced the instruments of peace, we renew our pledge of support—to prevent it from becoming merely a forum for invective—to strengthen its shield of the new and the weak—and to enlarge the area in which its writ may run.

Finally, to those nations who would make themselves our adversary, we offer not a pledge but a request: that both sides begin anew the quest for peace, before the dark powers of destruction unleashed by science engulf all humanity in planned or accidental self-destruction.

We dare not tempt them with weakness. For only when our arms are sufficient beyond doubt can we be certain beyond doubt that they will never be employed.

But neither can two great and powerful groups of nations take comfort from our present course—both sides overburdened by the cost of modern weapons, both rightly alarmed by the steady spread of the deadly atom, yet both racing to alter that uncertain balance of terror that stays the hand of mankind's final war.

So let us begin anew—remembering on both sides that civility is not a sign of weakness, and sincerity is always subject to proof. Let us never negotiate out of fear. But let us never fear to negotiate.

Let both sides explore what problems unite us instead of belaboring those problems which divide us.

Let both sides, for the first time, formulate serious and precise proposals for the inspection and control of arms—and bring the absolute power to destroy other nations under the absolute control of all nations.

Let both sides seek to invoke the wonders of science instead of its terrors. Together let us explore the stars, conquer the deserts, eradicate disease, tap the ocean depths, and encourage the arts and commerce.

Let both sides unite to heed in all corners of the earth the command of Isaiah—to "undo the heavy burdens [and] let the oppressed go free."

And if a beachhead of cooperation may push back the jungle of suspicion, let both sides join in creating a new endeavor, not a new balance of power, but a new world of law, where the strong are just and the weak secure and the peace preserved.

All this will not be finished in the first one hundred days. Nor will it be finished in the first one thousand days, nor in the life of this administration, nor even perhaps in our lifetime on this planet. But let us begin.

In your hands, my fellow citizens, more than mine, will rest the final success or failure of our course. Since this country was founded, each generation of Americans has been summoned to give testimony to its national loyalty. The graves of young Americans who answered the call to service surround the globe.

Now the trumpet summons us again—not as a call to bear arms, though arms we need—not as a call to battle, though embattled we are—but as a call to bear the burden of a long twilight struggle, year in and year out, "rejoicing in hope, patient in tribulation"—a struggle against the common enemies of man: tyranny, poverty, disease, and war itself.

Can we forge against these enemies a grand and global alliance, North and South, East and West, that can assure a more fruitful life for all mankind? Will you join in that historic effort?

In the long history of the world, only a few generations have been granted the role of defending freedom in its hour of maximum danger. I do not shrink from this responsibility—I welcome it. I do not believe that any of us would exchange places with any other people or any other generation. The energy, the faith, the devotion which we bring to this endeavor will light our country and all who serve it—and the glow from that fire can truly light the world.

And so, my fellow Americans: ask not what your country can do for you—ask what you can do for your country.

My fellow citizens of the world: ask not what America will do for you, but what together we can do for the freedom of man.

Finally, whether you are citizens of America or citizens of the world, ask of us here the same high standards of strength and sacrifice which we ask of you. With a good conscience our only sure reward, with history the final judge of our deeds, let us go forth to lead the land we love, asking His blessing and His help, but knowing that here on earth God's work must truly be our own.

THE TIMES THEY ARE A-CHANGIN'

C. 1963

Bob Dylan (1941–), born Robert Allen Zimmerman in Duluth, Minnesota, is one of the most influential musicians of the twentieth century. Heir to the socially conscious folk tradition of Woody Guthrie, Dylan became known in the early 1960s for political ballads, such as "Blowin' in the Wind," "A Hard Rain's A-Gonna Fall," and "The Times They Are A-Changin'." At the same time, he released the first of many albums featuring realistic love songs and personal explorations. These include *The Freewheelin' Bob Dylan* (1963), *Bringing It All Back Home* (1965), and *Blonde on Blonde* (1966). His immeasurable influence on other musicians has continued to this day, particularly through such later albums as *Blood on the Tracks* (1975) and *Desire* (1976). Dylan won his first Album of the Year Grammy in 1998 for *Time Out of Mind*.

Come gather 'round people
Wherever you roam
And admit that the waters
Around you have grown
And accept it that soon
You'll be drenched to the bone.
If your time to you
Is worth savin'
Then you better start swimmin'
Or you'll sink like a stone
For the times they are a-changin'.

Come writers and critics
Who prophesize with your pen
And keep your eyes wide
The chance won't come again
And don't speak too soon
For the wheel's still in spin
And there's no tellin' who
That it's namin'.
For the loser now
Will be later to win
For the times they are a-changin'.

Come senators, congressmen
Please heed the call
Don't stand in the doorway
Don't block up the hall
For he that gets hurt
Will be he who has stalled
There's a battle outside
And it is ragin'.
It'll soon shake your windows
And rattle your walls
For the times they are a-changin'.

Come mothers and fathers
Throughout the land
And don't criticize
What you can't understand
Your sons and your daughters
Are beyond your command
Your old road is
Rapidly agin'.
Please get out of the new one
If you can't lend your hand
For the times they are a-changin'.

The line it is drawn
The curse it is cast
The slow one now
Will later be fast
As the present now
Will later be past
The order is
Rapidly fadin'.
And the first one now
Will later be last
For the times they are a-changin'.

FIRST WORDS SPOKEN BY A MAN ON THE MOON

JULY 20, 1969

In the late 1950s and early 1960s, the cold war rivalry between the United States and the Soviet Union entered outer space as the Russians launched the first satellite and the first manned spacecraft. On May 25, 1961, President Kennedy called the country to action and committed the United States to sending a man to the moon within the decade. On July 20, 1969, Apollo 11 astronauts Neil Armstrong and Buzz Aldrin planted an American flag on the moon's surface, leaving a plaque that read, "Here men from the planet earth first set foot upon the moon July 1969 A.D. We came in peace for all mankind."

EAGLE (the lunar module): Houston, Tranquility Base here. The Eagle has landed.

HOUSTON: Roger, Tranquility, we copy you on the ground. You've got a bunch of guys about to turn blue. We're breathing again. Thanks a lot.

TRANQUILITY BASE: Thank you.

HOUSTON: You're looking good here.

TRANQUILITY BASE: A very smooth touchdown.

NEIL ARMSTRONG, Astronaut Edwin E. Aldrin Jr., Sea of Tranquility, Moon, 1969.

HOUSTON: Eagle, you are stay for T1. [The first step in the lunar operation.] Over.

TRANQUILITY BASE: Roger. Stay for T1. . . .

APOLLO CONTROL: The next major stay-no stay will be for the T2 event. That is at 21 minutes 26 seconds after initiation of power descent. . . .

APOLLO CONTROL: We have an unofficial time for that touchdown of 102 hours, 45 minutes, 42 seconds and we will update that. . . .

APOLLO CONTROL: We're now less than four minutes from our next stay-no stay. It will be for one complete revolution of the command module.

One of the first things that Armstrong and Aldrin will do after getting their next stay-no stay will be to remove their helmets and gloves.

HOUSTON: Eagle, you are stay for T2. Over. . . .

ARMSTRONG: Okay, Houston, I'm on the porch.

HOUSTON: Roger, Neil.

HOUSTON: Columbia, Columbia, This is Houston. One minute, 30 seconds LOS, all systems go. Over.

ALDRIN: Halt where you are a minute, Neil.

ARMSTRONG AND ALDRIN: Okay. Everything's nice and straight in here. Okay, can you pull the door open a little more? Right. . . .

HOUSTON: We can see you coming down the ladder now.

ARMSTRONG: Okay. I just checked getting back up to that first step. It didn't collapse too far. But it's adequate to get back up. It's a pretty good little jump.

ARMSTRONG: I'm at the foot of the ladder. The LM foot beds are only depressed in the surface about one or two inches, although the surface appears to be very, very fine-grained as you get close to it. It's almost like a powder. It's very fine. I'm going to step off the LM now.

That's one small step for man, one giant leap for mankind.

The surface is fine and powdery. I can pick it up loosely with my toe. It does adhere in fine layers like powdered charcoal to the sole and the sides of my boots. I only go in a small fraction of an inch, maybe an eighth of an inch but I can see the footprints of my boots and the treads in the fine sandy particles. . . .

HOUSTON: Oh, that looks beautiful from here, Neil.

ARMSTRONG: It has a stark beauty all its own. It's like much of the high desert of the United States. It's different but it's very pretty out here. . . .

FAREWELL ADDRESS

JANUARY 11, 1989

Ronald Reagan (1911–) was born into a hard luck life in Illinois and moved to California, where he became a successful movie actor before entering politics. Although a Democrat in his youth, he became a committed Republican before being elected governor of California in 1966. His election as president in 1980 represented a triumph for the conservative movement he championed. Eight years later in his Farewell Address, he emphasized its hallmarks: economic freedom, tax relief and deficit spending, a military build-up, and détente with the Soviet Union.

My fellow Americans:

This is the 34th time I'll speak to you from the Oval Office and the last. We've been together 8 years now, and soon it'll be time for me to go. But before I do, I wanted to share some thoughts, some of which I've been saving for a long time. . . .

One of the things about the Presidency is that you're always somewhat apart. You spend a lot of time going by too fast in a car someone else is driving, and seeing the people through tinted glass—the parents holding up a child, and the wave you saw too late and couldn't return. And so many times I wanted to stop and reach out from behind the glass, and connect. Well, maybe I can do a little of that tonight. . . .

You know, down the hall and up the stairs from this office is the part of the White House where the President and his family live. There are a few favorite windows I have up there that I like to stand and look out of early in the morning. The view is over the grounds here to the Washington Monument, and then the Mall and the Jefferson Memorial. But on mornings when the humidity is low, you can see past the Jefferson to the river, the Potomac, and the Virginia shore. Someone said that's the view Lincoln had when he saw the smoke rising from the Battle of Bull Run. I see more prosaic things: the grass on the banks, the morning traffic as people make their way to work, now and then a sailboat on the river.

I've been thinking a bit at that window. I've been reflecting on what the past 8 years have meant and mean. And the image that comes to mind like a refrain is a nautical one—a small story about a big ship, and a refugee, and a sailor. It was back in the early eighties, at the height of the boat people. And the sailor was hard at work on the carrier *Midway*, which was patrolling the South China Sea. The sailor, like most American servicemen, was young, smart, and fiercely observant. The crew spied on the horizon a leaky little boat. And crammed inside were refugees from

Indochina hoping to get to America. The *Midway* sent a small launch to bring them to the ship and safety. As the refugees made their way through the choppy seas, one spied the sailor on deck, and stood up, and called out to him. He yelled, "Hello, American sailor. Hello, freedom man."

A small moment with a big meaning, a moment the sailor, who wrote it in a letter, couldn't get out of his mind. And, when I saw it, neither could I. Because that's what it was to be an American in the 1980's. We stood, again, for freedom. I know we always have, but in the past few years the world again—and in a way, we ourselves—rediscovered it. . . .

Well, back in 1980, when I was running for President, it was all so different. Some pundits said our programs would result in catastrophe. Our views on foreign affairs would cause war. Our plans for the economy would cause inflation to soar and bring about economic collapse. I even remember one highly respected economist saying, back in 1982, that "The engines of economic growth have shut down here, and they're likely to stay that way for years to come." Well, he and the other opinion leaders were wrong. The fact is, what they called "radical" was really "right." What they called "dangerous" was just "desperately needed."

And in all of that time I won a nickname, "The Great Communicator." But I never thought it was my style or the words I used that made a difference: it was the content. I wasn't a great communicator, but I communicated great things, and they didn't spring full blown from my brow, they came from the heart of a great nation—from our experience, our wisdom, and our belief in the principles that have guided us for two centuries. They called it the Reagan revolution. Well, I'll accept that, but for me it always seemed more like the great rediscovery, a rediscovery of our values and our common sense.

Common sense told us that when you put a big tax on something, the people will produce less of it. So, we cut the people's tax rates, and the people produced more than ever before. . . .

Common sense also told us that to preserve the peace, we'd have to become strong again after years of weakness and confusion. So, we rebuilt our defenses, and this New Year we toasted the new peacefulness around the globe. . . .

The lesson of all of this was, of course, that because we're a great nation, our challenges seem complex. It will always be this way. But as long as we remember our first principles and believe in ourselves, the future will always be ours. And something else we learned: Once you begin a great movement, there's no telling where it will end. We meant to change a nation, and instead, we changed a world.

Countries across the globe are turning to free markets and free speech and turning away from the ideologies of the past. For them, the great rediscovery of the 1980's has been that, lo and behold, the moral way of government is the practical way of government: Democracy, the profoundly good, is also the profoundly productive. . . .

Finally, there is a great tradition of warnings in Presidential farewells, and I've got one that's been on my mind for some time. But oddly enough it starts with one of the things I'm proudest of in the past 8 years: the resurgence of national pride that I called the new patriotism. This national feeling is good, but it won't count for much, and it won't last unless it's grounded in thoughtfulness and knowledge.

An informed patriotism is what we want. And are we doing a good enough job teaching our children what America is and what she represents in the long history of the world? Those of us who are over 35 or so years of age grew up in a different America. We were taught, very directly, what it means to be an American. And we absorbed, almost in the air, a love of country and an appreciation of its institutions. If you didn't get these things from your family you got them from the neighborhood, from the father down the street who fought in Korea or the family who lost someone at Anzio. Or you could get a sense of patriotism from school. And if all else failed you could get a sense of patriotism from the popular culture. The movies celebrated democratic values and implicitly reinforced the idea that America was special. TV was like that, too, through the mid-sixties.

But now, we're about to enter the nineties, and some things have changed. Younger parents aren't sure that an unambivalent appreciation of America is the right thing to teach modern children. And as for those who create the popular culture, well-grounded patriotism is no longer the style. Our spirit is back, but we haven't reinstitutionalized it. We've got to do a better job of getting across that America is freedom—freedom of speech, freedom of religion, freedom of enterprise. And freedom is special and rare. It's fragile; it needs production [protection].

So, we've got to teach history based not on what's in fashion but what's important—why the Pilgrims came here, who Jimmy Doolittle was, and what those 30 seconds over Tokyo meant. You know, 4 years ago on the 40th anniversary of D–day, I read a letter from a young woman writing to her late father, who'd fought on Omaha Beach. Her name was Lisa Zanatta Henn, and she said, "we will always remember, we will never forget what the boys of Normandy did." Well, let's help her keep her word. If we forget what we did, we won't know who we are. I'm warning of an eradication of the American memory that could result, ultimately, in an erosion of the American spirit. Let's start with some basics: more attention to American history and a greater emphasis on civic ritual.

And let me offer lesson number one about America: All great change in America begins at the dinner table. So, tomorrow night in the kitchen I hope the talking begins. And children, if your parents haven't been teaching you what it means to be an American, let 'em know and nail 'em on it. That would be a very American thing to do.

And that's about all I have to say tonight, except for one thing. The past few days when I've been at the window upstairs, I've thought a bit of the "shining city upon a hill." The phrase comes from John Winthrop, who wrote it to describe the America he imagined. What he imagined was important because he was an early Pilgrim, an early freedom man. He journeyed here on what today we'd call a little wooden boat; and like the other Pilgrims, he was looking for a home that would be free.

I've spoken of the shining city all my political life, but I don't know if I ever quite communicated what I saw when I said it. But in my mind it was a tall, proud city built on rocks stronger than oceans, wind-swept, God-blessed, and teeming with people of all kinds living in harmony and peace; a city with free ports that hummed with commerce and creativity. And if there had to be city walls, the walls had doors and the doors were open to anyone with the will and the heart to get here. That's how I saw it, and see it still.

And how stands the city on this winter night? More prosperous, more secure, and happier than it was 8 years ago. But more than that: After 200 years, two centuries, she still stands strong and true on the granite ridge, and her glow has held steady no matter what storm. And she's still a beacon, still a magnet for all who must have freedom, for all the pilgrims from all the lost places who are hurtling through the darkness, toward home.

We've done our part. And as I walk off into the city streets, a final word to the men and women of the Reagan revolution, the men and women across America who for 8 years did the work that brought America back. My friends: We did it. We weren't just marking time. We made a difference. We made the city stronger, we made the city freer, and we left her in good hands. All in all, not bad, not bad at all.

PORTRAITS OF AMERICANS

CHARLES HARBUTT, "Mark Twain Fence Painting Contest," Hannibal, Missouri, July 1963.

JUST AS AMERICA has been animated by a special sense of mission, so too have Americans had a sense of their own unique qualities. Of course, it is difficult to define the character of a nation, least of all America, whose society has been created by so many diverse peoples. Yet there has always been a tradition of observing and chronicling our collective attributes.

Early on, foreign observers like de Crèvecoeur and de Tocqueville came from Europe to observe the process by which a new nationality was being formed and to describe its peculiarities. Later, homegrown skeptics like Henry Adams, Mark Twain, and H. L. Mencken chronicled with enthusiasm the hunger for power and the occasional hypocrisy of late-nineteenth- and early-twentieth-century American society. Recently, writers like Gloria Anzaldúa have described the difficult process of maintaining a cultural and linguistic identity within mainstream America. Although we continue to define our notions of what it means to be American, our sense that it is special has never faded.

These selections are intended to be entertaining as well as insightful. Social and political scientists have written much about the process of becoming American and about the American character. The selections here do not represent those disciplines but instead draw upon the work of social critics, humorists, and poets to give a flavor of the contradictions and complexity of American society—what H. L. Mencken called "the greatest show on earth."

YANKEE DOODLE

1755

There are many theories about the origin of the tune of this song, and of the term "Yankee." We do know that they were combined into America's first patriotic song by a British Army doctor in New York, Richard Shuckburg. At first it was sung by British troops deriding the colonists, but during the Revolution Americans adopted it with pride as a marching song and it has remained popular since.

Yankee Doodle went to town,
A-ridin' on a pony,
Stuck a feather in his cap
And called it Macaroni.

CHORUS:
Yankee Doodle, keep it up,
Yankee Doodle Dandy,
Mind the music and the step
And with the girls be handy.

Father and I went down to camp,
Along with Captain Gooding;
And there we saw the men and boys
As thick as hasty pudding.

And there we saw a thousand men,
As rich as Squire David;
And what they wasted every day,
I wish it could be saved.

And there was Captain Washington
Upon a slapping stallion,
A-giving orders to his men;
I guess there was a million.

And there I saw a little keg,
Its head was made of leather;
They knocked upon it with two sticks
To call the men together.

And there I saw a swamping gun,
As big as a log of maple,
Upon a mighty little cart,
A load for father's cattle.

And every time they fired it off
It took a horn of powder,
And made a noise like father's gun,
Only a nation louder.

I can't tell you half I saw,
They kept up such a smother,
So I took my hat off, made a bow
And scampered home to mother.

Yankee Doodle is the tune
Americans delight in,
'Twill do to whistle, sing or play
And just the thing for fightin'.

J. HECTOR ST. JOHN DE CRÈVECOEUR

LETTERS FROM AN AMERICAN FARMER

1782

French aristocrat J. Hector St. John de Crèvecoeur (1735–1813) was one of the earliest chroniclers of rural American society for a European audience hungry for information about the young republic. After military service in French Canadian territory, de Crèvecoeur traveled in Ohio and the Great Lakes region and worked as a surveyor in Pennsylvania. He later settled on a farm in New York, where he wrote the popular and influential *Letters from an American Farmer*. A believer in Franco-American exchange, de Crèvecoeur introduced European crops such as alfalfa to America and the American potato to France.

What then is the American, this new man? He is either an European, or the descendant of an European, hence that strange mixture of blood, which you will find in no other country. I could point out to you a family whose grandfather was an Englishman, whose wife was Dutch, whose son married a French woman, and whose present four sons now have four wives of different nations. *He* is an American, who, leaving behind him all his ancient prejudices and manners, receives new ones from the new mode of life he has embraced, the new government he obeys, and the new rank he holds. He became an American by being received in the broad lap of our great *Alma Mater.* Here individuals of all nations are melted into a new race of men, whose labor and posterity will one day cause great changes in the world. Americans are the western pilgrims, who are carrying along with them that great mass of arts, sciences, vigor, and industry which began long since in the east; they will finish the great circle. The Americans were once scattered all over Europe; here they are incorporated into one of the finest systems of population which has ever appeared, and which will hereafter become distinct by the power of the different climates they inhabit. The American ought therefore to love his country much better than that wherein he or his forefathers were born. Here the rewards of his industry follow with equal steps the progress of his labor; his labor is founded on the basis of nature, *self-interest*; can it want a stronger allurement? Wives and children, who before in vain demanded of him a morsel of bread, now, fat and frolicsome, gladly help their father to clear those fields whence exuberant crops are to arise to feed and clothe them all; without any part being claimed, either by a despotic prince, a rich abbot, or a mighty lord. Here religion demands but little of him; a small voluntary salary to the minister, and gratitude to God; can he refuse these? The American is a new man, who acts upon new principles; he must therefore entertain new ideas, and form new opinions. From involuntary idleness, servile dependence, penury, and useless labor, he has passed to toils of a very different nature, rewarded by ample subsistence.

ALEXIS DE TOCQUEVILLE

DEMOCRACY IN AMERICA

1835

French aristocrat, politician, and political philosopher Alexis de Tocqueville (1805–1859) traveled to the United States in 1831 to study the reforms of the American prison system. Traveling the country for nine months, de Tocqueville observed the American character through its political institutions and the habits and customs of its citizenry. His two-part treatise, *Democracy in America*, remains one of the earliest and most insightful commentaries on American political and social institutions and way of life.

. . . How does it happen that in the United States, where the inhabitants have only recently immigrated to the land which they now occupy, and brought neither customs nor traditions with them there; where they met one another for the first time with no previous acquaintance; where, in short, the instinctive love of country can scarcely exist; how does it happen that everyone takes as zealous an interest in the affairs of his township, his county, and the whole state as if they were his own? It is because everyone, in his sphere, takes an active part in the government of society. . . .

It is unnecessary to study the institutions and the history of the Americans in order to know the truth of this remark, for their manners render it sufficiently evident. As the American participates in all that is done in his country, he thinks himself obliged to defend whatever may be censured in it; for it is not only his country that is then attacked, it is himself. The consequence is that his national pride resorts to a thousand artifices and descends to all the petty tricks of personal vanity.

Nothing is more embarrassing in the ordinary intercourse of life than this irritable patriotism of the Americans. A stranger may be well inclined to praise many of the institutions of their country, but he begs permission to blame some things in it, a permission that is inexorably refused. America is therefore a free country in which, lest anybody should be hurt by your remarks, you are not allowed to speak freely of private individuals or of the state, of the citizens or of the authorities, of public or of private undertakings, or, in short, of anything at all except, perhaps, the climate and the soil; and even then Americans will be found ready to defend both as if they had co-operated in producing them. . . .

It is not impossible to conceive the surprising liberty that the Americans enjoy; some idea may likewise be formed of their extreme equality; but the political activity that pervades the United States must be seen in order to be understood. No sooner do you set foot upon American ground than you are stunned by a kind of tumult; a confused clamor is heard on every side, and a thousand simultaneous voices demand the satisfaction of their social wants. Everything is in motion around you; here the people of one quarter of a town are met to decide upon the building of a church; there the election of a representative is going on; a little farther, the delegates of a district are hastening to the town in order to consult upon some local improvements; in another place, the laborers of a village quit their plows to deliberate upon the project of a road or a public school. Meetings are called for the sole purpose of declaring their disapprobation of the conduct of the government; while in other assemblies citizens salute the authorities of the day as the fathers of their country. Societies are formed which regard drunkenness as the principal cause of the evils of the state, and solemnly bind themselves to give an example of temperance.

The great political agitation of American legislative bodies which is the only one that attracts the attention of foreigners, is a mere episode, or a sort of continuation, of that universal movement which originates in the lowest classes of the people and extends successively to all the ranks of society. It is impossible to spend more effort in the pursuit of happiness.

It is difficult to say what place is taken up in the life of an inhabitant of the United States by his concern for politics. To take a hand in the regulation of society and to discuss it is his biggest concern and, so to speak, the only pleasure an American knows. This feeling pervades the most trifling habits of life; even the women frequently attend public meetings and listen to political harangues as a recreation from their household labors. Debating clubs are, to a certain extent, a substitute for theatrical entertainments: an American cannot converse, but he can discuss, and his talk falls into a dissertation. He speaks to you as if he was addressing a meeting; and if he should chance to become warm in the discussion, he will say "Gentlemen" to the person with whom he is conversing.

In some countries the inhabitants seem unwilling to avail themselves of the political privileges which the law gives them; it would seem that they set too high a value upon their time to spend it on the interests of the community; and they shut themselves up in a narrow selfishness, marked out by four sunk fences and a quickset hedge. But if an American were condemned to confine his activity to his own affairs, he would be robbed of one half of his existence; he would feel an immense void in the life which he is accustomed to lead, and his wretchedness would be unbearable. I am persuaded that if ever a despotism should be established in America, it will be more difficult to overcome the habits that freedom has formed than to conquer the love of freedom itself.

The *Primary Colors* of its day, the satirical novel *Democracy* depicted late-nineteenth-century Washington society from an insider's point of view, prompting lively speculation as to the identity of its author. Henry Adams (1838–1918), descendant of John Adams and John Quincy Adams, was a leading intellectual and historian of the time. He is best remembered today for his autobiography, *The Education of Henry Adams*, which won the Pulitzer Prize in 1919.

For reasons which many persons thought ridiculous, Mrs. Lightfoot Lee decided to pass the winter in Washington. She was in excellent health, but she said that the climate would do her good. In New York she had troops of friends, but she suddenly became eager to see again the very small number of those who lived on the Potomac. It was only to her closest intimates that she honestly acknowledged herself to be tortured by *ennui*. Since her husband's death, five years before, she had lost her taste for New York society; she had felt no interest in the price of stocks, and very little in the men who dealt in them; she had become serious. . . .

Was it ambition—real ambition—or was it mere restlessness that made Mrs. Lightfoot Lee so bitter against New York and Philadelphia, Baltimore and Boston, American life in general and all life in particular? What did she want? Not social position, for she herself was an eminently respectable Philadelphian by birth; her father a famous clergyman; and her husband had been equally irreproachable, a descendant of one branch of the Virginia Lees, which had drifted to New York in search of fortune, and had found it, or enough of it to keep the young man there. His widow had her own place in society which no one disputed. Though not brighter than her neighbours, the world persisted in classing her among clever women; she had wealth, or at least enough of it to give her all that money can give by way of pleasure to a sensible woman in an American city; she had her house and her carriage; she dressed well; her table was good, and her furniture was never allowed to fall behind the latest standard of decorative art. She had travelled in Europe, and after several visits, covering some years of time, had returned home, carrying in one hand, as it were, a green-grey landscape, a remarkably pleasing specimen of Corot, and in the other some bales of Persian and Syrian rugs and embroideries, Japanese bronzes and porcelain. With this she declared Europe to be exhausted, and she frankly avowed that she was American to the tips of her fingers; she neither knew nor greatly cared whether America or Europe were best to live in; she had no violent love for either, and she had no objection to abusing both; but she meant to get all that American life had to offer, good or bad, and to drink it down to the dregs, fully determined that whatever there was in it she would have, and that whatever could be made out of it she would manufacture. "I know," said she, "that America produces petroleum and pigs; I have seen both on the steamers; and I am told it produces silver and gold. There is choice enough for any woman." . . .

Here, then, was the explanation of her restlessness, discontent, ambition,—call it what you will. It was the feeling of a passenger on an ocean steamer whose mind will not give him rest until he has been in the engine-room and talked with the engineer. She wanted to see with her own eyes the action of primary forces; to touch with her own hand the massive machinery of society; to measure with her own mind the capacity of the motive power. She was bent upon getting to the heart of the great American mystery of democracy and government. She cared little where her pursuit might lead her, for she put no extravagant value upon life, having already, as she said, exhausted at least two lives, and being fairly hardened to insensibility in the process. "To lose a husband and a baby," said she, "and keep one's courage and reason, one must become very hard or very soft. I am now pure steel. You may beat my heart with a trip-hammer and it will beat the trip-hammer back again."

Perhaps after exhausting the political world she might try again elsewhere; she did not pretend to say where she might then go, or what she should do; but at present she meant to see what amusement there might be in politics. Her friends asked what kind of amusement she expected to find among the illiterate swarm of ordinary people who in Washington represented constituencies so dreary that in comparison New York was a New Jerusalem, and Broad Street a grove of Academe. She replied that if Washington society were so bad as this, she should have gained all she wanted, for it would be a pleasure to return,—precisely the feeling she longed for. In her own mind, however, she frowned on the idea of seeking for men. What she wished to see, she thought, was the clash of interests, the interests of forty millions of people and a whole continent, centering at Washington; guided, restrained, controlled, or unrestrained and uncontrollable, by men of ordinary mould; the tremendous forces of government, and the machinery of society, at work. What she wanted, was POWER. . . .

THE PICTURE OF DORIAN GRAY

1891

Oscar Wilde (1854–1900), Irish author, aesthete, and wit, is most famous today for his plays, such as *An Ideal Husband* (1895) and *The Importance of Being Earnest* (1895), as well as his humorous epigrams and witticisms. Arriving in America to begin a lecture tour, Wilde said he had "nothing to declare but my genius." His novel *The Picture of Dorian Gray* (1891) tells the story of a man who remains young and beautiful while his portrait becomes disfigured through age and decay.

"Dry-goods! What are American Dry-goods?" asked the Duchess, raising her large hands in wonder, and accentuating the verb.

"American novels," answered Lord Henry, helping himself to some quail.

The Duchess looked puzzled.

"Don't mind him, my dear," whispered Lady Agatha. "He never means anything that he says."

"When America was discovered," said the Radical member, and he began to give some wearisome facts. Like all people who try to exhaust a subject, he exhausted his listeners. The Duchess sighed, and exercised her privilege of interruption. "I wish to goodness it never had been discovered at all!" she exclaimed. "Really, our girls have no chance nowadays. It is most unfair."

"Perhaps, after all, America never has been discovered," said Mr. Erskine; "I myself would say that it had merely been detected."

"Oh! but I have seen specimens of the inhabitants," answered the Duchess, vaguely. "I must confess that most of them are extremely pretty. And they dress well, too. They get all their dresses in Paris. I wish I could afford to do the same."

"They say that when good Americans die they go to Paris," chuckled Sir Thomas, who had a large wardrobe of Humour's cast-off clothes.

"Really! And where do bad Americans go to when they die?" inquired the Duchess.

"They go to America," murmured Lord Henry.

Sir Thomas frowned. "I am afraid that your nephew is prejudiced against that great country," he said to Lady Agatha. "I have travelled all over it, in cars provided by the directors, who, in such matters, are extremely civil. I assure you that it is an education to visit."

"But must we really see Chicago in order to be educated?" asked Mr. Erskine, plaintively. "I don't feel up to the journey."

Sir Thomas waved his hand. "Mr. Erskine of Treadley has the world on his shelves. We practical men like to see things, not to read about them. The Americans are an extremely interesting people. They are absolutely reasonable. I think that is their distinguishing characteristic. Yes, Mr. Erskine, an absolutely reasonable people. I assure you there is no nonsense about the Americans."

"How dreadful!" cried Lord Henry. "I can stand brute force, but brute reason is quite unbearable. There is something unfair about its use. It is hitting below the intellect."

DANGERS OF THE DRESS SUIT IN POLITICS

1905

George Washington Plunkitt was one of the most colorful and powerful ward bosses of New York's Tammany Hall, the party organization known for its system of political patronage, graft, and corruption. Plunkitt saw no harm in his system, however, once remarking, "There's an honest graft, and I'm an example of how it works. I might sum up the whole thing by sayin', 'I seen my opportunities and I took 'em. . . .'" His observations on the art of urban politics were delivered at the shoeshine stand outside the Tweed Courthouse and recorded by journalist William L. Riordon.

Puttin' on style don't pay in politics. The people won't stand for it. If you've got an achin' for style, sit down on it till you have made your pile and landed a Supreme Court Justiceship with a fourteen-year term at $17,500 a year, or some job of that kind. Then you've got about all you can get out of politics, and you can afford to wear a dress suit all day and sleep in it all night if you have a mind to. But, before you have caught onto your life meal ticket, be simple. Live like your neighbors even if you have the means to live better. Make the poorest man in your district feel that he is your equal, or even a bit superior to you.

Above all things, avoid a dress suit. You have no idea of the harm that dress suits have done in politics. They are not so fatal to young politicians as civil service reform and drink, but they have scores of victims. I will mention one sad case. After the big Tammany victory in 1897, Richard Croker went down to Lakewood to make up the slate of offices for Mayor Van Wyck to distribute. All the district leaders and many more Tammany men went down there, too, to pick up anything good that was goin'. There was nothin' but dress suits at dinner at Lakewood, and Croker wouldn't let any Tammany men go to dinner without them. Well, a bright young West Side politician, who held a three-thousand-dollar job in one of the departments, went to Lakewood to ask Croker for something better. He wore a dress suit for the first time in his life. It was his undoin'. He got stuck on himself. He thought he looked too beautiful for anything, and when he came home he was a changed man. As soon as he got to his house every evenin' he put on that dress suit and set around in it until bedtime. That didn't satisfy him long. He wanted others to see how beautiful he was in a dress suit; so he joined dancin' clubs and began goin' to all the balls that was given in town. Soon he began to neglect his family. Then he took to drinkin', and didn't pay any attention to his political work in the district. The end came in less than a year. He was dismissed from the department and went to the dogs. The other day I met him rigged out almost like a hobo, but he still had a dress-suit vest on. When I asked him what he was doin', he said: "Nothin' at present, but I got a promise of a job enrollin' voters at Citizens' Union headquarters." Yes, a dress suit had brought him that low! . . .

Now, nobody ever saw me puttin' on any style. I'm the same Plunkitt I was when I entered politics forty years ago. That is why the people of the district have confidence in me. If I went into the stylish business, even I, Plunkitt, might be thrown down in the district. That was shown pretty clearly in the senatorial fight last year. A day before the election, my enemies circulated a report that I had ordered a $10,000 automobile and a $125 dress suit. I sent out contradictions as fast as I could, but I wasn't able to stamp out the infamous slander before the votin' was over, and I suffered some at the polls. The people wouldn't have minded much if I had been accused of robbin' the city treasury, for they're used to slanders of that kind in campaigns, but the automobile and the dress suit were too much for them.

Another thing that people won't stand for is showin' off your learnin'. That's just puttin' on style in another way. If you're makin' speeches in a campaign, talk the language the people talk. Don't try to show how the situation is by quotin' Shakespeare. Shakespeare was all right in his way, but he didn't know anything about Fifteenth District politics. If you know Latin and Greek and have a hankerin' to work them off on somebody, hire a stranger to come to your house and listen to you for a couple of hours; then go out and talk the language of the Fifteenth to the people. I know it's an awful temptation, the hankerin' to show off your learnin'. I've felt it myself, but I always resist it. I know the awful consequences.

DOROTHEA LANGE, **McLennan County Courthouse, Waco, Texas, 1938.**

ALBERT VON TILZER AND JACK NORWORTH

TAKE ME OUT TO THE BALL GAME

1908

While riding a train in New York one day in 1908, composer and vaudevillian Jack Norworth (1879–1959) saw a poster announcing a baseball game at the Polo Grounds. Although he had never attended a major league game, Norworth jotted down the lines to a new song. Songwriter and former shoe salesman Albert Von Tilzer (1878–1956) contributed the melody, and a new American anthem was created.

Katie Casey was baseball mad,
Had the fever and had it bad;
Just to root for the home town crew, ev'ry sou, Katie blew
On a Saturday, her young beau
Called to see if she'd like to go,
To see a show but Miss Kate said, "No,
I'll tell you what you can do":

  Chorus:

Take me out to the ball game,
Take me out with the crowd
Buy me some peanuts and crackerjack,
I don't care if I never get back.
Let me root, root, root for the home team,
If they don't win it's a shame
For it's one, two, three strikes you're out,
At the old ball game.

Katie Casey saw all the games,
Knew the players by their first names;
Told the umpire he was wrong, all along, good and strong
When the score was just two to two,
Katie Casey knew just what to do,
Just to cheer up the boys she knew,
She made the gang sing this song:

  Repeat Chorus

Joe DiMaggio, Griffith Stadium, Washington, D.C., 1941.

H. L. MENCKEN

On Being an American

1922

Influential social critic, humorist, and essayist, H. L. Mencken (1880–1956) was above all a newspaperman. A columnist and editor for such Baltimore newspapers as the *Morning Herald, Evening Herald,* and the Baltimore *Sun,* he authored a major study of the American language as well as numerous other books. Mencken championed American writers such as Theodore Dreiser, Sherwood Anderson, Eugene O'Neill, and Sinclair Lewis. This essay appeared in the collection *Prejudices, Fourth Series.*

. . . It is my contention that, if this definition be accepted, there is no country on the face of the earth wherein a man roughly constituted as I am—a man of my general weaknesses, vanities, appetites, prejudices, and aversions—can be so happy, or even one-half so happy, as he can be in these free and independent states. Going further, I lay down the proposition that it is a sheer physical impossibility for such a man to live in These States and *not* be happy—that it is as impossible to him as it would be to a schoolboy to weep over the burning down of his schoolhouse. If he says that he isn't happy here, then he either lies or is insane. . . . Here, more than anywhere else that I know of or have heard of, the daily panorama of human existence, of private and communal folly—the unending procession of governmental extortions and chicaneries, of commercial brigandages and throat-slittings, of theological buffooneries, or aesthetic ribaldries, of legal swindles and harlotries, of miscellaneous rogueries, villainies, imbecilities, grotesqueries, and extravagances—is so inordinately gross and preposterous, so perfectly brought up to the highest conceivable amperage, so steadily enriched with an almost fabulous daring and originality, that only the man who was born with a petrified diaphragm fails to laugh himself to sleep every night, and to awake every morning with all the eager, unflagging expectation of a Sunday-school superintendent touring the Paris peep-shows. . . . The *boobus Americanus* is a bird that knows no closed season. . . .

In the older countries, where competence is far more general and competition is thus more sharp, the thing is often cruelly difficult, and sometimes almost impossible. But in the United States it is absurdly easy, given ordinary luck. Any man with a superior air, the intelligence of a stockbroker, and the resolution of a hat-check girl—in brief, any man who believes in himself enough, and with sufficient cause, to be called a journeyman—can cadge enough money, in this glorious commonwealth of morons, to make life soft for him.

And if a lining for the purse is thus facilely obtainable, given a reasonable prudence and resourcefulness, then balm for the ego is just as unlaboriously got, given ordinary dignity and decency. . . . Here is a country in which all political thought and activity are concentrated upon the scramble for jobs—in which the normal politician, whether he be a President or a village road supervisor, is willing to renounce any principle, however precious to him, and to adopt any lunacy, however offensive to him, in order to keep his place at the trough. . . . Here is a land in which women rule and men are slaves. Train your women to get your slippers for you, and your ill fame will match Galileo's or Darwin's. Once more, here is the Paradise of backslappers, of democrats, of mixers, of go-getters. . . .

2

All of which may be boiled down to this: that the United States is essentially a commonwealth of third-rate men—that distinction is easy here because the general level of culture, of information, of taste and judgment, of ordinary competence is so low. No sane man, employing an American plumber to repair a leaky drain, would expect him to do it at the first trial, and in precisely the same way no sane man, observing an American Secretary of State in negotiation with Englishmen and Japs, would expect him to come off better than second best. Third-rate men, of course, exist in all countries, but it is only here that they are in full control of the state, and with it of all the national standards. The land was peopled, not by the hardy adventurers of legend, but simply by incompetents who could not get on at home, and the lavishness of nature that they found here, the vast ease with which they could get livings, confirmed and augmented their native incompetence. No American colonist, even in the worst days of the Indian wars, ever had to face such hardships as ground down the peasants of Central Europe during the Hundred Years War, nor even such hardships as oppressed the English lower classes during the century before the Reform Bill of 1832. In most of the colonies, indeed, the seldom saw any Indians at all; the one thing that made life difficult for him was his congenital dunderheadedness. The winning of the West, so rhetorically celebrated in American romance, cost the lives of fewer men that the single battle of Tannenberg, and the victory was much easier and surer. The immigrants who have come in since those early days have been, if anything, of even lower grade than their forerunners. The old notion that the United States is peopled by the offspring of brave, idealistic and liberty loving minorities, who revolted against injustice, bigotry and mediavalism at home—this notion is fast succumbing to the alarmed study that has been given of late to the immigration of recent years. The truth is that the majority of non-Anglo-Saxon immigrants since the Revolution, like the majority of Anglo-Saxon immigrants before the Revolution, have been, not the superior men of their native lands, but the botched and unfit: Irishmen starving to death in Ireland, Germans unable to weather the *Sturm und Drang* of the post-Napoleonic reorganization, Italians weed-grown on exhausted soil, Scandinavians run to all bone and no brain, Jews too incompetent to swindle even the barbarous peasants of Russia, Poland, and Romania. Here and there among the immigrants, of course, there may be a bravo, or even a superman—e.g., the ancestors of Volstead, Ponzi, Jack Dempsey, Schwab, Daugherty, Debs, Pershing—but the average newcomer is, and always has been, simply a poor fish.

Nor is there much soundness in the common assumption, so beloved of professional idealists and wind-machines, that the people of America constitute "the youngest of the great peoples." . . . What gives it a certain specious plausibility is the fact that the American Republic, compared to a few other existing governments, is relatively young. But the American Republic is not necessarily identical with the American people; they might overturn it tomorrow and set up a monarchy, and still remain the same people. The truth is that as a distinct nation, they go back fully three hundred years, and that even their government is older than those of most other nations, e.g., France, Italy, Germany, Russia. Moreover, it is absurd to say that there is anything properly describable as youthfulness in the American outlook. . . . All the characteristics of senescence are in it: a great distrust of ideas, an habitual timorousness, a harsh fidelity to a few fixed beliefs, a touch of mysticism. The average American is a prude and a Methodist under his skin, and the fact is never more evident than when he is trying to disprove it. . . . If you would penetrate the causes thereof, simply go down to Ellis Island and look at the next shipload of immigrants. You will not find the spring of youth in their step; you will find the shuffling of exhausted men. From such exhausted men the American stock has sprung. It was easier for them to survive here than it was where they came from, but that ease, though it made them feel stronger, did not actually strengthen them. It left them what they were when they came: weary peasants, eager only for the comfortable security of a pig in a sty. Out of that eagerness has issued many of the noblest manifestations of American *Kultur*: the national hatred of war, the pervasive suspicion of the aims and intents of all other nations, the short way with heretics and disturbers of the peace, the unshakable belief in devils, the implacable hostility to every novel idea and point of view.

All these ways of thinking are the marks of the peasant. . . . He likes money and knows how to amass property, but his cultural development is but little above that of the domestic animals. He is intensely and cocksurely moral, but his morality and his self-interest are crudely identical. . . . He is a violent nationalist and patriot, but he admires rogues in office and always beats the tax-collector if he can. He has immovable opinions about all the great affairs of state, but nine-tenths of them are sheer imbecilities. He is violently jealous of what he conceives to be his rights, but brutally disregardful of the other fellow's. . . . This man, whether city or country bred, is the normal Americano—the 100 percent. . . . He exists in all countries, but here alone he rules. . . .

All the while I have been forgetting the third of my reasons for remaining so faithful a citizen of the Federation, despite all the lascivious inducements from expatriates to follow them beyond the seas, and all the surly suggestions from patriots that I succumb. It is the reason which grows out of my mediaeval but unashamed taste for the bizarre and indelicate, my congenital weakness for comedy of the grosser varieties. The United States, to my eye, is incomparably the greatest show on earth.

AS REGARDS PATRIOTISM

C. 1900

In addition to writing novels such as *The Adventures of Huckleberry Finn*, *The Prince and the Pauper*, and *A Connecticut Yankee in King Arthur's Court*, Mark Twain (1835–1910) was a journalist, humorist, and outspoken social critic. This biting essay was written in opposition to American imperialism in the Philippines.

It is agreed, in this country, that if a man can arrange his religion so that it perfectly satisfies his conscience, it is not incumbent upon him to care whether the arrangement is satisfactory to anyone else or not.

In Austria and some other countries this is not the case. There the state arranges a man's religion for him, he has no voice in it himself.

Patriotism is merely a religion—love of country, worship of country, devotion to the country's flag and honor and welfare.

In absolute monarchies it is furnished from the throne, cut and dried, to the subject; in England and America it is furnished, cut and dried, to the citizen by the politician and the newspaper.

The newpaper-and-politician-manufactured patriot often gags in private over his dose; but he takes it, and keeps it on his stomach the best he can. Blessed are the meek.

Sometimes, in the beginning of an insane shabby political upheaval, he is strongly moved to revolt, but he doesn't do it—he knows better. He knows that his maker would find out—the maker of his patriotism, the windy and incoherent six-dollar subeditor of his village newspaper—and would bray out in print and call him a traitor. And how dreadful that would be. It makes him tuck his tail between his legs and shiver. We all know—the reader knows it quite well—that two or three years ago nine-tenths of the human tails in England and America performed just that act. Which is to say, nine-tenths of the patriots in England and America turned traitor to keep from being called traitor. Isn't it true? You know it to be true. Isn't it curious?

Yet it was not a thing to be very seriously ashamed of. A man can seldom—very, very seldom—fight a winning fight against his training; the odds are too heavy. For many a year—perhaps always—the training of the two nations had been dead against independence in political thought, persistently inhospitable toward patriotism manufactured on a man's own premises, patriotism reasoned out in the man's own head and fire-assayed and tested and proved in his own conscience. The resulting patriotism was a shopworn product procured at second hand. The patriot did not know just how or when or where he got his opinions, neither did he care, so long as he was with what seemed the majority—which was the main thing, the safe thing, the comfortable thing. Does the reader believe he knows three men who have actual reasons for their pattern of patriotism—and can furnish them? Let him not examine, unless he wants to be disappointed. He will be likely to find that his men got their patriotism at the public trough, and had no hand in its preparation themselves.

Training does wonderful things. It moved the people of this country to oppose the Mexican War; then moved them to fall in with what they supposed was the opinion of the majority—majority patriotism is the customary patriotism—and go down there and fight. Before the Civil War it made the North indifferent to slavery and friendly to the slave interest; in that interest it made Massachusetts hostile to the American flag, and she would not allow it to be hoisted on her State house—in her eyes it was the flag of a faction. Then by and by, training swung Massachusetts the other way, and she went raging South to fight under that very flag and against that aforetime protected interest of hers.

There is nothing that training cannot do. Nothing is above its reach or below it. It can turn bad morals to good, good morals to bad; it can destroy principles, it can recreate them; it can debase angels to men and lift men to angelship. And it can do any one of these miracles in a year—even in six months.

Then men can be trained to manufacture their own patriotism. They can be trained to labor it out in their own heads and hearts and in the privacy and independence of their own premises. It can train them to stop taking it by command, as the Austrian takes his religion.

EDNA ST. VINCENT MILLAY

I LIKE AMERICANS

1924

Winner of the Pulitzer Prize for poetry in 1923, Edna St. Vincent Millay (1892–1950) represented the newly independent, free-thinking woman of the 1920s. She was brilliant, beautiful, and immensely popular. Her poetry readings were sold-out, theatrical events. Known as "Vincent," Millay was born in Maine, educated at Vassar, and lived abroad and among the bohemian artistic society of Greenwich Village. Her best-known poems include "Renascence," "First Fig," "Second Fig," and "The Ballad of the Harp-Weaver."

I like Americans.

You may say what you will, they are the nicest people in the world.

They sleep with their windows open.

Their bathtubs are never dry.

They are not grown up yet. They still believe in Santa Claus.

They are terribly in earnest.

But they laugh at everything. . . .

I like Americans.

They give the matches free. . . .

I like Americans.

They are the only men in the world, the sight of whom in their shirt-sleeves is not
    rumpled, embryonic and agonizing. . . .

I like Americans.

They carry such pretty umbrellas.

The Avenue de l'Opéra on a rainy day is just an avenue on a rainy day.

But Fifth Avenue on a rainy day is an old-fashioned garden under a shower. . . .

They are always rocking the boat.

I like Americans.

They either shoot the whole nickel, or give up the bones.

You may say what you will, they are the nicest people in the world.

Crossing the Columbia River, Oregon, 1932.

F. SCOTT FITZGERALD

THE GREAT GATSBY

1925

Francis Scott Key Fitzgerald (1896–1940), whose novels and short stories defined the Jazz Age lifestyle of the Roaring Twenties, was born in St. Paul, Minnesota, and attended Princeton University. His first novel, *This Side of Paradise*, was published in 1920 to instant acclaim. His masterpiece, *The Great Gatsby* (1925), a tragic portrait of complex characters destroyed in pursuit of the American Dream, is considered one of the greatest American novels. Fitzgerald also pursued a career as a Hollywood screenwriter, and with his wife, Zelda, was the center of the flamboyant American expatriate community in France during the 1920s. Fitzgerald's other novels include *Tender Is the Night* (1934) and *The Last Tycoon*, published in 1941 after his death.

There was music from my neighbor's house through the summer nights. In his blue gardens men and girls came and went like moths among the whisperings and the champagne and the stars. At high tide in the afternoon I watched his guests diving from the tower of his raft, or taking the sun on the hot sand of his beach while his two motor-boats slit the waters of the Sound, drawing aquaplanes over cataracts of foam. On week-ends his Rolls-Royce became an omnibus, bearing parties to and from the city between nine in the morning and long past midnight, while his station wagon scampered like a brisk yellow bug to meet all trains. And on Mondays eight servants, including an extra gardener, toiled all day with mops and scrubbing-brushes and hammers and garden-shears, repairing the ravages of the night before.

Every Friday five crates of oranges and lemons arrived from a fruiterer in New York—every Monday these same oranges and lemons left his back door in a pyramid of pulpless halves. There was a machine in the kitchen which could extract the juice of two hundred oranges in half an hour if a little button was pressed two hundred times by a butler's thumb.

At least once a fortnight a corps of caterers came down with several hundred feet of canvas and enough colored lights to make a Christmas tree of Gatsby's enormous garden. On buffet tables, garnished with glistening hors-d'œuvre, spiced baked hams crowded against salads of harlequin designs and pastry pigs and turkeys bewitched to a dark gold. In the main hall a bar with a real brass rail was set up, and stocked with gins and liquors and with cordials so long forgotten that most of his female guests were too young to know one from another.

By seven o'clock the orchestra has arrived—no thin five-piece affair, but a whole pitful of oboes and trombones and saxophones and viols and cornets and piccolos, and low and high drums. The last swimmers have come in from the beach now and are dressing up-stairs; the cars from New York are parked five deep in the drive, and already the halls and salons and verandas are gaudy with primary colors, and hair shorn in strange new ways, and shawls beyond the dreams of Castile. The bar is in full swing, and floating rounds of cocktails permeate the garden outside, until the air is alive with chatter and laughter, and casual innuendo and introductions forgotten on the spot, and enthusiastic meetings between women who never knew each other's names.

The lights grow brighter as the earth lurches away from the sun, and now the orchestra is playing yellow cocktail music, and the opera of voices pitches a key higher. Laughter is easier minute by minute, spilled with prodigality, tipped out at a cheerful word. The groups change more swiftly, swell with new arrivals, dissolve and form in the same breath; already there are wanderers, confident girls who weave here and there among the stouter and more stable, become for a sharp, joyous moment the center of a group, and then, excited with triumph, glide on through the sea-change of faces and voices and color under the constantly changing light.

Suddenly one of these gypsies, in trembling opal, seizes a cocktail out of the air, dumps it down for courage and, moving her hands like Frisco, dances out alone on the canvas platform. A momentary hush; the orchestra leader varies his rhythm obligingly for her, and there is a burst of chatter as the erroneous news goes around that she is Gilda Gray's understudy from the *Follies*. The party has begun.

AMERICAN NAMES

1927

Stephen Vincent Benét (1898–1943), a gifted poet born in Bethlehem, Pennsylvania, and educated at Yale and in Paris, is best remembered for his short story "The Devil and Daniel Webster" and for "John Brown's Body," a multilayered epic poem about the Civil War for which he won the Pulitzer Prize in 1929. His 1931 patriotic collection, *Ballads and Poems*, included "American Names," one of his most popular poems.

I have fallen in love with American names,
The sharp names that never get fat,
The snakeskin-titles of mining-claims,
The plumed war-bonnet of Medicine Hat,
Tucson and Deadwood and Lost Mule Flat.

Seine and Piave are silver spoons,
But the spoonbowl-metal is thin and worn,
There are English counties like hunting-tunes
Played on the keys of a postboy's horn,
But I will remember where I was born.

I will remember Carquinez Straits,
Little French Lick and Lundy's Lane,
The Yankee ships and the Yankee dates
And the bullet-towns of Calamity Jane.
I will remember Skunktown Plain.

I will fall in love with a Salem tree
And a rawhide quirt from Santa Cruz,
I will get me a bottle of Boston sea
And a blue-gum nigger to sing me blues.
I am tired of loving a foreign muse.

Rue des Martyrs and Bleeding-Heart-Yard,
Senlis, Pisa, and Blindman's Oast,
It is a magic ghost you guard

But I am sick for a newer ghost,
Harrisburg, Spartanburg, Painted Post.

Henry and John were never so
And Henry and John were always right?
Granted, but when it was time to go
And the tea and the laurels had stood all night,
Did they never watch for Nantucket Light?

I shall not rest quiet in Montparnasse.
I shall not lie easy at Winchelsea.
You may bury my body in Sussex grass,
You may bury my tongue at Champmédy.
I shall not be there. I shall rise and pass.
Bury my heart at Wounded Knee.

JOHN DOS PASSOS

THE 42ND PARALLEL

1930

John Dos Passos (1896–1970), born in Chicago to a Portuguese American family, first became prominent in literary circles after World War I. His trilogy *U.S.A.* (1930, 1932, 1936) is his best-known work, interweaving biography, narrative, quotations from periodicals of the day, and stream-of-consciousness technique into a portrait of American society from 1900 to the 1930s.

U.S.A.

The young man walks fast by himself through the crowd that thins into the night streets; feet are tired from hours of walking; eyes greedy for warm curve of faces, answering flicker of eyes, the set of a head, the lift of a shoulder, the way hands spread and clench; blood tingles with wants; mind is a beehive of hopes buzzing and stinging; muscles ache for the knowledge of jobs, for the roadmender's pick and shovel work, the fisherman's knack with a hook when he hauls on the slithery net from the rail of the lurching trawler, the swing of the bridgeman's arm as he slings down the whitehot rivet, the engineer's slow grip wise on the throttle, the dirt-farmer's use of his whole body when, whoaing the mules, he yanks the plow from the furrow. The young man walks by himself searching through the crowd with greedy eyes, greedy ears taut to hear, by himself, alone.

The streets are empty. People have packed into subways, climbed into streetcars and buses; in the stations they've scampered for suburban trains; they've filtered into lodgings and tenements, gone up in elevators into apartmenthouses. In a showwindow two sallow windowdressers in their shirtsleeves are bringing out a dummy girl in a red evening dress, at a corner welders in masks lean into sheets of blue flame repairing a cartrack, a few drunk bums shamble along, a sad street-walker fidgets under an arclight. From the river comes the deep rumbling whistle of a steamboat leaving dock. A tug hoots far away.

The young man walks by himself, fast but not fast enough, far but not far enough (faces slide out of sight, talk trails into tattered scraps, footsteps tap fainter in alleys); he must catch the last subway, the streetcar, the bus, run up the gangplanks of all the steamboats, register at all the hotels, work in the cities, answer the wantads, learn the trades, take up the jobs, live in all the boardinghouses, sleep in all the beds. One bed is not enough, one job is not enough, one life is not enough. At night, head swimming with wants, he walks by himself alone.

No job, no woman, no house, no city.

Only the ears busy to catch the speech are not alone; the ears are caught tight, linked tight by the tendrils of phrased words, the turn of a joke, the singsong fade of a story, the gruff fall of a sentence; linking tendrils of speech twine through the city blocks, spread over pavements, grow out along broad parked avenues, speed with the trucks leaving on their long night runs over roaring highways, whisper down sandy byroads past wornout farms, joining up cities and fillingstations, roundhouses, steamboats, planes groping along airways; words call out on mountain pastures, drift slow down rivers widening to the sea and the hushed beaches.

It was not in the long walks through jostling crowds at night that he was less alone, or in the training camp at Allentown, or in the day on the docks at Seattle, or in the empty reek of Washington City hot boyhood summer nights, or in the meal on Market Street, or in the swim off the red rocks at San Diego, or in the bed full of fleas in New Orleans, or in the cold razorwind off the lake, or in the gray faces trembling in the grind of gears in the street under Michigan Avenue, or in the smokers of limited expresstrains, or walking across country, or riding up the dry mountain canyons, or the night without a sleepingbag among frozen beartracks in the Yellowstone, or canoeing Sundays on the Quinnipiac;

but in his mother's words telling about longago, in his father's telling about when I was a boy, in the kidding stories of uncles, in the lies the kids told at school, the hired man's yarns, the tall tales the doughboys told after taps;

it was speech that clung to the ears, the link that tingled in the blood; U.S.A.

U.S.A. is the slice of a continent. U.S.A. is a group of holding companies, some aggregations of trade unions, a set of laws bound in calf, a radio network, a chain of moving picture theatres, a column of stockquotations rubbed out and written in by a Western Union boy on a blackboard, a public-library full of old newspapers and dogeared historybooks with protests scrawled on the margins in pencil. U.S.A. is the world's greatest rivervalley fringed with mountains and hills, U.S.A. is a set of bigmouthed officials with too many bankaccounts. U.S.A. is a lot of men buried in their uniforms in Arlington Cemetery. U.S.A. is the letters at the end of an address when you are away from home. But mostly U.S.A. is the speech of the people.

KOSTI RUOHOMAA, "Three Quarter Century Club" picnic, Portland, Maine, 1947.

You're the Top

1934

Cole Porter (1891–1964), born into an affluent family and educated at Yale and Harvard, went on to become one of the musical theater's greatest lyricists and composers. He celebrated the high society of his day in a series of smash Broadway musicals such as *Anything Goes* (1934), *Kiss Me Kate* (1948), and *Silk Stockings* (1955). He also had a successful Hollywood career, composing movie scores for *Born to Dance* (1936) and *High Society* (1956). Among his best-known songs are "Night and Day," "Let's Do It," and "It's Too Darn Hot."

(Verse 1)

At words poetic, I'm so pathetic

That I always have found it best,

Instead of getting 'em off my chest,

To let 'em rest unexpressed.

I hate parading my serenading

As I'll probably miss a bar,

But if this ditty is not so pretty,

At least it'll tell you how great you are.

(Chorus 1)

You're the top! You're the Colosseum,

You're the top! You're the Louvre Museum,

You're a melody from a symphony by Strauss,

You're a Bendel bonnet, a Shakespeare sonnet,

You're Mickey Mouse.

You're the Nile, You're the Tow'r of Pisa,

You're the smile on the Mona Lisa.

I'm a worthless check, a total wreck, a flop,

But if, Baby, I'm the bottom,

You're the top!

(Verse 2)

Your words poetic are not pathetic

On the other hand, boy, you shine

And I can feel after every line

A thrill divine down my spine.

Now gifted humans like Vincent Youmans
Might think that your song is bad,
But for a person who's just rehearsin'
Well I gotta say this my lad:

(Chorus 2)
You're the top! You're Mahatma Gandhi.
You're the top! You're Napoleon brandy.
You're the purple light of a summer night in Spain,
You're the National Gall'ry, You're Garbo's sal'ry,
You're cellophane.
You're sublime, You're a turkey dinner.
You're the time of the Derby winner.
I'm a toy balloon that is fated soon to pop.
But if, Baby, I'm the bottom,
You're the top!

(Chorus 3)
You're the top! You're a Ritz hot toddy.
You're the top! You're a Brewster body.
You're the boats that glide on the sleepy Zuider Zee,
You're a Nathan Panning, You're Bishop Manning,
You're broccoli.
You're a prize, You're a night at Coney,
You're the eyes of Irene Bordoni,
I'm a broken doll, a fol-de-rol, a blop,
But if, Baby, I'm the bottom,
You're the top.

(Chorus 4)
You're the top! You're an Arrow collar.
You're the top! You're a Coolidge dollar.
You're the nimble tread of the feet of Fred Astaire,
You're an O'Neill drama, You're Whistler's mama,
You're Camembert.
You're a rose, You're Inferno's Dante,
You're the nose of the great Durante.
I'm just in the way, as the French would say
"De trop,"

But if, Baby, I'm the bottom,
You're the top.

(Chorus 5)
You're the top! You're a Waldorf salad.
You're the top! You're a Berlin ballad.
You're a baby grand of a lady and a gent.
You're an old Dutch master, You're Mrs. Astor,
You're Pepsodent.
You're romance, You're the steppes of Russia,
You're the pants on a Roxy usher.
I'm a lazy lout that's just about to stop,
But if Baby, I'm the bottom,
You're the top!

(Chorus 6)
You're the top! You're a dance in Bali.
You're the top! You're a hot tamale.
You're an angel, you're simply too, too, too diveen,
You're a Botticelli, You're Keats, You're Shelley,
You're Ovaltine.
You're a boon, You're the dam at Boulder,
You're the moon over Mae West's shoulder.
I'm a nominee of the G.O.P. or GOP,
But if, Baby, I'm the bottom,
You're the top!

(Chorus 7)
You're the top! You're the Tower of Babel.
You're the top! You're the Whitney Stable.
By the River Rhine, You're a sturdy stein of beer
You're a dress from Saks's, You're next year's taxes,
You're stratosphere.
You're my thoist, You're a Drumstick Lipstick,
You're da foist in da Irish svispstick,
I'm a frightened frog that can find no log to hop,
But if, Baby, I'm the bottom,
You're the top!

THOMAS WOLFE

THE STORY OF A NOVEL

1936

The novels of Thomas Wolfe (1900–1938) chronicle the classic American journey of a young Southerner who travels north and to Europe in search of himself. Wolfe's autobiographical novels, *Look Homeward, Angel* (1929) and *Of Time and the River* (1935), are characterized by lyrical descriptions of place and the author's search for meaning and faith. In *The Story of a Novel*, Wolfe describes the process of writing his second novel.

The life of the artist at any epoch of man's history has not been an easy one. And here in America, it has often seemed to me, it may well be the hardest life that man has ever known. I am not speaking of some frustration in our native life, some barrenness of spirit, some arid Philistinism which contends against the artist's life and which prevents his growth. I do not speak of these things because I do not put the same belief in them that I once did. I am speaking as I have tried to speak from first to last in the concrete terms of the artist's actual experience, of the nature of the physical task before him. It seems to me that the task is one whose physical proportions are vaster and more difficult here than in any other nation on the earth. It is not merely that in the cultures of Europe and of the Orient the American artist can find no antecedent scheme, no structural plan, no body of tradition that can give his own work the validity and truth that it must have. It is not merely that he must make somehow a new tradition for himself, derived from his own life and from the enormous space and energy of American life, the structure of his own design; it is not merely that he is confronted by these problems; it is even more than this, that the labor of a complete and whole articulation, the discovery of an entire universe and of a complete language, is the task that lies before him.

Such is the nature of the struggle to which henceforth our lives must be devoted. Out of the billion forms of America, out of the savage violence and the dense complexity of all its swarming life; from the unique and single substance of this land and life of ours, must we draw the power and energy of our own life, the articulation of our speech, the substance of our art.

For here it seems to me in hard and honest ways like these we may find the tongue, the language, and the conscience that as men and artists we have got to have. Here, too, perhaps, must we who have no more than what we have, who know no more than what we know, who are no more than what we are, find our America. Here, at this present hour and moment of my life, I seek for mine.

TRUMAN CAPOTE

HOLLYWOOD

1950

Novelist, screenwriter, and literary celebrity Truman Capote (1924–1984) was born in New Orleans and spent his childhood with family relatives in Alabama and in New York City after his mother remarried. His first novel, *Other Voices, Other Rooms* (1948), brought him early acclaim, and *In Cold Blood* (1966), the chilling tale of the murder of a Kansas family, launched Capote into fame and stardom. Possessing a keen reporter's eye, a decade earlier Capote had published a collection of travel essays, *Local Color* (1950), from which this selection is taken.

Approaching Los Angeles, at least by air, is like, I should imagine, crossing the surface of the moon: prehistoric shapes, looming in stone ripples and corroded, leer upward, and paleozoic fish swim in the shadowy pools between desert mountains: burned and frozen, there is no living thing, only rock that was once a bird, bones that are sand, ferns turned to fiery stone. At last a welcoming fleet of clouds; we have crept between a sorcerer's passage, snow is on the mountains, yet flowers color the land, a summer sun juxtaposes December's winter sea, down, down, the plane splits through plumed, gold, incredible air. Oh, moaned Thelma, I can't stand it, she said, and poured a cascade of Chiclets into her mouth. Thelma had boarded the plane in Chicago; she was a young Negro girl, rather pretty, beautifully dressed, and it was the most wonderful thing that would ever happen to her, this trip to California. "I know it's going to be grand. Three years I've been ushering at the Lola Theatre on State Street just to save the fare. My auntie tells the cards, and she said—Thelma, honey, head for Hollywood 'cause there's a job as private secretary to a movie actress just waiting for you. She didn't say what actress, though. I hope it's not Esther Williams. I don't like swimming much."

Later on she asked if I was trying for film work, and because the idea seemed to please her, I said yes. On the whole she was very encouraging, and assured me that as soon as she was established as a private secretary, thereby having access to the ears of the great, she would not forget me, would indeed give me every assistance.

At the airport I helped with her luggage, and eventually we shared a taxi. It came about then that she had no place specific to go, she simply wanted the driver to let her off in the "middle" of Hollywood. It was a long drive, and she sat all the way on the edge of the seat, unbearably watchful. But there was not so much to see as she'd imagined. "It don't look correct," she said finally, quite as if we'd been played a wretched trick, for here again, though in disguise, was the surface of the moon, the noplace of everywhere; but how very correct, after all, that here at continent's end we should find only a dumping ground for all that is most exploitedly American: oil pumps pounding like the heartbeat of demons, avenues of used-car lots, supermarkets, motels, the gee dad I never knew a Chevrolet gee dad gee mom whiz wham of publicity, the biggest, broadest, best, sprawled and helplessly etherized by immaculate sunshine and sound of sea and unearthly sweetness of flowers blooming in December.

During the drive the sky had grown ash-colored, and as we turned into the laundered sparkle of Wilshire Boulevard, Thelma, giving her delicate feathered hat a protective touch, grumbled at the possibility of rain. Not a chance, said the driver, just wind blowing in dust from the desert. These words were not out of his mouth before the palm trees shivered under a violent downpour. But Thelma had no place to go, except into the street, so we left her standing there, rain pulling her costume apart. When a traffic light stopped us at the corner, she ran up and stuck her head in the window. "Look here, honey, remember what I say, you get hungry or anything you just find where I'm at." Then, with a lovely smile, "And listen, honey, lotsa luck!"

WALKER PERCY

THE LAST GENTLEMAN

1966

Walker Percy (1916–1990), a Southerner, was trained as a physician and psychiatrist before he contracted tuberculosis in 1942 and was confined to a sanatorium for two years. His first novel, *The Moviegoer* (1961), won the National Book Award. His later works include *The Last Gentleman* (1966), *Lancelot* (1977), and *The Second Coming* (1980). A Catholic and an existentialist, Percy used his novels to explore language, faith, and the search for a meaningful life.

New York is full of people from small towns who are quite content to live obscure lives in some out-of-the-way corner of the city. Here there is no one to keep track. Though such a person might have come from a long line of old settlers and a neighborhood rich in memories, now he chooses to live in a flat on 231st Street, pick up the paper and milk on the doorstep every morning, and speak to the elevator man. In Southern genealogies there is always mention of a cousin who went to live in New York in 1922 and not another word. One hears that people go to New York to seek their fortunes, but many go to seek just the opposite.

In his case, though, it was part of a family pattern. Over the years his family had turned ironical and lost its gift for action. It was an honorable and violent family, but gradually the violence had been deflected and turned inward. The great grandfather knew what was what and said so and acted accordingly and did not care what anyone thought. He even wore a pistol in a holster like a Western hero and once met the Grand Wizard of the Ku Klux Klan in a barbershop and invited him then and there to shoot it out in the street. The next generation, the grandfather, seemed to know what was what but he was not really so sure. He was brave but he gave much thought to the business of being brave. He too would have shot it out with the Grand Wizard if only he could have made certain it was the thing to do. The father was a brave man too and he said he didn't care what others thought, but he did care. More than anything else, he wished to act with honor and to be thought well of by other men. So living for him was a strain. He became ironical. For him it was not a small thing to walk down the street on an ordinary September morning. In the end he was killed by his own irony and sadness and by the strain of living out an ordinary day in a perfect dance of honor.

As for the present young man, the last of the line, he did not know what to think. So he became a watcher and a listener and a wanderer. He could not get enough of watching. Once when he was a boy, a man next door had gone crazy and had sat out in his back yard pitching gravel around and hollering out to his enemies in a loud angry voice. The boy watched him all day, squatted down and watched him, his mouth open and drying. It seemed to him that if he could figure out what was wrong with the man he would learn the great secret of life.

Like many young men in the South, he became overly subtle and had trouble ruling out the possible. They are not like an immigrant's son in Passaic who decides to become a dentist and that is that. Southerners have trouble ruling out the possible. What happens to a man to whom all things seem possible and every course of action open? Nothing of course. Except war. If a man lives in the sphere of the possible and waits for something to happen, what he is waiting for is war—or the end of the world. That is why Southerners like to fight and make good soldiers. In war the possible becomes actual through no doing of one's own.

HOW TO TAME A WILD TONGUE

1987

Gloria Anzaldúa (1942–), writer, poet, lecturer, and political activist, grew up working the fields of rural Texas and Arkansas alongside her immigrant Mexican family. She taught the children of migrant workers before becoming one of the first writers to explore the Hispanic struggle to negotiate the social and linguistic rules of the dominant Anglo culture. In "How to Tame a Wild Tongue" (1987), Anzaldúa writes in both Spanish and English, intertwining the two cultures.

"We're going to have to control your tongue," the dentist says, pulling out all the metal from my mouth. Silver bits plop and tinkle into the basin. My mouth is a motherlode.

The dentist is cleaning out my roots. I get a whiff of the stench when I gasp. "I can't cap that tooth yet, you're still draining," he says.

"We're going to have to do something about your tongue," I hear the anger rising in his voice. My tongue keeps pushing out the wads of cotton, pushing back the drills, the long thin needles. "I've never seen anything as strong or as stubborn," he says. And I think, how do you tame a wild tongue, train it to be quiet, how do you bridle and saddle it? How do you make it lie down?

> *Who is to say that robbing a people of*
> *its language is less violent than war?*
> —RAY GWYN SMITH

I remember being caught speaking Spanish at recess—that was good for three licks on the knuckles with a sharp ruler. I remember being sent to the corner of the classroom for "talking back" to the Anglo teacher when all I was trying to do was tell her how to pronounce my name. "If you want to be American, speak 'American.' If you don't like it, go back to Mexico where you belong."

"I want you to speak English. *Pa' hallar buen trabajo tienes que saber hablar el inglés bien. Qué vale toda tu educación si todavía hablas inglés con un* 'accent,' " my mother would say, mortified that I spoke English like a Mexican. At Pan American University, I, and all Chicano students, were required to take two speech classes. Their purpose: to get rid of our accents.

Attacks on one's form of expression with the intent to censor are a violation of the First Amendment. *El Anglo con cara de inocente nos arrancó la lengua.* Wild tongues can't be tamed, they can only be cut out. . . .

So if you want to really hurt me, talk badly about my language. Ethnic identity is twin skin to linguistic identity—I am my language. Until I can take pride in my language, I cannot take pride in myself. Until I can accept as legitimate Chicano Texas Spanish, Tex-Mex and all the other languages I speak, I cannot accept the legitimacy of myself. Until I am free to write bilingually and to switch codes without having always to translate, while I still have to speak English or Spanish when I would rather speak Spanglish, and as long as I have to accommodate the English speakers rather than having them accommodate me, my tongue will be illegitimate. . . .

Nosotros los Chicanos straddle the borderlands. On one side of us, we are constantly exposed to the Spanish of the Mexicans, on the other side we hear the Anglos' incessant clamoring so that we forget our language. Among ourselves we don't say *nosotros los americanos, o nosotros los españoles, o nosotros los hispanos*. We say *nosotros los mexicanos* (by *mexicanos* we do not mean citizens of Mexico; we do not mean a national identity, but a racial one). We distinguish between *mexicanos del otro lado* and *mexicanos de este lado*. Deep in our hearts we believe that being Mexican has nothing to do with which country one lives in. Being Mexican is a state of soul—not one of mind, not one of citizenship. Neither eagle nor serpent, but both. And like the ocean, neither animal respects borders.

> Dime con quien andas y te diré quien eres.
> *(Tell me who your friends are and I'll tell you who you are.)*
> —MEXICAN SAYING

. . . Chicanos and other people of color suffer economically for not acculturating. This voluntary (yet forced) alienation makes for psychological conflict, a kind of dual identity—we don't identify with the Anglo-American cultural values and we don't totally identify with the Mexican cultural values. We are a synergy of two cultures with various degrees of Mexicanness or Angloness. I have so internalized the borderland conflict that sometimes I feel like one cancels out the other and we are zero, nothing, no one. *A veces no soy nada ni nadie. Pero hasta cuando no lo soy, lo soy.*

When not copping out, when we know we are more than nothing, we call ourselves Mexican, referring to race and ancestry; *mestizo* when affirming both our Indian and Spanish (but we hardly ever own our Black ancestry); Chicano when referring to a politically aware people born and/or raised in the U.S.; Raza when referring to Chicanos; *tejanos* when we are Chicanos from Texas.

Chicanos did not know we were a people until 1965 when Ceasar Chavez and the farmworkers united and *I Am Joaquín* was published and *la Raza Unida* party was formed in Texas. With the recognition, we became a distinct people. Something momentous happened to the Chicano soul—we became aware of our reality and acquired a name and a language (Chicano Spanish) that reflected that reality. Now that we had a name, some of the fragmented pieces began to fall together—who we were, what we were, how we had evolved. We began to get glimpses of what we might eventually become.

Yet the struggle of identities continues, the struggle of borders is our reality still. One day the inner struggle will cease and a true integration take place. In the meantime, *tenémos que hacer la lucha. ¿Quién está protegiendo los ranchos de mi gente? ¿Quién está tratando de cerrar la fisura entre la india y el blanco en nuestra sangre? El Chicano, si, el Chicano que anda como un ladrón en su propia casa.*

Los Chicanos, how patient we seem, how very patient. There is the quiet of the Indian about us. We know how to survive. When other races have given up their tongue, we've kept ours. We know what it is to live under the hammer blow of the dominant *norteamericano* culture. But more than we count the blows, we count the days the weeks the years the centuries the eons until the white laws and commerce and customs will rot in deserts they've created, lie bleached. *Humildes* yet proud, *quietos* yet wild, *nosotros los mexicanos-Chicanos* will walk by the crumbling ashes as we go about our business. Stubborn, persevering, impenetrable as stone, yet possessing a malleability that renders us unbreakable, we, the *mestizas* and *mestizos*, will remain.

ANNA QUINDLEN

A COUNTRY AND A CONUNDRUM

2002

Journalist, novelist, and mother, Anna Quindlen (1953–) is one of America's best-known writers. She won a Pulitzer Prize in 1992 for her *New York Times* column "Public and Private" and is the author of three best-selling novels, *Object Lessons, One True Thing,* and *Black and Blue,* as well as *A Short Guide to a Happy Life.*

OUT OF MANY, ONE? HOW IN THE WORLD CAN THAT POSSIBLY WORK? JUST WATCH US.

America is an improbable idea. A mongrel nation built of ever changing disparate parts, it is held together by a notion, the notion that all men are created equal, though everyone knows that most men consider themselves better than someone. "Of all the nations in the world, the United States was built in nobody's image," the historian Daniel Boorstin wrote. That's because it was built of bits and pieces that seem discordant, like the crazy quilts that have been one of its great folk art forms, velvet and calico and checks and brocades.

Out of many, one. That is the ideal.

The reality is often quite different, a great nationl striving consisting frequently of failure. Many of the oft-told stories of the most pluralistic nation on earth are stories, not of tolerance, but of bigotry. Slavery and sweatshops, the burning of crosses and the ostracism of the other. Children learn in social studies class and in the news of the lynching of blacks, the denial of rights to women, the murders of gay men. It is difficult to know how to persuade them that this amounts to "crown thy good with brotherhood," that amid all the failures is something spectacularly successful. Perhaps they understand it at this moment, when enormous tragedy, as it so often does, demands a time of reflection on enormous blessings.

This is a nation founded on a conundrum, what Mario Cuomo has characterized as "community added to individualism." These two are our defining ideals; they are also in constant conflict. Historians today bemoan the ascendancy of a kind of prideful apartheid in America, saying that the clinging to ethnicity, in background and custom, has undermined the concept of unity. These historians must have forgotten the past, or have gilded it. The New York of my children is no more Balkanized, probably less so, than the Philadelphia of my father, in which Jewish boys would walk several blocks out of their way to avoid the Irish divide of Chester

Avenue. (I was the product of a mixed marriage, across barely bridgeable lines: an Italian girl, an Irish boy. How quaint it seems now, how incendiary then.) The Brooklyn of Francie Nolan's famous tree, the Newark of which Portnoy complained, even the uninflected WASP suburbs of Cheever's characters: they are ghettos, pure and simple. Do the Cambodians and the Mexicans in California coexist less easily today than did the Irish and Italians of Massachusetts a century ago? You know the answer.

What is the point of this splintered whole? What is the point of a nation in which Arab cabbies chauffeur Jewish passengers through the streets of New York—and in which Jewish cabbies chauffeur Arab passengers, too, and yet speak in theory of hatred, one for the other? What is the point of a nation in which one part seems to be always on the verge of fisticuffs with another, blacks and whites gays and straights, left and right, Pole and Chinese and Puerto Rican and Slovenian? Other countries with such divisions have in fact divided into new nations with new names, but not this one, impossibly interwoven even in its hostilities.

Once these disparate parts were held together by a common enemy, by the fault lines of the world wars and the electrified fence of communism. With the end of the cold war there was the creeping concern that without a focus for hatred and distrust, a sense of national identity would evaporate, that the left side of the hyphen—African-American, Mexican-American, Irish-American—would overwhelm the right. And slow-growing domestic traumas like economic unrest and increasing crime seemed more likely to emphasize division than community. Yet in 1994, the overwhelming majority of those surveyed by the National Opinion Research Center agreed with this statement: "The U.S. is a unique country that stands for something special in the world."

One of the things that it stands for is this vexing notion that a great nation can consist entirely of refugees from other nations, that people of different, even warring religions and cultures can live, if not side by side, then on either side of the country's Chester Avenues. Faced with this diversity there is little point in trying to isolate anything remotely resembling a national character, but there are two strains of behavior that, however tenuously, abet the concept of unity.

There is that Calvinist undercurrent in the American psyche that loves the difficult, the demanding, that sees mastering the impossible, whether it be prairie or subway, as a test of character, and so glories in the struggle of this fractured coalescing. And there is a grudging fairness among the citizens of the United States that eventually leads most to admit that, no matter what the English-only advocates try to suggest, the new immigrants are not so different from our own parents or grandparents. Lionel Castillo, former director of the Immigration and Naturalization Service and himself the grandson of Mexican immigrants, once told the writer Studs Terkel proudly, "The old neighborhood Ma-Pa stores are still around. They are not Italian or Jewish or Eastern European any more. Ma and Pa are now Korean, Vietnamese, Iraqi, Jordanian, Latin American. They live in the store. They work seven days a week. Their kids are doing well in school. They're making it. Sound familiar?"

Tolerance is the word used most often when this kind of coexistence succeeds, but tolerance is a vanilla pudding word, standing for little more than the allowance of letting others live unremarked and unmolested. Pride seems excessive, given the American willingness to endlessly complain about them, them being whoever is new, different, unknown or currently under suspicion. But patriotism is partly taking pride in this unlikely ability to throw all of us together in a country that across its length and breadth is as different as a dozen countries, and still be able to call it by one name. When photographs of the faces of all of those who died in the World Trade Center destruction are assembled in one place, it will be possible to trace in the skin color, the shape of the eyes and the noses, the texture of the hair, a map of the world. These are the representatives of a mongrel nation that somehow, at times like this, has one spirit. Like many improbable ideas, when it actually works, it's a wonder.

MARK SHAW, Jacqueline Kennedy and Caroline Kennedy, Hyannis Port, Massachusetts, 1959.

RULE OF LAW

GEORGE TAMES, Studying the Constitution, The National Archives Building, Washington, D.C., 1964.

OLIVER WENDELL HOLMES JR., the great Supreme Court justice and son of the poet, captured the genius of our government when he wrote of the Constitution, "It is an experiment, as all life is an experiment." Now the oldest written Constitution in the world, it has succeeded in part because it provides within it the mechanism for peaceful change. Its structure prevents the abuse of power by any one of the three branches of government, and protects the rights of minorities. Throughout our history, it has provided the stability and flexibility necessary for democracy to thrive. These selections show the Constitution in action and reflect the deep commitment Americans feel to the rule of law.

Today, we assume that the Constitution must always have seemed like the inspired creation of a collective genius. We take for granted the separation of powers, the system of checks and balances that we learn about in school, often with our eyes glazing over. But, in fact, the Constitution was drafted in 1787 because our early government was falling apart, and even then, some of our founding fathers like Thomas Jefferson and Patrick Henry originally opposed its ratification, believing that its strong central government could overwhelm the states, bringing a return to tyranny. They also objected that it did not provide sufficient protection for individual rights. Others, like Benjamin Franklin and James Madison, supported the Constitution but believed a Bill of Rights should be added (which was done in 1789 and ratified in 1791). In the landmark Supreme Court decision *Marbury v. Madison*, Chief Justice John Marshall set forth the principle of judicial review, which placed the judicial branch on a par with the executive and legislative branches and continues to play a critical role in preserving our freedom and democracy.

Other documents show our reliance on the rule of law in times of crisis. In his First Inaugural Address, Abraham Lincoln makes a powerful argument that the Union is perpetual, the Constitution is its fundamental law, and secession is illegal. He attempted to reassure Southerners that their constitutional rights had not been violated and that war would come only as a result of their aggression. One month later, on April 12, Confederate forces attacked Fort Sumter and the Civil War began.

A century later, the civil rights movement used the law to transform American society and force America to live up to the promises of the Declaration of Independence, the Constitution, and the Civil War. In March 1965, after a young black man was shot and killed during an Alabama march for the right to vote, the civil rights leadership decided to march from Selma to Montgomery to dramatize their struggle to participate in the democratic process. Governor George Wallace and Sheriff Jim Clark forbade the march and deputized a posse of local white men to enforce the prohibition. They beat the marchers with nightsticks and bullwhips. But the nation had witnessed the events on television, and eight days later, President Johnson, speaking before a joint session of Congress, condemned the violence and called for the passage of the Voting Rights Act, which was signed into law on August 6, 1965.

The day when I feel most proud to be an American is not the Fourth of July, but Election Day. The right to vote is perhaps the most critical right in a democracy, the means by which we can create the kind of society that truly represents America. A woman who had been the victim of FBI harassment and who had sacrificed twenty years fighting for her First Amendment rights once said to me, "It is up to us to create a government that is close to our heart's desire. Because," she added, "if you don't do it, somebody else will." One only has to look at the lengths to which people went to deny others the right to vote to understand that we should never take its importance for granted, nor forget that it is an opportunity as well as an obligation.

The Constitution also provides for an orderly transfer of power in extraordinary circumstances. The resignation of President Richard Nixon, under the threat of impeachment proceedings, and his subsequent pardon by President Gerald Ford show how our Constitution provides stability in times of crisis. The election of 2000 challenged our system as few events have, putting the right to vote itself on trial, as well as the power of judicial review. However, our acceptance of the process and eventual outcome renewed our belief in the rule of law.

The Constitution of the United States

1787

Americans were reluctant to submit to a strong central authority after throwing off the tyranny of the British king; hence, our first attempt at constructing a national government—the 1777 Articles of Confederation—was so weak that it proved unworkable. On the second try, in 1787, delegates to the Constitutional Convention drafted a document providing for a stronger national government that could levy taxes and provide for the common defense. The Constitution sets forth the relationship between the states and the federal government and divides federal power among the executive, legislative, and judicial branches. It has been amended numerous times, most significantly to add a Bill of Rights in 1791, and to end slavery, enfranchise African Americans, and provide due process of law after the Civil War. It is the world's oldest written constitution.

We, the People of the United States, in Order to form a more perfect Union, establish Justice, insure domestic Tranquility, provide for the common defence, promote the general Welfare, and secure the Blessings of Liberty to ourselves and our Posterity, do ordain and establish this Constitution for the United States of America.

ARTICLE I

Section 1. All legislative Powers herein granted shall be vested in a Congress of the United States, which shall consist of a Senate and House of Representatives.

Section 2. [1] The House of Representatives shall be composed of Members chosen every second Year by the People of the several States, and the Electors in each State shall have the Qualifications requisite for Electors of the most numerous Branch of the State Legislature.

[2] No Person shall be a Representative who shall not have attained to the age of twenty five Years, and been seven Years a Citizen of the United States, and who shall not, when elected, be an inhabitant of that State in which he shall be chosen.

[3] Representatives and direct Taxes shall be apportioned among the several States which may be included within this Union, according to their respective Numbers, which shall be determined by adding to the whole Number of free Persons, including those bound to Service for a Term of Years, and excluding Indians not taxed, three fifths of all other Persons. The actual Enumeration shall be made within three Years after the first Meeting of the Congress of the United States, and within every subsequent Term of ten Years, in such a Manner as they shall by Law direct. The Number of Representatives shall not exceed one for every thirty Thousand, but each State shall have at Least one Representative; and until such enumeration shall

be made, the State of New Hampshire shall be entitled to chuse three, Massachusetts eight, Rhode Island and Providence Plantations one, Connecticut five, New York six, New Jersey four, Pennsylvania eight, Delaware one, Maryland six, Virginia ten, North Carolina five, South Carolina five, and Georgia three.

[4] When vacancies happen in the Representation from any State, the Executive Authority thereof shall issue Writs of Election to fill such Vacancies.

[5] The House of Representatives shall chuse their Speaker and other Officers; and shall have the sole Power of Impeachment.

Section 3. [1] The Senate of the United States shall be composed of two Senators from each State, chosen by the Legislature thereof, for six Years; and each Senator shall have one Vote.

[2] Immediately after they shall be assembled in Consequence of the first Election, they shall be divided as equally as may be into three Classes. The Seats of the Senators of the first Class shall be vacated at the Expiration of the Second Year, of the second Class at the Expiration of the fourth Year, and of the third Class at the Expiration of the sixth Year, so that one third may be chosen every second Year; and if Vacancies happen by Resignation, or otherwise, during the Recess of the Legislature of any State, the Executive thereof may make temporary Appointments until the next Meeting of the Legislature, which shall then fill such Vacancies.

[3] No Person shall be a Senator who shall not have attained to the Age of thirty Years, and been nine Years a Citizen of the United States, and who shall not, when elected, be an Inhabitant of that State for which he shall be chosen.

[4] The Vice President of the United States shall be President of the Senate, but shall have no Vote, unless they be equally divided.

[5] The Senate shall chuse their other Officers, and also a President pro tempore, in the Absence of the Vice President, or when he shall exercise the Office of the President of the United States.

[6] The Senate shall have the sole Power to try all Impeachments. When sitting for that Purpose, they shall be on Oath or Affirmation. When the President of the United States is tried, the Chief Justice shall preside: And no Person shall be convicted without the Concurrence of two thirds of the Members present.

[7] Judgment in Cases of Impeachment shall not extend further than to removal from Office, and disqualification to hold and enjoy any Office of honor, Trust, or Profit under the United States: but the Party convicted shall nevertheless be liable and subject to Indictment, Trial, Judgment, and Punishment, according to Law.

Section 4. [1] The Times, Places and Manner of holding Elections for Senators and Representatives, shall be prescribed in each State by the Legislature thereof; but the Congress may at any time by Law make or alter such Regulations, except as to the Places of chusing Senators.

[2] The Congress shall assemble at least once in every Year, and such meeting shall be on the first Monday in December, unless they shall by Law appoint a different Day.

Section 5. [1] Each House shall be the Judge of the Elections, Returns, and Qualifications of its own Members, and a Majority of each shall constitute a Quorum to do Business; but a smaller Number may adjourn from day to day, and may be authorized to compel the Attendance of absent Members, in such Manner, and under such Penalties as each House may provide.

[2] Each House may determine the Rules of its Proceedings, punish its Members for disorderly Behaviour, and, with the Concurrence of two thirds, expel a Member.

[3] Each House shall keep a journal of its Proceedings, and from time to time publish the same, excepting such Parts as may in their Judgment require Secrecy; and the Yeas and Nays of the Members of either House on any question shall, at the Desire of one fifth of those Present, be entered on the Journal.

[4] Neither House, during the session of Congress, shall, without the Consent of the other, adjourn for more than three days, nor to any other Place than that in which the two Houses shall be sitting.

Section 6. [1] The Senators and Representatives shall receive a Compensation for their Services, to be ascertained by Law, and paid out of the Treasury of the United States. They shall in all Cases, except Treason, Felony and Breach of the Peace, be privileged from Arrest during their Attendance at the Session of their respective Houses, and in going to and returning from the same; and for any Speech or Debate in either House, they shall not be questioned in any other Place.

[2] No Senator or Representative shall, during the Time for which he was elected, be appointed to any civil Office under the Authority of the United States, which shall have been created, or the Emoluments whereof shall have been encreased during such time; and no Person holding any Office under the United States shall be a Member of either House during his Continuance in Office.

Section 7. [1] All Bills for raising Revenue shall originate in the House of Representatives; but the Senate may propose or concur with Amendments as on other Bills.

[2] Every Bill which shall have passed the House of Representatives and the Senate, shall, before it becomes a Law, be presented to the President of the United States; If he approves he shall sign it, but if not he shall return it, with his Objec-

tions, to that House in which it shall have originated, who shall enter the Objections at large on their Journal, and proceed to reconsider it. If after such Reconsideration two thirds of that House shall agree to pass the Bill, it shall be sent together with the Objections, to the other House, by which it shall likewise be reconsidered, and if approved by two thirds of that House, it shall become a Law. But in all such Cases the Votes of both Houses shall be determined by yeas and Nays, and the Names of the Persons voting for and against the Bill shall be entered on the Journal of each House respectively. If any Bill shall not be returned by the President within ten Days (Sundays excepted) after it shall have been presented to him, the Same shall be a Law, in like Manner as if he had signed it, unless the Congress by their Adjournment prevent its Return, in which Case it shall not be a Law.

[3] Every Order, Resolution, or Vote, to Which the Concurrence of the Senate and the House of Representatives may be necessary (except on a question of Adjournment) shall be presented to the President of the United States; and before the same shall take Effect, shall be approved by him, or being disapproved by him, shall be repassed by two thirds of the Senate and House of Representatives, according to the Rules and Limitations prescribed in the Case of a Bill.

Section 8. [1] The Congress shall have Power to lay and collect Taxes, Duties, Imposts, and Excises, to pay the Debts and provide for the common Defence and general Welfare of the United States; but all Duties, Imposts, and Excises shall be uniform throughout the United States;

[2] To borrow Money on the credit of the United States;

[3] To regulate Commerce with foreign Nations, and among the several States, and with the Indian Tribes;

[4] To establish an uniform Rule of Naturalization, and uniform Laws on the subject of Bankruptcies throughout the United States;

[5] To coin Money, regulate the Value thereof, and of foreign Coin, and fix the Standard of Weights and Measures;

[6] To provide for the Punishment of counterfeiting the Securities and current Coin of the United States;

[7] To Establish Post Offices and Post Roads;

[8] To promote the Progress of Science and useful Arts, by securing for limited Times to Authors and Inventors the exclusive Right to their respective Writings and Discoveries;

[9] To constitute Tribunals inferior to the supreme Court;

[10] To define and punish Piracies and Felonies committed on the high Seas, and Offences against the Law of Nations;

[11] To declare War, grant Letters of Marque and Reprisal, and make Rules concerning Captures on Land and Water;

[12] To raise and support Armies, but no Appropriation of Money to that Use shall be for a longer Term than two Years;

[13] To provide and maintain a Navy;

[14] To make Rules for the Government and Regulation of the land and naval Forces;

[15] To provide for calling forth the Militia to execute the Laws of the Union, suppress Insurrections and repel Invasions;

[16] To provide for organizing, arming, and disciplining, the Militia, and for governing such Part of them as may be employed in the Service of the United States, reserving to the States respectively, the Appointment of the Officers, and the Authority of training the Militia according to the discipline prescribed by Congress;

[17] To exercise exclusive Legislation in all Cases whatsoever, over such District (not exceeding ten Miles square) as may, by Cession of particular States, and the Acceptance of Congress, become the Seat of the Government of the United States, and to exercise like Authority over all Places purchased by the Consent of the Legislature of the State in which the Same shall be, for the Erection of Forts, Magazines, Arsenals, dock-Yards, and other needful Buildings—And

[18] To make all Laws which shall be necessary and proper for carrying into Execution the foregoing Powers, and all other Powers vested by this Constitution in the Government of the United States, or in any Department or Officer thereof.

Section 9. [1] Migration or Importation of Such Persons as any of the States now existing shall think proper to admit, shall not be prohibited by the Congress prior to the Year one thousand eight hundred and eight, but a Tax or duty may be imposed on such Importation, not exceeding ten dollars for each Person.

[2] The Privilege of the Writ of Habeas Corpus shall not be suspended, unless when in Cases of Rebellion or Invasion the public Safety may require it.

[3] No Bill of Attainder or ex post facto Law shall be passed.

[4] No Capitation, or other direct, Tax shall be laid, unless in Proportion to the Census or Enumeration herein before directed to be taken.

[5] No Tax or Duty shall be laid on Articles exported from any State.

[6] No Preference shall be given by any Regulation of Commerce or Revenue to the Ports of one State over those of another: nor shall Vessels bound to, or from, one State be obliged to enter, clear, or pay Duties in another.

[7] No Money shall be drawn from the Treasury, but in Consequence of Appropriations made by Law; and a regular Statement and Account of the Receipts and

Expenditures of all public Money shall be published from time to time.

[8] No Title of Nobility shall be granted by the United States: And no Person holding any Office of Profit or Trust under them, shall, without the Consent of the Congress, accept of any present, Emolument, Office, or Title, of any kind whatever, from any King, Prince, or foreign State.

Section 10. [1] No State shall enter into any Treaty, Alliance, or Confederation; grant Letters of Marque and Reprisal; coin Money; emit Bills of Credit; make any Thing but gold and silver Coin a Tender in Payment of Debts; pass any Bill of Attainder, ex post facto Law, or Law impairing the Obligation of Contracts, or grant any Title of Nobility.

[2] No State shall, without the Consent of the Congress, lay any Imposts or Duties on Imports or Exports, except what may be absolutely necessary for executing its inspection Laws; and the net Produce of all Duties and Imposts laid by any State on Imports or Exports, shall be for the Use of the Treasury of the United States; and all such Laws shall be subject to the Revision and Controul of the Congress.

[3] No State shall, without the Consent of the Congress, lay any Duty of Tonnage, keep Troops, or Ships of War in time of Peace, enter into any Agreement or Compact with another State, or with a foreign Power, or engage in War, unless actually invaded, or in such imminent Danger as will not admit of delay.

ARTICLE II

Section 1. [1] The executive Power shall be vested in a President of the United States of America. He shall hold his Office during the Term of four Years, and, together with the Vice President, chosen for the same Term, be elected as follows:

[2] Each State shall appoint, in such Manner as the Legislature thereof may direct, a Number of Electors, equal to the whole Number of Senators and Representatives to which the State may be entitled in the Congress; but no Senator or Representative, or Person holding an Office of Trust or Profit under the United States, shall be appointed an Elector.

[3] The Electors shall meet in their respective States, and vote by Ballot for two Persons, of whom one at least shall not be an Inhabitant of the same State with themselves. And they shall make a List of all the Persons voted for, and of the Number of Votes for each; which List they shall sign and certify, and transmit sealed to the Seat of the Government of the United States, directed to the President of the Senate. The President of the Senate shall, in the Presence of the Senate and House of Representatives, open all the Certificates, and the Votes shall then be counted. The Person having the greatest Number of Votes shall be the President, if such

Number be a Majority of the whole Number of Electors appointed; and if there be more than one who have such Majority, and have an equal Number of Votes, then the House of Representatives shall immediately chuse by Ballot one of them for President; and if no Person have a Majority, then from the five highest on the List the said House shall in like Manner chuse the President. But in chusing the President, the Votes shall be taken by States, the Representation from each State having one Vote; A quorum for this Purpose shall consist of a Member or Members from two thirds of the States, and a Majority of all the States shall be necessary to a Choice. In every Case, after the Choice of the President, the Person having the greatest Number of Votes of the Electors shall be the Vice President. But if there should remain two or more who have equal Votes, the Senate shall chuse from them by Ballot the Vice President.

[4] The Congress may determine the Time of chusing the Electors, and the Day on which they shall give their Votes; which Day shall be the same throughout the United States.

[5] No person except a natural born Citizen, or a Citizen of the United States, at the time of the Adoption of this Constitution, shall be eligible to the Office of President; neither shall any Person be eligible to that Office who shall not have attained to the Age of thirty five Years, and been fourteen Years a Resident within the United States.

[6] In case of the removal of the President from Office, or of his Death, Resignation or Inability to discharge the Powers and Duties of the said Office, the Same shall devolve on the Vice President, and the Congress may by Law provide for the Case of Removal, Death, Resignation or Inability, both of the President and Vice President, declaring what Officer shall then act as President, and such Officer shall act accordingly, until the Disability be removed, or a President shall be elected.

[7] The President shall, at stated Times, receive for his Services, a Compensation, which shall neither be increased nor diminished during the Period for which he shall have been elected, and he shall not receive within that Period any other Emolument from the United States, or any of them.

[8] Before he enter on the Execution of his Office, he shall take the following Oath or Affirmation: "I do solemnly swear (or affirm) that I will faithfully execute the Office of President of the United States, and will to the best of my Ability, preserve, protect and defend the Constitution of the United States."

Section 2. [1] The President shall be Commander in Chief of the Army and Navy of the United States, and of the militia of the several States, when called into the actual Service of the United States; he may require the Opinion, in writing, of the principal Officer in each of the executive Departments, upon any Subject relating to the Duties of their respective Offices, and he shall have Power to grant Reprieves and Pardons for Offenses against the United States, except in Cases of Impeachment.

[2] He shall have Power, by and with the Advice and Consent of the Senate, to make Treaties, provided two thirds of the Senators present concur; and he shall nominate, and by and with the Advice and Consent of the Senate, shall appoint Ambassadors, other public Ministers and Consuls, Judges of the supreme Court, and all other Officers of the United States, whose Appointments are not herein otherwise provided for, and which shall be established by Law; but the Congress may by Law vest the Appointment of such inferior Officers, as they think proper, in the President alone, in the Courts of Law, or in the Heads of Departments.

[3] The President shall have Power to fill up all Vacancies that may happen during the Recess of the Senate, by granting Commissions which shall expire at the End of their next Session.

Section 3. He shall from time to time give to the Congress Information of the State of the Union, and recommend to their Consideration such Measures as he shall judge necessary and expedient; he may, on extraordinary Occasions, convene both Houses, or either of them, and in Case of Disagreement between them, with Respect to the Time of Adjournment, he may adjourn them to such Time as he shall think proper; he shall receive Ambassadors and other public Ministers; he shall take Care that the Laws be faithfully executed, and shall Commission all the Officers of the United States.

Section 4. The President, Vice President, and all civil Officers of the United States, shall be removed from Office on Impeachment for, and Conviction of, Treason, Bribery, or other high Crimes and Misdemeanors.

ARTICLE III

Section 1. The judicial Power of the United States, shall be vested in one supreme Court, and in such inferior Courts as the Congress may from time to time ordain and establish. The Judges, both of the supreme and inferior Courts, shall hold their Offices during good Behaviour, and shall, at stated Times, receive for their Services a Compensation, which shall not be diminished during their Continuance in Office.

Section 2. [1] The judicial Power shall extend to all Cases, in Law and Equity, arising under this Constitution, the Laws of the United States, and Treaties made, or which shall be made, under their Authority;—to all Cases affecting Ambassadors, other public Ministers and Consuls;—to all Cases of admiralty and maritime Jurisdiction;—to Controversies to which the United States shall be a Party;—to Controversies between two or more States;—between a State and Citizens of another State;—between Citizens of different States;—between Citizens of the same State claiming Lands under the Grants of different States, and between a State, or the Citizens thereof, and foreign States, Citizens or Subjects.

[2] In all Cases affecting Ambassadors, other public Ministers and Consuls, and those in which a State shall be a Party, the supreme Court shall have original Jurisdiction. In all the other Cases before mentioned, the supreme Court shall have appellate Jurisdiction, both as to Law and Fact, with such Exceptions, and under such Regulations as the Congress shall make.

[3] The trial of all Crimes, except in Cases of Impeachment, shall be by Jury; and such Trial shall be held in the State where the said Crimes shall have been committed; but when not committed within any State, the Trial shall be at such Place or Places as the Congress may by Law have directed.

Section 3. [1] Treason against the United States, shall consist only in levying War against them, or, in adhering to their Enemies, giving them Aid and Comfort. No Person shall be convicted of Treason unless on the Testimony of two Witnesses to the same overt Act, or on Confession in open Court.

[2] The Congress shall have Power to declare the Punishment of Treason, but no Attainder of Treason shall work Corruption of Blood, or Forfeiture except during the Life of the Person attained.

ARTICLE IV

Section 1. Full Faith and Credit shall be given in each State to the public Acts, Records, and judicial Proceedings of every other State. And the Congress may by general Laws prescribe the Manner in which such Acts, Records and Proceedings shall be proved, and the Effect thereof.

Section 2. [1] The Citizens of each State shall be entitled to all Privileges and Immunities of Citizens in the several States.

[2] A Person charged in any State with Treason, Felony, or other Crime, who shall flee from Justice, and be found in another State, shall on demand of the executive Authority of the State from which he fled, be delivered up, to be removed to the State having Jurisdiction of the Crime.

[3] No Person held to Service or Labour in one State, under the Laws thereof, escaping into another, shall, in consequence of any Law or Regulation therein, be discharged from such Service or Labour, but shall be delivered up on Claim of the Party to whom such Service or Labour may be due.

Section 3. [1] New States may be admitted by the Congress into this Union; but no new State shall be formed or erected within the Jurisdiction of any other State; nor any State be formed by the Junction of two or more States, or Parts of States, without the Consent of the Legislatures of the States concerned as well as of the Congress.

[2] The Congress shall have Power to dispose of and make all needful Rules and Regulations respecting the Territory or other Property belonging to the United States; and nothing in this Constitution shall be so construed as to Prejudice any Claims of the United States, or of any particular State.

Section 4. The United States shall guarantee to every State in this Union a Republican Form of Government, and shall protect each of them against Invasion; and on Application of the Legislature, or of the Executive (when the Legislature cannot be convened), against domestic Violence.

ARTICLE V

The Congress, whenever two thirds of both Houses shall deem it necessary, shall propose Amendments to this Constitution, or, on the Application of the legislatures of two thirds of the several States, shall call a Convention for proposing Amendments, which, in either Case, shall be valid to all Intents and Purposes, as part of this Constitution, when ratified by the Legislatures of three fourths of the several States, or by Conventions in three fourths thereof, as the one or the other Mode of Ratification may be proposed by the Congress; Provided that no Amendment which may be made prior to the Year One thousand eight hundred and eight shall in any Manner affect the first and fourth Clauses in the Ninth Section of the first Article; and that no State, without its Consent, shall be deprived of its equal Suffrage in the Senate.

ARTICLE VI

[1] All Debts contracted and Engagements entered into, before the Adoption of this Constitution, shall be as valid against the United States under this Constitution, as under the Confederation.

[2] This Constitution, and the Laws of the United States which shall be made in Pursuance thereof; and all Treaties made, or which shall be made, under the Authority of the United States, shall be the supreme Law of the Land; and the Judges in every State shall be bound thereby, any Thing in the Constitution or Laws of any State to the Contrary notwithstanding.

[3] The Senators and Representatives before mentioned, and the Members of the several State Legislatures, and all executive and judicial Officers, both of the United States and of the several States, shall be bound by Oath or Affirmation, to

support this Constitution; but no religious Test shall ever be required as a Qualification to any Office or public Trust under the United States.

ARTICLE VII

The Ratification of the Conventions of nine States shall be sufficient for the Establishment of this Constitution between the States so ratifying the Same.
Articles in Addition to, and Amendment of, the Constitution of the United States of America, Proposed by Congress, and Ratified by the Legislatures of the Several States Pursuant to the Fifth Article of the original Constitution.

AMENDMENT I [1791]

Congress shall make no law respecting an establishment of religion, or prohibiting the free exercise thereof; or abridging the freedom of speech, or of the press; or the right of the people peaceably to assemble, and to petition the Government for a redress of grievances.

AMENDMENT II [1791]

A well regulated Militia, being necessary to the security of a free State, the right of the people to keep and bear Arms, shall not be infringed.

AMENDMENT III [1791]

No Soldier shall, in time of peace be quartered in any house, without the consent of the owner, nor in time of war, but in a manner to be prescribed by law.

AMENDMENT IV [1791]

The right of the people to be secure in their persons, houses, papers, and effects, against unreasonable searches and seizures, shall not be violated, and no Warrants shall issue, but upon probable cause, supported by Oath or affirmation, and particularly describing the place to be searched, and the persons or things to be seized.

AMENDMENT V [1791]

No person shall be held to answer for a capital, or otherwise infamous crime, unless on a presentment or indictment of a Grand Jury, except in cases arising in the land or naval forces, or in the Militia, when in actual service in time of War or public danger; nor shall any person be subject for the same offence to be twice put in jeopardy of life or limb; nor shall be compelled in any criminal case to be a witness against himself, nor be deprived of life, liberty, or property, without due process of law; nor shall private property be taken for public use, without just compensation.

AMENDMENT VI [1791]

In all criminal prosecutions, the accused shall enjoy the right to a speedy and public trial, by an impartial jury of the State and district wherein the crime shall have been committed, which district shall have been previously ascertained by law, and to be informed of the nature and cause of the accusation; to be confronted with the witnesses before him; to have compulsory process for obtaining witnesses in his favor, and to have the Assistance of Counsel for his defence.

AMENDMENT VII [1791]

In Suits at common law, where the value in controversy shall exceed twenty dollars, the right of trial by jury shall be preserved, and no fact tried by jury, shall be otherwise re-examined in any Court of the United States, than according to the rules of the common law.

AMENDMENT VIII [1791]

Excessive bail shall not be required, nor excessive fines imposed, nor cruel and unusual punishments inflicted.

AMENDMENT IX [1791]

The enumeration in the Constitution, of certain rights, shall not be construed to deny or disparage others retained by the people.

AMENDMENT X [1791]

The powers not delegated to the United States by the Constitution, nor prohibited by it to the States, are reserved to the States respectively, or to the people.

AMENDMENT XI [1798]

The Judicial power of the United States shall not be construed to extend to any suit in law or equity, commenced or prosecuted against one of the United States by Citizens of another State, or by Citizens or Subjects of any Foreign State.

AMENDMENT XII [1804]

The Electors shall meet in their respective states and vote by ballot for President and Vice-President, one of whom, at least, shall not be an inhabitant of the same state with themselves; they shall name in their ballots the person voted for as President, and in distinct ballots the person voted for as Vice-President, and they shall make distinct lists of all persons voted for as President, and of all persons voted for as Vice-President, and of the number of votes for each, which lists they shall sign and certify, and transmit sealed to the seat of the government of the United States, directed to the President of the Senate;—The President of the Senate shall, in the presence of the Senate and House of Representatives, open all the certificates and the votes shall then be counted;—The person having the greatest number of votes for President, shall be the President, if such number be a majority of the whole number of Electors appointed; and if no person have such majority, then from the persons having the highest numbers not exceeding three on the list of those voted for as President, the House of Representatives shall choose immediately, by ballot, the President. But in choosing the President, the votes shall be taken by states, the representation from each state having one vote; a quorum for this purpose shall consist of a member or members from two-thirds of the states, and a majority of all the states shall be necessary to a choice. And if the House of Representatives shall not choose a President whenever the right of choice shall devolve upon them, before the fourth day of March next following, then the Vice-President shall act as President, as in the case of the death or other constitutional disability of the President.—The person having the greatest number of votes as Vice-President shall be the Vice-President, if such number be a majority of the whole number of Electors appointed, and if no person have a majority, then from the two highest numbers on the list, the Senate shall choose the Vice-President; a quorum for the purpose shall consist of two-thirds of the whole number of Senators, and a majority of the whole number shall be necessary to a choice. But no person constitutionally ineligible to the office of President shall be eligible to that of Vice-President of the United States.

AMENDMENT XIII [1865]

Section 1. Neither slavery nor involuntary servitude, except as punishment for crime whereof the party shall have been duly convicted, shall exist within the United States, or any place subject to their jurisdiction.

Section 2. Congress shall have power to enforce this article by appropriate legislation.

AMENDMENT XIV [1868]

Section 1. All persons born or naturalized in the United States, and subject to the jurisdiction thereof, are citizens of the United States and of the State wherein they reside. No State shall make or enforce any law which shall abridge the privileges or immunities of citizens of the United States; nor shall any State deprive any person of life, liberty, or property, without due process of law; nor deny to any person within its jurisdiction the equal protection of the laws.

Section 2. Representatives shall be apportioned among the several States according to their respective numbers, counting the whole number of persons in each State, excluding Indians not taxed. But when the right to vote at any election for the choice of electors for President and Vice President of the United States, Representatives in Congress, the Executive and Judicial officers of a State, or the members of the Legislature thereof, is denied to any of the male inhabitants of such State, being twenty-one years of age, and citizens of the United States, or in any way abridged, except for participation in rebellion, or other crime, the basis of representation therein shall be reduced in the proportion which the number of such male citizens shall bear to the whole numbers of male citizens twenty-one years of age in such State.

Section 3. No person shall be a Senator or Representative in Congress, or elector of President and Vice President, or hold any office, civil or military, under the United States, or under any State, who having previously taken an oath, as a member of Congress, or as an officer of the United States, or a member of any State legislature, or as an executive or judicial officer of any State, to support the Constitution of the United States, shall have engaged in insurrection or rebellion against the same, or given aid or comfort to the enemies thereof. But Congress may by a vote of two-thirds of each House, remove such disability.

Section 4. The validity of the public debt of the United States, authorized by law, including debts incurred for payment of pensions and bounties for services in suppressing insurrection or rebellion, shall not be questioned. But neither the United States nor any State shall assume or pay any debt or obligation incurred in aid of insurrection or rebellion against the United States, or any claim for the loss or emancipation of any slave; but all such debts, obligations, and claims shall be held illegal and void.

Section 5. The Congress shall have power to enforce, by appropriate legislation, the provisions of this article.

AMENDMENT XV [1870]

Section 1. The right of citizens of the United States to vote shall not be denied or abridged by the United States or by any State on account of race, color, or previous condition of servitude.

Section 2. The Congress shall have power to enforce this article by appropriate legislation.

AMENDMENT XVI [1913]

The Congress shall have power to lay and collect taxes on incomes, from whatever source derived, without apportionment among the several States, and without regard to any census or enumeration.

AMENDMENT XVII [1913]

Section 1. The Senate of the United States shall be composed of two Senators from each State, elected by the people thereof, for six years; and each Senator shall have one vote. The electors in each State shall have the qualifications requisite for electors of the most numerous branch of the State legislatures.

Section 2. When vacancies happen in the representation of any State in the Senate, the executive authority of such State shall issue writs of election to fill such vacancies: *Provided,* That the legislature of any State may empower the executive thereof to make temporary appointments until the people fill the vacancies by election as the legislature may direct.

Section 3. This amendment shall not be so construed as to affect the election or term of any Senator chosen before it becomes valid as part of the Constitution.

AMENDMENT XVIII [1919]

Section 1. After one year from the ratification of this article the manufacture, sale, or transportation of intoxicating liquors within, the importation thereof into, or the exportation thereof from the United States and all territory subject to the jurisdiction thereof for beverage purposes is hereby prohibited.

Section 2. The Congress and the several States shall have concurrent power to enforce this article by appropriate legislation.

Section 3. This article shall be inoperative unless it shall have been ratified as an amendment to the Constitution by the legislatures of the several States, as provided in the Constitution, within seven years from the date of the submission hereof to the States by the Congress.

AMENDMENT XIX [1920]

Section 1. The right of citizens of the United States to vote shall not be denied or abridged by the United States or by any State on account of sex.

Section 2. The Congress shall have the power to enforce this article by appropriate legislation.

AMENDMENT XX [1933]

Section 1. The terms of the President and Vice President shall end at noon on the 20th day of January, and the terms of Senators and Representatives at noon on the 3d day of January, of the years in which such terms would have ended if this article had not been ratified; and the terms of their successors shall then begin.

Section 2. The Congress shall assemble at least once in every year, and such meeting shall begin at noon on the 3d day of January, unless they shall by law appoint a different day.

Section 3. If, at the time fixed for the beginning of the term of the President, the President elect shall have died, the Vice President elect shall become President. If a President shall not have been chosen before the time fixed for the beginning of his term, or if the President elect shall have failed to qualify, then the Vice President elect shall act as President until a President shall have qualified; and the Congress may by law provide for the case wherein neither a President elect nor a Vice President elect shall have qualified, declaring who shall then act as President, or the manner in which one who is to act shall be selected, and such person shall act accordingly until a President or Vice President shall have qualified.

Section 4. The Congress may by law provide for the case of the death of any of the persons from whom the House of Representatives may choose a President whenever the right of choice shall have devolved upon them, and for the case of the death of any of the persons from whom the Senate may choose a Vice President whenever the right of choice shall have devolved upon them.

Section 5. Sections 1 and 2 shall take effect on the 15th day of October following the ratification of this article.

Section 6. This article shall be inoperative unless it shall have been ratified as an amendment to the Constitution by the legislatures of three-fourths of the several States within seven years from the date of its submission.

AMENDMENT XXI [1933]

Section 1. The eighteenth article of amendment to the Constitution of the United States is hereby repealed.

Section 2. The transportation or importation into any State, Territory, or possession of the United States for delivery or use therein of intoxicating liquors, in violation of the laws thereof, is hereby prohibited.

Section 3. This article shall be inoperative unless it shall have been ratified as an amendment to the Constitution by conventions in the several States, as provided in the Constitution, within seven years from the date of the submission thereof to the States by the Congress.

AMENDMENT XXII [1951]

Section 1. No person shall be elected to the office of the President more than twice, and no person who has held the office of President, or acted as President, for more than two years of a term to which some other person was elected President shall be elected to the office of the President more than once. But this article shall not apply to any person holding the office of President when this article was proposed by the Congress, and shall not prevent any person who may be holding the office of President, or acting as President, during the term within which this article becomes operative from holding the office of President or acting as President during the remainder of such term.

Section 2. This article shall be inoperative unless it shall have been ratified as an amendment to the Constitution by the legislatures of three fourths of the several States within seven years from the date of its submission to the States by the Congress.

AMENDMENT XXIII [1961]

Section 1. The District constituting the seat of Government of the United States shall appoint in such manner as the Congress may direct:

A number of electors of President and Vice President equal to the whole number of Senators and Representatives in Congress to which the District would be entitled if it were a State, but in no event more than the least populous state; they shall be in addition to those appointed by the states, but shall be considered, for the purpose of the election of President and Vice President, to be electors appointed by a State; and they shall meet in the District and perform such duties as provided by the twelfth article of amendment.

Section 2. The Congress shall have power to enforce this article by appropriate legislation.

AMENDMENT XXIV [1964]

Section 1. The right of citizens of the United States to vote in any primary or other election for President or Vice President, for electors for President or Vice President, or for Senator or Representative in Congress, shall not be denied or abridged by the United States or any State by reason of failure to pay any poll tax or other tax.

Section 2. The Congress shall have power to enforce this article by appropriate legislation.

AMENDMENT XXV [1967]

Section 1. In case of the removal of the President from office or of his death or resignation, the Vice President shall become President.

Section 2. Whenever there is a vacancy in the office of the Vice President, the President shall nominate a Vice President who shall take office upon confirmation by a majority vote of both Houses of Congress.

Section 3. Whenever the President transmits to the President pro tempore of the

Senate and the Speaker of the House of Representatives his written declaration that he is unable to discharge the powers and duties of his office, and until he transmits to them a written declaration to the contrary, such powers and duties shall be discharged by the Vice President as Acting President.

Section 4. Whenever the Vice President and a majority of either the principal officers of the executive departments or of such other body as Congress may by law provide, transmit to the President pro tempore of the Senate and the Speaker of the House of Representatives their written declaration that the President is unable to discharge the powers and duties of his office, the Vice President shall immediately assume the powers and duties of the office as Acting President.

Thereafter, when the President transmits to the President pro tempore of the Senate and the Speaker of the House of Representatives his written declaration that no inability exists, he shall resume the powers and duties of his office unless the Vice President and a majority of either the principal officers of the executive department or of such other body as Congress may by law provide, transmit within four days to the President pro tempore of the Senate and the Speaker of the House of Representatives their written declaration that the President is unable to discharge the powers and duties of his office. Thereupon Congress shall decide the issue, assembling within forty-eight hours for that purpose if not in session. If the Congress, within twenty-one days after receipt of the latter written declaration, or, if Congress is not in session, within twenty-one days after Congress is required to assemble, determines by two-thirds vote of both houses that the President is unable to discharge the powers and duties of his office, the Vice President shall continue to discharge the same as Acting President; otherwise, the President shall resume the powers and duties of his office.

AMENDMENT XXVI [1971]

Section 1. The right of citizens of the United States, who are eighteen years of age or older, to vote shall not be denied or abridged by the United States or any State on account of age.

Section 2. The Congress shall have the power to enforce this article by appropriate legislation.

AMENDMENT XXVII [1992]

Section 1. No law, varying the compensation for the services of the Senators and Representatives, shall take effect, until an election of Representatives shall have intervened.

THE CONSTITUTIONAL CONVENTION, SPEECH AT THE CONCLUSION OF ITS DELIBERATIONS

SEPTEMBER 17, 1787

Benjamin Franklin (1706–1790), one of America's greatest statesmen and inventors, was also one of the few Founding Fathers to serve as a delegate to both the Continental Congress (where he was a member of the drafting committee for the Declaration of Independence) and the Constitutional Convention of 1787. Franklin began working as an apprentice printer at the age of ten; from 1732 to 1757 published *Poor Richard's Almanack*, known for its proverbs extolling thrift and industry; and wrote one of the greatest American autobiographies. He also invented bifocals, the Franklin stove, and the lightning rod. A witty ladies' man, he enjoyed serving as American minister to France after the Revolution and helped negotiate the peace treaty with Great Britain in 1781. His support of the Constitution was critical to its acceptance.

MR. PRESIDENT,

I confess, that I do not entirely approve of this Constitution at present; but, Sir, I am not sure I shall never approve it; for, having lived long, I have experienced many instances of being obliged, by better information or fuller consideration, to change my opinions even on important subjects, which I once thought right, but found to be otherwise. It is therefore that, the older I grow, the more apt I am to doubt my own judgment of others. Most men, indeed, as well as most sects in religion, think themselves in possession of all truth, and that wherever others differ from them, it is so far error. Steele, a Protestant, in a dedication, tells the Pope, that the only difference between our two churches in their opinions of the certainty of their doctrine, is, the Romish Church is *infallible*, and the Church of England is *never in the wrong*. But, though many private Persons think almost as highly of their own infallibility as of that of their Sect, few express it so naturally as a certain French Lady, who, in a little dispute with her sister, said, "But I meet with nobody but myself that is *always* in the right." "*Je ne trouve que moi qui aie toujours raison.*"

In these sentiments, Sir, I agree to this Constitution, with all its faults—if they are such; because I think a general Government necessary for us, and there is no *form* of government but what may be a blessing to the people, if well administered; and I believe, farther, that this is likely to be well administered for a course of years, and can only end in despotism, as other forms have done before it, when the people shall become so corrupted as to need despotic government, being incapable of any other. I doubt, too, whether any other Convention we can obtain, may be able to make a better constitution; for, when you assemble a number of men, to have the advantage of their joint wisdom, you inevitably assemble with those men all their prejudices, their passions, their errors of opinion, their local interests, and their selfish views. From such an assembly can a *perfect* production be expected? It therefore astonished me, Sir, to find this system approaching so near to perfection as it does; and I think it will astonish our enemies, who are waiting with confidence to hear, that our councils are confounded like those of the builders of Babel, and that our States are on the point of separation, only to meet hereafter for the purpose of cutting one another's throats. Thus I consent, Sir, to this Constitution, because I expect no better, and because I am not sure that it is not the best. The opinions I have had of its *errors* I sacrifice to the public good. I have never whispered a syllable of them abroad. Within these walls they were born, and here they shall die. If every one of us, in returning to our Constituents, were to report the objections he has had to it, and endeavour to gain Partisans in support of them, we might prevent its being generally received, and thereby lose all the salutary effects and great advantages resulting naturally in our favour among foreign nations, as well as among ourselves, from our real or apparent unanimity. Much of the strength and efficiency of any government, in procuring and securing happiness to the people, depends on *opinion*, on the general opinion of the goodness of that government, as well as of the wisdom and integrity of its governors. I hope, therefore, for our own sakes, as a part of the people, and for the sake of our posterity, that we shall act heartily and unanimously in recommending this Constitution, wherever our Influence may extend, and turn our future thoughts and endeavours to the means of having it *well administered*.

On the whole, Sir, I cannot help expressing a wish, that every member of the Convention who may still have objections to it, would with me on this occasion doubt a little of his own infallibility, and, to make *manifest* our *unanimity*, put his name to this Instrument.

Marbury v. Madison
5 U.S. 137

1803

The facts of this case involved a political dispute over last-minute judicial commissions made by the outgoing administration of John Adams that were opposed by incoming president Thomas Jefferson. But its significance is much greater. In his opinion, Chief Justice John Marshall (1755–1835) articulated the principle of judicial review, which gives the Supreme Court the power to declare an Act of Congress unconstitutional. Marshall thereby bolstered the strength of the judicial branch of government and established the Supreme Court as the ultimate arbiter of the rule of law. Marshall, a cousin and political antagonist of Thomas Jefferson, served as chief justice of the Supreme Court from 1801 to 1835. The eldest of fifteen children, Marshall was born in a Virginia log cabin, served as an officer in the American Revolution, was elected to Congress in 1799, and served as secretary of state under John Adams before being appointed to the Supreme Court, which he dominated for many years with his eloquence, integrity, and legal reasoning. In a series of decisions, Marshall bolstered the strength of the federal government in its early critical years, and carved out a powerful role for the Supreme Court.

. . . The constitution vests the whole judicial power of the United States in one supreme court, and such inferior courts as congress shall, from time to time, ordain and establish. This power is expressly extended to all cases arising under the laws of the United States; and consequently, in some form, may be exercised over the present case; because the right claimed is given by a law of the United States. . . .

That the people have an original right to establish, for their future government, such principles as, in their opinion, shall most conduce to their own happiness, is the basis, on which the whole American fabric has been erected. The exercise of this original right is a very great exertion; nor can it, nor ought it to be frequently repeated. The principles, therefore, so established, are deemed fundamental. And as the authority, from which they proceed, is supreme, and can seldom act, they are designed to be permanent. . . .

The government of the United States is of the latter description. The powers of the legislature are defined, and limited; and that those limits may not be mistaken, or forgotten, the constitution is written. To what purpose are powers limited, and to what purpose is that limitation committed to writing, if these limits may, at any time, be passed by those intended to be restrained? The distinction, between a government with limited and unlimited powers, is abolished, if those limits do not confine the persons on whom they are imposed, and if acts prohibited and acts allowed, are of equal obligation. It is a proposition too plain to be contested, that the constitution controls any legislative act repugnant to it; or, that the legislature may alter the constitution by an ordinary act.

Between these alternatives there is no middle ground. The constitution is either a superior, paramount law, unchangeable by ordinary means, or it is on a level with ordinary legislative acts, and like other acts, is alterable when the legislature shall please to alter it. . . .

Certainly all those who have framed written constitutions contemplate them as forming the fundamental and paramount law of the nation, and consequently the theory of every such government must be, that an act of the legislature, repugnant to the constitution, is void.

This theory is essentially attached to a written constitution, and is consequently to be considered, by this court, as one of the fundamental principles of our society. It is not therefore to be lost sight of in the further consideration of this subject. . . .

It is emphatically the province and duty of the judicial department to say what the law is. Those who apply the rule to particular cases, must of necessity expound and interpret that rule. If two laws conflict with each other, the courts must decide on the operation of each. . . .

From these, and many other selections which might be made, it is apparent, that the framers of the constitution contemplated that instrument, as a rule for the government of courts, as well as of the legislature. . . .

It is also not entirely unworthy of observation, that in declaring what shall be the supreme law of the land, the constitution itself is first mentioned; and not the laws of the United States generally, but those only which shall be made in pursuance of the constitution, have that rank.

Thus, the particular phraseology of the constitution of the United States confirms and strengthens the principle, supposed to be essential to all written constitutions, that a law repugnant to the constitution is void; and that courts, as well as other departments, are bound by that instrument.

HENRY DAVID THOREAU

CIVIL DISOBEDIENCE

1849

Thoreau (1817–1862), Harvard-educated Massachusetts author and naturalist, spent a night in jail after refusing to pay a poll tax in support of the Mexican War, which he believed represented an effort to extend slavery. This essay, based on Thoreau's experience, was not immediately popular, although it has had enormous twentieth-century impact, influencing both Gandhi's tactics in the struggle for Indian independence and Martin Luther King Jr.'s leadership of the civil rights movement. Both campaigns used civil disobedience in their non-violent resistance to authority.

. . . How does it become a man to behave toward his American government to-day? I answer, that he cannot without disgrace be associated with it. I cannot for an instant recognize that political organization as *my* government which is the *slave's* government also.

All men recognize the right of revolution; that is, the right to refuse allegiance to, and to resist, the government, when its tyranny or its inefficiency are great and unendurable. But almost all say that such is not the case now. But such was the case, they think, in the Revolution of '75. If one were to tell me that this was a bad government because it taxed certain foreign commodities brought to its ports, it is most probable that I should not make an ado about it, for I can do without them. All machines have their friction; and possibly this does enough good to counterbalance the evil. At any rate, it is a great evil to make a stir about it. But when the friction comes to have its machine, and oppression and robbery are organized, I say, let us not have such a machine any longer. In other words, when a sixth of the population of a nation which has undertaken to be the refuge of liberty are slaves, and a whole country is unjustly overrun and conquered by a foreign army, and subjected to military law, I think that it is not too soon for honest men to rebel and revolutionize. What makes this duty the more urgent is the fact, that the country so overrun is not our own, but ours is the invading army. . . .

Under a government which imprisons any unjustly, the true place for a just man is also a prison. . . .

I have paid no poll-tax for six years. I was put into a jail once on this account, for one night; and, as I stood considering the walls of solid stone, two or three feet thick, the door of wood and iron, a foot thick, and the iron grating which strained the light, I could not help being struck with the foolishness of that institution which treated me as if I were mere flesh and blood and bones, to be locked up. I wondered

Antiwar protest,
New York, 1972.

that it should have concluded at length that this was the best use it could put me to, and had never thought to avail itself of my services in some way. I saw that, if there was a wall of stone between me and my townsmen, there was a still more difficult one to climb or break through, before they could get to be as free as I was. I did not for a moment feel confined, and the walls seemed a great waste of stone and mortar. I felt as if I alone of all my townsmen had paid my tax. They plainly did not know how to treat me, but behaved like persons who are underbred. In every threat and in every compliment there was a blunder; for they thought that my chief desire was to stand the other side of that stone wall. I could not but smile to see how industriously they locked the door on my meditations, which followed them out again without let or hindrance, and *they* were really all that was dangerous. As they could not reach me, they had resolved to punish my body; just as boys, if they cannot come at some person against whom they have a spite, will abuse his dog. I saw that the State was half-witted, that it was timid as a lone woman with her silver spoons, and that it did not know its friends from its foes, and I lost all my remaining respect for it, and pitied it.

Thus the State never intentionally confronts a man's sense, intellectual or moral, but only his body, his senses. It is not armed with superior wit or honesty, but with superior physical strength. I was not born to be forced. I will breathe after my own fashion. Let us see who is the strongest. . . .

The authority of government, even such as I am willing to submit to,—for I will cheerfully obey those who know and can do better than I, and in many things even those who neither know nor can do so well,—is still an impure one: to be strictly just, it must have the sanction and consent of the governed. It can have no pure right over my person and property but what I concede to it. The progress from an absolute to a limited monarchy, from a limited monarchy to a democracy, is a progress toward a true respect for the individual. Even the Chinese philosopher was wise enough to regard the individual as the basis of the empire. Is a democracy, such as we know it, the last improvement possible in government? Is it not possible to take a step further towards recognizing and organizing the rights of man? There will never be a really free and enlightened State, until the State comes to recognize the individual as a higher and independent power, from which all its own power and authority are derived, and treats him accordingly. I please myself with imagining a State at last which can afford to be just to all men, and to treat the individual with respect as a neighbor; which even would not think it inconsistent with its own repose, if a few were to live aloof from it, not meddling with it, nor embraced by it, who fulfilled all the duties of neighbors and fellowmen. A State which bore this kind of fruit, and suffered it to drop off as fast as it ripened, would prepare the way for a still more perfect and glorious State, which also I have imagined, but not yet anywhere seen.

ABRAHAM LINCOLN

FIRST INAUGURAL ADDRESS

MARCH 4, 1861

Abraham Lincoln (1809–1865) was elected president on November 6, 1860, after campaigning to prevent the spread of slavery. When he delivered his First Inaugural Address, the nation was on the verge of war. Seven states had already seceded from the Union. Lincoln made a powerful argument that the Union was perpetual, and secession illegal, even as he attempted to reassure the South that the federal government would not start war. One month later, on April 12, Confederate forces attacked Fort Sumter, and the Civil War began. On April 14, Lincoln began the mobilization of 75,000 militiamen.

Fellow-citizens of the United States:

In compliance with a custom as old as the government itself, I appear before you to address you briefly, and to take, in your presence, the oath prescribed by the Constitution of the United States, to be taken by the President "before he enters on the execution of his office."

I do not consider it necessary at present for me to discuss those matters of administration about which there is no special anxiety or excitement.

Apprehension seems to exist among the people of the Southern States, that by the accession of a Republican Administration, their property, and their peace, and personal security, are to be endangered. There has never been any reasonable cause for such apprehension. Indeed, the most ample evidence to the contrary has all the while existed, and been open to their inspection. It is found in nearly all the published speeches of him who now addresses you. I do but quote from one of those speeches when I declare that "I have no purpose, directly or indirectly, to interfere with the institution of slavery in the States where it exists. I believe I have no lawful right to do so, and I have no inclination to do so." Those who nominated and elected me did so with full knowledge that I had made this, and many similar declarations, and had never recanted them. And more than this, they placed in the platform, for my acceptance, and as a law to themselves, and to me, the clear and emphatic resolution which I now read:

"*Resolved*, That the maintenance inviolate of the rights of the States, and especially the right of each State to order and control its own domestic institutions according to its own judgment exclusively, is essential to that balance of power on which the perfection and endurance of our political fabric depend; and we denounce the lawless invasion by armed force of the soil of any State or Territory, no matter under what pretext, as among the gravest of crimes."

I now reiterate these sentiments: and in doing so, I only press upon the public attention the most conclusive evidence of which the case is susceptible, that the property, peace and security of no section are to be in any wise endangered by the now incoming Administration. I add too, that all the protection which, consistently with the Constitution and the laws, can be given, will be cheerfully given to all the States when lawfully demanded, for whatever cause—as cheerfully to one section as to another. . . .

I hold, that in contemplation of universal law, and of the Constitution, the Union of these States is perpetual. Perpetuity is implied, if not expressed, in the fundamental law of all national governments. It is safe to assert that no government proper ever had a provision in its organic law for its own termination. Continue to execute all the express provisions of our national Constitution, and the Union will endure forever—it being impossible to destroy it, except by some action not provided for in the instrument itself.

GEORGE TAMES, The Lincoln Memorial, Washington, D.C., 1959.

Again, if the United States be not a government proper, but an association of States in the nature of contract merely, can it, as a contract, be peaceably unmade, by less than all the parties who made it? One party to a contract may violate it—break it, so to speak; but does it not require all to lawfully rescind it?

Descending from these general principles, we find the proposition that, in legal contemplation, the Union is perpetual, confirmed by the history of the Union itself. The Union is much older than the Constitution. It was formed in fact, by the Articles of Association in 1774. It was matured and continued by the Declaration of Independence in 1776. It was further matured and the faith of all the then thirteen States expressly plighted and engaged that it should be perpetual, by the Articles of Confederation in 1778. And finally, in 1787, one of the declared objects for ordaining and establishing the Constitution, was *"to form a more perfect Union."*

But if the destruction of the Union, by one, or by a part only, of the States, be lawfully possible, the Union is *less* perfect than before the Constitution, having lost the vital element of perpetuity.

It follows from these views that no State, upon its own mere motion, can lawfully get out of the Union,—that *resolves* and *ordinances* to that effect are legally void, and that acts of violence, within any State or States, against the authority of the United States, are insurrectionary or revolutionary, according to circumstances.

I therefore consider that in view of the Constitution and the laws, the Union is unbroken; and to the extent of my ability I shall take care, as the Constitution itself expressly enjoins upon me, that the laws of the Union be faithfully executed in all the States. Doing this I deem to be only a simple duty on my part; and I shall perform it, so far as practicable, unless my rightful masters, the American people, shall withhold the requisite means, or, in some authoritative manner, direct the contrary. I trust this will not be regarded as a menace, but only as the declared purpose of the Union that it will constitutionally defend and maintain itself.

In doing this there needs to be no bloodshed or violence; and there shall be none, unless it be forced upon the national authority. The power confided to me will be used to hold, occupy, and possess the property and places belonging to the government, and to collect the duties and imposts; but beyond what may be necessary for these objects, there will be no invasion—no using of force against or among the people anywhere. Where hostility to the United States, in any interior locality, shall be so great and so universal, as to prevent competent resident citizens from holding the Federal offices, there will be no attempt to force obnoxious strangers among the people for that object. While the strict legal right may exist in the government to enforce the exercise of these offices, the attempt to do so would be so irritating, and so nearly impracticable withal, that I deem it better to forego, for the time, the uses of such offices. . . .

That there are persons in one section or another who seek to destroy the Union at all events, and are glad of any pretext to do it, I will neither affirm or deny; but if there be such, I need address no word to them. To those, however, who really love the Union, may I not speak?

Before entering upon so grave a matter as the destruction of our national fabric, with all its benefits, its memories and its hopes, would it not be wise to ascertain precisely why we do it? Will you hazard so desperate a step, while there is any possibility that any portion of the ills you fly from have no real existence? Will you, while the certain ills you fly to, are greater than all the real ones you fly from? Will you risk the commission of so fearful a mistake?

All profess to be content in the Union, if all constitutional rights can be maintained. Is it true, then, that any right, plainly written in the Constitution, has been denied? I think not. Happily the human mind is so constituted, that no party can reach to the audacity of doing this. Think, if you can, of a single instance in which a plainly written provision of the Constitution has ever been denied. If, by the mere force of numbers, a majority should deprive a minority of any clearly written constitutional right, it might, in a moral point of view, justify revolution—certainly would, if such a right were a vital one. But such is not our case. All the vital rights of minorities, and of individuals, are so plainly assured to them, by affirmations and negations, guarantees and prohibitions, in the Constitution, that controversies never arise concerning them. But no organic law can ever be framed with a provision specifically applicable to every question which may occur in practical administration. No foresight can anticipate, nor any document of reasonable length contain express provisions for all possible questions. Shall fugitives from labor be surrendered by national or by State authority? The Constitution does not expressly say. *May* Congress prohibit slavery in the territories? The Constitution does not expressly say. *Must* Congress protect slavery in the territories? The Constitution does not expressly say.

From questions of this class spring all our constitutional controversies, and we divide upon them into majorities and minorities. If the minority will not acquiesce, the majority must, or the government must cease. There is no other alternative; for continuing the government is acquiescence on one side or the other. If a minority, in such case, will secede rather than acquiesce, they make a precedent which, in turn, will divide and ruin them; for a minority of their own will secede from them whenever a majority refuses to be controlled by such minority. . . .

Plainly, the central idea of secession, is the essence of anarchy. A majority, held in restraint by constitutional checks and limitations, and always changing easily with deliberate changes of popular opinions and sentiments, is the only true sovereign of a free people. Whoever rejects it, does, of necessity, fly to anarchy or to despotism. Unanimity is impossible; the rule of a minority, as a permanent arrangement, is wholly inadmissible; so that, rejecting the majority principle, anarchy or despotism in some form is all that is left. . . .

One section of our country believes slavery is *right*, and ought to be extended, while the other believes it is *wrong*, and ought not to be extended. This is the only substantial dispute. The fugitive slave clause of the Constitution, and the law for the suppression of the foreign slave trade, are each as well enforced, perhaps, as any law can ever be in a community where the moral sense of the people imperfectly supports the law itself. The great body of the people abide by the dry legal obligation in both cases, and a few break over in each. This, I think, cannot be perfectly cured; and it would be worse in both cases *after* the separation of the sections, than before. The foreign slave trade, now imperfectly suppressed, would be ultimately revived without restriction, in one section; while fugitive slaves, now only partially surrendered, would not be surrendered at all, by the other.

Physically speaking, we cannot separate. We cannot remove our respective sections from each other, nor build an impassable wall between them. A husband and wife may be divorced, and go out of the presence, and beyond the reach of each other; but the different parts of our country cannot do this. They cannot but remain face to face; and intercourse, either amicable or hostile, must continue between them. Is it possible, then, to make that intercourse more advantageous or more satisfactory, *after* separation than *before*? Can aliens make treaties easier than friends can make laws? Can treaties be more faithfully enforced between aliens than laws can among friends? Suppose you go to war, you cannot fight always; and when, after much loss on both sides, and no gain on either, you cease fighting, the identical old questions, as to terms of intercourse, are again upon you.

This country, with its institutions, belongs to the people who inhabit it. Whenever they shall grow weary of the existing government, they can exercise their *constitutional* right of amending it, or their *revolutionary* right to dismember or overthrow it. I cannot be ignorant of the fact that many worthy and patriotic citizens are desirous of having the national Constitution amended. While I make no recommendation of amendments, I fully recognize the rightful authority of the people over the whole subject to be exercised in either of the modes prescribed in the instrument itself; and I should under existing circumstances favor rather than oppose a fair opportunity being afforded the people to act upon it. . . .

Abraham Lincoln outside his home, Springfield, Illinois, August 1860.

Why should there not be a patient confidence in the ultimate justice of the people? Is there any better or equal hope, in the world? In our present differences, is either party without faith of being in the right? If the Almighty Ruler of nations, with his eternal truth and justice, be on your side of the North or on yours of the South, that truth, and that justice, will surely prevail, by the judgment of this great tribunal, the American people. . . .

My countrymen, one and all, think calmly and *well*, upon this whole subject. Nothing valuable can be lost by taking time. If there be an object to *hurry* any of you, in hot haste, to a step which you would never take *deliberately*, that object will be frustrated by it. Such of you as are now dissatisfied, still have the old Constitution unimpaired, and, on the sensitive point, the laws of your own framing under it; while the new administration will have no immediate power, if it would, to change either. If it were admitted that you who are dissatisfied, hold the right side in the dispute, there still is no single good reason for precipitate action. Intelligence, patriotism, Christianity, and a firm reliance on Him, who has never yet forsaken this favored land, are still competent to adjust, in the best way, all our present difficulty.

In *your* hands, my dissatisfied fellow-countrymen, and not in *mine*, is the momentous issue of civil war. The government will not assail *you*. You can have no conflict, without being yourselves the aggressors. *You* have no oath registered in Heaven to destroy the government, while *I* shall have the most solemn one to "preserve, protect and defend" it.

I am loth to close. We are not enemies, but friends. We must not be enemies. Though passion may have strained, it must not break our bonds of affection. The mystic chords of memory, stretching from every battlefield, and patriot grave, to every living heart and hearth-stone, all over this broad land, will yet swell the chorus of the Union, when again touched, as surely they will be, by the better angels of our nature.

The United States of America v. Susan B. Anthony

1873

Susan B. Anthony (1820–1906), the daughter of Quaker abolitionists, was a founder, along with Elizabeth Cady Stanton (1815–1902), of the National Woman Suffrage Association in 1869. In 1872, Anthony walked into a Rochester, New York, polling station and voted, despite the fact that it was illegal for women to do so at the time. She was fined $100, which she refused to pay. Anthony's leadership and tireless advocacy paved the way for the adoption of the Nineteenth Amendment, which gave women the right to vote, in 1920.

THE PROSECUTION

D. A. Richard Crowley: May it please the Court and Gentlemen of the Jury: . . . The defendant, Miss Susan B. Anthony . . . voted for a representative in the Congress of the United States, to represent the 29th Congressional District of this State, and also for a representative at large for the State of New York to represent the State in the Congress of the United States. At that time she was a woman. I suppose there will be no question about that . . . whatever Miss Anthony's intentions may have been—whether they were good or otherwise—she did not have a right to vote upon that question, and if she did vote without having a lawful right to vote, then there is no question but what she is guilty of violating a law of the United States. . . .

Conceded, that on the 5th day of November, 1872, Miss Susan B. Anthony was a woman.

THE INSPECTORS' TESTIMONY

Q: Did you see her vote?

A: [Beverly W. Jones]: Yes, sir. . . .

Q: She was not challenged on the day she voted?

A: No, sir.

Cross-examination by Defense Attorney, Judge Henry Selden

Q: Prior to the election, was there a registry of voters in that district made?

A: Yes, sir.

Q: Were you one of the officers engaged in making that registry?

A: Yes, sir.

Q: When the registry was being made did Miss Anthony appear before the Board of Registry and claim to be registered as a voter?

A: She did.

Q: Was there any objection made, or any doubt raised as to her right to vote?

A: There was.

Q: On what ground?

A: On the ground that the Constitution of the State of New York did not allow women to vote.

Q: What was the defect in her right to vote as a citizen?

A: She was not a male citizen.

Q: That she was a woman?

A: Yes, sir. . . .

Q: Did the Board consider the question of her right to registry, and decide that she was entitled to registry as a voter?

A: Yes, sir.

Q: And she was registered accordingly?

A: Yes, sir. . . .

Q: Won't you state what Miss Anthony said, if she said anything, when she came there and offered her name for registration?

A: She stated that she did not claim any rights under the Constitution of the State of New York; she claimed her right under the Constitution of the United States.

Q: Did she name any particular amendment?

A: Yes, sir; she cited the XIV amendment.

Q: Under that she claimed her right to vote?

A: Yes, sir. . . .

THE DEFENSE

Attorney, Judge Henry R. Selden: The only alleged ground of illegality of the defendant's vote is that she is a woman. If the same act had been done by her brother under the same circumstances, the act would have been not only innocent, but honorable and laudable; but having been done by a woman it is said to be a crime. . . . I believe this is the first instance in which a woman has been arraigned in a criminal court merely on account of her sex. . . . Another objection is, that the right to hold office must attend the right to vote, and that women are not qualified to discharge the duties of responsible offices. I beg leave to answer this objection by asking one or more questions. How many of the male bipeds who do our voting are qualified to hold high offices? . . . Another objection is that engaging in political controversies is not consistent with the feminine character. Upon that subject, women themselves are the best judges, and if political duties should be found inconsistent with female delicacy, we may rest assured that women will either effect a change in the character of political contests, or decline to engage in them. . . .

THE COURT: The question, gentlemen of the jury . . . is wholly a question or questions of law, and I have decided as a question of law, in the first place, that under the XIV Amendment, which Miss Anthony claims protects her, she was not protected in a right to vote. And I have decided also that her belief and the advice which she took do not protect her in the act which she committed. If I am right in this, the result must be a verdict on your part of guilty, and I therefore direct that you find a verdict of guilty.

MR. SELDEN: That is a direction no Court has power to make in a criminal case.

THE COURT: Take the verdict, Mr. Clerk. . . .

THE NEXT DAY

THE COURT: The prisoner will stand up. Has the prisoner anything to say why sentence shall not be pronounced?

MISS ANTHONY: Yes, your honor, I have many things to say; for in your ordered verdict of guilty, you have trampled underfoot every vital principle of our government. My natural rights, my civil rights, my political rights, are all alike ignored. Robbed of the fundamental privilege of citizenship, I am degraded from the status of a citizen to that of a subject; and not only myself individually, but all of my sex, are, by your honor's verdict, doomed to political subjection under this so-called Republican government.

JUDGE HUNT: The Court can not listen to a rehearsal of arguments the prisoner's counsel has already consumed three hours in presenting.

MISS ANTHONY: May it please your honor, I am not arguing the question, but simply stating the reasons why sentence can not, in justice, be pronounced against me. Your denial of my citizen's right to vote is the denial of my right of consent as one of the governed, the denial of my right of representation as one of the taxed, the denial of my right to a trial by a jury of my peers as an offender against the law, therefore, the denial of my sacred rights to life, liberty, property, and—

JUDGE HUNT: The Court can not allow the prisoner to go on.

MISS ANTHONY: But your honor will not deny me this one and only poor privilege of protest against this high-handed outrage upon my citizen's rights. May it please the Court to remember that since the day of my arrest last November, this is the first time that either myself or any person of my disfranchised class has been allowed a word of defense before judge or jury—

JUDGE HUNT: The prisoner must sit down; the Court can not allow it.

MISS ANTHONY: All my prosecutors, from the 8th Ward corner grocery politician, who entered the complaint, to the United States Marshal, Commissioner, District Attorney, District Judge, your honor on the bench, not one is my peer, but each and all are my political sovereigns; and had your honor submitted my case to the jury, as was clearly your duty, even then I should have had just cause of protest, for not one of those men was my peer; but, native or foreign, white or black, rich or poor, educated or ignorant, awake or asleep, sober or drunk, each and every man of them was my political superior; hence, in no sense, my peer. . . .

JUDGE HUNT: The Court must insist—the prisoner has been tried according to the established forms of law.

MISS ANTHONY: Yes, your honor, but by forms of law all made by men, interpreted by men, administered by men, in favor of men, and against women; and hence, your honor's ordered verdict of guilty, against a United States citizen for the exercise of "that citizen's right to vote," simply because that citizen was a woman and not a man. But, yesterday, the same manmade forms of law declared it a crime punishable with $1,000 fine and six months' imprisonment, for you, or me, or any of us, to give a cup of cold water, a crust of bread, or a night's shelter to a panting fugitive as he was tracking his way to Canada. And every man or woman in whose veins coursed a drop of human sympathy violated that wicked law, reckless of consequences, and was justified in so doing. As then the slaves who got their freedom must take it over, or under, or through the unjust forms of law, precisely so now must women, to get their right to a voice in this Government, take it; and I have taken mine, and mean to take it at every possible opportunity.

JUDGE HUNT: The Court orders the prisoner to sit down. It will not allow another word.

MISS ANTHONY: When I was brought before your honor for trial, I hoped for a broad and liberal interpretation of the Constitution and its recent amendments, that should declare all United States citizens under its protecting aegis—that should declare equality of rights the national guarantee to all persons born or naturalized in the United States. But failing to get this justice—failing, even, to get a trial by a jury *not* of my peers—I ask not leniency at your hands—but rather the full rigors of the law.

JUDGE HUNT: The Court must insist—*[Here the prisoner sat down.]* The prisoner will stand up. *[Here Miss Anthony arose again.]* The sentence of the Court is that you pay a fine of $100 and the costs of the prosecution.

MISS ANTHONY: May it please your honor, I shall never pay a dollar of your unjust penalty. All the stock in trade I possess is a $10,000 debt, incurred by publishing my paper—*The Revolution*—four years ago, the sole object of which was to educate all women to do precisely as I have done, rebel against your man-made, unjust, unconstitutional forms of law, that tax, fine, imprison, and hang women, while they deny them the right of representation in the Government; and I shall work on with might and main to pay every dollar of that honest debt, but not a penny shall go to this unjust claim. And I shall earnestly and persistently continue to urge all women to the practical recognition of the old revolutionary maxim that "Resistance to tyranny is obedience to God."

JUDGE HUNT: Madam, the Court will not order you committed until the fine is paid.

HARPER LEE

TO KILL A MOCKINGBIRD

1960

Born in Monroeville, Alabama, Harper Lee achieved literary immortality with her Pulitzer Prize–winning novel, *To Kill a Mockingbird*. The novel, set in small-town Alabama, tells the story of the young narrator's father, lawyer Atticus Finch, who courageously defended a black man wrongly accused of raping a white woman. The 1962 film of the same name starring Gregory Peck won three Academy Awards.

"You can just take that back, boy!"

This order, given by me to Cecil Jacobs, was the beginning of a rather thin time for Jem and me. My fists were clenched and I was ready to let fly. Atticus had promised me he would wear me out if he ever heard of me fighting any more; I was far too old and too big for such childish things, and the sooner I learned to hold in, the better off everybody would be. I soon forgot.

Cecil Jacobs made me forget. He had announced in the schoolyard the day before that Scout Finch's daddy defended niggers. I denied it, but told Jem.

"What'd he mean sayin' that?" I asked.

"Nothing," Jem said. "Ask Atticus, he'll tell you."

"Do you defend niggers, Atticus?" I asked him that evening.

"Of course I do. Don't say nigger, Scout. That's common."

"'s what everybody at school says."

"From now on it'll be everybody less one—"

"Well if you don't want me to grow up talkin' that way, why do you send me to school?"

My father looked at me mildly, amusement in his eyes. Despite our compromise, my campaign to avoid school had continued in one form or another since my first day's dose of it: the beginning of last September had brought on sinking spells, dizziness, and mild gastric complaints. I went so far as to pay a nickel for the privilege of rubbing my head against the head of Miss Rachel's cook's son, who was afflicted with a tremendous ringworm. It didn't take.

But I was worrying another bone. "Do all lawyers defend n-Negroes, Atticus?"

"Of course they do, Scout."

"Then why did Cecil say you defended niggers? He made it sound like you were runnin' a still."

Atticus sighed. "I'm simply defending a Negro—his name's Tom Robinson. He lives in that little settlement beyond the town dump. He's a member of Calpurnia's church, and Cal knows his family well. She says they're clean-living folks. Scout, you aren't old enough to understand some things yet, but there's been some high talk around town to the effect that I shouldn't do much about defending this man. It's a peculiar case—it won't come to trial until summer session. John Taylor was kind enough to give us a postponement . . ."

"If you shouldn't be defendin' him, then why are you doin' it?"

"For a number of reasons," said Atticus. "The main one is, if I didn't I couldn't hold up my head in town, I couldn't represent this county in the legislature, I couldn't even tell you or Jem not to do something again."

"You mean if you didn't defend that man, Jem and me wouldn't have to mind you any more?"

"That's about right."

"Why?"

"Because I could never ask you to mind me again. Scout, simply by the nature of the work, every lawyer gets at least one case in his lifetime that affects him personally. This one's mine, I guess. You might hear some ugly talk about it at school, but do one thing for me if you will: you just hold your head high and keep those fists down. No matter what anybody says to you, don't you let 'em get your goat. Try fighting with your head for a change . . . it's a good one, even if it does resist learning."

"Atticus, are you going to win it?"

"No, honey."

"Then why—"

"Simply because we were licked a hundred years before we started is no reason for us not to try to win," Atticus said.

GEORGE TAMES, Voting, Little Rock, Arkansas, 1957.

LETTER FROM BIRMINGHAM CITY JAIL

APRIL 16, 1963

Known as the "most segregated city in the South," with parks, playgrounds, swimming pools, restaurants, theaters, hotels, and elevators all segregated by race and no black police or firefighters, Birmingham, Alabama, became a target of the civil rights movement in the spring of 1963. A campaign of sit-ins, boycotts, rallies, and mass meetings was planned. In January 1963, eight white clergymen published an open letter to Martin Luther King Jr. (1929–1968), accusing him of fomenting civil unrest and urging him to call off the demonstrations. On Good Friday, Dr. King was arrested for defying a state court order prohibiting demonstrations. He wrote this essay in reply on scraps of paper, which were smuggled out of his cell.

. . . Beyond this, I am in Birmingham because injustice is here. Just as the eighth century prophets left their little villages and carried their "thus saith the Lord" far beyond the boundaries of their hometowns; and just as the Apostle Paul left his little village of Tarsus and carried the gospel of Jesus Christ to practically every hamlet and city of the Graeco-Roman world, I too am compelled to carry the gospel of freedom beyond my particular hometown. . . .

Moreover, I am cognizant of the interrelatedness of all communities and states. I cannot sit idly by in Atlanta and not be concerned about what happens in Birmingham. Injustice anywhere is a threat to justice everywhere. We are caught in an inescapable network of mutuality, tied in a single garment of destiny. Whatever affects one directly affects all indirectly. Never again can we afford to live with the narrow, provincial "outside agitator" idea. Anyone who lives in the United States can never be considered an outsider anywhere in this country.

You deplore the demonstrations that are presently taking place in Birmingham. But I am sorry that your statement did not express a similar concern for the conditions that brought the demonstrations into being. I am sure that each of you would want to go beyond the superficial social analyst who looks merely at effects, and does not grapple with underlying causes. I would not hesitate to say that it is unfortunate that so-called demonstrations are taking place in Birmingham at this time, but I would say in more emphatic terms that it is even more unfortunate that the white power structure of this city left the Negro community with no other alternative. . . .

You may well ask, "Why direct action? Why sit-ins, marches, etc.? Isn't negotiation a better path?" You are exactly right in your call for negotiation. Indeed, this is the purpose of direct action. Nonviolent direct action seeks to create such a crisis and establish such creative tension that a community that has constantly refused to

REV. WYATT TEE WALKER, Martin Luther King Jr., Birmingham, Alabama, 1963.

negotiate is forced to confront the issue. It seeks so to dramatize the issue that it can no longer be ignored. I just referred to the creation of tension as a part of the work of the nonviolent resister. This may sound rather shocking. But I must confess that I am not afraid of the word tension. I have earnestly worked and preached against violent tension, but there is a type of constructive nonviolent tension that is necessary for growth. . . .

We know through painful experience that freedom is never voluntarily given by the oppressor; it must be demanded by the oppressed. Frankly, I have never yet engaged in a direct action movement that was "well-timed," according to the timetable of those who have not suffered unduly from the disease of segregation. For years now I have heard the word "Wait!" It rings in the ear of every Negro with a piercing familiarity. This "Wait" has almost always meant "Never." It has been a tranquilizing thalidomide, relieving the emotional stress for a moment, only to give birth to an ill-formed infant of frustration. We must come to see with the distinguished jurist of yesterday that "justice too long delayed is justice denied." We have waited for more than 340 years for our constitutional and God-given rights. The nations of Asia and Africa are moving with jetlike speed toward the goal of political independence, and we still creep at horse and buggy pace toward the gaining of a cup of coffee at a lunch counter. I guess it is easy for those who have never felt the stinging darts of segregation to say, "Wait." But when you have seen vicious mobs lynch your mothers and fathers at will and drown your sisters and brothers at whim; when you have seen hate-filled policemen curse, kick, brutalize and even kill your black brothers and sisters with impunity; when you see the vast majority of your twenty million Negro brothers smothering in an airtight cage of poverty in the midst of an affluent society; when you suddenly find your tongue twisted and your speech stammering as you seek to explain to your six-year-old daughter why she can't go to the public amusement park that has just been advertised on television, and see tears welling up in her little eyes when she is told that Funtown is closed to colored children, and see the depressing clouds of inferiority begin to form in her little mental sky, and see her begin to distort her little personality by unconsciously developing a bitterness toward white people; when you have to concoct an answer for a five-year-old son asking in agonizing pathos: "Daddy, why do white people treat colored people so mean?"; when you take a cross-country drive and find it necessary to sleep night after night in the uncomfortable corners of your automobile because no motel will accept you; when you are humiliated day in and day out by nagging signs reading "white" and "colored"; when your first name becomes "nigger" and your middle name becomes "boy" (however old you are) and your last name becomes "John," and when your wife and mother are never given the respected title "Mrs."; when you are harried by day and haunted by night by the fact that you are a Negro, living constantly at tiptoe stance never quite knowing what to expect next, and plagued with inner fears and outer resentments; when you are forever fighting a degenerating sense of "nobodiness"; then you will understand why we find it difficult to wait. There comes a time when the cup of endurance runs over, and men are no longer willing to be plunged into an abyss of injustice where they experience the blackness of corroding despair. I hope, sirs, you can understand our legitimate and unavoidable impatience.

You express a great deal of anxiety over our willingness to break laws. This is certainly a legitimate concern. Since we so diligently urge people to obey the Supreme Court's decision of 1954 outlawing segregation in the public schools, it is rather strange and paradoxical to find us consciously breaking laws. One may well ask, "How can you advocate breaking some laws and obeying others?" The answer is found in the fact that there are two types of laws: there are *just* and there are *unjust* laws. I would agree with Saint Augustine that "An unjust law is no law at all."

Now what is the difference between the two? How does one determine when a law is just or unjust? A just law is a man-made code that squares with the moral law or the law of God. An unjust law is a code that is out of harmony with the moral law. To put it in the terms of Saint Thomas Aquinas, an unjust law is a human law that is not rooted in eternal and natural law. Any law that uplifts human personality is just. Any law that degrades human personality is unjust. All segregation statutes are unjust because segregation distorts the soul and damages the personality. It gives the segregator a false sense of superiority, and the segregated a false sense of inferiority. . . .

Let us turn to a more concrete example of just and unjust laws. An unjust law is a code that a majority inflicts on a minority that is not binding on itself. This is difference made legal. On the other hand a just law is a code that a majority compels a minority to follow that it is willing to follow itself. This is sameness made legal.

Let me give another explanation. An unjust law is a code inflicted upon a minority which that minority had no part in enacting or creating because they did not have the unhampered right to vote. Who can say that the legislature of Alabama which set up the segregation laws was democratically elected? Throughout the state of Alabama all types of conniving methods are used to prevent Negroes from becoming registered voters and there are some counties without a single Negro registered to vote despite the fact that the Negro constitutes a majority of the population. Can any law set up in such a state be considered democratically structured?

These are just a few examples of unjust and just laws. There are some instances when a law is just on its face and unjust in its application. For instance, I was arrested Friday on a change of parading without a permit. Now there is nothing wrong with an ordinance which requires a permit for a parade, but when the ordinance is used to preserve segregation and to deny citizens the First Amendment privilege of peaceful assembly and peaceful protest, then it becomes unjust.

I hope you can see the distinction I am trying to point out. In no sense do I advocate evading or defying the law as the rabid segregationist would do. This would lead to anarchy. One who breaks an unjust law must do it *openly*, *lovingly* (not hatefully as the white mothers did in New Orleans when they were seen on television screaming, "nigger, nigger, nigger"), and with a willingness to accept the penalty. I submit that an individual who breaks a law that conscience tells him is unjust, and willingly accepts the penalty by staying in jail to arouse the conscience of the community over its injustice, is in reality expressing the very highest respect for law. . . .

I must close now. But before closing I am impelled to mention one other point in your statement that troubled me profoundly. You warmly commended the Birmingham police force for keeping "order" and "preventing violence." I don't believe you would have so warmly commended the police force if you had seen its angry violent dogs literally biting six unarmed, nonviolent Negroes. I don't believe you would so quickly commend the policemen if you would observe their ugly and inhuman treatment of Negroes here in the city jail; if you would watch them push and curse old Negro women and young Negro girls; if you would see them slap and kick old Negro men and young boys; if you will observe them, as they did on two occasions, refuse to give us food because we wanted to sing our grace together. I'm sorry that I can't join you in your praise for the police department. . . .

I wish you had commended the Negro sit-inners and demonstrators of Birmingham for their sublime courage, their willingness to suffer and their amazing discipline in the midst of the most inhuman provocation. One day the South will recognize its real heroes. They will be the James Merediths, courageously and with a majestic sense of purpose facing jeering and hostile mobs and the agonizing loneliness that characterizes the life of the pioneer. They will be old, oppressed, battered Negro women, symbolized in a seventy-two-year-old woman of Montgomery, Alabama, who rose up with a sense of dignity and with her people decided not to ride the segregated buses, and responded to one who inquired about her tiredness with ungrammatical profundity: "My feet is tired, but my soul is rested." They will be the young high school and college students, young ministers of the gospel and a host of their elders courageously and nonviolently sitting-in at lunch counters and willingly going to jail for conscience's sake. One day the South will know that when these disinherited children of God sat down at lunch counters they were in reality standing up for the best in the American dream and the most sacred values in our Judeo-Christian heritage, and thusly, carrying our whole nation back to those great wells of democracy which were dug deep by the Founding Fathers in the formulation of the Constitution and the Declaration of Independence. . . .

LYNDON B. JOHNSON

SPECIAL MESSAGE TO THE CONGRESS: THE AMERICAN PROMISE

MARCH 15, 1965

Lyndon Baines Johnson (1908–1973) was born into a Texas farming family and taught high school before pursuing a career in politics. First elected to Congress in 1937, he served in the navy in World War II, and was elected to the Senate in 1948. He rapidly rose to power, becoming a master legislator and Senate majority leader. He served as vice president under John F. Kennedy. Johnson became president after Kennedy's assassination and was reelected in 1964. He pushed hard for the Civil Rights Act of 1964, and the Voting Rights Act of 1965, as well as medicare and other social welfare legislation known as the Great Society. In foreign affairs, Johnson increased American involvement in Vietnam, which cost him much popular support, and he declined to seek a second full term.

President Johnson delivered this speech to Congress on prime-time television just a few days after the nation witnessed the brutal beating by police of unarmed civil rights marchers in Selma, Alabama, in March 1965. Johnson called on Congress to pass the Voting Rights Act, which outlawed literacy tests and other barriers to the enfranchisement of African Americans and authorized federal examiners to register black voters. The Voting Rights Act was passed in 1965 and signed by Johnson in the same Senate chamber where Abraham Lincoln had signed the Emancipation Proclamation. By the end of the year, more than 250,000 African Americans had registered to vote for the first time.

. . . At times history and fate meet at a single time in a single place to shape a turning point in man's unending search for freedom. So it was at Lexington and Concord. So it was a century ago at Appomattox. So it was last week in Selma, Alabama.

There, long-suffering men and women peacefully protested the denial of their rights as Americans. Many were brutally assaulted. One good man, a man of God, was killed.

There is no cause for pride in what has happened in Selma. There is no cause for self-satisfaction in the long denial of equal rights of millions of Americans. But there is cause for hope and for faith in our democracy in what is happening here tonight.

For the cries of pain and the hymns and protests of oppressed people have summoned into convocation all the majesty of this great Government—the Government of the greatest Nation on earth.

Our mission is at once the oldest and the most basic of this country: to right wrong, to do justice, to serve man.

In our time we have come to live with moments of great crisis. Our lives have been marked with debate about great issues; issues of war and peace, issues of prosperity and depression. But rarely in any time does an issue lay bare the secret heart

Martin Luther King Jr., Robert F. Kennedy, Roy Wilkins, and Lyndon B. Johnson,
after meeting at White House to discuss civil rights legislation and upcoming
March on Washington, 1963.

of America itself. Rarely are we met with a challenge, not to our growth or abundance, our welfare or our security, but rather to the values and the purposes and the meaning of our beloved Nation.

The issue of equal rights for American Negroes is such an issue. And should we defeat every enemy, should we double our wealth and conquer the stars, and still be unequal to this issue, then we will have failed as a people and as a nation.

For with a country as with a person, "What is a man profited, if he shall gain the whole world, and lose his own soul?"

There is no Negro problem. There is no Southern problem. There is no Northern problem. There is only an American problem. And we are met here tonight as Americans—not as Democrats or Republicans—we are met here as Americans to solve that problem.

This was the first nation in the history of the world to be founded with a purpose. The great phrases of that purpose still sound in every American heart, North and South: "All men are created equal"—"government by consent of the governed"—"give me liberty or give me death." Well, those are not just clever words, or those are not just empty theories. In their name Americans have fought and died for two centuries, and tonight around the world they stand there as guardians of our liberty, risking their lives.

Those words are a promise to every citizen that he shall share in the dignity of man. This dignity cannot be found in a man's possessions; it cannot be found in his power, or in his position. It really rests on his right to be treated as a man equal in opportunity to all others. It says that he shall share in freedom, he shall choose his leaders, educate his children, and provide for his family according to his ability and his merits as a human being.

To apply any other test—to deny a man his hopes because of his color or race, his religion or the place of his birth—is not only to do injustice, it is to deny America and to dishonor the dead who gave their lives for American freedom.

Our fathers believed that if this noble view of the rights of man was to flourish, it must be rooted in democracy. The most basic right of all was the right to choose your own leaders. The history of this country, in large measure, is the history of the expansion of that right to all of our people.

Many of the issues of civil rights are very complex and most difficult. But about this there can and should be no argument. Every American citizen must have an equal right to vote. There is no reason which can excuse the denial of that right. There is no duty which weighs more heavily on us than the duty we have to ensure that right.

Yet the harsh fact is that in many places in this country men and women are kept from voting simply because they are Negroes.

Every device of which human ingenuity is capable has been used to deny this right. The Negro citizen may go to register only to be told that the day is wrong, or the hour is late, or the official in charge is absent. And if he persists, and if he manages to present himself to the registrar, he may be disqualified because he did not spell out his middle name or because he abbreviated a word on the application.

And if he manages to fill out an application he is given a test. The registrar is the sole judge of whether he passes this test. He may be asked to recite the entire Constitution, or explain the most complex provisions of State law. And even a college degree cannot be used to prove that he can read and write.

For the fact is that the only way to pass these barriers is to show a white skin.

Experience has clearly shown that the existing process of law cannot overcome systematic and ingenious discrimination. No law that we now have on the books—

and I have helped to put three of them there—can ensure the right to vote when local officials are determined to deny it.

In such a case our duty must be clear to all of us. The Constitution says that no person shall be kept from voting because of his race or his color. We have all sworn an oath before God to support and to defend that Constitution. We must now act in obedience to that oath.

Wednesday I will send to Congress a law designed to eliminate illegal barriers to the right to vote. . . .

This bill will strike down restrictions to voting in all elections—Federal, State, and local—which have been used to deny Negroes the right to vote.

This bill will establish a simple, uniform standard which cannot be used, however ingenious the effort, to flout our Constitution.

It will provide for citizens to be registered by officials of the United States Government if the State officials refuse to register them.

It will eliminate tedious, unnecessary lawsuits which delay the right to vote.

Finally, this legislation will ensure that properly registered individuals are not prohibited from voting.

I will welcome the suggestions from all of the Members of Congress—I have no doubt that I will get some—on ways and means to strengthen this law and to make it effective. But experience has plainly shown that this is the only path to carry out the command of the Constitution.

To those who seek to avoid action by their National Government in their own communities; who want to and who seek to maintain purely local control over elections, the answer is simple:

Open your polling places to all your people. Allow men and women to register and vote whatever the color of their skin. Extend the rights of citizenship to every citizen of this land.

There is no constitutional issue here. The command of the Constitution is plain.

There is no moral issue. It is wrong—deadly wrong—to deny any of your fellow Americans the right to vote in this country.

There is no issue of States rights or national rights. There is only the struggle for human rights. . . .

But even if we pass this bill, the battle will not be over. What happened in Selma is part of a far larger movement which reaches into every section and State of America. It is the effort of American Negroes to secure for themselves the full blessings of American life.

Their cause must be our cause too. Because it is not just Negroes, but really it is all of us, who must overcome the crippling legacy of bigotry and injustice.

And we shall overcome.

As a man whose roots go deeply into Southern soil I know how agonizing racial feelings are. I know how difficult it is to reshape the attitudes and the structure of our society.

But a century has passed, more than a hundred years, since the Negro was freed. And he is not fully free tonight.

It was more than a hundred years ago that Abraham Lincoln, a great President of another party, signed the Emancipation Proclamation, but emancipation is a proclamation and not a fact.

A century has passed, more than a hundred years, since equality was promised. And yet the Negro is not equal.

A century has passed since the day of promise. And the promise is unkept.

The time of justice has now come. I tell you that I believe sincerely that no force can hold it back. It is right in the eyes of man and God that it should come. And when it does, I think that day will brighten the lives of every American.

For Negroes are not the only victims. How many white children have gone un-educated, how many white families have lived in stark poverty, how many white lives have been scarred by fear, because we have wasted our energy and our substance to maintain the barriers of hatred and terror?

So I say to all of you here, and to all in the Nation tonight, that those who appeal to you to hold on to the past do so at the cost of denying you your future.

This great, rich, restless country can offer opportunity and education and hope to all: black and white, North and South, sharecropper and city dweller. These are the enemies: poverty, ignorance, disease. They are the enemies and not our fellow man, not our neighbor. And these enemies too, poverty, disease and ignorance, we shall overcome. . . .

DUNCAN V. LOUISIANA
391 U.S. 145

1968

In this case, the Supreme Court held that anyone accused of a crime punishable by at least two years in prison is entitled to a trial by jury. After reviewing the history of trial by jury, the Court concluded that it was a fundamental right under the Fourteenth Amendment's guarantee of due process of law. The opinion was written by Byron White (1917–2002), who joined the Court in 1962. The right to a fair trial was also bolstered by the Court's landmark decision *Gideon v. Wainwright*, which guaranteed a right to counsel for someone accused of a serious crime.

MR. JUSTICE WHITE delivered the opinion of the Court.

. . . Appellant, Gary Duncan, was convicted of simple battery in the Twenty-fifth Judicial District Court of Louisiana. Under Louisiana law simple battery is a misdemeanor, punishable by a maximum of two years' imprisonment and a $300 fine. Appellant sought trial by jury, but because the Louisiana Constitution grants jury trials only in cases in which capital punishment or imprisonment at hard labor may be imposed, the trial judge denied the request. . . .

Appellant was 19 years of age when tried. While driving on Highway 23 in Plaquemines Parish on October 18, 1966, he saw two younger cousins engaged in a conversation by the side of the road with four white boys. Knowing his cousins, Negroes who had recently transferred to a formerly all-white high school, had reported the occurrence of racial incidents at the school, Duncan stopped the car, got out, and approached the six boys. At trial the white boys and a white onlooker testified, as did appellant and his cousins. The testimony was in dispute on many points, but the witnesses agreed that appellant and the white boys spoke to each other, that appellant encouraged his cousins to break off the encounter and enter his car, and that appellant was about to enter the car himself for the purpose of driving away with his cousins. The whites testified that just before getting in the car appellant slapped Herman Landry, one of the white boys, on the elbow. The Negroes testified that appellant had not slapped Landry, but had merely touched him. The trial judge concluded that the State had proved beyond a reasonable doubt that Duncan had committed simple battery, and found him guilty. . . .

The position of Louisiana, on the other hand, is that the Constitution imposes upon the States no duty to give a jury trial in any criminal case, regardless of the seriousness of the crime or the size of the punishment which may be imposed. Because we believe that trial by jury in criminal cases is fundamental to the American scheme of justice, we hold that the Fourteenth Amendment guarantees a right of jury trial in all criminal cases which—were they to be tried in a federal court—would come within the Sixth Amendment's guarantee. Since we consider the appeal before us to be such a case, we hold that the Constitution was violated when appellant's demand for jury trial was refused. . . .

The history of trial by jury in criminal cases has been frequently told. It is sufficient for present purposes to say that by the time our Constitution was written, jury trial in criminal cases had been in existence in England for several centuries and carried impressive credentials traced by many to Magna Carta. Its preservation and proper operation as a protection against arbitrary rule were among the major objectives of the revolutionary settlement which was expressed in the Declaration and Bill of Rights of 1689. . . .

Jury trial came to America with English colonists, and received strong support from them. Royal interference with the jury trial was deeply resented. Among the resolutions adopted by the First Congress of the American Colonies (the Stamp Act Congress) on October 19, 1765—resolutions deemed by their authors to state "the most essential rights and liberties of the colonists"—was the declaration:

"That trial by jury is the inherent and invaluable right of every British subject in these colonies."

The First Continental Congress, in the resolve of October 14, 1774, objected to trials before judges dependent upon the Crown alone for their salaries and to trials in England for alleged crimes committed in the colonies; the Congress therefore declared:

"That the respective colonies are entitled to the common law of England, and more especially to the great and inestimable privilege of being tried by their peers of the vicinage, according to the course of that law."

The Declaration of Independence stated solemn objections to the King's making "Judges dependent on his Will alone, for the tenure of their offices, and the amount and payment of their salaries," to his "depriving us in many cases, of the benefits of Trial by Jury," and to his "transporting us beyond Seas to be tried for pretended offenses." The Constitution itself, in Art. III, § 2, commanded:

"The Trial of all Crimes, except in Cases of Impeachment, shall be by Jury; and such Trial shall be held in the State where the said Crimes shall have been committed."

Objections to the Constitution because of the absence of a bill of rights were met by the immediate submission and adoption of the Bill of Rights. Included was the Sixth Amendment which, among other things, provided:

"In all criminal prosecutions, the accused shall enjoy the right to a speedy and public trial, by an impartial jury of the State and district wherein the crime shall have been committed." . . .

The constitutions adopted by the original States guaranteed jury trial. Also, the constitution of every State entering the Union thereafter in one form or another protected the right to jury trial in criminal cases.

Even such skeletal history is impressive support for considering the right to jury trial in criminal cases to be fundamental to our system of justice, an importance frequently recognized in the opinions of this Court. . . .

The guarantees of jury trial in the Federal and State Constitutions reflect a profound judgment about the way in which law should be enforced and justice administered. A right to jury trial is granted to criminal defendants in order to prevent oppression by the Government. Those who wrote our constitutions knew from history and experience that it was necessary to protect against unfounded criminal charges brought to eliminate enemies and against judges too responsive to the voice of higher authority. The framers of the constitutions strove to create an independent judiciary but insisted upon further protection against arbitrary action. Providing an accused with the right to be tried by a jury of his peers gave him an inestimable safeguard against the corrupt or overzealous prosecutor and against the compliant, biased, or eccentric judge. If the defendant preferred the common-sense judgment of a jury to the more tutored but perhaps less sympathetic reaction of the single judge, he was to have it. Beyond this, the jury trial provisions in the Federal and State Constitutions reflect a fundamental decision about the exercise of official power—a reluctance to entrust plenary powers over the life and liberty of the citizen to one judge or to a group of judges. Fear of unchecked power, so typical of our State and Federal Governments in other respects, found expression in the criminal law in this insistence upon community participation in the determination of guilt or innocence. The deep commitment of the Nation to the right of jury trial in serious criminal cases as a defense against arbitrary law enforcement qualifies for protection under the Due Process Clause of the Fourteenth Amendment, and must therefore be respected by the States.

BARBARA JORDAN

OPENING STATEMENT TO THE HOUSE JUDICIARY COMMITTEE, PROCEEDINGS ON IMPEACHMENT OF RICHARD NIXON

JULY 25, 1974

As a member of the House Judiciary Committee, Barbara Jordan (1936–1996), a lawyer and the first black woman elected to the Texas State Senate, opened the televised hearings of the House Judiciary Committee's impeachment proceedings of President Richard Nixon. The Watergate scandal had erupted following an inquiry into the break-in of the Democratic Party Headquarters at the Watergate Office Building in Washington, D.C. The subsequent investigation revealed a widespread criminal conspiracy that implicated the president and his top advisers. In her statement, Jordan combined constitutional history and a critique of Nixon's actions into a powerful oratorical presentation that made her a nationally known figure.

. . . Earlier today we heard the beginning of the Preamble to the Constitution of the United States, "We, the people." It is a very eloquent beginning. But when that document was completed, on the seventeenth of September in 1787, I was not included in that "We, the people." I felt somehow for many years that George Washington and Alexander Hamilton just left me out by mistake. But through the process of amendment, interpretation, and court decision I have finally been included in "We, the people."

Today, I am an inquisitor. I believe hyperbole would not be fictional and would not overstate the solemness that I feel right now. My faith in the Constitution is whole, it is complete, it is total. I am not going to sit here and be an idle spectator to the diminution, the subversion, the destruction of the Constitution.

"Who can so properly be the inquisitors for the nation as the representatives of the nation themselves?" (*Federalist*, no. 65.) The subject of its jurisdiction are those offenses which proceed from the misconduct of public men. That is what we are talking about. In other words, the jurisdiction comes from the abuse of violation of some public trust. It is wrong, I suggest, it is a misreading of the Constitution for any member here to assert that for a member to vote for an article of impeachment means that that member must be convinced that the president should be removed from office. The Constitution doesn't say that. The powers relating to impeachment are an essential check in the hands of this body, the legislature, against and upon the encroachment of the executive. In establishing the division between the two branches of the legislature, the House and the Senate, assigning to the one the right to accuse and to the other the right to judge, the framers of this Constitution were very astute. They did not make the accusers and the judges the same person.

We know the nature of impeachment. We have been talking about it awhile now. "It is chiefly designed for the president and his high ministers" to somehow be called into account. It is designed to "bridle" the executive if he engages in excesses. "It is designed as a method of national inquest into the conduct of public men." (Hamilton, *Federalist*, no. 65.) The framers confined in the Congress the power if need be, to remove the president in order to strike a delicate balance between a president swollen with power and grown tyrannical, and preservation of the independence of the executive. The nature of impeachment is a narrowly channeled exception to the separation-of-powers maxim; the federal convention of 1787 said that. It limited impeachment to high crimes and misdemeanors and discounted and opposed the term "maladministration." "It is to be used only for great misdemeanors," so it was said in the North Carolina ratification convention. And in the Virginia ratification convention: "We do not trust our liberty to a particular branch. We need one branch to check the others." . . .

Of the impeachment process, it was Woodrow Wilson who said that "nothing short of the grossest offenses against the plain law of the land will suffice to give them speed and effectiveness. Indignation so great as to overgrow party interest may secure a conviction; but nothing else can."

Common sense would be revolted if we engaged upon this process for petty reasons. Congress has a lot to do. Appropriations, tax reform, health insurance, campaign finance reform, housing, environmental protection, energy sufficiency, mass transportation. Pettiness cannot be allowed to stand in the face of such overwhelming problems. So today we are not being petty. We are trying to be big because the task we have before us is a big one. . . .

At this point I would like to juxtapose a few of the impeachment criteria with some of the president's actions.

Impeachment criteria: James Madison, from the Virginia ratification convention. "If the president be connected in any suspicious manner with any person and there be grounds to believe that he will shelter him, he may be impeached."

We have heard time and time again that the evidence reflects payment to the defendants of money. The president had knowledge that these funds were being paid and that these were funds collected for the 1972 presidential campaign.

We know that the president met with Mr. Henry Petersen twenty-seven times to discuss matters related to Watergate and immediately thereafter met with the very persons who were implicated in the information Mr. Petersen was receiving and transmitting to the president. The words are "if the president be connected in any suspicious manner with any person and there be grounds to believe that he will shelter that person, he may be impeached."

Justice Story: "Impeachment is intended for occasional and extraordinary cases where a superior power acting for the whole people is put into operation to protect their rights and rescue their liberties from violations."

We know about the Huston plan. We know about the break-in of the psychiatrist's office. We know that there was absolute complete direction in August 1971 when the president instructed Ehrlichman to "do whatever is necessary." This instruction led to a surreptitious entry into Dr. Fielding's office.

"Protect their rights." "Rescue their liberties from violation."

The South Carolina ratification convention impeachment criteria: those are impeachable "who behave amiss or betray their public trust."

Beginning shortly after the Watergate break-in and continuing to the present time, the president has engaged in a series of public statements and actions designed to thwart the lawful investigation by government prosecutors. Moreover, the president has made public announcements and assertions bearing on the Watergate case which the evidence will show he knew to be false.

These assertions, false assertions, impeachable, those who misbehave. Those who "behave amiss or betray their public trust."

James Madison again at the Constitutional Convention: "A president is impeachable if he attempts to subvert the Constitution."

The Constitution charges the president with the task of taking care that the laws be faithfully executed, and yet the president has counseled his aides to commit perjury, willfully disregarded the secrecy of grand jury proceedings, concealed surreptitious entry, attempted to compromise a federal judge while publicly displaying his cooperation with the processes of criminal justice.

"A president is impeachable if he attempts to subvert the Constitution."

If the impeachment provision in the Constitution of the United States will not reach the offenses charged here, then perhaps that eighteenth-century Constitution should be abandoned to a twentieth-century paper shredder. Has the president committed offenses and planned and directed and acquiesced in a course of conduct which the Constitution will not tolerate? That is the question. We know that. We know the question. We should now forthwith proceed to answer the question. It is reason, and not passion, which must guide our deliberations, guide our debate, and guide our decision.

REMARKS ON TAKING THE OATH OF OFFICE

AUGUST 9, 1974

After serving in the Navy in World War II, Gerald Ford (1913–) returned to Grand Rapids, Michigan, to practice law and enter politics. He was elected to Congress in 1948, served as minority leader from 1965 to 1973, and became vice president when Spiro Agnew resigned in disgrace. Ford became the nation's first appointed president when President Nixon resigned rather than face impeachment. Ford's decision to pardon Nixon was extremely controversial. Many believe it cost him the presidency, but Ford maintains that the pardon was necessary for American society to move beyond the Watergate scandal.

The oath that I have taken is the same oath that was taken by George Washington and by every president under the Constitution. But I assume the presidency under extraordinary circumstances never before experienced by Americans. This is an hour of history that troubles our minds and hurts our hearts.

Therefore, I feel it is my first duty to make an unprecedented compact with my countrymen. Not an inaugural address, not a fireside chat, not a campaign speech— just a little straight talk among friends. And I intend it to be the first of many.

I am acutely aware that you have not elected me as your president by your ballots, and so I ask you to confirm me as your president with your prayers. And I hope that such prayers will also be the first of many.

If you have not chosen me by secret ballot, neither have I gained office by any secret promises. I have not campaigned either for the presidency or the vice-presidency. I have not subscribed to any partisan platform. I am indebted to no man, and only to one woman—my dear wife—as I begin this very difficult job.

I have not sought this enormous responsibility, but I will not shirk it. Those who nominated and confirmed me as vice president were my friends and are my friends. They were of both parties, elected by all the people and acting under the Constitution in their name. It is only fitting then that I should pledge to them and to you that I will be the president of all the people.

Thomas Jefferson said the people are the only sure reliance for the preservation of our liberty. And down the years, Abraham Lincoln renewed this American article of faith asking, "Is there any better way or equal hope in the world?"

I intend, on Monday next, to request of the speaker of the House of Representatives and the president pro tempore of the Senate the privilege of appearing before the Congress to share with my former colleagues and with you, the American people, my views on the priority business of the nation and to solicit your views and their views. And may I say to the Speaker and the others, if I could meet with you right after these remarks, I would appreciate it.

Even though this is late in an election year, there is no way we can go forward except together and no way anybody can win except by serving the people's urgent needs. We cannot stand still or slip backwards. We must go forward now together.

To the peoples and the governments of all friendly nations, and I hope that could encompass the whole world, I pledge an uninterrupted and sincere search for peace. America will remain strong and united, but its strength will remain dedicated to the safety and sanity of the entire family of man, as well as to our own precious freedom.

I believe that truth is the glue that holds government together, not only our government but civilization itself. That bond, though strained, is unbroken at home and abroad.

In all my public and private acts as your president, I expect to follow my instincts of openness and candor with full confidence that honesty is always the best policy in the end.

My fellow Americans, our long national nightmare is over.

Our Constitution works; our great Republic is a government of laws and not of men. Here the people rule. But there is a higher power, by whatever name we honor him, who ordains not only righteousness but love, not only justice but mercy.

As we bind up the internal wounds of Watergate, more painful and more poisonous than those of foreign wars, let us restore the golden rule to our political process, and let brotherly love purge our hearts of suspicion and of hate.

In the beginning, I asked you to pray for me. Before closing, I ask again your prayers, for Richard Nixon and for his family. May our former president, who brought peace to millions, find it for himself. May God bless and comfort his wonderful wife and daughters, whose love and loyalty will forever be a shining legacy to all who bear the lonely burdens of the White House.

I can only guess at those burdens, although I have witnessed at close hand the tragedies that befell three presidents and the lesser trials of others.

With all the strength and all the good sense I have gained from life, with all the confidence my family, my friends, and my dedicated staff impart to me, and with the good will of countless Americans I have encountered in recent visits to forty states, I now solemnly reaffirm my promise I made to you last December 6: to uphold the Constitution, to do what is right as God gives me to see the right, and to do the very best I can for America.

God helping me, I will not let you down.

Thank you.

BUSH V. GORE
531 U.S. 98

2000

Article II of the Constitution sets forth the process by which the president and the vice president are chosen, the system known as the Electoral College. In the presidential election of 2000, although Al Gore received approximately 550,000 more popular votes than George W. Bush, the electoral votes were undecided for thirty-five days, due to discrepancies in the Florida vote tallies. In this opinion, the second 5–4 decision involving the election results, the Supreme Court held that the recount of votes ordered by the Florida Supreme Court gave some votes more weight than others, thereby violating the equal protection guarantee of the Constitution, and certified Bush as the forty-third president. The opinion in this case was issued per curiam (for the court).

Per Curiam.

On November 8, 2000, the day following the Presidential election, the Florida Division of Elections reported that petitioner Bush had received 2,909,135 votes, and respondent Gore had received 2,907,351 votes, a margin of 1,784 for Governor Bush. Because Governor Bush's margin of victory was less than "one-half of a percent . . . of the votes cast," an automatic machine recount was conducted under §102.141(4) of the election code, the results of which showed Governor Bush still winning the race but by a diminished margin. Vice President Gore then sought manual recounts in Volusia, Palm Beach, Broward, and Miami-Dade Counties, pursuant to Florida's election protest provisions. A dispute arose concerning the deadline for local county canvassing boards to submit their returns to the Secretary of State (Secretary). The secretary declined to waive the November 14 deadline imposed by statutes. The Florida Supreme Court, however, set the deadline at November 26. We granted certiorari and vacated the Florida Supreme Court's decision, finding considerable uncertainty as to the grounds on which it was based. On December 11, the Florida Supreme Court issued a decision on remand reinstating that date. On November 26, the Florida Elections Canvassing Commission certified the results of the election and declared Governor Bush the winner of Florida's 25 electoral votes. On November 27, Vice President Gore, pursuant to Florida's contest provisions, filed a complaint in Leon County Circuit Court contesting the certification. He sought relief pursuant to § 102.168(3)(c), which provides that "[r]eceipt of a number of illegal votes or rejection of a number of legal votes sufficient to change or place in doubt the result of the election" shall be grounds for a contest. The Circuit Court denied relief, stating that

Vice President Gore failed to meet his burden of proof. He appealed to the First District Court of Appeal, which certified the matter to the Florida Supreme Court. Accepting jurisdiction, the Florida Supreme Court affirmed in part and reversed in part. The court held that the Circuit Court had been correct to reject Vice President Gore's challenge to the results certified in Nassau County and his challenge to the Palm Beach County Canvassing Board's determination that 3,300 ballots cast in that county were not, in the statutory phrase, "legal votes." . . .

The petition presents the following questions: whether the Florida Supreme Court established new standards for resolving Presidential election contests, thereby violating Art. II, § 1, cl. 2, of the United States Constitution and failing to comply with 3 U.S.C. § 5, and whether the use of standardless manual recounts violates the Equal Protection and Due Process Clauses. With respect to the equal protection question, we find a violation of the Equal Protection Clause.

The closeness of this election, and the multitude of legal challenges which have followed in its wake, have brought into sharp focus a common, if heretofore unnoticed, phenomenon. Nationwide statistics reveal that an estimated 2% of ballots cast do not register a vote for President for whatever reason, including deliberately choosing no candidate at all or some voter error, such as voting for two candidates or insufficiently marking a ballot. . . .

This case has shown that punchcard balloting machines can produce an unfortunate number of ballots which are not punched in a clean, complete way by the voter. After the current counting, it is likely legislative bodies nationwide will examine ways to improve the mechanisms and machinery for voting.

The individual citizen has no federal constitutional right to vote for electors for the President of the United States unless and until the state legislature chooses a statewide election as the means to implement its power to appoint members of the Electoral College. . . .

History has now favored the voter, and in each of the several States the citizens themselves vote for Presidential electors. When the state legislature vests the right to vote for President in its people, the right to vote as the legislature has prescribed is fundamental; and one source of its fundamental nature lies in the equal weight accorded to each vote and the equal dignity owed to each voter. The State, of course, after granting the franchise in the special context of Article II, can take back the power to appoint electors. . . .

The right to vote is protected in more than the initial allocation of the franchise. Equal protection applies as well to the manner of its exercise. Having once granted the right to vote on equal terms, the State may not, by later arbitrary and disparate treatment, value one person's vote over that of another. . . .

There is no difference between the two sides of the present controversy on these basic propositions. . . . The question before us, however, is whether the recount procedures the Florida Supreme Court has adopted are consistent with its obligation to avoid arbitrary and disparate treatment of the members of its electorate.

Much of the controversy seems to revolve around ballot cards designed to be perforated by a stylus but which, either through error or deliberate omission, have not been perforated with sufficient precision for a machine to register the perforations. In some cases a piece of the card—a chad—is hanging, say, by two corners. In other cases there is no separation at all, just an indentation.

The Florida Supreme Court has ordered that the intent of the voter be discerned from such ballots. . . .

The recount mechanisms implemented in response to the decisions of the Florida Supreme Court do not satisfy the minimum requirement for nonarbitrary treatment of voters necessary to secure the fundamental right. Florida's basic command for the count of legally cast votes is to consider the "intent of the voter." This is unobjectionable as an abstract proposition and a starting principle. The problem inheres in the absence of specific standards to ensure its equal application. The formulation of uniform rules to determine intent based on these recurring circumstances is practicable and, we conclude, necessary. . . .

The want of those rules here has led to unequal evaluation of ballots in various respects. As seems to have been acknowledged at oral argument, the standards for accepting or rejecting contested ballots might vary not only from county to county but indeed within a single county from one recount team to another. . . .

In addition, the recounts in these three counties were not limited to so-called undervotes but extended to all of the ballots. The distinction has real consequences. A manual recount of all ballots identifies not only those ballots which show no vote but also those which contain more than one, the so-called overvotes. Neither category will be counted by the machine. This is not a trivial concern. At oral argument, respondents estimated there are as many as 110,000 overvotes statewide. As a result, the citizen whose ballot was not read by a machine because he failed to vote for a candidate in a way readable by a machine may still have his vote counted in a manual recount; on the other hand, the citizen who marks two candidates in a way discernible by the machine will not have the same opportunity to have his vote count, even if a manual examination of the ballot would reveal the requisite indicia of intent. Furthermore, the citizen who marks two candidates, only one of which is discernible by the machine, will have his vote counted even though it should have been read as an invalid ballot. The State Supreme Court's inclusion of vote counts based on these variant standards exemplifies concerns with the remedial processes that were under way. . . .

The recount process is inconsistent with the minimum procedures necessary to protect the fundamental right of each voter in the special instance of a statewide recount under the authority of a single state judicial officer. Our consideration is limited to the present circumstances, for the problem of equal protection in election processes generally presents many complexities. The question before the Court is not whether local entities, in the exercise of their expertise, may develop different systems for implementing elections. Instead, we are presented with a situation where a state court with the power to assure uniformity has ordered a statewide recount with minimal procedural safeguards. When a court orders a statewide remedy, there must be at least some assurance that the rudimentary requirements of equal treatment and fundamental fairness are satisfied. . . .

The Supreme Court of Florida has said that the legislature intended the State's electors to "participat[e] fully in the federal electoral process," as provided in 3 U.S.C. § 5. That statute, in turn, requires that any controversy or contest that is designed to lead to a conclusive selection of electors be completed by December 12. That date is upon us, and there is no recount procedure in place under the State Supreme Court's order that comports with minimal constitutional standards. Because it is evident that any recount seeking to meet the December 12 date will be unconstitutional for the reasons we have discussed, we reverse the judgment of the Supreme Court of Florida ordering a recount to proceed. Seven Justices of the Court agree that there are constitutional problems with the recount ordered by the Florida Supreme Court that demand a remedy. The only disagreement is as to the remedy. . . .

None are more conscious of the vital limits on judicial authority than are the Members of this Court, and none stand more in admiration of the Constitution's design to leave the selection of the President to the people, through their legislatures, and to the political sphere. When contending parties invoke the process of the courts, however, it becomes our unsought responsibility to resolve the federal and constitutional issues the judicial system has been forced to confront. . . .

FREEDOM

CARTER JONES, "Hay Play Day,"
Yorktown Heights, New York, 1961.

WHEN ASKED TO NAME the quality that best defines America, people most often say freedom. It is the principle on which our country was founded, and remains the reason why people around the world want to come to America today. The tension between freedom and power has marked our history ever since the Declaration of Independence, when Thomas Jefferson set forth the ideal of liberty as an inalienable right. This seems remarkable when one considers that in 1770 the total population of the thirteen colonies was approximately 2,312,000, of whom roughly 462,000 were slaves. In this section, some of the most heart-wrenching writings about freedom are by those to whom it was denied. These are all the more powerful since slaves were largely prohibited from learning to read and write.

At the other end of the spectrum, leaders like Franklin Roosevelt and Ronald Reagan have articulated the universal aspects of freedom. In his Four Freedoms speech, delivered when the world was battling the spread of totalitarianism, Roosevelt set forth a vision of the human spirit that committed the United States to defend freedom and democracy around the world. Forty years later, Ronald Reagan presided over the end of the cold war and gave one of his most inspiring speeches to Russian students whose countrymen had for generations been denied such liberties.

Our government is one of limited powers, granted to it by "We the People," and may not infringe upon the rights and freedoms of each individual. Only four hundred words long, the Bill of Rights forms the most comprehensive protection of individual liberty ever written. In many ways it is a document responding to the fear of tyranny from which the United States had just become liberated. Yet its language and the values it protects—freedom of speech and religion, the right to a fair trial and due process of law, the right to privacy—are timeless. As Americans, we often take these rights for granted—until the moment comes when they are threatened. Each generation is reminded that these rights bring responsibilities, and only if we are willing to fight for our freedoms will they be preserved. The war on terrorism is the most recent such moment.

The First Amendment protects freedom of speech and the press, speech that criticizes the government and speech that we may find offensive, even un-American. During and after World War I, anarchists and socialists were imprisoned for criticizing the war effort, and although the protestors received harsh prison sentences that shock our modern notions of free speech, the eloquent defenses of free speech in *Abrams v. U.S.* and *Whitney v. California* played a critical role in advancing civil liberties. Today, when it comes to political protest, only speech that is likely to incite "imminent lawless action" can be suppressed. Likewise, in the landmark free press decision *New York Times Co. v. Sullivan*, the Supreme Court safeguarded the public's right to know by promoting "uninhibited, wide open robust debate" on public issues and protecting the freedom to publish without undue fear of reprisal, acknowledging that some errors are the price we pay for living in a free society.

Freedom of religion is also protected by the First Amendment. Historically, the right to worship according to one's own beliefs brought many early settlers to America. We remain a deeply religious country, yet often struggle to live up to our own ideals. Chief Red Jacket's 1805 plea that his people be free to practice their religion and my father's attack on religious bigotry during the 1960 campaign, separated by 150 years, show the power of faith and the continuing importance of tolerance. The First Amendment also prohibits the government from "establishing" religion or favoring one religion over another. Thomas Jefferson wrote that the First Amendment creates "a wall of separation between church and state," yet the boundaries of this prohibition are often difficult to define. The debates surrounding religion in the public schools show how the issue continues to divide the Court and the country. School prayer was first prohibited by the Supreme Court in the 1962 decision *Engel v. Vitale*, yet the issue continues to be litigated, and the controversial 2002 decision allowing parents to use publicly funded vouchers to pay for parochial school tuition was seen as the most important redefinition of the church-state relationship in forty years.

The Fourth Amendment protects our right to be secure in "our persons, places, houses and effects" and to be free from "unreasonable search and seizure." In the eighteenth century, British troops, armed with the notorious writs of assistance, could enter and ransack the homes of the colonists. The issue was a rallying point for those seeking independence from Great Britain. After Massachusetts lawyer James Otis gave a five-hour speech of protest, in 1761, John Adams wrote, "Otis was a flame of fire! Then and there was the first act of opposition to the arbitrary claims of Great Britain. Then and there the child Independence was born. In fifteen years, namely in 1776, he grew up to manhood, and declared himself free."

Today, we live in a very different world, yet the timeless values of the Bill of Rights still protect us from unwarranted government intrusion. Its principles determine the circumstances under which the government is allowed to collect and compile comprehensive data banks of personal information for national security purposes, regulate video surveillance on our streets, conduct airport security precautions, test safety workers or students for drugs, and maintain or invade medical confidentiality. As these difficult cases show, important health or safety concerns often outweigh individual rights.

When I was researching books on the Bill of Rights and the right to privacy, my coauthor and I spent time with Native Americans seeking to practice their religion in their sacred ancestral high country and keep the wilderness free from development. We interviewed death row inmates who believed they had been denied a fair trial, and we talked to Ku Klux Klan members who claimed that free speech meant airing their own public access television show. We spoke with a couple whose house had been ransacked by federal agents, and women who had been strip-searched by the police in violation of the Fourth Amendment. We deepened our understanding of the debate surrounding the right to choose and how destructive it can be when the rights of the child are pitted against those of the mother. These cases were not easy. None of the people involved thought they would ever have to fight for their rights. All had to relive painful experiences to do so, yet when their rights were threatened, they shouldered the difficult responsibility, on behalf of all of us, rather than risk losing our fundamental freedoms.

The future will bring new challenges to civil liberties. Our rights will be preserved for future generations only if we are informed and committed to the values upon which our country was founded.

THOMAS JEFFERSON

THE DECLARATION OF INDEPENDENCE

1776

On July 2, 1776, the Continental Congress voted upon a resolution introduced by Virginia, that "these colonies are, and of right, ought to be, free and independent states." The young Virginia lawyer and planter Thomas Jefferson served as chairman of the committee—which also included John Adams and Benjamin Franklin—appointed to draft a declaration. Building upon the ideas of enlightenment philosopher John Locke, and English and colonial declarations of rights, Jefferson wrote for the world and for the ages. For the first time in history, principles of freedom and equality became the political foundations for a nation.

When in the course of human events it becomes necessary for one people to dissolve the political bands which have connected them with another, and to assume among the powers of the earth, the separate and equal station to which the Laws of Nature and of Nature's God entitle them, a decent respect to the opinions of mankind requires that they should declare the causes which impel them to the separation.

We hold these truths to be self-evident, that all men are created equal, that they are endowed by their Creator with certain unalienable rights, that among these are life, liberty and the pursuit of happiness. That to secure these rights, governments are instituted among men, deriving their just powers from the consent of the governed. That whenever any form of government becomes destructive of these ends, it is the right of the people to alter or to abolish it, and to institute new government, laying its foundation on such principles and organizing its powers in such form, as to them shall seem most likely to effect their safety and happiness. Prudence, indeed, will dictate that governments long established should not be changed for light and transient causes; and accordingly all experience hath shown, that mankind are more disposed to suffer, while evils are sufferable, than to right themselves by abolishing the forms to which they are accustomed. But when a long train of abuses and usurpations, pursuing invariably the same object, evinces a design to reduce them under absolute despotism, it is their right, it is their duty, to throw off such government, and to provide new guards for their future security. Such has been the patient sufferance of these Colonies; and such is now the necessity which constrains them to alter their former systems of government. The history of the present King of Great Britain is a history of repeated injuries and unsurpations, all having, in direct object, the establishment of an absolute tyranny over these States. To prove this, let facts be submitted to a candid world.

WILLIAM HUTCHINGS.

LEMUEL COOK

ALEXANDER MILLENER.

ADAM LINK.

DANIEL WALDO.

Revolutionary War veterans, 1864.

He has refused his assent to laws, the most wholesome and necessary for the public good.

He has forbidden his Governors to pass laws of immediate and pressing importance, unless suspended in their operation till his assent should be obtained; and when so suspended, he has utterly neglected to attend to them.

He has refused to pass other laws for the accommodation of large districts of people, unless those people would relinquish the right of representation in the legislature, a right inestimable to them and formidable to tyrants only.

He has called together legislative bodies at places unusual, uncomfortable, and distant from the depository of their public records, for the sole purpose of fatiguing them into compliance with his measures.

He has dissolved representative houses repeatedly, for opposing with manly firmness his invasions on the rights of the people.

He has refused for a long time, after such dissolutions, to cause others to be elected; whereby the legislative powers, incapable of annihilation, have returned to the people at large for their exercise; the State remaining in the meantime exposed to all the dangers of invasion from without and convulsions within.

He had endeavoured to prevent the population of these states; for that purpose obstructing the laws of naturalization of foreigners; refusing to pass others to encourage their migration hither, and raising the conditions of new appropriations of lands.

He has obstructed the administration of justice, by refusing his assent to laws for establishing judiciary powers.

He had made judges dependent on his will alone, for the tenure of their offices, and the amount and payment of their salaries.

He has erected a multitude of new offices, and sent hither swarms of officers to harass our people, and eat out their substance.

He has kept among us, in times of peace, standing armies without the consent of our legislatures.

He has affected to render the military independent of, and superior to, the civil power.

He has combined with others to subject us to a jurisdiction foreign to our constitution, and unacknowledged by our laws; giving his assent to their acts of pretended legislation:

For quartering large bodies of armed troops among us:

For protecting them, by a mock trial, from punishment for any murders which they should commit on the inhabitants of these States:

For cutting off our trade with all parts of the world:

For imposing taxes on us without our consent:

For depriving us, in many cases, of the benefit of trial by jury:

For transporting us beyond seas to be tried for pretended offences:

For abolishing the free system of English laws in a neighbouring Province, establishing therein an arbitrary government, and enlarging its boundaries so as to render it at once an example and fit instrument for introducing the same absolute rule into these Colonies:

For taking away our Charters, abolishing our most valuable laws, and altering fundamentally the forms of our governments:

For suspending our own legislatures, and declaring themselves invested with power to legislate for us in all cases whatsoever.

He has abdicated government here, by declaring us out of his protection and waging war against us.

He has plundered our seas, ravaged our coasts, burnt our towns, and destroyed the lives of our people.

He is, at this time, transporting large armies of foreign mercenaries to complete the works of death, desolation and tyranny, already begun, with circumstances of cruelty and perfidy scarcely paralleled in the most barbarous ages, and totally unworthy the head of a civilized nation.

He has constrained our fellow citizens taken captive on the high seas to bear arms against their country, to become the executioners of their friends and brethren, or to fall themselves by their hands.

He has excited domestic insurrections amongst us, and has endeavoured to bring on the inhabitants of our frontiers, the merciless Indian savages, whose known rule of warfare is an undistinguished destruction of all ages, sexes, and conditions.

In every stage of these oppressions we have petitioned for redress in the most humble terms: our repeated petitions have been answered only by repeated injury. A prince whose character is thus marked by every act which may define a tyrant is unfit to be the ruler of a free people.

Nor have we been wanting in attention to our British brethren. We have warned them from time to time of attempts by their legislature to extend an unwarrantable jurisdiction over us. We have reminded them of the circumstances of our emigration and settlement here. We have appealed to their native justice and magnanimity, and we have conjured them by the ties of our common kindred to disavow these usurpations, which would inevitably interrupt our connections and correspondence. They too have been deaf to the voice of justice and of consanguinity. We must, therefore, acquiesce in the necessity, which denounces our separation, and hold them, as we hold the rest of mankind, enemies in war, in peace, friends.

We, therefore, the Representatives of the United States of America, in General Congress assembled, appealing to the Supreme Judge of the world for the rectitude of our intentions, do, in the name, and by authority of the good people of these Colonies, solemnly publish and declare, That these United Colonies are, and of right ought to be, Free and Independent States; that they are absolved from all allegiance to the British Crown, and that all political connection between them and the State of Great Britain, is and ought to be totally dissolved; and that as Free and Independent States, they have full power to levy war, conclude peace, contract alliances, establish commerce, and to do all other acts and things which Independent States may of right do. And for the support of this declaration, with a firm reliance on the protection of Divine Providence, we mutually pledge to each other our lives, our fortunes, and our sacred honor.

BUT, MISTER ADAMS
(FROM THE BROADWAY MUSICAL *1776*)

1964

Songwriter Sherman Edwards spent nine and a half years researching material for *1776*, the award-winning Broadway musical based upon the creation of the Declaration of Independence that won three Tony Awards, had a run of 1,217 performances, and was released on film in 1972. Edwards's song "But, Mr. Adams" is set in Philadelphia during 1776 when a Committee of Five, composed of John Adams, Thomas Jefferson, Roger Sherman, Benjamin Franklin, and Robert Livingston, was appointed by the Continental Congress to draft a statement proclaiming independence from Great Britain. At the insistence of Massachusetts's John Adams, Virginian Thomas Jefferson became the principal author of the draft document that would later become America's Declaration of Independence. Jefferson's original draft was adopted almost in its entirety; however, a paragraph highly critical of King George III for sanctioning slavery and the slave trade was deleted at the demand of Georgian and South Carolinian delegates. The Declaration was adopted unanimously on July 2 and ratified on July 4.

Adams:	All right, gentlemen, let's get on with it.
	Which of us will write our Declaration of Independence?
Franklin:	Mr. Adams, I say you should write it
	To your legal mind and brilliance we defer
Adams:	Is that so? Well, if I'm the one to do it
	They'll run their quill pens through it
	I'm obnoxious and disliked, you know that, sir
Franklin:	Yes, I know
Adams:	But I say you should write it Franklin, yes you
Franklin:	Hell, no!
Adams:	Yes, you, Dr. Franklin, you!
Franklin:	But,
Adams:	You!
Franklin:	But,
Adams:	You!
Franklin:	But, Mr. Adams! But, Mr. Adams,
	The things I write are only light extemporania!
	I won't put politics on paper; it's a mania!
	So I refuse to use the pen in Pennsylvania!
Liberals:	Pennsylvania, Pennsylvania, refuse to use the pen!
Adams:	Mr. Sherman, I say you should write it.

	You are never controversial as it were
Sherman:	That is true.
Adams:	Whereas if I'm the one to do it
	They'll run their quill pens through it.
	I'm obnoxious and disliked, you know that, sir
Sherman:	Yes, I do!
Adams:	Then I say you should write it, Roger. Yes, you.
Sherman:	Good heavens, no!
Adams:	Yes you, Roger Sherman, you!
Sherman:	But,
Adams:	You!
Sherman:	But,
Adams:	You!
Sherman:	But, Mr. Adams! But, Mr. Adams,
	I cannot write with any style or proper etiquette!
	I don't know a participle from a predicate!
	I am just a simple cobbler from Connecticut!
Liberals:	Connecticut, Connecticut, a simple cobbler, he!
Adams:	Mr. Livingston, maybe you should write it.
	You have many friends and you're a diplomat.
Franklin:	Oh, that word!
Adams:	Whereas if I'm the one to do it
	They'll run their quill pens through it.
Liberals:	He's obnoxious and disliked. Did you know that?
Livingston:	I hadn't heard.
Adams:	So I say you should write it, Robert, yes, you!
Livingston:	Not me, Johnny!
Adams:	Yes, you, Robert Livingston, you!
Livingston:	But,
Adams:	You!
Livingston:	But,
Adams:	You!
Livingston:	But! Mr. Adams, dear Mr. Adams,
	I've been presented with a new son by the noble stork.
	So I am going home to celebrate and pop the cork
	With all the Livingstons together back in old New York!

Liberals:	New York, New York. Livingston's going to pop a cork
Adams:	Well, Mr. Jefferson?
Jefferson:	Mr. Adams, leave me alone!
(Liberals:	La la la la, etc.)
Adams:	Mr. Jefferson.
Jefferson:	Mr. Adams, I have not seen my wife for the past six months. I beg you, man,
Adams:	And we solemnly declare that we will preserve our liberties, Being with one mind resolved to die free men rather than to live slaves.
	Thomas Jefferson on the necessity of taking up arms, 1775.
	Magnificent! You write ten times better than any man in Congress, including me.
	Now then, sir, will you be a patriot or a lover?
(Jefferson:	Lover!)
Adams:	No!
Jefferson:	But I burn, Mister A.
Adams:	So do I, Mister J.!
Jefferson:	You?
1st Congressman:	You do?
2nd Congressman:	John! Who'd have thought it!
Adams:	Mr. Jefferson, dear Mr. Jefferson
	I'm only forty-one. I still have my virility,
	And I can romp through Cupid's Grove with great agility.
	But life is more than sexual combustibility!
Liberals:	Bustibility, bustibility, combustibili-
Jefferson:	Quiet!
	Mr. Adams, damn you, Mr. Adams,
	You're obnoxious and disliked; that cannot be denied
	Once again you stand between me and my lovely bride?
Liberals:	Lovely bride.
Jefferson:	Oh, Mr. Adams, you are driving me to homicide.
Liberals:	Homicide, homicide. We may see murder yet!

SAMUEL FRANCIS SMITH

AMERICA

1832

The words to "America," or "My Country 'Tis of Thee," were written by a young Massachu-setts divinity student, Samuel Francis Smith (1808–1895), in 1832, to the melody of the British national anthem, "God Save the King."

1.

My country! 'tis of thee,
Sweet land of liberty,
Of thee I sing;
Land where my fathers died,
Land of the Pilgrims' pride,
From ev'ry mountain side
Let freedom ring.

2.

My native country, thee,
Land of the noble free,
Thy name I love;
I love thy rocks and rills;
Thy woods and templed hills;
My heart with rapture thrills
Like that above.

3.

Let music swell the breeze,
And ring from all the trees
Sweet Freedom's song;
Let mortal tongues awake,
Let all that breathe partake,
Let rocks their silence break,
The sound prolong.

4.
Our fathers' God, to Thee,
Author of liberty,
To Thee we sing;
Long may our land be bright
With Freedom's holy light;
Protect us by Thy might,
Great God, our King.

FRED R. CONRAD, Celebrating the Statue of Liberty's centenary, New York, 1986.

If I Had a Country, I Should Be a Patriot

SEPTEMBER 24, 1847

Frederick Douglass (1817–1895) was born Frederick Augustus Washington Bailey in Maryland, to a slave mother and, it is believed, her white master. Douglass taught himself to read and eventually arranged to flee to the North in 1838. He joined the Massachusetts Anti-Slavery Society, founded by William Lloyd Garrison, and impressed his colleagues with his oratorical skill. Douglass's powerful autobiography, *Narrative of the Life of Frederick Douglass*, brought him fame. He fled to England, and was able to return only after English friends paid for his freedom. Shortly afterward, in 1847, Douglass gave this address in Syracuse, New York.

Ours is a glorious land, and from across the Atlantic we welcome those who are stricken by the storms of despotism. Yet the damning fact remains, there is not a rood of earth under the stars and the eagle on your flag, where a man of my complexion can stand free. There is no mountain so high, no plain so extensive, no spot so sacred, that it can secure to me the right of liberty. Wherever waves the star-spangled banner there the bondman may be arrested and hurried back to the jaws of Slavery. This is your "land of the free," your "home of the brave." . . .

I never knew what freedom was till I got beyond the limits of the American eagle. When I first rested my head on a British Island, I felt that the eagle might scream, but from its talons and beak I was free, at least for a time. . . .

I know this kind of talk is not agreeable to what are called patriots. Indeed some have called me a traitor. . . . Two things are necessary to make a traitor. One is, he shall have a country. I believe if I had a country, I should be a patriot. I think I have all the feelings necessary—all the moral material, to say nothing about the intellectual. I do not know that I ever felt the emotion, but sometimes thought I had a glimpse of it. When I have been delighted with the little brook that passes by the cottage in which I was born, with the woods and the fertile fields, I felt a sort of glow which I suspect resembles a little what they call patriotism. I can look with some admiration on your wide lakes, your fertile fields, your enterprise, your industry, your many lovely institutions. I can read with pleasure your Constitution to establish justice and secure the blessings of liberty to posterity. Those are precious sayings to my mind.

But when I remember that the blood of four sisters and one brother is making fat the soil of Maryland and Virginia—when I remember that an aged grandmother . . . reared twelve children for the Southern [slave] market, and these one after another . . . were torn from her bosom—when I remember that when she became too much racked for toil, she was turned out by a professed Christian master to grope her way in the darkness of old age, literally to die with none to help her, and the institutions of this country sanctioning and sanctifying this crime, I have no words of eulogy, I have no patriotism. How can I love a country where the blood of my own blood, the flesh of my own flesh, is now toiling under the lash? . . .

No, I make no pretension to patriotism. So long as my voice can be heard on this or the other side of the Atlantic, I will hold up America to the lightning scorn of moral indignation. In doing this, I shall feel myself discharging the duty of a true patriot; for he is a lover of his country who rebukes and does not excuse its sins.

LETTER TO PRESIDENT LINCOLN

AUGUST 25, 1864

Annie Davis's letter to President Lincoln in August of 1864 reflected the predicament of many slaves in border states. The Emancipation Proclamation, issued by President Lincoln in January of 1863, applied only to slaves in states rebelling against the Union. While the institution of slavery was on the verge of collapse, slaves in states loyal to the Union and slaves in southern states already under Union control were not freed.

Belair [*Md.*]

Mr president   It is my Desire to be free. to go to see my people on the eastern shore.   my mistress wont let me   you will please let me know if we are free. and what i can do.   I write to you for advice.   please send me word this week. or as soon as possible and oblidge.

SYMPATHY

1893

Dunbar (1872–1906), the son of former slaves from Ohio, wrote poems in black dialect and standard English. Although he published extensively and attracted a national audience with *Lyrics of Lowly Life* in 1896, he never made enough money to quit his job as an elevator operator. Today he is regarded as one of the most influential poets of the African American tradition and in the field of American poetry.

I know what the caged bird feels, alas!
When the sun is bright on the upland slopes;
When the wind stirs soft through the springing grass
And the river flows like a stream of glass;
When the first bird sings and the first bud opes,
And the faint perfume from its chalice steals—
I know what the caged bird feels!

I know why the caged bird beats his wing
Till its blood is red on the cruel bars;
For he must fly back to his perch and cling
When he fain would be on the bough a-swing;
And a pain still throbs in the old, old scars
And they pulse again with a keener sting—

I know why he beats his wing!
I know why the caged bird sings, ah me,
When his wing is bruised and his bosom sore,—
When he beats his bars and he would be free;
It is not a carol of joy or glee,
But a prayer that he sends from his heart's deep core,
But a plea, that upward to Heaven he flings—
I know why the caged bird sings!

E. B. WHITE

FREEDOM

JULY 1940

Elwyn Brooks White (1899–1985) is best known for his classic children's books, *Stuart Little* (1945), *Charlotte's Web* (1952), and *The Trumpet of the Swan* (1970). He was also a writer and editor at *The New Yorker* magazine and a leading midcentury essayist and humorist. Students know him as the final authority on literary style, from his revision of William Strunk Jr.'s *The Elements of Style*. This essay was published in the collection *One Man's Meat* (1942).

I have often noticed on my trips to the city that people have recut their clothes to follow the fashion. On my last trip, however, it seemed to me that people had remodeled their ideas too—taken in their convictions a little at the waist, shortened the sleeves of their resolve, and fitted themselves out in a new intellectual ensemble copied from a smart design out of the very latest page of history. It seemed to me they had strung along with Paris a little too long.

I confess to a disturbed stomach. I feel sick when I find anyone adjusting his mind to the new tyranny that is succeeding abroad. Because of its fundamental strictures, fascism does not seem to me to admit of any compromise or any rationalization, and I resent the patronizing air of persons who find in my plain belief in freedom a sign of immaturity. If it is boyish to believe that a human being should live free, then I'll gladly arrest my development and let the rest of the world grow up.

I shall report some of the strange remarks I heard in New York. One man told me that he thought perhaps the Nazi ideal was a sounder ideal than our constitutional system "because have you ever noticed what fine alert young faces the young German soldiers have in the newsreel?" He added: "Our American youngsters spend all their time at the movies—they're a mess." That was his summation of the case, his interpretation of the new Europe. Such a remark leaves me pale and shaken. If it represents the peak of our intelligence, then the steady mark of despotism will not receive any considerable setback at our shores.

Another man informed me that our democratic notion of popular government was decadent and not worth bothering about—"because England is really rotten and the industrial towns there are a disgrace." That was the only reason he gave for the hopelessness of democracy; and he seemed mightily pleased with himself, as though he were more familiar than most with the anatomy of decadence, and had detected subtler aspects of the situation than were discernible to the rest of us.

Another man assured me that anyone who took *any* kind of government seriously was a gullible fool. You could be sure, he said, that there is nothing but corruption "because of the way Clemenceau acted at Versailles." He said it didn't make any difference really about this war. It was just another war. Having relieved himself of this majestic bit of reasoning, he subsided.

Another individual, discovering signs of zeal creeping into my blood, berated me for having lost my detachment, my pure skeptical point of view. He announced that he wasn't going to be swept away by all this nonsense, but would prefer to remain in the role of innocent bystander, which he said was the duty of any intelligent person. (I noticed, however, that he phoned later to qualify his remark, as though he had lost some of his innocence in the cab on the way home.)

Those are just a few samples of the sort of talk that seemed to be going round—talk that was full of defeatism and disillusion and sometimes of a too studied innocence. Men are not merely annihilating themselves at a great rate these days, but they are telling one another enormous lies, grandiose fibs. Such remarks as I heard are fearfully disturbing in their cumulative effect. They are more destructive than dive bombers and mine fields, for they challenge not merely one's immediate position but one's main defenses. They seemed to me to issue either from persons who could never have really come to grips with freedom, so as to understand her, or from renegades. Where I expected to find indignation, I found paralysis, or a sort of dim acquiescence, as in a child who is dully swallowing a distasteful pill. I was advised of the growing anti-Jewish sentiment by a man who seemed to be watching the phenomenon of intolerance not through tears of shame but with a clear intellectual gaze, as through a well-ground lens.

The least a man can do at such a time is to declare himself and tell where he stands. I believe in freedom with the same burning delight, the same faith, the same intense abandon that attended its birth on this continent more than a century and a half ago. I am writing my declaration rapidly, much as though I were shaving to catch a train. Events abroad give a man a feeling of being pressed for time. Actually I do not believe I am pressed for time, and I apologize to the reader for a false impression that may be created. I just want to tell, before I get slowed down, that I am in love with freedom and that it is an affair of long standing and that it is a fine state to be in, and that I am deeply suspicious of people who are beginning to adjust to fascism and dictators merely because they are succeeding in war. From such adaptable natures a smell rises. I pinch my nose.

For as long as I can remember I have had a sense of living somewhat freely in a natural world. I don't mean I enjoyed freedom of action, but my existence seemed to have the quality of freeness. I traveled with secret papers pertaining to a divine conspiracy. Intuitively I've always been aware of the vitally important pact that a man has with himself, to be all things to himself, and to be identified with all things, to stand self-reliant, taking advantage of his haphazard connection with a planet, riding his luck, and following his bent with the tenacity of a hound. My first and greatest love affair was with this thing we call freedom, this lady of infinite allure, this dangerous and beautiful and sublime being who restores and supplies us all.

It began with the haunting intimation (which I presume every child receives) of his mystical inner life; of God in man; of nature publishing herself through the "I." This elusive sensation is moving and memorable. It comes early in life: a boy, we'll say, sitting on the front steps on a summer night, thinking of nothing in particular, suddenly hearing as with a new perception and as though for the first time the pulsing sound of crickets, overwhelmed with the novel sense of identification with the natural company of insects and grass and night, conscious of a faint answering cry to the universal perplexing question: "What is 'I'?" Or a little girl, returning from the grave of a pet bird and leaning with her elbows on the windowsill, inhaling the unfamiliar draught of death, suddenly seeing herself as part of the complete story. Or an older youth, encountering for the first time a great teacher who by some chance word or mood awakens something and the youth beginning to breathe as an individual and conscious of strength in his vitals. I think the sensation must develop in many men as a feeling of identity with God—an eruption of the spirit caused by allergies and the sense of divine existence as distinct from mere animal existence. This is the beginning of the affair with freedom.

But a man's free condition is of two parts: the instinctive freeness he experiences as an animal dweller on a planet, and the practical liberties he enjoys as a privileged member of human society. The latter is, of the two, more generally understood, more widely admired, more violently challenged and discussed. It is the practical and apparent side of freedom. The United States, almost alone today, offers the liberties and the privileges and the tools of freedom. In this land the citizens are still invited to write their plays and books, to paint their pictures, to meet for discussion, to dissent as well as to agree, to mount soapboxes in the public square, to enjoy education in all subjects without censorship, to hold court and judge one another, to compose music, to talk politics with their neighbors without wondering whether the secret police are listening, to exchange ideas as well as goods, to kid the government when it needs kidding, and to read real news of real events instead of phony news manufactured by a paid agent of the state. This is a fact and should give every person pause.

To be free, in a planetary sense, is to feel that you belong to earth. To be free, in a social sense, is to feel at home in a democratic framework. In Adolf Hitler, although he is a freely flowering individual, we do not detect either type of sensibility. From reading his book I gather that his feeling for earth is not a sense of communion but a driving urge to prevail. His feeling for men is not that they co-exist, but that they are capable of being arranged and standardized by a superior intellect—that their existence suggests not a fulfillment of their personalities but a submersion of their personalities in the common racial destiny. His very great absorption in the destiny of the German people somehow loses some of its effect when you discover, from his writings, in what vast contempt he holds *all* people. "I learned," he wrote, ". . . to gain an insight into the unbelievably primitive opinions and arguments of the people." To him the ordinary man is a primitive, capable only of being used and led. He speaks continually of people as sheep, halfwits, and impudent fools—the same people from whom he asks the utmost in loyalty, and to whom he promises the ultimate in prizes.

Here in America, where our society is based on belief in the individual, not contempt for him, the free principle of life has a chance of surviving. I believe that it must and will survive. To understand freedom is an accomplishment all men may acquire who set their minds in that direction; and to love freedom is a tendency many Americans are born with. To live in the same room with freedom, or in the same hemisphere, is still a profoundly shaking experience for me.

One of the earliest truths (and to him most valuable) that the author of *Mein Kempf* discovered was that it is not the written word, but the spoken word, that in heated moments moves great masses of people to noble or ignoble action. The written word, unlike the spoken word, is something every person examines privately and judges calmly by his own intellectual standards, not by what the man standing next to him thinks. "I know," wrote Hitler, "that one is able to win people far more by the spoken than by the written word. . . ." Later he adds contemptuously: "For let it be said to all knights of the pen and to all the political dandies, especially of today: the greatest changes in this world have never yet been brought about by a goose quill! No, the pen has always been reserved to motivate these changes theoretically."

Luckily I am not out to change the world—that's being done for me, and at a great clip. But I know that the free spirit of man is persistent in nature; it recurs, and has never successfully been wiped out, by fire or flood. I set down the above remarks merely (in the words of Mr. Hitler) to motivate that spirit, theoretically. Being myself a knight of the goose quill, I am under no misapprehension about "winning people"; but I am inordinately proud these days of the quill, for it has shown itself, historically, to be the hypodermic that inoculates men and keeps the germ of freedom always in circulation, so that there are individuals in every time in every land who are the carriers, the Typhoid Marys, capable of infecting others by mere contact and example. These persons are feared by every tyrant—who shows his fear by burning the books and destroying the individuals. A writer goes about his task today with the extra satisfaction that comes from knowing that he will be the first to have his head lopped off—even before the political dandies. In my own case this is a double satisfaction, for if freedom were denied me by force of earthly circumstance, I am the same as dead and would infinitely prefer to go into fascism without my head than with it, having no use for it any more and not wishing to be saddled with so heavy an encumbrance.

as freedom is a breakfastfood

1940

An inventive, experimental poet, E. E. Cummings (1894–1962) used the visual appearance of the words on the page as part of his poetic composition. He incorporated romantic imagery and a modern irony into his work. This poem represents an exploration of personal freedom against the backdrop of an increasingly powerful mass culture.

as freedom is a breakfastfood
or truth can live with right and wrong
or molehills are from mountains made
—long enough and just so long
will being pay the rent of seem
and genius please the talentgang
and water most encourage flame

as hatracks into peachtrees grow
or hopes dance best on bald men's hair
and every finger is a toe
and any courage is a fear
—long enough and just so long
will the impure think all things pure
and hornets wail by children stung

or as the seeing are the blind
and robins never welcome spring
nor flatfolk prove their world is round
nor dingsters die at break of dong
and common's rare and millstones float
—long enough and just so long
tomorrow will not be too late

worms are the words but joy's the voice
down shall go which and up come who
breasts will be breasts thighs will be thighs

deeds cannot dream what dreams can do
—time is a tree(this life one leaf)
but love is the sky and i am for you
just so long and long enough

ARTHUR LEIPZIG, "Chalk Games," Brooklyn, New York, 1950.

FRANKLIN DELANO ROOSEVELT

STATE OF THE UNION ADDRESS

JANUARY 6, 1941

In this address, known as the Four Freedoms speech, FDR committed the United States to the war effort, though our nation did not become officially involved until the Japanese attack on Pearl Harbor eleven months later. Roosevelt outlined the lend-lease program of wartime aid to our allies, strengthened American commitment to preserving the free world against totalitarianism, and immortalized the fundamental rights of a free society.

I address you, the Members of the Seventy-seventh Congress, at a moment unprecedented in the history of the Union. I use the word "unprecedented," because at no previous time has American security been as seriously threatened from without as it is today. . . .

Every realist knows that the democratic way of life is at this moment being directly assailed in every part of the world—assailed either by arms, or by secret spreading of poisonous propaganda by those who seek to destroy unity and promote discord in nations that are still at peace.

During sixteen long months this assault has blotted out the whole pattern of democratic life in an appalling number of independent nations, great and small. The assailants are still on the march, threatening other nations, great and small.

Therefore, as your President, performing my constitutional duty to "give to the Congress information of the state of the Union," I find it, unhappily, necessary to report that the future and the safety of our country and of our democracy are overwhelmingly involved in events far beyond our borders.

Armed defense of democratic existence is now being gallantly waged in four continents. If that defense fails, all the population and all the resources of Europe, Asia, Africa and Australasia will be dominated by the conquerors. Let us remember that the total of those populations and their resources in those four continents greatly exceeds the sum total of the population and the resources of the whole of the Western Hemisphere—many times over.

In times like these it is immature—and incidentally, untrue—for anybody to brag that an unprepared America, single-handed, and with one hand tied behind its back, can hold off the whole world.

No realistic American can expect from a dictator's peace international generosity, or return of true independence, or world disarmament, or freedom of expression, or freedom of religion—or even good business.

Such a peace would bring no security for us or for our neighbors. "Those, who would give up essential liberty to purchase a little temporary safety, deserve neither liberty nor safety."

As a nation, we may take pride in the fact that we are softhearted; but we cannot afford to be soft-headed.

We must always be wary of those who with sounding brass and a tinkling cymbal preach the "ism" of appeasement.

We must especially beware of that small group of selfish men who would clip the wings of the American eagle in order to feather their own nests.

I have recently pointed out how quickly the tempo of modern warfare could bring into our very midst the physical attack which we must eventually expect if the dictator nations win this war.

There is much loose talk of our immunity from immediate and direct invasion from across the seas. Obviously, as long as the British Navy retains its power, no such danger exists. Even if there were no British Navy, it is not probable that any enemy would be stupid enough to attack us by landing troops in the United States from across thousands of miles of ocean, until it had acquired strategic bases from which to operate.

But we learn much from the lessons of the past years in Europe—particularly the lesson of Norway, whose essential seaports were captured by treachery and surprise built up over a series of years.

The first phase of the invasion of this Hemisphere would not be the landing of regular troops. The necessary strategic points would be occupied by secret agents and their dupes—and great numbers of them are already here, and in Latin America.

As long as the aggressor nations maintain the offensive, they—not we—will choose the time and the place and the method of their attack.

That is why the future of all the American Republics is today in serious danger.

That is why this Annual Message to the Congress is unique in our history.

That is why every member of the Executive Branch of the Government and every member of the Congress faces great responsibility and great accountability.

The need of the moment is that our actions and our policy should be devoted primarily—almost exclusively—to meeting this foreign peril. For all our domestic problems are now a part of the great emergency.

Just as our national policy in internal affairs has been based upon a decent respect for the rights and the dignity of all our fellow men within our gates, so our national policy in foreign affairs has been based on a decent respect for the rights and dignity of all nations, large and small. And the justice of morality must and will win in the end. Our national policy is this:

First, by an impressive expression of the public will and without regard to partisanship, we are committed to all-inclusive national defense.

Second, by an impressive expression of the public will and without regard to partisanship, we are committed to full support of all those resolute peoples, everywhere, who are resisting aggression and are thereby keeping war away from our hemisphere. By this support, we express our determination that the democratic cause shall prevail; and we strengthen the defense and the security of our own nation.

Third, by an impressive expression of the public will and without regard to partisanship, we are committed to the proposition that principles of morality and considerations for our own security will never permit us to acquiesce in a peace dictated by aggressors and sponsored by appeasers. We know that enduring peace cannot be bought at the cost of other people's freedom.

In the recent national election there was no substantial difference between the two great parties in respect to that national policy. No issue was fought out on this line before the American electorate. Today it is abundantly evident that American citizens everywhere are demanding and supporting speedy and complete action in recognition of obvious danger.

Therefore, the immediate need is a swift and driving increase in our armament production.

Leaders of industry and labor have responded to our summons. Goals of speed have been set. In some cases these goals are being reached ahead of time; in some cases we are on schedule; in other cases there are slight but not serious delays; and in some cases—and I am sorry to say very important cases—we are all concerned by the slowness of the accomplishment of our plans.

The Army and Navy, however, have made substantial progress during the past year. Actual experience is improving and speeding up our methods of production with every passing day. And today's best is not good enough for tomorrow.

I am not satisfied with the progress thus far made. The men in charge of the program represent the best in training, in ability, and in patriotism. They are not satisfied with the progress thus far made. None of us will be satisfied until the job is done.

No matter whether the original goal was set too high or too low, our objective is quicker and better results. To give you two illustrations:

We are behind schedule in turning out finished airplanes; we are working day and night to solve the innumerable problems and to catch up.

We are ahead of schedule in building warships but we are working to get even further ahead of that schedule.

To change a whole nation from a basis of peacetime production of implements of peace to a basis of wartime production of implements of war is no small task. And the greatest difficulty comes at the beginning of the program, when new tools, new plant facilities, new assembly lines, and new ship ways must first be constructed before the actual materiel begins to flow steadily and speedily from them.

The Congress, of course, must rightly keep itself informed at all times of the progress of the program. However, there is certain information, as the Congress itself will readily recognize, which, in the interests of our own security and those of the nations that we are supporting, must of needs be kept in confidence.

New circumstances are constantly begetting new needs for our safety. I shall ask this Congress for greatly increased new appropriations and authorizations to carry on what we have begun.

I also ask this Congress for authority and for funds sufficient to manufacture additional munitions and war supplies of many kinds, to be turned over to those nations which are now in actual war with aggressor nations.

Our most useful and immediate role is to act as an arsenal for them as well as for ourselves. They do not need man power, but they do need billions of dollars worth of the weapons of defense.

The time is near when they will not be able to pay for them all in ready cash. We cannot, and we will not, tell them that they must surrender, merely because of present inability to pay for the weapons which we know they must have.

I do not recommend that we make them a loan of dollars with which to pay for these weapons—a loan to be repaid in dollars.

I recommend that we make it possible for those nations to continue to obtain war materials in the United States, fitting their orders into our own program. Nearly all their materiel would, if the time ever came, be useful for our own defense.

Taking counsel of expert military and naval authorities, considering what is best for our own security, we are free to decide how much should be kept here and how much should be sent abroad to our friends who by their determined and heroic resistance are giving us time in which to make ready our own defense.

For what we send abroad, we shall be repaid within a reasonable time following the close of hostilities, in similar materials, or, at our option, in other goods of many kinds, which they can produce and which we need.

Let us say to the democracies: "We Americans are vitally concerned in your defense of freedom. We are putting forth our energies, our resources and our organizing powers to give you the strength to regain and maintain a free world. We shall send you, in ever-increasing numbers, ships, planes, tanks, guns. This is our purpose and our pledge."

In fulfillment of this purpose we will not be intimidated by the threats of dictators that they will regard as a breach of international law or as an act of war our aid to the democracies which dare to resist their aggression. Such aid is not an act of war, even if a dictator should unilaterally proclaim it so to be.

When the dictators, if the dictators, are ready to make war upon us, they will not wait for an act of war on our part. They did not wait for Norway or Belgium or the Netherlands to commit an act of war.

Their only interest is in a new one-way international law, which lacks mutuality in its observance, and, therefore, becomes an instrument of oppression.

The happiness of future generations of Americans may well depend upon how effective and how immediate we can make our aid felt. No one can tell the exact character of the emergency situations that we may be called upon to meet. The Nation's hands must not be tied when the Nation's life is in danger.

We must all prepare to make the sacrifices that the emergency—almost as serious as war itself—demands. Whatever stands in the way of speed and efficiency in defense preparations must give way to the national need.

A free nation has the right to expect full cooperation from all groups. A free nation has the right to look to the leaders of business, of labor, and of agriculture to take the lead in stimulating effort, not among other groups but within their own groups.

The best way of dealing with the few slackers or trouble makers in our midst is, first, to shave them by patriotic example, and, if that fails, to use the sovereignty of Government to save Government.

As men do not live by bread alone, they do not fight by armaments alone. Those who man our defenses, and those behind them who build our defenses, must have the stamina and the courage which come from unshakable belief in the manner of life which they are defending. The mighty action that we are calling for cannot be based on a disregard of all things worth fighting for.

The Nation takes great satisfaction and much strength from the things which have been done to make its people conscious of their individual stake in the preservation of democratic life in America. Those things have toughened the fibre of our people, have renewed their faith and strengthened their devotion to the institutions we make ready to protect.

Certainly this is no time for any of us to stop thinking about the social and economic problems which are the root cause of the social revolution which is today a supreme factor in the world.

For there is nothing mysterious about the foundations of a healthy and strong democracy. The basic things expected by our people of their political and economic systems are simple. They are:

Equality of opportunity for youth and for others.

Jobs for those who can work.

Security for those who need it.

The ending of special privilege for the few.

The preservation of civil liberties for all.

The enjoyment of the fruits of scientific progress in a wider and constantly rising standard of living.

These are the simple, basic things that must never be lost sight of in the turmoil and unbelievable complexity of our modern world. The inner and abiding strength of our economic and political systems is dependent upon the degree to which they fulfull these expectations.

Many subjects connected with our social economy call for immediate improvement. As examples:

We should bring more citizens under the coverage of old-age pensions and unemployment insurance.

We should widen the opportunities for adequate medical care.

We should plan a better system by which persons deserving or needing gainful employment may obtain it.

I have called for personal sacrifice. I am assured of the willingness of almost all Americans to respond to that call.

A part of the sacrifice means the payment of more money in taxes. In my Budget Message I shall recommend that a greater portion of this great defense program be paid for from taxation than we are paying today. No person should try, or be allowed, to get rich out of this program; and the principle of tax payments in accordance with ability to pay should be constantly before our eyes to guide our legislation.

If the Congress maintains these principles, the voters, putting patriotism ahead of pocketbooks, will give you their applause.

In the future days, which we seek to make secure, we look forward to a world founded upon four essential human freedoms.

The first is freedom of speech and expression—everywhere in the world.

The second is freedom of every person to worship God in his own way—everywhere in the world.

The third is freedom from want—which, translated into world terms, means economic understandings which will secure to every nation a healthy peacetime life for its inhabitants—everywhere in the world.

The fourth is freedom from fear—which, translated into world terms, means a world-wide reduction of armaments to such a point and in such a thorough fashion that no nation will be in a position to commit an act of physical aggression against any neighbor—anywhere in the world.

That is no vision of a distant millennium. It is a definite basis for a kind of world attainable in our own time and generation. That kind of world is the very antithesis of the so-called new order of tyranny which the dictators seek to create with the crash of a bomb.

To that new order we oppose the greater conception—the moral order. A good society is able to face schemes of world domination and foreign revolutions alike without fear.

Since the beginning of our American history, we have been engaged in change—in a perpetual peaceful revolution—a revolution which goes on steadily, quietly adjusting itself to changing conditions—without the concentration camp or the quick-lime in the ditch. The world order which we seek is the cooperation of free countries, working together in a friendly, civilized society.

This nation has placed its destiny in the hands and heads and hearts of its millions of free men and women; and its faith in freedom under the guidance of God. Freedom means the supremacy of human rights everywhere. Our support goes to those who struggle to gain those rights or keep them. Our strength is our unity of purpose. To that high concept there can be no end save victory.

JUDGE LEARNED HAND

ADDRESS AT "I AM AN AMERICAN" DAY, CENTRAL PARK, NEW YORK

MAY 21, 1944

Learned Hand (1872–1961) served as a federal judge from 1909 until 1951. Nicknamed the "Tenth Justice of the Supreme Court" for his many influential decisions, Hand became known as a defender of free speech and liberty in his more than two thousand opinions. Hand's long tenure as a federal judge rendered him one of the most frequently cited judges in our legal history. His address, often referred to as "The Spirit of Liberty," was noted for its emphasis on tolerance in the midst of wartime.

We have gathered here to affirm a faith, a faith in a common purpose, a common conviction, a common devotion. Some of us have chosen America as the land of our adoption; the rest have come from those who did the same. For this reason we have some right to consider ourselves a picked group, a group of those who had the courage to break from the past and brave the dangers and the loneliness of a strange land.

What was the object that nerved us, or those who went before us, to this choice? We sought liberty; freedom from oppression, freedom from want, freedom to be ourselves. This we then sought; this we now believe that we are by way of winning.

What do we mean when we say that first of all we seek liberty? I often wonder whether we do not rest our hopes too much upon constitutions, upon laws and upon courts. These are false hopes; believe me, these are false hopes. Liberty lies in the hearts of men and women; when it dies there, no constitution, no law, no court can save it; no constitution, no law, no court can even do much to help it. While it lies there it needs no constitution, no law, no court to save it.

And what is this liberty which must lie in the hearts of men and women? It is not the ruthless, the unbridled will; it is not freedom to do as one likes. That is the denial of liberty, and leads straight to its overthrow. A society in which men recognize no check upon their freedom soon becomes a society where freedom is the possession of only a savage few; as we have learned to our sorrow.

What, then, is the spirit of liberty? I cannot define it; I can only tell you my own faith. The spirit of liberty is the spirit which is not too sure that it is right; the spirit of liberty is the spirit which seeks to understand the minds of other men and women; the spirit of liberty is the spirit which weighs their interests alongside its own without bias; the spirit of liberty remembers that not even a sparrow falls to earth unheeded.

The spirit of liberty is the spirit of Him who, near two thousand years ago, taught mankind that lesson it has never learned, but has never quite forgotten; that there may be a kingdom where the least shall be heard and considered side by side with the greatest.

And now . . . in the spirit of that America for which our young men are at this moment fighting and dying; in that spirit of liberty and of America I ask you to rise and with me pledge our faith in the glorious destiny of our beloved country. I now ask you to raise your hands and repeat with me this pledge:

I pledge allegiance to the flag of the United States of America, and to the Republic for which it stands—one nation, indivisible, with liberty and justice for all.

FRED SASS, "I Am an American" Day, Times Square, New York, 1946.

I'VE GOT THE LIGHT OF FREEDOM

In July of 1963, legendary folksinger Pete Seeger (1919–), who has won the Grammy, a Kennedy Center artistic honor, and has been inducted into the Rock and Roll Hall of Fame, joined Bob Dylan, Theodore Bikel, and others in a music festival supporting a voter registration drive organized by freedom fighters in Greenwood, Mississippi. One of the most popular songs of the festival was "I've Got the Light of Freedom," which quickly became an anthem of the civil rights movement. In addition to his work for civil rights, Seeger has been involved in peace movements and the labor movement, and he is a strong supporter of the environment.

I've got the light of freedom,
I'm going to let it shine,
I've got the light of freedom,
I'm going to let it shine.

I've got the light of freedom,
I'm going to let it shine.
Let it shine, let it shine, let it shine.

RONALD REAGAN

ADDRESS TO STUDENTS, MOSCOW STATE UNIVERSITY

MAY 31, 1988

Throughout his career, Ronald Reagan was a strong anti-Communist and believer in the free-market economy. He was famous for calling the Soviet Union the "evil empire," and by the end of his second term, the Berlin Wall had been torn down and the centralized economy of the Soviet Union was disintegrating. Reagan delivered this address in Moscow standing underneath a portrait of Lenin.

. . . Standing here before a mural of your revolution, I want to talk about a very different revolution that is taking place right now, quietly sweeping the globe, without bloodshed or conflict. Its effects are peaceful, but they will fundamentally alter our world, shatter old assumptions, and reshape our lives.

It's easy to underestimate because it's not accompanied by banners or fanfare. It has been called the technological or information revolution, and as its emblem, one might take the tiny silicon chip—no bigger than a fingerprint. One of these chips has more computing power than a roomful of old-style computers. . . .

Like a chrysalis, we're emerging from the economy of the Industrial Revolution—an economy confined to and limited by the Earth's physical resources—into . . . an era in which there are no bounds on human imagination and the freedom to create is the most precious natural resource.

Think of that little computer chip. Its value isn't in the sand from which it is made, but in the microscopic architecture designed into it by ingenious human minds. Or take the example of the satellite relaying this broadcast around the world, which replaces thousands of tons of copper mined from the Earth and molded into wire. In the new economy, human invention increasingly makes physical resources obsolete. We're breaking through the material conditions of existence to a world where man creates his own destiny. Even as we explore the most advanced reaches of science, we're returning to the age-old wisdom of our culture, a wisdom contained in the book of Genesis in the Bible: In the beginning was the spirit, and it was from this spirit that the material abundance of creation issued forth.

But progress is not foreordained. The key is freedom—freedom of thought, freedom of information, freedom of communication. . . .

Some people, even in my own country, look at the riot of experiment that is the free market and see only waste. What of all the entrepreneurs that fail? Well, many do, particularly the successful ones. Often several times. And if you ask them the secret of their success, they'll tell you, it's all that they learned in their struggles along the way—yes, it's what they learned from failing. Like an athlete in competition, or a scholar in pursuit of the truth, experience is the greatest teacher. . . .

We Americans make no secret of our belief in freedom. In fact, it's something of a national pastime. Every four years the American people choose a new president, and 1988 is one of those years. At one point there were 13 major candidates running in the two major parties, not to mention all the others, including the Socialist and Libertarian candidates—all trying to get my job.

About 1,000 local television stations, 8,500 radio stations, and 1,700 daily newspapers, each one an independent, private enterprise, fiercely independent of the government, report on the candidates, grill them in interviews, and bring them together for debates. In the end, the people vote—they decide who will be the next president.

But freedom doesn't begin or end with elections. Go to any American town, to take just an example, and you'll see dozens of churches, representing many different beliefs—in many places synagogues and mosques—and you'll see families of every conceivable nationality, worshipping together.

Go into any schoolroom, and there you will see children being taught the Declaration of Independence, that they are endowed by their Creator with certain inalienable rights—among them life, liberty, and the pursuit of happiness—that no government can justly deny—the guarantees in their Constitution for freedom of speech, freedom of assembly, and freedom of religion.

Go into any courtroom and there will preside an independent judge, beholden to no government power. There every defendant has the right to a trial by a jury of his peers, usually 12 men and women—common citizens, they are the ones, the only ones, who weigh the evidence and decide on guilt or innocence. In that court, the accused is innocent until proven guilty, and the word of a policeman, or any official, has no greater legal standing than the word of the accused.

Go to any university campus, and there you'll find an open, sometimes heated discussion of the problems in American society and what can be done to correct them. Turn on the television, and you'll see the legislature conducting the business of government right there before the camera, debating and voting on the legislation that will become the law of the land. March in any demonstration, and there are many of them—the people's right of assembly is guaranteed in the Constitution and protected by the police. Go into any union hall, where the members know their right to strike is protected by law. . . .

But freedom is even more than this: Freedom is the right to question, and change the established way of doing things. It is the continuing revolution of the marketplace. It is the understanding that allows us to recognize shortcomings and seek solutions. It is the right to put forth an idea, scoffed at by the experts, and watch it catch fire among the people. It is the right to follow your dream, to stick to your conscience, even if you're the only one in a sea of doubters.

Freedom is the recognition that no single person, no single authority or government has a monopoly on the truth, but that every individual life is infinitely precious, that every one of us put on this earth has been put here for a reason and has something to offer. . . .

Democracy is less a system of government than it is a system to keep government limited, unintrusive: A system of constraints on power to keep politics and government secondary to the important things in life, the true sources of value found only in family and faith.

But I hope you know I go on about these things not simply to extol the virtues of my own country, but to speak to the true greatness of the heart and soul of your land. Who, after all, needs to tell the land of Dostoevsky about the quest for truth, the home of Kandinsky and Scriabin about imagination, the rich and noble culture of the Uzbek man of letters, Alisher Navio, about beauty and heart?

The great culture of your diverse land speaks with a glowing passion to all humanity. Let me cite one of the most eloquent contemporary passages on human freedom. It comes, not from the literature of America, but from this country, from one of the greatest writers of the twentieth century, Boris Pasternak, in the novel *Dr. Zhivago*. He writes, "I think that if the beast who sleeps in man could be held down by threats—any kind of threat, whether of jail or of retribution after death—then the highest emblem of humanity would be the lion tamer in the circus with his whip, not the prophet who sacrificed himself. But this is just the point—what has for centuries raised man above the beast is not the cudgel, but an inward music—the irresistible power of unarmed truth."

The irresistible power of unarmed truth. Today the world looks expectantly to signs of change, steps toward greater freedom in the Soviet Union. . . .

Your generation is living in one of the most exciting, hopeful times in Soviet history. It is a time when the first breath of freedom stirs the air and the heart beats to the accelerated rhythm of hope, when the accumulated spiritual energies of a long silence yearn to break free.

I am reminded of the famous passage near the end of Gogol's *Dead Souls*. Comparing his nation to a speeding troika, Gogol asks what will be its destination. But he writes, "There was no answer save the bell pouring forth marvelous sound."

We do not know what the conclusion of this journey will be, but we're hopeful that the promise of reform will be fulfilled. In this Moscow spring, this May 1988, we may be allowed that hope—that freedom, like the fresh green sapling planted over Tolstoi's grave, will blossom forth at last in the rich fertile soil of your people and culture. We may be allowed to hope that the marvelous sound of a new openness will keep rising through, ringing through, leading to a new world of reconciliation, friendship, and peace. . . .

FREEDOM OF SPEECH AND OF THE PRESS

Socialist Party candidate Eugene V. Debs campaigning for president, 1912.

STATEMENT AT TRIAL OF JOHN PETER ZENGER

1735

In 1735, John Peter Zenger, publisher of the *New York Weekly Journal,* was imprisoned and put on trial for attacking the policies of the royal governor, William Cosby. At his trial, attorney Andrew Hamilton (1676–1741) established truth as a defense against libel, won an acquittal for Zenger, and scored an important victory for freedom of the press. The trial was called "the morning star of liberty" by New York's Chief Justice (and later New Jersey's governor) Lewis Morris.

. . . There is heresy in law as well as in religion, and both have changed very much; and we well know that it is not two centuries ago that a man would have burned as a heretic for owning such opinions in matters of religion as are publicly written and printed at this day. They were fallible men, it seems, and we take the liberty, not only to differ from them in religious opinion, but to condemn them and their opinions too; and I must presume that in taking these freedoms in thinking and speaking about matters of faith or religion, we are in the right; for, though it is said there are very great liberties of this kind taken in New York, yet I have heard of no information preferred by Mr. Attorney for any offenses of this sort. From which I think it is pretty clear that in New York a man may make very free with his God, but he must take special care what he says of his Governor. It is agreed upon by all men that this is a reign of liberty, and while men keep within the bounds of truth, I hope they may with safety both speak and write their sentiments of the conduct of men of power; I mean of that part of their conduct only which affects the liberty or property of the people under their administration; were this to be denied, then the next step may make them slaves. For what notions can be entertained of slavery beyond that of suffering the greatest injuries and oppressions without the liberty of complaining; or if they do, to be destroyed, body and estate, for so doing?

It is said, and insisted upon by Mr. Attorney, that government is a sacred thing; that it is to be supported and reverenced; it is government that protects our persons and estates; that prevents treasons, murders, robberies, riots, and all the train of evils that overturn kingdoms and states and ruin particular persons; and if those in the administration, especially the supreme magistrates, must have all their conduct censured by private men, government cannot subsist. This is called a licentiousness not to be tolerated. It is said that it brings the rulers of the people into contempt so that their authority is not regarded, and so that in the end the laws cannot be put in execution. These, I say, and such as these, are the general topics insisted upon by men in power and their advocates. But I wish it might be considered at the same time how often it has happened that the abuse of power has been the primary cause of these evils, and that it was the injustice and oppression of these great men which has commonly brought them into contempt with the people. The craft and art of such men are great, and who that is the least acquainted with history or with law can be ignorant of the specious pretenses which have often been made use of by men in power to introduce arbitrary rule and destroy the liberties of a free people. . . .

If a libel is understood in the large and unlimited sense urged by Mr. Attorney, there is scarce a writing I know that may not be called a libel, or scarce any person safe from being called to account as a libeler, for Moses, meek as he was, libeled Cain; and who is it that has not libeled the devil? For, according to Mr. Attorney, it is no justification to say one has a bad name. . . . How must a man speak or write, or what must he hear, read, or sing? Or when must he laugh, so as to be secure from being taken up as a libeler? I sincerely believe that were some persons to go through the streets of New York nowadays and read a part of the Bible, if it were not known to be such, Mr. Attorney, with the help of his innuendoes, would easily turn it into a libel. As for instance: Isaiah 11:16: "The leaders of the people cause them to err, and they that are led by them are destroyed." But should Mr. Attorney go about to make this a libel, he would read it thus: "The leaders of the people" (*innuendo*, the Governor and council of New York) "cause them" (*innuendo*, the people of this province) "to err, and they" (the Governor and council meaning) "are destroyed" (*innuendo*, are deceived into the loss of their liberty), "which is the worst kind of destruction." . . .

The loss of liberty to a generous mind is worse than death; and yet we know there have been those in all ages who, for the sakes of preferment or some imaginary honor, have freely lent a helping hand to oppress, nay, to destroy, their country. This brings to my mind that saying of the immortal Brutus, when he looked upon the creatures of Caesar, who were very great men, but by no means good men: "You Romans," said Brutus, "if yet I may call you so, consider what you are doing; remember that you are assisting Caesar to forge those very chains which one day he will make yourselves wear." This is what every man that values freedom ought to consider; he should act by judgment and not by affection or self-interest; for where those prevail, no ties of either country or kindred are regarded; as, upon the other hand, the man who loves his country prefers its liberty to all other considerations, well knowing that without liberty life is a misery. . . .

Power may justly be compared to a great river; while kept within its bounds, it is both beautiful and useful, but when it overflows its banks, it is then too impetuous to be stemmed; it bears down all before it, and brings destruction and desolation wherever it comes. If, then, this be the nature of power, let us at least do our duty, and, like wise men who value freedom, use our utmost care to support liberty, the only bulwark against lawless power, which, in all ages, has sacrificed to its wild lust and boundless ambition the blood of the best men that ever lived.

I hope to be pardoned, sir, for my zeal upon this occasion. It is an old and wise caution that "when our neighbor's house is on fire, we ought to take care of our own." For though, blessed be God, I live in a government where liberty is well understood and freely enjoyed, yet experience has shown us all (I am sure it has to me) that a bad precedent in one government is soon set up for an authority in another; and therefore I cannot but think it mine and every honest man's duty that, while we pay all due obedience to men in authority, we ought, at the same time, to be upon our guard against power wherever we apprehend that it may affect ourselves or our fellow subjects.

I am truly very unequal to such an undertaking, on many accounts. And you see I labor under the weight of many years and am borne down with great infirmities of body; yet old and weak as I am, I should think it my duty, if required, to go to the utmost part of the land, where my service could be of any use in assisting to quench the flame of persecutions upon informations, set on foot by the government to deprive a people of the right of remonstrating, and complaining too, of the arbitrary attempts of men in power. Men who injure and oppress the people under their administration provoke them to cry out and complain, and then make that very complaint the foundation for new oppressions and prosecutions. I wish I could say there were no instances of this kind. But, to conclude, the question before the court, and you, gentlemen of the jury, is not of small nor private concern; it is not the cause of a poor printer, nor of New York alone, which you are now trying. No! It may, in its consequence, affect every free man that lives under a British government on the main continent of America. It is the best cause; it is the cause of liberty; and I make no doubt but your upright conduct, this day, will not only entitle you to the love and esteem of your fellow citizen, but every man who prefers freedom to a life of slavery will bless and honor you as men who have baffled the attempt of tyranny, and, by an impartial and uncorrupt verdict, have laid a noble foundation for securing to our-selves, our posterity, and our neighbors that to which nature and the laws of our country have given us a right—the liberty of both exposing and opposing arbitrary power (in these parts of the world at least) by speaking and writing truth. . . .

ABRAMS V. U.S.
250 U.S. 616

1919

This case involved a small group of anarchist Russian immigrants who were sentenced to fifteen to twenty years in prison under the Espionage Act for writing and distributing two leaflets attacking President Wilson. The Supreme Court upheld the harsh convictions. In a famous dissent, Justice Oliver Wendell Holmes (1841–1935) objected that the "surreptitious publishing of a silly leaflet by an unknown man" did not satisfy the "clear and present danger" test Holmes had articulated in an earlier opinion. Holmes, a Civil War veteran, renowned legal scholar, and chief justice of the Massachusetts Supreme Court before his appointment to the U.S. Supreme Court in 1902, set forth the bedrock principles underlying the freedom of speech: the power of truth, a belief in the free exchange of ideas, and government that allows room for growth and experiment. The views expressed by Holmes and Brandeis later became adopted by a majority of the Court.

MR. JUSTICE CLARKE delivered the opinion of the Court.

. . . Each of the first three counts charged the defendants with conspiring, when the United States was at war with the Imperial Government of Germany, to unlawfully utter, print, write and publish: In the first count, "disloyal, scurrilous and abusive language about the form of Government of the United States;" in the second count, language "intended to bring the form of Government of the United States into contempt, scorn, contumely and disrepute;" and in the third count, language "intended to incite, provoke and encourage resistance to the United States in said war." . . .

It was charged in each count of the indictment that it was a part of the conspiracy that the defendants would attempt to accomplish their unlawful purpose by printing, writing and distributing in the City of New York many copies of which, properly identified, were attached to the indictment.

All of the five defendants were born in Russia. They were intelligent, had considerable schooling, and at the time they were arrested they had lived in the United States terms varying from five to ten years, but none of them had applied for naturalization. Four of them testified as witnesses in their own behalf and of these, three frankly avowed that they were "rebels," "revolutionists," "anarchists," that they did not believe in government in any form, and they declared that they had no interest whatever in the Government of the United States. The fourth defendant testified that he was a "socialist" and believed in "a proper kind of government, not capitalistic," but in his classification the Government of the United States was "capitalistic."

It was admitted on the trial that the defendants had united to print and distribute the described circulars and that five thousand of them had been printed and distributed about the 22d day of August, 1918. The group had a meeting place in New York City, in rooms rented by defendant Abrams, under an assumed name, and there the subject of printing the circulars was discussed about two weeks before the defendants were arrested. The defendant Abrams, although not a printer, on July 27, 1918, purchased the printing outfit with which the circulars were printed and installed it in a basement room where the work was done at night. The circulars were distributed some by throwing them from a window of a building where one of the defendants was employed and others secretly, in New York City. . . .

The first of the two articles attached to the indictment is conspicuously headed, "The Hypocrisy of the United States and her Allies." After denouncing President Wilson as a hypocrite and a coward because troops were sent into Russia, it proceeds to assail our Government in general, saying:

"His [the President's] shameful, cowardly silence about the intervention in Russia reveals the hypocrisy of the plutocratic gang in Washington and vicinity."

Police raid of a Communist Party office, Boston, Massachusetts, 1919.

It continues:

"He [the President] is too much of a coward to come out openly and say: 'We capitalistic nations cannot afford to have a proletarian republic in Russia.' "

Among the capitalistic nations Abrams testified the United States was included.

Growing more inflammatory as it proceeds, the circular culminates in:

"The Russian Revolution cries: Workers of the World! Awake! Rise! Put down your enemy and mine!

"Yes! friends, there is only one enemy of the workers of the world and that is CAPITALISM."

This is clearly an appeal to the "workers" of this country to arise and put down by force the Government of the United States which they characterize as their "hypocritical," "cowardly" and "capitalistic" enemy.

It concludes:

"Awake! Awake, you Workers of the World!

"REVOLUTIONISTS." . . .

MR. JUSTICE HOLMES dissenting.

. . . In this case sentences of twenty years imprisonment have been imposed for the publishing of two leaflets that I believe the defendants had as much right to publish as the Government has to publish the Constitution of the United States now vainly invoked by them. Even if I am technically wrong and enough can be squeezed from these poor and puny anonymities to turn the color of legal litmus paper; I will add, even if what I think the necessary intent were shown; the most nominal punishment seems to me all that possibly could be inflicted, unless the defendants are to be made to suffer not for what the indictment alleges but for the creed that they avow—a creed that I believe to be the creed of ignorance and immaturity when honestly held, as I see no reason to doubt that it was held here, but which, although made the subject of examination at the trial, no one has a right even to consider in dealing with the charges before the Court.

Persecution for the expression of opinions seems to me perfectly logical. If you have no doubt of your premises or your power and want a certain result with all your heart you naturally express your wishes in law and sweep away all opposition. To allow opposition by speech seems to indicate that you think the speech impotent, as when a man says that he has squared the circle, or that you do not care whole-heartedly for the result, or that you doubt either your power or your premises. But when men have realized that time has upset many fighting faiths, they may come to believe even more than they believe the very foundations of their own conduct that the ultimate good desired is better reached by free trade in ideas—that the best test of truth is the power of the thought to get itself accepted in the competition of the market, and that truth is the only ground upon which their wishes safely can be carried out. That at any rate is the theory of our Constitution. It is an experiment, as all life is an experiment. Every year if not every day we have to wager our salvation upon some prophecy based upon imperfect knowledge. While that experiment is part of our system I think that we should be eternally vigilant against attempts to check the expression of opinions that we loathe and believe to be fraught with death, unless they so imminently threaten immediate interference with the lawful and pressing purposes of the law that an immediate check is required to save the country. I wholly disagree with the argument of the Government that the First Amendment left the common law as to seditious libel in force. History seems to me against the notion. I had conceived that the United States through many years had shown its repentance for the Sedition Act of 1798, by repaying fines that it imposed. Only the emergency that makes it immediately dangerous to leave the correction of evil counsels to time warrants making any exception to the sweeping command, "Congress shall make no law . . . abridging the freedom of speech." Of course I am speaking only of expressions of opinion and exhortations, which were all that were uttered here, but I regret that I cannot put into more impressive words my belief that in their conviction upon this indictment the defendants were deprived of their rights under the Constitution of the United States. . . .

WHITNEY V. CALIFORNIA
274 U.S. 357

1927

Charlotte Whitney was convicted under California's Criminal Syndicalism Act for attending a Communist Party convention. In his concurring opinion, Justice Louis D. Brandeis (1856–1941) objected that advocacy of revolution that does not pose an imminent danger to the public welfare should be protected by the constitutional guarantee of free speech. Together with Holmes's dissent in *Abrams*, Brandeis's eloquent defense of freedom of thought and ideas helped set the direction for the protection of free speech that the Supreme Court would eventually adopt in *Brandenburg v. Ohio* (1969). In *Brandenburg*, the Court held that freedom of speech cannot be suppressed by the government unless it presents a threat of imminent and likely lawless action. Brandeis, a successful Boston lawyer, and liberal advocate of social reform, revolutionized the practice of law by including in his arguments economic and sociological statistics, a technique later known as the "Brandeis brief." He was appointed to the U.S. Supreme Court in 1916.

MR. JUSTICE SANFORD delivered the opinion of the Court.

The defendant, a resident of Oakland, in Alameda County, California, had been a member of the Local Oakland branch of the Socialist Party. This Local sent delegates to the national convention of the Socialist Party held in Chicago in 1919, which resulted in a split between the "radical" group and the old-wing Socialists. The "radicals"—to whom the Oakland delegates adhered—being ejected, went to another hall, and formed the Communist Labor Party of America. . . . In its "Platform and Program" the Party declared . . . that its purpose was "to create a unified revolutionary working class movement in America," . . . for the overthrow of capitalist rule, the conquest of political power and the establishment of a working class government, the Dictatorship of the Proletariat . . .

Shortly thereafter the Local Oakland withdrew from the Socialist Party, and sent accredited delegates, including the defendant, to a convention held in Oakland in November, 1919, for the purpose of organizing a California branch of the Communist Labor Party. The defendant, after taking out a temporary membership in the Communist Labor Party, attended this convention as a delegate and took an active part in its proceedings. She was elected a member of the Credentials Committee, and, as its chairman, made a report to the convention upon which the delegates were seated. She was also appointed a member of the Resolutions Committee, and as such signed the following resolution in reference to political action, among others proposed by the Committee: "The C.L.P. of California fully recognizes the value of political action as a means of spreading communist propaganda. . . .

Therefore, we again urge the workers who are possessed of the right of franchise to cast their votes for the party which represents their immediate and final interest—the C.L.P.—at all elections, being fully convinced of the utter futility of obtaining any real measure of justice or freedom under officials elected by parties owned and controlled by the capitalist class." . . .

After this action, the defendant, without, so far as appears, making any protest, remained in the convention until it adjourned. She later attended as an alternate member one or two meetings of the State Executive Committee in San Jose and San Francisco, and stated, on the trial, that she was then a member of the Communist Labor Party. She also testified that it was not her intention that the Communist Labor Party of California should be an instrument of terrorism or violence, and that it was not her purpose or that of the Convention to violate any known law. . . .

We cannot hold that, as here applied, the Act is an unreasonable or arbitrary exercise of the police power of the State, unwarrantably infringing any right of free speech, assembly or association, or that those persons are protected from punishment by the due process clause who abuse such rights by joining and furthering an organization thus menacing the peace and welfare of the State.

We find no repugnancy in the Syndicalism Act as applied in this case to either the due process or equal protection clauses of the Fourteenth Amendment on any of the grounds upon which its validity has been here challenged.

MR. JUSTICE BRANDEIS, concurring.

Miss Whitney was convicted of the felony of assisting in organizing, in the year 1919, the Communist Labor Party of California, of being a member of it, and of assembling with it. These acts are held to constitute a crime, because the party was formed to teach criminal syndicalism. The statute which made these acts a crime restricted the right of free speech and of assembly theretofore existing. . . .

The mere act of assisting in forming a society for teaching syndicalism, of becoming a member of it, or of assembling with others for that purpose is given the dynamic quality of crime. There is guilt although the society may not contemplate immediate promulgation of the doctrine.

Thus the accused is to be punished, not for contempt, incitement or conspiracy, but for a step in preparation, which, if it threatens the public order at all, does so only remotely. The novelty in the prohibition introduced is that the statute aims, not at the practice of criminal syndicalism, nor even directly at the preaching of it, but at association with those who propose to preach it. . . .

Those who won our independence believed that the final end of the State was to make men free to develop their faculties; and that in its government the deliberative forces should prevail over the arbitrary. They valued liberty both as an end and as a means. They believed liberty to be the secret of happiness and courage to be the secret of liberty. They believed that freedom to think as you will and to speak as you think are means indispensable to the discovery and spread of political truth; that without free speech and assembly discussion would be futile; that with them, discussion affords ordinarily adequate protection against the dissemination of noxious doctrine; that the greatest menace to freedom is an inert people; that public discussion is a political duty; and that this should be a fundamental principle of the American government. They recognized the risks to which all human institutions are subject. But they knew that order cannot be secured merely through fear of punishment for its infraction; that it is hazardous to discourage thought, hope and imagination; that fear breeds repression; that repression breeds hate; that hate menaces stable government; that the path of safety lies in the opportunity to discuss freely supposed grievances and proposed remedies; and that the fitting remedy for evil counsels is a good ones. Believing in the power of reason as applied through public discussion, they eschewed silence coerced by law—the argument of force in its worst form. Recognizing the occasional tyrannies of governing majorities, they amended the Constitution so that free speech and assembly should be guaranteed.

Fear of serious injury cannot alone justify suppression of free speech and assembly. Men feared witches and burnt women. It is the function of speech to free men from the bondage of irrational fears. To justify suppression of free speech there must be reasonable ground to fear that serious evil will result if free speech is practiced. There must be reasonable ground to believe that the danger apprehended is imminent. There must be reasonable ground to believe that the evil to be prevented is a serious one. Every denunciation of existing law tends in some measure to increase the probability that there will be violation of it. Condonation of a breach enhances the probability. Expressions of approval add to the probability. Propagation of the criminal state of mind by teaching syndicalism increases it. Advocacy of law-breaking heightens it still further. But even advocacy of violation, however, reprehensible morally, is not a justification for denying free speech where the advocacy falls sort of incitement and there is nothing to indicate that the advocacy would be immediately acted on. The wide difference between advocacy and incitement, between preparation and attempt, between assembling and conspiracy, must be borne in mind. In order to support a finding of clear and present danger it must be shown either that immediate serious violence was to be expected or was advocated, or that the past conduct furnished reason to believe that such advocacy was then contemplated.

Those who won our independence by revolution were not cowards. They did not fear political change. They did not exalt order at the cost of liberty. To courageous, self-reliant men, with confidence in the power of free and fearless reasoning applied through the processes of popular government, no danger flowing from speech can be deemed clear and present, unless the incidence of the evil apprehended is so imminent that it may befall before there is opportunity for full discussion. If there be time to expose through discussion the falsehood and fallacies, to avert the evil by the processes of education, the remedy to be applied is more speech, not enforced silence. Only an emergency can justify repression. Such must be the rule if authority is to be reconciled with freedom. Such, in my opinion, is the command of the Constitution. It is therefore always open to Americans to challenge a law abridging free speech and assembly by showing that there was no emergency justifying it. . . .

The fact that speech is likely to result in some violence or in destruction of property is not enough to justify its suppression. There must be the probability of serious injury to the State. Among free men, the deterrents ordinarily to be applied to prevent crime are education and punishment for violations of the law, not abridgment of the rights of free speech and assembly. . . .

Whether in 1919, when Miss Whitney did the things complained of, there was in California such clear and present danger of serious evil, might have been made the important issue in the case. She might have required that the issue be determined either by the court or the jury. She claimed below that the statute as applied to her violated the Federal Constitution; but she did not claim that it was void because there was no clear and present danger of serious evil, nor did she request that the existence of these conditions of a valid measure thus restricting the rights of free speech and assembly be passed upon by the court or a jury. On the other hand, there was evidence on which the court or jury might have found that such danger existed. I am unable to assent to the suggestion in the opinion of the Court that assembling with a political party, formed to advocate the desirability of a proletarian revolution by mass action at some date necessarily far in the future, is not a right within the protection of the Fourteenth Amendment. In the present case, however, there was other testimony which tended to establish the existence of a conspiracy, on the part of members of the International Workers of the World, to commit present serious crimes; and likewise to show that such a conspiracy would be furthered by the activity of the society of which Miss Whitney was a member. Under these circumstances the judgment of the state court cannot be disturbed.

MARGARET CHASE SMITH

REMARKS TO THE SENATE IN SUPPORT OF A DECLARATION OF CONSCIENCE

JUNE 1, 1950

The international cold war struggle against communism came to be personified at home by Wisconsin senator Joseph R. McCarthy (1908–1957). From 1950 to 1954, McCarthy alleged that the U.S. government was infiltrated with communists disloyal to the United States. His accusations, combined with investigations conducted by the House Un-American Activities Committee, destroyed the reputations of individuals both within and outside of government. This condemnation of McCarthy and his tactics was drafted and delivered on behalf of seven Republican senators by the Senate's only woman, Margaret Chase Smith of Maine (1897–1995). Smith began her career as a teacher and newspaperwoman, and was Maine's first congresswoman from 1940 to 1948. She served in the Senate from 1949 to 1973.

Mr. President, I would like to speak briefly and simply about a serious national condition. It is a national feeling of fear and frustration that could result in national suicide and the end of everything that we Americans hold dear. It is a condition that comes from the lack of effective leadership either in the legislative branch or the executive branch of our Government. That leadership is so lacking that serious and responsible proposals are being made that national advisory commissions be appointed to provide such critically needed leadership.

I speak as briefly as possible because too much harm has already been done with irresponsible words of bitterness and selfish political opportunism. I speak as simply as possible because the issue is too great to be obscured by eloquence. I speak simply and briefly in the hope that my words will be taken to heart.

Mr. President, I speak as a Republican. I speak as a woman. I speak as a United States Senator. I speak as an American.

The United States Senate has long enjoyed world-wide respect as the greatest deliberative body in the world. But recently that deliberative character has too often been debased to the level of a forum of hate and character assassination sheltered by the shield of congressional immunity.

It is ironical that we Senators can in debate in the Senate, directly or indirectly, by any form of words, impute to any American who is not a Senator any conduct or motive unworthy or unbecoming an American—and without that non-Senator American having any legal redress against us—yet if we say the same thing in the Senate about our colleagues we can be stopped on the grounds of being out of order.

It is strange that we can verbally attack anyone else without restraint and with full protection, and yet we hold ourselves above the same type of criticism here on the Senate floor. Surely the United States Senate is big enough to take self-criticism and self-appraisal. Surely we should be able to take the same kind of character attacks that we "dish out" to outsiders.

I think that it is high time for the United States Senate and its Members to do some real soul searching and to weigh our consciences as to the manner in which we are performing our duty to the people of America and the manner in which we are using or abusing our individual powers and privileges.

I think it is high time that we remembered that we have sworn to uphold and defend the Constitution. I think it is high time that we remembered that the Constitution, as amended speaks not only of the freedom of speech but also of trial by jury instead of trial by accusation.

Whether it be a criminal prosecution in court or a character prosecution in the Senate, there is little practical distinction when the life of a person has been ruined.

Those of us who shout the loudest about Americanism in making character assassinations are all too frequently those who, by our own words and acts, ignore some of the basic principles of Americanism—

The right to criticize.

The right to hold unpopular beliefs.

The right to protest.

The right of independent thought.

The exercise of these rights should not cost one single American citizen his reputation or his right to a livelihood nor should he be in danger of losing his reputation or livelihood merely because he happens to know someone who holds unpopular beliefs. Who of us does not? Otherwise none of us could call our souls our own. Otherwise thought control would have set in.

The American people are sick and tired of being afraid to speak their minds lest they be politically smeared as Communists or Fascists by their opponents. Freedom of speech is not what it used to be in America. It has been so abused by some that it is not exercised by others.

The American people are sick and tired of seeing innocent people smeared and guilty people whitewashed. But there have been enough proved cases, such as the Amerasia case, the Hiss case, the Coplon case, the Gold case, to cause Nation-wide distrust and strong suspicion that there may be something to the unproved, sensational accusations.

As a Republican, I say to my colleagues on this side of the aisle that the Republican Party faces a challenge today that is not unlike the challenge which it faced back in Lincoln's day. The Republican Party so successfully met that challenge that it emerged from the Civil War as the champion of a united nation—in addition to being a party which unrelentingly fought loose spending and loose programs.

Today our country is being psychologically divided by the confusion and the suspicions that are bred in the United States Senate to spread like cancerous tentacles of "know nothing, suspect everything" attitudes. Today we have a Democratic administration which has developed a mania for loose spending and loose programs. History is repeating itself—and the Republican Party again has the opportunity to emerge as the champion of unity and prudence.

The record of the present Democratic administration has provided us with sufficient campaign issues without the necessity of resorting to political smears. America is rapidly losing its position as leader of the world simply because the Democratic administration has pitifully failed to provide effective leadership.

The Democratic administration has completely confused the American people by its daily contradictory grave warnings and optimistic assurances, which show the people that our Democratic administration has no idea of where it is going.

The Democratic administration has greatly lost the confidence of the American people by its complacency to the threat of communism here at home and the leak of vital secrets to Russia through key officials of the Democratic administration. There are enough proved cases to make this point without diluting our criticism with unproved charges.

Surely these are sufficient reasons to make it clear to the American people that it is time for a change and that a Republican victory is necessary to the security of the country. Surely it is clear that this Nation will continue to suffer so long as it is governed by the present ineffective Democratic administration.

Yet to displace it with a Republican regime embracing a philosophy that lacks political integrity or intellectual honesty would prove equally disastrous to the Nation. The Nation sorely needs a Republican victory. But I do not want to see the Republican Party ride to political victory on the Four Horsemen of Calumny—fear, ignorance, bigotry, and smear.

I doubt if the Republican Party could do so, simply because I do not believe the American people will uphold any political party that puts political exploitation above national interest. Surely we Republicans are not so desperate for victory.

I do not want to see the Republican Party win that way. While it might be a fleeting victory for the Republican Party, it would be a more lasting defeat for the American people. Surely it would ultimately be suicide for the Republican Party and the two-party system that has protected our American liberties from the dictatorship of a one-party system.

As members of the minority party, we do not have the primary authority to formulate the policy of our Government. But we do have the responsibility of rendering constructive criticism, of clarifying issues, of allaying fears by acting as responsible citizens.

As a woman, I wonder how the mothers, wives, sisters, and daughters feel about the way in which members of their families have been politically managed in Senate debate—and I use the word "debate" advisedly.

As a United States Senator, I am not proud of the way in which the Senate has been made a publicity platform for irresponsible sensationalism. I am not proud of the reckless abandon in which unproved charges have been hurled from this side of the aisle. I am not proud of the obviously staged, undignified countercharges which have been attempted in retaliation from the other side of the aisle.

I do not like the way the Senate has been made a rendezvous for vilification, for selfish political gain at the sacrifice of individual reputations and national unity. I am not proud of the way we smear outsiders from the floor of the Senate and hide behind the cloak of congressional immunity and still place ourselves beyond criticism on the floor of the Senate.

As an American, I am shocked at the way Republicans and Democrats alike are playing directly into the Communist design of "confuse, divide, and conquer." As an American, I do not want a Democratic administration white wash or cover up any more than I want a Republican smear or witch hunt.

As an American, I condemn a Republican Fascist just as much as I condemn a Democrat Communist. I condemn a Democrat Fascist just as much as I condemn a Republican Communist. They are equally dangerous to you and me and to our country. As an American, I want to see our Nation recapture the strength and unity it once had when we fought the enemy instead of ourselves. . . .

New York Times Co. v. Sullivan
376 U.S. 254

1964

At the time of civil rights demonstrations in Montgomery, Alabama, the *New York Times* published an advertisement containing some false statements. Sullivan and other officials in the police department sued for defamation. In this landmark decision protecting freedom of the press, the Supreme Court held that a public official may not recover damages unless he proves that the defamatory statement was made with "actual malice—that is, with knowledge that it was false, or with reckless disregard for the truth." In effect, the Court recognized that certain errors, inaccuracies, and falsehoods are the price society pays for a free press.

. . . MR. JUSTICE BRENNAN delivered the opinion of the Court.

We are required in this case to determine for the first time the extent to which the constitutional protections for speech and press limit a State's power to award damages in a libel action brought by a public official against critics of his official conduct.

Respondent L. B. Sullivan is one of the three elected Commissioners of the City of Montgomery, Alabama. . . . He brought this civil libel action against the four individual petitioners, who are Negroes and Alabama clergymen, and against petitioner the New York Times Company. . . . A jury in the Circuit Court of Montgomery County awarded him damages of $500,000, the full amount claimed, against all the petitioners, and the Supreme Court of Alabama affirmed.

Respondent's complaint alleged that he had been libeled by statements in a full-page advertisement that was carried in the New York Times on March 29, 1960. Entitled "Heed Their Rising Voices," the advertisement began by stating that "As the whole world knows by now, thousands of Southern Negro students are engaged in widespread non-violent demonstrations in positive affirmation of the right to live in human dignity as guaranteed by the U.S. Constitution and the Bill of Rights." It went on to charge that "in their efforts to uphold these guarantees, they are being met by an unprecedented wave of terror by those who would deny and negate that document which the whole world looks upon as setting the pattern for modern freedom. . . ." Succeeding paragraphs purported to illustrate the "wave of terror" by describing certain alleged events. The text concluded with an appeal for funds for three purposes: support of the student movement, "the struggle for the right-to-vote," and the legal defense of Dr. Martin Luther King, Jr., leader of the movement, against a perjury indictment then pending in Montgomery. . . .

The text appeared over the names of 64 persons, many widely known for their activities in public affairs, religion, trade unions, and the performing arts. Below these names, and under a line reading "We in the south who are struggling daily for dignity and freedom warmly endorse this appeal," appeared the names of the four individual petitioners and of 16 other persons, all but two of whom were identified as clergymen in various Southern cities. The advertisement was signed at the bottom of the page by the "Committee to Defend Martin Luther King and the Struggle for Freedom in the South," and the officers of the Committee were listed.

Of the 10 paragraphs of text in the advertisement, the third and a portion of the sixth were the basis of respondent's claim of libel. They read as follows:

Third paragraph:

"In Montgomery, Alabama, after students sang 'My Country, 'Tis of Thee' on the State Capitol steps, their leaders were expelled from school, and truckloads of police armed with shotguns and tear-gas ringed the Alabama State College Campus. When the entire student body protested to state authorities by refusing to re-register, their dining hall was padlocked in an attempt to starve them into submission."

Sixth paragraph:

"Again and again the Southern violators have answered Dr. King's peaceful protests with intimidation and violence. They have bombed his home almost killing his wife and child. They have assaulted his person. They have arrested him seven times—for 'speeding,' 'loitering' and similar 'offenses.' And now they have charged him with 'perjury'—a *felony* under which they could imprison him for *ten years*. . . ."

Although neither of these statements mentions respondent by name, he contended that the word "police" in the third paragraph referred to him as the Montgomery Commissioner who supervised the Police Department, so that he was being accused of "ringing" the campus with police. He further claimed that the paragraph would be read as imputing to the police, and hence to him, the padlocking of the dining hall in order to starve the students into submission. As to the sixth paragraph, he contended that since arrests are ordinarily made by the police, the statement "They have arrested [Dr. King] seven times" would be read as referring to him; he further contended that the "They" who did the arresting would be equated with the "They" who committed the other described acts and with the "Southern violators." Thus, he argued, the paragraph would be read as accusing the Montgomery police, and hence him, of answering Dr. King's protests with "intimidation and violence," bombing his home, assaulting his person, and charging him with perjury. Respondent and six other Montgomery residents testified that they read some or all of the statements as referring to him in his capacity as Commissioner. . . .

It is uncontroverted that some of the statements contained in the two paragraphs were not accurate descriptions of events which occurred in Montgomery. Although Negro students staged a demonstration on the State Capitol steps, they sang the National Anthem and not "My Country, 'Tis of Thee." Although nine students were expelled by the State Board of Education, this was not for leading the demonstration at the Capitol, but for demanding service at a lunch counter in the Montgomery County Courthouse on another day. Not the entire student body, but most of it, had protested the expulsion, not by refusing to register, but by boycotting classes on a single day; virtually all the students did register for the ensuing semester. The campus dining hall was not padlocked on any occasion, and the only students who may have been barred from eating there were the few who had neither signed a preregistration application nor requested temporary meal tickets. Although the police were deployed near the campus in large numbers on three occasions, they did not at any time "ring" the campus, and they were not called to the campus in connection with the demonstration on the State Capitol steps, as the third paragraph implied. Dr. King had not been arrested seven times, but only four; and although he claimed to have been assaulted some years earlier in connection with his arrest for loitering outside a courtroom, one of the officers who made the arrest denied that there was such an assault. . . .

The cost of the advertisement was approximately $480, and it was published by the Times upon an order from a New York advertising agency acting for the signatory Committee. The agency submitted the advertisement with a letter from A. Philip Randolph, Chairman of the Committee, certifying that the persons whose names appeared on the advertisement had given their permission. Mr. Randolph was known to the Times' Advertising Acceptability Department as a responsible person, and in accepting the letter as sufficient proof of authorization it followed its established practice. . . .

Respondent relies heavily, as did the Alabama courts, on statements of this Court to the effect that the Constitution does not protect libelous publications. Those statements do not foreclose our inquiry here. . . .

Like insurrection, contempt, advocacy of unlawful acts, breach of the peace, obscenity, solicitation of legal business, and the various other formulae for the repression of expression that have been challenged in this Court, libel can claim no talismanic immunity from constitutional limitations. It must be measured by standards that satisfy the First Amendment. . . .

Thus we consider this case against the background of a profound national commitment to the principle that debate on public issues should be uninhibited, robust, and wide-open, and that it may well include vehement, caustic, and sometimes unpleasantly sharp attacks on government and public officials. The present advertisement, as an expression of grievance and protest on one of the major public issues of our time, would seem clearly to qualify for the constitutional protection. The question is whether it forfeits that protection by the falsity of some of its factual statements and by its alleged defamation of respondent.

Authoritative interpretations of the First Amendment guarantees have consistently refused to recognize an exception for any test of truth—whether administered by judges, juries, or administrative officials—and especially one that puts the burden of proving truth on the speaker. The constitutional protection does not turn upon "the truth, popularity, or social utility of the ideas and beliefs which are offered." As Madison said, "Some degree of abuse is inseparable from the proper use of every thing; and in no instance is this more true than in that of the press." In *Cantwell v. Connecticut*, the Court declared:

"In the realm of religious faith, and in that of political belief, sharp differences arise. In both fields the tenets of one man may seem the rankest error to his neighbor. To persuade others to his own point of view, the pleader, as we know, at times, resorts to exaggeration, to vilification of men who have been, or are, prominent in church or state, and even to false statement. But the people of this nation have ordained in the light of history, that, in spite of the probability of excesses and abuses, these liberties are, in the long view, essential to enlightened opinion and right conduct on the part of the citizens of a democracy." . . .

The constitutional guarantees require, we think, a federal rule that prohibits a public official from recovering damages for a defamatory falsehood relating to his official conduct unless he proves that the statement was made with "actual malice"— that is, with knowledge that it was false or with reckless disregard of whether it was false or not. . . .

We hold today that the Constitution delimits a State's power to award damages for libel in actions brought by public officials against critics of their official conduct. Since this is such an action, the rule requiring proof of actual malice is applicable. . . .

Applying these standards, we consider that the proof presented to show actual malice lacks the convincing clarity which the constitutional standard demands, and hence that it would not constitutionally sustain the judgment for respondent under the proper rule of law. . . .

FREEDOM OF RELIGION

JACK MANNING, Commandment Keepers Ethiopian Hebrews Congregation, Harlem, New York, 1964.

JOHN NEWTON

AMAZING GRACE

1779, 1829 (LAST STANZA)

The words to "Amazing Grace" were written by John Newton (1725–1807), an English sailor and sea captain whose ship plied the slave trade. Newton underwent a religious conversion during a violent high-seas storm in 1748 and eventually became a minister in the Church of England. "Amazing Grace" appeared in the 1779 *Olney Hymnal*, which Newton wrote with poet William Cowper. The melody is of unknown origin.

1.

Amazing grace! How sweet the sound

That saved a wretch like me;

I once was lost, but now am found,

Was blind, but now I see.

2.

'Twas grace that taught my heart to fear,

And grace my fears relieved;

How precious did that grace appear

The hour I first believed.

. . .

MARION POST WOLCOTT, Baptism, Morehead, Kentucky, 1940.

CHIEF RED JACKET

Speech Against Missionaries' Efforts to Baptize Members of the Seneca Tribe

1805

Red Jacket was the chief of the Seneca Nation. His Senecan name was Otetiani, which he later changed to Sagoyewatha when he became chief. He supported the British during the American Revolution, hence the name Red Jacket. However, he eventually sought peace with the U.S. government and supported the United States against Britain in the War of 1812. Red Jacket fought hard to preserve Native American customs and resisted European values and missionary efforts. Toward the end of his life, he was deposed as chief, defended himself before a tribunal council, and was reinstated.

Friend and Brother, it was the will of the Great Spirit that we should meet together this day. . . .

Brother, this council fire was kindled by you. It was at your request that we came together at this time. We have listened with attention to what you have said. You requested us to speak our minds freely. This gives us great joy; for we now consider that we stand upright before you and can speak what we think. All have heard your voice, and all speak to you now as one man. Our minds are agreed. . . .

Brother, listen to what we say.

There was a time when our forefathers owned this great island. Their seats extended from the rising to the setting sun. The Great Spirit had made it for the use of Indians. He had created the buffalo, the deer, and other animals for food. He had made the bear and the beaver. Their skins served us for clothing. He had scattered them over the country and taught us how to take them. He had caused the earth to produce corn for bread. All this he had done for his red children because he loved them. If we had some disputes about our hunting ground, they were generally settled without the shedding of much blood.

But an evil day came upon us. Your forefathers crossed the great water and landed on this island. Their numbers were small. They found friends and not enemies. They told us they had fled from their own country for fear of wicked men and had come here to enjoy their religion. They asked for a small seat. We took pity on them, granted their request, and they sat down among us. We gave them corn and meat; they gave us poison in return.

Brother, our seats were once large and yours were small. You have now become a great people, and we have scarcely a place left to spread our blankets. You have got our country, but are not satisfied; you want to force your religion upon us.

Brother, continue to listen.

You say that you are sent to instruct us how to worship the Great Spirit agreeably to his mind; and, if we do not take hold of the religion which you white people teach, we shall be unhappy hereafter. You say that you are right and we are lost. How do we know this to be true?

We understand that your religion is written in a book. If it was intended for us, as well as you, why has not the Great Spirit given to us, and not only to us, but why did he not give to our forefathers the knowledge of that book, with the means of understanding it rightly. We only know what you tell us about it. How shall we know when to believe, being so often deceived by the white people?

Brother, you say there is but one way to worship and serve the Great Spirit. If there is but one religion, why do you white people differ so much about it? Why do not all agree, as you can all read the book?

Brother, we do not understand these things. We are told that your religion was given to your forefathers and has been handed down from father to son. We also have a religion which was given to our forefathers and has been handed down to us, their children. We worship in that way. It teaches us to be thankful for all the favors we receive, to love each other, and to be united. We never quarrel about religion. . . .

Brother, we do not wish to destroy your religion or take it from you. We only want to enjoy our own.

SPEECH TO THE GREATER HOUSTON
MINISTERIAL ASSOCIATION

SEPTEMBER 12, 1960

In 1960, many people doubted that a Catholic could be elected president. A crucial primary victory in the predominantly Protestant state of West Virginia gave John Kennedy's candidacy increased momentum. In this speech, delivered to a group of ministers in the heart of the Bible Belt, Kennedy tackled the religious issue head-on. In an extremely close election that November, he became the first Catholic to be elected president.

. . . While the so-called religious issue is necessarily and properly the chief topic here tonight, I want to emphasize from the outset that we have far more critical issues to face in the 1960 election; the spread of Communist influence, until it now festers ninety miles off the coast of Florida; the humiliating treatment of our President and Vice-President by those who no longer respect our power; the hungry children I saw in West Virginia, the old people who cannot pay their doctor bills, the families forced to give up their farms; an America with too many slums, with too few schools, and too late to the moon and outer space.

These are the real issues which should decide this campaign. And they are not religious issues—for war and hunger and ignorance and despair know no religious barriers.

But because I am a Catholic, and no Catholic has ever been elected President, the real issues in this campaign have been obscured—perhaps deliberately, in some quarters less responsible than this. So it is apparently necessary for me to state once again—not what kind of church I believe in, for that should be important only to me—but what kind of America I believe in.

I believe in an America where the separation of church and state is absolute—where no Catholic prelate would tell the President (should he be Catholic) how to act, and no Protestant minister would tell his parishioners for whom to vote—where no church or church school is granted any public funds or political preference—and where no man is denied public office merely because his religion differs from the President who might appoint him or the people who might elect him.

I believe in an America that is officially neither Catholic, Protestant, nor Jewish—where no public official either requests or accepts instructions on public policy from the pope, the National Council of Churches, or any other ecclesiastical source—where no religious body seeks to impose its will directly or indirectly upon the general populace or the public acts of its officials—and where religious liberty is so indivisible that an act against one church is treated as an act against all.

For while this year it may be a Catholic against whom the finger of suspicion is pointed, in other years it has been, and may someday be again, a Jew—or a Quaker—or a Unitarian—or a Baptist. It was Virginia's harassment of Baptist preachers, for example, that helped lead to Jefferson's Statute of Religious Freedom. Today I may be the victim—but tomorrow it may be you—until the whole fabric of our harmonious society is ripped at a time of great national peril.

Finally, I believe in an America where religious intolerance will someday end—where all men and all churches are treated as equal—where every man has the same right to attend or not attend the church of his choice—where there is no Catholic vote, no anti-Catholic vote, no bloc voting of any kind—and where Catholics, Protestants, and Jews, at both the lay and pastoral level, will refrain from those attitudes of disdain and division which have so often marred their works in the past, and promote instead the American ideal of brotherhood. . . .

This is the kind of America I believe in—and this is the kind I fought for in the South Pacific, and the kind my brother died for in Europe. No one suggested then that we might have a "divided loyalty," that we did "not believe in liberty," or that we belonged to a disloyal group that threatened the "freedoms for which our forefathers died."

And in fact this is the kind of America for which our forefathers died—when they fled here to escape religious test oaths that denied office to members of less favored churches—when they fought for the Constitution, the Bill of Rights, and the Virginia Statute of Religious Freedom—and when they fought at the shrine I visited today, the Alamo. For side by side with Bowie and Crockett died McCafferty and Bailey and Carey—but no one knows whether they were Catholics or not. For there was no religious test at the Alamo.

I ask you tonight to follow in that tradition—to judge me on the basis of my record of fourteen years in Congress—on my declared stands against an ambassador to the Vatican, against unconstitutional aid to parochial schools, and against any boycott of the public schools (which I have attended myself)—instead of judging me on the basis of these pamphlets and publications we all have seen that carefully select quotations out of context from the statements of Catholic leaders, usually in other countries, frequently in other centuries, and always omitting, of course, the statement of the American bishops in 1948 which strongly endorsed church-state separation, and which more nearly reflects the views of almost every American Catholic.

I do not consider these other quotations binding upon my public acts—why should you? But let me say, with respect to other countries, that I am wholly opposed to the state being used by any religious group, Catholic or Protestant, to compel, prohibit, or persecute the free exercise of any other religion. And I hope that you and I condemn with equal fervor those nations which deny their Presidency to Protestants and those which deny it to Catholics. . . .

But let me stress again that these are my views—for, contrary to common newspaper usages I am not the Catholic candidate for President. I am the Democratic Party's candidate for President who happens also to be a Catholic. I do not speak for my church on public matters—and the Church does not speak for me.

Whatever issue may come before me as President—on birth control, divorce, censorship, gambling, or any other subject—I will make my decision in accordance with these views, in accordance with what my conscience tells me to be the national interest, and without regard to outside religious pressures or dictates. And no power or threat of punishment could cause me to decide otherwise.

But if the time should ever come—and I do not concede any conflict to be even remotely possible—when my office would require me to either violate my conscience or violate the national interest, then I would resign the office; and I hope any conscientious public servant would do the same.

But I do not intend to apologize for these views to my critics of either Catholic or Protestant faith—nor do I intend to disavow either my views or my church in order to win this election.

If I should lose on the real issues, I shall return to my seat in the Senate, satisfied that I had tried my best and was fairly judged. But if this election is decided on the basis that forty million Americans lost their chance of being President on the day they were baptized, then it is the whole nation that will be the loser, in the eyes of Catholics and non-Catholics around the world, in the eyes of history, and in the eyes of our own people.

But if, on the other hand, I should win the election, then I shall devote every effort of mind and spirit to fulfilling the oath of the Presidency—practically identical, I might add, to the oath I have taken for fourteen years in the Congress. For, without reservation, I can "solemnly swear that I will faithfully execute the office of President of the United States, and will to the best of my ability preserve, protect, and defend the Constitution . . . so help me God."

ENGEL V. VITALE
370 U.S. 421

1962

Under the First Amendment, freedom of religion has two aspects: Government may not prohibit the "free exercise" of our beliefs, nor may it "establish," or sponsor religion, or favor one religion over another. As Thomas Jefferson described, the First Amendment creates a "wall of separation" between church and state. *Engel v. Vitale* represents the first in a series of cases declaring school prayer unconstitutional. This decision placed the Supreme Court squarely in the middle of the continuing debate over the role of religion in our public life, a battle that is often fought in the schools. The opinion was written by Justice Hugo Black (1886–1971), a former Alabama senator who became known for his strong defense of freedom of speech and religion after his appointment to the Court in 1937.

MR. JUSTICE BLACK delivered the opinion of the Court.

. . . The respondent Board of Education of Union Free School District No. 9, New Hyde Park, New York, acting in its official capacity under state law, directed the School District's principal to cause the following prayer to be said aloud by each class in the presence of a teacher at the beginning of each school day:

"Almighty God, we acknowledge our dependence upon Thee, and we beg Thy blessings upon us, our parents, our teachers and our Country." . . .

Shortly after the practice of reciting the Regents' prayer was adopted by the School District, the parents of ten pupils brought this action in a New York State Court insisting that use of this official prayer in the public schools was contrary to the beliefs, religions, or religious practices of both themselves and their children. . . .

We think that by using its public school system to encourage recitation of the Regents' prayer, the State of New York has adopted a practice wholly inconsistent with the Establishment Clause. There can, of course, be no doubt that New York's program of daily classroom invocation of God's blessings as prescribed in the Regents' prayer is a religious activity. It is a solemn avowal of divine faith and supplication for the blessings of the Almighty. The nature of such a prayer has always been religious, none of the respondents has denied this . . .

The petitioners contend among other things that the state laws requiring or permitting use of the Regents' prayer must be struck down as a violation of the Establishment Clause because that prayer was composed by governmental officials as a part of a governmental program to further religious beliefs. For this reason, petitioners argue, the State's use of the Regents' prayer in its public school system breaches the constitutional wall of separation between Church and State. We agree with that contention since we think that the constitutional prohibition against laws respecting an establishment of religion must at least mean that in this country it is no part of the business of government to compose official prayers for any group of the American people to recite as a part of a religious program carried on by government.

It is a matter of history that this very practice of establishing governmentally composed prayers for religious services was one of the reasons which caused many of our early colonists to leave England and seek religious freedom in America. . . .

It is an unfortunate fact of history that when some of the very groups which had most strenuously opposed the established Church of England found themselves sufficiently in control of colonial governments in this country to write their own prayers into law, they passed laws making their own religion the official religion of their respective colonies. Indeed, as late as the time of the Revolutionary War, there were established churches in at least eight of the thirteen former colonies and established religions in at least four of the other five. But the successful Revolution against English political domination was shortly followed by intense opposition to the practice of establishing religion by law. This opposition crystallized rapidly into an effective political force in Virginia where the minority religious groups such as Presbyterians, Lutherans, Quakers and Baptists had gained such strength that the adherents to the established Episcopal Church were actually a minority themselves. In 1785–1786, those opposed to the established Church, led by James Madison and Thomas Jefferson, who, though themselves not members of any of these dissenting religious groups, opposed all religious establishments by law on grounds of principle, obtained the enactment of the famous "Virginia Bill for Religious Liberty" by which all religious groups were placed on an equal footing so far as the State was concerned. Similar though less far-reaching legislation was being considered and passed in other States. . . .

By the time of the adoption of the Constitution, our history shows that there was a widespread awareness among many Americans of the dangers of a union of Church and State. These people knew, some of them from bitter personal experience, that one of the greatest dangers to the freedom of the individual to worship in his own way lay in the Government's placing its official stamp of approval upon one particular kind of prayer or one particular form of religious services. They knew the anguish, hardship and bitter strife that could come when zealous religious groups struggled with one another to obtain the Government's stamp of approval from each

King, Queen, or Protector that came to temporary power. The Constitution was intended to avert a part of this danger by leaving the government of this country in the hands of the people rather than in the hands of any monarch. But this safeguard was not enough. Our Founders were no more willing to let the content of their prayers and their privilege of praying whenever they pleased be influenced by the ballot box than they were to let these vital matters of personal conscience depend upon the succession of monarchs. The First Amendment was added to the Constitution to stand as a guarantee that neither the power nor the prestige of the Federal Government would be used to control, support or influence the kinds of prayer the American people can say—that the people's religions must not be subjected to the pressures of government for change each time a new political administration is elected to office. Under that Amendment's prohibition against governmental establishment of religion, as reinforced by the provisions of the Fourteenth Amendment, government in this country, be it state or federal, is without power to prescribe by law any particular form of prayer which is to be used as an official prayer in carrying on any program of governmentally sponsored religious activity.

There can be no doubt that New York's state prayer program officially establishes the religious beliefs embodied in the Regents' prayer. The respondents' argument to the contrary, which is largely based upon the contention that the Regents' prayer is "non-denominational" and the fact that the program, as modified and approved by state courts, does not require all pupils to recite the prayer but permits those who wish to do so to remain silent or be excused from the room, ignores the essential nature of the program's constitutional defects. Neither the fact that the prayer may be denominationally neutral nor the fact that its observance on the part of the students is voluntary can serve to free it from the limitations of the Establishment Clause, as it might from the Free Exercise Clause, of the First Amendment, both of which are operative against the States by virtue of the Fourteenth Amendment. Although these two clauses may in certain instances overlap, they forbid two quite different kinds of governmental encroachment upon religious freedom. The Establishment Clause, unlike the Free Exercise Clause, does not depend upon any showing of direct governmental compulsion and is violated by the enactment of laws which establish an official religion whether those laws operate directly to coerce nonobserving individuals or not. This is not to say, of course, that laws officially prescribing a particular form of religious worship do not involve coercion of such individuals. When the power, prestige and financial support of government is placed behind a particular religious belief, the indirect coercive pressure upon religious minorities to conform to the prevailing officially approved religion is plain. But the purposes underlying the Establishment Clause go much further than that. Its first and most immediate purpose rested on the belief that a union of government and religion tends to destroy government and to degrade religion. . . .

It has been argued that to apply the Constitution in such a way as to prohibit state laws respecting an establishment of religious services in public schools is to indicate a hostility toward religion or toward prayer. Nothing, of course, could be more wrong. The history of man is inseparable from the history of religion. And perhaps it is not too much to say that since the beginning of that history many people have devoutly believed that "More things are wrought by prayer than this world dreams of." It was doubtless largely due to men who believed this that there grew up a sentiment that caused men to leave the cross-currents of officially established state religions and religious persecution in Europe and come to this country filled with the hope that they could find a place in which they could pray when they pleased to the God of their faith in the language they chose. And there were men of this same faith in the power of prayer who led the fight for adoption of our Constitution and also for our Bill of Rights with the very guarantees of religious freedom that forbid the sort of governmental activity which New York has attempted here. These men knew that the First Amendment, which tried to put an end to governmental control of religion and of prayer, was not written to destroy either. They knew rather that it was written to quiet well-justified fears which nearly all of them felt arising out of an awareness that governments of the past had shackled men's tongues to make them speak only the religious thoughts that government wanted them to speak and to pray only to the God that government wanted them to pray to. It is neither sacrilegious nor antireligious to say that each separate government in this country should stay out of the business of writing or sanctioning official prayers and leave that purely religious function to the people themselves and to those the people choose to look to for religious guidance. . . .

MEYER LIEBOWITZ, **Pentecostal Church, Harlem, New York, 1969.**

ZELMAN V. SIMMONS-HARRIS
122 S. CT. 2460

2002

Hailed as the most important ruling on religion in the public schools since *Engel v. Vitale*, this 5–4 decision concluded that a plan allowing public money to be used for religious school tuition did not violate the First Amendment's prohibition against government "establishment of religion." The Court found that Cleveland's voucher program allowed parents to make private educational choices for their children, and was therefore neutral with respect to religion. Chief Justice William Rehnquist (1924–), who was appointed to the Supreme Court in 1971 by President Nixon after serving as an assistant attorney general, wrote the opinion.

CHIEF JUSTICE REHNQUIST delivered the opinion of the Court.

The state of Ohio has established a pilot program designed to provide educational choices to families with children who reside in the Cleveland City School District. The question presented is whether this program offends the Establishment Clause of the United States Constitution. We hold that it does not.

There are more than 75,000 children enrolled in the Cleveland City School District. The majority of these children are from low-income and minority families. Few of these families enjoy the means to send their children to any school other than inner-city public school. For more than a generation, however, Cleveland's public schools have been among the worst performing public schools in the Nation. In 1995, a Federal District Court declared a "crisis of magnitude" and placed the entire Cleveland school district under state control. Shortly thereafter, the state auditor found that Cleveland's public schools were in the midst of a "crisis that is perhaps unprecedented in the history of American education." Cleveland City School District Performance Audit 2-1 (Mar. 1996). The district had failed to meet any of the 18 state standards for minimal acceptable performance. Only 1 in 10 ninth graders could pass a basic proficiency examination, and students at all levels performed at a dismal rate compared with students in other Ohio public schools. More than two-thirds of high school students either dropped or failed out before graduation. Of those students who managed to reach their senior year, one of every four still failed to graduate. Of those students who did graduate, few could read, write, or compute at levels comparable to their counterparts in other cities.

It is against this backdrop that Ohio enacted, among other initiatives, its Pilot Project [*9] Scholarship Program. . . .

The program provides two basic kinds of assistance to parents of children in a covered district. First, the program provides *tuition aid* for students in kindergarten through third grade, expanding each year through eighth grade, to attend a participating public or private school of their parent's choosing. Second, the program provides tutorial aid for students who choose to remain enrolled in public school. . . .

Tuition aid is distributed to parents according to financial need. Families with incomes below 200% of the poverty line are given priority and are eligible to receive 90% of private school tuition up to $2,250. For these lowest-income families, participating private schools may not charge a parental co-payment greater than $250. For all other families, the program pays 75% of tuition costs, up to $1,875, with no co-payment cap. . . . Where tuition aid is spent depends solely upon where parents who receive tuition aid choose to enroll their child. If parents choose a private school, checks are made payable to the parents who then endorse the checks over to the chosen school.

The tutorial aid portion of the program provides tutorial assistance through grants to any student in a covered district who chooses to remain in public school. Parents arrange for registered tutors to provide assistance to their children and then submit bills for those services to the State for payment. Students from low-income families receive 90% of the amount charged for such assistance up to $360. All other students receive 75% of that amount. . . .

The program has been in operation within the Cleveland City School District since the 1996–1997 school year. In the 1999–2000 school year, 56 private schools participated in the program, 46 (or 82%) of which had a religious affiliation. None of the public schools in districts adjacent to Cleveland have elected to participate. More than 3,700 students participated in the scholarship program, most of whom (96%) enrolled in religiously affiliated schools. Sixty percent of these students were from families at or below the poverty line. In the 1998–1999 school year, approximately 1,400 Cleveland public school students received tutorial aid. This number was expected to double during the 1999–2000 school year. . . .

The Establishment Clause of the First Amendment, applied to the States through the Fourteenth Amendment, prevents a State from enacting laws that have the "purpose" or "effect" of advancing or inhibiting religion. There is no dispute that the program challenged here was enacted for the valid secular purpose of providing educational assistance to poor children in a demonstrably failing public school system. Thus, the question presented is whether the Ohio program nonetheless has the forbidden "effect" of advancing or inhibiting religion.

To answer that question, our decisions have drawn a consistent distinction between government programs that provide aid directly to religious schools, and programs of true private choice, in which government aid reaches religious schools only as a result of the genuine and independent choices of private individuals. . . .

[Our previous cases] *Mueller, Witters,* and *Zobrest* thus make clear that where a government aid program is neutral with respect to religion, and provides assistance directly to a broad class of citizens who, in turn, direct government aid to religious schools wholly as a result of their own genuine and independent private choice, the program is not readily subject to challenge under the Establishment Clause. . . .

In sum, the Ohio program is entirely neutral with respect to religion. It provides benefits directly to a wide spectrum of individuals, defined only by financial need and residence in a particular school district. It permits such individuals to exercise genuine choice among options public and private, secular and religious. The program is therefore a program of true private choice. In keeping with an unbroken line of decisions rejecting challenges to similar programs, we hold that the program does not offend the Establishment Clause.

THE RIGHT TO BE LET ALONE

ERNST HAAS, **Refugees, New York, 1951.**

JAMES OTIS

STATEMENT AGAINST THE WRITS OF ASSISTANCE, BOSTON

1761

A prominent Boston lawyer, Otis (1725–1783) resigned his prestigious position as advocate general of the admiralty court to oppose the notorious British writs of assistance, which placed virtually no limits on the ability of British customs officers to search for smuggled goods. Otis lost the case, but his arguments laid the foundation for the Fourth Amendment's prohibition against unreasonable search and seizure. Otis's prominent career ended when he was struck on the head during a quarrel with a British officer and was rendered insane.

May it please your honors, I was desired by one of the court to look into the books, and consider the question now before them concerning writs of assistance. I have, accordingly, considered it, and now appear not only in obedience to your order, but likewise in behalf of the inhabitants of this town, who have presented another petition, and out of regard to the liberties of the subject. And I take this opportunity to declare that, whether under a fee or not (for in such a cause as this I despise a fee), I will to my dying day oppose with all the powers and faculties God has given me all such instruments of slavery, on the one hand, and villainy, on the other, as this writ of assistance is.

It appears to me the worst instrument of arbitrary power, the most destructive of English liberty and the fundamental principles of law, that ever was found in an English lawbook. . . . I shall not think much of my pains in this cause, as I engaged in it from principle. I was solicited to argue this cause as Advocate General; and because I would not, I have been charged with desertion from my office. To this charge I can give a very sufficient answer. I renounced that office, and I argue this cause from the same principle; and I argue it with the greater pleasure, as it is in favor of British liberty. . . .

Your honors will find in the old books concerning the office of a justice of the peace precedents of general warrants to search suspected houses. But in more modern books you will find only special warrants to search such and such houses, specially named, in which the complainant has before sworn that he suspects his goods are concealed; and will find it adjudged that special warrants only are legal. In the same manner I rely on it that the writ prayed for in this petition, being general, is illegal. It is a power that places the liberty of every man in the hands of every petty officer. I say I admit that special writs of assistance, to search special places, may be granted to certain persons on oath; but I deny that the writ now prayed for can be granted, for I beg leave to make some observations on the writ itself, before I proceed to other acts of Parliament. In the first place, the writ is universal, being directed "to all and singular justices, sheriffs, constables, and all other officers and subjects"; so that, in short, it is directed to every subject in the king's dominions. Everyone with this writ may be a tyrant; if this commission be legal, a tyrant in a legal manner, also, may control, imprison, or murder anyone within the realm. In the next place, it is perpetual; there is no return. A man is accountable to no person for his doings. Every man may reign secure in his petty tyranny, and spread terror and desolation around him, until the trump of the archangel shall excite different emotions in his soul. In the third place, a person with this writ, in the daytime, may enter all houses, shops, etc., at will, and command all to assist him. Fourthly, by this writ, not only deputies, etc., but even their menial servants, are allowed to lord it over us. What is this but to have the curse of Canaan with a witness on us; to be the servant of servants, the most despicable of God's creation? Now, one of the most essential branches of English liberty is the freedom of one's house. A man's house is his castle; and whilst he is quiet, he is as well guarded as a prince in his castle. This writ, if it should be declared legal, would totally annihilate this privilege. Customhouse officers may enter our houses when they please; we are commanded to permit their entry. Their menial servants may enter, may break locks, bars, and everything in their way; and whether they break through malice or revenge, no man, no court, can inquire. Bare suspicion without oath is sufficient. This wanton exercise of this power is not a chimerical suggestion of a heated brain. I will mention some facts. Mr. Pew had one of these writs, and when Mr. Ware succeeded him, he indorsed this writ over to Mr. Ware; so that these writs are negotiable from one officer to another; and so your honors have no opportunity of judging the persons to whom this vast power is delegated. Another instance is this: Mr. Justice Walley had called this same Mr. Ware before him, by a constable, to answer for a breach of the Sabbath Day Acts, or that of profane swearing. As soon as he had finished, Mr. Ware asked him if he had done. He replied: "Yes." "Well, then," said Mr. Ware, "I will show you a little of my power. I command you to permit me to search your house for uncustomed goods"; and went on to search the house from the garret to the cellar, and then served the constable in the same manner! But to show another absurdity in this writ, if it should be established, I insist upon it that every person, by the 14th of Charles II, has this power as well as the customhouse officers. The words are: "It shall be lawful for any person or persons authorized," etc. What a scene does this open! Every man prompted by revenge, ill humor, or wantonness to inspect the inside of his neighbor's house may get a writ of assistance. Others will ask it from self-defense; one arbitrary exertion will provoke another, until society be involved in tumult and in blood. . . .

OLMSTEAD V. U.S.
277 U.S. 438

1928

Eventually overruled, this case shows the Supreme Court grappling with the implications of new technology, holding that private telephone conversations were not protected by the Fourth Amendment. However, the case is primarily known for Justice Brandeis's stirring defense of individual liberty and the right to privacy. Although the right to privacy is not explicitly mentioned in the Constitution, Brandeis called it the "right to be let alone—the right most valued by civilized man."

MR. CHIEF JUSTICE TAFT delivered the opinion of the Court.

. . . The evidence in the records discloses a conspiracy of amazing magnitude to import, possess and sell liquor unlawfully. It involved the employment of not less than fifty persons, of two seagoing vessels for the transportation of liquor to British Columbia, of smaller vessels for coastwise transportation to the State of Washington, the purchase and use of a ranch beyond the suburban limits of Seattle, with a large underground cache for storage and a number of smaller caches in that city, the maintenance of a central office manned with operators, the employment of executives, salesmen, deliverymen, dispatchers, scouts, bookkeepers, collectors and an attorney. In a bad month sales amounted to $176,000; the aggregate for a year must have exceeded two millions of dollars.

Olmstead was the leading conspirator and the general manager of the business. He made a contribution of $10,000 to the capital; eleven others contributed $1,000 each. The profits were divided one-half to Olmstead and the remainder to the other eleven. Of the several offices in Seattle the chief one was in a large office building. In this there were three telephones on three different lines. There were telephones in an office of the manager in his own home, at the homes of his associates, and at other places in the city. Communication was had frequently with Vancouver, British Columbia. Times were fixed for the deliveries of the "stuff," to places along Puget Sound near Seattle and from there the liquor was removed and deposited in the caches already referred to. One of the chief men was always on duty at the main office to receive orders by telephones and to direct their filling by a corps of men stationed in another room—the "bull pen." The call numbers of the telephones were given to those known to be likely customers. At times the sales amounted to 200 cases of liquor per day.

The information which led to the discovery of the conspiracy and its nature and extent was largely obtained by intercepting messages on the telephones of the conspirators by four federal prohibition officers. Small wires were inserted along the ordinary telephone wires from the residences of four of the petitioners and those leading from the chief office. The insertions were made without trespass upon any property of the defendants. They were made in the basement of the large office building. The taps from house lines were made in the streets near the houses. . . .

The Fourth Amendment provides—"The right of the people to be secure in their persons, houses, papers, and effects against unreasonable searches and seizures shall not be violated; and no warrants shall issue but upon probable cause, supported by oath or affirmation and particularly describing the place to be searched and the persons or things to be seized." And the Fifth: "No person . . . shall be compelled, in any criminal case, to be a witness against himself." . . .

The United States takes no such care of telegraph or telephone messages as of mailed sealed letters. The Amendment does not forbid what was done here. There was no searching. There was no seizure. The evidence was secured by the use of the sense of hearing and that only. There was no entry of the houses of offices of the defendants. . . .

The reasonable view is that one who installs in his house a telephone instrument with connecting wires intends to project his voice to those quite outside, and that the wires beyond his house and messages while passing over them are not within the protection of the Fourth Amendment. Here those who intercepted the projected voices were not in the house of either party to the conversation. . . .

We think, therefore, that the wire tapping here disclosed did not amount to a search or seizure within the meaning of the Fourth Amendment. . . .

MR. JUSTICE BRANDEIS, dissenting.

The defendants were convicted of conspiring to violate the National Prohibition Act. Before any of the persons now charged had been arrested or indicted, the telephones by means of which they habitually communicated with one another and with others had been tapped by federal officers. To this end, a lineman of long experience in wire-tapping was employed, on behalf of the Government and at its expense. He tapped eight telephones, some in the homes of the persons charged, some in their offices. Acting on behalf of the Government and in their official capacity, at least six other prohibition agents listened over the tapped wires and reported the messages taken. Their operations extended over a period of nearly five months. The type-written record of the notes of conversations overheard occupies 775 typewritten pages. By objections seasonably made and persistently renewed, the defendants objected to the admission of the evidence obtained by wire-tapping, on the ground that the Government's wire-tapping constituted an unreasonable search and seizure, in violation of the Fourth Amendment; and that the use as evidence of the conversations overheard compelled the defendants to be witnesses against themselves, in violation of the Fifth Amendment. . . .

When the Fourth and Fifth Amendments were adopted, "the form that evil had theretofore taken," had been necessarily simple. Force and violence were then the only means known to man by which a Government could directly effect self-incrimination. It could compel the individual to testify—a compulsion effected, if need be, by torture. It could secure possession of his papers and other articles incident to his private life—a seizure effected, if need be, by breaking and entry. Protection against such invasion of "the sanctities of a man's home and the privacies of life" was provided in the Fourth and Fifth Amendments by specific language. But "time works changes, brings into existence new conditions and purposes." Subtler and more far-reaching means of invading privacy have become available to the Government. Discovery and invention have made it possible for the Government, by means far more effective than stretching upon the rack, to obtain disclosure in court of what is whispered in the closet.

Moreover, "in the application of a constitution, our contemplation cannot be only of what has been but of what may be." The progress of science in furnishing the Government with means of espionage is not likely to stop with wire-tapping. Ways may some day be developed by which the Government, without removing papers from secret drawers, can reproduce them in court, and by which it will be enabled to expose to a jury the most intimate occurrences of the home. Advances in the psychic and related sciences may bring means of exploring unexpressed beliefs, thoughts and emotions. "That places the liberty of every man in the hands of every petty officer" was said by James Otis of much lesser intrusions than these. To Lord Camden, a far slighter intrusion seemed "subversive of all the comforts of society." Can it be that the Constitution affords no protection against such invasions of individual security? . . .

The makers of our Constitution undertook to secure conditions favorable to the pursuit of happiness. They recognized the significance of man's spiritual nature, of his feelings and of his intellect. They knew that only a part of the pain, pleasure and satisfactions of life are to be found in material things. They sought to protect Americans in their beliefs, their thoughts, their emotions and their sensations. They conferred, as against the Government, the right to be let alone—the most comprehensive of rights and the right most valued by civilized men. To protect that right, every unjustifiable intrusion by the Government upon the privacy of the individual, whatever the means employed, must be deemed a violation of the Fourth Amendment. And the use, as evidence in a criminal proceeding, of facts ascertained by such intrusion must be deemed a violation of the Fifth.

Applying to the Fourth and Fifth Amendments the established rule of construction, the defendants' objections to the evidence obtained by wire-tapping must, in my opinion, be sustained. It is, of course, immaterial where the physical connection with the telephone wires leading into the defendants' premises was made. And it is also immaterial that the intrusion was in aid of law enforcement. Experience should teach us to be most on our guard to protect liberty when the Government's purposes are beneficent. Men born to freedom are naturally alert to repel invasion of their liberty by evil-minded rulers. The greatest dangers to liberty lurk in insidious encroachment by men of zeal, well-meaning but without understanding. . . .

Decency, security and liberty alike demand that government officials shall be subjected to the same rules of conduct that are commands to the citizen. In a government of laws, existence of the government will be imperilled if it fails to observe the law scrupulously. Our Government is the potent, the omnipresent teacher. For good or for ill, it teaches the whole people by its example. Crime is contagious. If the Government becomes a lawbreaker, it breeds contempt for law; it invites every man to become a law unto himself; it invites anarchy. To declare that in the administration of the criminal law the end justifies the means—to declare that the Government may commit crimes in order to secure the conviction of a private criminal—would bring terrible retribution. Against that pernicious doctrine this Court should resolutely set its face.

Planned Parenthood of Southeastern Pennsylvania v. Casey
505 U.S. 833

1992

Twenty years after *Roe v. Wade*, following a series of cases restricting its scope and with at least three justices committed to overturning it, the Supreme Court reaffirmed *Roe's* underlying validity. The Court gave weight to the fact that a generation of women had come of age relying on the availability of reproductive choice and held that a law restricting abortion before fetal viability is unconstitutional if it places an "undue burden" on a woman seeking to exercise her right. The opinion was written by Justice Sandra Day O'Connor (1930–), who served as a judge on the Arizona Court of Appeals before becoming the first woman Supreme Court justice in 1981.

JUSTICE O'CONNOR, JUSTICE KENNEDY, and JUSTICE SOUTER announced the judgment of the Court and delivered the opinion of the Court.

Liberty finds no refuge in a jurisprudence of doubt. Yet 19 years after our holding that the Constitution protects a woman's right to terminate her pregnancy in its early stages, *Roe* v. *Wade*, that definition of liberty is still questioned. Joining the respondents as *amicus curiae*, the United States, as it has done in five other cases in the last decade, again asks us to overrule *Roe*.

After considering the fundamental constitutional questions resolved by *Roe*, principles of institutional integrity, and the rule of *stare decisis*, we are led to conclude this: the essential holding of *Roe* v. *Wade* should be retained and once again reaffirmed.

It must be stated at the outset and with clarity that *Roe's* essential holding, the holding we reaffirm, has three parts. First is a recognition of the right of the woman to choose to have an abortion before viability and to obtain it without undue interference from the State. Before viability, the State's interests are not strong enough to support a prohibition of abortion or the imposition of a substantial obstacle to the woman's effective right to elect the procedure. Second is a confirmation of the State's power to restrict abortions after fetal viability, if the law contains exceptions for pregnancies which endanger the woman's life or health. And third is the principle that the State has legitimate interests from the outset of the pregnancy in protecting the health of the woman and the life of the fetus that may become a child. These principles do not contradict one another; and we adhere to each. . . .

Constitutional protection of the woman's decision to terminate her pregnancy derives from the Due Process Clause of the Fourteenth Amendment. It declares that no State shall "deprive any person of life, liberty, or property, without due process of law." The controlling word in the cases before us is "liberty." Although a literal reading of the Clause might suggest that it governs only the procedures by which a State may deprive persons of liberty, for at least 105 years, since *Mugler* v. *Kansas*, the Clause has been understood to contain a substantive component as well, one "barring certain government actions regardless of the fairness of the procedures used to implement them." . . .

The inescapable fact is that adjudication of substantive due process claims may call upon the Court in interpreting the Constitution to exercise that same capacity which by tradition courts always have exercised: reasoned judgment. Its boundaries are not susceptible of expression as a simple rule. That does not mean we are free to invalidate state policy choices with which we disagree; yet neither does it permit us to shrink from the duties of our office. . . .

Men and women of good conscience can disagree, and we suppose some always shall disagree, about the profound moral and spiritual implications of terminating a pregnancy, even in its earliest stage. Some of us as individuals find abortion offensive to our most basic principles of morality, but that cannot control our decision. Our obligation is to define the liberty of all, not to mandate our own moral code. The underlying constitutional issue is whether the State can resolve these philosophic questions in such a definitive way that a woman lacks all choice in the matter, except perhaps in those rare circumstances in which the pregnancy is itself a danger to her own life or health, or is the result of rape or incest. . . .

Our law affords constitutional protection to personal decisions relating to marriage, procreation, contraception, family relationships, child rearing, and education. Our cases recognize "the right of the *individual,* married or single, to be free from unwarranted governmental intrusion into matters so fundamentally affecting a person as the decision whether to bear or beget a child." Our precedents "have respected the private realm of family life which the state cannot enter." These matters, involving the most intimate and personal choices a person may make in a lifetime, choices central to personal dignity and autonomy, are central to the liberty protected by the Fourteenth Amendment. At the heart of liberty is the right to define one's own concept of existence, of meaning, of the universe, and of the mystery of human life. Beliefs about these matters could not define the attributes of personhood were they formed under compulsion of the State.

These considerations begin our analysis of the woman's interest in terminating her pregnancy but cannot end it, for this reason: though the abortion decision may originate within the zone of conscience and belief, it is more than a philosophic exercise. Abortion is a unique act. It is an act fraught with consequences for others: for the woman who must live with the implications of her decision; for the persons who perform and assist in the procedure; for the spouse, family, and society which must confront the knowledge that these procedures exist, procedures some deem nothing short of an act of violence against innocent human life; and, depending on one's beliefs, for the life or potential life that is aborted. Though abortion is conduct, it does not follow that the State is entitled to proscribe it in all instances. That is because the liberty of the woman is at stake in a sense unique to the human condition and so unique to the law. The mother who carries a child to full term is subject to anxieties, to physical constraints, to pain that only she must bear. That these sacrifices have from the beginning of the human race been endured by woman with a pride that ennobles her in the eyes of others and gives to the infant a bond of love cannot alone be grounds for the State to insist she make the sacrifice. Her suffering is too intimate and personal for the State to insist, without more, upon its own vision of the woman's role, however dominant that vision has been in the course of our history and our culture. The destiny of the woman must be shaped to a large extent on her own conception of her spiritual imperatives and her place in society. . . .

The obligation to follow precedent begins with necessity, and a contrary necessity marks its outer limit. With Cardozo, we recognize that no judicial system could do society's work if it eyed each issue afresh in every case that raised it. Indeed, the very concept of the rule of law underlying our own Constitution requires such continuity over time that a respect for precedent is, by definition, indispensable. At the other extreme, a different necessity would make itself felt if a prior judicial ruling should come to be seen so clearly as error that its enforcement was for that very reason doomed. . . .

Although *Roe* has engendered opposition, it has in no sense proven "unworkable," representing as it does a simple limitation beyond which a state law is unenforceable. While *Roe* has, of course, required judicial assessment of state laws affecting the exercise of the choice guaranteed against government infringement, and although the need for such review will remain as a consequence of today's decision, the required determinations fall within judicial competence. . . .

To eliminate the issue of reliance that easily, however, one would need to limit cognizable reliance to specific instances of sexual activity. But to do this would be simply to refuse to face the fact that for two decades of economic and social developments, people have organized intimate relationships and made choices that define their views of themselves and their places in society, in reliance on the availability of abortion in the event that contraception should fail. The ability of women to participate equally in the economic and social life of the Nation has been facilitated by their ability to control their reproductive lives. The Constitution serves human values, and while the effect of reliance on *Roe* cannot be exactly measured, neither can the certain cost of overruling *Roe* for people who have ordered their thinking and living around that case be dismissed. . . .

The sum of the precedential enquiry to this point shows *Roe*'s underpinnings unweakened in any way affecting its central holding. While it has engendered disapproval, it has not been unworkable. An entire generation has come of age free to assume *Roe*'s concept of liberty in defining the capacity of women to act in society, and to make reproductive decisions; no erosion of principle going to liberty or personal autonomy has left *Roe*'s central holding a doctrinal remnant; *Roe* portends no developments at odds with other precedent for the analysis of personal liberty; and no changes of fact have rendered viability more or less appropriate as the point at which the balance of interests tips. Within the bounds of normal *stare decisis* analysis, then, and subject to the considerations on which it customarily turns, the stronger argument is for affirming *Roe*'s central holding, with whatever degree of personal reluctance any of us may have, not for overruling it. . . .

The root of American governmental power is revealed most clearly in the instance of the power conferred by the Constitution upon the Judiciary of the United States and specifically upon this Court. As Americans of each succeeding generation are rightly told, the Court cannot buy support for its decisions by spending money and, except to a minor degree, it cannot independently coerce obedience to its decrees. The Court's power lies, rather, in its legitimacy, a product of substance and perception that shows itself in the people's acceptance of the Judiciary as fit to determine what the Nation's law means and to declare what it demands. . . .

The underlying substance of this legitimacy is of course the warrant for the Court's decisions in the Constitution and the lesser sources of legal principle on which the Court draws. That substance is expressed in the Court's opinions, and our contemporary understanding is such that a decision without principled justification would be no judicial act at all. But even when justification is furnished by apposite legal principle, something more is required. Because not every conscientious claim of principled justification will be accepted as such, the justification claimed must be beyond dispute. The Court must take care to speak and act in ways that allow people to accept its decisions on the terms the Court claims for them, as grounded truly in principle, not as compromises with social and political pressures having, as such, no bearing on the principled choices that the Court is obliged to make. Thus, the Court's legitimacy depends on making legally principled decisions under circumstances in which their principled character is sufficiently plausible to be accepted by the Nation. . . .

Where, in the performance of its judicial duties, the Court decides a case in such a way as to resolve the sort of intensely divisive controversy reflected in *Roe* and those rare, comparable cases, its decision has a dimension that the resolution of the normal case does not carry. It is the dimension present whenever the Court's interpretation of the Constitution calls the contending sides of a national controversy to end their national division by accepting a common mandate rooted in the Constitution.

The Court is not asked to do this very often, having thus addressed the Nation only twice in our lifetime, in the decisions of *Brown* and *Roe*. But when the Court does act in this way, its decision requires an equally rare precedential force to counter the inevitable efforts to overturn it and to thwart its implementation. Some of those efforts may be mere unprincipled emotional reactions; others may proceed from principles worthy of profound respect. But whatever the premises of opposition may be, only the most convincing justification under accepted standards of precedent could suffice to demonstrate that a later decision overruling the first was anything but a surrender to political pressure, and an unjustified repudiation of the principle on which the Court staked its authority in the first instance. So to overrule under fire in the absence of the most compelling reason to reexamine a watershed decision would subvert the Court's legitimacy beyond any serious question. . . .

From what we have said so far it follows that it is a constitutional liberty of the woman to have some freedom to terminate her pregnancy. We conclude that the basic decision in *Roe* was based on a constitutional analysis which we cannot now repudiate. The woman's liberty is not so unlimited, however, that from the outset the State cannot show its concern for the life of the unborn, and at a later point in fetal development the State's interest in life has sufficient force so that the right of the woman to terminate the pregnancy can be restricted.

That brings us, of course, to the point where much criticism has been directed at *Roe*, a criticism that always inheres when the Court draws a specific rule from what in the Constitution is but a general standard. We conclude, however, that the urgent claims of the woman to retain the ultimate control over her destiny and her body, claims implicit in the meaning of liberty, require us to perform that function. Liberty must not be extinguished for want of a line that is clear. And it falls to us to give some real substance to the woman's liberty to determine whether to carry her pregnancy to full term. . . .

The second reason is that the concept of viability, as we noted in *Roe*, is the time at which there is a realistic possibility of maintaining and nourishing a life outside the womb, so that the independent existence of the second life can in reason and all fairness be the object of state protection that now overrides the rights of the woman. Consistent with other constitutional norms, legislatures may draw lines which appear arbitrary without the necessity of offering a justification. But courts may not. We must justify the lines we draw. And there is no line other than viability which is more workable. . . . The viability line also has, as a practical matter, an element of fairness. In some broad sense it might be said that a woman who fails to act before viability has consented to the State's intervention on behalf of the developing child.

The woman's right to terminate her pregnancy before viability is the most central principle of *Roe v. Wade*. It is a rule of law and a component of liberty we cannot renounce. . . .

Though the woman has a right to choose to terminate or continue her pregnancy before viability, it does not at all follow that the state is prohibited from taking steps to ensure that this choice is thoughtful and informed. Even in the earliest stages of pregnancy, the State may enact rules and regulations designed to encourage her to know that there are philosophic and social arguments of great weight that can be brought to bear in favor of continuing the pregnancy to full term and that there are procedures and institutions to allow adoption of unwanted children as well as a certain degree of state assistance if the mother chooses to raise the child herself. "'The Constitution does not forbid a State or city, pursuant to democratic processes, from expressing a preference for normal childbirth.'" It follows that States are free to enact laws to provide a reasonable framework for a woman to make a decision that has such profound and lasting meaning. This, too, we find consistent with *Roe*'s central premises, and indeed the inevitable consequence of our holding that the State has an interest in protecting the life of the unborn. . . .

The very notion that the State has a substantial interest in potential life leads to the conclusion that not all regulations must be deemed unwarranted. Not all burdens on the right to decide whether to terminate a pregnancy will be undue. In our view, the undue burden standard is the appropriate means of reconciling the State's interest with the woman's constitutionally protected liberty. . . .

A finding of an undue burden is a shorthand for the conclusion that a state regulation has the purpose or effect of placing a substantial obstacle in the path of a woman seeking an abortion of a nonviable fetus. A statute with this purpose is invalid because the means chosen by the State to further the interest in potential life must be calculated to inform the woman's free choice, not hinder it. And a statute which, while furthering the interest in potential life or some other valid state interest, has the effect of placing a substantial obstacle in the path of a woman's choice cannot be considered a permissible means of serving its legitimate ends. To the extent that the opinions of the Court or of individual Justices use the undue burden standard in a manner that is inconsistent with this analysis, we set out what in our view should be the controlling standard. In our considered judgment, an undue burden is an unconstitutional burden. Understood another way, we answer the question, left open in previous opinions discussing the undue burden formulation, whether a law designed to further the State's interest in fetal life which imposes an undue burden on the woman's decision before fetal viability could be constitutional. The answer is no.

Some guiding principles should emerge. What is at stake is the woman's right to make the ultimate decision, not a right to be insulated form all others in doing so. Regulations which do no more than create a structural mechanism by which the State, or the parent or guardian of a minor, may express profound respect for the life of the unborn are permitted, if they are not a substantial obstacle to the woman's exercise of the right to choose. Unless it has that effect on her right of choice, a state measure designed to persuade her to choose childbirth over abortion will be upheld if reasonably related to that goal. Regulations designed to foster the health of a woman seeking an abortion are valid if they do not constitute an undue burden. . . .

Our Constitution is a covenant running from the first generation of Americans to us and then to future generations. It is a coherent succession. Each generation must learn anew that the Constitution's written terms embody ideas and aspirations that must survive more ages than one. We accept our responsibility not to retreat from interpreting the full meaning of the covenant in light of all our precedents. We invoke it once again to define the freedom guaranteed by the Constitution's own promise, the promise of liberty.

EQUALITY

VOTES FOR US
WHEN
WE ARE WOMEN

Suffragettes, Long Island,
New York, 1913.

"WE HOLD THESE truths to be self-evident—that all men are created equal." With these words, the Declaration of Independence committed the United States at its birth to the promise of equality. That ideal has defined our history and is one we are still struggling to reach. It took the Civil War and the civil rights movement to begin to fulfill our country's promise to African Americans. Women were denied the vote until 1920, and not until the 1970s did they enter the workforce in large numbers, backed by Supreme Court decisions reinforcing equality of opportunity. More recently, our society has begun expanding the Declaration's promise to other victims of discrimination, ethnic minorities, the disabled, and gay men and women. The progress made in our society has inspired an international human rights movement. This section contains documents representing these social transformations.

Within our national concept of equality, there are tensions. Some believe the goal should be equal opportunity and access, others define equality by results. In addition, as the concept of equality embraces different groups, we must seek to maintain and celebrate our diversity. The process by which we resolve these conflicts will define our society for years to come.

Modern American society was transformed by the civil rights movement, just as the struggle for emancipation, the Civil War, and the woman's suffrage movement transformed nineteenth-century America. Education was the battleground in Little Rock, Arkansas, and in Alabama, Mississippi, and New Orleans, and remains a fulcrum in the fight for equality. The movement was led by parents who believed so strongly that they were willing to put their children in danger, and by children who by the power of their example showed us the way toward a better, more peaceful society. That vision of America has never been more eloquently defined than by

Martin Luther King Jr. in the speech he gave at the March on Washington in August 1963. "I say to you today, my friends, that in spite of the difficulties and frustrations of the moment I still have a dream. It is a dream deeply rooted in the American dream. I have a dream that one day this nation will rise up and live out the true meaning of its creed: 'We hold these truths to be self-evident; that all men are created equal.'"

Today's education battles involve equal access to education, affirmative action, and funding discrepancies between rich and poor children. To understand these issues, it is helpful to re-read the historic 1954 decision *Brown v. Board of Education*, in which the Supreme Court declared that separate could not be equal. Fifty years after *Brown*, President Clinton, who grew up during the Little Rock crisis, makes an eloquent case for a renewed national commitment to the principle of equality and illuminates the benefits that have accrued to all Americans.

In my family, like many others, it is easy to see how much our society has changed just in the lifetimes of the people I have known. I have often thought about how ironic it is that my grandmother, who spent her childhood campaigning with her father, Honey Fitz, the mayor of Boston, and who was the source of the political talent in our family, was thirty years old before she could vote in a presidential election. By that time she had three children, one of whom overcame religious discrimination to become the first Catholic president and put the power of the federal government on the side of civil rights. As attorney general, my uncle Bobby led that effort, and as a senator he crusaded for the rights of the disadvantaged in Appalachia, in Mississippi, and in the fields of California. This commitment continued as my uncle Teddy led the fight in the Congress for the Americans with Disabilities Act, and my aunt Eunice Shriver founded Special Olympics, an international athletic program for the mentally retarded. I saw my mother go back to work in the 1970s when my brother and I were in college, like so many women of her generation who faced the demands of a workplace they had left twenty years before. Now my children are growing up when it is possible to take these hard-won opportunities for granted, yet the challenges of balancing work and family remain, and the fight for equal opportunity, equal access, and equal pay continues.

Fannie Lou Hamer's speech ends with a story about some children who bring a bird to a wise old man. When they ask him if the bird is alive or dead, he places the bird in their hands and says, "It is up to you." The future is up to each of us, and we all have a responsibility to ensure that the promise of equal rights is fulfilled for ourselves and for our children.

ABIGAIL ADAMS

LETTER TO JOHN ADAMS

MARCH 31, 1776

John Adams (1735–1826), farmer, Boston lawyer, revolutionary patriot, and second president of the United States, carried on a remarkable correspondence with his wife, Abigail Smith Adams (1744–1818), during the many years that his political and diplomatic responsibilities took him away from home. Though Abigail had little formal schooling, she was intelligent, witty, and an astute judge of character. Her letters are an important chronicle of the early Republic and she is remembered as one of our most distinguished First Ladies. During the beginnings of the American Republic, Adams played a crucial role in the establishment of the new nation: He was the first to propose the creation of an American navy; the nomination of George Washington as head of the Continental Army; the selection of Thomas Jefferson to draft the Declaration of Independence; and the appointment of John Marshall as chief justice of the Supreme Court. During the critical spring of 1776, as the movement for independence gathered force, Abigail wrote to her husband in Philadelphia expressing the hope that any call for independence would include equal rights for "the ladies." This exchange between John and Abigail followed.

. . . I long to hear that you have declared an independancy—and by the way in the new Code of Laws which I suppose it will be necessary for you to make I desire you would Remember the Ladies, and be more generous and favourable to them than your ancestors. Do not put such unlimited power into the hands of the Husbands. Remember all Men would be tyrants if they could. If perticular care and attention is not paid to the Laidies we are determined to foment a Rebelion, and will not hold ourselves bound by any Laws in which we have no voice, or Representation.

That your Sex are Naturally Tyrannical is a Truth so thoroughly established as to admit of no dispute, but such of you as wish to be happy willingly give up the harsh title of Master for the more tender and endearing one of Friend. Why then, not put it out of the power of the vicious and the Lawless to use us with cruelty and indignity with impunity. Men of Sense in all Ages abhor those customs which treat us only as the vassals of your Sex. Regard us then as Beings placed by providence under your protection and in immitation of the Supreem Being make use of that power only for our happiness.

JOHN ADAMS

LETTER TO ABIGAIL ADAMS

APRIL 14, 1776

. . . As to your extraordinary Code of Laws, I cannot but laugh. We have been told that our Struggle has loosened the bands of Government every where. That Children and Apprentices were disobedient—that schools and Colledges were grown turbulent—that Indians slighted their Guardians and Negroes grew insolent to their Masters. But your Letter was the first Intimation that another Tribe more numerous and powerfull than all the rest were grown discontented.—This is rather too coarse a Compliment but you are so saucy, I wont blot it out.

Depend upon it, We know better than to repeal our Masculine systems. Altho they are in full Force, you know they are little more than Theory. We dare not exert our Power in its full Latitude. We are obliged to go fair, and softly, and in Practice you know We are the subjects. We have only the Name of Masters, and rather than give up this, which would compleatly subject Us to the Despotism of the Peticoat, I hope General Washington, and all our brave Heroes would fight. I am sure every good Politician would plot, as long as he would against Despotism, Empire, Monarchy, Aristocracy, Oligarchy, or Ochlocracy.—A fine Story indeed. I begin to think the Ministry as deep as they are wicked. After stirring up Tories, Landjobbers, Trimmers, Bigots, Canadians, Indians, Negroes, Hanoverians, Hessians, Russians, Irish Roman Catholicks, Scotch Renegadoes, at last they are stimulated the [Ladies] to demand new Priviledges and threaten to rebell.

DECLARATION OF SENTIMENTS AND RESOLUTIONS, SENECA FALLS CONVENTION

1848

Elizabeth Cady Stanton (1815–1902) and Lucretia Mott (1793–1880) were active in the abolitionist movement, only to experience discrimination on the basis of gender. They organized a convention of protest at Seneca Falls in New York in 1848 where a manifesto, modeled after the Declaration of Independence, was adopted. The grievances and resolutions, written by Stanton, which the delegates accepted, delineated the lack of opportunity that American women faced in politics, education, marriage, religion, and the workplace. Stanton worked tirelessly for women's suffrage for the next fifty years.

When, in the course of human events, it becomes necessary for one portion of the family of man to assume among the people of the earth a position different from that which they have hitherto occupied, but one to which the laws of nature and of nature's God entitle them, a decent respect to the opinions of mankind requires that they should declare the causes that impel them to such a course.

We hold these truths to be self-evident: that all men and women are created equal; that they are endowed by their Creator with certain inalienable rights, that among these are life, liberty, and the pursuit of happiness; that to secure these rights governments are instituted, deriving their just powers from the consent of the governed. Whenever any form of government becomes destructive of these ends, it is the right of those who suffer from it to refuse allegiance to it, and to insist upon the institution of a new government, laying its foundation on such principles, and organizing its powers in such form as to them shall seem most likely to effect their safety and happiness. Prudence, indeed, will dictate that governments long established should not be changed for light and transient causes; and accordingly, all experience hath shown that mankind are more disposed to suffer, while evils are sufferable, than to right themselves by abolishing the forms to which they were accustomed. But when a long train of abuses and usurpations, pursuing invariably the same object, evinces a design to reduce them under absolute despotism, it is their duty to throw off such government and to provide new guards for their future security. Such has been the patient sufferance of the women under this government, and such is now the necessity which constrains them to demand the equal station to which they are entitled.

The history of mankind is a history of repeated injuries and usurpations on the part of man toward woman, having in direct object the establishment of an absolute tyranny over her. To prove this, let facts be submitted to a candid world.

He has never permitted her to exercise her inalienable right to the elective franchise.

He has compelled her to submit to laws, in the formation of which she had no voice.

He has withheld from her rights which are given to the most ignorant and degraded men—both natives and foreigners.

Having deprived her of this first right of a citizen, the elective franchise, thereby leaving her without representation in the halls of legislation, he has oppressed her on all sides.

He has made her, if married, in the eye of the law, civilly dead.

He has taken from her all right in property, even to the wages she earns.

He has made her, morally, an irresponsible being, as she can commit many crimes with impunity, provided they be done in the presence of her husband. In the covenant of marriage, she is compelled to promise obedience to her husband, he becoming, to all intents and purposes, her master—the law giving him power to deprive her of her liberty, and to administer chastisement.

He has so framed the laws of divorce, as to what shall be the proper causes of divorce; in case of separation, to whom the guardianship of the children shall be given; as to be wholly regardless of the happiness of women—the law, in all cases, going upon a false supposition of the supremacy of man, and giving all power into his hands.

After depriving her of all rights as a married woman, if single and the owner of property, he has taxed her to support a government which recognizes her only when her property can be made profitable to it.

He has monopolized nearly all the profitable employments, and from those she is permitted to follow, she receives but a scanty remuneration.

He closes against her all the avenues to wealth and distinction, which he considers most honorable to himself. As a teacher of theology, medicine, or law, she is not known.

He has denied her the facilities for obtaining a thorough education—all colleges being closed against her.

He allows her in Church, as well as State, but a subordinate position, claiming Apostolic authority for her exclusion from the ministry, and, with some exceptions, from any public participation in the affairs of the Church.

He has created a false public sentiment, by giving to the world a different code of morals for men and women, by which moral delinquencies which exclude women from society, are not only tolerated but deemed of little account in man.

He has usurped the prerogative of Jehovah himself, claiming it as his right to assign for her a sphere of action, when that belongs to her conscience and to her God.

He has endeavored, in every way that he could, to destroy her confidence in her own powers, to lessen her self-respect, and to make her willing to lead a dependent and abject life.

Now, in view of this entire disfranchisement of one-half the people of this country, their social and religious degradation,—in view of the unjust laws above mentioned, and because women do feel themselves aggrieved, oppressed, and fraudulently deprived of their most sacred rights, we insist that they have immediate admission to all the rights and privileges which belong to them as citizens of the United States.

In entering upon the great work before us, we anticipate no small amount of misconception, misrepresentation, and ridicule; but we shall use every instrumentality within our power to effect our object. We shall employ agents, circulate tracts, petition the state and national legislatures, and endeavor to enlist the pulpit and the press in our behalf. We hope this Convention will be followed by a series of Conventions, embracing every part of the country.

Firmly relying upon the final triumph of the Right and True, we do this day affix our signatures to this declaration. *[Names followed.]*

RESOLUTIONS

Whereas, The great precept of nature is conceded to be, "that man shall pursue his own true and substantial happiness." Blackstone, in his *Commentaries* remarks, that this law of Nature being coeval with mankind, and dictated by God himself, is of course superior in obligation to any other. It is binding over all the globe, in all countries, and at all times; no human laws are of any validity if contrary to this, and such of them as are valid, derive all their force, and all their validity, and all their authority, mediately and immediately, from this original; therefore,

Resolved, That such laws as conflict, in any way, with the true and substantial happiness of woman, are contrary to the great precept of nature, and of no validity; for this is "superior in obligation to any other."

Resolved, That all laws which prevent woman from occupying such a station in society as her conscience shall dictate, or which place her in a position inferior to that of man, are contrary to the great precept of nature, and therefore of no force or authority.

Resolved, That woman is man's equal—was intended to be so by the Creator, and the highest good of the race demands that she should be recognized as such.

Resolved, That the women of this country ought to be enlightened in regard to the laws under which they live, that they may no longer publish their degradation, by declaring themselves satisfied with their present position, nor their ignorance, by asserting that they have all the rights they want.

Resolved, That inasmuch as man, while claiming for himself intellectual superiority, does not accord to woman moral superiority, it is pre-eminently his duty to encourage her to speak, and teach, as she has an opportunity, in all religious assemblies.

Resolved, That the same amount of virtue, delicacy, and refinement of behavior, that is required of woman in the social state, should also be required of man, and the same transgressions should be visited with equal severity on both man and woman.

Resolved, That the objection of indelicacy and impropriety, which is so often brought against woman when she addresses a public audience, comes with a very ill-grace from those who encourage, by their attendance, her appearance on the stage, in the concert or in feats of the circus.

Resolved, That woman has too long rested satisfied in the circumscribed limits which corrupt customs and a perverted application of the Scriptures have marked out for her, and that it is time she should move in the enlarged sphere which her great Creator has assigned her.

Resolved, That it is the duty of the women of this country to secure to themselves their sacred right to the elective franchise.

Resolved, That the equality of human rights results necessarily from the fact of the identity of the race in capabilities and responsibilities.

Resolved, therefore, That, being invested by the Creator with the same capabilities, and the same consciousness of responsibility for their exercise, it is demonstrably the right and duty of woman, equally with man, to promote every righteous cause, by every righteous means; and especially in regard to the great subjects of morals and religions, it is self-evidently her right to participate with her brother in teaching them, both in private and in public, by writing and by speaking, by any instrumentalities proper to be used, and in any assemblies proper to be held; and this being a self-evident truth, growing out of the divinely implanted principles of human nature, any custom or authority adverse to it, whether modern or wearing the hoary sanction of antiquity, is to be regarded as a self-evident falsehood, and at war with mankind.

Resolved, That the speedy success of our cause depends upon the zealous and untiring efforts of both men and women, for the overthrow of the monopoly of the pulpit, and for the securing to woman an equal participation with men in the various trades, professions, and commerce.

SOJOURNER TRUTH

AIN'T I A WOMAN?

MAY 1851

Sojourner Truth was born into slavery c. 1797 and given the name of Isabella Baumfree by her master. With the help of Quakers she gained her freedom in 1826 and became a powerful speaker for the abolitionist cause. In 1843 she took the name "Sojourner Truth," an indication of her willingness to embark upon a nationwide quest for justice. Sojourner Truth delivered her most famous address, "Ain't I a Woman?" at a convention in Akron, Ohio.

Well, children, where there is so much racket there must be something out of kilter. I think that between the niggers of the South and the women at the North, all talking about rights, the white men will be in a fix pretty soon. But what's all this here talking about?

That man over there say that women needs to be helped into carriages, and lifted over ditches, and to have the best place everywhere. Nobody ever helps me into carriages, or over mud-puddles, or gives me any best place! . . . And ain't I a woman?

Look at me! Look at my arm! I have ploughed, and planted, and gathered into barns, and no man could head me! And ain't I a woman?

I could work as much and eat as much as a man—when I could get it—and bear the lash as well! And ain't I a woman?

I have borne thirteen children, and seen most of them sold off to slavery, and when I cried out with my mother's grief, none but Jesus heard me! And ain't I a woman?

Then they talks about this thing in their head; what's this they call it? ("Intellect," someone whispers near.) That's it, honey. What's that got to do with women's rights or niggers' rights? If my cup won't hold but a pint, and yours holds a quart, wouldn't you be mean not to let me have my little half-measure full? (. . . and the cheering was long and loud.)

Then that little man in black there, he say women can't have as much rights as men, because Christ wasn't a woman! Where did your Christ come from? . . . Where did your Christ come from? From God and a woman! Men had nothing to do with Him. . . .

If the first woman God ever made was strong enough to turn the world upside down all alone, these women together . . . ought to be able to turn it back, and get it right side up again! And now that they are asking to do it, the men better let them! (Long, continuous cheering greets this.)

Obliged to you for hearing me, and now old Sojourner has got nothing more to say.

LIFT EVERY VOICE AND SING

1900

Educator, poet, diplomat, and civil rights activist, James Weldon Johnson (1871–1938) was born in Florida, where he and his brother, John Rosamond (1873–1954), were first exposed to music by their mother. James became the first African American admitted to the Florida bar, and served as American consul to Venezuela and Nicaragua (1906–1913). He was a founding member and secretary of the NAACP from 1916 to 1930, and author of several books, including the 1912 novel *The Autobiography of an Ex-Coloured Man*, before becoming a professor at Fisk University. Rosamond pursued a career in music, performing in the United States and Europe, composing several hundred songs, and editing several collections of African American songs and spirituals. In 1900, the brothers collaborated on a song for a school ceremony celebrating the birthday of Abraham Lincoln. The powerful composition, "Lift Every Voice and Sing," became known as the "Black National Anthem."

Lift ev'ry voice and sing,
Till earth and heaven ring,
Ring with the harmonies of Liberty;
Let our rejoicing rise
High as the list'ning skies,
Let it resound loud as the rolling sea.
Sing a song full of the faith that the dark past has taught us,
Sing a song full of the hope that the present has brought us;
Facing the rising sun of our new day begun,
Let us march on till victory is won.

Stony the road we trod,
Bitter the chast'ning rod,
Felt in the days when hope unborn had died;
Yet with a steady beat,
Have not our weary feet
Come to the place for which our fathers sighed?
We have come over a way that with tears has been watered.
We have come, treading our path through the blood of the slaughtered,
Out from the gloomy past,
Till now we stand at last
Where the white gleam of our bright star is cast.

God of our weary years,
God of our silent tears,
Thou who hast brought us thus far on the way;
Thou who hast by Thy might,
Led us into the light,
Keep us forever in the path, we pray.
Lest our feet stray from the places, our God, where we met Thee,
Lest our hearts, drunk with the wine of the world, we forget Thee;
Shadowed beneath Thy hand,
May we forever stand,
True to our God,
True to our native land.

JEANNETTE RANKIN

SPEECH IN CONGRESS ON WOMEN'S RIGHTS AND WARTIME SERVICE

JANUARY 10, 1918

Jeannette Rankin (1880–1973), a lifelong pacifist and the first woman to serve in Congress, was the only legislator to vote against U.S. entry into both World War I and World War II. Her commitment to principle cost her elections, not once but twice. First elected to Congress from Montana in 1916, Rankin lobbied for women's suffrage and helped draft the constitutional amendment giving women the vote, which was ratified in 1920. In April 1917, only four days after she took her seat, she cast one of twenty-six votes against World War I; the following year she was defeated in a race for the Senate. Reelected to Congress in 1940, she cast the lone vote against U.S. involvement in World War II, following the Japanese attack on Pearl Harbor. As late as 1968, Rankin was speaking out against war, joining a march against American involvement in Vietnam.

Mr. Speaker, we are facing today a question of political evolution. International circumstances have forced this question to an issue. Our country is in a state of war; the nation has had a terrible shock. The result has been a sudden change in our national consciousness. The things we have been taking for granted for years are suddenly assuming a new significance for us. . . .

We have men—men for the army, for the navy, for the air; men for the industries, the mines, the fields; men for the government. And the national leaders are now reaching out and drawing men of talent, picking those with the best minds, with expert knowledge, and with broad perspective to aid in war work.

But something is still lacking in the completeness of our national effort. With all our abundance of coal, with our great stretches of idle, fertile land, babies are dying from cold and hunger; soldiers have died for lack of a woolen shirt.

Might it not be that men who have spent their lives thinking in terms of commercial profit find it hard to adjust themselves to thinking in terms of human needs?

Might it not be that a great force which has always been thinking in terms of human needs, and that always will think in terms of human needs, has not been mobilized?

Is it not possible that the women of the country have something of value to give the country at this time?

It would be strange indeed if the women of this country, through all these years, had not developed an intelligence, a feeling, a spiritual force to themselves which they hold in readiness to give the world. It would be strange indeed if the influence of women through direct participation in the political struggles, through which all social and industrial development proceeds, would not lend a certain virility, a certain influx of new strength and understanding and sympathy and ability to the exhausting effort we are now making to meet the problem before us. . . .

Today as never before, the nation needs its women—needs the work of their hands and their hearts and their minds. Their energy must be utilized in the most effective service they can give. Are we now going to refuse these women the opportunity to serve, in the face of their plea—in the face of the nation's great need? Are you, gentlemen, representing the South, you who have struggled with your Negro problem for half a century, going to retaliate after fifty years for the injustice you believe that was done you so long ago? Have you not learned, in your struggle for adjustment in the South, to be broad and fair and open-minded in dealing with another franchise problem that concerns the whole nation? . . .

We declared war, not state by state, but by federal action. We mobilized and equipped our army, not state by state, but through Congress. Shall our women, our home defense, be our only fighters in the struggle for democracy who shall be denied federal action?

It is time for our old political doctrines to give way to the new visions, the new aspects of national and international relations which have come to us already since the war began. For we have had new visions; we have been aroused to a new way of looking at things. Our president, with his wisdom and astuteness, has helped us to penetrate new problems, to analyze situations, to make fine distinctions. He startled us by urging us to distinguish between the German government and the German people. We who have been steeped in democratic ideals since the days when our forefathers signed the Declaration of Independence find it difficult to think of government as something separate from the people.

Yet as we learn to make this distinction for Germany, will not our minds revert to our own situation and be puzzled? How can people in other countries who are trying to grasp our plan of democracy avoid stumbling over our logic when we deny the first steps in democracy to our women? May they not see a distinction between the government of the United States and the women of the United States?

Deep down in the hearts of the American people is a living faith in democracy. Sometimes it is not expressed in the most effective way. Sometimes it seems almost forgotten. But when the test comes, we find it still there, groping and aspiring and helping men and women to understand each other and their common need. It is our national religion and it prompts in us the desire for that measure of justice which is based on equal opportunity, equal protection, equal freedom for all. In our hearts we know that desire can be realized only when "those who submit to authority have a voice in their own government"—whether that government be political, industrial or social.

Today there are men and women in every field of endeavor who are bending all their energies toward a realization of this dream of universal justice. They believe that we are waging a war for democracy. The farmer who knows the elements of democracy becomes an idealist when he contemplates the possibility of feeding the world during this crisis. The woman who knits all day to keep from thinking of the sacrifice she is making wonders what this democracy is which she is denied and for which she is asked to give. The miner is dreaming his dreams of industrial democracy as he goes about 2,000 feet underground, bringing forth from the rock precious metals to help in the prosecution of the war.

The girl who works in the Treasury no long works until she is married. She knows not that she will work on and on and on. The war has taken from her opportunities for the joys that young girls look forward to. Cheerfully and willingly, she makes her sacrifice. And she will pay to the very end in order that the future need not find women paying again for the same cause.

The boys at the front know something of the democracy for which they are fighting. These courageous lads who are paying with their lives testified to the sincerity of their fight when they sent home their ballots in the New York election, and voted two to one in favor of woman suffrage and democracy at home.

These are the people of the nation. These are the fiber and sinew of war—the mother, the farmer, the miner, the industrial worker, the soldier. These are the people who are giving their all for the cause of democracy. These are the people who are resting their faith in the Congress of the United States because they believe that Congress knows what democracy means. These people will not fight in vain.

Can we afford to allow these men and women to doubt for a single instant the sincerity of our protestations of democracy? How shall we answer their challenge, gentlemen? How shall we explain to them the meaning of democracy if the same Congress that voted for war to make the world safe for democracy refuses to give this small measure of democracy to the women of our country?

COUNTEE CULLEN

INCIDENT

1925

Countee Cullen (1903–1946) was raised in New York City and began writing poetry when he was fourteen years old. He subsequently earned a Phi Beta Kappa key from New York University and an M.A. from Harvard University. He became a leading figure in the Harlem Renaissance after the publication of *Color* (1925), his first collection of poetry, which won critical acclaim. Cullen taught at New York's Frederick Douglass Junior High School until his death in 1946.

Once riding in old Baltimore,
    Heart-filled, head-filled with glee,
I saw a Baltimorean
    Keep looking straight at me.

Now I was eight and very small,
    And he was no whit bigger,
And so I smiled, but he poked out
    His tongue, and called me, "Nigger."

I saw the whole of Baltimore
    From May until December;
Of all the things that happened there
    That's all that I remember.

NAACP headquarters, New York, 1936.

LANGSTON HUGHES

MERRY-GO-ROUND

1942

In 1926, Langston Hughes, the most visible poet of the Harlem Renaissance, published his first book of poetry, *The Weary Blues*, to critical raves. Awarded the Guggenheim Fellowship in 1935, he edited the groundbreaking anthologies *The Poetry of the Negro* (with Arna Bontemps), and *New Negro Poets: USA*. In addition to writing plays, children's books, and newspaper sketches, he published numerous books of poetry, including *Shakespeare in Harlem* (1942) and *Ask Your Mama: Twelve Moods for Jazz* (1961).

Where is the Jim Crow section
On this merry-go-round,
Mister, cause I want to ride?
Down South where I come from
White and colored
Can't sit side by side.
Down South on the train
There's a Jim Crow car.
On the bus we're put in the back—
But there ain't no back
To a merry-go-round!
Where's the horse
For a kid that's black?

ELEANOR ROOSEVELT

CAN A WOMAN EVER BE
PRESIDENT OF THE UNITED STATES?

1935

Eleanor Roosevelt (1884–1962) was the niece of Theodore Roosevelt and, in 1905, married her cousin Franklin D. Roosevelt, who became governor of New York in 1929 and, four years later, president of the United States. Not content to be merely a White House hostess, she transformed the role of the First Lady. During the Depression she worked tirelessly on behalf of New Deal legislation to aid the nation's poor, unemployed, and downtrodden, and also campaigned vigorously for the passage of civil rights legislation. In 1946, President Truman appointed her as a delegate to the United Nations, where she served as chair of the Human Rights Commission. Shortly before her death in 1962, President John F. Kennedy appointed her to lead a Commission on the Status of Women.

"Can a woman be elected President of the United States?" This question is asked me over and over again, and though I cannot see why people should be unusually interested in the answer, I have to acknowledge that they are.

When my boys were at school, a master who was fond of emphasizing certain distinctions in the use of words invariably answered the small boy's question, "Can I go to the village?" by, "You *can* go to the village, but you *may* not."

The same answer seems to me applicable! Can a woman be elected President? Certainly, a woman can be elected President—in all probability, some time a woman will be—but she *may* not, in my opinion, be elected at the present time or in the near future. This is not a criticism of women or of their capacity, but I believe in facing facts.

I read an interview given by a certain lady not long ago in which she was reported to have said that a woman could be a better President than a man because women had intuition.

Women have always been credited with a greater degree of this particular quality, but what is intuition? Intuition is simply the development of the sensitive side of one's nature to meet some particular need. Intuition unaccompanied by experience and trained judgment is far more dangerous than a slow process of reasoning, for it leads to snap judgments, prejudices and stubbornness.

Women have, as a rule, a more sensitive make-up than men, and because of the lives they have led they respond more quickly to their surroundings. It has been their job to live with men as peacefully as possible, and to help their children adjust themselves to their environment. They have used their wits to make life more pleasant and agreeable, and to achieve their own ends without friction.

A wise commentator on politics said in print not long ago that if the present trend toward humanitarian interests in government held through the next few years, in all probability there *would* be a woman President, because the interests of government would more nearly coincide with the usual interests of women. That is perhaps a reasonable conjecture, but even granting the premise, I doubt that the conclusion will prove correct in the near future.

Before we analyze the Presidency today and consider the qualifications it requires, we must reckon with certain things in human nature which take long years to change. There have been great women in history who have ruled nations, but these nations were bred to the tradition of hereditary rulers, and were accustomed to the thought that it was blood and not sex that counted in rulers.

We in this country, because only a short time ago it required brute strength to preserve life, still have a subconscious feeling that man is the natural defender and bearer of burdens. Many of us realize that the Presidency does not require today certain of the attributes of the early pioneer. Many of us know that the kind of strength women possess would enable them to bear the physical strain of the Presidency. But people in general do not like the idea of a woman as Chief Executive—and if they dislike it from the physical standpoint, how much less do they like it when they consider mental and emotional questions!

When men wish to pay a woman a great compliment, they usually say her mind works like a man's, or that she has the executive ability of a man, and this attitude is so ingrained that women frequently say the same thing about each other.

Women are usually credited with being more emotional than men; less able to hold an objective point of view; more given to injecting the personal note. My own experience leads me to believe that men are as temperamental as women and as apt to be personal and lose the objective view. Some men, however, can combine feeling and emotion with the ability to stand off and view situations as though they themselves were not involved. I have known only a few women who were able to do this.

It may well be that the greater imaginative sympathy inherent in women will make a woman a better President than a man of equal ability, for she will understand more easily many situations in which the unfortunates of the world find themselves. The general public, however, believes that good hard common sense is what is really needed, and attributes this particular quality only to men.

Time will show, I think that women are capable of attending to detail and are able to think clearly even when their emotions are involved, but until this has been proved, there is little use in pushing women into positions which will be made untenable for them by prejudice.

By and large, men and women in the country today would vote for a man against a woman for President, no matter what her qualifications might be. I, for one, am glad that this is so, for when a woman assumes this great responsibility, other women throughout the country should be qualified to help her carry the burden of that office.

This will require a far more general development of interest in public questions, past and present, and more willingness to serve in public positions than we have yet seen. Until women have had more legislative training, they will lack a very necessary experience. It is far more difficult to induce women to run for public office, or even to accept appointive office, than it is to secure men to fill the same positions.

This is not all timidity and modesty. There is a certain amount of selfishness in it—a feeling among women that their responsibilities have run along different lines and that they must not drop their age-old duties. Of course, they not only must not, but they *cannot*. They ignore the fact that performing these duties has been made a great deal easier than it was even fifty years ago, and therefore that they are quite able to keep on with the old and take on the new. . . .

Now let us look at woman's qualifications.

There are unquestionably women today with sufficient education to pass on the score of education alone. It is only a very short time, comparatively speaking, since women have had responsibility as citizens. Now it is thought that many women do not care to assume this responsibility. This may be true, but the same can be said of men. Taken by and large, however, you will find more men than women discussing questions of public policy when they get together.

With many of our Presidents, it was never felt that they were the only men of their generation who could have been elected to the office, and that must hold true in the future for women. Before a woman may serve the country usefully as President—not to speak of being elected—we women as a whole shall have to be more willing to master subjects which we have considered uninteresting; we shall have to be willing to perform tasks which we have shunned in the past; we shall, I believe, have to reach the point in industry and in government where the sex line is practically removed.

If the race is to go on, there must always be certain differences in the sexes which cause the fundamental attraction between men and women, but if women are to do the same work and occupy the same positions as men, these differences must be confined to private life. In the world outside, it will have to be a question of ability.

The vast majority of women have not as yet attained the power to be objective about their work and impersonal in their business contacts. They must learn to stand criticism and disagreement without allowing personal feeling to enter into their evaluations of that criticism. They must freely grant the other person's right to a different point of view. Men generally are none too capable of doing this, but great men do it, and their training and work make them realize the necessity of it. Women are doing it more and more, but they still have some distance to travel on this particular road.

I am enormously interested in the development and advancement of women. I am enormously interested in the contributions which women can make to the advancement of the world; but this does not blind me to the fact that there are still things which men have been better trained to do by custom and experience.

The training which women have had will, I think, in the future fit them to do certain things better than men have done them. For instance, women understand human suffering better than men, and they will worker harder to eliminate it. Women bear pain better than men, and they have greater sympathy for those in pain.

However, they should not take positions before they are prepared to fill them. The failures which some women have made when they have taken prominent positions have done incalculable harm to the political usefulness of women as a whole. It has always seemed to me very unfair that these failures should be so much dwelt on and so rarely forgotten, for as a rule the woman involved either did what men told her to do or did the same things which had been done by men for many years. They were unfortunate in being in the positions they occupied at a time when public opinion as to proper conduct was changing.

That, however, does not alter the fact that women cannot afford to fail in any work which they undertake, particularly if it is work of a public character. They must stand on their own feet and make no excuses. They should come up from the bottom and learn their jobs in public life step by step. Above all, they must learn to take other women with them. They must learn that only in proportion as women as a whole are educated in public affairs will individual women succeed in positions of importance.

Even more important, women must realize that attaining their objectives will always count for more with them than their personal success, for fundamentally women work for causes better than for the fulfillment of their own ambitions. This is a weakness if it causes them to be discouraged easily and to abandon their personal careers, but it is a tremendous strength if they keep their courage and maintain a certain indifference to their personal achievement. We will do well not to rush unprepared into action.

When women are prepared and do assume leadership and command a following regardless of sex, I believe that the advance of the human race toward the goal of human happiness will be more rapid than it has ever been.

BROWN V. BOARD OF EDUCATION
347 U.S. 483

1954

One of the most important Supreme Court decisions in American history, *Brown* struck down racial segregation in public schools and overruled *Plessy v. Ferguson*, the infamous 1896 decision that had upheld "separate but equal" and formed the cornerstone of Jim Crow segregation. *Brown* was argued by Thurgood Marshall (1908–1993), who became the first African American justice of the U.S. Supreme Court in 1967. The culmination of a long strategic legal battle by the NAACP Legal Defense and Educational Fund under Marshall's leadership, *Brown* paved the way for decisions striking down racial discrimination in voting, employment, and housing and ignited the broader civil rights movement. The unanimous opinion was written by Chief Justice Warren (1891–1974), a former governor of California, and Republican vice presidential candidate, who joined the Court in 1953. Warren presided over a Court known for its landmark decisions in the areas of civil liberties and criminal justice, as well as civil rights.

MR. CHIEF JUSTICE WARREN delivered the opinion of the Court.

. . . These cases come to us from the States of Kansas, South Carolina, Virginia, and Delaware. They are premised on different facts and different local conditions, but a common legal question justifies their consideration together in this consolidated opinion. . . .

In each of these cases, minors of the Negro race, through their legal representatives, seek the aid of the courts in obtaining admission to the public schools of their community on a nonsegregated basis. In each instance, they had been denied admission to schools attended by white children under laws requiring or permitting segregation according to race. This segregation was alleged to deprive the plaintiffs of the equal protection of the laws under the Fourteenth Amendment. In each of the cases other than the Delaware case, a three-judge federal district court denied relief to the plaintiffs on the so-called "separate but equal" doctrine announced by this Court in *Plessy v. Ferguson*. Under that doctrine, equality of treatment is accorded when the races are provided substantially equal facilities, even though these facilities are separate. . . .

The plaintiffs contend that segregated public schools are not "equal" and cannot be made "equal," and that hence they are deprived of the equal protection of the laws. Because of the obvious importance of the question presented, the Court took jurisdiction. . . .

Reargument was largely devoted to the circumstances surrounding the adop-

JOSEPH SCHERSCHEL, Integration, Texarkana College, Texarkana, Texas, 1956.

tion of the Fourteenth Amendment in 1868. It covered exhaustively consideration of the Amendment in Congress, ratification by the states, then existing practices in racial segregation, and the views of proponents and opponents of the Amendment. This discussion and our own investigation convince us that, although these sources cast some light, it is not enough to resolve the problem with which we are faced. At best, they are inconclusive. The most avid proponents of the post-War Amendments undoubtedly intended them to remove all legal distinctions among "all persons born or naturalized in the United States." Their opponents, just as certainly, were antagonistic to both the letter and the spirit of the Amendments and wished them to have the most limited effect. What others in Congress and the state legislatures had in mind cannot be determined with any degree of certainty.

An additional reason for the inconclusive nature of the Amendment's history, with respect to segregated schools, is the status of public education at that time. In the South, the movement toward free common schools, supported by general taxation, had not yet taken hold. Education of white children was largely in the hands of private groups. Education of Negroes was almost nonexistent, and practically all of the race were illiterate. In fact, any education of Negroes was forbidden by law in some states. Today, in contrast, many Negroes have achieved outstanding success in the arts and sciences as well as in the business and professional world. It is true that public school education at the time of the Amendment had advanced further in the North, but the effect of the Amendment on Northern States was generally ignored in the congressional debates. Even in the North, the conditions of public education did not approximate those existing today. The curriculum was usually rudimentary; ungraded schools were common in rural areas; the school term was but three months a year in many states; and compulsory school attendance was virtually unknown. As a consequence, it is not surprising that there should be so little in the history of the Fourteenth Amendment relating to its intended effect on public education.

In the first cases in this Court construing the Fourteenth Amendment, decided shortly after its adoption, the Court interpreted it as proscribing all state-imposed discriminations against the Negro race. . . . The doctrine of "separate but equal" did not make its appearance in this Court until 1896 in the case of *Plessy v. Ferguson*, involving not education but transportation. American courts have since labored with the doctrine for over half a century. . . .

In the instant cases, that question is directly presented. Here, . . . there are findings below that the Negro and white schools involved have been equalized, or are being equalized, with respect to buildings, curricula, qualifications and salaries of teachers, and other "tangible" factors. Our decision, therefore, cannot turn on merely a comparison of these tangible factors in the Negro and white schools involved in each of the cases. We must look instead to the effect of segregation itself on public education.

In approaching this problem, we cannot turn the clock back to 1868 when the Amendment was adopted, or even to 1896 when *Plessy v. Ferguson* was written. We must consider public education in the light of its full development and its present place in American life throughout the Nation. Only in this way can it be determined if segregation in public schools deprives these plaintiffs of the equal protection of the laws.

Today, education is perhaps the most important function of state and local governments. Compulsory school attendance laws and the great expenditures for education both demonstrate our recognition of the importance of education to our

Ruby Bridges entering school, New Orleans, Louisiana, 1960.

democratic society. It is required in the performance of our most basic public responsibilities, even service in the armed forces. It is the very foundation of good citizenship. Today it is a principal instrument in awakening the child to cultural values, in preparing him for later professional training, and in helping him to adjust normally to his environment. In these days, it is doubtful that any child may reasonably be expected to succeed in life if he is denied the opportunity of an education. Such an opportunity, where the state has undertaken to provide it, is a right which must be made available to all on equal terms.

We come then to the question presented: Does segregation of children in public schools solely on the basis of race, even though the physical facilities and other "tangible" factors may be equal, deprive the children of the minority group of equal educational opportunities? We believe that it does. . . .

We conclude that in the field of public education the doctrine of "separate but equal" has no place. Separate educational facilities are inherently unequal. Therefore, we hold that the plaintiffs and others similarly situated for whom the actions have been brought are, by reason of the segregation complained of, deprived of the equal protection of the laws guaranteed by the Fourteenth Amendment. . . .

BROWN V. BOARD OF EDUCATION
347 U.S. 483

1954

MR. CHIEF JUSTICE WARREN delivered the opinion of the Court.

These cases were decided on May 17, 1954. The opinions of that date, declaring the fundamental principle that racial discrimination in public education is unconstitutional, are incorporated herein by reference. All provisions of federal, state, or local law requiring or permitting such discrimination must yield to this principle. There remains for consideration the manner in which relief is to be accorded. . . .

Full implementation of these constitutional principles may require solution of varied local school problems. School authorities have the primary responsibility for elucidating, assessing, and solving these problems; courts will have to consider whether the action of school authorities constitutes good faith implementation of the governing constitutional principles. Because of their proximity to local conditions and the possible need for further hearings, the courts which originally heard these cases can best perform this judicial appraisal. Accordingly, we believe it appropriate to remand the cases to those courts. . . .

While giving weight to these public and private considerations, the courts will require that the defendants make a prompt and reasonable start toward full compliance with our May 17, 1954, ruling. Once such a start has been made, the courts may find that additional time is necessary to carry out the ruling in an effective manner. The burden rests upon the defendants to establish that such time is necessary in the public interest and is consistent with good faith compliance at the earliest practicable date. . . .

The judgments below, except that in the Delaware case, are accordingly reversed and the cases are remanded to the District Courts to take such proceedings and enter such orders and decrees consistent with this opinion as are necessary and proper to admit to public schools on a racially nondiscriminatory basis with all deliberate speed the parties to these cases.

THE CHICAGO *DEFENDER* SENDS A MAN TO LITTLE ROCK, FALL 1957

1960

In 1957, the Central High School of Little Rock, Arkansas, was under court order to integrate. Initial compliance gave way to violent resistance, and the lives of the Little Rock Nine (African American students chosen to integrate the high school) were in jeopardy, causing President Eisenhower to mobilize the National Guard. Brooks wrote this poem after being sent to Little Rock by the Chicago *Defender* to cover the story.

In Little Rock the people bear
Babes, and comb and part their hair
And watch the want ads, put repair
To roof and latch. While wheat toast burns
A woman waters multiferns.

Time upholds or overturns
The many, tight, and small concerns.

In Little Rock the people sing
Sunday hymns like anything,
Through Sunday pomp and polishing.
And after testament and tunes,
Some soften Sunday afternoons
With lemon tea and Lorna Doones.

I forecast
And I believe
Come Christmas Little Rock will cleave
To Christmas tree and trifle, weave,
From laugh and tinsel, texture fast.

In Little Rock is baseball; Barcarolle.
That hotness in July . . . the uniformed figures raw and implacable
And not intellectual,
Batting the hotness or clawing the suffering dust.

The Open Air Concert, on the special twilight green . . .
When Beethoven is brutal or whispers to ladylike air.
Blanket-sitters are solemn, as Johann troubles to lean
To tell them what to mean . . .
There is love, too, in Little Rock. Soft women softly
Opening themselves in kindness,
Or, pitying one's blindness,
Awaiting one's pleasure
In Azure
Glory with anguished rose at the root . . .
To wash away old semidiscomfitures.
They reteach purple and unsullen blue.
The wispy soils go. And uncertain
Half-havings have they clarified to sures.

In Little Rock they know
Not answering the telephone is a way of rejecting life,

GEORGE TAMES, Students, Little Rock, Arkansas, 1957.

That it is our business to be bothered, is our business
To cherish bores or boredom, be polite
To lies and love and many-faceted fuzziness.

I scratch my head, massage the hate-I-had.
I blink across my prim and pencilled pad.
The saga I was sent for is not down.
Because there is a puzzle in this town.
The biggest News I do not dare
Telegraph to the Editor's chair:
"They are like people everywhere."
The angry Editor would reply
In hundred harryings of Why.

And true, they are hurling spittle, rock,
Garbage and fruit in Little Rock.
And I saw coiling storm a-writhe
On bright madonnas. And a scythe
Of men harassing brownish girls.
(The bows and barrettes in the curls
And braids declined away from joy.)

I saw a bleeding brownish boy . . .
The lariat lynch-wish I deplored.
The loveliest lynchee was our Lord.

JOHN F. KENNEDY

TELEVISED ADDRESS TO THE NATION

JUNE 11, 1963

In 1963, when cities across the South were burning with the long-delayed promise of civil rights, and local police attacked the nonviolent civil rights demonstrators with fire hoses and police dogs, President Kennedy put the full power of the federal government behind the struggle for integration. In a televised address to the nation, he issued a moral challenge to Americans and announced that he would send to Congress legislation outlawing discrimination in all public facilities. This legislation would become the Civil Rights Act of 1964, passed after his death.

This afternoon, following a series of threats and defiant statements, the presence of Alabama National Guardsmen was required on the University of Alabama to carry out the final and unequivocal order of the United States District Court of the Northern District of Alabama. That order called for the admission of two clearly qualified young Alabama residents who happened to have been born Negro.

That they were admitted peacefully on the campus is due in good measure to the conduct of the students of the University of Alabama, who met their responsibilities in a constructive way.

I hope that every American, regardless of where he lives, will stop and examine his conscience about this and other related incidents. This nation was founded by men of many nations and backgrounds. It was founded on the principle that all men are created equal, and that the rights of every man are diminished when the rights of one man are threatened.

Today we are committed to a worldwide struggle to promote and protect the rights of all who wish to be free. When Americans are sent to Vietnam or West Berlin, we do not ask for whites only. It ought to be possible, therefore, for American students of any color to attend any public institution they select without having to be backed up by troops.

It ought to be possible for American consumers of any color to receive equal service in places of public accommodation, such as hotels and restaurants and theaters and retail stores, without being forced to resort to demonstrations in the street. It ought to be possible for American citizens of any color to register and to vote in a free election without interference or fear of reprisal.

It ought to be possible, in short, for every American to enjoy the privileges of being American without regard to his race or his color. In short, every American ought to have the right to be treated as he would wish to be treated, as one would wish his children to be treated. But this is not the case today.

The Negro baby born in America today, regardless of the section of the nation in which he is born, has about one half as much chance of completing high school as a white baby born in the same place on the same day, one third as much chance of completing college, one third as much chance of becoming a professional man, twice as much chance of becoming unemployed, about one seventh as much chance of earning $10,000 a year or more, a life expectancy which is seven years shorter, and the prospects of earning only half as much.

This is not a sectional issue. Difficulties over segregation and discrimination exist in every city, in every state of the Union, producing in many cities a rising tide of discontent that threatens the public safety. Nor is this a partisan issue. In a time of domestic crisis men of goodwill and generosity should be able to unite regardless of party or politics. This is not even a legal or legislative issue alone. It is better to settle these matters in the courts than on the streets, and new laws are needed at every level, but law alone cannot make men see right.

We are confronted primarily with a moral issue. It is as old as the Scriptures and is as clear as the American Constitution.

The heart of the question is whether all Americans are to be afforded equal rights and equal opportunities, whether we are going to treat our fellow Americans as we want to be treated. If an American, because his skin is dark, cannot eat lunch in a restaurant open to the public, if he cannot send his children to the best public school available, if he cannot vote for the public officials who represent him, if, in short, he cannot enjoy the full and free life which all of us want, then who among us would be content to have the color of his skin changed and stand in his place? Who among us would then be content with the counsels of patience and delay?

One hundred years of delay have passed since President Lincoln freed the slaves, yet their heirs, their grandsons, are not fully free. They are not yet freed from the bonds of injustice. They are not yet freed from social and economic oppression. And this nation, for all its hopes and all its boasts, will not be fully free until all its citizens are free.

We preach freedom around the world, and we mean it, and we cherish our freedom here at home; but are we to say to the world, and, much more importantly, to each other, that this is a land of the free except for the Negroes; that we have no second-class citizens except Negroes; that we have no class or caste system, no ghettos, no master race, except with respect to Negroes?

Now the time has come for this nation to fulfill its promise. The events in Birmingham and elsewhere have so increased the cries for equality that no city or state or legislative body can prudently choose to ignore them.

The fires of frustration and discord are burning in every city, North and South, where legal remedies are not at hand. Redress is sought in the streets, in demonstrations, parades, and protests which create tensions and threaten violence and threaten lives.

We face, therefore, a moral crisis as a country and as a people. It cannot be met by repressive police action. It cannot be left to increased demonstrations in the streets. It cannot be quieted by token moves or talk. It is a time to act in the Congress, in your state and local legislative bodies and, above all, in all of our daily lives.

It is not enough to pin the blame on others, to say this is a problem of one section of the country or another, or deplore the facts that we face. A great change is at hand, and our task, our obligation, is to make that revolution, that change, peaceful and constructive for all.

Those who do nothing are inviting shame as well as violence. Those who act boldly are recognizing right as well as reality.

Next week I shall ask the Congress of the United States to act, to make a commitment it has not fully made in this century to the proposition that race has no place in American life or law. The federal judiciary has upheld that proposition in a series of forthright cases. The executive branch has adopted that proposition in the conduct of its affairs, including the employment of federal personnel, the use of federal facilities, and the sale of federally financed housing.

But there are other necessary measures which only the Congress can provide, and they must be provided at this session. The old code of equity law under which we live commands for every wrong a remedy, but in too many communities, in too many parts of the country, wrongs are inflicted on Negro citizens and there are no remedies at law. Unless the Congress acts, their only remedy is in the street.

I am, therefore, asking the Congress to enact legislation giving all Americans the right to be served in facilities which are open to the public—hotels, restaurants, theaters, retail stores, and similar establishments.

This seems to me to be an elementary right. Its denial is an arbitrary indignity that no American in 1963 should have to endure. But many do.

I have recently met with scores of business leaders urging them to take voluntary action to end this discrimination, and I have been encouraged by their response. In the last two weeks over seventy-five cities have seen progress made in desegregating these kinds of facilities. But many are unwilling to act alone, and for this reason, nationwide legislation is needed if we are to move this problem from the streets to the courts.

ABBIE ROWE, John F. Kennedy delivers address on civil rights, Washington, D.C., 1963.

I am also asking Congress to authorize the federal government to participate more fully in lawsuits designed to end segregation in public education. We have succeeded in persuading many districts to desegregate voluntarily. Dozens have admitted Negroes without violence. Today a Negro is attending a state-supported institution in every one of our fifty states. But the pace is very slow.

Too many Negro children entering segregated grade schools at the time of the Supreme Court's decision nine years ago will enter segregated high schools this fall, having suffered a loss which can never be restored. The lack of an adequate education denies the Negro a chance to get a decent job.

The orderly implementation of the Supreme Court decision, therefore, cannot be left solely to those who may not have the economic resources to carry the legal action or who may be subject to harassment.

Other features will also be requested, including greater protection for the right to vote. But legislation, I repeat, cannot solve this problem alone. It must be solved in the homes of every American in every community across our country.

In this respect, I want to pay tribute to those citizens, North and South, who have been working in their communities to make life better for all. They are acting not out of a sense of legal duty but out of a sense of human decency. Like our soldiers and sailors in all parts of the world, they are meeting freedom's challenge on the firing line, and I salute them for their honor and their courage.

My fellow Americans, this is a problem which faces us all—in every city of the North as well as the South. Today there are Negroes, unemployed—two or three times as many compared to whites—with inadequate education, moving into the large cities, unable to find work, young people particularly out of work and without hope, denied equal rights, denied the opportunity to eat at a restaurant or lunch counter or go to a movie theater, denied the right to a decent education. . . . It seems to me that these are matters which concern us all, not merely Presidents or congressmen or governors, but every citizen of the United States.

This is one country. It has become one country because all the people who came here had an equal chance to develop their talents.

We cannot say to ten percent of the population that you can't have that right; that your children can't have the chance to develop whatever talents they have; that the only way that they are going to get their rights is to go into the streets and demonstrate. I think we owe them and we owe ourselves a better country than that.

Therefore, I am asking for your help in making it easier for us to move ahead and to provide the kind of equality of treatment which we would want ourselves; to give a chance for every child to be educated to the limit of his talents.

As I have said before, not every child has an equal talent or an equal ability or an equal motivation, but they should have the equal right to develop their talent and their ability and their motivation, to make something of themselves.

We have a right to expect that the Negro community will be responsible and will uphold the law; but they have a right to expect that the law will be fair, that the Constitution will be color blind, as Justice Harlan said at the turn of the century.

This is what we are talking about. This is a matter which concerns this country and what it stands for, and in meeting it I ask the support of all our citizens.

ADDRESS AT THE MARCH ON WASHINGTON

AUGUST 28, 1963

Martin Luther King Jr., a Baptist minister, was the founder of the Southern Christian Leadership Conference and the leader of the Montgomery, Alabama, bus boycott, 1955–1956. He delivered this immortal address in front of 200,000 people at the March on Washington in 1963, though its impact continues to the present day. Inspired by Gandhi, King led the nonviolent civil rights movement and won international recognition, including the Nobel Peace Prize in 1964. King, who had expanded his crusade for civil rights to one against poverty and other forms of injustice, was killed in Memphis, Tennessee, in April 1968.

Five score years ago, a great American, in whose symbolic shadow we stand, signed the Emancipation Proclamation. This momentous decree came as a great beacon light of hope to millions of Negro slaves who had been seared in the flames of withering injustice. It came as a joyous daybreak to end the long night of captivity.

But one hundred years later, we must face the tragic fact that the Negro is still not free. One hundred years later, the life of the Negro is still sadly crippled by the manacles of segregation and the chains of discrimination. One hundred years later, the Negro lives on a lonely island of poverty in the midst of a vast ocean of material prosperity. One hundred years later, the Negro is still languished in the corners of American society and finds himself an exile in his own land. So we have come here today to dramatize an appalling condition.

In a sense we have come to our nation's Capital to cash a check. When the architects of our republic wrote the magnificent words of the Constitution and the Declaration of Independence, they were signing a promissory note to which every American was to fall heir. This note was a promise that all men would be guaranteed the unalienable rights of life, liberty, and the pursuit of happiness.

It is obvious today that America has defaulted in this promissory note insofar as her citizens of color are concerned. Instead of honoring this sacred obligation, America has given the Negro people a bad check; a check which has come back marked "insufficient funds." But we refuse to believe that the bank of justice is bankrupt. We refuse to believe that there are insufficient funds in the great vaults of opportunity of this nation. So we have come to cash this check—a check that will give us upon demand the riches of freedom and the security of justice.

We have also come to this hallowed spot to remind America of the fierce urgency of *now*. This is not time to engage in the luxury of cooling off or to take the tranquilizing drug of gradualism. *Now* is the time to make real the promises of democracy. *Now* is the time to rise from the dark and desolate valley of segregation to the sunlit path of racial justice. *Now* is the time to open the doors of opportunity to all of God's children. *Now* is the time to lift our nation from the quicksands of racial injustice to the solid rock of brotherhood.

It would be fatal for the nation to overlook the urgency of the moment and to underestimate the determination of the Negro. This sweltering summer of the Negro's legitimate discontent will not pass until there is an invigorating autumn of freedom and equality. Nineteen sixty-three is not an end, but a beginning. Those who hope that the Negro needed to blow off steam and will now be content will have a rude awakening if the nation returns to business as usual. There will be neither rest nor tranquillity in America until the Negro is granted his citizenship rights. The whirlwinds of revolt will continue to shake the foundations of our nation until the bright day of justice emerges.

But there is something that I must say to my people who stand on the warm threshold which leads into the palace of justice. In the process of gaining our rightful place we must not be guilty of wrongful deeds. Let us not seek to satisfy our thirst for freedom by drinking from the cup of bitterness and hatred. We must forever conduct our struggle on the high plane of dignity and discipline. We must not allow our creative protest to degenerate into physical violence. Again and again we must rise to the majestic heights of meeting physical force with soul force.

The marvelous new militancy which has engulfed the Negro community must not lead us to a distrust of all white people, for many of our white brothers, as evidenced by their presence here today, have come to realize that their freedom is inextricably bound to our freedom. We cannot walk alone.

And as we walk, we must make the pledge that we shall march ahead. We cannot turn back. There are those who are asking the devotees of civil rights, "When will you be satisfied?"

We can never be satisfied as long as the Negro is the victim of the unspeakable horrors of police brutality.

We can never be satisfied as long as our bodies, heavy with fatigue of travel, cannot gain lodging in the motels of the highways and the cities.

We cannot be satisfied as long as the Negro's basic mobility is from a smaller ghetto to a larger one.

We can never be satisfied as long as a Negro in Mississippi cannot vote and a Negro in New York believes he has nothing for which to vote.

No, no, we are not satisfied, and we will not be satisfied until justice rolls down like waters and righteousness like a mighty stream.

I am not unmindful that some of you have come here out of great trials and tribulations. Some of you have come fresh from narrow jail cells. Some of you have come from areas where your quest for freedom left you battered by the storms of persecution and staggered by the winds of police brutality. You have been the veterans of creative suffering. Continue to work with the faith that unearned suffering is redemptive.

Go back to Mississippi, go back to Alabama, go back to South Carolina, go back to Georgia, go back to Louisiana, go back to the slums and ghettos of our Northern cities, knowing that somehow this situation can and will be changed. Let us not wallow in the valley of despair.

I say to you today, my friends, that in spite of the difficulties and frustrations of the moment I still have a dream. It is a dream deeply rooted in the American dream.

I have a dream that one day this nation will rise up and live out the true meaning of its creed: "We hold these truths to be self-evident; that all men are created equal."

I have a dream that one day on the red hills of Georgia the sons of former slaves and the sons of former slaveowners will be able to sit down together at the table of brotherhood.

I have a dream that one day even the state of Mississippi, a desert state sweltering with the heat of injustice and oppression, will be transformed into an oasis of freedom and justice.

I have a dream that my four little children will one day live in a nation where they will not be judged by the color of their skin but by the content of their character.

I have a dream today.

I have a dream that one day the state of Alabama, whose governor's lips are presently dripping with the words of interposition and nullification, will be transformed into a situation where little black boys and black girls will be able to join hands with little white boys and girls and walk together as sisters and brothers.

I have a dream today.

I have a dream that one day every valley shall be exalted, every hill and mountain shall be made low, the rough places will be made plain, and the crooked places will be made straight, and the glory of the Lord shall be revealed, and all flesh shall see it together.

This is our hope. This is the faith with which I return to the South. With this faith we will be able to hew out of the mountain of despair a stone of hope. With this faith we will be able to transform the jangling discords of our nation into a beautiful symphony of brotherhood.

With this faith we will be able to work together, to pray together, to struggle together, to go to jail together, to stand up for freedom together, knowing that we will be free one day.

This will be the day when all of God's children will be able to sing with new meaning, "My country 'tis of thee, sweet land of liberty, of thee I sing. Land where my father died, land of the Pilgrims' pride, from every mountainside, let freedom ring."

And if America is to be a great nation, this must become true. So let freedom ring from the prodigious hilltops of New Hampshire. Let freedom ring from the mighty mountains of New York. Let freedom ring from the heightening Alleghenies of Pennsylvania!

Let freedom ring from the snowcapped Rockies of Colorado! Let freedom ring from the curvaceous peaks of California! But not only that; let freedom ring from Stone Mountain of Georgia! Let freedom ring from Lookout Mountain of Tennessee!

Let freedom ring from every hill and molehill of Mississippi. From every mountainside, let freedom ring.

When we let freedom ring, when we let it ring from every village and every hamlet, from every state and every city, we will be able to speed up that day when all of God's children, black men and white men, Jews and Gentiles, Protestants and Catholics, will be able to join hands and sing in the words of the old Negro spiritual, "Free at last! Free at last! Thank God Almighty, we are free at last!"

BETTY FRIEDAN

THE FEMININE MYSTIQUE

1963

After graduating from Smith College, Betty Friedan (1921–) went to New York, where she worked as a journalist and freelance writer. Her most influential book, *The Feminine Mystique*, was based on interviews with a number of American women, largely white and middle class, who had sacrificed education and professional opportunity for a life of domesticity. Friedan founded the National Organization for Women in 1966, serving as its first president, and later organized the Women's Political Caucus.

The problem lay buried, unspoken, for many years in the minds of American women. It was a strange stirring, a sense of dissatisfaction, a yearning that women suffered in the middle of the twentieth century in the United States. Each suburban wife struggled with it alone. As she made the beds, shopped for groceries, matched slipcover material, ate peanut butter sandwiches with her children, chauffeured Cub Scouts and Brownies, lay beside her husband at night—she was afraid to ask even of herself the silent question—"Is this all?"

For over fifteen years there was no word of this yearning in the millions of words written about women, for women, in all the columns, books and articles by experts telling women their role was to seek fulfillment as wives and mothers. Over and over women heard in voices of tradition and of Freudian sophistication that they could desire no greater destiny than to glory in their own femininity. Experts told them how to catch a man and keep him, how to breastfeed children and handle their toilet training, how to cope with sibling rivalry and adolescent rebellion; how to buy a dishwasher, bake bread, cook gourmet snails, and build a swimming pool with their own hands; how to dress, look, and act more feminine and make marriage more exciting; how to keep their husband from dying young and their sons from growing into delinquents. They were taught to pity the neurotic, unfeminine, unhappy women who wanted to be poets or physicists or presidents. They learned that truly feminine women do not want careers, higher education, political rights—the independence and the opportunities that the old-fashioned feminists fought for. Some women, in their forties and fifties, still remembered painfully giving up those dreams, but most of the younger women no longer even thought about them. A thousand expert voices applauded their femininity, their adjustment, their new maturity. All they had to do was devote their lives from earliest girlhood to finding a husband and bearing children. . . .

WILLIAM E. SAURO, **Women's Strike for Equality**, New York, 1970.

The feminine mystique says that the highest value and the only commitment for women is to the fulfillment of their own femininity. It says that the great mistake of Western culture, through most of its history, has been the undervaluation of this femininity. It says this femininity is so mysterious and intuitive and close to the creation and origin of life that man-made science may never be able to understand it. But however special and different, it is in no way inferior to the nature of man; it may even in certain respects be superior. The mistake, says the mystique, the root of women's troubles in the past is that women envied men, women tried to be like men, instead of accepting their own nature, which can find fulfillment only in sexual passivity, male domination, and nurturing maternal love. . . .

The logic of the feminine mystique redefined the very nature of woman's problem. When woman was seen as a human being of limitless human potential, equal to man, anything that kept her from realizing her full potential was a problem to be solved: barriers to higher education and political participation, discrimination or prejudice in law or morality. But now that woman is seen only in terms of her sexual role, the barriers to the realization of her full potential, the prejudices which deny her full participation in the world, are no longer problems. The only problems

now are those that might disturb her adjustment as a housewife. So career is a problem, education is a problem, political interest, even the very admission of women's intelligence and individuality is a problem. And finally there is the problem that has no name, a vague undefined wish for "something more" than washing dishes, ironing, punishing and praising the children. . . .

It . . . is time to stop giving lip service to the idea that there are no battles left to be fought for women in America, that women's rights have already been won. It is ridiculous to tell girls to keep quiet when they enter a new field, or an old one, so the men will not notice they are there. In almost every professional field, in business and in the arts and sciences, women are still treated as second-class citizens. It would be a great service to tell girls who plan to work in society to expect this subtle, uncomfortable discrimination—tell them not to be quiet, and hope it will go away, but fight it. A girl should not expect special privileges because of her sex, but neither should she "adjust" to prejudice and discrimination.

She must learn to compete then, not as a woman, but as a human being. Not until a great many women move out of the fringes into the mainstream will society itself provide the arrangements for their new life plan.

THE SPECIAL PLIGHT AND THE ROLE OF THE BLACK WOMAN

MAY 7, 1971

Fannie Lou Hamer (1917–1977), one of twenty children born to a poor Mississippi share-cropping family, began picking cotton at the age of six. Arrested for attempting to register to vote, she became a tireless civil rights activist. Undeterred by repeated beatings and arrests, Hamer was a field leader for the Student Non-Violent Coordinating Committee and an organizer of the Mississippi Freedom Democratic Party, which eventually succeeded in winning black representation in the Mississippi delegation to the Democratic Convention in 1968.

The special plight and the role of black women is not something that just happened three years ago. We've had a special plight for 350 years. My grandmother had it. My grandmother was a slave. She died in 1960. She was 136 years old. She died in Mount Bayou, Mississippi.

It's been a special plight for the black woman. I remember my uncles and some of my aunts—and that's why it really tickled me when you talked about integration. Because I'm very black, but I remember some of my uncles and some of my aunts was as white as anybody in here, and blue-eyed, and some kind of green-eyed—and my grandfather didn't do it, you know. So what the folks is fighting at this point is what they started. They started unloading the slave ships of Africa, that's when they started. And right now, sometimes, you know I work for the liberation of all people, because when I liberate myself, I'm liberating other people. But you know, sometimes I really feel more sorrier for the white woman than I feel for ourselves because she been caught up in this thing, caught up feeling very special, and folks, I'm going to put it on the line, because my job is not to make people feel comfortable— (drowned out by applause). You've been caught up in this thing because, you know, you worked my grandmother, and after that you worked my mother, and then finally you got hold of me. And you really thought, people—you might try and cool it now, but I been watching you, baby. You thought that you was *more* because you was a woman, and especially a white woman, you had this kind of angel feeling that you were untouchable. You know that? There's nothing under the sun that made you believe that you was just like me, that under this white pigment of skin is red blood, just like under this black skin of mine. So we was used as black women over and over and over. You know, I remember a time when I was working around white people's house, and one thing that would make me mad as hell, after I would be done slaved all day long, this white woman would get on the phone, calling some of her friends, and said, "You know, I'm tired, because *we* have been working," and I said, "That's a damn lie." You're not used to that kind of language, honey, but I'm gone tell you where it's *at.* So all of these things was happening because you *had* more. You had been put on a pedestal, and then not only put on a pedestal, but you had been put in something like a ivory castle. So what happened to you, we have busted the castle open and whacking like hell for the pedestal. And when you hit the ground, you're gone have to fight like hell, like we've been fighting all this time. . . .

We have a job as black women, to support whatever is right, and to bring in justice where we've had so much injustice. Some people say, well, I work for $24 per week. That's not true in my case, I work sometimes for $15 per week. I remember my mother working for 25 and 30 cents per day. But we are organizing ourselves now, because we don't have any other choice. . . .

A few years ago throughout the country the middle-class black woman—I used to say not really black women, but the middle-class colored women, c-u-l-l-u-d, didn't even respect the kind of work that I was doing. But you see now, baby, whether you have a Ph.D., D.D., or no D, we're in this bag together. And whether you're from Morehouse or Nohouse, we're still in this bag together. Not to fight to try to liberate ourselves from the men—this is another trick to get us fighting among ourselves—but to work together with the black man, then we will have a better chance to just act as human beings, and to be treated as human beings in our sick society.

I would like to tell you in closing a story of an old man. This old man was very wise, and he could answer questions that was almost impossible for people to answer. So some people went to him one day, two young people, and said, "We're going to trick this guy today. We're going to catch a bird and we're going to carry it to this old man. And we're going to ask him, 'This that we hold in our hands today, is it alive or is it dead?' If he says 'Dead,' we're going to turn it loose and let it fly. But if he says, 'Alive,' we're going to crush it." So they walked up to this old man, and they said, "This that we hold in our hands today, is it alive or is it dead?" He looked at the young people and he smiled. And he said, "It's in your hands."

Frontiero v. Richardson
411 U.S. 677

1973

Decided during the heyday of the women's movement, this decision was one of the first to uphold a claim of gender discrimination. In *Frontiero* the Court struck down a federal law awarding spousal support benefits to married men in the military but not to married military women and indicated that it would scrutinize such claims as carefully as those based on race, although in later years it retreated somewhat from this protective standard. The case on behalf of Sharron Frontiero, an Air Force lieutenant, was argued by the ACLU's pioneering women's rights attorney Ruth Bader Ginsburg (1933–), who became the second female Supreme Court justice in 1993.

The question before us concerns the right of a female member of the uniformed services to claim her spouse as a "dependent" for the purposes of obtaining increased quarters allowances and medical and dental benefits on an equal footing with male members. A serviceman may claim his wife as a "dependent" without regard to whether she is in fact dependent upon him for any part of her support. A servicewoman, on the other hand, may not claim her husband as a "dependent" unless he is in fact dependent upon her for over one-half of his support. Thus, the question for decision is whether this difference in treatment constitutes an unconstitutional discrimination against servicewomen in violation of the Due Process Clause of the Fifth Amendment. . . .

Appellant Sharron Frontiero, a lieutenant in the United States Air Force, sought increased quarters allowances, and housing and medical benefits for her husband, appellant Joseph Frontiero, on the ground that he was her "dependent." Although such benefits would automatically have been granted with respect to the wife of a male member of the uniformed services, appellant's application was denied because she failed to demonstrate that her husband was dependent on her for more than one-half of his support. . . . Appellants then commenced this suit, contending that, by making this distinction, the statutes unreasonably discriminate on the basis of sex in violation of the Due Process Clause of the Fifth Amendment. In essence, appellants asserted that the discriminatory impact of the statutes is twofold: first, as a procedural matter, a female member is required to demonstrate her spouse's dependency, while no such burden is imposed upon male members; and, second, as a substantive matter, a male member who does not provide more than one-half of his wife's support receives benefits, while a similarly situated female member is denied such benefits. Appellants therefore sought a permanent injunction against the continued enforcement of these statutes and an order directing the appellees to provide

Lieutenant Frontiero with the same housing and medical benefits that a similarly situated male member would receive. . . .

There can be no doubt that our Nation has had a long and unfortunate history of sex discrimination. Traditionally, such discrimination was rationalized by an attitude of "romantic paternalism" which, in practical effect, put women, not on a pedestal, but in a cage. Indeed, this paternalistic attitude became so firmly rooted in our national consciousness that, 100 years ago, a distinguished Member of this Court was able to proclaim:

"Man is, or should be, woman's protector and defender. The natural and proper timidity and delicacy which belongs to the female sex evidently unfits it for many of the occupations of civil life. . . .

". . . The paramount destiny and mission of woman are to fulfil the noble and benign offices of wife and mother. This is the law of the Creator." . . .

As a result of notions such as these, our statute books gradually became laden with gross, stereotyped distinctions between the sexes and, indeed, throughout much of the 19th century the position of women in our society was, in many respects, comparable to that of blacks under the pre–Civil War slave codes. Neither slaves nor women could hold office, serve on juries, or bring suit in their own names, and married women traditionally were denied the legal capacity to hold or convey property or to serve as legal guardians of their own children. And although blacks were guaranteed the right to vote in 1870, women were denied even that right—which is itself "preservative of other basic civil and political rights"—until adoption of the Nineteenth Amendment half a century later. . . .

It is true, of course, that the position of women in America has improved markedly in recent decades. Nevertheless, it can hardly be doubted that, in part because of the high visibility of the sex characteristic, women still face pervasive, although at times more subtle, discrimination in our educational institutions, in the job market and, perhaps not conspicuously, in the political arena. . . .

With these considerations in mind, we can only conclude that classifications based upon sex, like classifications based upon race, alienage, or national origin, are inherently suspect, and must therefore be subjected to strict judicial scrutiny. Applying the analysis mandated by that stricter standard of review, it is clear that the statutory scheme now before us is constitutionally invalid. . . .

We therefore conclude that, by according differential treatment to male and female members of the uniformed services for the sole purpose of achieving administrative convenience, the challenged statutes violate the Due Process Clause of the Fifth Amendment insofar as they require a female member to prove the dependency of her husband.

STATEMENT ON AMERICANS WITH DISABILITIES ACT

MAY 9, 1989

Edward M. Kennedy (1932–) was elected to his brother John F. Kennedy's Senate seat from Massachusetts in 1962. Over the past forty years he has become one of history's most effective senators, working tirelessly for national health insurance, working families, a living wage, education reform, Social Security and Medicare for senior citizens, environmental protection, fair housing, immigration reform, and civil rights. He led the fight for the passage of the Americans with Disabilities Act of 1990, often considered the disabled community's bill of rights.

I am pleased to join in sponsoring of the Americans with Disabilities Act. 43 million Americans with disabilities deserve the opportunity to be first class citizens in our society.

The road to discrimination is paved with good intentions. For years, because of our concern for the less fortunate, we have tolerated a status of second class citizenship for our disabled fellow citizens.

The Americans with Disabilities Act will end this American Apartheid. It will roll back the unthinking and unacceptable practices by which disabled Americans today are segregated, excluded, and fenced off from fair participation in our society by mindless biased attitudes and senseless physical barriers.

JANET DURRANS, Road race, Stamford, Connecticut, 2001.

The timing of this bill has special significance in the history of civil rights. This year we celebrate the 25th anniversary of the Civil Rights Act of 1964. That legislation helped bring about one of the greatest peaceful transformations in our history for millions of Americans who were victims of racial discrimination, and this legislation can do the same for millions of citizens who are disabled.

The Americans with Disabilities Act applies to both the public sector and the private sector. It prohibits discrimination on the basis of disability in employment, public accommodations, transportation and communications. Its goal is nothing less than to give every disabled American a fair share of the American dream.

The removal of physical barriers and access to reasonable accommodations are among the most essential elements of this measure. The lunch counter sit-ins of the early 1960's led to the great public accommodations title of the 1964 Act. But if the students demonstrating at those lunch counters had been in wheelchairs, they could not have made it through the door of the establishment. If Rosa Parks had been disabled, she could not have boarded the bus at all.

Accessible transportation is the linchpin for integration of the disabled. It does little good to open the doors of institutions, to provide rehabilitation and early intervention programs, if the disabled can not even leave their homes and move freely in society. Disabled Americans deserve a better future in their communities than to be relegated to sitting in front of television sets in their homes.

Reliance on paratransit facilities often means no transit at all. Paratransit is called a "demand-response" system, but to many of the disabled it is a "beg-deny" system. Hundreds and sometimes thousands of disabled citizens in every city languish on paratransit waiting lists, hoping for rides which are denied, or which are provided under strict limitations—only to see the doctor, or only until 3:00 p.m. on weekdays, or only 5 trips a month. The restrictions are endless. Under these conditions, no human being can work, raise a family, or function normally in society.

In every era, society is confronted with the challenge of dealing with those who are disabled. All too often, out of fear and misunderstanding, the reaction is to shun those who are afflicted. Half a century ago, our response to the polio epidemic was to close swimming pools and instruct children to avoid the water fountain at their school. Many Americans once felt compelled to whisper when mentioning cancer in their family—fearing that it might be transmitted through casual contact. Even today, young adults suffering from an acute phase of multiple sclerosis are treated as drunk, and older Americans with unrecognized Alzheimer's Disease are rebuked for behavior beyond their control. Most recently, we have seen the impact of fear and misinformation in the treatment of people with AIDS. I have heard from

ALBERT FENN, Child guiding his deaf and blind parents, 1957.

individuals and families whose homes have been torched and whose lives have been threatened.

In every case, science, public health and painful experience have shown that the appropriate reaction is not to fear or to isolate, but to reach out with assistance, understanding, and support.

In no instance is this response more essential than in the epidemic of AIDS. Beyond the fundamental issues of fairness and justice for individuals, protections against discrimination for people with HIV disease are essential to protect the public health. We cannot expect to bring this devastating scourge under control unless we make it possible for individuals who believe that they may be infected to come forward for counseling and testing.

If the price of seeking professional medical guidance is the potential loss of employment, public accommodations, and vital services—we cannot possibly expect those at greatest risk to participate in prevention and treatment programs.

The legislation that we are introducing today is designed not only to protect individuals with disabilities—but to protect the general public health and the integrity of our society.

Some will argue that it costs too much to implement this bill. But I reply, it costs too much to go on without it. We are spending billions of dollars today in the federal budget on programs that make disabled citizens dependent, not independent.

We need a new way of thinking. The short term cost of this legislation is far less than the long-term gain. Disabled does not mean unable.

Vast resources can be saved by making disabled Americans productive Americans. They deserve to participate in the promise of America too. May the enactment of this legislation be the first of many steps in a new effort by Congress and the Administration to redeem that promise.

ADDRESS TO THE FOURTH UN WORLD CONFERENCE ON WOMEN, BEIJING, CHINA

SEPTEMBER 5, 1993

Born in Illinois, Hillary Rodham (1947–) graduated from Wellesley College and received a law degree from Yale University. Prior to her marriage to William J. Clinton, Rodham published papers arguing for closer judicial scrutiny of children's rights. As First Lady, Hillary Clinton led the effort, ultimately unsuccessful, to provide national health insurance for all Americans and continued to speak out on behalf of children and families, both in the United States and around the world. She became the first First Lady to be elected to office when she became the junior senator from New York in 2001.

This is truly a celebration—a celebration on the contributions women make in every aspect of life: in the home, on the job, in their communities, as mothers, wives, sisters, daughters, learners, workers, citizens and leaders.

It is also a coming together, much the way women come together every day in every country. We come together in fields and in factories. In village markets and supermarkets. In living rooms and board rooms.

Whether it is while playing with our children in the park, or washing clothes in a river, or taking a break at the office water cooler, we come together and talk about our aspirations and concerns. And time and again, our talk turns to our children and our families.

However different we may be, there is far more that unites us than divides us. We share a common future. And we are here to find common ground so that we may help bring new dignity and respect to women and girls all over the world—and in so doing, bring new strength and stability to families as well.

By gathering in Beijing, we are focusing world attention on issues that matter most in the lives of women and their families: access to education, health care, jobs, and credit, the chance to enjoy basic legal and human rights and participate fully in the political life of their countries. . . .

What we are learning around the world is that, if women are healthy and educated, their families will flourish. If women are free from violence, their families will flourish. If women have a chance to work and earn as full and equal partners in society, their families will flourish.

And when families flourish, communities and nations will flourish.

That is why every woman, every man, every child, every family, and every nation on our planet has a stake in the discussion that takes place here. . . .

Women comprise more than half the world's population. Women are 70 percent of the world's poor, and two-thirds of those who are not taught to read and write. Women are the primary caretakers for most of the world's children and elderly. Yet much of the work we do is not valued—not by economists, not by historians, not by popular culture and not by government leaders.

At this very moment, as we sit here, women around the world are giving birth, raising children, cooking meals, washing clothes, cleaning houses, planting crops, working on assembly lines, running companies, and running countries.

Women are also dying from diseases that should have been prevented or treated; they are watching their children succumb to malnutrition caused by poverty and economic deprivation; they are being denied the right to go to school by their own fathers and brothers; they are being forced into prostitution, and they are being barred from the ballot box and the bank lending office.

Those of us with the opportunity to be here have the responsibility to speak for those who could not.

As an American, I want to speak up for women in my own country—women who are raising children on the minimum wage, women who can't afford health care or child care, women whose lives are threatened by violence, including violence in their own homes. I want to speak up for mothers who are fighting for good schools, safe neighborhoods, clean air and clean airwaves; for older women, some of them widows, who have raised their families and now find that their skills and life experiences are not valued in the workplace, for women who are working all night as nurses, hotel clerks, and fast food chefs so that they can be at home during the day with their kids; and for women everywhere who simply don't have enough time to do everything they are called upon to do each day.

Speaking to you today, I speak for them, just as each of us speaks for women around the world who are denied the chance to go to school, or see a doctor, or own property, or have a say about the direction of their lives, simply because they are women.

The truth is that most women around the world work both inside and outside the home, usually by necessity.

We need to understand that there is no formula for how women should lead their lives. That is why we must respect the choices that each woman makes for herself and her family. Every woman deserves the chance to realize her God-given potential. We must also recognize that women will never gain full dignity until their human rights are respected and protected. . . .

Tragically, women are most often the ones whose human rights are violated. Even in the late 20th century, the rape of women continues to be used as an instrument of armed conflict. Women and children make up a large majority of the world's refugees. And when women are excluded from the political process, they become even more vulnerable to abuse.

I believe that, on the eve of a new millennium, it is time to break our silence. It is time for us to say here in Beijing, and the world to hear, that it is no longer acceptable to discuss women's rights as separate from human rights. These abuses have continued because, for too long, the history of women has been a history of silence.

Even today, there are those who are trying to silence our words. The voices of this conference and of the women at Huairou must be heard loud and clear: It is a violation of human rights when babies are denied food, or drowned, or suffocated, or their spines broken, simply because they are girls.

It is a violation of human rights when women and girls are sold into the slavery of prostitution.

It is a violation of human rights when women are doused with gasoline, set on fire and burned to death because their marriage dowries are deemed too small.

It is a violation of human rights when individual women are raped in their own communities and when thousands of women are subjected to rape as a tactic or prize of war.

It is a violation of human rights when a leading cause of death worldwide among women ages 14 to 44 is the violence they are subjected to in their own homes.

It is a violation of human rights when young girls are brutalized by the painful and degrading practice of genital mutilation.

It is a violation of human rights when women are denied the right to plan their own families, and that includes being forced to have abortions or being sterilized against their will.

If there is one message that echoes forth from this conference, it is that human rights are women's rights, and women's rights are human rights. Let us not forget that among those rights are the right to speak freely and the right to be heard.

Women must enjoy the right to participate fully in the social and political lives of their countries if we want freedom and democracy to thrive and endure.

It is indefensible that many women in non-governmental organizations who wished to participate in this conference have not been able to attend—or have been prohibited from fully taking part.

Let me be clear: Freedom means the right of people to assemble, organize, and debate openly. It means respecting the views of those who may disagree with the views of their governments. It means not taking citizens away from their loved ones and jailing them, mistreating them, or denying them their freedom or dignity because of the peaceful expression of their ideas and opinions. . . .

In my country, we recently celebrated the 75th anniversary of women's suffrage. It took 150 years after the signing of our Declaration of Independence for women to win the right to vote. It took 72 years of organized struggle on the part of many courageous women and men. It was one of America's most divisive philosophical wars. But it was also a bloodless war. Suffrage was achieved without a shot fired. . . .

We have seen peace prevail in most places for a half century. We have avoided another world war. But we have not solved older, deeply rooted problems that continue to diminish the potential of half the world's population.

Now it is time to act on behalf of women everywhere.

If we take bold steps to better the lives of women, we will be taking bold steps to better the lives of children and families too. Families rely on mothers and wives for emotional support and care; families rely on women for labor in the home; and increasingly, families rely on women for income needed to raise healthy children and care for other relatives. As long as discrimination and inequities remain so commonplace around the world—as long as girls and women are valued less, fed less, fed last, overworked, underpaid, not schooled and subjected to violence in and out of their homes—the potential of the human family to create a peaceful, prosperous world will not be realized.

Let this conference be our, and the world's, call to action. . . .

WILLIAM JEFFERSON CLINTON

REMARKS ON AFFIRMATIVE ACTION

JULY 19, 1995

After living with his grandparents in Hope, Arkansas, while his mother worked as a nurse in New Orleans, Bill Clinton (1946–) attended Georgetown University, was a Rhodes scholar at Oxford University, and received a law degree from Yale University. Returning home to pursue a career in politics, Clinton was elected governor of Arkansas in 1978 and 1982, and catapulted to the presidency in 1992. Strong support for civil rights and affirmative action were hallmarks of Clinton's administration.

. . . Our challenge is twofold: first, to restore the American dream of opportunity and the American value of responsibility; and second, to bring our country together amid all our diversity into a stronger community, so that we can find common ground and move forward as one.

More than ever these two endeavors are inseparable. I am absolutely convinced we cannot restore economic opportunity or solve our social problems unless we find a way to bring the American people together. To bring our people together we must openly and honestly deal with the issues that divide us. Today I want to discuss one of those issues: affirmative action.

It is, in a way, ironic that this issue should be divisive today, because affirmative action was begun 25 years ago by a Republican president with bipartisan support. It began simply as a means to an end of enduring national purpose equal opportunity for all Americans.

So let us today trace the roots of affirmative action in our never ending search for equal opportunity. Let us determine what it is and what it isn't. Let us see where it's worked and where it hasn't, and ask ourselves what we need to do now. Along the way, let us remember always that finding common ground as we move toward the 21st century depends fundamentally on our shared commitment to equal opportunity for all Americans. It is a moral imperative, a constitutional mandate, and a legal necessity. . . .

Beyond all else, our country is a set of convictions: We hold these truths to be self-evident: that all men are created equal; that they are endowed by their Creator with certain inalienable rights; that among these are life, liberty and the pursuit of happiness.

Our whole history can be seen first as an effort to preserve these rights, and then as an effort to make them real in the lives of all our citizens. We know that from the beginning, there was a great gap between the plain meaning of our creed and the meaner reality of our daily lives. Back then, only white male property-owners could vote. Black slaves were not even counted as whole people, and Native Americans were regarded as little more than an obstacle to our great national progress. No wonder Thomas Jefferson, reflecting on slavery, said he trembled to think God is just.

On the 200th anniversary of our great Constitution, Justice Thurgood Marshall, the grandson of a slave, said, "The government our founders devised was defective from the start, requiring several amendments, a civil war, and momentous social transformation to attain the system of constitutional government and its respect for the individual freedoms and human rights we hold as fundamental today." . . .

Thirty years ago in this city, you didn't see many people of color or women making their way to work in the morning in business clothes, or serving in substantial numbers in powerful positions in Congress or at the White House, or making executive decisions every day in businesses. In fact, even the employment want ads were divided, men on one side and women on the other.

It was extraordinary then to see women or people of color as television news anchors, or, believe it or not, even in college sports. There were far fewer women or minorities as job supervisors, or firefighters, or police officers, or doctors, or lawyers, or college professors, or in many other jobs that offer stability and honor and integrity to family life.

A lot has changed, and it did not happen as some sort of random evolutionary drift. It took hard work and sacrifices and countless acts of courage and conscience by millions of Americans. It took the political courage and statesmanship of Democrats and Republicans alike, the vigilance and compassion of courts and advocates in and out of government committed to the Constitution and to equal protection and to equal opportunity. It took the leadership of people in business who knew that in the end we would all be better. It took the leadership of people in labor unions who knew that working people had to be reconciled. . . .

How did this happen? Fundamentally, because we opened our hearts and minds and changed our ways. But not without the pressure of court decisions, legislation, executive action, and the power of examples in the public and private sector. Along the way we learned that laws alone do not change society; that old habits and thinking patterns are deeply ingrained and die hard; that more is required to really open the doors of opportunity. Our search to find ways to move more quickly to equal opportunity led to the development of what we now call affirmative action.

The purpose of affirmative action is to give our nation a way to finally address the systemic exclusion of individuals of talent on the basis of their gender or race from opportunities to develop, perform, achieve and contribute. Affirmative action is an effort to develop a systematic approach to open the doors of education, employment and business development opportunities to qualified individuals who happen to be members of groups that have experienced longstanding and persistent discrimination.

It is a policy that grew out of many years of trying to navigate between two unacceptable pasts. One was to say simply that we declared discrimination illegal and that's enough. We saw that that way still relegated blacks with college degrees to jobs as railroad porters, and kept women with degrees under a glass ceiling with a lower paycheck.

The other path was simply to try to impose change by leveling draconian penalties on employers who didn't meet certain imposed, ultimately arbitrary, and sometimes unachievable quotas. That, too, was rejected out of a sense of fairness.

So with affirmative action a middle ground was developed that would change an inequitable status quo gradually, but firmly, by building the pool of qualified applicants for college, for contracts, for jobs, and giving more people the chance to learn, work and earn. When affirmative action is done right, it is flexible, it is fair, and it works.

I know some people are honestly concerned about the times affirmative action doesn't work, when it's done in the wrong way. And I know there are times when some employers don't use it in the right way. They may cut corners and treat a flexible goal as a quota. They may give opportunities to people who are unqualified instead of those who deserve it. They may, in so doing, allow a different kind of discrimination. When this happens, it is also wrong. But it isn't affirmative action, and it is not legal. . . .

Let me be clear about what affirmative action must not mean and what I won't allow it to be. It does not mean the unjustified preference of the unqualified over the qualified of any race or gender. It doesn't mean numerical quotas. It doesn't mean and I don't favor rejection or selection of any employee or student solely on the basis of race or gender without regard to merit. . . .

Let me say that affirmative action has also done more than just open the doors of opportunity to individual Americans. Most economists who study it agree that affirmative action has also been an important part of closing gaps in economic opportunity in our society, thereby strengthening the entire economy. . . .

Now, there are those who say, my fellow Americans, that even good affirmative action programs are no longer needed; that it should be enough to resort to the courts or the Equal Employment Opportunity Commission in cases of actual, provable, individual discrimination because there is no longer any systematic discrimination in our society. In deciding how to answer that let us consider the facts.

The unemployment rate for African Americans remains about twice that of whites. The Hispanic rate is still much higher. Women have narrowed the earnings gap, but still make only 72 percent as much as men do for comparable jobs. The average income for an Hispanic woman with a college degree is still less than the average income of a white man with a high school diploma.

According to the recently completed Glass Ceiling Report, sponsored by Republican members of Congress, in the nation's largest companies only six tenths of one percent of senior management positions are held by African Americans, four tenths of a percent by Hispanic Americans, three tenths of a percent by Asian Americans; women hold between three and five percent of these positions. White males make up 43 percent of our work force, but hold 95 percent of these jobs.

Just last week, the Chicago Federal Reserve Bank reported that black home loan applicants are more than twice as likely to be denied credit as whites with the same qualifications; and that Hispanic applicants are more than one and a half times as likely to be denied loans as whites with the same qualifications.

Last year alone the federal government received more than 90,000 complaints of employment discrimination based on race, ethnicity or gender. Less than three percent were for reverse discrimination.

Evidence abounds in other ways of the persistence of the kind of bigotry that can affect the way we think if we're not conscious of it, in hiring and promotion and business and educational decisions. . . .

Now, let's get to the other side of the argument. If affirmative action has worked and if there is evidence that discrimination still exists on a wide scale in ways that are conscious and unconscious, then why should we get rid of it as many people are urging? Some question the effectiveness or the fairness of particular affirmative action programs. I say to all of you, those are fair questions, and they prompted the review of our affirmative action programs, about which I will talk in a few moments.

Some question the fundamental purpose of the effort. There are people who honestly believe that affirmative action always amounts to group preferences over individual merit; that affirmative action always leads to reverse discrimination; that ultimately, therefore, it demeans those who benefit from it and discriminates against those who are not helped by it.

I just have to tell you that all of you have to decide how you feel about that, and all of our fellow countrymen and women have to decide as well. But I believe if there are no quotas, if we give no opportunities to unqualified people, if we have no reverse discrimination, and if, when the problem ends, the program ends, that criticism is wrong. . . .

Affirmative action did not cause the great economic problems of the American middle class. And because most minorities or women are either members of that middle class or people who are poor who are struggling to get into it, we must also admit that affirmative action alone won't solve the problems of minorities and women who seek to be a part of the American Dream. To do that, we have to have an economic strategy that reverses the decline in wages and the growth of poverty among working people. Without that, women, minorities, and white males will all be in trouble in the future.

But it is wrong to use misunderstandings about affirmative action to stir up anxieties of the middle class to divert the American people from the real causes of their economic distress the sweeping historic changes taking all the globe in its path, and the specific policies or lack of them in our own country which have aggravated those challenges. It is simply wrong to play politics with the issue of affirmative action and divide our country at a time when, if we're really going to change things, we have to be united. . . .

If we're going to empower America, we have to do more than talk about it, we have to do it. And we surely have learned that we cannot empower all Americans by a simple strategy of taking opportunity away from some Americans.

So to those who use this as a political strategy to divide us, we must say, no. We must say, no. But to those who raise legitimate questions about the way affirmative action works, or who raise the larger question about the genuine problems and anxieties of all the American people and their sense of being left behind and treated unfairly, we must say, yes, you are entitled to answers to your questions. . . .

Now, that's why I ordered this review of all of our affirmative action programs; a review to look at the facts, not the politics of affirmative action. This review concluded that affirmative action remains a useful tool for widening economic and educational opportunity. The model used by the military, the Army in particular, . . . has been especially successful because it emphasizes education and training, ensuring that it has a wide pool of qualified candidates for every level of promotion. . . .

Now, college presidents will tell you that the education their schools offer actually benefit from diversity; colleges where young people get the education and make the personal and professional contacts that will shape their lives. If their colleges look like the world they're going to live and work in, and they learn from all different kinds of people things that they can't learn in books, our systems of higher education are stronger. . . .

This review also found that the executive order on employment practices of large federal contractors also has helped to bring more fairness and inclusion into the work force. . . .

We also looked at the way we awarded procurement contracts under the programs known as set asides. There's no question that these programs have helped to build up firms owned by minorities and women, who historically had been excluded from the old boy networks in these areas. It has helped a new generation of entrepreneurs to flourish, opening new paths to self reliance and an economic growth in which all of us ultimately share. Because of the set asides, businesses ready to compete have had a chance to compete, a chance they would not have otherwise had.

But as with any government program, set asides can be misapplied, misused, even intentionally abused. There are critics who exploit that fact as an excuse to abolish all these programs, regardless of their effects. I believe they are wrong, but I also believe, based on our factual review, we clearly need some reform. So first, we should crack down on those who take advantage of everyone else through fraud and abuse. We must crack down on fronts and pass throughs, people who pretend to be eligible for these programs and aren't. That is wrong. . . .

Second, we must, and we will, comply with the Supreme Court's Adarand decision of last month. Now, in particular, that means focusing set aside programs on particular regions and business sectors where the problems of discrimination or exclusion are provable and are clearly requiring affirmative action. . . .

What the Supreme Court ordered the federal government to do was to meet the same more rigorous standard for affirmative action programs that state and local governments were ordered to meet several years ago. And the best set aside programs under that standard have been challenged and have survived.

Third, beyond discrimination we need to do more to help disadvantaged people and distressed communities, no matter what their race or gender. There are places in our country where the free enterprise system simply doesn't reach. It simply isn't working to provide jobs and opportunity. . . .

Today, I am directing all our agencies to comply with the Supreme Court's Adarand decision, and also to apply the four standards of fairness to all our affirmative action programs that I have already articulated: No quotas in theory or practice; no illegal discrimination of any kind, including reverse discrimination; no preference for people who are not qualified for any job or other opportunity; and as soon as a program has succeeded, it must be retired. Any program that doesn't meet these four principles must be eliminated or reformed to meet them.

But let me be clear: Affirmative action has been good for America.

Affirmative action has not always been perfect, and affirmative action should not go on forever. It should be changed now to take care of those things that are wrong, and it should be retired when its job is done. I am resolved that that day will come. But the evidence suggests, indeed, screams that that day has not yet come.

The job of ending discrimination in this country is not over. That should not be surprising. We had slavery for centuries before the passage of the 13th, 14th and 15th Amendments. We waited another hundred years for the civil rights legislation. Women have had the vote less than a hundred years. We have always had difficulty with these things, as most societies do. But we are making more progress than many people.

Based on the evidence, the job is not done. So here is what I think we should do. We should reaffirm the principle of affirmative action and fix the practices. We should mend it, but don't end it. . . .

If properly done, affirmative action can help us come together, go forward and grow together. It is in our moral, legal and practical interest to see that every person can make the most of his life. In the fight for the future, we need all hands on deck and some of those hands still need a helping hand.

In our national community we're all different, we're all the same. We want liberty and freedom. We want the embrace of family and community. We want to make the most of our own lives and we're determined to give our children a better one. Today there are voices of division who would say forget all that. Don't you dare. Remember we're still closing the gap between our founders' ideals and our reality. But every step along the way has made us richer, stronger and better. And the best is yet to come.

BAKER V. STATE
170 VT. 194

1999

In 1999, a unanimous Vermont Supreme Court ruled that under the "common benefits clause" of the Vermont Constitution, Vermont must guarantee the same protection to gay and lesbian partners that it does to heterosexual couples. This decision made Vermont the first state to provide such constitutional protection and led to the authorization of civil unions. The decision illustrates a principle of federalism, in which state courts are free to interpret their state constitutions to provide greater protection for individual rights than does the U.S. Constitution.

. . . May the State of Vermont exclude same-sex couples from the benefits and protections that its laws provide to opposite-sex married couples? That is the fundamental question we address in this appeal, a question that the Court well knows arouses deeply-felt religious, moral, and political beliefs. Our constitutional responsibility to consider the legal merits of issues properly before us provides no exception for the controversial case. The issue before the Court, moreover, does not turn on the religious or moral debate over intimate same-sex relationships, but rather on the statutory and constitutional basis for the exclusion of same-sex couples from the secular benefits and protections offered married couples.

We conclude that under the Common Benefits Clause of the Vermont Constitution, which, in pertinent part, reads, "That government is, or ought to be, instituted for the common benefit, protection, and security of the people, nation, or community, and not for the particular emolument or advantage of any single person, family, or set of persons, who are a part only of that community," plaintiffs may not be deprived of the statutory benefits and protections afforded persons of the opposite sex who choose to marry. We hold that the State is constitutionally required to extend to same-sex couples the common benefits and protections that flow from marriage under Vermont law. Whether this ultimately takes the form of inclusion within the marriage laws themselves or a parallel "domestic partnership" system or some equivalent statutory alternative, rests with the Legislature. Whatever system is chosen, however, must conform with the constitutional imperative to afford all Vermonters the common benefit, protection, and security of the law.

Plaintiffs are three same-sex couples who have lived together in committed relationships for periods ranging from four to twenty-five years. Two of the couples have raised children together. Each couple applied for a marriage license from their respective town clerk, and each was refused a license as ineligible under the applicable state marriage laws. . . .

In considering this issue, it is important to emphasize at the outset that it is the Common Benefits Clause of the Vermont Constitution we are construing, rather than its counterpart, the Equal Protection Clause of the Fourteenth Amendment to the United States Constitution. It is altogether fitting and proper that we do so. Vermont's constitutional commitment to equal rights was the product of the successful effort to create an independent republic and a fundamental charter of government, the Constitution of 1777, both of which preceded the adoption of the Fourteenth Amendment by nearly a century. . . .

The words of the Common Benefits Clause are revealing. While they do not, to be sure, set forth a fully-formed standard of analysis for determining the constitutionality of a given statute, they do express broad principles which usefully inform that analysis. Chief among these is the principle of inclusion. . . .

The historical origins of the Vermont Constitution thus reveal that the framers, although enlightened for their day, were not principally concerned with civil rights for African-Americans and other minorities, but with equal access to public benefits and protections for the community as a whole. The concept of equality at the core of the Common Benefits Clause was not the eradication of racial or class distinctions, but rather the elimination of artificial governmental preferments and advantages. The Vermont Constitution would ensure that the law uniformly afforded every Vermonter its benefit, protection, and security so that social and political preeminence would reflect differences of capacity, disposition, and virtue, rather than governmental favor and privilege. . . .

It is beyond dispute that the State has a legitimate and long-standing interest in promoting a permanent commitment between couples for the security of their children. It is equally undeniable that the State's interest has been advanced by extending formal public sanction and protection to the union, or marriage, of those couples considered capable of having children, i.e., men and women. And there is no doubt that the overwhelming majority of births today continue to result from natural conception between one man and one woman. . . .

It is equally undisputed that many opposite-sex couples marry for reasons unrelated to procreation, that some of these couples never intend to have children, and that others are incapable of having children. Therefore, if the purpose of the statutory exclusion of same-sex couples is to "further the link between procreation and child rearing," it is significantly under-inclusive. The law extends the benefits and protections of marriage to many persons with no logical connection to the stated governmental goal.

Furthermore, while accurate statistics are difficult to obtain, there is no dispute that a significant number of children today are actually being raised by same-sex parents, and that increasing numbers of children are being conceived by such parents through a variety of assisted-reproductive techniques. . . .

Thus, with or without the marriage sanction, the reality today is that increasing numbers of same-sex couples are employing increasingly efficient assisted-reproductive techniques to conceive and raise children. The Vermont Legislature has not only recognized this reality, but has acted affirmatively to remove legal barriers so that same-sex couples may legally adopt and rear the children conceived through such efforts. . . . The State has also acted to expand the domestic relations laws to safeguard the interests of same-sex parents and their children when such couples terminate their domestic relationship.

Therefore, to the extent that the State's purpose in licensing civil marriage was, and is, to legitimize children and provide for their security, the statutes plainly exclude many same-sex couples who are no different from opposite-sex couples with respect to these objectives. If anything, the exclusion of same-sex couples from the legal protections incident to marriage exposes their children to the precise risks that the State argues the marriage laws are designed to secure against. In short, the marital exclusion treats persons who are similarly situated for purposes of the law, differently. . . .

While the laws relating to marriage have undergone many changes during the last century, largely toward the goal of equalizing the status of husbands and wives, the benefits of marriage have not diminished in value. On the contrary, the benefits and protections incident to a marriage license under Vermont law have never been greater. . . .

Thus, viewed in the light of history, logic, and experience, we conclude that none of the interests asserted by the State provides a reasonable and just basis for the continued exclusion of same-sex couples from the benefits incident to a civil marriage license under Vermont law. Accordingly, in the faith that a case beyond the imagining of the framers of our Constitution may, nevertheless, be safely anchored in the values that infused it, we find a constitutional obligation to extend to plaintiffs the common benefit, protection, and security that Vermont law provides opposite-sex married couples. . . .

While many have noted the symbolic or spiritual significance of the marital relation, it is plaintiffs' claim to the secular benefits and protections of a singularly human relationship that, in our view, characterizes this case. The State's interest in extending official recognition and legal protection to the professed commitment of two individuals to a lasting relationship of mutual affection is predicated on the belief that legal support of a couple's commitment provides stability for the individuals, their family, and the broader community. . . . The extension of the Common Benefits Clause to acknowledge plaintiffs as Vermonters who seek nothing more, nor less, than legal protection and security for their avowed commitment to an intimate and lasting human relationship is simply, when all is said and done, a recognition of our common humanity.

THE INDIVIDUAL

JACQUES LOWE, John F. Kennedy,
Coos Bay, Oregon, 1959.

THE PURSUIT OF happiness was one of the inalienable rights upon which this country was founded. For each of us this pursuit leads to its own particular journey, intertwining solitary moments and engagement with the world. We may combine these elements differently, but as Americans there are some experiences that we share.

We celebrate the artist, who questions power and asks life's difficult questions. In a speech honoring Robert Frost, my father said, "When power leads man toward arrogance, poetry reminds him of his limitations. When power narrows the area of man's concern, poetry reminds him of the richness and diversity of his existence. When power corrupts, poetry cleanses—for art establishes the basic human truth that must serve as the touchstone of our judgment." William Faulkner's Nobel Prize acceptance speech celebrates the anguish of creation, and the role of conscience in an often dehumanized modern world.

We celebrate the nonconformist. In Henry David Thoreau's words, "Why should we be in such desperate haste to succeed, and in such desperate enterprises? If a man does not keep pace with his companions, perhaps it is because he hears a different drummer. Let him step to the music which he hears, however measured or far away."

We celebrate the creative spirit, which recognized or not, has shaped our civilization. Alice Walker writes of her mother, who worked hard to feed and clothe her family yet found time to plant and care for a garden that expressed who she truly was. "I notice that it is only when my mother is working in her flowers that she is radiant. Almost to the point of being invisible—except as a Creator: hand and eye. She is involved in work her soul must have. Ordering the universe in the image of her personal conception of Beauty . . . she has handed down respect for the possibilities—and the will to grasp them."

We also honor those with moral courage. When Lillian Hellman appeared before the House Committee on Un-American Activities and refused to name names, it signaled that the tyranny of the McCarthy era witch-hunts was not invincible. A different kind of personal fortitude was required by the central character in Ralph Ellison's *Invisible Man*. The inner strength of the young black narrator enables him to overcome the life of rejection and fear to which he is condemned by a racist society, and emerge from his social isolation to engage with the world.

When we face moments of crisis in our lives, personal or public, we are fortunate to be able to draw strength from those who struggled with the same conflicts. In "The Road Not Taken," Robert Frost describes a life-changing moment of decision. The rewards of serving others are defined by Martin Luther King Jr. in his speech "The Drum Major Instinct." In this context, I often think of my uncle Robert Kennedy's speech against injustice in South Africa, when he said, "Each time a man stands up for an ideal, or acts to improve the lot of others, or strikes out against injustice, he sends forth a tiny ripple of hope, and crossing each other from a million centers of energy and daring those ripples build a current which can sweep down the mightiest walls of oppression and resistance."

JOSEPH BRACKETT

SIMPLE GIFTS

1848

The Shakers, led by Mother Ann Lee, were members of an English religious sect who immigrated to America, founding a colony in upstate New York in 1776. In the first half of the nineteenth century, the movement had grown to include eighteen communities in eight states. The members were known for the singing, dancing, and trembling produced by their religious fervor—hence the name "Shaker." Those who joined utopian Shaker communities gave up their worldly possessions and lived a celibate, self-sufficient, and austere life consecrated to God. Today, the Shakers are primarily known for their elegantly simple furniture, design, and handicrafts. "Simple Gifts" was composed in 1848 by Shaker elder Joseph Brackett and has influenced many later American composers, most notably Aaron Copland, whose 1944 ballet *Appalachian Spring* incorporates its melody.

'Tis the gift to be simple, 'tis the gift to be free,

'Tis the gift to come down where we ought to be,

And when we find ourselves in the place just right,

'Twill be in the valley of love and delight.

When true simplicity is gain'd,

To bow and to bend we shan't be asham'd,

To turn, turn will be our delight

'Till by turning, turning we come round right.

RALPH WALDO EMERSON

SELF-RELIANCE

1841

Born in Boston, poet, essayist, and lecturer Emerson (1803–1882) was the leading proponent of transcendentalism, a school of thought based on the mystical union of nature and the importance of individual intuition and self-knowledge. Influenced by German philosophy, Oriental teachings, the mystical writings of Swedenborg, and the poetry of Coleridge, Carlyle, and Wordsworth (whom Emerson met in Europe), Emerson's work has had a lasting impact on American thought. His lectures were first published in a collection of essays in 1841. Emerson was also an outspoken abolitionist in the years preceding the Civil War.

. . . To believe your own thought, to believe that what is true for you in your private heart is true for all men,—that is genius. Speak your latent conviction, and it shall be the universal sense; for the inmost in due time becomes the outmost,—and our first thought is rendered back to us by the trumpets of the Last Judgment. . . .

There is a time in every man's education when he arrives at the conviction that envy is ignorance; that imitation is suicide; that he must take himself for better, for worse, as his portion; that though the wide universe is full of good, no kernel of nourishing corn can come to him but through his soil bestowed on that plot of ground which is given to him to till. The power which resides in him is new in nature, and none but he knows what that is which he can do, nor does he know until he has tried. . . .

Whoso would be a man must be a nonconformist. He who would gather immortal palms must not be hindered by the name of goodness, but must explore if it be goodness. Nothing is at last sacred but the integrity of your own mind. Absolve you to yourself, and you shall have the suffrage of the world. . . .

Virtues are, in the popular estimate, rather the exception than the rule. There is the man *and* his virtues. Men do what is called a good action, as some piece of courage or charity, much as they would pay a fine in expiation of daily nonappearance on parade. Their works are done as an apology or extenuation of their living in the world,—as invalids and the insane pay a high board. Their virtues are penances. I do not wish to expiate, but to live. My life is for itself and not for a spectacle. . . .

What I must do is all that concerns me, not what the people think. This rule, equally arduous in actual and in intellectual life, may serve for the whole distinction between greatness and meanness. It is the harder, because you will always find those who think they know what is your duty better than you know it. It is easy in the world to live after the world's opinion; it is easy in solitude to live after our own; but the great man is he who in the midst of the crowd keeps with perfect sweetness the independence of solitude. . . .

A foolish consistency is the hobgoblin of little minds, adored by little statesmen and philosophers and divines. With consistency a great soul has simply nothing to do. He may as well concern himself with his shadow on the wall. Speak what you think now in hard words, and to-morrow speak what to-morrow thinks in hard words again, though it contradict every thing you said to-day.—"Ah, so you shall be sure to be misunderstood."—Is it so bad, then, to be misunderstood? Pythagoras was misunderstood, and Socrates, and Jesus, and Luther, and Copernicus, and Galileo, and Newton, and every pure and wise spirit that ever took flesh. To be great is to be misunderstood. . . .

Your genuine action will explain itself, and will explain your other genuine actions. Your conformity explains nothing. Act singly, and what you have already done singly will justify you now. Greatness appeals to the future. If I can be firm enough to-day to do right, and scorn eyes, I must have done so much right before as to defend me now. Be it how it will, do right now. Always scorn appearances, and you always may. The force of character is cumulative.

JOHN VACHON, **Riding the ranch, Lyman County, South Dakota, 1940.**

MARION POST WOLCOTT,
Shenandoah Valley, Virginia, 1941.

WALDEN

In 1845, Emerson's most famous disciple, Henry David Thoreau, wanted some time to write and reflect. With Emerson's permission, Thoreau spent less than $28.00 to build a cabin on land Emerson owned on the shore of Walden Pond, near Concord, Massachusetts, in which he lived for two years. Out of that experience came *Walden*, one of the most influential books in American literature. In *Walden*, Thoreau examines the meaning of life, the virtues of simplicity and respect for nature, and the importance of remaining true to one's self.

The mass of men lead lives of quiet desperation. What is called resignation is confirmed desperation. From the desperate city you go into the desperate country, and have to console yourself with the bravery of minks and muskrats. A stereotyped but unconscious despair is concealed even under what are called the games and amusements of mankind. There is no play in them, for this comes after work. But it is a characteristic of wisdom not to do desperate things.

When we consider what, to use the words of the catechism, is the chief end of man, and what are the true necessaries and means of life, it appears as if men had deliberately chosen the common mode of living because they preferred it to any other. Yet they honestly think there is no choice left. But alert and healthy natures remember that the sun rose clear. It is never too late to give up our prejudices. No way of thinking or doing, however ancient, can be trusted without proof. What every body echoes or in silence passes by as true to-day may turn out to be falsehood to-morrow, mere smoke of opinion, which some had trusted for a cloud that would sprinkle fertilizing rain on their fields. What old people say you cannot do you try and find that you can. Old deeds for old people, and new deeds for new. . . .

When first I took up my abode in the woods, that is, began to spend my nights as well as days there, which, by accident, was on Independence Day, or the fourth of July, 1845, my house was not finished for winter, but was merely a defence against the rain, without plastering or chimney, the walls being of rough weather-stained boards, with wide chinks, which made it cool at night. The upright white hewn studs and freshly planed door and window casings gave it a clean and airy look, especially in the morning, when its timbers were saturated with dew, so that I fancied that by noon some sweet gum would exude from them. To my imagination it retained throughout the day more or less of this auroral character, reminding me of a certain house on a mountain which I had visited the year before. This was an airy and unplastered cabin, fit to entertain a travelling god, and where a goddess might trail her garments. The winds which passed over my dwelling were such as sweep over the ridges of mountains, bearing the broken strains, or celestial parts only, of terrestrial music. The morning wind forever blows, the poem of creation is uninterrupted; but few are the ears that hear it. . . .

We must learn to reawaken and keep ourselves awake, not by mechanical aids, but by an infinite expectation of the dawn, which does not forsake us in our soundest sleep. I know of no more encouraging fact than the unquestionable ability of man to elevate his life by a conscious endeavor. It is something to be able to paint a particular picture, or to carve a statue, and so to make a few objects beautiful; but it is far more glorious to carve and paint the very atmosphere and medium through which we look, which morally we can do. To affect the quality of the day, that is the highest of arts. Every man is tasked to make his life, even in its details, worthy of the contemplation of his most elevated and critical hour. If we refused, or rather used up, such paltry information as we get, the oracles would distinctly inform us how this might be done.

I went to the woods because I wished to live deliberately, to front only the essential facts of life, and see if I could not learn what it had to teach, and not, when I came to die, discover that I had not lived. I did not wish to live what was not life, living is so dear; nor did I wish to practise resignation, unless it was quite necessary. I wanted to live deep and suck out all the marrow of life, to live so sturdily and Spartan-like as to put to rout all that was not life, to cut a broad swath and shave close, to drive life into a corner, and reduce it to its lowest terms, and, if it proved to be mean, why then to get the whole and genuine meanness of it, and publish its meanness to the world; or if it were sublime, to know it by experience, and be able to give a true account of it in my next excursion. For most men, it appears to me, are in a strange uncertainty about it, whether it is of the devil or of God, and have *somewhat hastily* concluded that it is the chief end of man here to "glorify God and enjoy him forever."

Still we live meanly, like ants; though the fable tells us that we were long ago changed into men; like pygmies we fight with cranes; it is error upon error, and clout upon clout, and our best virtue has for its occasion a superfluous and evitable wretchedness. Our life is frittered away by detail. An honest man has hardly need to count more than his ten fingers, or in extreme cases he may add his ten toes, and lump the rest. Simplicity, simplicity, simplicity! I say, let your affairs be as two or three, and not a hundred or a thousand; instead of a million count half a dozen, and keep your accounts on your thumb nail. In the midst of this chopping sea of civilized life, such are the clouds and storms and quick-sands and thousand-and-one items to be allowed for, that a man has to live, if he would not founder and go to the bottom and not make his port at all, by dead reckoning, and he must be a great calculator indeed who succeeds. Simplify, simplify. . . .

I left the woods for as good a reason as I went there. Perhaps it seemed to me that I had several more lives to live, and could not spare any more time for that one. It is remarkable how easily and insensibly we fall into a particular route, and make a beaten track for ourselves. I had not lived there a week before my feet wore a path from my door to the pond-side; and though it is five or six years since I trod it, it is still quite distinct. It is true, I fear that others may have fallen into it, and so helped to keep it open. The surface of the earth is soft and impressible by the feet of men; and so with the paths which the mind travels. How worn and dusty, then, must be the highways of the world, how deep the ruts of tradition and conformity! I did not wish to take a cabin passage, but rather to go before the mast and on the deck of the world, for there I could best see the moonlight amid the mountains. I do not wish to go below now.

I learned this, at least, by my experiment; that if one advances confidently in the direction of his dreams, and endeavors to live the life which he has imagined, he will meet with a success unexpected in common hours. He will put some things behind, will pass an invisible boundary; new, universal, and more liberal laws will begin to establish themselves around and within him; or the old laws be expanded, and interpreted in his favor in a more liberal sense, and he will live with the license of a higher order of beings. In proportion as he simplifies his life, the laws of the universe will appear less complex, and solitude will not be solitude, nor poverty poverty, nor weakness weakness. If you have built castles in the air, your work need not be lost; that is where they should be. Now put the foundations under them. . . .

Some are dinning in our ears that we Americans, and moderns generally, are intellectual dwarfs compared with the ancients, or even the Elizabethan men. But what is that to the purpose? A living dog is better than a dead lion. Shall a man go and hang himself because he belongs to the race of pygmies, and not be the biggest pygmy that he can? Let every one mind his own business, and endeavor to be what he was made.

Why should we be in such desperate haste to succeed, and in such desperate enterprises? If a man does not keep pace with his companions, perhaps it is because he hears a different drummer. Let him step to the music which he hears, however measured or far away. It is not important that he should mature as soon as an apple-tree or an oak. Shall he turn his spring into summer? If the condition of things which we were made for is not yet, what were any reality which we can substitute? We will not be shipwrecked on a vain reality. Shall we with pains erect a heaven of blue glass over ourselves, though when it is done we shall be sure to gaze still at the true ethereal heaven far above, as if the former were not? . . .

The life in us is like the water in the river. It may rise this year higher than man has ever known it, and flood the parched uplands; even this may be the eventful year, which will drown out all our muskrats. It was not always dry land where we dwell. I see far inland the banks which the stream anciently washed, before science began to record its freshets. Every one has heard the story which has gone the rounds of New England, of a strong and beautiful bug which came out of the dry leaf of an old table of apple-tree wood, which had stood in a farmer's kitchen for sixty years, first in Connecticut, and afterward in Massachusetts,—from an egg deposited in the living tree many years earlier still, as appeared by counting the annual layers beyond it; which was heard gnawing out for several weeks, hatched perchance by the heat of an urn. Who does not feel his faith in a resurrection and immortality strengthened by hearing of this? Who knows what beautiful and winged life, whose egg has been buried for ages under many concentric layers of woodenness in the dead dry life of society, deposited at first in the alburnum of the green and living tree, which has been gradually converted into the semblance of its well-seasoned tomb,—heard perchance gnawing out now for years by the astonished family of man, as they sat round the festive board,—may unexpectedly come forth from amidst society's most trivial and handselled furniture, to enjoy its perfect summer life at last!

I do not say that John or Jonathan will realize all this; but such is the character of that morrow which mere lapse of time can never make to dawn. The light which puts out our eyes is darkness to us. Only that day dawns to which we are awake. There is more day to dawn. The sun is but a morning star.

SIOUX

SONGS OF THE SACRED MYSTERIES

1869

These songs and many others were collected by Stephen Return Riggs and his son Alfred
Longley Riggs, who worked as missionaries among the Sioux. Stephen Riggs became a
leading authority on Siouan languages, preparing "The Grammar and Dictionary of the
Dakota Language" for the Smithsonian (1852) and translating the Bible into the language of
the Dakotas in 1879. According to Alfred Riggs, this sun-dance song was chanted by a devotee
seeking divine acceptance. After a night of feverish dancing and worship, the chorus prays on
behalf of the warrior-devotee and the sun bursts forth. The devotee is further tested and the
song ends with an offering of swan's down dyed red, a sacred article favored by the god who is
referred to as Grandfather.

In the home of mysterious life I lie;
In the home of mysterious life I lie;
In the home of mystery, may I grow into mystery;
In the home of mysterious life I lie.

Shooting an arrow, I come;
Shooting an arrow, I come;
In the east my father sings for me:—I come,
Shooting an arrow, I come.

Having those, may I come;
Having those four souls, may I make my camp-fires.

The day that is determined for me;
May it come earthward.

I have four souls;
Holy boy! I give them to thee.

Sun-gazer, where have you gone?
Behold your friend!

The day to see thee;
May it come.

JOHN C. GRABILL, Sioux encampment, Dakota Territory, c. 1891.

Encrowned with glory,
I come forth resplendent.

Sounding Cloud, my friend!
Do you want water?

    I sing to a Spirit;
    This is the Thunder.

Lo! a cloud is let down from above!
Father! shall I fly upon it?

    Across the lake mysteriously I lie;
    Across the lake mysteriously I lie;
That, decoying some soul, I may eat him alive.
    So may it be.

    This wakan' I whirled,
    This wakan' I whirled,
    This house I levelled.

    This wakan' I whirled,
    This house I levelled,
    This wakan' I whirled.

Grandfather made me mysterious medicine;
    That is true.
Being of mystery, grown in the water,
    He gave it to me.
To grandfather's face wave the imploring hand;
Holding a quadruped, wave the imploring hand.

    In red down he made it for me;
    In red down he made it for me;
He of the water, he of the mysterious countenance,
    Gave it to me,
    Grandfather!

W. E. B. DU BOIS

THE SORROW SONGS
(FROM *THE SOULS OF BLACK FOLK*)

1903

W. E. B. Du Bois (1868–1963) received his Ph.D. in 1895 from Harvard before cofounding in 1909 the organization that became the National Association for the Advancement of Colored People. A pioneering civil rights leader and prolific author, Du Bois split with Booker T. Washington, who advocated vocational training and education, and instead worked for full political, economic, and social equality for African Americans. Du Bois taught economics and history at Atlanta University for many years, edited the NAACP magazine *Crisis*, worked for black liberation worldwide, and became a member of the Communist Party in 1961 before moving to Ghana, where he lived for the last two years of his life.

. . . Through all the sorrow of the Sorrow Songs there breathes a hope—a faith in the ultimate justice of things. The minor cadences of despair change often to triumph and calm confidence. Sometimes it is faith in life, sometimes a faith in death, sometimes assurance of boundless justice in some fair world beyond. But whichever it is, the meaning is always clear: that sometime, somewhere, men will judge men by their souls and not by their skins. Is such a hope justified? Do the Sorrow Songs sing true?

The silently growing assumption of this age is that the probation of races is past, and that the backward races of to-day are of proven inefficiency and not worth the saving. Such an assumption is the arrogance of peoples irreverent toward Time and ignorant of the deeds of men. A thousand years ago such an assumption, easily possible, would have made it difficult for the Teuton to prove his right to life. Two thousand years ago such dogmatism, readily welcome, would have scouted the idea of blond races ever leading civilization. So woefully unorganized is sociological knowledge that the meaning of progress, the meaning of "swift" and "slow" in human doing, and the limits of human perfectability, are veiled, unanswered sphinxes on the shores of science. Why should Æschylus have sung two thousand years before Shakespeare was born? Why has civilization flourished in Europe, and flickered, flamed, and died in Africa? So long as the world stands meekly dumb before such questions, shall this nation proclaim its ignorance and unhallowed prejudices by denying freedom of opportunity to those who brought the Sorrow Songs to the Seats of the Mighty?

Your country? How came it yours? Before the Pilgrims landed we were here. Here we have brought our three gifts and mingled them with yours: a gift of story and song—soft, stirring melody in an ill-harmonized and unmelodious land; the gift of sweat and brawn to beat back the wilderness, conquer the soil, and lay the foundations of this vast economic empire two hundred years earlier than your weak hands could have done it; the third, a gift of the Spirit. Around us the history of the land has centred for thrice a hundred years; out of the nation's heart we have called all that was best to throttle and subdue all that was worst; fire and blood, prayer and sacrifice, have billowed over this people, and they have found peace only in the altars of the God of Right. Nor has our gift of the Spirit been merely passive. Actively we have woven ourselves with the very warp and woof of this nation,—we fought their battles, shared their sorrow, mingled our blood with theirs, and generation after generation have pleaded with a headstrong, careless people to despise not Justice, Mercy, and Truth, lest the nation be smitten with a curse. Our song, our toil, our cheer, and warning have been given to this nation in blood-brotherhood. Are not these gifts worth the giving? Is not this work and striving? Would America have been America without her Negro people?

HENRI CARTIER-BRESSON, Picking cotton, South Carolina, 1960.

Even so is the hope that sang in the songs of my fathers well sung. If somewhere in this whirl and chaos of things there dwells Eternal Good, pitiful yet masterful, then anon in His good time America shall rend the Veil and the prisoned shall go free. Free, free as the sunshine trickling down the morning into these high windows of mine, free as yonder fresh young voices welling up to me from the caverns of brick and mortar below—swelling with song, instinct with life, tremulous treble and darkening bass. My children, my little children, are singing to the sunshine, and thus they sing:

Let us cheer the weary traveller,
Cheer the weary traveller,
Let us cheer the weary traveller
Along the heavenly way,

And the traveller girds himself, and sets his face toward the Morning, and goes his way.

THE ROAD NOT TAKEN

1916

Robert Frost (1874–1963), considered by many the greatest American twentieth-century poet, was awarded the Pulitzer Prize for poetry four times (1924, 1931, 1937, and 1943). Although he was born in San Francisco, Frost's work chronicles the landscape, seasons, and character of rural New England while exploring the larger questions of life's meaning and complexity. This immortal poem was published in the collection *Mountain Interval*. At a writers' conference in 1953, Frost described its creation: "One stanza of 'The Road Not Taken' was written while I was sitting on a sofa in the middle of England; was found three or four years later and I couldn't bear not to finish it. I wasn't thinking about myself there, but about a friend who had gone off to war, a person who, whichever road he went, would be sorry he didn't go the other. He was hard on himself that way."

Two roads diverged in a yellow wood,
And sorry I could not travel both
And be one traveler, long I stood
And looked down one as far as I could
To where it bent in the undergrowth;

Then took the other, as just as fair,
And having perhaps the better claim,
Because it was grassy and wanted wear;
Though as for that the passing there
Had worn them really about the same,

And both that morning equally lay
In leaves no step had trodden black.
Oh, I kept the first for another day!
Yet knowing how way leads on to way,
I doubted if I should ever come back.

I shall be telling this with a sigh
Somewhere ages and ages hence:
Two roads diverged in a wood, and I—
I took the one less traveled by,
And that has made all the difference.

RALPH ELLISON

INVISIBLE MAN

1947

Ralph Ellison (1914–1994) was born in Oklahoma City and came to New York as a young man. His experiences formed the basis for his first novel, *Invisible Man*, which chronicles a young black man's journey through an often hostile white society in search of himself and a life of meaning. Hailed as a masterpiece, *Invisible Man* won the National Book Award. From 1970 until his death, Ellison was the Albert Schweitzer Professor at New York University.

EPILOGUE

Let me be honest with you—a feat which, by the way, I find of the utmost difficulty. When one is invisible he finds such problems as good and evil, honesty and dishonesty, of such shifting shapes that he confuses one with the other, depending upon who happens to be looking through him at the time. Well, now I've been trying to look through myself, and there's a risk in it. I was never more hated than when I tried to be honest. Or when, even as just now I've tried to articulate exactly what I felt to be the truth. No one was satisfied—not even I. . . .

So I took to the cellar; I hibernated. I got away from it all. But that wasn't enough. I couldn't be still even in hibernation. Because, damn it, there's the mind, the *mind*. It wouldn't let me rest. Gin, jazz and dreams were not enough. . . .

I'm not blaming anyone for this state of affairs, mind you; nor merely crying *mea culpa*. The fact is that you carry part of your sickness within you, at least I do as an invisible man. I carried my sickness and though for a long time I tried to place it in the outside world, the attempt to write it down shows me that at least half of it lay within me. . . .

Whence all this passion toward conformity anyway?—diversity is the word. Let man keep his many parts and you'll have no tyrant states. Why, if they follow this conformity business they'll end up by forcing me, an invisible man, to become white, which is not a color but the lack of one. Must I strive toward colorlessness? But seriously, and without snobbery, think of what the world would lose if that should happen. America is woven of many strands; I would recognize them and let it so remain. It's "winner take nothing" that is the great truth of our country or of any country. Life is to be lived, not controlled; and humanity is won by continuing to play in face of certain defeat. Our fate is to become one, and yet many—This is not prophecy, but description. . . .

HENRI CARTIER-BRESSON,
New York, 1947.

So it is that now I denounce and defend, or feel prepared to defend. I condemn and affirm, say no and say yes, say yes and say no. . . .

And I defend because in spite of all I find that I love. In order to get some of it down I *have* to love. I sell you no phony forgiveness, I'm a desperate man—but too much of your life will be lost, its meaning lost, unless you approach it as much through love as through hate. So I approach it through division. So I denounce and I defend and I hate and I love. . . .

In going underground, I whipped it all except the mind, the *mind*. And the mind that has conceived a plan of living must never lose sight of the chaos against which that pattern was conceived. That goes for societies as well as for individuals. Thus, having tried to give pattern to the chaos which lives within the pattern of your certainties, I must come out, I must emerge. And there's still a conflict within me: With Louis Armstrong one half of me says, "Open the window and let the foul air out," while the other says, "It was good green corn before the harvest." Of course Louie was kidding, *he* wouldn't have thrown old Bad Air out, because it would have broken up the music and the dance, when it was the good music that came from the bell of old Bad Air's horn that counted. Old Bad Air is still around with his music and his dancing and his diversity, and I'll be up and around with mine. And, as I said before, a decision has been made. I'm shaking off the old skin and I'll leave it here in the hole. I'm coming out, no less invisible without it, but coming out nevertheless. And I suppose it's damn well time. Even hibernations can be overdone, come to think of it. Perhaps that's my greatest social crime, I've overstayed my hibernation, since there's a possibility that even an invisible man has a socially responsible role to play.

"Ah," I can hear you say, "so it was all a build-up to bore us with his buggy jiving. He only wanted us to listen to him rave!" But only partially true: Being invisible and without substance, a disembodied voice, as it were, what else could I do? What else but try to tell you what was really happening when your eyes were looking through? And it is this which frightens me:

Who knows but that, on the lower frequencies, I speak for you?

WILLIAM FAULKNER

ADDRESS UPON RECEIVING THE NOBEL PRIZE

DECEMBER 10, 1950

William Faulkner (1897–1962), whose novels describe the fictional rural southern society of Yoknapatawpha County, received the Nobel Prize for literature for 1949. Known for his complex narrative structure, rich lyrical language, and tragic characters, Faulkner portrayed the racial tensions and social decay of the post–Civil War South in such influential novels as *The Sound and the Fury* (1929), *As I Lay Dying* (1930), and *Light in August* (1932). He won the Pulitzer Prize for *A Fable* in 1954 and *The Reivers* in 1962. His Nobel Prize acceptance speech addresses the role of the artist and the triumph of the human spirit against the backdrop of the nuclear age.

. . . Our tragedy today is a general and universal physical fear so long sustained by now that we can even bear it. There are no longer problems of the spirit. There is only the question, When will I be blown up? Because of this, the young man or woman writing today has forgotten the problems of the human heart in conflict with itself which alone can make good writing because only that is worth writing about, worth the agony and the sweat.

He must learn them again. He must teach himself that the basest of all things is to be afraid; and, teaching himself that, forget it forever, leaving no room in his work-shop for anything but the old verities and truths of the heart, the old universal truths lacking which any story is ephemeral and doomed—love and honor and pity and pride and compassion and sacrifice. Until he does so, he labors under a curse. He writes not of love but of lust, of defeats in which nobody loses anything of value, of victories without hope and, worst of all, without pity or compassion. His griefs grieve on no universal bones, leaving no scars. He writes not of the heart but of the glands.

Until he relearns these things, he will write as though he stood among and watched the end of man. I decline to accept the end of man. It is easy enough to say that man is immortal simply because he will endure: that when the last ding-dong of doom has clanged and faded from the last worthless rock hanging tideless in the last red and dying evening, that even then there will still be one more sound: that of his puny inexhaustible voice, still talking. I refuse to accept this. I believe that man will not merely endure: he will prevail. He is immortal, not because he alone among crea-tures has an inexhaustible voice, but because he has a soul, a spirit capable of com-passion and sacrifice and endurance. The poet's, the writer's, duty is to write about these things. It is his privilege to help man endure by lifting his heart, by reminding him of the courage and honor and hope and pride and compassion and pity and sac-rifice which have been the glory of his past. The poet's voice need not merely be the record of man, it can be one of the props, the pillars to help him endure and prevail.

LETTER TO THE HOUSE COMMITTEE ON UN-AMERICAN ACTIVITIES, AND REPLY (FROM *SCOUNDREL TIME*)

1952

In the early 1950s the fear of communism was rampant. Our nation was engaged in the cold war struggle with the Soviet Union, China had fallen to the Communists in 1949, and American soldiers were fighting in Korea. At home, Senator Joe McCarthy was broadening his investigations into Communist infiltration of the federal government, and since 1947 the House Un-American Activities Committee had been investigating "subversives" in the entertainment industry, calling to testify nearly one hundred witnesses, including Pete Seeger, Elia Kazan, and Lee J. Cobb. In 1952, playwright Lillian Hellman (1905–1984) was subpoenaed. She offered a stinging rebuke to the committee in the form of an open letter. In her memoir *Scoundrel Time*, she describes the devastating effect of these investigations on her life and career. Along with three hundred others, she was "blacklisted" and prohibited from working in Hollywood for more than ten years.

Dear Mr. Wood:

As you know, I am under subpoena to appear before your Committee on May 21, 1952.

I am most willing to answer any questions about myself. I have nothing to hide from your Committee and there is nothing in my life of which I am ashamed. I have been advised by counsel that under the Fifth Amendment I have a constitutional privilege to decline to answer any questions about my political opinions, activities, and associations, on the grounds of self-incrimination. I do not wish to claim this privilege. I am ready and willing to testify before the representatives of our Government as to my own opinions and my own actions, regardless of any risks or consequences to myself.

But I am advised by counsel that if I answer the Committee's questions about myself, I must also answer questions about other people and that if I refuse to do so, I can be cited for contempt. My counsel tells me that if I answer questions about myself, I will have waived my rights under the Fifth Amendment and could be forced legally to answer questions about others. This is very difficult for a layman to understand. But there is one principle that I do understand: I am not willing, now or in the future, to bring bad trouble to people who, in my past association with them, were completely innocent of any talk or any action that was disloyal or subversive. I do not like subversion or disloyalty in any form, and if I had ever seen any, I would have considered it my duty to have reported it to the proper authorities. But to hurt innocent people whom I knew many years ago in order to save myself is, to me, inhuman and indecent and dishonorable. I cannot and will not cut my conscience to fit this year's fashions, even though I long ago came to the conclusion that I was not a political person and could have no comfortable place in any political group.

I was raised in an old-fashioned American tradition and there were certain homely things that were taught to me: to try to tell the truth, not to bear false witness, not to harm my neighbor, to be loyal to my country, and so on. In general, I respected these ideals of Christian honor and did as well with them as I knew how. It is my belief that you will agree with these simple rules of human decency and will not expect me to violate the good American tradition from which they spring. I would, therefore, like to come before you and speak of myself.

I am prepared to waive the privilege against self-incrimination and to tell you everything you wish to know about my views or actions if your Committee will agree to refrain from asking me to name other people. If the Committee is unwilling to give me this assurance, I will be forced to plead the privilege of the Fifth Amendment at the hearing.

A reply to this letter would be appreciated.

Sincerely yours,
Lillian Hellman

The answer to the letter is as follows:

Dear Miss Hellman:

Reference is made to your letter dated May 19, 1952, wherein you indicate that in the event the Committee asks you questions regarding your association with other individuals you will be compelled to rely upon the Fifth Amendment in giving your answers to the Committee questions.

In this connection, please be advised that the Committee cannot permit witnesses to set forth the terms under which they will testify.

We have in the past secured a great deal of information from persons in the entertainment profession who cooperated wholeheartedly with the Committee. The Committee appreciates any information furnished it by persons who have been members of the Communist Party. The Committee, of course, realizes that a great number of persons who were members of the Communist Party at one time honestly felt that it was not a subversive organization. However, on the other hand, it should be pointed out that the contributions made to the Communist Party as a whole by persons who were not themselves subversive made it possible for those members of the Communist Party who were and still are subversives to carry on their work.

The Committee has endeavored to furnish a hearing to each person identified as a Communist engaged in work in the entertainment field in order that the record could be made clear as to whether they were still members of the Communist Party. Any persons identified by you during the course of Committee hearings will be afforded the opportunity of appearing before the Committee in accordance with the policy of the Committee.

Sincerely yours,
John S. Wood, Chairman

. . . Was I a member of the Communist Party, had I been, what year had I stopped being? How could I harm such people as Martin Berkeley by admitting I had known them, and so on. At times I couldn't follow the reasoning, at times I understood full well that in refusing to answer questions about membership in the Party I had, of course, trapped myself into a seeming admission that I once had been.

But in the middle of one of the questions about my past, something so remarkable happened that I am to this day convinced that the unknown gentleman who spoke had a great deal to do with the rest of my life. A voice from the press gallery had been for at least three or four minutes louder than the other voices. (By this time, I think, the press had finished reading my letter to the committee and were discussing it.) The loud voice had been answered by a less loud voice, but no words could be distinguished. Suddenly a clear voice said, "Thank God somebody finally had the guts to do it."

It is never wise to say that something is the best minute of your life, you must be forgetting, but I still think that unknown voice made the words that helped to save me. (I had been sure that not only did the elderly ladies in the room disapprove of me, but the press would be antagonistic.) Wood rapped his gavel and said angrily, "If that occurs again, I will clear the press from these chambers."

"You do that, sir," said the same voice.

Mr. Wood spoke to somebody over his shoulder and the somebody moved around to the press section, but that is all that happened. To this day I don't know the name of the man who spoke, but for months later, almost every day I would say to myself, I wish I could tell him that I had really wanted to say to Mr. Wood: "There is no Communist menace in this country and you know it. You have made cowards into liars, an ugly business, and you made me write a letter in which I acknowledged your power. I should have gone into your Committee room, given my name and address, and walked out." Many people have said they liked what I did, but I don't much, and if I hadn't worried about rats in jail, and such. . . . Ah, the bravery you tell yourself was possible when it's all over, the bravery of the staircase. . . .

Life had changed and there were many people who did not call me. But there were others, a few friends, a few half-strangers, who made a point of asking me for dinner or who sent letters. That was kind, because I knew that some of them were worried about the consequences of seeing me.

But the mishmash of those years, beginning before my congressional debut and for years after, took a heavy penalty. My belief in liberalism was mostly gone. I think I have substituted for it something private called, for want of something that should be more accurate, decency. And yet certain connecting strings have outworn many knives, perhaps because the liberal connections had been there for thirty years and that's a long time. There was nothing strange about my problem, it is native to our time; but it is painful for a nature that can no longer accept liberalism not to be able to accept radicalism. One sits uncomfortably on a too comfortable cushion. Many of us now endlessly jump from one side to another and endlessly fall in space. The American creative world is not only equal but superior in talent to their colleagues in other countries, but they have given no leadership, written no words of new theory in a country that cries out for belief and, because it has none, finds too many people acting in strange and aimless violence.

But there were other penalties in that year of 1952: life was to change sharply in ordinary ways. We were to have enough money for a few years and then we didn't have any, and that was to last for a while, with occasional windfalls. I saw that coming the day the subpoena was first served. It was obvious, as I have said, the farm had to be sold. I knew I would now be banned from writing movies, that the theater was as uncertain as it always had been, and I was slow and usually took two years to write a play. Hammett's radio, television and book money was gone forever. I could have broken up the farm in small pieces and made a fortune—I had had an offer that made that possible—and I might have accepted it except for Hammett, who said, "No, I won't have it that way. Let everybody else mess up the land. Why don't you and I leave it alone?," a fine sentiment with which I agree and have forever regretted listening to. More important than the sale of the farm, I knew that a time of my life had ended and the faster I put it away the easier would be an altered way of living, although I think the sale of the farm was the most painful loss of my life. It was, perhaps, more painful to Hammett, although to compare the pains of the loss of beloved land one has worked oneself, a house that fits because you have made it fit thinking you would live in it forever, is a foolish guess-game.

DAY OF AFFIRMATION, CAPE TOWN UNIVERSITY

JUNE 6, 1966

Robert F. Kennedy (1925–1968) was a lawyer, chief counsel to the Senate Investigations Subcommittee, manager of his brother's 1960 presidential campaign, attorney general (1961–1963), and U.S. senator from New York (1965–1968). As attorney general, he served as President Kennedy's closest adviser on international affairs as well as domestic issues, particularly civil rights.

In 1966, he accepted an invitation to be the keynote speaker at South Africa's annual Day of Affirmation of Academic and Human Freedom at the University of Cape Town. Apartheid was firmly in place, and the South African government opposed the visit, delaying Kennedy's visa for five months, denying travel permits for foreign journalists to accompany him, and cutting the wires to loudspeakers that had been set up for the overflow crowd during the speech. Nevertheless, Kennedy delivered an inspirational address in which he challenged the students to fight injustice and oppression and work to bring about social change in their country. In his campaign for the presidency two years later, Robert Kennedy returned to the themes of moral courage, the power of the human spirit, and the quest for social justice present in this speech.

. . . This is a Day of Affirmation, a celebration of liberty. We stand here in the name of freedom.

At the heart of that Western freedom and democracy is the belief that the individual man, the child of God, is the touchstone of value, and all society, groups, the state, exist for his benefit. Therefore the enlargement of liberty for individual human beings must be the supreme goal and the abiding practice of any Western society.

The first element of this individual liberty is the freedom of speech: the right to express and communicate ideas, to set oneself apart from the dumb beasts of field and forest; to recall governments to their duties and obligations; above all, the right to affirm one's membership and allegiance to the body politic—to society—to the men with whom we share our land, our heritage, and our children's future.

Hand in hand with freedom of speech goes the power to be heard, to share in the decisions of government which shape men's lives. Everything that makes man's life worthwhile—family, work, education, a place to rear one's children and a place to rest one's head—all this depends on decisions of government; all can be swept away by a government which does not heed the demands of its people. Therefore, the essential humanity of men can be protected and preserved only where government must answer—not just to the wealthy, not just to those of a particular religion, or a particular race, but to all its people.

And even government by the consent of the governed, as in our own Constitu-

Robert F. Kennedy in Soweto,
South Africa, 1966.

tion, must be limited in its power to act against its people; so that there may be no interference with the right to worship, or with the security of the home; no arbitrary imposition of pains or penalties by officials high or low; no restrictions on the freedom of men to seek education or work or opportunity of any kind, so that each man may become all he is capable of becoming. . . .

We must recognize the full human equality of all of our people—before God, before the law, and in the councils of government. We must do this, not because it is economically advantageous, although it is; not because of the laws of God command it, although they do; not because people in other lands wish it so. We must do it for the single and fundamental reason that it is the right thing to do. . . .

All do not develop in the same manner, or at the same pace. Nations, like men, often march to the beat of different drummers, and the precise solutions of the United States can neither be dictated nor transplanted to others. What is important is that all nations must march toward increasing freedom; toward justice for all; toward a society strong and flexible enough to meet the demands of all its own people, and a world of immense and dizzying change. . . .

Our answer is the world's hope; it is to rely on youth. The cruelties and obstacles of this swiftly changing planet will not yield to obsolete dogmas and outworn slogans. It cannot be moved by those who cling to a present which is already dying, who prefer the illusion of security to the excitement and danger which comes with even the most peaceful progress.

This world demands the qualities of youth; not a time of life but a state of mind, a temper of the will, a quality of the imagination, a predominance of courage over timidity, of the appetite for adventure over the love of ease. It is a revolutionary world we live in, and thus, as I have said in Latin America and Asia, in Europe and in the United States, it is young people who must take the lead. Thus you, and your young compatriots everywhere, have had thrust upon you a greater burden of responsibility than any generation that has ever lived.

"There is," said an Italian philosopher, "nothing more difficult to take in hand, more perilous to conduct, or more uncertain in its success than to take the lead in the introduction of a new order of things." Yet this is the measure of the task of your generation, and the road is strewn with many dangers.

First, is the danger of futility: the belief there is nothing one man or one woman can do against the enormous array of the world's ills—against misery and ignorance, injustice and violence. Yet many of the world's greatest movements, of thought and action, have flowed from the work of a single man. A young monk began the Protestant Reformation, a young general extended an empire from Macedonia to the borders of the earth, and a young woman reclaimed the territory of France. It was a young Italian explorer who discovered the New World, and the thirty-two-year-old Thomas Jefferson who proclaimed that all men are created equal.

"Give me a place to stand," said Archimedes, "and I will move the world." These men moved the world, and so can we all. Few will have the greatness to bend history itself; but each of us can work to change a small portion of events, and in the total of all those acts will be written the history of this generation. Thousands of Peace Corps volunteers are making a difference in isolated villages and city slums in dozens of countries. Thousands of unknown men and women in Europe resisted the occupation of the Nazis and many died, but all added to the ultimate strength and freedom of their countries. It is from numberless diverse acts of courage and belief that human history is shaped. Each time a man stands up for an ideal, or acts to improve the lot of others, or strikes out against injustice, he sends forth a tiny ripple of hope, and crossing each other from a million different centers of energy and daring those ripples build a current which can sweep down the mightiest walls of oppression and resistance. . . .

The second danger is that of expediency; of those who say that hopes and beliefs must bend before immediate necessities. Of course, if we would act effectively we must deal with the world as it is. We must get things done. But if there was one thing President Kennedy stood for that touched the most profound feelings of young people around the world, it was the belief that idealism, high aspirations, and deep convictions are not incompatible with the most practical and efficient of programs— that there is no basic inconsistency between ideals and realistic possibilities, no separation between the deepest desires of heart and mind and the rational application of human effort to human problems. . . .

A third danger is timidity. Few men are willing to brave the disapproval of their fellows, the censure of their colleagues, the wrath of their society. Moral courage is a rarer commodity than bravery in battle or great intelligence. Yet it is the one essential, vital quality of those who seek to change a world which yields most painfully to change. Aristotle tells us that "At the Olympic games it is not the finest and the strongest men who are crowned, but they who enter the lists. . . . So too in the life of the honorable and the good it is they who act rightly who win the prize." I believe that in this generation those with the courage to enter the moral conflict will find themselves with companions in every corner of the world.

For the fortunate among us, the fourth danger is comfort, the temptation to follow the easy and familiar paths of personal ambition and financial success so grandly spread before those who have the privilege of education. But that is not the road history has marked out for us. There is a Chinese curse which says "May he live in interesting times." Like it or not we live in interesting times. They are times of danger and uncertainty; but they are also more open to the creative energy of men than any other time in history. And everyone here will ultimately be judged—will ultimately judge himself—on the effort he has contributed to building a new world society and the extent to which his ideals and goals have shaped that effort. . . .

And I hope you will often take heart from the knowledge that you are joined with fellow young people in every land, they struggling with their problems and you with yours, but all joined in a common purpose; that, like the young people of my own country and of every country I have visited, you are all in many ways more closely united to the brothers of your time than to the older generations of any of these nations; and that you are determined to build a better future. . . .

The Drum Major Instinct

Five years after the inspirational "I Have a Dream" speech, King's hopes for a social transformation remained unfulfilled. In early 1968, as the nation was engulfed in antiwar protests and race riots, King planned a poor people's march on Washington, D.C. On February 4—only two months before his assassination—Martin Luther King delivered this speech to the congregation at Ebenezer Baptist Church in Atlanta. A moving exhortation to service, it is also a prophetic eulogy for King's own life and work.

This morning I would like to use as a subject from which to preach "The Drum Major Instinct." And our text for the morning is taken from a very familiar passage in the tenth chapter as recorded by Saint Mark; beginning with the thirty-fifth verse of that chapter, we read these words: "And James and John . . . came unto him saying, 'Master, we would that thou shouldest do for us whatsoever we shall desire.' And he said unto them, 'What would ye that I should do for you?' And they said unto him, 'Grant unto us that we may sit one on thy right hand, and the other on thy left hand in thy glory.' . . . And Jesus said unto them, '. . . To sit on my right hand and on my left hand is not mine to give, but it shall be given to them for whom it is prepared.'"

And then, Jesus goes on toward the end of that passage to say, "But so shall it not be among you, but whosoever will be great among you, shall be your servant; and whosoever of you will be the chiefest, shall be servant of all." The setting is clear. James and John are making a specific request of the master. They had dreamed, as most Hebrews dreamed, of a coming king of Israel who would set Jerusalem free. And establish his kingdom on Mount Zion, and in righteousness rule the world. And they thought of Jesus as this kind of king, and they were thinking of that day when Jesus would reign supreme as this new king of Israel. And they were saying now, "when you establish your kingdom, let one of us sit on the right hand, and the other on the left hand of your throne."

Now very quickly, we would automatically condemn James and John, and we would say they were selfish. Why would they make such a selfish request? But before we condemn them too quickly, let us look calmly and honestly at ourselves, and we will discover that we too have those same basic desires for recognition, for importance, that same desire for intention, that same desire to be first. Of course the other disciples got mad with James and John, and you could understand why, but we must understand that we have some of the same James and John qualities. And there is, deep down within all of us, an instinct. It's a kind of drum major instinct—a desire to be out front, a desire to lead the parade, a desire to be first. And it is something that runs a whole gamut of life.

And so before we condemn them, let us see that we all have the drum major instinct. We all want to be important, to surpass others, to achieve distinction, to lead the parade. . . .

And you know, we begin early to ask life to put us first. Our first cry as baby was a bid for attention. And all through childhood the drum major impulse or instinct is a major obsession. Children ask life to grant them first place. They are a little bundle of ego. And they have innately the drum major impulse, or the drum major instinct.

Now in adult life, we still have it, and we really never get by it. We like to do something good. And you know, we like to be praised for it. Now if you don't believe that, you just go on living life, and you will discover very soon that you like to be praised. Everybody likes it, as a matter of fact. And somehow this warm glow we feel when we are praised, or when our name is in print, is something of the vitamin A to our ego. Nobody is unhappy when they are praised, even if they know they don't deserve it, and even if they don't believe it. The only unhappy people about praise is when that praise is going too much toward somebody else. But everybody likes to be praised, because of this real drum major instinct.

Now the presence of the drum major instinct is why so many people are joiners. You know there are some people who just join everything. And it's really a quest for attention, and recognition, and importance. And they get names that give them that impression. . . .

There comes a time that the drum major instinct can become destructive. And that's where I want to move now. I want to move to the point of saying that if this instinct is not harnessed, it becomes a very dangerous, pernicious instinct. For instance, if it isn't harnessed, it causes one's personality to become distorted. I guess that's the most damaging aspect of it—what it does to the personality. If it isn't harnessed, you will end up day in and day out trying to deal with your ego problem by boasting. . . .

And then it does other things to the personality. It causes you to lie about who you know sometimes. There are some people who are influence peddlers. And in their attempt to deal with the drum major instinct, they have to try to identify with the so-called big name people. . . .

And the other thing is that it causes one to engage ultimately in activities that are merely used to get attention. Criminologists tell us that some people are driven to crime because of this drum major instinct. They don't feel that they are getting enough attention through the normal channels of social behavior, and others turn to anti-social behavior in order to get attention, in order to feel important. . . .

And then the final great tragedy of the distorted personality is the fact that when one fails to harness this instinct, he ends by trying to push others down in order to push himself up. And whenever you do that, you engage in some of the most vicious activities. You will spread evil, vicious, lying gossip on people, because you are trying to pull them down in order to push yourself up. . . .

Now the other thing is that it leads to tragic—and we've see it happen so often—tragic race prejudice. . . . Do you know that a lot of the race problem grows out of the drum major instinct? A need that some people have to feel superior. A need that some people have to feel that they are first, and to feel that their white skin ordained them to be first. And they have said it over and over again in ways that we see with our own eyes. In fact, not too long ago, a man down in Mississippi said that God was a charter member of the White Citizens Council. And so God being the charter member means that everybody who's in that has a kind of divinity, a kind of superiority.

And think of what has happened in history as a result of this perverted use of the drum major instinct. It has led to the most tragic prejudice, the most tragic expressions of man's inhumanity to man. . . .

And we have perverted the drum major instinct. But let me rush on to my conclusion, because I want you to see what Jesus was really saying. What was the answer that Jesus gave these men? It's very interesting. One would have thought that Jesus would have said, "You are out of your place. You are selfish. Why would you raise such a question?"

But that isn't what Jesus did. He did something altogether different. He said in substance, "Oh, I see, you want to be first. You want to be great. You want to be important. You want to be significant. Well you ought to be. If you're going to be my disciple, you must be." . . .

And he transformed the situation by giving a new definition of greatness. And you know how he said it? He said now, "Brethren, I can't give you greatness. And really, I can't make you first." This is what Jesus said to James and John. You must earn it. True greatness comes not by favoritism, but by fitness. And the right hand and the left are not mine to give, they belong to those who are prepared.

And so Jesus gave us a new norm of greatness. If you want to be important—wonderful. If you want to be recognized—wonderful. If you want to be great—wonderful. But recognize that he who is greatest among you shall be your servant. That's your new definition of greatness. And this morning, the thing that I like about it . . . by giving that definition of greatness, it means that everybody can be great. Because everybody can serve. You don't have to have a college degree to serve. You don't have to make your subject and your verb agree to serve. You don't have to know about Plato and Aristotle to serve. You don't have to know Einstein's theory of relativity to serve. You don't have to know the second theory of thermodynamics in physics to serve. You only need a heart full of grace. A soul generated by love. And you can be that servant. . . .

This morning, you can be on his right hand and his left hand if you serve. It's the only way in.

Every now and then I guess we all think realistically about that day when we will be victimized with what is life's final common denominator—that something we call death. We all think about it. And every now and then I think about my own death, and I think about my own funeral. And I don't think of it in a morbid sense. Every now and then I ask myself, "What is it that I would want said?" And I leave the word to you this morning. . . .

I'd like somebody to mention that day, that Martin Luther King, Jr., tried to give his life serving others. I'd like for somebody to say that day, that Martin Luther King, Jr., tried to love somebody. I want you to say that day, that I tried to be right on the war question. I want you to be able to say that day, that I did try to feed the hungry. And I want you to be able to say that day, that I did try, in my life, to clothe those who were naked. I want you to say, on that day, that I did try, in my life, to visit those who were in prison. I want you to say that I tried to love and serve humanity.

Yes, if you want to say that I was a drum major, say that I was a drum major for justice; say that I was a drum major for peace; I was a drum major for righteousness. And all of the other shallow things will not matter. I won't have any money to leave behind. I won't have the fine and luxurious things of life to leave behind. But I just want to leave a committed life behind. . . .

IN SEARCH OF OUR MOTHERS' GARDENS

1974

Poet, essayist, civil rights activist, and author Alice Walker (1944–) published an anthology of speeches, book reviews, essays, and articles written between 1966 and 1982 titled *In Search of Our Mothers' Gardens*. Published a year after *The Color Purple* (1982), for which she won the Pulitzer Prize, the collection sets forth Walker's views on racism and sexism.

> I described her own nature and temperament. Told how they needed a larger life for their expression . . . I pointed out that in lieu of proper channels, her emotions had over-flowed into paths that dissipated them. I talked, beautifully I thought, about an art that would be born, an art that would open the way for women the likes of her. I asked her to hope, and build up an inner life against the coming of that day . . . I sang, with a strange quiver in my voice, a promise song.—*Jean Toomer, "Avey,"* CANE

. . . When the poet Jean Toomer walked through the South in the early twenties, he discovered a curious thing: black women whose spirituality was so intense, so deep, so *unconscious*, that they were themselves unaware of the richness they held. They stumbled blindly through their lives: creatures so abused and mutilated in body, so dimmed and confused by pain, that they considered themselves unworthy even of hope. In the selfless abstractions their bodies became to the men who used them, they became more than "sexual objects," more even than mere women: they became "Saints." Instead of being perceived as whole persons, their bodies became shrines: what was thought to be their minds became temples suitable for worship. These crazy Saints stared out at the world, wildly, like lunatics—or quietly, like suicides; and the "God" that was in their gaze was as mute as a great stone.

Who were these Saints? These crazy, loony, pitiful women?

Some of them, without a doubt, were our mothers and grandmothers.

In the still heat of the post-Reconstruction South, this is how they seemed to Jean Toomer: exquisite butterflies trapped in an evil honey, toiling away their lives in an era, a century, that did not acknowledge them except as "the *mule* of the world." They dreamed dreams that no one knew—not even themselves, in any coherent fashion—and saw visions no one could understand. They wandered or sat about the countryside crooning lullabies to ghosts, and drawing the mother of Christ in charcoal on courthouse walls.

They forced their minds to desert their bodies and their striving spirits sought to rise, like frail whirlwinds from the hard red clay. And when those frail whirlwinds fell, in scattered particles, upon the ground, no one mourned. Instead, men lit candles to celebrate the emptiness that remained, as people do who enter a beautiful but vacant space to resurrect a God.

Our mothers and grandmothers, some of them: moving to music not yet written. And they waited.

They waited for a day when the unknown thing that was in them would be made known; but guessed, somehow in their darkness, that on the day of their revelation they would be long dead. Therefore to Toomer they walked, and even ran, in slow motion. For they were going nowhere immediate, and the future was not yet within their grasp. And men took our mothers and grandmothers, "but got no pleasure from it." So complex was their passion and their calm.

To Toomer, they lay vacant and fallow as autumn fields, with harvest time never in sight: and he saw them enter loveless marriages, without joy; and become prostitutes, without resistance; and become mothers of children, without fulfillment.

For these grandmothers and mothers of ours were not Saints, but Artists; driven to a numb and bleeding madness by the springs of creativity in them for which there was no release. They were Creators, who lived lives of spiritual waste, because they were so rich in spirituality—which is the basis of Art—that the strain of enduring their unused and unwanted talent drove them insane. Throwing away this spirituality was their pathetic attempt to lighten the soul to a weight their work-worn, sexually abused bodies could bear.

What did it mean for a black woman to be an artist in our grandmothers' time? In our great-grandmothers' day? It is a question with an answer cruel enough to stop the blood.

Did you have a genius of a great-great-grandmother who died under some ignorant and depraved white overseer's lash? Or was she required to bake biscuits for a lazy backwater tramp, when she cried out in her soul to paint watercolors of sunsets, or the rain falling on the green and peaceful pasturelands? Or was her body broken and forced to bear children (who were more often than not sold away from her)—eight, ten, fifteen, twenty children—when her one joy was the thought of modeling heroic figures of rebellion, in stone or clay?

How was the creativity of the black woman kept alive, year after year and century after century, when for most of the years black people have been in America, it was a punishable crime for a black person to read or write? And the freedom to paint, to sculpt, to expand the mind with action did not exist. Consider, if you can bear to imagine it, what might have been the result if singing, too, had been forbidden by law. Listen to the voices of Bessie Smith, Billie Holiday, Nina Simone, Roberta Flack, and Aretha Franklin, among others, and imagine those voices muzzled for life. Then you may begin to comprehend the lives of our "crazy," "Sainted" mothers and grandmothers. The agony of the lives of women who might have been Poets, Novelists, Essayists, and Short-Story Writers (over a period of centuries), who died with their real gifts stifled within them. . . .

How they did it—those millions of black women who were not Phillis Wheatley, or Lucy Terry or Frances Harper or Zora Hurston or Nella Larsen or Bessie Smith; or Elizabeth Catlett, or Katherine Dunham, either—brings me to the title of this essay, "In Search of Our Mothers' Gardens," which is a personal account that is yet shared, in its theme and its meaning, by all of us. I found, while thinking about the far-reaching world of the creative black woman, that often the truest answer to a question that really matters can be found very close.

Black women are called, in the folklore that so aptly identifies one's status in society, "the *mule* of the world," because we have been handed the burdens that everyone else—*everyone* else refused to carry. We have also been called "Matriarchs," "Superwomen," and "Mean and Evil Bitches." Not to mention "Castraters" and "Sapphire's Mama." When we have pleaded for understanding, our character has been distorted; when we have asked for simple caring, we have been handed empty inspirational appellations, then stuck in the farthest corner. . . .

In the late 1920s my mother ran away from home to marry my father. Marriage, if not running away, was expected of seventeen-year-old girls. By the time she was twenty, she had two children and was pregnant with a third. Five children later, I was born. And this is how I came to know my mother: she seemed a large, soft, loving-eyed woman who was rarely impatient in our home. Her quick, violent temper was on view only a few times a year, when she battled with the white landlord who had the misfortune to suggest to her that her children did not need to go to school.

She made all the clothes we wore, even my brothers' overalls. She made all the towels and sheets we used. She spent the summers canning vegetables and fruits. She spent the winter evenings making quilts enough to cover all our beds.

During the "working" day, she labored beside—not behind—my father in the fields. Her day began before sunup, and did not end until late at night. There was never a moment for her to sit down, undisturbed, to unravel her own private thoughts; never a time free from interruption—by work or the noisy inquiries of her many children. And yet, it is to my mother—and all our mothers who were not famous—that I went in search of the secret of what has fed that muzzled and often mutilated, but vibrant, creative spirit that the black woman has inherited, and that pops out in wild and unlikely places to this day.

But when, you will ask, did my overworked mother have time to know or care about feeding the creative spirit?

The answer is so simple that many of us have spent years discovering it. We have constantly looked high, when we should have looked high—and low.

And so it is, certainly, with my own mother. Unlike "Ma" Rainey's songs, which retained their creator's name even while blasting forth from Bessie Smith's mouth, no song or poem will bear my mother's name. Yet so many of the stories that I write, that we all write, are my mother's stories. Only recently did I fully realize this: that through years of listening to my mother's stories of her life, I have absorbed not only the stories themselves, but something of the manner in which she spoke, something of the urgency that involves the knowledge that her stories—like her life—must be recorded. It is probably for this reason that so much of what I have written is about characters whose counterparts in real life are so much older than I am.

But the telling of these stories, which came from my mother's lips as naturally as breathing, was not the only way my mother showed herself as an artist. For stories, too, were subject to being distracted, to dying without conclusion. Dinners must be started, and cotton must be gathered before the big rains. The artist that was and is my mother showed itself to me only after many years. This is what I finally noticed:

Like Mem, a character in *The Third Life of Grange Copeland*, my mother adorned with flowers whatever shabby house we were forced to live in. And not just your typical straggly country stand of zinnias, either. She planted ambitious gardens—and still does—with over fifty different varieties of plants that bloom profusely from early March until late November. Before she left home for the fields, she watered her flowers, chopped up the grass, and laid out new beds. When she returned from the fields she might divide clumps of bulbs, dig a cold pit, uproot and replant roses, or prune branches from her taller bushes or trees—until night came and it was too dark to see.

Whatever she planted grew as if by magic, and her fame as a grower of flowers spread over three counties. Because of her creativity with her flowers, even my memories of poverty are seen through a screen of blooms—sunflowers, petunias, roses, dahlias, forsythia, spirea, delphiniums, verbena . . . and on and on.

And I remember people coming to my mother's yard to be given cuttings from her flowers; I hear again the praise showered on her because whatever rocky soil she landed on, she turned into a garden. A garden so brilliant with colors, so original in its design, so magnificent with life and creativity, that to this day people drive by our house in Georgia—perfect strangers and imperfect strangers—and ask to stand or walk among my mother's art.

I notice that it is only when my mother is working in her flowers that she is radiant, almost to the point of being invisible—except as Creator: hand and eye. She is involved in work her soul must have. Ordering the universe in the image of her personal conception of Beauty.

Her face, as she prepares the Art that is her gift, is a legacy of respect she leaves to me, for all that illuminates and cherishes life. She has handed down respect for the possibilities—and the will to grasp them.

For her, so hindered and intruded upon in so many ways, being an artist has still been a daily part of her life. This ability to hold on, even in very simple ways, is work black women have done for a very long time. . . .

Guided by my heritage of a love of beauty and a respect for strength—in search of my mother's garden, I found my own.

And perhaps in Africa over two hundred years ago, there was just such a mother; perhaps she painted vivid and daring decorations in oranges and yellows and greens on the walls of her hut; perhaps she sang—in a voice like Roberta Flack's—*sweetly* over the compounds of her village; perhaps she wove the most stunning mats or told the most ingenious stories of all the village storytellers. Perhaps she was herself a poet—though only her daughter's name is signed to the poems that we know. . . .

WAR AND PEACE

RAY MEWS, Lance Cpl. Perron
Shinneman comes home,
Sioux Falls, South Dakota, 1966.

SEPTEMBER 11 CHANGED our world, forcing us to take stock of who we are as a nation and what values we cherish. The idea of "America" became personal. As we mourned those who died, we drew strength from the courage of those who tried to save them, and from each other. Often the greatest source of strength during a difficult time is the feeling that we are not alone. Out of the overwhelming heartbreak came the miracle of connectedness. This shared outpouring of grief, resolve, and love helped to heal our country and connected us to friends, to neighbors, to those who risk their lives to protect us, and most of all, to our children.

When I walked out of church the Sunday following the tragedy, people were humming "America, the Beautiful," and asking each other if they could remember all the verses of "The Star-Spangled Banner." We turn and return to the words we share, words that have inspired Americans in the past, and that have been passed down to us. Knowing that they aided our parents and grandparents in overcoming the horrors of war helps give us the confidence that we need to fight our generation's battle for freedom and democracy.

In wartime, our greatest leaders have articulated a vision for America that requires sacrifice but exalts our spirit. Abraham Lincoln's Second Inaugural Address, delivered when the enemy was just outside of Washington, is perhaps the greatest speech in American history. The brutality and horror of the three-day battle of Gettysburg, in which nearly 51,000 people were killed or wounded, was also transformed by Lincoln's healing words. The leadership of Presidents Franklin D. Roosevelt and Harry S. Truman during World War II, along with military leaders like Dwight D. Eisenhower, unified the country, just as George W. Bush responded to the September 11 attack with words of courage and determination. Americans come together in wartime, and these bonds of national unity form our enduring destiny.

Although the shared sacrifice of wartime unifies our nation, wars produce wrenching dissent. Those who disagree with a national wartime commitment are often considered unpatriotic even though they may be pursuing an alternate, honestly held belief about what is best for our country. There is a tension between support for America in times of crisis and the obligation to speak out on matters of vital national importance. The documents and photographs from the antiwar movement of the 1960s and 1970s as well as contemporary questions show that we do not have to give up our freedom in order to defend it.

Reading this section, one is struck by the sobering realization that much less material has entered the popular culture dealing with the hard work of achieving peace. Interestingly, the cold war, when the specter of total annihilation somehow made war seem less likely, seemed to allow some opportunity to reflect. In President Kennedy's speech at American University, he said, "Genuine peace must be a product of many nations, the sum of many acts. It must be dynamic, not static, changing to meet the challenge of each new generation. For peace is a process, a way of solving problems. . . . So, let us not be blind to our differences—but let us also direct attention to our common interests and to the means by which those differences can be resolved. And if we cannot now end our differences, at least we can help make the world safe for diversity. For in the final analysis, our most basic common link is that we all inhabit this small planet. We all breathe the same air. We all cherish our children's future. And we are all mortal."

Those words were put into practice during President Nixon's breakthrough opening in Chinese relations, President Carter's Camp David Accords, and President Clinton's intervention in the Balkans. The steps to peace are never easy but these courageous actions made the world smaller and America safer.

SPEECH AFTER DEFEAT BY THE VIRGINIA MILITIA

1774

When members of his tribe and family were killed by white settlers, Mingo Chief Logan (c. 1725–1780) led several tribes in an uprising against the Virginia militia, sent by Royal Governor Lord Dunmore. Though facing defeat, Chief Logan refused to negotiate a settlement. In his *Notes on the State of Virginia*, Thomas Jefferson distinguished Chief Logan's statement as one of the most eloquent in history. "I may challenge the orations of Demosthenes and Cicero, and of any more eminent orator, if Europe has furnished more eminent, to produce a single passage, superior to the speech of Logan, a Mingo Chief."

I appeal to any white man to say, if ever he entered Logan's cabin hungry, and he gave him not meat: if ever he came cold and naked, and he cloathed him not. During the course of the last long and bloody war Logan remained idle in his cabin, an advocate for peace. Such was my love for the whites, that my countrymen pointed as they passed, and said, "Logan is the friend of white man." I had even thought to have lived with you, but for the injuries of one man. Colonel Cresap, the last spring, in cold blood, and unprovoked, murdered all the relations of Logan, not even sparing my women and children. There runs not a drop of my blood in the veins of any living creature. This called on me for revenge. I have sought it: I have killed many; I have fully glutted my vengeance: for my country I rejoice at the beams of peace. But do not harbour a thought that mine is the joy of fear. Logan never felt fear. He will not turn on his heel to save his life. Who is there to mourn for Logan?—Not one.

PATRICK HENRY

SPEECH TO THE SECOND VIRGINIA CONVENTION

MARCH 23, 1775

Delivered three weeks before the American Revolution began at the Battles of Concord and Lexington, this speech ends with Henry's immortal words, "Give me liberty or give me death!" A lawyer and planter from Virginia, Henry (1736–1799) first gained recognition as an opponent of British colonial rule when he proposed that the Virginia House of Burgesses oppose the Stamp Act (1765), the British law intended to raise colonial revenue in spite of colonial protests that it amounted to "taxation without representation." In 1776, Henry helped draft instructions to Virginia's delegates to the Second Continental Congress supporting a Declaration of Independence. In 1787, however, he refused to attend the Constitutional Convention, fearing that the creation of a strong central government would threaten individual freedom.

. . . I have but one lamp by which my feet are guided; and that is the lamp of experience. I know of no way of judging of the future but by the past. And judging by the past, I wish to know what there has been in the conduct of the British ministry for the last ten years to justify those hopes with which gentlemen have been pleased to solace themselves and the House? Is it that insidious smile with which our petition has been lately received? Trust it not, sir; it will prove a snare to your feet. Suffer not yourselves to be betrayed with a kiss. Ask yourselves how this gracious reception of our petition comports with these warlike preparations which cover our waters and darken our land. Are fleets and armies necessary to a work of love and reconciliation? Have we shown ourselves so unwilling to be reconciled, that force must be called in to win back our love? Let us not deceive ourselves, sir. These are the implements of war and subjugation; the last arguments to which kings resort. I ask gentlemen, sir, what means this martial array, if its purpose be not to force us to submission? Can gentlemen assign any other possible motives for it? Has Great Britain any enemy, in this quarter of the world, to call for all this accumulation of navies and armies? No, sir, she has none. They are meant for us; they can be meant for no other. They are sent over to bind and rivet upon us those chains which the British ministry have been so long forging. And what have we to oppose to them? Shall we try argument? Sir, we have been trying that for the last ten years. Have we anything new to offer on the subject? Nothing. We have held the subject up in every light of which it is capable; but it has been all in vain. Shall we resort to entreaty and humble supplication? What terms shall we find which have not been already exhausted? Let us not, I beseech you, sir, deceive ourselves longer. Sir, we have done everything that could be done to avert the storm which is now coming on. We have petitioned; we have remonstrated; we have supplicated; we have prostrated ourselves before the tyrannical hands of the ministry and parliament. Our petitions have been slighted; our remonstrances have produced additional violence and insult; our supplications have been disregarded; and we have been spurned, with contempt, from the foot of the throne. In vain, after these things, may we indulge the fond hope of peace and reconciliation. There is no longer any room for hope. If we wish to be free—if we mean to preserve inviolate those inestimable privileges for which we have been so long contending—if we mean not basely to abandon the noble struggle in which we have been so long engaged, and which we have pledged ourselves never to abandon until the glorious object of our contest shall be obtained, we must fight! I repeat it, sir, we must fight! An appeal to arms and to the God of Hosts is all that is left us!

They tell us, sir, that we are weak; unable to cope with so formidable an adversary. But when shall we be stronger? Will it be the next week, or the next year? Will it be when we are totally disarmed, and when a British guard shall be stationed in every house? Shall we gather strength by irresolution and inaction? Shall we acquire the means of effectual resistance by lying supinely on our backs, and hugging the delusive phantom of hope, until our enemies shall have bound us hand and foot? Sir, we are not weak, if we make a proper use of the means which the God of nature hath placed in our power. Three millions of people, armed in the holy cause of liberty, and in such a country as that which we possess, are invincible by any force which our enemy can send against us. Besides, sir, we shall not fight our battles alone. There is a just God who presides over the destinies of nations; and who will raise friends to fight our battles for us. The battle, sir, is not to the strong alone; it is to the vigilant, the active, the brave. Besides, sir, we have no election. If we were base enough to desire it, it is now too late to retire from the contest. There is no retreat but in submission and slavery! Our chains are forged! Their clanking may be heard on the plains of Boston! The war is inevitable—and let it come! I repeat it, sir, let it come!

It is in vain, sir, to extenuate the matter. Gentlemen may cry peace, peace—but there is no peace. The war is actually begun! The next gale that sweeps from the North will bring to our ears the clash of resounding arms! Our brethren are already in the field! Why stand we here idle? What is it that gentlemen wish? What would they have? Is life so dear, or peace so sweet, as to be purchased at the price of chains and slavery? Forbid it, Almighty God! I know not what course others may take; but as for me, give me liberty, or give me death!

THOMAS PAINE

COMMON SENSE

FEBRUARY 14, 1776

Encouraged by Benjamin Franklin, Thomas Paine (1737–1809) emigrated from England to Philadelphia in 1774, where he became an outspoken advocate of independence. His pamphlet, "Common Sense," became an instant best-seller, with 500,000 copies in print by the time the Second Continental Congress declared independence. While serving in the Continental Army, Paine wrote the first of sixteen pamphlets published as *The American Crisis*, in which he urged Americans to support Washington's army in spite of the heavy losses it was sustaining. Those essays are famous for the lines, "These are the times that try men's souls. The summer soldier and the sunshine patriot will, in this crisis, shrink from the service of their country; but he that stands it now, deserves the love and thanks of man and woman."

. . . Volumes have been written on the subject of the struggle between England and America. Men of all ranks have embarked in the controversy, from different motives, and with various designs; but all have been ineffectual, and the period of debate is closed. Arms, as the last resource, decide the contest; the appeal was the choice of the king, and the continent hath accepted the challenge. . . .

I have heard it asserted by some, that as America hath flourished under her former connexion with Great-Britain, that the same connexion is necessary towards her future happiness, and will always have the same effect. Nothing can be more fallacious than this kind of argument. We may as well assert that because a child has thrived upon milk, that it is never to have meat, or that the first twenty years of our lives is to become a precedent for the next twenty. But even this is admitting more than is true, for I answer roundly, that America would have flourished as much, and probably much more, had no European power had any thing to do with her. The commerce, by which she hath enriched herself are the necessaries of life, and will always have a market while eating is the custom of Europe.

But she has protected us, say some. That she hath engrossed us is true, and defended the continent at our expence as well as her own is admitted, and she would have defended Turkey from the same motive, viz, the sake of trade and dominion.

Alas, we have been long led away by ancient prejudices, and made large sacrifices to superstition. We have boasted the protection of Great-Britain, without considering, that her motive was *interest* not *attachment*; that she did not protect us from *our enemies* on *our account*, but from *her enemies* on *her own account*, from those who had no quarrel with us on any *other account*, and who will always be our enemies on the *same account*. Let Britain wave her pretensions to the continent, or the continent throw off the dependence, and we should be at peace with France and Spain were they at war with Britain. The miseries of Hanover last war ought to warn us against connexions. . . .

But Britain is the parent country, say some. Then the more shame upon her conduct. Even brutes do not devour their young, nor savages make war upon their families; wherefore the assertion, if true, turns to her reproach; but it happens not to be true, or only partly so, and the phrase *parent* or *mother country* hath been jesuitically adopted by the king and his parasites, with a low papistical design of gaining an unfair bias on the credulous weakness of our minds. Europe, and not England, is the parent country of America. This new world hath been the asylum for the persecuted lovers of civil and religious liberty from *every part* of Europe. Hither have they fled, not from the tender embraces of the mother, but from the cruelty of the monster; and it is so far true of England, that the same tyranny which drove the first emigrants from home, pursues their descendants still. . . .

I challenge the warmest advocate for reconciliation, to shew, a single advantage that this continent can reap, by being connected with Great Britain. I repeat the challenge, not a single advantage is derived. Our corn will fetch its price in any market in Europe, and our imported goods must be paid for buy them where we will.

But the injuries and disadvantages we sustain by that connection, are without number; and our duty to mankind at large, as well as to ourselves, instruct us to renounce the alliance: Because, any submission to, or dependance on Great-Britain, tends directly to involve this continent in European wars and quarrels; and sets us at variance with nations, who would otherwise seek our friendship; and against whom, we have neither anger nor complaint. As Europe is our market for trade, we ought to form no partial connection with any part of it. It is the true interest of America to steer clear of European contentions, which she never can do, while by her dependance on Britain, she is made the make-weight in the scale of British politics.

Europe is too thickly planted with kingdoms to be long at peace, and whenever a war breaks out between England and any foreign power, the trade of America goes to ruin, *because of her connection with Britain.* The next war may not turn out like the last, and should it not, the advocates for reconciliation now will be wishing for separation then, because, neutrality in that case, would be a safer convoy than a man of war. Every thing that is right or natural pleads for separation. The blood of the slain, the weeping voice of mature cries, 'TIS TIME TO PART. . . .

But where says some is the King of America? I'll tell you Friend, he reigns above, and doth not make havoc of mankind like the Royal Brute of Britain. Yet that we may not appear to be defective even in earthly honors, let a day be solemnly set apart for proclaiming the charter; let it be brought forth placed on the divine law, the word of God; let a crown be placed thereon, by which the world may know, that so far as we approve of monarchy, that in America THE LAW IS KING. For as in absolute governments the King is law, so in free countries the law *ought* to be King; and there ought to be no other. But lest any ill use should afterwards arise, let the crown at the conclusion of the ceremony be demolished, and scattered among the people whose right it is.

A government of our own is our natural right: And when a man seriously reflects on the precariousness of human affairs, he will become convinced, that it is infinitely wiser and safer, to form a constitution of our own in a cool deliberate manner, while we have it in our power, than to trust such an interesting event to time and chance. . . .

Ye that tell us of harmony and reconciliation, can ye restore to us the time that is past? Can ye give to prostitution its former innocence? Neither can ye reconcile Britain and America. The last cord now is broken, the people of England are presenting addresses against us. There are injuries which nature cannot forgive; she would cease to be nature if she did. As well can the lover forgive the ravisher of his mistress, as the continent forgive the murders of Britain. The Almighty hath implanted in us these unextinguishable feelings for good and wise purposes. They are the guardians of his image in our hearts. They distinguish us from the herd of common animals. The social compact would dissolve, and justice be extirpated from the earth, or have only a casual existence were we callous to the touches of affection. The robber, and the murderer, would often escape unpunished, did not the injuries which our tempers sustain, provoke us into justice.

O ye that love mankind! Ye that dare oppose, not only the tyranny, but the tyrant, stand forth! Every spot of the old world is overrun with oppression. Freedom hath been hunted round the globe. Asia; and Africa; have long expelled her.— Europe regards her like a stranger, and England hath given her warning to depart, O! receive the fugitive, and prepare in time as asylum for mankind!

PAUL REVERE'S RIDE

1863

Paul Revere (1735–1818) was a silversmith and political leader in colonial Boston. He was also skilled in engraving, bell founding, and dentistry. He was a member of the Sons of Liberty and played a role in the Boston Tea Party. Along with Samuel Prescott and William Dawes, he rode to warn the colonists in Concord and Lexington that the British Army was being sent to attack. Although Revere was captured on the way, he is the most famous of the three, having been immortalized in Longfellow's poem.

Listen, my children, and you shall hear
Of the midnight ride of Paul Revere,
On the eighteenth of April, in Seventy-five;
Hardly a man is now alive
Who remembers that famous day and year.

He said to his friend, "If the British march
By land or sea from the town to-night,
Hang a lantern aloft in the belfry arch
Of the North Church tower as a signal light,—
One, if by land, and two, if by sea;
And I on the opposite shore will be,
Ready to ride and spread the alarm
Through every Middlesex village and farm,
For the country-folk to be up and to arm."

Then he said, "Good night!" and with muffled oar
Silently rowed to the Charlestown shore,
Just as the moon rose over the bay,
Where swinging wide at her moorings lay
The Somerset, British man-of-war;
A phantom ship, with each mast and spar
Across the moon like a prison bar,
And a huge black hulk, that was magnified
By its own reflection in the tide.

Meanwhile, his friend, through alley and street,
Wanders and watches with eager ears,
Till in the silence around him he hears
The muster of men at the barrack door,
The sound of arms, and the tramp of feet,
And the measured tread of the grenadiers,
Marching down to their boats on the shore.

Then he climbed the tower of the Old North Church,
By the wooden stairs, with stealthy tread,
To the belfry-chamber overhead,
And startled the pigeons from their perch
On the sombre rafters, that round him made
Masses and moving shapes of shade,—
By the trembling ladder, steep and tall,
To the highest window in the wall,
Where he paused to listen and look down
A moment on the roofs of the town,
And the moonlight flowing over all.

Beneath, in the churchyard, lay the dead,
In their night-encampment on the hill,
Wrapped in silence so deep and still
That he could hear, like a sentinel's tread,
The watchful night-wind, as it went
Creeping along from tent to tent,
And seeming to whisper, "All is well!"
A moment only he feels the spell
Of the place and the hour, and the secret dread
Of the lonely belfry and the dead;
For suddenly all his thoughts are bent
On a shadowy something far away,
Where the river widens to meet the bay,—
A line of black that bends and floats
On the rising tide, like a bridge of boats.

Meanwhile, impatient to mount and ride,
Booted and spurred, with a heavy stride
On the opposite shore walked Paul Revere.
Now he patted his horse's side,
Now gazed at the landscape far and near,
Then, impetuous, stamped the earth,
And turned and tightened his saddle-girth;
But mostly he watched with eager search
The belfry-tower of the Old North Church,
As it rose above the graves on the hill,
Lonely and spectral and sombre and still.
And lo! as he looks, on the belfry's height
A glimmer, and then a gleam of light!
He springs to the saddle, the bridle he turns,
But lingers and gazes, till full on his sight
A second lamp in the belfry burns!

A hurry of hoofs in a village street,
A shape in the moonlight, a bulk in the dark,
And beneath, from the pebbles, in passing, a spark
Struck out by a steed flying fearless and fleet:
That was all! And yet, through the gloom and the light,
The fate of a nation was riding that night;
And the spark struck out by that steed, in his flight,
Kindled the land into flame with its heat.

He has left the village and mounted the steep,
And beneath him, tranquil and broad and deep,
Is the Mystic, meeting the ocean tides;
And under the alders, that skirt its edge,
Now soft on the sand, now loud on the ledge,
Is heard the tramp of his steed as he rides.

It was twelve by the village clock
When he crossed the bridge into Medford town.
He heard the crowing of the cock,

And the barking of the farmer's dog,
And felt the damp of the river fog,
That rises after the sun goes down.

It was one by the village clock,
When he galloped into Lexington.
He saw the gilded weathercock
Swim in the moonlight as he passed,
And the meeting-house windows, blank and bare,
Gaze at him with a spectral glare,
As if they already stood aghast
At the bloody work they would look upon.

It was two by the village clock,
When he came to the bridge in Concord town.
He heard the bleating of the flock,
And the twitter of birds among the trees,
And felt the breath of the morning breeze
Blowing over the meadows brown.
And one was safe and asleep in his bed
Who at the bridge would be first to fall,
Who that day would be lying dead,
Pierced by a British musket-ball.

You know the rest. In the books you have read,
How the British Regulars fired and fled,—
How the farmers gave them ball for ball,
From behind each fence and farm-yard wall,
Chasing the red-coats down the lane,
Then crossing the fields to emerge again
Under the trees at the turn of the road,
And only pausing to fire and load.

So through the night rode Paul Revere;
And so through the night went his cry of alarm
To every Middlesex village and farm,—
A cry of defiance and not of fear,

A voice in the darkness, a knock at the door,
And a word that shall echo forevermore!
For, borne on the night-wind of the Past,
Through all our history, to the last,
In the hour of darkness and peril and need,
The people will waken and listen to hear
The hurrying hoof-beats of that steed,
And the midnight message of Paul Revere.

THE MONROE DOCTRINE

1823

In the early 1820s, President James Monroe (1758–1831) and his secretary of state, John Quincy Adams (1767–1848), became alarmed that the European powers, primarily Great Britain, Spain, and France, might attempt to recolonize territory in the Western Hemisphere. On December 2, 1823, Monroe issued one of the most important principles of American foreign policy, declaring that henceforth the Americas were to be free from "future colonization by any European powers."

. . . It was stated at the commencement of the last session, that a great effort was then making in Spain and Portugal, to improve the condition of the people of those countries, and that it appeared to be conducted with extraordinary moderation. It need scarcely be remarked, that the result has been, so far, very different from what was then anticipated. Of events in that quarter of the globe, with which we have so much intercourse, and from which we derive our origin, we have always been anxious and interested spectators. The citizens of the United States cherish sentiments the most friendly, in favor of the liberty and happiness of their fellow men on that side of the Atlantic. In the wars of the European powers, in matters relating to themselves, we have never taken any part, nor does it comport with our policy, so to do. It is only when our rights are invaded, or seriously menaced, that we resent injuries, or make preparation for our defence. With the movements in this hemisphere, we are, of necessity, more immediately connected, and by causes which must be obvious to all enlightened and impartial observers. The political system of the allied powers is essentially different, in this respect from that of America. This difference proceeds from that which exists in their respective governments. And to the defence of our own, which has been achieved by the loss of so much blood and treasure, and matured by the wisdom of their most enlightened citizens, and under which we have enjoyed unexampled felicity, this whole nation is devoted. We owe it, therefore, to candor, and to the amicable relations existing between the United States and those powers, to declare, that we should consider any attempt on their part to extend their system to any portion of this hemisphere, as dangerous to our peace and safety. With the existing colonies or dependencies of any European power, we have not interfered, and shall not interfere. But with the governments who have declared their independence, and maintained it, and whose independence we have, on great consideration, and on just principles, acknowledged, we could not view any interposition for the purpose of oppressing them, or controlling, in any other manner, their destiny, by any European power, in any other light than as the manifestation of an unfriendly disposition towards the United States. In the war between those new governments and Spain, we declared our neutrality at the time of their recognition, and to this we have adhered, and shall continue to adhere, provided no change shall occur, which, in the judgment of the competent authorities of this government, shall make a corresponding change, on the part of the United States, indispensable to their security.

Our policy, in regard to Europe, which was adopted at an early stage of the wars which have so long agitated that quarter of the globe, nevertheless remains the same, which is, not to interfere in the internal concerns of any of its powers; to consider the government *de facto* as the legitimate government for us; to cultivate friendly relations with it, and to preserve those relations by a frank, firm, and manly policy; meeting, in all instances, the just claims of every power; submitting to injuries from none. But, in regard to these continents, circumstances are eminently and conspicuously different. It is impossible that the allied powers should extend their political system to any portion of either continent, without endangering our peace and happiness: nor can any one believe that our Southern Brethren, if left to themselves, would adopt it of their own accord. It is equally impossible, therefore, that we should behold such interposition, in any form, with indifference. If we look to the comparative strength and resources of Spain and those new governments, and their distance from each other, it must be obvious that she can never subdue them. It is still the true policy of the United States to leave the parties to themselves, in the hope that other powers will pursue the same course.

JULIA WARD HOWE

THE BATTLE HYMN OF THE REPUBLIC

1861

Julia Ward Howe (1819–1910) and her husband, Samuel, were leading philanthropists and abolitionists in pre–Civil War Boston. She was also an active supporter of women's suffrage and the world peace movement, and the first woman member of the American Academy of Arts and Letters. In late 1861, after hearing soldiers sing "John Brown's Body" on a visit to a Union Army camp on the Potomac, Howe was inspired to write "The Battle Hymn of the Republic," set to the same rousing tune. Soon after its publication in the *Atlantic Monthly* in February 1862, it was adopted by Union soldiers as a marching tune. It is said that President Abraham Lincoln wept when he first heard the song.

Mine eyes have seen the glory of the coming of the Lord;
He is trampling out the vintage where the grapes of wrath are stored;
He hath loosed the fateful lightning of His terrible swift sword;
 His truth is marching on.

I have seen Him in the watch-fires of a hundred circling camps;
They have builded Him an altar in the evening dews and damps;
I can read His righteous sentence by the dim and flaring lamps:
 His day is marching on.

I have read a fiery gospel writ in burnished rows of steel:
"As ye deal with my contemners, so with you my grace shall deal;
Let the Hero, born of woman, crush the serpent with his heel,
 Since God is marching on."

He has sounded forth the trumpet that shall never call retreat;
He is sifting out the hearts of men before His judgment-seat:
Oh, be swift, my soul, to answer Him! be jubilant, my feet!
 Our God is marching on.

In the beauty of the lilies Christ was born across the sea,
With a glory in his bosom that transfigures you and me:
As he died to make men holy, let us die to make men free,
 While God is marching on.

HERMAN MELVILLE

SHILOH, A REQUIEM

APRIL 1862

Herman Melville (1819–1891) is best known for his masterpiece *Moby-Dick*, but he also wrote short stories and poetry, including this poem, which was published in a collection of Civil War poems titled *Battle-Pieces and Aspects of the War* (1866). The two-day Battle of Shiloh, an important Union victory, was fought in April 1862 near Shiloh Church in Tennessee. With over 23,000 killed or wounded, Shiloh alone caused more casualties than any previous American war. The Civil War, in which nearly 600,000 died, remains the bloodiest conflict in American history.

Skimming lightly, wheeling still,
    The swallows fly low
Over the field in clouded days,
    The forest-field of Shiloh—
Over the field where April rain
Solaced the parched ones stretched in pain
Through the pause of night
That followed the Sunday fight
    Around the church of Shiloh—
The church so lone, the log-built one,
That echoed to many a parting groan
    And natural prayer
    Of dying foemen mingled there—
Foemen at morn, but friends at eve—
    Fame or country least their care:
(What like a bullet can undeceive!)
    But now they lie low,
While over them the swallows skim,
    And all is hushed at Shiloh.

FINAL EMANCIPATION PROCLAMATION

JANUARY 1, 1863

Born in Kentucky, Lincoln moved to Illinois as a young man and was first elected to state political office in 1834. He was elected president of the United States in 1860 and was reelected in 1864. Lincoln viewed slavery as immoral and initially opposed its extension into new territories. In 1862, however, in the midst of the Civil War, he also began to view emancipation as a military necessity, recognizing that freed slaves would weaken the South and provide manpower for the North. The Emancipation Proclamation was limited in scope, applying only to the states within the Confederacy. Nonetheless, the announcement of the Proclamation gave new meaning to the Civil War and to the abolitionist cause. Slavery was abolished throughout the United States with the passage of the Thirteenth Amendment to the Constitution in 1865.

Whereas, on the twenty-second day of September, in the year of our Lord one thousand eight hundred and sixty-two a proclamation was issued by the President of the United States, containing, among other things, the following, to wit:

"That on the first day of January, in the year of our Lord one thousand eight hundred and sixty-three, all persons held as slaves within any state, or designated part of a state, the people whereof shall then be in rebellion against the United States, shall be then, thenceforward and forever free; and the Executive Government of the United States, including the military and naval authority thereof, will recognize and maintain the freedom of such persons, and will do no act or acts to repress such persons, or any of them, in any efforts they may make for their actual freedom.

"That the executive will, on the first day of January aforesaid, by proclamation, designate the states and parts of states, if any, in which the people thereof, respectively, shall then be in rebellion against the United States, and the fact that any state, or the people thereof, shall on that day be in good faith represented in the Congress of the United States by members chosen thereto, at elections wherein a majority of the qualified voters of such state shall have participated, shall, in the absence of strong countervailing testimony, be deemed conclusive evidence that such state, and the people thereof, are not then in rebellion against the United States."

Now, therefore I, Abraham Lincoln, President of the United States, by virtue of the power in me vested as Commander-in-Chief, of the Army and Navy of the United States in time of actual armed rebellion against authority and government of the United States, and as a fit and necessary war measure for suppressing said rebellion, do on this first day of January, in the year of our Lord one thousand eight hundred and

G. H. COYELLER, Civil War veterans, c. 1910.

sixty-three, and in accordance with my purpose so to do publicly proclaimed for the full period of one hundred days, from the day first above mentioned, order and designate as the States and parts of States wherein the people thereof respectively, are this day in rebellion against the United States, the following, to wit:

Arkansas, Texas, Louisiana (except the Parishes of St. Bernard, Plaquemine, Jefferson, St. Johns, St. Charles, St. James, Ascension, Assumption, Terrebonne, Lafourche, St. Mary, St. Martin, and Orleans, including the City of New Orleans), Mississippi, Alabama, Florida, Georgia, South-Carolina, North-Carolina, and Virginia, (except the forty-eight counties designated as West Virginia and also the counties of Berkeley, Accomac, Northampton, Elizabeth City, York, Princess-Ann, and Norfolk, including the cities of Norfolk & Portsmouth; and which excepted parts are for the present left precisely as if this proclamation were not issued).

And by virtue of the power and for the purpose aforesaid I do order and declare that all persons held as slaves within said designated States, and parts of States are and henceforward shall be free; and that the Executive government of the United

States, including the military and naval authorities thereof, will recognize and maintain the freedom of said persons.

And I hereby enjoin upon the people so declared to be free to abstain from all violence, unless in necessary self-defense; and I recommend to them that in all cases when allowed, they labor faithfully for reasonable wages.

And I further declare and make known, that such persons of suitable condition, will be received into the armed services of the United States to garrison forts, positions, stations and other places, and to man vessels of all sorts in said service.

And upon this act sincerely believed to be an act of justice, warranted by the Constitution upon military necessity, I invoke the considerate judgment of mankind, and the gracious favor of Almighty God. . . .

ABRAHAM LINCOLN

GETTYSBURG ADDRESS

NOVEMBER 19, 1863

The Battle of Gettysburg was a crucial victory for the Union and the bloodiest battle of the Civil War. Fifty-one thousand soldiers were killed or wounded in three days. After Gettysburg, the South was no longer able to mount an offensive campaign north of Virginia. Four months later, Abraham Lincoln visited the site to dedicate a cemetery for those who had fallen in battle. After the main speaker, renowned orator Edward Everett, gave a speech that lasted two hours, Lincoln spoke for only two minutes. In one of the briefest yet most eloquent eulogies of all time, Lincoln connected the Civil War to the Declaration of Independence and articulated the significance of the Civil War for freedom and democracy.

Fourscore and seven years ago our fathers brought forth on this continent a new nation, conceived in liberty, and dedicated to the proposition that all men are created equal.

Now we are engaged in a great civil war, testing whether that nation, or any nation so conceived and so dedicated, can long endure. We are met on a great battlefield of that war. We have come to dedicate a portion of that field as a final resting-place for those who here gave their lives that the nation might live. It is altogether fitting and proper that we should do this. But, in a larger sense, we cannot dedicate—we cannot consecrate—we cannot hallow—this ground. The brave men, living and dead, who struggled here have consecrated it, far above our poor power to add or detract. The world will little note, nor long remember, what we say here, but it can never forget what they did here. It is for us the living, rather, to be dedicated here to the unfinished work which they who fought here have thus far so nobly advanced. It is rather for us to be here dedicated to the great task remaining before us—that from these honored dead we take increased devotion to that cause for which they gave the last full measure of devotion—that we here highly resolve that these dead shall not have died in vain—that this nation, under God, shall have a new birth of freedom and that government of the people, by the people, for the people, shall not perish from the earth.

Richmond, Virginia, 1865.

ABRAHAM LINCOLN

SECOND INAUGURAL ADDRESS

MARCH 4, 1865

When Lincoln delivered this address on March 4, 1865, the Civil War was all but over. Confederate General Robert E. Lee surrendered his army five weeks later. Rooted in his religious beliefs, weaving together past, present, and future, the mere 703 words of this address redeemed the suffering of the Civil War and offered reconciliation and hope to a wounded nation. The speech was not immediately popular in the North or South, but Lincoln considered it his greatest speech, and over time many have come to agree. Lincoln was assassinated six weeks later, on April 15, 1865.

At this second appearing to take the oath of the presidential office there is less occasion for an extended address than there was at the first. Then a statement, somewhat in detail, of a course to be pursued seemed fitting and proper. Now, at the expiration of four years, during which public declarations have been constantly called forth on every point and phase of the great contest which still absorbs the attention and engrosses the energies of the nation, little that is new could be presented. The progress of our arms, upon which all else chiefly depends, is as well known to the public as to myself, and it is, I trust, reasonably satisfactory and encouraging to all. With high hope for the future, no prediction in regard to it is ventured.

On the occasion corresponding to this four years ago all thoughts were anxiously directed to an impending civil war. All dreaded it; all sought to avert it. While the inaugural address was being delivered from this place, devoted altogether to *saving* the Union without war, insurgent agents were in the city seeking to *destroy* it without war—seeking to dissolve the Union and divide effects by negotiation. Both parties deprecated war, but one of them would *make* war rather than let the nation survive, and the other would *accept* war rather than let it perish, and the war came.

One-eighth of the whole population were colored slaves, not distributed generally over the Union, but localized in the southern part of it. These slaves constituted a peculiar and powerful interest. All knew that this interest was somehow the cause of war. To strengthen, perpetuate, and extend this interest was the object for which the insurgents would rend the Union even by war, while the government claimed no right to do more than to restrict the territorial enlargement of it. Neither party expected for the war the magnitude or the duration which it has already attained. Neither anticipated that the *cause* of the conflict might cease with or even before the conflict itself should cease. Each looked for an easier triumph, and a result less fundamental and astounding. Both read the same Bible and pray to the same God, and each invokes his aid against the other. It may seem strange that any men should dare to ask a just God's assistance in wringing their bread from the sweat of other men's faces, but let us judge not, that we be not judged. The prayers of both could not be answered. That of neither has been answered fully. The Almighty has his own purposes. "Woe unto the world because of offenses; for it must needs be that offenses come, but woe to that man by whom the offense cometh." If we shall suppose that American slavery is one of those offenses which, in the providence of God, must needs come, but which, having continued through his appointed time, he now wills to remove, and that he gives to both North and South this terrible war as the woe due to those by whom the offense came, shall we discern therein any departure from those divine attributes which the believers in a living God always ascribe to him? Fondly do we hope, fervently do we pray, that this mighty scourge of war may speedily pass away. Yet, if God wills that it continue until all the wealth piled by the bondsman's two hundred and fifty years of unrequited toil shall be sunk, and until every drop of blood drawn with the lash shall be paid by another drawn with the sword, as was said three thousand years ago, so still it must be said "the judgments of the Lord are true and righteous altogether."

With malice toward none, with charity for all, with firmness in the right as God gives us to see the right, let us strive on to finish the work we are in, to bind up the nation's wounds, to care for him who shall have borne the battle and for his widow and his orphan, to do all which may achieve and cherish a just and lasting peace among ourselves and with all nations.

ULYSSES S. GRANT

MEMOIRS

1885–1886

Ulysses S. Grant (1822–1885) was born in Ohio and graduated from West Point. Forced to resign from the army for excessive drinking, Grant suffered a series of business failures before rejoining the army when the Civil War broke out. A brilliant strategist and courageous commander, Grant led his troops to a magnificent victory at Vicksburg in July 1863, when the Union troops effectively divided Confederate forces and caused them to lose control of the Mississippi River. In 1864, President Lincoln gave General Grant command of the Army of the Potomac, and on April 9, 1865, Grant accepted the surrender of General Robert E. Lee at Appomattox. In 1866, Grant became the first U.S. citizen since George Washington to hold the rank of full general. In 1868, he was elected president of the United States, serving two terms until 1877. His presidency was plagued by scandal and corruption—kickbacks, bribery, and greed. In 1884, after losing his savings in a fraudulent investment scheme, Grant began writing his memoirs in an effort to pay off lingering debts and to provide for his family. A year later, Grant finished his manuscript a few days before his death from throat cancer. Published posthumously with the help of Mark Twain, the memoirs are considered a classic American narrative and important military chronicle.

I had known General Lee in the old army, and had served with him in the Mexican War; but did not suppose, owing to the difference in our age and rank, that he would remember me; while I would more naturally remember him distinctly, because he was the chief of staff of General Scott in the Mexican War.

When I left camp that morning I had not expected so soon the result that was then taking place, and consequently was in rough garb. I was without a sword, as I usually was when on horseback on the field, and wore a soldier's blouse for a coat, with the shoulder straps of my rank to indicate to the army who I was. When I went into the house I found General Lee. We greeted each other, and after shaking hands took our seats. I had my staff with me, a good portion of whom were in the room during the whole of the interview.

What General Lee's feelings were I do not know. As he was a man of much dignity, with an impassible face, it was impossible to say whether he felt inwardly glad that the end had finally come, or felt sad over the result, and was too manly to show it. Whatever his feelings, they were entirely concealed from my observation; but my own feelings, which had been quite jubilant on the receipt of his letter, were sad and depressed. I felt like anything rather than rejoicing at the downfall of a foe who had fought so long and so valiantly.

CHIEF JOSEPH

SURRENDER TO THE U.S. ARMY

1877

The mid-nineteenth-century discovery of gold in Oregon began a life of struggle and bloodshed for Nez Percé Chief Joseph (c. 1840–1904) and his people. When settlers encroached upon the Nez Percé reservation, he led his people to the Idaho territory. In a skirmish over land, a member of the tribe killed a white settler, and Chief Joseph, fearing retaliation, fled with his people. During the summer of 1877, the Nez Percé clashed with the U.S. Army in the mountainous terrain of the Rockies, almost escaping to Canada, only to be captured that fall. Chief Joseph's surrender was recorded and published in the November 11, 1877, issue of *Harper's Weekly*.

Tell General Howard I know his heart. What he told me before, I have it in my heart. I am tired of fighting. Our chiefs are killed; Looking-Glass is dead, Ta-Hool-Hool-Shute is dead. The old men are all dead. It is the young men who say yes or no. He who led on the young men is dead. It is cold, and we have no blankets; the little children are freezing to death. My people, some of them, have run away to the hills, and have no blankets, no food. No one knows where they are—perhaps freezing to death. I want to have time to look for my children, and see how many of them I can find. Maybe I shall find them among the dead. Hear me, my chiefs! I am tired; my heart is sick and sad. From where the sun now stands I will fight no more forever.

The Marines' Song

1891

While the authorship of the lyrics for "The Marines' Song" is unknown, Marine Corps Colonel A. S. McLemore believed the tune originated in the comic opera *Genevieve de Brabant*, while others believe the tune came from a Spanish folk song. In 1929, the Marine Corps adopted the song as its official hymn. The "Halls of Montezuma" refers to the Marine landing in 1847 in the Mexican War and "the shores of Tripoli" to their attack on the Barbary Coast pirates during Thomas Jefferson's administration.

From the Halls of Montezuma
To the shores of Tripoli
We fight our country's battles
On the land as on the sea.
First to fight for right and freedom
And to keep our honor clean;
We are proud to claim the title
Of United States Marines.

Our flag's unfurled to every breeze
From dawn to setting sun;
We have fought in every clime and place
Where we could take a gun.
In the snow of far-off Northern lands
And in sunny tropic scenes;
You will find us always on the job—
The United States Marines.

Here's health to you and to our Corps
Which we are proud to serve;
In many a strife we've fought for life
And never lost our nerve.
If the Army and the Navy
Ever look on Heaven's scenes,
They will find the streets are guarded
By United States Marines.

STEPHEN CRANE

DO NOT WEEP, MAIDEN, FOR WAR IS KIND

1899

Stephen Crane (1871–1900), the fourteenth child of a Methodist minister, moved to New York City in 1890 and lived in poverty while he pursued a career as a freelance writer. The realistic depiction of slum life in his first novel, *Maggie: A Girl of the Streets* (1893), was a product of his own observations. Though Crane never served in battle, his most famous work, *The Red Badge of Courage* (1895), is the Civil War story of a young soldier under fire. His short stories in *The Open Boat and Other Tales* (1898) and *The Monster and Other Stories* (1899), and epigrammatic symbolic free verse, including the collection *War Is Kind* (1899), in which this poem first appeared, earned Crane a reputation as a modern master before his death of tuberculosis at age twenty-eight.

Do not weep, maiden, for war is kind.
Because your lover threw wild hands toward the sky
And the affrighted steed ran on alone,
Do not weep.
War is kind.

    Hoarse, booming drums of the regiment
    Little souls who thirst for fight,
    These men were born to drill and die
    The unexplained glory flies above them
    Great is the battle-god, great, and his kingdom—
    A field where a thousand corpses lie.

Do not weep, babe, for war is kind.
Because your father tumbled in the yellow trenches,
Raged at his breast, gulped and died,
Do not weep.
War is kind.

    Swift, blazing flag of the regiment
    Eagle with crest of red and gold,
    These men were born to drill and die
    Point for them the virtue of slaughter

Make plain to them the excellence of killing
And a field where a thousand corpses lie.

Mother whose heart hung humble as a button
On the bright splendid shroud of your son,
Do not weep.
War is kind.

. . .

EDMUND L. GRUBER

THE CAISSON SONG

1907

"The Caisson Song" was written by artillery First Lieutenant (later elevated to Brigadier General) Edmund L. Gruber (1879–1941) while he was stationed in the Philippines in 1908. Composer and conductor John Philip Sousa wrote music to accompany the lyrics in 1917, renaming it "The Field Artillery Song." The tune became a popular marching song with U.S. troops in both world wars, and in 1952, it was adopted with revised lyrics as the official U.S. Army song, retitled "The Army Goes Rolling Along."

Over hill, over dale, we have hit the dusty trail,
And those caissons go rolling along.
In and out, hear them shout, "Counter march and right about!"
And those caissons go rolling along.

    Chorus:
Then it's hi! hi! hee! in the field artillery,
Sound off your numbers loud and strong.
Where e'er you go you will always know
That those caissons are rolling along.
Keep them rolling! And those caissons go rolling along.
Then it's Battery Halt!

Through the storm, through the night, up to where the doughboys fight.
All our caissons go rolling along.
At zero we'll be there, answering every call and flare,
While our caissons go rolling along.

Cavalry, boot to boot, we will join in the pursuit,
While the caissons go rolling along.
Action Front, at a trot; volley fire with shell and shot,
While those caissons go rolling along.

But if fate me should call, and in action I should fall,
And those caissons go rolling along.

WOODROW WILSON

WAR MESSAGE TO CONGRESS

APRIL 2, 1917

Woodrow Wilson (1856–1924) taught government and political theory at Princeton University prior to assuming the presidency of that institution. As a leading progressive, he became governor of New Jersey in 1910 and, two years later, was elected president of the United States (1913–1921). After the outbreak of World War I, Wilson struggled to keep the United States from being drawn into the European conflict. However, after a German submarine sank the *Lusitania* in 1915, killing 1,200 people, including 128 Americans, public opinion turned against Germany. In 1917, when Germany violated its pledge not to attack unarmed ships and resumed submarine warfare, Wilson asked Congress for a declaration of war. Eventually, over 1 million American soldiers served in World War I, and the protracted conflict, which ended in 1918, cost more than 10 million lives.

. . . On the third of February last I officially laid before you the extraordinary announcement of the imperial German government that on and after the first day of February it was its purpose to put aside all restraints of law or of humanity and use its submarines to sink every vessel that sought to approach either the ports of Great Britain and Ireland or the western coasts of Europe or any of the ports controlled by the enemies of Germany within the Mediterranean. That had seemed to be the object of the German submarine warfare earlier in the war, but since April of last year the imperial government had somewhat restrained the commanders of its undersea craft in conformity with its promise then given to us that passenger boats should not be sunk and that due warning would be given to all other vessels which its submarines might seek to destroy, when no resistance was offered or escape attempted, and care taken that their crews were given at least a fair chance to save their lives in their open boats. The precautions taken were meager and haphazard enough, as was proved in distressing instance after instance in the progress of the cruel and unmanly business, but a certain degree of restraint was observed. The new policy has swept every restriction aside. Vessels of every kind, whatever their flag, their character, their cargo, their destination, their errand, have been ruthlessly sent to the bottom without warning and without thought of help or mercy for those on board, the vessels of friendly neutrals along with those of belligerents. Even hospital ships and ships carrying relief to the sorely bereaved and stricken people of Belgium, though the latter were provided with safe conduct through the proscribed areas by the German government itself and were distinguished by unmistakable marks of identity, have been sunk with the same reckless lack of compassion or of principle.

I was for a little while unable to believe that such things would in fact be done by any government that had hitherto subscribed to the humane practices of civilized nations. International law had its origin in the attempt to set up some law which would be respected and observed upon the seas, where no nation had right of dominion and where lay the free highways of the world. By painful stage after stage has that law been built up, with meager enough results, indeed, after all was accomplished that could be accomplished, but always with a clear view, at least, of what the heart and conscience of mankind demanded. This minimum of right the German government has swept aside under the plea of retaliation and necessity and because it had no weapons which it could use at sea except these which it is impossible to employ as it is employing them without throwing to the winds all scruples of humanity or of respect for the understandings that were supposed to underlie the intercourse of the world. I am not now thinking of the loss of property involved, immense and serious as that is, but only of the wanton and wholesale destruction of the lives of noncombatants, men, women, and children, engaged in pursuits which have always, even in the darkest periods of modern history, been deemed innocent and legitimate. Property can be paid for; the lives of peaceful and innocent people cannot be. The present German submarine warfare against commerce is a warfare against mankind.

It is a war against all nations. American ships have been sunk, American lives taken, in ways which it has stirred us very deeply to learn of, but the ships and people of other neutral and friendly nations have been sunk and overwhelmed in the waters in the same way. There has been no discrimination. The challenge is to all mankind. Each nation must decide for itself how it will meet it. The choice we make for ourselves must be made with a moderation of counsel and a temperateness of judgment befitting our character and our motives as a nation. We must put excited feeling away. Our motive will not be revenge or the victorious assertion of the physical might of the nation, but only the vindication of right, of human right, of which we are only a single champion. . . .

With a profound sense of the solemn and even tragical character of the step I am taking and of the grave responsibilities which it involves, but in unhesitating obedience to what I deem my constitutional duty, I advise that the Congress declare the recent course of the imperial German government to be in fact nothing less than war against the government and people of the United States; that it formally accept the status of belligerent which has thus been thrust upon it; and that it take immediate steps not only to put the country in a more thorough state of defense but also to exert all its power and employ all its resources to bring the government of the German Empire to terms and end the war. . . .

I have exactly the same things in mind now that I had in mind when I addressed the Senate on the twenty-second of January last; the same that I had in mind when I addressed the Congress on the third of February and on the twenty-sixth of February. Our object now, as then, is to vindicate the principles of peace and justice in the life of the world as against selfish and autocratic power and to set up amongst the really free and self-governed peoples of the world such a concert of purpose and of action as will henceforth ensure the observance of those principles. Neutrality is no longer feasible or desirable where the peace of the world is involved and the freedom of its peoples, and the menace to that peace and freedom lies in the existence of autocratic governments backed by organized force which is controlled wholly by their will, not by the will of their people. We have seen the last of neutrality in such circumstances. We are at the beginning of an age in which it will be insisted that the same standards of conduct and of responsibility for wrong done shall be observed among nations and their governments that are observed among the individual citizens of civilized states.

We have no quarrel with the German people. We have no feeling toward them but one of sympathy and friendship. It was not upon their impulse that their government acted in entering this war. It was not with their previous knowledge or approval. It was a war determined upon as wars used to be determined upon in the old, unhappy days when peoples were nowhere consulted by their rulers and wars were provoked and waged in the interest of dynasties or of little groups of ambitious men who were accustomed to use their fellow men as pawns and tools. . . .

A steadfast concert for peace can never be maintained except by a partnership of democratic nations. No autocratic government could be trusted to keep faith within it or observe its covenants. It must be a league of honor, a partnership of opinion. Intrigue would eat its vitals away; the plottings of inner circles who could plan what they would and render account to no one would be a corruption seated at its very heart. Only free peoples can hold their purpose and their honor steady to a common end and prefer the interests of mankind to any narrow interest of their own. . . .

We are accepting this challenge of hostile purpose because we know that in such a government, following such methods, we can never have a friend; and that in the presence of its organized power, always lying in wait to accomplish we know not what purpose, there can be no assured security for the democratic governments of the world. We are now about to accept gage of battle with this natural foe to liberty and shall, if necessary, spend the whole force of the nation to check and nullify its pretensions and its power. We are glad, now that we see the facts with no veil of false pretense about them, to fight thus for the ultimate peace of the world and for the liberation of its peoples, the German peoples included: for the rights of nations great and small and the privilege of men everywhere to choose their way of life and of obedience. *The world must be made safe for democracy.* Its peace must be planted upon the tested foundations of political liberty. We have no selfish ends to serve. We desire no conquest, no dominion. We seek no indemnities for ourselves, no material compensation for the sacrifices we shall freely make. We are but one of the champions of the rights of mankind. We shall be satisfied when those rights have been made as secure as the faith and the freedom of nations can make them.

Just because we fight without rancor and without selfish object, seeking nothing for ourselves but what we shall wish to share with all free peoples, we shall, I feel confident, conduct our operations as belligerents without passion and ourselves observe with proud punctilio the principles of right and of fair play we profess to be fighting for. . . .

It is a distressing and oppressive duty, gentlemen of the Congress, which I have performed in thus addressing you. There are, it may be, many months of fiery trial and sacrifice ahead of us. It is a fearful thing to lead this great peaceful people into war, into the most terrible and disastrous of wars, civilization itself seeming to be in the balance. But the right is more precious than peace, and we shall fight for the things which we have always carried nearest our hearts—for democracy, for the right of those who submit to authority to have a voice in their own governments, for the rights and liberties of small nations, for a universal dominion of right by such a concert of free peoples as shall bring peace and safety to all nations and make the world itself at last free. To such a task we can dedicate our lives and our fortunes, everything that we are and everything that we have, with the pride of those who know that the day has come when America is privileged to spend her blood and her might for the principles that gave her birth and happiness and the peace which she has treasured. God helping her, she can do no other.

GEORGE M. COHAN

OVER THERE

1917

During World War I, George M. Cohan (1878–1942) turned his prodigious talents to the support of the American war effort in Europe with the song "Over There." Written to instill patriotism and encourage young men to enlist, the song was in sharp contrast to one of the most popular hits of 1915, "I Didn't Raise My Boy to Be a Soldier," and the campaign promises of Woodrow Wilson to keep America out of war. Cohan received a special Congressional Medal of Honor in 1941 in recognition of "You're a Grand Old Flag" (1906) and "Over There."

Johnnie get your gun, get your gun, get your gun,
Take it on the run, on the run, on the run;
Hear them calling you and me;
Ev'ry son of liberty.
Hurry right away, no delay, go today,
Make your daddy glad, to have had such a lad,
Tell your sweetheart not to pine,
To be proud her boy's in line.

CHORUS:
Over there, over there,
Send the word, send the word over there,
That the Yanks are coming,
the Yanks are coming,
The drums rum-tumming ev'ry where—
So prepare, say a pray'r,
Send the word, send the word to beware,
We'll be over, we're coming over,
And we won't come back till it's over over there.

Johnnie get your gun, get your gun, get your gun,
Johnnie show the Hun, you're a son-of-a-gun,
Hoist the flag and let her fly,
Like true heroes, do or die.
Pack your little kit, show your grit, do your bit,
Soldiers to the ranks from the towns and the tanks,
Make your mother proud of you,
And to liberty be true.

THE UNKNOWN SOLDIER

After World War I, each of the Allies took steps to create their own tomb for the unknown soldier in recognition of the veterans who gave their lives in the war. The American Tomb of the Unknown Soldier in Arlington National Cemetery was dedicated on November 11, 1921, three years after the armistice. That soldier was brought over from a battlefield in France and was subsequently joined by unidentified soldiers from World War II and the Korean and Vietnam Wars.

There's a graveyard near the White House
    Where the Unknown Soldier lies,
And the flowers there are sprinkled
    With the tears from mother's eyes.

I stood there not so long ago
    With roses for the brave,
And suddenly I heard a voice
    Speak from out the grave:

"I am the Unknown Soldier,"
    The spirit voice began,
"And I think I have the right
    To ask some questions man to man.

"Are my buddies taken care of?
    Was their victory so sweet?
Is that big reward you offered
    Selling pencils on the street?

"Did they really win the freedom
    They battled to achieve?
Do you still respect that Croix de Guerre
    Above that empty sleeve?

"Does a gold star in the window
    Now mean anything at all?
I wonder how my old girl feels
    When she hears a bugle call.

"And that baby who sang
    'Hello, Central, give me no man's land'—
Can they replace her daddy
    With a military band?

"I wonder if the profiteers
    Have satisfied their greed?
I wonder if a soldier's mother
    Ever is in need?

"I wonder if the kings, who planned it all
    Are really satisfied?
They played their game of checkers
    And eleven million died.

"I am the Unknown Soldier
    And maybe I died in vain,
But if I were alive and my country called,
    I'd do it all over again."

W. H. AUDEN

SEPTEMBER 1, 1939

1941

Wystan Hugh Auden (1907–1973), born in England and educated at Oxford, was prominent in 1930s left-wing intellectual circles. He lived in Germany during the early days of Nazism, joined the Republican cause as a stretcher bearer in the Spanish Civil War, moved to New York in 1939, and became an American citizen in 1946. Auden published many collections of poetry, including *The Age of Anxiety*, for which he received a Pulitzer Prize in 1948. He was awarded the National Medal for Literature in 1967. This poem achieved a renewed popularity after the destruction of the World Trade Center.

I sit in one of the dives
On Fifty-second Street
Uncertain and afraid
As the clever hopes expire
Of a low dishonest decade:
Waves of anger and fear
Circulate over the bright
And darkened lands of the earth,
Obsessing our private lives;
The unmentionable odour of death
Offends the September night.

Accurate scholarship can
Unearth the whole offence
From Luther until now
That has driven a culture mad,
Find what occurred at Linz,
What huge imago made
A psychopathic god:
I and the public know
What all schoolchildren learn,
Those to whom evil is done
Do evil in return.

Exiled Thucydides knew
All that a speech can say
About Democracy,
And what dictators do,
The elderly rubbish they talk
To an apathetic grave;
Analysed all in his book,
The enlightenment driven away,
The habit-forming pain,
Mismanagement and grief:
We must suffer them all again.

Into this neutral air
Where blind skyscrapers use
Their full height to proclaim
The strength of Collective Man,
Each language pours its vain
Competitive excuse:
But who can live for long
In an euphoric dream;
Out of the mirror they stare,
Imperialism's face
And the international wrong.

Faces along the bar
Cling to their average day:
The lights must never go out,
The music must always play,
All the conventions conspire
To make this fort assume
The furniture of home;
Lest we should see where we are,
Lost in a haunted wood,
Children afraid of the night
Who have never been happy or good.

The windiest militant trash
Important Persons shout
Is not so crude as our wish:
What mad Nijinsky wrote
About Diaghilev
Is true of the normal heart;
For the error bred in the bone
Of each woman and each man
Craves what it cannot have,
Not universal love
But to be loved alone.

From the conservative dark
Into the ethical life
The dense commuters come,
Repeating their morning vow;
'I *will* be true to the wife,
I'll concentrate more on my work,'
And helpless governors wake
To resume their compulsory game:
Who can release them now,
Who can reach the deaf,
Who can speak for the dumb?

Defenceless under the night
Our world in stupor lies;
Yet, dotted everywhere,
Ironic points of light
Flash out wherever the Just
Exchange their messages:
May I, composed like them
Of Eros and of dust,
Beleaguered by the same
Negation and despair,
Show an affirming flame.

FRANKLIN DELANO ROOSEVELT

WAR MESSAGE TO CONGRESS

DECEMBER 8, 1941

Franklin Delano Roosevelt grew up in New York State, was educated at Harvard College and Columbia Law School, and served as assistant secretary of the navy during World War I and governor of New York before being elected to the presidency for the first of four terms in 1932. In 1939 and 1940, FDR recognized the dangers of fascism, and before the United States was officially at war, arranged for U.S. assistance to the Allies, called "lend-lease." When Japan attacked Pearl Harbor, the nation immediately rallied behind Roosevelt, joining Great Britain, the Soviet Union, and China against the Axis powers.

Mr. Vice-President, Mr. Speaker, members of the Senate and the House of Representatives:

Yesterday, December 7, 1941—a date which will live in infamy—the United States of America was suddenly and deliberately attacked by naval and air forces of the empire of Japan.

The United States was at peace with that nation and, at the solicitation of Japan, was still in conversation with its government and its emperor looking toward the maintenance of peace in the Pacific.

Indeed, one hour after Japanese air squadrons had commenced bombing in the American island of Oahu the Japanese ambassador to the United States and his colleague delivered to our secretary of state a formal reply to a recent American message. And, while this reply stated that it seemed useless to continue the existing diplomatic negotiations, it contained no threat or hint of war or of armed attack.

It will be recorded that the distance of Hawaii from Japan makes it obvious that the attack was deliberately planned many days or even weeks ago. During the intervening time the Japanese government has deliberately sought to deceive the United States by false statements and expressions of hope for continued peace.

The attack yesterday on the Hawaiian Islands has caused severe damage to American naval and military forces. I regret to tell you that very many American lives have been lost. In addition, American ships have been reported torpedoed on the high seas between San Francisco and Honolulu.

Yesterday the Japanese government also launched an attack against Malaya.

Last night Japanese forces attacked Hong Kong.

Last night Japanese forces attacked Guam.

Last night Japanese forces attacked the Philippine Islands.

Last night Japanese forces attacked Wake Island.

And this morning the Japanese attacked Midway Island.

Japan has therefore undertaken a surprise offensive extending throughout the Pacific area. The facts of yesterday and today speak for themselves. The people of the United States have already formed their opinions and well understand the implications to the very life and safety of our nation.

As commander in chief of the army and navy I have directed that all measures be taken for our defense, that always will our whole nation remember the character of the onslaught against us.

No matter how long it may take us to overcome this premeditated invasion, the American people, in their righteous might, will win through to absolute victory.

I believe that I interpret the will of the Congress and of the people when I assert that we will not only defend ourselves to the uttermost but will make it very certain that this form of treachery shall never again endanger us.

Hostilities exist. There is no blinking at the fact that our people, our territory, and our interests are in grave danger.

With confidence in our armed forces, with the unbounding determination of our people, we will gain the inevitable triumph. So help us God.

I ask that the Congress declare that since the unprovoked and dastardly attack by Japan on Sunday, December 7, 1941, a state of war has existed between the United States and the Japanese Empire.

MARGARET BOURKE-WHITE, The Homefront, Gary, Indiana, 1943.

ROBERT FROST

THE GIFT OUTRIGHT

1942

Born in San Francisco, four-time Pulitzer Prize–winning poet Robert Frost spent most of his life in New England, as a farmer, poet, and professor. In January 1963, Frost was invited to read at the presidential inauguration of John F. Kennedy, the first time a poet had been so honored. Though he wrote a special poem for the occasion, the glare of the sun prevented him from reading it. Instead, Frost recited his classic poem "The Gift Outright." At the request of the president, Frost changed the last line from "Such as she was, such as she would become" to "Such as she was, such as she will become."

The land was ours before we were the land's.
She was our land more than a hundred years
Before we were her people. She was ours
In Massachusetts, in Virginia,
But we were England's, still colonials,
Possessing what we still were unpossessed by,
Possessed by what we now no more possessed.
Something we were withholding made us weak
Until we found out that it was ourselves
We were withholding from our land of living,
And forthwith found salvation in surrender.
Such as we were we gave ourselves outright
(The deed of gift was many deeds of war)
To the land vaguely realizing westward,
But still unstoried, artless, unenhanced,
Such as she was, such as she would become.

GEORGE SILK, Inauguration of John F. Kennedy, Washington, D.C., 1961.

WALLACE STEVENS

MARTIAL CADENZA

1954

Born in Reading, Pennsylvania, and educated at Harvard, Wallace Stevens (1879–1955) worked in an insurance company throughout his career. He published *Harmonium*, his first book of poems, in 1923. He won the National Book Award for poetry in 1951 and again in 1955. Stevens sought to use images from nature juxtaposed with his brilliant philosophical insights to create a unique style that made him one of the most influential poets of his generation.

I

Only this evening I saw again low in the sky
The evening star, at the beginning of winter, the star
That in spring will crown every western horizon,
Again . . . as if it came back, as if life came back,
Not in a later son, a different daughter, another place,
But as if evening found us young, still young,
Still walking in a present of our own.

II

It was like sudden time in a world without time,
This world, this place, the street in which I was,
Without time: as that which is not has no time,
Is not, or is of what there was, is full
Of the silence before the armies, armies without
Either trumpets or drums, the commanders mute, the arms
On the ground, fixed fast in a profound defeat.

III

What had this star to do with the world it lit
With the blank skies over England, over France
And above the German camps? It looked apart.
Yet it is this that shall maintain—Itself
Is time, apart from any past, apart
From any future, the ever-living and being,
The ever-breathing and moving, the constant fire,

IV

The present close, the present realized,
Not the symbol but that for which the symbol stands,
The vivid thing in the air that never changes,
Though the air change. Only this evening I saw it again,
At the beginning of winter, and I walked and talked
Again, and lived and was again, and breathed again
And moved again and flashed again, time flashed again.

DWIGHT D. EISENHOWER

THE GREAT CRUSADE

JUNE 6, 1944

Dwight D. Eisenhower (1890–1969) was born in Texas, raised in Kansas, and educated at West Point. He trained troops in Pennsylvania during World War I and spent part of his military career in the 1930s in the Philippines. In 1942, he received command of the American Expeditionary Force in the European Theater and led the campaign in North Africa and Sicily; in 1944, he was in charge of Operation Overlord, the invasion of Normandy—the largest amphibious invasion in history, when 129,000 Allied troops landed in a surprise attack on Normandy and embarked on the final liberation of Europe. Eisenhower became the commander of the North Atlantic Treaty Organization in 1951. He was elected president in 1952 and in 1956.

Soldiers, Sailors and Airmen of the Allied Expeditionary Forces: You are about to embark upon the Great Crusade, toward which we have striven these many months. The eyes of the world are upon you. The hopes and prayers of liberty-loving people everywhere march with you. In company with our brave Allies and brothers-in-arms on other Fronts you will bring about the destruction of the German war machine, the elimination of Nazi tyranny over oppressed peoples of Europe, and security for ourselves in a free world.

Your task will not be an easy one. Your enemy is well trained, well equipped and battle-hardened. He will fight savagely.

But this is the year 1944! Much has happened since the Nazi triumphs of 1940–41. The United Nations have inflicted upon the Germans great defeats, in open battle, man-to-man. Our air offensive has seriously reduced their strength in the air and their capacity to wage war on the ground. Our Home Fronts have given us an overwhelming superiority in weapons and munitions of war, and placed at our disposal great reserves of trained fighting men. The tide has turned! The free men of the world are marching together to Victory!

I have full confidence in your courage, devotion to duty and skill in battle. We will accept nothing less than full victory!

Good Luck! And let us all beseech the blessing of Almighty God upon this great and noble undertaking.

WALTER ROSENBLUM, D-Day, Normandy, France, 1944.

ROBERT SARGENT, D-Day, Normandy, France, 1944.

J. ROBERT OPPENHEIMER

ON THE ATOMIC BOMB

1945

J. Robert Oppenheimer (1904–1967) grew up in New York City and attended Harvard University, from which he graduated summa cum laude. A theoretical physicist whose early work was concerned with quantum theory and nuclear physics, in 1942 Oppenheimer became the director of the Manhattan Project, the top-secret effort to develop an atomic bomb, located at Los Alamos, New Mexico. Oppenheimer later grew concerned about its destructive potential, and strongly advocated civilian control of atomic energy. He opposed the development of the hydrogen bomb. In 1953, he was suspended from the U.S. Atomic Energy Commission as an alleged security risk, though many doubted the validity of the accusations.

We waited until the blast had passed, walked out of the shelter and then it was extremely solemn. We knew the world would not be the same. A few people laughed, a few people cried. Most people were silent. I remembered the line from the Hindu scripture, the *Bhagavad-Gita:* Vishnu is trying to persuade the Prince that he should do his duty and to impress him he takes on his multi-armed form and says, "Now I am become Death, the destroyer of worlds." I suppose we all thought that, one way or another.

ALBERT EINSTEIN

The Fateful Decision

1948

Born in Germany and educated in Switzerland, Einstein (1879–1955) is considered the most brilliant scientist of the twentieth century. Decades before the atomic bomb, he was making vital contributions toward defining a theory of relativity as well as quantum theory, culminating in his 1905 paper, "On Electrodynamics of Moving Bodies." In 1933, recognizing the dangers facing a Jew in Germany, Einstein accepted an invitation to the Institute for Advanced Study at Princeton University. In 1939, at the suggestion of other scientists, he wrote to FDR urging consideration of a government effort to develop an atomic bomb. In 1945, as the end of World War II appeared near, Einstein grew increasingly concerned about the dangers of nuclear proliferation. He issued another plea to President Roosevelt, this time to halt further work on a nuclear arsenal, fearing that a global arms race could prove catastrophic for the world.

This is a time in which men and women are called upon to consider the possibility of the greatest disaster in the history of modern civilization.

All about us we see the wreckage of what were once the great hopes held by mankind for the building of peace. The gulf between East and West, which men of good will have labored to close, is widening daily. Some people voice the belief that no reconciliation is possible and that only another world war can resolve the present conflict. To this, we scientists reply that it is no longer possible to decide any issue by war since atomic warfare can effect no solution but would cause unprecedented death and devastation to both sides.

Times such as ours have always bred defeatism and despair. But there remain, nonetheless, some few among us who believe man has within him the capacity to meet and overcome even the greatest challenges of his time. If we want to avoid defeat, we must wish to know the truth and be courageous enough to act upon it. If we get to know the truth and have courage, we need not despair.

We scientists have ample evidence that the time of decision has come, and that what we do, or fail to do, within the next few years, will determine the fate of our civilization. Man must come to recognize that his fate is linked with that of his fellow men throughout the world. Great ideas have often been expressed in very simple words. In the shadow of the atomic bomb it has become even more apparent that all men are, indeed, brothers. If we recognize and act upon this simple truth, mankind may proceed to a higher level of human development. But should the angry passions of a nationalistic world engulf us any further, we are doomed.

We consider it the task of the scientists to be untiring in their explanation of these truths to the American people that they may understand what is at stake. Equipped with real understanding, the American people will reject war and will want to seek a peaceful solution; they will come to realize that real security in the world can only come through the creation of a supranational body, a government of the world with powers adequate to preserve the peace.

Each of us, whether a scientist who helped make possible the release of atomic energy, or whether a citizen of the nation which first applied that knowledge for war purposes, is responsible for whatever use is made of this tremendous new force in the future: our generation will have to make the most fateful decision in the recorded history of the human race. Our collective determination can ensure that this formidable achievement of man's intellect will, instead of destroying humanity, be utilized for the benefit of future generations. I believe that mankind is capable of reason and courage and will choose the path of peace.

HARRY S. TRUMAN

ADDRESS TO THE NATION ON KOREA

APRIL 11, 1951

Harry Truman (1884–1972) was born on a farm in Missouri. He served in World War I as captain of an artillery unit, and ran a haberdashery business before entering politics. As a senator from Missouri, he was chosen to be FDR's running mate in 1944. Roosevelt died only three months into his term, leaving Truman to face the challenges of ending the war, planning the future of Europe, and containing the growing threat of Soviet power. In 1950, when North Korea invaded the South, President Truman organized a U.S. and UN effort to repel the invaders. One of the most dramatic tests of his leadership was when the People's Republic of China came to the aid of North Korea, and Douglas MacArthur, World War II hero and popular commander of the UN/U.S./South Korean forces, advocated bombing of Manchuria. Fearing a wider conflict with both China and the Soviet Union, Truman opposed these actions. When MacArthur appealed to Republican leaders in Congress, Truman fired MacArthur for insubordination. Later recognized as courageous, Truman's decision was widely criticized at the time.

I want to talk to you tonight about what we are doing in Korea and about our policy in the Far East. In the simplest terms what we are doing in Korea is this: We are trying to prevent a third world war.

I think most people in this country recognized that fact last June. And they warmly supported the decision of the government to help the Republic of Korea against the communist aggressors. Now, many persons, even some who applauded our decision to defend Korea, have forgotten the basic reasons for our action. It is right for us to be in Korea now. It was right last June. It is right today. I want to remind you why this is true.

The communists in the Kremlin are engaged in a monstrous conspiracy to stamp out freedom all over the world. If they were to succeed, the United States would be numbered among their principal victims. It must be clear to everyone that the United States cannot and will not sit idly by and await foreign conquest. The only question is: When is the best time to meet the threat and how?

The best time to meet the threat is in the beginning. It is easier to put out a fire in the beginning when it is small than after it has become a roaring blaze. And the best way to meet the threat of aggression is for the peace-loving nations to act together. If they don't act together, they are likely to be picked off, one by one. If they had followed the right policies in the 1930s—if the free countries had acted together to crush the aggression of the dictators, and if they had acted in the beginning, when the aggression was small—there probably would have been no World War II.

If history has taught us anything, it is that aggression anywhere in the world is a threat to the peace everywhere in the world. When that aggression is supported by the cruel and selfish rulers of a powerful nation who are bent on conquest, it becomes a clear and present danger to the security and independence of every free nation. This is a lesson that most people in this country have learned thoroughly. This is the basic reason why we have joined in creating the United Nations. And, since the end of World War II, we have been putting that lesson into practice. We're working with other free nations to check the aggressive designs of the Soviet Union before they can result in a third world war. . . .

The aggression against Korea is the boldest and most dangerous move the communists have yet made. The attack on Korea was part of a greater plan for conquering all of Asia. I would like to read to you from a secret intelligence report which came to us after the attack. I have that report right here. It is a report of a speech a communist army officer in North Korea gave to a group of spies and saboteurs last May, one month before South Korea was invaded. The report shows in great detail how this invasion was a part of a carefully prepared plot. Here is part of what the communist officer, who had been trained in Moscow, told his men: "Our forces," he said, "are scheduled to attack South Korean forces about the middle of June. . . . The coming attack on South Korea marks the first step toward the liberation of Asia." Notice that he used the word *liberation*. This is communist double-talk meaning conquest. . . .

That's what the communist leaders are telling their people, and that is what they've been trying to do. They want to control all Asia from the Kremlin. This plan of conquest is in flat contradiction to what we believe. We believe that Korea belongs to the Koreans. We believe that India belongs to the Indians. We believe that all nations of Asia should be free to work out their affairs in their own way. This is the basis of peace in the Far East, and it is the basis of peace of everywhere else. . . .

The question we have had to face is whether the communist plan of conquest can be stopped without a general war. Our government and other countries associated with us in the United Nations believe that the best chance of stopping it without a general war is to meet the attack in Korea and defeat it there. That is what we have been doing. It is a difficult and bitter task, but so far it has been successful. So far, we have prevented World War III. So far, by fighting a limited war in Korea, we have prevented aggression from succeeding and bringing on a general war. And the ability of the whole free world to resist communist aggression has been greatly improved.

We have taught the enemy a lesson. He has found out that aggression is not cheap or easy. Moreover, men all over the world who want to remain free have been given new courage and new hope. They know now that the champions of freedom

AL CHANG, Haktong-ni Area, Korea, 1950.

can stand up and fight, and that they *will* stand up and fight. Our resolute stand in Korea is helping the forces of freedom now fighting in Indochina and other countries in that part of the world. It has already slowed down the timetable of conquest. . . .

The communist side must now choose its course of action. The communist rulers may press the attack against us. They may take further action which will spread the conflict. They have that choice and with it the awful responsibility for what may follow. The communists also have the choice of a peaceful settlement which could lead to general relaxation of the tensions in the Far East. The decision is theirs, because the forces of the United Nations will strive to limit the conflict if possible.

We do not want to see the conflict in Korea extended. We are trying to prevent a world war, not to start one. And the best way to do that is to make it plain that we and the other free countries will continue to resist the attack. But you may ask why can't we take other steps to punish the aggressor. Why don't we bomb Manchuria and China itself? Why don't we assist the Chinese nationalist troops to land on the mainland of China?

If we were to do these things, we would be running a very grave risk of starting a general war. If that were to happen, we would have brought about the exact situation we are trying to prevent. If we were to do these things, we would become entangled in a vast conflict on the continent of Asia, and our task would become immeasurably more difficult all over the world. What would suit the ambitions of the Kremlin better than for our military forces to be committed to a full-scale war with Red China? It may well be that, in spite of our best efforts, the communists may spread the war. But it would be wrong—tragically wrong—for us to take the initiative in extending the war. . . .

A number of events have made it evident that General MacArthur did not agree with that policy. I have therefore considered it essential to relieve General MacArthur so that there would be no doubt or confusion as to the real purpose and aim of our policy. It was with the deepest personal regret that I found myself compelled to take this action. General MacArthur is one of our greatest military commanders. But the cause of world peace is more important than any individual.

The change in commands in the Far East means no change whatever in the policy of the United States. We will carry on the fight in Korea with vigor and determination in an effort to bring the war to a speedy and successful conclusion. The new commander, Lieutenant General Matthew Ridgway, has already demonstrated that he has the good qualities of military leadership needed for the task.

We are ready, at any time, to negotiate for a restoration of peace in the area. But we will not engage in appeasement. We are only interested in real peace. Real peace can be achieved through a settlement based on the following factors: One, the fighting must stop. Two, concrete steps must be taken to insure that the fighting will not break out again. Three, there must be an end of the aggression. A settlement founded upon these elements would open the way for the unification of Korea and the withdrawal of all foreign forces.

In the meantime, I want to be clear about our military objective. We are fighting to resist an outrageous aggression in Korea. We are trying to keep the Korean conflict from spreading to other areas. But at the same time we must conduct our military activities so as to insure the security of our forces. This is essential if they are to continue the fight until the enemy abandons its ruthless attempts to destroy the Republic of Korea. That is our military objective—to repel attack and to restore peace.

In the hard fighting in Korea, we are proving that collective action among nations is not only a high principle but a workable means of resisting aggression. Defeat of aggression in Korea may be the turning point in the world's search for a practical way of achieving peace and security.

The struggle of the United Nations in Korea is a struggle for peace. The free nations have united their strength in an effort to prevent a third world war. That war can come if the communist rulers want it to come. But this nation and its allies will not be responsible for its coming. We do not want to widen the conflict. We will use every effort to prevent that disaster. And in so doing, we know that we are following the great principles of peace, freedom, and justice.

DWIGHT D. EISENHOWER

FAREWELL ADDRESS

JANUARY 17, 1961

As president, Dwight D. Eisenhower presided over the cold war and the growing arms race between the United States and the Soviet Union. Eisenhower's illustrious military career, which included service in both world wars and culminated in his leadership of NATO, gave added weight to his concerns about the increasing power of the military-industrial complex in civilian society, and his farewell address took on a prophetic importance.

My fellow Americans:

Three days from now, after half a century in the service of our country, I shall lay down the responsibilities of office as, in traditional and solemn ceremony, the authority of the Presidency is vested in my successor.

This evening I come to you with a message of leave-taking and farewell, and to share a few final thoughts with you, my countrymen.

We now stand ten years past the midpoint of a century that has witnessed four major wars among great nations. Three of these involved our own country. Despite these holocausts America is today the strongest, the most influential and most productive nation in the world. Understandably proud of this pre-eminence, we yet realize that America's leadership and prestige depend, not merely upon our unmatched material progress, riches and military strength, but on how we use our power in the interests of world peace and human betterment.

Throughout America's adventure in free government, our basic purposes have been to keep the peace; to foster progress in human achievement, and to enhance liberty, dignity, and integrity among people and among nations. To strive for less would be unworthy of a free and religious people. Any failure traceable to arrogance, or our lack of comprehension or readiness to sacrifice, would inflict upon us grievous hurt both at home and abroad.

Progress toward these noble goals is persistently threatened by the conflict now engulfing the world. It commands our whole attention, absorbs our very beings. We face a hostile ideology—global in scope, atheistic in character, ruthless in purpose, and insidious in method. Unhappily the danger it poses promises to be of indefinite duration. To meet it successfully, there is called for, not so much the emotional and transitory sacrifices of crisis, but rather those which enable us to carry forward steadily, surely, and without complaint the burdens of a prolonged and complex struggle—with liberty at stake. Only thus shall we remain, despite every provocation, on our charted course toward permanent peace and human betterment.

Crises there will continue to be. In meeting them, whether foreign or domestic, great or small, there is a recurring temptation to feel that some spectacular and costly action could become the miraculous solution to all current difficulties. A huge increase in newer elements of our defense; development of unrealistic programs to cure every ill in agriculture; a dramatic expansion in basic and applied research—these and many other possibilities, each possibly promising in itself, may be suggested as the only way to the road we wish to travel.

But each proposal must be weighed in the light of a broader consideration: the need to maintain balance in and among national programs—balance between the private and the public economy, balance between cost and hoped for advantage—balance between the clearly necessary and the comfortably desirable; balance between our essential requirements as a nation and the duties imposed by the nation upon the individual; balance between action of the moment and the national welfare of the future. Good judgment seeks balance and progress; lack of it eventually finds imbalance and frustration.

The record of many decades stands as proof that our people and their government have, in the main, understood these truths and have responded to them well, in the face of stress and threat. But threats, new in kind or degree, constantly arise. I mention two only.

A vital element in keeping the peace is our military establishment. Our arms must be mighty, ready for instant action, so that no potential aggressor may be tempted to risk his own destruction.

Our military organization today bears little relation to that known by any of my predecessors in peace time, or indeed by the fighting men of World War II or Korea.

Until the latest of our world conflicts, the United States had no armaments industry. American makers of plowshares could, with time and as required, make swords as well. But now we can no longer risk emergency improvisation of national defense; we have been compelled to create a permanent armaments industry of vast proportions. Added to this, three and a half million men and women are directly engaged in the defense establishment. We annually spend on military security more than the net income of all United States corporations.

This conjunction of an immense military establishment and a large arms industry is new in the American experience. The total influence—economic, political, even spiritual—is felt in every city, every state house, every office of the Federal government. We recognize the imperative need for this development. Yet we must not fail to comprehend its grave implications. Our toil, resources and livelihood are all involved; so is the very structure of our society.

In the councils of government, we must guard against the acquisition of unwarranted influence, whether sought or unsought, by the military-industrial complex. The potential for the disastrous rise of misplaced power exists and will persist.

We must never let the weight of this combination endanger our liberties or democratic processes. We should take nothing for granted. Only an alert and knowledgeable citizenry can compel the proper meshing of huge industrial and military machinery of defense with our peaceful methods and goals, so that security and liberty may prosper together.

Akin to, and largely responsible for the sweeping changes in our industrial-military posture, has been the technological revolution during recent decades.

In this revolution, research has become central; it also becomes more formalized, complex, and costly. A steadily increasing share is conducted for, by, or at the direction of, the Federal government.

Today, the solitary inventor, tinkering in his shop, has been overshadowed by task forces of scientists in laboratories and testing fields. In the same fashion, the free university, historically the fountainhead of free ideas and scientific discovery, has experienced a revolution in the conduct of research. Partly because of the huge costs involved, a government contract becomes virtually a substitute for intellectual curiosity. For every old blackboard there are now hundreds of new electronic computers.

The prospect of domination of the nation's scholars by Federal employment, project allocations, and the power of money is ever present and is gravely to be regarded.

Yet, in holding scientific research and discovery in respect, as we should, we must also be alert to the equal and opposite danger that public policy could itself become the captive of a scientific-technological elite.

It is the task of statesmanship to mold, to balance, and to integrate these and other forces, new and old, within the principles of our democratic system—ever aiming toward the supreme goals of our free society.

Another factor in maintaining balance involves the element of time. As we peer into society's future, we—you and I, and our government—must avoid the impulse to live only for today, plundering, for our own ease and convenience, the precious resources of tomorrow. We cannot mortgage the material assets of our grandchildren without risking the loss also of their political and spiritual heritage. We want democracy to survive for all generations to come, not to become the insolvent phantom of tomorrow.

Down the long lane of the history yet to be written America knows that this world of ours, ever growing smaller, must avoid becoming a community of dreadful fear and hate, and be, instead, a proud confederation of mutual trust and respect.

Such a confederation must be one of equals. The weakest must come to the conference table with the same confidence as do we, protected as we are by our moral, economic, and military strength. That table, though scarred by many past frustrations, cannot be abandoned for the certain agony of the battlefield.

Disarmament, with mutual honor and confidence, is a continuing imperative. Together we must learn how to compose difference, not with arms, but with intellect and decent purpose. Because this need is so sharp and apparent I confess that I lay down my official responsibilities in this field with a definite sense of disappointment. As one who has witnessed the horror and the lingering sadness of war—as one who knows that another war could utterly destroy this civilization which has been so slowly and painfully built over thousands of years—I wish I could say tonight that a lasting peace is in sight.

Happily, I can say that war has been avoided. Steady progress toward our ultimate goal has been made. But, so much remains to be done. As a private citizen, I shall never cease to do what little I can to help the world advance along that road.

So—in this my last good night to you as your President—I thank you for the many opportunities you have given me for public service in war and peace. I trust that in that service you find some things worthy; as for the ret of it, I know you will find ways to improve performance in the future.

You and I—my fellow citizens—need to be strong in our faith that all nations, under God, will reach the goal of peace with justice. May we be ever unswerving in devotion to principle, confident but humble with power, diligent in pursuit of the Nation's great goals.

To all the peoples of the world, I once more give expression to America's prayerful and continuing inspiration:

We pray that peoples of all faiths, all races, all nations, may have their great human needs satisfied; that those now denied opportunity shall come to enjoy it to the full; that all who yearn for freedom may experience its spiritual blessings; that those who have freedom will understand, also, its heavy responsibilities; that all who are insensitive to the needs of others will learn charity; that the scourges of poverty, disease and ignorance will be made to disappear from the earth, and that, in the goodness of time, all peoples will come to live together in a peace guaranteed by the binding force of mutual respect and love.

BOB DYLAN

BLOWIN' IN THE WIND

1962

Bob Dylan (1941–), folk singer and writer, carried on the "troubadour" tradition of Woody Guthrie. He turned songwriting into poetry for the postwar generation, emerging as one of the most talented and appreciated American songwriters in the last forty years. "Blowin' in the Wind" is perhaps Dylan's most famous ballad, written and recorded in 1962. It was adopted as a central anthem of the civil rights and Vietnam protest movements.

How many roads must a man walk down
Before you call him a man?
Yes, 'n' how many seas must a white dove sail
Before she sleeps in the sand?
Yes, 'n' how many times must the cannon balls fly
Before they're forever banned?
The answer, my friend, is blowin' in the wind,
The answer is blowin' in the wind.

How many times must a man look up
Before he can see the sky?
Yes, 'n' how many ears must one man have
Before he can hear people cry?
Yes 'n' how many deaths will it take till he knows
That too many people have died?
The answer, my friend, is blowin' in the wind,
The answer is blowin' in the wind.

How many years can a mountain exist
Before it's washed to the sea?
Yes, 'n' how many years can some people exist
Before they're allowed to be free?
Yes, 'n' how many times can a man turn his head,
Pretending he just doesn't see?
The answer, my friend, is blowin' in the wind,
The answer is blowin' in the wind.

JOHN F. KENNEDY

COMMENCEMENT ADDRESS AT AMERICAN UNIVERSITY

JUNE 10, 1963

In 1962, when he discovered that the Soviets were building offensive nuclear missile bases in Cuba, President Kennedy resisted calls for an immediate air strike and pursued a course of diplomacy that averted the catastrophe of nuclear war. His brilliant judgment during the Cuban Missile Crisis led to a new chapter in Soviet-American relations, making it possible to negotiate the first treaty banning the testing of nuclear weapons in the atmosphere, outer space, and underwater. In this speech, which he gave the summer after the Cuban Missile Crisis, President Kennedy spoke of peace.

. . . I have chosen this time and this place to discuss a topic on which ignorance too often abounds and the truth is too rarely perceived—yet it is the most important topic on earth: world peace.

What kind of peace do I mean? What kind of peace do we seek? Not a Pax Americana enforced on the world by American weapons of war. Not the peace of the grave or the security of the slave. I am talking about genuine peace, the kind of peace that makes life on earth worth living, the kind that enables men and nations to grow and to hope and to build a better life for their children—not merely peace for Americans but peace for all men and women—not merely peace in our time but peace for all time.

I speak of peace because of the new face of war. Total war makes no sense in an age when great powers can maintain large and relatively invulnerable nuclear forces and refuse to surrender without resort to those forces. It makes no sense in an age when a single nuclear weapon contains almost ten times the explosive force delivered by all of the allied air forces in the Second World War. It makes no sense in an age when the deadly poisons produced by a nuclear exchange would be carried by wind and water and soil and seed to the far corners of the globe and to generations yet unborn. . . .

I speak of peace, therefore, as the necessary rational end of rational men. I realize that the pursuit of peace is not as dramatic as the pursuit of war—and frequently the words of the pursuer fall on deaf ears. But we have no more urgent task. . . .

First: Let us examine our attitude toward peace itself. Too many of us think it is impossible. Too many think it unreal. But that is a dangerous, defeatist belief. It leads to the conclusion that war is inevitable—that mankind is doomed—that we are gripped by forces we cannot control.

We need not accept that view. Our problems are manmade—therefore, they can be solved by man. And man can be as big as he wants. No problem of human destiny is beyond human beings. Man's reason and spirit have often solved the seemingly unsolvable—and we believe they can do it again. . . .

Let us focus instead on a more practical, more attainable peace—based not on a sudden revolution in human nature but on a gradual evolution in human institutions—on a series of concrete actions and effective agreements which are in the interest of all concerned. There is no single, simple key to this peace—no grand or magic formula to be adopted by one or two powers. Genuine peace must be the product of many nations, the sum of many acts. It must be dynamic, not static, changing to meet the challenge of each new generation. For peace is a process—a way of solving problems. . . .

So let us persevere. Peace need not be impracticable, and war need not be inevitable. By defining our goal more clearly, by making it seem more manageable

John F. Kennedy in Berlin, Germany, 1963.

and less remote, we can help all peoples to see it, to draw hope from it, and to move irresistibly toward it.

Second: Let us reexamine our attitude toward the Soviet Union. . . .

Today, should total war ever break out again—no matter how—our two countries would become the primary targets. It is an ironic but accurate fact that the two strongest powers are the two in the most danger of devastation. All we have built, all we have worked for, would be destroyed in the first 24 hours. And even in the cold war, which brings burdens and dangers to so many countries, including this Nation's closest allies—our two countries bear the heaviest burdens. For we are both devoting massive sums of money to weapons that could be better devoted to combating ignorance, poverty, and disease. We are both caught up in a vicious and dangerous cycle in which suspicion on one side breeds suspicion on the other, and new weapons beget counterweapons. . . .

So, let us not be blind to our differences—but let us also direct attention to our common interests and to the means by which those differences can be resolved. And if we cannot end now our differences, at least we can help make the world safe for diversity. For, in the final analysis, our most basic common link is that we all inhabit this small planet. We all breathe the same air. We all cherish our children's future. And we are all mortal.

Third: Let us reexamine our attitude toward the cold war, remembering that we are not engaged in a debate, seeking to pile up debating points. We are not here distributing blame or pointing the finger of judgment. We must deal with the world as it is, and not as it might have been had the history of the last 18 years been different.

We must, therefore, persevere in the search for peace in the hope that constructive changes within the Communist bloc might bring within reach solutions which now seem beyond us. We must conduct our affairs in such a way that it becomes in the Communists' interest to agree on a genuine peace. Above all, while defending our own vital interests, nuclear powers must avert those confrontations which bring an adversary to a choice of either a humiliating retreat or a nuclear war. To adopt that kind of course in the nuclear age would be evidence only of the bankruptcy of our policy—or of a collective death-wish for the world. . . .

Meanwhile, we seek to strengthen the United Nations, to help solve its financial problems, to make it a more effective instrument for peace, to develop it into a genuine world security system—a system capable of resolving disputes on the basis of law, of insuring the security of the large and the small, and of creating conditions under which arms can finally be abolished.

At the same time we seek to keep peace inside the non-Communist world, where many nations, all of them our friends, are divided over issues which weaken Western unity, which invite Communist intervention or which threaten to erupt into war. . . .

Speaking of other nations, I wish to make one point clear. We are bound to many nations by alliances. Those alliances exist because our concern and theirs substantially overlap. Our commitment to defend Western Europe and West Berlin, for example, stands undiminished because of the identity of our vital interests. The United States will make no deal with the Soviet Union at the expense of other nations and other peoples, not merely because they are our partners, but also because their interests and ours converge.

Our interests converge, however, not only in defending the frontiers of freedom, but in pursuing the paths of peace. It is our hope—and the purpose of allied policies—to convince the Soviet Union that she, too, should let each nation choose in its own future, so long as that choice does not interfere with the choices of others. The Communist drive to impose their political and economic system on others is the primary cause of world tension today. For there can be no doubt that, if all nations could refrain from interfering in the self-determination of others, the peace would be much more assured.

This will require a new effort to achieve world law—a new context for world discussions. It will require increased understanding between the Soviets and ourselves. And increased understanding will require increased contact and communication. One step in this direction is the proposed arrangement for a direct line between Moscow and Washington, to avoid on each side the dangerous delays, misunderstandings, and misreadings of the other's actions which might occur at a time of crisis.

We have also been talking in Geneva about other first-step measures of arms control, designed to limit the intensity of the arms race and to reduce the risks of accidental war. . . .

The one major area of these negotiations where the end is in sight, yet where a fresh start is badly needed, is in a treaty to outlaw nuclear tests. The conclusion of such a treaty, so near and yet so far, would check the spiraling arms race in one of its most dangerous areas. It would place the nuclear powers in a position to deal more effectively with one of the greatest hazards which man faces in 1963, the further spread of nuclear arms. It would increase our security—it would decrease the prospects of war. Surely this goal is sufficiently important to require our steady pursuit, yielding neither to the temptation to give up the whole effort nor the temptation to give up our insistence on vital and responsible safeguards.

I am taking this opportunity, therefore, to announce two important decisions in this regard.

First: Chairman Khrushchev, Prime Minister Macmillan, and I have agreed that high-level discussions will shortly begin in Moscow looking toward early agreement on a comprehensive test ban treaty. Our hopes must be tempered with the caution of history—but with our hopes go the hopes of all mankind.

Second: To make clear our good faith and solemn convictions on the matter, I now declare that the United States does not propose to conduct nuclear tests in the atmosphere so long as other states do not do so. We will not be the first to resume. Such a declaration is no substitute for a formal binding treaty, but I hope it will help us achieve one. Nor would such a treaty be a substitute for disarmament, but I hope it will help us achieve it.

Finally, my fellow Americans, let us examine our attitude toward peace and freedom here at home. The quality and spirit of our own society must justify and support our efforts abroad. We must show it in the dedication of our own lives—as many of you who are graduating today will have a unique opportunity to do, by serving without pay in the Peace Corps abroad or in the proposed National Service Corps here at home.

But wherever we are, we must all, in our daily lives, live up to the age-old faith that peace and freedom walk together. In too many of our cities today, the peace is not secure because freedom is incomplete.

It is the responsibility of the executive branch at all levels of government—local, State, and National—to provide and protect that freedom for all of our citizens by all means within their authority. It is the responsibility of the legislative branch at all levels, wherever that authority is not now adequate, to make it adequate. And it is the responsibility of all citizens in all sections of this country to respect the rights of all others and to respect the law of the land.

All this is not unrelated to world peace. "When a man's ways please the Lord," the Scriptures tell us, "he maketh even his enemies to be at peace with him." And is not peace, in the last analysis, basically a matter of human rights—the right to live out our lives without fear of devastation—the right to breathe air as nature provided it—the right of future generations to a healthy existence?

While we proceed to safeguard our national interests, let us also safeguard human interests. And the elimination of war and arms is clearly in the interest of both. No treaty, however much it may be to the advantage of all, however tightly it may be worded, can provide absolute security against the risks of deception and evasion. But it can—if it is sufficiently effective in its enforcement and if it is sufficiently in the interests of its signers—offer far more security and far fewer risks than an unabated, uncontrolled, unpredictable arms race.

The United States, as the world knows, will never start a war. We do not want a war. We do not now expect a war. This generation of Americans has already had enough—more than enough—of war and hate and oppression. We shall be prepared if others wish it. We shall be alert to try to stop it. But we shall also do our part to build a world of peace where the weak are safe and the strong are just. We are not helpless before that task or hopeless of its success. Confident and unafraid, we labor on—not toward a strategy of annihilation but toward a strategy of peace.

VIETNAM VETERANS AGAINST THE WAR

1971

After attending Yale University, John Kerry (1943–) served as a decorated navy lieutenant in the Vietnam War. Disillusioned, he returned to the United States and helped found the Vietnam Veterans Against the War, on behalf of whom he testified before the Senate Foreign Relations Committee. Kerry became a senator in 1985, where he is known for his expertise on foreign policy matters.

It is impossible to describe to you exactly what did happen in Detroit—the emotions in the room and the feelings of the men who were reliving their experiences in Vietnam. They relived the absolute horror of what this country, in a sense, made them do.

They told stories that at times they had personally raped, cut off ears, cut off heads, taped wires from portable telephones to human genitals and turned up the power, cut off limbs, blown up bodies, randomly shot at civilians, razed villages in fashion reminiscent of Genghis Khan, shot cattle and dogs for fun, poisoned food stocks, and generally ravaged the countryside of South Vietnam in addition to the normal ravage of war and the normal and very particular ravaging which is done by the applied bombing power of this country.

We call this investigation the Winter Soldier Investigation. The term Winter Soldier is a play on words of Thomas Paine's in 1776 when he spoke of the Sunshine Patriots and summertime soldiers who deserted at Valley Forge because the going was rough.

We who have come here to Washington have come here because we feel we have to be winter soldiers now. We would come back to this country, we could be quiet, we could hold our silence, we could not tell what went on in Vietnam, but we feel because of what threatens this country, not the reds, but the crimes which we are committing that threaten it, that we have to speak out. . . .

In our opinion and from our experience, there is nothing in South Vietnam which could happen that realistically threatens the United States of America. And to attempt to justify the loss of one American life in Vietnam, Cambodia or Laos by linking such loss to the preservation of freedom, which those misfits supposedly abuse, is to us the height of criminal hypocrisy, and it is that kind of hypocrisy which we feel has torn this country apart.

We found that not only was it a civil war, an effort by a people who had for years been seeking their liberation from any colonial influence whatsoever, but also we found that the Vietnamese whom we had enthusiastically molded after our own image were hard put to take up the fight against the threat we were supposedly saving them from.

We found most people didn't even know the difference between communism and democracy. They only wanted to work in rice paddies without helicopters strafing them and bombs with napalm burning their villages and tearing their country apart. They wanted everything to do with the war, particularly with this foreign presence of the United States of America, to leave them alone in peace, and they practiced the art of survival by siding with whichever military force was present at a particular time, be it Viet Cong, North Vietnamese or American.

We found also that all too often American men were dying in those rice paddies for want of support from their allies. We saw first hand how monies from American taxes were used for a corrupt dictatorial regime. We saw that many people in this country had a one-sided idea of who was kept free by our flag, and blacks provided the highest percentage of casualties. We saw Vietnam ravaged equally by American bombs and search and destroy missions, as well as by Viet Cong terrorism and yet we listened while this country tried to blame all of the havoc on the Viet Cong.

We rationalized destroying villages in order to save them. We saw America lose her sense of morality as she accepted very coolly a My Lai and refused to give up the image of American soldiers who hand out chocolate bars and chewing gum.

We learned the meaning of free fire zones, shooting anything that moves, and we watched while America placed a cheapness on the lives of Orientals.

We watched the United States' falsification of body counts, in fact the glorification of body counts. We listened while month after month we were told the back of the enemy was about to break. We fought using weapons against "oriental human beings." We fought using weapons against those people which I do not believe this country would dream of using were we fighting in the European theater. We watched while men charged up hills because a general said that hill was to be taken, and after losing one platoon or two platoons they marched away to leave the hill for reoccupation by the North Vietnamese. We watched pride allow the most unimportant battles to be blown into extravaganzas, because we couldn't lose, and we couldn't retreat, and because it didn't matter how many American bodies were lost to prove that point, and so there were Hamburger Hills and Khe Sanhs and Hill 81s and Fire Base 6s, and so many others.

Now we are told that the men who fought there must watch quietly while American lives are lost so that we can exercise the incredible arrogance of Vietnamizing the Vietnamese.

Each day to facilitate the process by which the United States washes her hands of Vietnam someone has to give up his life so that the United States doesn't have to admit something that the entire world already knows, so that we can't say that we have made a mistake. Somone has to die so that President Nixon won't be, and these are his words, "the first President to lose a war."

We are asking Americans to think about that because how do you ask a man to be the last man to die in Vietnam? How do you ask a man to be the last man to die for a mistake? . . . We are here in Washington also to say that the problem of this war is not just a question of war and diplomacy. It is part and parcel of everything that we are trying as human beings to communicate to people in this country—the question of racism whic is rampant in the military, and so many other questions such as the use of weapons; the hypocrisy in our taking umbrage at the Geneva Conventions and using that as justification for a continuation of this war when we are more guilty than any other body of violations of those Geneva Conventions: in the use of free fire zones, harassment interdiction fire, search and destroy missions, the bombings, the torture of prisoners, the killing of prisoners, all accepted policy by many units in South Vietnam. That is what we are trying to say. It is part and parcel of everything.

An American Indian friend of mine who lives in the Indian Nation of Alcatraz put it to me very succintly. He told me how as a boy on an Indian reservation he had

CONSTANTINE MANOS, Soldier's funeral, South Carolina, 1966.

watched television and he used to cheer the cowboys when they came in and shot the Indians, and then suddenly one day he stopped in Vietnam and he said "my God, I am doing to these people the very same thing that was done to my people," and he stopped. And that is what we are trying to say, that we think this thing has to end.

We are here to ask, and we are here to ask vehemently, where are the leaders of our country. Where is the leadership? We're here to ask where are McNamara, Rostow, Bundy, Gilpatrick, and so many others. Where are they now that we, the men they sent off to war, have returned. These are commanders who have deserted their troops. And there is no more serious crime in the laws of war. The Army says they never leave their wounded. The marines say they never leave even their dead. These men have left all the casualties and retreated behind a pious shield of public rectitude. They've left the real stuff of their reputations bleaching behind behind them in the sun in this country. . . .

We wish that a merciful God could wipe away our own memories of that service as easily as this administration has wiped away their memories of us. But all that they have done and all that they can do by this denial is to make more clear than ever our own determination to undertake one last mission—to search out and destroy the last vestige of this barbaric war, to pacify our own hearts, to conquer the hate and the fear that have driven this country these last ten years and more. And more. And so when thirty years from now our brothers go down the street without a leg, without an arm, or a face, and small boys ask why, we will be able to say "Vietnam" and not mean a desert, not a filthy obscene memory, but mean instead the place where America finally turned and where soldiers like us helped it in the turning.

BORN IN THE U.S.A.

1984

Bruce Springsteen (1949–) grew up in the blue-collar town of Freehold, New Jersey. In the early 1970s he formed the E Street Band. "Born in the U.S.A.," an ironic hymn to those who served in Vietnam and one of Springsteen's most famous songs from the album of the same name, was released in 1984.

Born down in a dead man's town
The first kick I took was when I hit the ground
You end up like a dog that's been beat too much
Till you spend half your life just covering up

Born in the U.S.A.
I was born in the U.S.A.
I was born in the U.S.A.
Born in the U.S.A.

Got in a little hometown jam
So they put a rifle in my hand
Sent me off to a foreign land
To go and kill the yellow man

Born in the U.S.A.
I was born in the U.S.A.
I was born in the U.S.A.
I was born in the U.S.A.
Born in the U.S.A.

Come back home to the refinery
Hiring man says "Son, if it was up to me"
Went down to see my V.A. man
He said "Son, don't you understand"

I had a brother at Khe Sahn fighting off the Viet Cong
They're still there, he's all gone

He had a woman he loved in Saigon
I got a picture of him in her arms now

Down in the shadow of the penitentiary
Out by the gas fires of the refinery
I'm ten years burning down the road
Nowhere to run ain't got nowhere to go

Born in the U.S.A.
I was born in the U.S.A.
Born in the U.S.A.
I'm a long gone Daddy in the U.S.A.
Born in the U.S.A.
Born in the U.S.A.
Born in the U.S.A.
I'm a cool rocking Daddy in the U.S.A.

WAYNE MILLER, Antiwar protest, Berkeley, California, 1965.

ON THE RAINY RIVER
(FROM *THE THINGS THEY CARRIED*)

1990

A native of a small Minnesota town, Vietnam veteran Tim O'Brien (1946–) won immediate acclaim for his fictionalized accounts of soldiering in Southeast Asia. He was among the first Vietnam combat veterans to write of his experiences, publishing his memoir *If I Die in a Combat Zone, Tie Me Up and Send Me Home* in 1973, the same year that the last American troops evacuated Vietnam. His novel *Going After Cacciato* won the National Book Award in 1979. It was followed by the internationally acclaimed books *The Things They Carried* (1990) and *In the Lake of the Woods* (1994).

This is one story I've never told before. Not to anyone. Not to my parents, not to my brother or sister, not even to my wife. To go into it, I've always thought, would only cause embarrassment for all of us, a sudden need to be elsewhere, which is the natural response to a confession. Even now, I'll admit, the story makes me squirm. For more than twenty years I've had to live with it, feeling the shame, trying to push it away, and so by this act of remembrance, by putting the facts down on paper, I'm hoping to relieve at least some of the pressure on my dreams. Still, it's a hard story to tell. All of us, I suppose, like to believe that in a moral emergency we will behave like the heroes of our youth, bravely and forthrightly, without thought of personal loss or discredit. Certainly that was my conviction back in the summer of 1968. Tim O'Brien: a secret hero. The Lone Ranger. If the stakes ever became high enough— if the evil were evil enough, if the good were good enough—I would simply tap a secret reservoir of courage that had been accumulating inside me over the years. Courage, I seemed to think, comes to us in finite quantities, like an inheritance, and by being frugal and stashing it away and letting it earn interest, we steadily increase our moral capital in preparation for that day when the account must be drawn down. It was a comforting theory. It dispensed with all those bothersome little acts of daily courage; it offered hope and grace to the repetitive coward; it justified the past while amortizing the future.

In June of 1968, a month after graduating from Macalester College, I was drafted to fight a war I hated. I was twenty-one years old. Young, yes, and politically naive, but even so the American war in Vietnam seemed to me wrong. Certain blood was being shed for uncertain reasons. I saw no unity of purpose, no consensus on matters of philosophy or history or law. The very facts were shrouded in uncertainty: Was it a civil war? A war of national liberation or simple aggression? Who started it, and when, and why? What really happened to the USS *Maddox* on that dark night in the Gulf of Tonkin? Was Ho Chi Minh a Communist stooge, or a nationalist savior, or both, or neither? What about the Geneva Accords? What about SEATO and the Cold War? What about dominoes? America was divided on these and a thousand other issues, and the debate had spilled out across the floor of the United States Senate and into the streets, and smart men in pinstripes could not agree on even the most fundamental matters of public policy. The only certainty that summer was moral confusion. It was my view then, and still is, that you don't make war without knowing why. Knowledge, of course, is always imperfect, but it seemed to me that when a nation goes to war it must have reasonable confidence in the justice and imperative of its cause. You can't fix your mistakes. Once people are dead, you can't make them undead.

In any case those were my convictions, and back in college I had taken a modest stand against the war. Nothing radical, no hothead stuff, just ringing a few doorbells for Gene McCarthy, composing a few tedious, uninspired editorials for the campus newspaper. Oddly, though, it was almost entirely an intellectual activity. I brought some energy to it, of course, but it was the energy that accompanies almost any abstract endeavor; I felt no personal danger; I felt no sense of an impending crisis in my life. Stupidly, with a kind of smug removal that I can't begin to fathom, I assumed that the problems of killing and dying did not fall within my special province.

The draft notice arrived on June 17, 1968. It was a humid afternoon, I remember, cloudy and very quiet, and I'd just come in from a round of golf. My mother and father were having lunch out in the kitchen. I remember opening up the letter, scanning the first few lines, feeling the blood go thick behind my eyes. I remember a sound in my head. It wasn't thinking, just a silent howl. A million things all at once—I was too *good* for this war. Too smart, too compassionate, too everything. It couldn't happen. I was above it. I had the world dicked—Phi Beta Kappa and summa cum laude and president of the student body and a full-ride scholarship for grad studies at Harvard. A mistake, maybe—a foul-up in the paperwork. I was no soldier. I hated Boy Scouts. I hated camping out. I hated dirt and tents and mosquitoes. The sight of blood made me queasy, and I couldn't tolerate authority, and I didn't know a rifle from a slingshot. . . .

I remember the rage in my stomach. Later it burned down to a smoldering self-pity, then to numbness. At dinner that night my father asked what my plans were. "Nothing," I said. "Wait." . . .

At some point in mid-July I began thinking seriously about Canada. The border lay a few hundred miles north, an eight-hour drive. Both my conscience and my instincts were telling me to make a break for it, just take off and run like hell and never stop. In the beginning the idea seemed purely abstract, the word Canada printing itself out in my head; but after a time I could see particular shapes and images, the sorry details of my own future—a hotel room in Winnipeg, a battered old suitcase, my father's eyes as I tried to explain myself over the telephone. I could almost hear his voice, and my mother's. Run, I'd think. Then I'd think, Impossible. Then a second later I'd think, *Run*. . . .

I was bitter, sure. But it was so much more than that. The emotions went from outrage to terror to bewilderment to guilt to sorrow and then back again to outrage. I felt a sickness inside me. Real disease. . . .

I drove north. . . .

For a while I just drove, not aiming at anything, then in the late morning I began looking for a place to lie low for a day or two. I was exhausted, and scared sick, and around noon I pulled into an old fishing resort called the Tip Top Lodge. Actually it was not a lodge at all, just eight or nine tiny yellow cabins clustered on a peninsula that jutted northward into the Rainy River. The place was in sorry shape. There was a dangerous wooden dock, an old minnow tank, a flimsy tar paper boathouse along the shore. The main building, which stood in a cluster of pines on high ground, seemed to lean heavily to one side, like a cripple, the roof sagging toward Canada. Briefly, I thought about turning around, just giving up, but then I got out of the car and walked up to the front porch.

The man who opened the door that day is the hero of my life. How do I say this without sounding sappy? Blurt it out—the man saved me. He offered exactly what I needed, without questions, without any words at all. He took me in. He was there at the critical time—a silent, watchful presence. Six days later, when it ended, I was unable to find a proper way to thank him, and I never have, and so, if nothing else, this story represents a small gesture of gratitude twenty years overdue.

Even after two decades I can close my eyes and return to that porch at the Tip Top Lodge. I can see the old guy staring at me. Elroy Berdahl: eighty-one years old, skinny and shrunken and mostly bald. He wore a flannel shirt and brown work pants. In one hand, I remember, he carried a green apple, a small paring knife in the other. His eyes had the bluish gray color of a razor blade, the same polished shine, and as he peered up at me I felt a strange sharpness, almost painful, a cutting sensation, as if his gaze were somehow slicing me open. In part, no doubt, it was my own sense of guilt, but even so I'm absolutely certain that the old man took one look and went right to the heart of things—a kid in trouble. . . .

We spent six days together at the Tip Top Lodge. Just the two of us. Tourist season was over, and there were no boats on the river, and the wilderness seemed to withdraw into a great permanent stillness. What I remember more than anything is the man's willful, almost ferocious silence. In all that time together, all those hours, he never asked the obvious questions: Why was I there? Why alone? Why so preoccupied? If Elroy was curious about any of this, he was careful never to put it into words. . . .

My hunch, though, is that he already knew. At least the basics. After all, it was 1968, and guys were burning draft cards, and Canada was just a boat ride away. Elroy Berdahl was no hick. His bedroom, I remember, was cluttered with books and newspapers. He killed me at the Scrabble board, barely concentrating, and on those occasions when speech was necessary he had a way of compressing large thoughts into small, cryptic packets of language. One evening, just at sunset, he pointed up at an owl circling over the violet-lighted forest to the west.

"Hey, O'Brien," he said. "There's Jesus."

The man was sharp—he didn't miss much. Those razor eyes. Now and then he'd catch me staring out at the river, at the far shore, and I could almost hear the tumblers clicking in his head. Maybe I'm wrong, but I doubt it.

One thing for certain, he knew I was in desperate trouble. And he knew I couldn't talk about it. The wrong word—or even the right word—and I would've disappeared. I was wired and jittery. My skin felt too tight. After supper one evening I vomited and went back to my cabin and lay down for a few moments and then vomited again; another time, in the middle of the afternoon, I began sweating and couldn't shut it off. I went through whole days feeling dizzy with sorrow. I couldn't sleep; I couldn't lie still. At night I'd toss around in bed, half awake, half dreaming, imagining how I'd sneak down to the beach and quietly push one of the old man's boats out into the river and start paddling my way toward Canada. There were times when I thought I'd gone off the psychic edge. I couldn't tell up from down, I was just falling, and late in the night I'd lie there watching weird pictures spin through my head. Getting chased by the Border Patrol—helicopters and searchlights and barking dogs—I'd be crashing through the woods, I'd be down on my hands and knees—people shouting out my name—the law closing in on all sides—my hometown draft board and the FBI and the Royal Canadian Mounted Police. It all seemed crazy and impossible. Twenty-one years old, an ordinary kid with all the ordinary dreams and ambitions, and all I wanted was to live the life I was born to—a mainstream life—I loved baseball and hamburgers and cherry Cokes—and now I was off on the margins of exile, leaving my country forever, and it seemed so impossible and terrible and sad.

I'm not sure how I made it through those six days. Most of it I can't remember. On two or three afternoons, to pass some time, I helped Elroy get the place ready for winter, sweeping down the cabins and hauling in the boats, little chores that kept my body moving. The days were cool and bright. The nights were very dark. One morning the old man showed me how to split and stack firewood, and for several hours we just worked in silence out behind his house. At one point, I remember, Elroy put down his maul and looked at me for a long time, his lips drawn as if framing a difficult question, but then he shook his head and went back to work. The man's self-control was amazing. He never pried. He never put me in a position that required lies or denials. . . . Simple politeness was part of it. But even more than that, I think, the man understood that words were insufficient. . . . I was ashamed to be there at the Tip Top Lodge. I was ashamed of my conscience, ashamed to be doing the right thing.

Some of this Elroy must've understood. Not the details, of course, but the plain fact of crisis. . . .

On my last full day, the sixth day, the old man took me out fishing on the Rainy River. . . . All around us, I remember, there was a vastness to the world, an unpeopled rawness, just the trees and the sky and the water reaching out toward nowhere. . . .

For a time I didn't pay attention to anything, just feeling the cold spray against my face, but then it occurred to me that at some point we must've passed into Canadian waters, across that dotted line between two different worlds, and I remember a sudden tightness in my chest as I looked up and watched the far shore come at me. This wasn't a daydream. It was tangible and real. As we came in toward land, Elroy cut the engine, letting the boat fishtail lightly about twenty yards off shore. The old man didn't look at me or speak. Bending down, he opened up his tackle box and busied himself with a bobber and a piece of wire leader, humming to himself, his eyes down.

It struck me then that he must've planned it. I'll never be certain, of course, but I think he meant to bring me up against the realities, to guide me across the river and to take me to the edge and to stand a kind of vigil as I chose a life for myself.

I remember staring at the old man, then at my hands, then at Canada. The shoreline was dense with brush and timber. I could see tiny red berries on the bushes. I could see a squirrel up in one of the birch trees, a big crow looking at me from a boulder along the river. That close—twenty yards—and I could see the delicate latticework of the leaves, the texture of the soil, the browned needles beneath the pines, the configurations of geology and human history. Twenty yards. I could've done it. I could've jumped and started swimming for my life. Inside me, in my chest, I felt a terrible squeezing pressure. Even now, as I write this, I can still feel that tightness. And I want you to feel it—the wind coming off the river, the waves, the silence, the wooded frontier. You're at the bow of a boat on the Rainy River. You're twenty-one years old, you're scared, and there's a hard squeezing pressure in your chest.

What would you do?

Would you jump? Would you feel pity for yourself? Would you think about your family and your childhood and your dreams and all you're leaving behind? Would it hurt? Would it feel like dying? Would you cry, as I did?

I tried to swallow it back. I tried to smile, except I was crying.

Now, perhaps, you can understand why I've never told this story before. It's not just the embarrassment of tears. That's part of it, no doubt, but what embarrasses me much more, and always will, is the paralysis that took my heart. A moral freeze: I couldn't decide, I couldn't act, I couldn't comport myself with even a pretense of modest human dignity.

All I could do was cry. Quietly, not bawling, just the chest-chokes.

At the rear of the boat Elroy Berdahl pretended not to notice. He held a fishing rod in his hands, his head bowed to hide his eyes. He kept humming a soft, monotonous little tune. Everywhere, it seemed, in the trees and water and sky, a great worldwide sadness came pressing down on me, a crushing sorrow, sorrow like I had never known it before. And what was so sad, I realized, was that Canada had become a pitiful fantasy. Silly and hopeless. It was no longer a possibility. Right then, with the shore so close, I understood that I would not do what I should do. I would not swim away from my hometown and my country and my life. I would not be brave. That old image of myself as a hero, as a man of conscience and courage, all that was just a threadbare pipe dream. . . .

It was as if there were an audience to my life, that swirl of faces along the river, and in my head I could hear people screaming at me. Traitor! they yelled. Turncoat! Pussy! I felt myself blush. I couldn't tolerate it. I couldn't endure the mockery, or the disgrace, or the patriotic ridicule. Even in my imagination, the shore just twenty yards away, I couldn't make myself be brave. It had nothing to do with morality. Embarrassment, that's all it was.

And right then I submitted.

I would go to the war—I would kill and maybe die—because I was embarrassed not to. . . .

Around noon, when I took my suitcase out to the car, I noticed that his old black pickup truck was no longer parked in front of the house. I went inside and waited for a while, but I felt a bone certainty that he wouldn't be back. In a way, I thought, it was appropriate. I washed up the breakfast dishes, left his two hundred dollars on the kitchen counter, got into the car, and drove south toward home.

The day was cloudy. I passed through towns with familiar names, through the pine forests and down to the prairie, and then to Vietnam, where I was a soldier, and then home again. I survived, but it's not a happy ending. I was a coward. I went to the war.

RICHARD M. NIXON

REMARKS UPON RETURNING FROM THE PEOPLE'S REPUBLIC OF CHINA

FEBRUARY 28, 1972

As a congressman and senator from California during the 1940s and early '50s, Richard M. Nixon (1913–1994) achieved widespread recognition for his vigorous battle against communism at home and abroad. He was elected to the vice presidency in 1952 and 1956 on the Republican ticket with Dwight D. Eisenhower. Defeated by John F. Kennedy in the presidential election of 1960, Nixon retired to the practice of law until he returned to politics and was elected president in 1968 and again by a landslide in 1972. Nixon campaigned on a promise to end the Vietnam War, which he did in 1973 after a controversial extension of the war into Laos and Cambodia. In 1972, Nixon became the first American president to visit the People's Republic of China, and began the normalization of diplomatic relations. These remarks were delivered upon his return from that historic visit, which he described as "the week that changed the world." Nixon also worked to reduce cold war tension with the Soviet Union, initiating strategic arms limitation talks in 1969.

At home, Nixon's presidency was dominated by the Watergate scandal. On August 9, 1974, he resigned in disgrace after the release of tape recordings of his conversations confirmed his role in the cover-up of illegal activity. He was the first president to do so.

Remarks of the President at Andrews Air Force Base.

. . . I want to express my very deep appreciation, and the appreciation of all of us, for this wonderfully warm welcome that you have given us and for the support that we have had on the trip that we have just completed from Americans of both political parties and all walks of life across this land.

Because of the superb efforts of the hardworking members of the press who accompanied us—they got even less sleep than I did—millions of Americans in this past week have seen more of China than I did. Consequently, tonight I would like to talk to you not about what we saw but about what we did, to sum up the results of the trip and to put it in perspective.

When I announced this trip last July, I described it as a journey for peace. In the last 30 years, Americans have in three different wars gone off by the hundreds of thousands to fight, and some to die, in Asia and in the Pacific. One of the central motives behind my journey to China was to prevent that from happening a fourth time to another generation of Americans.

As I have often said, peace means more than the mere absence of war. In a technical sense, we were at peace with the People's Republic of China before this trip, but a gulf of almost 12,000 miles and 22 years of noncommunication and hostility separated the United States of America from the 750 million people who live in the People's Republic of China, and that is one-fourth of all the people in the world.

As a result of this trip, we have started the long process of building a bridge across that gulf, and even now we have something better than the mere absence of war. Not only have we completed a week of intensive talks at the highest levels, we have set up a procedure whereby we can continue to have discussions in the future. We have demonstrated that nations with very deep and fundamental differences can learn to discuss those differences calmly, rationally, and frankly, without compromising their principles. This is the basis of a structure for peace, where we can talk about differences rather than fight about them.

The primary goal of this trip was to reestablish communication with the People's Republic of China after a generation of hostility. We achieved that goal. Let me turn now to our joint communiqué.

We did not bring back any written or unwritten agreements that will guarantee peace in our time. We did not bring home any magic formula which will make unnecessary the efforts of the American people to continue to maintain the strength so that we can continue to be free.

We made some necessary and important beginnings, however, in several areas. We entered into agreements to expand cultural, educational, and journalistic contacts between the Chinese and the American people. We agreed to work to begin and broaden trade between our two countries. We have agreed that the communications that have now been established between our governments will be strengthened and expanded.

Most important, we have agreed on some rules of international conduct which will reduce the risk of confrontation and war in Asia and in the Pacific.

We agreed that we are opposed to domination of the Pacific area by any one power. We agreed that international disputes should be settled without the use of the threat of force and we agreed that we are prepared to apply this principle to our mutual relations.

With respect to Taiwan, we stated our established policy that our forces overseas will be reduced gradually as tensions ease, and that our ultimate objective is to withdraw our forces as a peaceful settlement is achieved.

We have agreed that we will not negotiate the fate of other nations behind their backs, and we did not do so at Peking. There were no secret deals of any kind. We have done all this without giving up any United States commitment to any other country.

In our talks, the talks that I had with the leaders of the People's Republic and that the Secretary of State had with the office of the Government of the People's Republic in the foreign affairs area, we both realized that a bridge of understanding that spans almost 12,000 miles and 22 years of hostility can't be built in one week of discussions. But we have agreed to begin to build that bridge, recognizing that our work will require years of patient effort. We made no attempt to pretend that major differences did not exist between our two governments, because they do exist.

This communiqué was unique in honestly setting forth differences rather than trying to cover them up with diplomatic doubletalk.

One of the gifts that we left behind in Hangchow was a planted sapling of the American redwood tree. As all Californians know, and as most Americans know, redwoods grow from saplings into the giants of the forest. But the process is not one of days or even years; it is a process of centuries.

Just as we hope that those saplings, these tiny saplings that we left in China, will grow one day into mighty redwoods, so we hope, too, that the seeds planted on this journey for peace will grow and prosper into a more enduring structure for peace and security in the Western Pacific.

But peace is too urgent to wait for centuries. We must seize the moment to move toward that goal now, and this is what we have done on this journey.

As I am sure you realize, it was a great experience for us to see the timeless wonders of ancient China, the changes that are being made in modern China. And one fact stands out, among many others, from my talks with the Chinese leaders. It is their total belief, their total dedication, to their system of government. That is their right, just as it is the right of any country to choose the kind of government it wants.

But as I return from this trip, just as has been the case on my return from other trips abroad which have taken me to over 80 countries, I come back to America with an even stronger faith in our system of government.

As I flew across America today, all the way from Alaska, over the Rockies, the Plains, and then on to Washington, I thought of the greatness of our country and, most of all, I thought of the freedom, the opportunity, the progress that 200 million Americans are privileged to enjoy. I realized again this is a beautiful country. And tonight my prayer and my hope is that as a result of this trip, our children will have a better chance to grow up in a peaceful world.

WILLIAM JEFFERSON CLINTON

REMARKS AT MICHIGAN STATE UNIVERSITY

MAY 5, 1995

After the first bombing of the World Trade Center on February 26, 1993, the tragic bombing of a federal office building in Oklahoma City in April of 1995, and the attacks on U.S. embassies in Africa in 1998, terrorism took hold of the American consciousness. President Clinton addressed the issue of domestic terrorism and condemned violence as a means of political change in this powerful speech.

. . . And so, my fellow Americans, it falls to your generation to make your historic choices for America. This is a very new and different time. But the basic question before us is as old as our country: Will we face up to the problems and seize our opportunities with confidence and courage?. . .

In this, the 20th century, millions of lives were lost in wars between nations, and in efforts by totalitarian dictatorships to stamp out the light of liberty among their subjects. In the 21st century, bloody wars of ethnic and tribal hatred will be fought still in some parts of the world. But with freedom and democracy advancing, the real threat to our security will be rooted in the fact that all the forces that are lifting us up and opening unparalleled opportunity for us contain a dark underside. For open societies are characterized by free and rapid movements of people and technology and information. And that very wonder makes them very, very vulnerable to the forces of organized destruction and evil. So the great security challenge for your future in the 21st century will be to determine how to beat back the dangers while keeping the benefits of this new time.

The dark possibilities of our age are visible now in the smoke, the horror and the heartbreak of Oklahoma City. As the long and painful search and rescue effort comes to an end with 165 dead, 467 injured, and two still unaccounted for, our prayers are with those who lost their loved ones, and with the brave and good people of Oklahoma City, who have moved with such strength and character to deal with this tragedy.

But that threat is not isolated. And you must not believe it is. We see that threat again in the bombing of the World Trade Center in New York; in the nerve gas attack in the Tokyo subway; in the terrorist assault on innocent civilians in the Middle East; in the organized crime plaguing the former Soviet Union now that the heavy hand of communism has been lifted. We see it even on the Internet, where people exchange information about bombs and terrorism, even as children learn from sources all around the world.

My fellow Americans, we must respond to this threat in ways that preserve both our security and our freedom. Appeasement of organized evil is not an option for the next century any more than it was in this century. Like the vigilant generations that brought us victory in World War II and the Cold War, we must stand our ground. In this high-tech world, we must make sure that we have the high-tech tools to confront the high-tech forces of destruction and evil. . . .

We can do this without undermining our constitutional rights. In fact, the failure to act will undermine those rights. For no one is free in America where parents have to worry when they drop off their children for day care, or when you are the target of assassination simply because you work for our government. No one is free in America when large numbers of our fellow citizens must always be looking over their shoulders.

It is with this in mind that I would like to say something to the paramilitary groups and to others who believe the greatest threat to America comes not from terrorists from within our country or beyond our borders, but from our own government.

I want to say this to the militias and to others who believe this, to those nearby and those far away: I am well aware that most of you have never violated the law of the land. I welcome the comments that some of you have made recently condemning the bombing in Oklahoma City. I believe you have every right, indeed you have the responsibility, to question our government when you disagree with its policies. And I will do everything in my power to protect your right to do so. . . .

So I ask you to hear me now. It is one thing to believe that the federal government has too much power and to work within the law to reduce it. It is quite another to break the law of the land and threaten to shoot officers of the law if all they do is their duty to uphold it.

It is one thing to believe we are taxed too much and work to reduce the tax burden. It is quite another to refuse to pay your taxes, though your neighbor pays his. It is one thing to believe we are over-regulated and to work to lessen the burden of regulation. It is quite another to slander our dedicated public servants, our brave police officers, even our rescue workers who have been called a hostile army of occupation.

This is a very free country. Those of you in the militia movements have broader rights here than you would in any other country in the entire world.

Do people who work for the government sometimes make mistakes? Of course they do. They are human. Almost every American has some experience with this—a rude tax collector, an arbitrary regulator, an insensitive social worker, an abusive law officer. As long as human beings make up our government there will be mistakes. But our Constitution was established by Americans determined to limit those abuses. And think of the limits—the Bill of Rights, the separation of powers, access to the courts, the right to take your case to the country through the media, and the right to vote people in or out of office on a regular basis.

But there is no right to resort to violence when you don't get your way. There is no right to kill people. There is no right to kill people who are doing their duty, or minding their own business, or children who are innocent in every way. Those are the people who perished in Oklahoma City. And those who claim such rights are wrong and un-American.

Whenever in our history people have believed that violence is a legitimate extension of politics they have been wrong. . . .

Freedom of political speech will never justify violence—never. Our founding fathers created a system of laws in which reason could prevail over fear. Without respect for this law there is no freedom.

So I say this to the militias and all others who believe that the greatest threat to freedom comes from the government instead of from those who would take away our freedom: If you say violence is an acceptable way to make change, you are wrong. If you say that government is in a conspiracy to take your freedom away, you are just plain wrong.

If you treat law enforcement officers who put their lives on the line for your safety every day like some kind of enemy army to be suspected, derided and, if they should enforce the law against you, to be shot, you are wrong. If you appropriate our sacred symbols for paranoid purposes and compare yourselves to colonial militias who fought for the democracy you now rail against, you are wrong.

How dare you suggest that we in the freest nation on Earth live in tyranny. How dare you call yourselves patriots and heroes.

I say to you, there is nothing patriotic about hating your country, or pretending that you can love your country but despise your government. There is nothing heroic about turning your back on America, or ignoring your own responsibilities. If you want to preserve your own freedom, you must stand up for the freedom of others with whom you disagree. But you also must stand up for the rule of law. You cannot have one without the other.

The real American heroes today are the citizens who get up every morning and have the courage to work hard and play by the rules—the mother who stays up the extra half hour after a long day's work to read her child a story; the rescue worker who digs with his hands in the rubble as the building crumbles about him; the neighbor who lives side-by-side with people different from himself; the government worker who quietly and efficiently labors to see to it that the programs we depend on are honestly and properly carried out; most of all, the parent who works long years for modest pay and sacrifices so that his or her children can have the education that you have had, and the chances you are going to have. I ask you never to forget that.

ADDRESS ON TERRORISM BEFORE
A JOINT MEETING OF CONGRESS

SEPTEMBER 20, 2001

George W. Bush (1946–), son of President George Bush, grew up in Texas and attended Yale University. He pursued a career in the oil business and owned a baseball team, but ultimately he switched to politics as his father had done before him. He was elected governor of Texas in 1992 and 1996. In the presidential election of 2000, although he lost the popular vote, he defeated Al Gore, becoming president in January 2001. Eight months later, he faced the all-consuming crisis of September 11 when terrorists destroyed the World Trade Center and attacked the Pentagon, resulting in the loss of over 3,000 lives.

Mr. Speaker, Mr. President pro tem, members of Congress and fellow Americans: In the normal course of events, presidents come to this chamber to report on the state of the union. Tonight, no such report is needed. It has already been delivered by the American people.

We have seen it in the courage of passengers who rushed terrorists to save others on the ground. . . .

We have seen the state of our union in the endurance of rescuers working past exhaustion. We've seen the unfurling of flags, the lighting of candles, the giving of blood, the saying of prayers in English, Hebrew and Arabic. We have seen the decency of a loving and giving people who have made the grief of strangers their own.

My fellow citizens, for the last nine days, the entire world has seen for itself the state of our union, and it is strong. . . .

America will never forget the sounds of our national anthem playing at Buckingham Palace, on the streets of Paris and at Berlin's Brandenburg Gate. We will not forget South Korean children gathering to pray outside our embassy in Seoul or the prayers of sympathy offered at a mosque in Cairo. We will not forget moments of silence and days of mourning in Australia and Africa and Latin America.

Nor will we forget the citizens of 80 other nations who died with our own: dozens of Pakistanis, more than 130 Israelis, more than 250 citizens of India, men and women from El Salvador, Iran, Mexico and Japan, and hundreds of British citizens. . . .

On Sept. 11, enemies of freedom committed an act of war against our country. Americans have known wars. But for the past 136 years they have been wars on foreign soil, except for one Sunday in 1941. Americans have known the casualties of war. But not at the center of a great city on a peaceful morning. Americans have known surprise attacks. But never before on thousands of civilians. All of this was brought upon us in a single day. And night fell on a different world, a world where freedom itself is under attack.

Americans have many questions tonight. Americans are asking, "Who attacked our country?"

The evidence we have gathered all points to a collection of loosely affiliated terrorist organizations known as Al Qaeda. They are some of the murderers indicted for bombing American Embassies in Tanzania and Kenya, and responsible for bombing the U.S.S. *Cole.*

Al Qaeda is to terror what the Mafia is to crime. But its goal is not making money; its goal is remaking the world and imposing its radical beliefs on people everywhere.

The terrorists practice a fringe form of Islamic extremism that has been rejected by Muslim scholars and the vast majority of Muslim clerics. A fringe movement that perverts the peaceful teaching of Islam. The terrorists' directive commands them to kill Christians and Jews, to kill all Americans and make no distinctions among military and civilians, including women and children. This group and its leader, a person named Osama bin Laden, are linked to many other organizations in different countries, including the Egyptian Islamic Jihad and the Islamic Movement of Uzbekistan.

There are thousands of these terrorists in more than 60 countries. They are recruited from their own nations and neighborhoods and brought to camps in places like Afghanistan, where they are trained in the tactics of terror. They are sent back to their homes or sent to hide in countries around the world to plot evil and destruction. The leadership of Al Qaeda has great influence in Afghanistan and supports the Taliban regime in controlling most of that country.

In Afghanistan we see Al Qaeda's vision for the world. Afghanistan's people have been brutalized. Many are starving and many have fled. Women are not allowed to attend school. You can be jailed for owning a television. Religion can be practiced only as their leaders dictate. A man can be jailed in Afghanistan if his beard is not long enough.

The United States respects the people of Afghanistan. After all, we are currently its largest source of humanitarian aid. But we condemn the Taliban regime. It is not only repressing its own people; it is threatening people everywhere by sponsoring and sheltering and supplying terrorists. By aiding and abetting murder, the Taliban regime is committing murder.

And tonight the United States of America makes the following demands on the Taliban:

- Deliver to United States authorities all the leaders of Al Qaeda who hide in your land.
- Release all foreign nationals, including American citizens, you have unjustly imprisoned.
- Protect foreign journalists, diplomats and aid workers in your country.
- Close immediately and permanently every terrorist training camp in Afghanistan and hand over every terrorist and every person in their support structure to appropriate authorities.
- Give the United States full access to terrorist training camps so we can make sure they are no longer operating.

These demands are not open to negotiation or discussion. The Taliban must act and act immediately. They will hand over the terrorists or they will share in their fate.

I also want to speak tonight directly to Muslims throughout the world. We respect your faith. It's practiced freely by many millions of Americans and by millions more in countries that America counts as friends. Its teachings are good and peaceful. And those who commit evil in the name of Allah blaspheme the name of Allah. The terrorists are traitors to their own faith, trying in effect to hijack Islam itself.

The enemy of America is not our many Muslim friends. It is not our many Arab friends. Our enemy is a radical network of terrorists and every government that supports them.

Our war on terror begins with Al Qaeda, but it does not end there. It will not end until every terrorist group of global reach has been found, stopped and defeated.

Americans are asking, "Why do they hate us?"

They hate what they see right here in this chamber, a democratically elected government. Their leaders are self-appointed. They hate our freedoms, our freedom of religion, our freedom of speech, our freedom to vote and assemble and disagree with each other. They want to overthrow existing governments in many Muslim countries, such as Egypt, Saudi Arabia and Jordan. They want to drive Israel out of the Middle East. They want to drive Christians and Jews out of vast regions of Asia and Africa.

These terrorists kill not merely to end lives but to disrupt and end a way of life. With every atrocity they hope that America grows fearful, retreating from the world and forsaking our friends. They stand against us because we stand in their way. We're not deceived by their pretenses to piety. We have seen their kind before. They are the heirs of all the murderous ideologies of the 20th century. By sacrificing human life to serve their radical visions, by abandoning every value except the will to power, they follow in the path of fascism, Nazism and totalitarianism. And they will follow that path all the way to where it ends in history's unmarked grave of discarded lies.

Americans are asking, "How will we fight and win this war?"

We will direct every resource at our command—every means of diplomacy, every tool of intelligence, every instrument of law enforcement, every financial influence and every necessary weapon of war—to the disruption and to the defeat of the global terror network. . . .

Americans should not expect one battle, but a lengthy campaign unlike any other we have ever seen. It may include dramatic strikes visible on TV and covert operations, secret even in success.

We will starve terrorists of funding, turn them one against another, drive them from place to place until there is no refuge or no rest. And we will pursue nations that provide aid or safe haven to terrorism.

Every nation in every region now has a decision to make. Either you are with us or you are with the terrorists.

From this day forward, any nation that continues to harbor or support terrorism will be regarded by the United States as a hostile regime.

Our nation has been put on notice: We're not immune from attack.

We will take defensive measures against terrorism to protect Americans. Today dozens of federal departments and agencies as well as state and local governments have responsibilities affecting homeland security. These efforts must be coordinated at the highest level.

So tonight I announce the creation of a cabinet-level position reporting directly to me, the Office of Homeland Security. . . .

And tonight a few miles from the damaged Pentagon, I have a message for our military: be ready. I've called the armed forces to alert and there is a reason. The hour is coming when America will act and you will make us proud.

This is not, however, just America's fight. And what is at stake is not just America's freedom. This is the world's fight, this is civilization's fight, this is the fight of all who believe in progress and pluralism, tolerance and freedom.

We ask every nation to join us. We will ask and we will need the help of police forces, intelligence service and banking systems around the world.

The United States is grateful that many nations and many international organizations have already responded with sympathy and with support. Nations from Latin America to Asia to Africa to Europe to the Islamic world.

LARRY TOWELL, World Trade Center, New York, September 11, 2001.

Perhaps the NATO charter reflects best the attitude of the world: an attack on one is an attack on all.

The civilized world is rallying to America's side. They understand that if this terror goes unpunished, their own cities, their own citizens, may be next. Terror unanswered can not only bring down buildings, it can threaten the stability of legitimate governments. And you know what? We're not going to allow it.

Americans are asking, "What is expected of us?"

I ask you to live your lives and hug your children. I know many citizens have fears tonight and I ask you to be calm and resolute, even in the face of a continuing threat. I ask you to uphold the values of America and remember why so many have come here.

We're in a fight for our principles and our first responsibility is to live by them. No one should be singled out for unfair treatment or unkind words because of their ethnic background or religious faith.

I ask you to continue to support the victims of this tragedy with your contributions. . . . The thousands of F.B.I. agents who are now at work in this investigation may need your cooperation. And I ask you to give it. I ask for your patience with the delays and inconveniences that may accompany tighter security. And for your patience in what will be a long struggle.

I ask your continued participation and confidence in the American economy. Terrorists attacked a symbol of American prosperity. They did not touch its source. America is successful because of the hard work and creativity and enterprise of our people. These were the true strengths of our economy before Sept. 11 and they are our strengths today.

And finally, please continue praying for the victims of terror and their families, for those in uniform and for our great country. Prayer has comforted us in sorrow and will help strengthen us for the journey ahead. . . .

After all that has just passed, all the lives taken and all the possibilities and hopes that died with them, it is natural to wonder if America's future is one of fear. Some speak of an age of terror. I know there are struggles ahead and dangers to face.

But this country will define our times, not be defined by them. As long as the United States of America is determined and strong, this will not be an age of terror. This will be an age of liberty here and across the world.

Great harm has been done to us. We have suffered great loss. And in our grief and anger, we have found our mission and our moment. Freedom and fear are at war. The advance of human freedom, the great achievement of our time and the great hope of every time, now depends on us. . . .

JIMMY CARTER

ADDRESS UPON RECEIVING THE NOBEL PRIZE

DECEMBER 10, 2002

James Earl Carter Jr. (1924–) was born and raised in Plains, Georgia, and later attended the U.S. Naval Academy while continuing to work on his family's peanut farm. He was elected governor of Georgia in 1970 and president in 1976. During his presidency he was instrumental in passage of the 1977 Panama Canal treaties, which transferred control of the canal back to Panama, and the signing of the Camp David Peace Accords between Egypt and Israel in 1978. Since leaving the presidency in 1981, Carter has been a tireless advocate of human rights, world peace, and humanitarian causes. In 1999, he was awarded the Presidential Medal of Freedom, and in 2002 he received the Nobel Peace Prize.

. . . The world has changed greatly since I left the White House. Now there is only one superpower, with unprecedented military and economic strength. The coming budget for American armaments will be greater than those of the next fifteen nations combined, and there are troops from the United States in many countries throughout the world. Our gross national economy exceeds that of the three countries that follow us, and our nation's voice most often prevails as decisions are made concerning trade, humanitarian assistance, and the allocation of global wealth. This dominant status is unlikely to change in our lifetimes.

Great American power and responsibility are not unprecedented, and have been used with restraint and great benefit in the past. We have not assumed that super strength guarantees super wisdom, and we have consistently reached out to the international community to ensure that our own power and influence are tempered by the best common judgment.

Within our country, ultimate decisions are made through democratic means, which tend to moderate radical or ill-advised proposals. Constrained and inspired by historic constitutional principles, our nation has endeavored for more than two hundred years to follow the now almost universal ideals of freedom, human rights, and justice for all. . . .

But instead of entering a millennium of peace, the world is now, in many ways, a more dangerous place. The greater ease of travel and communication has not been matched by equal understanding and mutual respect. There is a plethora of civil wars, unrestrained by rules of the Geneva Convention, within which an overwhelming portion of the casualties are unarmed civilians who have no ability to defend themselves. And recent appalling acts of terrorism have reminded us that no nations, even superpowers, are invulnerable.

It is clear that global challenges must be met with an emphasis on peace, in harmony with others, with strong alliances and international consensus. Imperfect as it may be, there is no doubt that this can best be done through the United Nations, which Ralph Bunche described here in this same forum as exhibiting a "fortunate flexibility"—not merely to preserve peace but also to make change, even radical change, without violence.

He went on to say: "To suggest that war can prevent war is a base play on words and a despicable form of warmongering. The objective of any who sincerely believe in peace clearly must be to exhaust every honorable recourse in the effort to save the peace. The world has had ample evidence that war begets only conditions that beget further war."

We must remember that today there are at least eight nuclear powers on earth, and three of them are threatening to their neighbors in areas of great international tension. For powerful countries to adopt a principle of preventive war may well set an example that can have catastrophic consequences.

If we accept the premise that the United Nations is the best avenue for the maintenance of peace, then the carefully considered decisions of the United Nations Security Council must be enforced. All too often, the alternative has proven to be uncontrollable violence and expanding spheres of hostility. . . .

I thought often during my years in the White House of an admonition that we received in our small school in Plains, Georgia, from a beloved teacher, Miss Julia Coleman. She often said: "We must adjust to changing times and still hold to unchanging principles."

When I was a young boy, this same teacher also introduced me to Leo Tolstoy's novel *War and Peace*. She interpreted that powerful narrative as a reminder that the simple human attributes of goodness and truth can overcome great power. She also taught us that an individual is not swept along on a tide of inevitability but can influence even the greatest human events. . . .

I am not here as a public official, but as a citizen of a troubled world who finds hope in a growing consensus that the generally accepted goals of society are peace, freedom, human rights, environmental quality, the alleviation of suffering, and the rule of law.

During the past decades, the international community, usually under the auspices of the United Nations, has struggled to negotiate global standards that can help us achieve these essential goals. They include: the abolition of land mines and chemical weapons; an end to the testing, proliferation, and further deployment of nuclear warheads; constraints on global warming; prohibition of the death penalty, at least for children; and an international criminal court to deter and to punish war crimes and genocide. Those agreements already adopted must be fully implemented, and others should be pursued aggressively.

We must also strive to correct the injustice of economic sanctions that seek to penalize abusive leaders but all too often inflict punishment on those who are already suffering from the abuse.

The unchanging principles of life predate modern times. I worship Jesus Christ, whom we Christians consider to be the Prince of Peace. As a Jew, he taught us to cross religious boundaries, in service and in love. He repeatedly reached out and embraced Roman conquerors, other Gentiles, and even the more despised Samaritans.

Despite theological differences, all great religions share common commitments that define our ideal secular relationships. I am convinced that Christians, Muslims, Buddhists, Hindus, Jews, and others can embrace each other in a common effort to alleviate human suffering and to espouse peace.

But the present era is a challenging and disturbing time for those who lives are shaped by religious faith based on kindness toward each other. We have been reminded that cruel and inhuman acts can be derived from distorted theological beliefs, as suicide bombers take the lives of innocent human beings, draped falsely in the cloak of God's will. With horrible brutality, neighbors have massacred neighbors in Europe, Asia, and Africa.

In order for us human beings to commit ourselves personally to the inhumanity of war, we find it necessary first to dehumanize our opponents, which is itself a violation of the beliefs of all religions. Once we characterize our adversaries as beyond the scope of God's mercy and grace, their lives lose all value. We deny personal responsibility when we plant landmines and, days or years later, a stranger to us—often a child—is crippled or killed. From a great distance, we launch bombs or missiles with almost total impunity, and never want to know the number or identity of the victims.

At the beginning of this new millennium I was asked to discuss, here in Oslo, the greatest challenge that the world faces. Among all the possible choices, I decided that the most serious and universal problem is the growing chasm between the richest and poorest people on earth. Citizens of the ten wealthiest countries are now seventy-five times richer than those who live in the ten poorest ones, and the separation is increasing every year, not only between nations but also within them. The results of this disparity are root causes of most of the world's unresolved problems, including starvation, illiteracy, environmental degradation, violent conflict, and unnecessary illnesses that range from Guinea worm to HIV/AIDS. . . .

Most work of The Carter Center is in remote villages in the poorest nations of

Africa, and there I have witnessed the capacity of destitute people to persevere under heartbreaking conditions. I have come to admire their judgment and wisdom, their courage and faith, and their awesome accomplishments when given a chance to use their innate abilities.

But tragically, in the industrialized world there is a terrible absence of understanding or concern about those who are enduring lives of despair and hopelessness. We have not yet made the commitment to share with others an appreciable part of our excessive wealth. This is a potentially rewarding burden that we should all be willing to assume.

. . . War may sometimes be a necessary evil. But no matter how necessary, it is always an evil, never a good. We will not learn how to live together in peace by killing each other's children.

The bond of our common humanity is stronger than the divisiveness of our fears and prejudices. God gives us the capacity for choice. We can choose to alleviate suffering. We can choose to work together for peace. We can make these changes— and we must.

WORK, OPPORTUNITY, AND INVENTION

ERNIE SISTO,
The Whitestone Bridge,
New York, 1953.

THE POLITICAL IDEALS of America have been supported by the economic miracle of the American dream. Other than the Native Americans, all those dreamers have come to America from other parts of the world. Some were brought against their will as slaves, others came seeking political or religious freedom, or fleeing poverty, hardship, and persecution in their countries of origin. The life they found here wasn't easy, yet for most it was better than what they had left behind. Whether they came in chains or in steerage, there was no turning back.

When they arrived, they went to work. Most immigrants were too poor to travel farther, settling near or in the cities where they landed and doing whatever they could to eke out a living. Some, like the Scandinavians and Germans, sought agricultural work similar to what they had done at home. The Irish worked on the docks, digging canals, and in the mills of the early Industrial Revolution; the Italians were masons, miners, and shopkeepers; Jewish immigrants found jobs for each other in sweatshops; and the Chinese built railroads. Today's immigrants work our farms, clean office buildings, and struggle just as their predecessors did.

Many immigrants passed by the Statue of Liberty, inscribed with Emma Lazarus's immortal poem, "Give me your tired, your poor, your huddled masses yearning to breathe free." Like 60 percent of all Americans, my children are descended from someone who came through Ellis Island. Strangers to each other, my husband's grandparents all fled neighboring Russian villages to escape the Czarist pogroms, traveled to Montana, and lived in Virginia before settling in New York, where his parents met working in the same office.

Although we celebrate our heritage as a nation of immigrants, each group faced hostility from those that preceded it, and often organized political resistance. The Know-Nothing Party was founded to incite anti-immigrant, anti-Catholic fears, the Ku Klux Klan terrorized immigrants as well as African Americans. In my own family, anti-Irish discrimination was not a thing of the past but a real and painful fact of life. My grandmother spoke often of the "No Irish Need Apply" signs that were part of her youth. My grandfather achieved financial success only after moving his family to New York in search of opportunity.

One of the central characters in the immigrant experience is the public school-teacher. In immigrant chronicles like *Barrio Boy* by Ernesto Galarza, these women became the symbol of America's welcoming arms. They taught citizenship and civic education, they taught English and how not to be afraid. This is as true today as it has been in the past. For example, the New York City public school system educates 1.1 million children who speak more than 140 different languages at home. They will follow the same process of becoming an American as have millions before them.

Some of the selections give a flavor of the immigrant experience, its hardship and hope, as experienced by people of different ethnic groups and generations. We hear the voices of those who have just arrived in America, like Manny Steen, an Irish immigrant who describes his first day in New York, and others, like Mario Puzo, who writes of his childhood in the Italian immigrant community of Hell's Kitchen.

America's success has been built on invention, the desire for wealth, and the ability to seize opportunity. This section includes the voices of American innovators: Thomas Edison, Wilbur Wright, Henry Ford, and Bill Gates. We also hear from a few who put it in perspective, from Andy Warhol to Arnold Schwarzenegger.

We also read testimony from those who work the land, whose ancient and natural way of life is disappearing, such as the heartbreaking dialogue between the members of the Ute tribe and the federal representative sent to explain the breakup of their reservation. John Steinbeck writes of migrant life, FDR speaks of hope during the Great Depression, Cesar Chavez empowers his people, and Robert Kennedy questions the rewards of materialism. Whether in times of sacrifice or success, we see the enduring power of the American dream, so strong that even a homeless child believes that he has a chance to grow up to be president.

EMMA LAZARUS

THE NEW COLOSSUS

1883

On October 28, 1886, the Statue of Liberty, a work of French sculptor Frédéric Auguste Bartholdi with structural help from Gustave Eiffel, was dedicated by President Grover Cleveland at Bedloe's Island in New York Harbor. Thousands filled the city streets celebrating the event. Standing 151 feet high, the statue was a gift from the people of France in celebration of the ideal of liberty. Three years earlier, as part of the effort to raise funds for the statue's 154-foot pedestal and foundation, Emma Lazarus (1849–1887) wrote a poem celebrating the statue's symbolism for immigrants seeking a new life in America. In 1903, the poem was inscribed on a memorial plaque in her honor on the pedestal she had helped make possible.

Not like the brazen giant of Greek fame,
With conquering limbs astride from land to land;
Here at our sea-washed, sunset gates shall stand
A mighty woman with a torch, whose flame
Is the imprisoned lightning, and her name
Mother of Exiles. From her beacon-hand
Glows world-wide welcome; her mild eyes command
The air-bridged harbor that twin cities frame.
"Keep, ancient lands, your storied pomp!" cries she
With silent lips. "Give me your tired, your poor,
Your huddled masses yearning to breathe free,
The wretched refuse of your teeming shore.
Send these, the homeless, tempest-tost to me,
I lift my lamp beside the golden door!"

HUANG ZUNXIAN

EXPULSION OF THE IMMIGRANTS

C. 1884

In the two decades following the discovery of gold in California in 1848, more than 125,000 Chinese immigrants made their way to America. By the late 1870s resentment among previously settled workers who were competing against the influx of "cheap" Chinese labor erupted into riots in the San Francisco area. In response, the federal government enacted the Chinese Exclusion Act in 1882, suspending Chinese immigration for ten years. Twenty years later, with anti-Chinese sentiment still running high, the prohibition was renewed. Stunned and hurt by the backlash, Chinese poet and diplomat Huang Zunxian (1848–1905) responded.

Alas! What crime have our people committed,

That they suffer this calamity in our nation's fortunes?

Five thousand years since the Yellow Emperor,

Our country today is exceedingly weak.

Demons and ghouls are hard to fathom;

Even worse than the woodland and monsters.

Who can say our fellow men have not met an inhuman fate,

In the end oppressed by another race?

Within the vastness of the six directions,

Where can our people find asylum?

When the Chinese first crossed the ocean,

They were the same as pioneers.

They lived in straw hovels, cramped as snail shells;

For protection gradually built bamboo fences.

Dressed in tatters, they cleared mountain forests;

Wilderness and waste turned into towns and villages.

Mountains of gold towered on high,

Which men could grab with their hands left and right.

Eureka! They return with a load full of gold,

All bragging this land is paradise.

They beckon and beg their families to come;

Legs in the rear file behind legs in the front.

Wearing short coats, they braid their queues;

Men carry bamboo rainhats, wear straw sandals.

Bartenders lead along cooks;
Some hold tailors' needles, others workmen's axes.
They clap with excitement, traveling overseas;
Everyone surnamed Wong creates confusion. . . .

Gradually the natives turned jealous.
Time to time spreading false rumors,
They say these Chinese paupers
Only wish to fill their money bags.
Soon as their feet touch the ground,
All the gold leaps out of the earth.
They hang ten thousand cash on their waists,
And catch the next boat back to China.
Which of them is willing to loosen his queue,
And do some hard labor for us?
Some say the Chinese are shiftless; . . .
Others say the Chinese are a bunch of hoodlums,
By nature all filthy and unclean.
Their houses are as dirty as dogs';
Their food even worse than pigs'.
All they need is a dollar a day;
Who is as scrawny as they are?
If we allow this cheap labor of theirs,
Then all of us are finished.
We see our own brothers being injured;
Who can stand these venomous vermin? . . .

From now on they set up a strict ban,
Establishing customs posts everywhere.
They have sealed all the gates tightly,
Door after door with guards beating alarms.
Chinese who leave are like magpies circling a tree,
Those staying like swallows nesting on curtains. . . .

Those who do not carry passports
Are arrested as soon as they arrive.
Anyone with a yellow-colored face

Is beaten even if guiltless.
I sadly recollect George Washington,
Who had the makings of a great ruler.
He proclaimed that in America,
There is a broad land to the west of the desert.
All kinds of foreigners and immigrants,
Are allowed to settle in these new lands.
The yellow, white, red, and black races
Are all equal with our native people.
Not even a hundred years till today,
But they are not ashamed to eat his words. . . .
The land of the red man is vast and remote;
I know you are eager to settle and open it.
The American eagle strides the heavens soaring,
With half of the globe clutched in his claw.
Although the Chinese arrived later,
Couldn't you leave them a little space? . . .

Grave, dignified, I arrive with my dragon banners,
Knock on the custom's gate, hesitant, doubtful.
Even if we emptied the water of four oceans,
it would be hard to wash this shame clean. . . .

(translation by J. D. Schmidt)

I HEAR AMERICA SINGING

1891

This poem by Walt Whitman (1819–1892) is a celebration of the industry and spirit of the American worker. Born on Long Island, New York, to a carpenter father and a Quaker mother, Whitman had little formal schooling as a youth and was mostly self-educated, reading the classics of Homer and Shakespeare. One of America's greatest poets, Whitman also worked as a teacher, a journalist for newspapers in New York and New Orleans, and during the Civil War, tended to wounded soldiers on both sides of the conflict. Whitman's most celebrated poems include "When Lilacs Last in the Dooryard Bloom'd," "Song of Myself," and "I Hear America Singing," which was included in an edition of one of his greatest works, *Leaves of Grass*.

I hear America singing, the varied carols I hear:
Those of mechanics—each one singing his, as it should be,
    blithe and strong;
The carpenter singing his, as he measures his plank or beam,
The mason singing his, as he makes ready for work, or
    leaves off work;
The boatman singing what belongs to him in his boat—the
    deckhand singing on the steamboat deck;
The shoemaker singing as he sits on his bench—the hatter
    singing as he stands;
The wood cutter's song—the ploughboy's on his way in the
    morning, or at noon intermission, or at sundown;
The delicious singing of the mother—or of the young wife
    at work—or of the girl sewing or washing—
Each singing what belongs to him or her and to none else;
The day what belongs to the day—at night, the party of
    young fellows, robust, friendly,
Singing, with open mouths, their strong melodious songs.

ANDREW J. RUSSELL, Completion of the transcontinental railroad, Promontory, Utah, 1869.

I've Been Working on the Railroad

The exact origins of this old American favorite are unknown. Some say it evolved in the South from an old African American melody in Louisiana, while Irish immigrant workers in the American West claim it as their own. The construction of a transcontinental railroad dominated the American imagination in the mid–nineteenth century. It was completed on May 10, 1869, when 1,086 miles of track laid by the Union Pacific Railroad met 689 miles of track laid by the Central Pacific Railroad at Promontory Summit, Utah.

I've been working on the railroad,
All the live-long day,
I've been working on the railroad,
Just to pass the time away.
Don't you hear the whistle blowing,
Rise up so early in the morn;
Don't you hear the captain shouting,
"Dinah, blow your horn!"

Dinah, won't you blow,
Dinah, won't you blow,
Dinah, won't you blow your horn.
Dinah, won't you blow
Dinah, won't you blow.
Dinah, won't you blow your horn.
Someone's in the kitchen with Dinah,
Someone's in the kitchen I know,
Someone's in the kitchen with Dinah,
Strummin' on the old banjo, and singin':
Fee-fi-fidd-lee-i-o,
Fee-fi-fidd-lee-i-o,
Fee-fi-fidd-lee-i-o,
Strummin' on the old banjo.

WILBUR WRIGHT

LETTER TO OCTAVE CHANUTE

MAY 13, 1900

On December 17, 1903 the Wright Brothers, Wilbur (1867–1912) and Orville (1871–1948), made the first controlled sustained flight in a power-driven airplane. The brothers honed their mechanical skills in their Dayton, Ohio, bicycle shop, where they spent the winter months constructing and experimenting with gliders, a wind tunnel, propeller design, and an engine. They shipped their invention to North Carolina's Outer Banks in search of a steady wind. On the historic morning, they made four short flights—the longest of which was fifty-nine seconds.

For some years I have been afflicted with the belief that flight is possible to man. My disease has increased in severity and I feel that it will soon cost me an increased amount of money if not my life. I have been trying to arrange my affairs in such a way that I can devote my entire time for a few months to experiment in this field.

My general ideas of the subject are similar [to] those held by most practical experimenters, to wit: that what is chiefly needed is skill rather than machinery. The

JOHN T. DANIELS, First flight, Kitty Hawk, North Carolina, 1903.

flight of the buzzard and similar sailors is a convincing demonstration of the value of skill and the partial needlessness of motors.

It is possible to fly without motors, but not without knowledge and skill. This I conceive to be fortunate, for man, by reason of his greater intellect, can more reasonably hope to equal birds in knowledge than to equal nature in the perfection of her machinery. . . .

My observation of the flight of buzzards leads me to believe that they regain their lateral balance when partly overturned by a gust of wind, by a torsion of the tips of the wings. If the rear edge of the right wing tip is twisted upward and the left downward the bird becomes an animated windmill and instantly begins to turn, a line from its head to its tail being the axis. It thus regains its level even if thrown on its beam's end, so to speak, as I have frequently seen them. I think the bird also in general retains its lateral equilibrium, partly by presenting its two wings at different angles to the wind, and partly by drawing in one wing, thus reducing its area. I incline to the belief that the first is the more important and usual method. . . .

My business [the bicycle shop] requires that my experimental work be confined to the months between September and January and I would be particularly thankful for advice as to a suitable locality where I could depend on winds of about 15 miles per hour without rain or too inclement weather. I am certain that such localities are rare. . . .

LEWIS W. HINE, Young mill-worker, Lancaster, South Carolina, 1908.

SPEECH AT THE CONVENTION OF THE NATIONAL AMERICAN WOMAN SUFFRAGE ASSOCIATION

JULY 22, 1905

Florence Kelley (1859–1932) was the daughter of a Republican congressman from Pennsylvania who took her to visit the newly constructed steel factories that were transforming the American economy. While the adults marveled at the revolutionary Bessemer process, Florence noticed that although it was two o'clock in the morning, dozens of little boys were carrying water to the steelworkers. She later wrote that to the adults intent on this "industrial novelty," the child laborers "were no more important than so many grains of sand in the molds." Her early interest developed into a lifetime battle against the exploitation of women and child laborers.

To-night while we sleep, several thousand little girls will be working in textile mills, all the night through, in the deafening noise of the spindles and looms spinning and weaving cotton and woolen, silks and ribbons for us to buy. . . . If the mothers and the teachers in Georgia could vote, would the Georgia Legislature have refused at every session for the last three years to stop the work in the mills of children under twelve years of age? . . .

Until the mothers in the great industrial States are enfranchised, we shall none of us be able to free our consciences from participation in this great evil. No one in this room to-night can feel free from such participation. The children make our shoes in the shoe factories; they knit our stockings, our knitted underwear in the knitting factories. They spin and weave our cotton underwear in the cotton mills. Children braid straw for our hats, they spin and weave the silk and velvet wherewith we trim our hats. They stamp buckles and metal ornaments of all kinds, as well as pins and hat-pins. Under the sweating system, tiny children make artificial flowers and neckwear for us to buy. They carry bundles of garments from the factories to the tenements, little beasts of burden, robbed of school life that they may work for us.

We do not wish this. We prefer to have our work done by men and women. But we are almost powerless. Not wholly powerless, however, are citizens who enjoy the right of petition. For myself, I shall use this power in every possible way until the right to the ballot is granted, and then I shall continue to use both.

What can we do to free our consciences? There is one line of action by which we can do much. We can enlist the workingmen on behalf of our enfranchisement just in proportion as we strive with them to free the children. No labor organization in this country ever fails to respond to an appeal for help in the freeing of the children.

UPTON SINCLAIR

THE JUNGLE

1906

Upton Sinclair (1878–1968), a native of Baltimore, Maryland, advanced his socialist agenda in the more than eighty books he wrote during his career. In 1904, Sinclair began work on one of his greatest and most influential works, *The Jungle*, a novel about the appalling work conditions inside a Chicago meatpacking plant, hoping to arouse sympathy for the plight of exploited immigrant laborers. The book shocked both the public and the government, and spurred passage of the Pure Food and Drug Act (1906) and the Meat Inspection Act (1906). "I aimed at the public's heart," Sinclair later said of the book, "and by accident I hit it in the stomach." He ran unsuccessfully for governor of California in 1934. His antifascist novel about the rise of Hitler, *Dragon's Teeth*, won the Pulitzer Prize in 1943.

Poor Jurgis was now an outcast and a tramp once more. He was crippled—he was as literally crippled as any wild animal which has lost its claws, or been torn out of its shell. He had been shorn, at one cut, of all those mysterious weapons whereby he had been able to make a living easily and to escape the consequences of his actions. He could no longer command a job when he wanted it; he could no longer steal with impunity—he must take his chances with the common herd; Nay, worse, he dared not mingle with the herd; he must hide by himself, for he was one marked out for destruction. His old companions would betray him, for the sake of the influence they would gain thereby; and he would be made to suffer, not merely for the offence he had committed, but for others which would be laid at his door, just as had been done for some poor devil on the occasion of that assault upon the 'country customer' by him and Duane.

And also he laboured under another handicap now. He had acquired new standards of living, which were not easily to be altered. When he had been out of work before he had been content if he could sleep in a doorway or under a truck out of the rain, and if he could get fifteen cents a day for saloon lunches. But now he desired all sorts of other things, and suffered because he had to do without them. He must have a drink now and then—a drink for its own sake, and apart from the food that came with it. The craving for it was strong enough to master every other consideration—he would have it, though it were his last nickel and he had to starve the balance of the day in consequence.

Jurgis became once more a besieger of factory gates. But never since he had been in Chicago had he stood less chance of getting a job than just then. For one thing, there was the economic crisis, the million or two of men who had been out of work in the spring and summer, and were not yet all back, by any means. And then there was the strike, with seventy thousand men and women all over the country idle for a couple of months—twenty thousand in Chicago, and many of them now seeking work throughout the city. It did not remedy matters that a few days later the strike was given up and about half the strikers went back to work; for every one taken on, there was a 'scab' who gave up and fled. The ten or fifteen thousand 'green' negroes, foreigners, and criminals were now being turned loose to shift for themselves. Everywhere Jurgis went he kept meeting them, and he was in an agony of fear lest some one of them should know that he was 'wanted'. He would have left Chicago, only by the time he had realized his danger he was almost penniless; and it would be better to go to gaol than to be caught out in the country in the winter-time.

At the end of about ten days Jurgis had only a few pennies left; and he had not yet found a job—not even a day's work at anything, not a chance to carry a satchel. Once again, as when he had come out of the hospital, he was bound hand and foot, and facing the grisly phantom of starvation. Raw, naked terror possessed him, a maddening passion that would never leave him, and that wore him down more quickly than the actual want of food. He was going to die of hunger! The field reached out its scaly arms for him—it touched him, its breath came into his face; and he would cry out for the awfulness of it; he would wake up in the night, shuddering, and bathed in perspiration, and start up and flee. He would walk, begging for work, until he was exhausted; he could not remain still—he would wander on, gaunt and haggard, gazing about him with restless eyes. Everywhere he went, from one end of the vast city to the other, there were hundreds of others like him; everywhere was the sight of plenty—and the merciless hand of authority waving them away. There is one kind of prison where the man is behind bars, and everything that he desires is outside; and there is another kind where the things are behind the bars, and the man is outside.

ELLIS ISLAND

1907

Harvard-educated Bostonian Henry James (1843–1916), whose richly textured, psychologically complex masterpieces *Daisy Miller* (1879), *The Portrait of a Lady* (1881), *The Ambassadors* (1903), and *The Golden Bowl* (1904) chronicle the arrival of the late-nineteenth-century American in Europe, returned home in 1904 after a twenty-year absence to find that his native country had changed dramatically. He was fascinated by the flood of new immigrants pouring into America— nearly 1 million in the year he returned. James collected his thoughts and observations about the new America for his book *The American Scene*, in which this selection appeared.

. . . In the Bay, the rest of the morning, the dense raw fog that delayed the big boat, allowing sight but of the immediate ice-masses through which it thumped its way, was not less of the essence. Anything blander, as a medium, would have seemed a mockery of the facts of the terrible little Ellis Island, the first harbour of refuge and stage of patience for the million or so of immigrants annually knocking at our official door. Before this door, which opens to them there only with a hundred forms and ceremonies, grindings and grumblings of the key, they stand appealing and waiting, marshalled, herded, divided, subdivided, sorted, sifted, searched, fumigated, for longer or shorter periods—the effect of all which prodigious process, an intendedly "scientific" feeding of the mill, is again to give the earnest observer a thousand more things to think of than he can pretend to retail. The impression of Ellis Island, in fine, would be—as I was to find throughout that so many of my impressions would be—a chapter by itself; and with a particular page for recognition of the degree in which the liberal hospitality of the eminent Commissioner of this wonderful service, to whom I had been introduced, helped to make the interest of the whole watched drama poignant and unforgettable. It is a drama that goes on, without a pause, day by day and year by year, this visible set of ingurgitation on the part of our body politic and social, and constituting really an appeal to amazement beyond that of any sword-swallowing or fire-swallowing of the circus. The wonder that one couldn't keep down was the thought that these two or three hours of one's own chance vision of the business were but as a tick or two of the mighty clock, the clock that never, never stops— least of all when it strikes, for a sign of so much winding-up, some louder hour of our national fate than usual. I think indeed that the simplest account of the action of Ellis Island on the spirit of any sensitive citizen who may have happened to "look in" is that he comes back from his visit not at all the same person that he went. He has eaten of the tree of knowledge, and the taste will be for ever in his mouth. He had thought he knew before, thought he had the sense of the degree in which it is his American fate to share the sanctity of his American consciousness, the intimacy of his American patriotism, with the inconceivable alien; but the truth had never come home to him with any such force. In the lurid light projected upon it by those courts of dismay it shakes him—or I like at least to imagine it shakes him—to the depths of his being; I like to think of him, I positively *have* to think of him, as going about ever afterwards with a new look, for those who can see it, in his face, the outward sign of the new chill in his heart. So is stamped, for detection, the questionably privileged person who has had an apparition, seen a ghost in his supposedly safe old house. Let not the unwary, therefore, visit Ellis Island.

Inspection of immigrants,
Ellis Island, New York, 1920.

ERNESTO GALARZA

BARRIO BOY

1971

Educator, social activist, poet, and author Ernesto Galarza (1905–1984) devoted his life to education, working to improve the plight of disadvantaged farmworkers, and raising awareness of Mexican American heritage and culture. Perhaps his most important work was *Barrio Boy*, which chronicled the story of his family's journey to America in the wake of the 1910 Mexican Revolution. It is a tale of hope and inspiration, in which they struggled to retain their roots in a strange new world.

. . . These were the boundaries of the lower part of town, for that was what everyone called the section of the city between Fifth Street and the river and from the railway yards to the Y-street levee. Nobody ever mentioned an upper part of town; at least, no one could see the difference because the whole city was built on level land. We were not lower topographically, but in other ways that distinguished between Them, the uppers, and Us, the lowers. Lower Sacramento was the quarter that people who made money moved away from. Those of us who lived in it stayed there because our problem was to make a living and not to make money. . . .

In Tucson, when I had asked my mother again if the Americans were having a revolution, the answer was: "No, but they have good schools, and you are going to one of them." We were by now settled at 418 L Street and the time had come for me to exchange a revolution for an American education.

The two of us walked south on Fifth Street one morning to the corner of Q Street and turned right. Half of the block was occupied by the Lincoln School. It was a three-story wooden building, with two wings that gave it the shape of a double-T connected by a central hall. It was a new building, painted yellow, with a shingled roof that was not like the red tile of the school in Mazatlán. I noticed other differences, none of them very reassuring.

We walked up the wide staircase hand in hand and through the door, which closed by itself. A mechanical contraption screwed to the top shut it behind us quietly.

Up to this point the adventure of enrolling me in the school had been carefully rehearsed. Mrs. Dodson had told us how to find it and we had circled it several times on our walks. Friends in the *barrio* explained that the director was called a principal, and that it was a lady and not a man. They assured us that there was always a person at the school who could speak Spanish. . . .

The principal half turned in the swivel chair to look at us over the pinch glasses crossed on the ridge of her nose. To do this she had to duck her head slightly as if she were about to step through a low doorway. . . .

As long as the questions continued, Doña Henriqueta could stay and I was secure. Now that they were over, Miss Hopley saw her to the door, dismissed our interpreter and without further ado took me by the hand and strode down the hall to Miss Ryan's first grade.

Miss Ryan took me to a seat at the front of the room, into which I shrank—the better to survey her. She was, to skinny, somewhat runty me, of a withering height when she patrolled the class. And when I least expected it, there she was, crouching by my desk, her blond radiant face level with mine, her voice patiently maneuvering me over the awful idiocies of the English language.

During the next few weeks Miss Ryan overcame my fears of tall, energetic teachers as she bent over my desk to help me with a word in the pre-primer. Step by step, she loosened me and my classmates from the safe anchorage of the desks for recitations at the blackboard and consultations at her desk. Frequently she burst into happy announcements to the whole class. "Ito can read a sentence," and small Japanese Ito, squint-eyed and shy, slowly read aloud while the class listened in wonder: "Come, Skipper, come. Come and run." The Korean, Portuguese, Italian, and Polish first graders had similar moments of glory, no less shining than mine the day I conquered "butterfly," which I had been persistently pronouncing in standard Spanish as boo-ter-flee. "Children," Miss Ryan called for attention. "Ernesto has learned how to pronounce *butterfly!*" And I proved it with a perfect imitation of Miss Ryan. From that celebrated success, I was soon able to match Ito's progress as a sentence reader with "Come, butterfly, come fly with me."

Like Ito and several other first graders who did not know English, I received private lessons from Miss Ryan in the closet, a narrow hall off the classroom with a door at each end. Next to one of these doors Miss Ryan placed a large chair for herself and a small one for me. Keeping an eye on the class through the open door she read with me about sheep in the meadow and a frightened chicken going to see the king, coaching me out of my phonetic ruts in words like *pasture, bow-wow-wow, hay,* and *pretty,* which to my Mexican ear and eye had so many unnecessary sounds and letters. She made me watch her lips and then close my eyes as she repeated words I found hard to read. When we came to know each other better, I tried interrupting to tell Miss Ryan how we said it in Spanish. It didn't work. She only said "oh" and went on with *pasture, bow-wow-wow,* and *pretty.* It was as if in that closet we were both discovering together the secrets of the English language and grieving together over the tragedies of Bo-Peep. The main reason I was graduated with honors from the first grade was that I had fallen in love with Miss Ryan. Her radiant, no-nonsense character made us either afraid not to love her or love her so we would not be afraid, I am not sure which. It was not only that we sensed she was with it, but also that she was with us.

Like the first grade, the rest of the Lincoln School was a sampling of the lower part of town where many races made their home. My pals in the second grade were Kazushi, whose parents spoke only Japanese; Matti, a skinny Italian boy; and Manuel, a fat Portuguese who would never get into a fight but wrestled you to the ground and just sat on you. Our assortment of nationalities included Koreans, Yugoslavs, Poles, Irish, and home-grown Americans.

Miss Hopley and her teachers never let us forget why we were at Lincoln: for those who were alien, to become good Americans; for those who were so born, to accept the rest of us. Off the school grounds we traded the same insults we heard from our elders. On the playground we were sure to be marched up to the principal's office for calling someone a wop, a chink, a dago, or a greaser. The school was not so much a melting pot as a griddle where Miss Hopley and her helpers warmed knowledge into us and roasted racial hatreds out of us.

Making us into Americans did not mean scrubbing away what made us originally foreign. The teachers called us as our parents did, or as close as they could pronounce our names in Spanish or Japanese. No one was ever scolded or punished for speaking in his native tongue on the playground. Matti told the class about his mother's down quilt, which she had made in Italy with the fine feathers of a thousand geese. Encarnación acted out how boys learned to fish in the Philippines. I astounded the third grade with the story of my travels on a stagecoach, which nobody else in the class had seen except in the museum at Sutter's Fort. After a visit to the Crocker Art Gallery and its collection of heroic paintings of the golden age of California, someone showed a silk scroll with a Chinese painting. Miss Hopley herself had a way of expressing wonder over these matters before a class, her eyes wide open until they popped slightly. It was easy for me to feel that becoming a proud American, as she said we should, did not mean feeling ashamed of being a Mexican.

HENRY FORD

MY LIFE AND WORK

1922

After a series of mechanical experiments and business arrangements, Henry Ford (1863–1947) launched the Ford Motor Company in 1903 and the Model T car in 1908. He adapted the conveyor belt and assembly line to automobiles, revolutionized mass production, and gained control of both raw materials and the means of production. By 1922, Ford was making an estimated $264,000 per day and was credited with producing 60 percent of America's automobiles. In the early years, Ford paid his workers high salaries of $5 per day, though he later became unpopular for his antiunion policies, isolationism, and anti-Semitism. Ford was a leading producer of war materiel during both world wars and ran unsuccessfully for the Senate in 1918. His autobiography, written with the help of his P.R. man, Samuel Crowther, is an American classic.

From the day the first motor car appeared on the streets it had to me appeared to be a necessity. It was this knowledge and assurance that led me to build to the one end—a car that would meet the wants of the multitudes. All my efforts were then and still are turned to the production of one car—one model. And, year following year, the pressure was, and still is, to improve and refine and make better, with an increasing reduction in price. The universal car, had to have these attributes:

1. Quality in material to give service in use. . . .
2. Simplicity in operation—because the masses are not mechanics.
3. Power in sufficient quantity.
4. Absolute reliability—because of the varied uses to which the cars would be put and the variety of roads over which they would travel.
5. Lightness. . . .
6. Control—to hold its speed always in hand, calmly and safely meeting every emergency and contingency either in the crowded streets of the city or on dangerous roads. The planetary transmission of the Ford gave this control and anybody could work it. That is the "why" of the saying: "Anybody can drive a Ford." It can turn around almost anywhere. . . .

The design which I settled upon was called "Model T." The important feature of the new model—which, if it were accepted, as I thought it would be, I intended to make the only model and then start into real production—was its simplicity. There were but four constructional units in the car—the power plant, the frame, the front axle, and the rear axle. All of these were easily accessible and they were designed so that no special skill would be required for their repair or replacement. I believed then, although I said very little about it because of the novelty of the idea, that it ought to be possible to have parts so simple and so inexpensive that the menace of expensive hand repair work would be entirely eliminated. The parts could be made so cheaply that it would be less expensive to buy new ones than to have old ones repaired. They could be carried in hardware shops just as nails or bolts are carried. I thought that it was up to me as the designer to make the car so completely simple that no one could fail to understand it. . . .

Therefore in 1909 I announced one morning, without any previous warning, that in the future we were going to build only one model, that the model was going to be "Model T," and that the chassis would be exactly the same for all cars, and I remarked:

"Any customer can have a car painted any colour that he wants so long as it is black." . . .

Along about April 1, 1913, we first tried the experiment of an assembly line. We tried it on assembling the fly-wheel magneto. We try everything in a little way first—we will rip out anything once we discover a better way, but we have to know absolutely that the new way is going to be better than the old before we do anything drastic.

I believe that this was the first moving line ever installed. The idea came in a general way from the overhead trolley that the Chicago packers use in dressing beef. We had previously assembled the fly-wheel magneto in the usual method. With one workman doing a complete job he could turn out from thirty-five to forty pieces in a nine-hour day, or about twenty minutes to an assembly. What he did alone was then spread into twenty-nine operations; that cut down the assembly time to thirteen minutes, ten seconds. Then we raised the height of the line eight inches—this was in 1914—and cut the time to seven minutes. Further experimenting with the speed that the work should move at cut the time down to five minutes. In short, the result is this: by the aid of scientific study one man is now able to do somewhat more than four did only a comparative few years ago. That line established the efficiency of the method and we now use it everywhere. The assembling of the motor, formerly done by one man, is now divided into eighty-four operations—those men do the work that three times their number formerly did. In a short time we tried out the plan on the chassis. . . .

THOMAS ALVA EDISON

THEY WON'T THINK

1921

Born in Milan, Ohio, Thomas Alva Edison (1847–1931) had little formal education, though he was a voracious reader. He spent his early years as a newspaper boy on trains (where he was given space in a baggage car to conduct experiments) and working in telegraph stations. Through his tireless hard work—he coined the phrase "Genius is 1 percent inspiration and 99 percent perspiration"—Edison was responsible for over 1,000 inventions that changed the American way of life. The electric lightbulb, the phonograph, and motion pictures were among the products of the "Wizard of Menlo Park."

Every man has some forte, something he can do better than he can do anything else. Many men, however, never find the job they are best suited for. And often this is because they do not think enough. Too many men drift lazily into any job, suited or unsuited for them; and when they don't get along well they blame everybody and everything but themselves.

Grouches are nearly always pinheads, small men who have never made any effort to improve their mental capacity.

The brain can be developed just the same as the muscles can be developed, if one will only take the pains to train the mind to think.

Why do so many men never amount to anything? Because they don't think. . . .

The man who doesn't make up his mind to cultivate the habit of thinking misses the greatest pleasure in life. He not only misses the greatest pleasure, but he cannot make the most of himself. All progress, all success, springs from thinking.

Of course, even the most concentrated thinking cannot solve every new problem that the brain can conceive. It usually takes me from five to seven years to perfect a thing. Some things I have been working on for twenty-five years—and some of them are still unsolved. My average would be about seven years. The incandescent light was the hardest one of all; it took many years not only of concentrated thought but also of world-wide research. The storage battery took eight years. It took even longer to perfect the phonograph. . . .

Many inventions are not suitable for the people at large because of their carelessness. Before a thing can be marketed to the masses, it must be made practically fool-proof. Its operation must be made extremely simple. That is one reason, I think, why the phonograph has been so universally adopted. Even a child can operate it.

Another reason, is that people are far more willing to pay for being amused than for anything else.

HAPPY DAYS ARE HERE AGAIN

1929

Ironically, this song was composed in the year the stock market crash sent a shock wave of economic devastation throughout the land. As America struggled to pull itself out of the depths of the Great Depression, the song became a symbol of renewed optimism, and Franklin D. Roosevelt adopted it as the theme song for his presidential campaign.

So long, sad times;
Go 'long, bad times!
We are rid of you at last.
Howdy, gay times!
Cloudy gray times,
You are now a thing of the past.

'Cause happy days are here again!
The skies above are clear again.
Let us sing a song of cheer again
Happy days are here again!

Altogether shout it now!
There's no one who can doubt it now,
So let's tell the world about it now
Happy days are here again!

Your cares and troubles are gone;
There'll be no more from now on.
Happy days are here again,
The skies above are clear again;
Let us sing a song of cheer again
Happy days are here again!

BROTHER, CAN YOU SPARE A DIME?

1932

On October 29, 1929, the U.S. stock market crashed, wiping out some $30 billion in stock capital and sending economic shock waves throughout America. Banks, businesses, and farms failed. Millions lost their jobs, their homes, their savings. Within three years, some 34 million people had no source of income. In 1932, songwriters E. Y. Harburg (1898–1981), who also wrote the lyrics for *The Wizard of Oz* and *Finian's Rainbow*, and Jay Gorney (1896–1990) composed this song, which captured America's disillusionment.

They used to tell me I was building a dream,
And so I followed the mob
When there was earth to plough or guns to bear
I was always there right there on the job.

They used to tell me I was building a dream
With peace and glory ahead
Why should I be standing in line
Just waiting for bread?

Once I built a railroad, made it run,
Made it race against time.
Once I built a railroad,
Now it's done
Brother, can you spare a dime?

Once I built a tower, to the sun.
Brick and rivet and lime,
Once I built a tower,
Now it's done,
Brother, can you spare a dime?

Once in khaki suits
Gee, we looked swell
Full of that Yankee Doodle-de-dum.
Half a million boots went sloggin' thru Hell,

I was the kid with the drum.
Say, don't you remember, they called me Al
It was Al all the time
Say, don't you remember I'm your Pal!
Buddy, can you spare a dime?

FRANKLIN DELANO ROOSEVELT

FIRST INAUGURAL ADDRESS

MARCH 4, 1933

When Franklin D. Roosevelt accepted the Democratic nomination for president in June 1932, the country was still in the depths of a cruel economic depression. Some 13 million people were out of work (a million in New York City alone), over 5,000 banks had failed, some 86,000 businesses had closed shop, and, tragically, 21,000 suicides had been recorded. After his election that November, Roosevelt quickly went to work to put in place the "New Deal" he had promised the American people during the campaign.

I am certain that my fellow Americans expect that on my induction into the Presidency I will address them with a candor and a decision which the present situation of our Nation impels. This is preeminently the time to speak the truth, the whole truth, frankly and boldly. Nor need we shrink from honestly facing conditions in our country today. This great Nation will endure as it has endured, will revive and will prosper. So, first of all, let me assert my firm belief that the only thing we have to fear is fear itself—nameless, unreasoning, unjustified terror which paralyzes needed efforts to convert retreat into advance. In every dark hour of our national life a leadership of frankness and vigor has met with that understanding and support of the people themselves which is essential to victory. I am convinced that you will again give that support to leadership in these critical days.

In such a spirit on my part and on yours we face our common difficulties. They concern, thank God, only material things. Values have shrunken to fantastic levels; taxes have risen; our ability to pay has fallen; government of all kinds is faced by serious curtailment of income; the means of exchange are frozen in the currents of trade; the withered leaves of industrial enterprise lie on every side; farmers find no markets for their produce; the savings of many years in thousands of families are gone.

More important, a host of unemployed citizens face the grim problem of existence, and an equally great number toil with little return. Only a foolish optimist can deny the dark realities of the moment.

Yet our distress comes from no failure of substance. We are stricken by no plague of locusts. Compared with the perils which our forefathers conquered because they believed and were not afraid, we have still much to be thankful for. Nature still offers her bounty and human efforts have multiplied it. Plenty is at our doorstep, but a generous use of it languishes in the very sight of the supply. Primarily this is because rulers of the exchange of mankind's goods have failed through their own stubbornness and their own incompetence, have admitted their failure, and have abdicated. Practices of the unscrupulous money changers stand indicted in the court of public opinion, rejected by the hearts and minds of men.

True they have tried, but their efforts have been cast in the pattern of an out-worn tradition. Faced by failure of credit they have proposed only the lending of more money. Stripped of the lure of profit by which to induce our people to follow their false leadership, they have resorted to exhortations, pleading tearfully for restored confidence. They know only the rules of a generation of self-seekers. They have no vision, and when there is no vision the people perish.

The money changers have fled from their high seats in the temple of our civilization. We may now restore that temple to the ancient truths. The measure of the restoration lies in the extent to which we apply social values more noble than mere monetary profit.

Happiness lies not in the mere possession of money; it lies in the joy of achievement, in the thrill of creative effort. The joy and moral stimulation of work no longer must be forgotten in the mad chase of evanescent profits. These dark days will be worth all they cost us if they teach us that our true destiny is not to be ministered unto but to minister to ourselves and to our fellow men.

Recognition of the falsity of material wealth as the standard of success goes hand in hand with the abandonment of the false belief that public office and high political position are to be valued only by the standards of pride of place and personal profit; and there must be an end to a conduct in banking and in business which too often has given to a sacred trust the likeness of callous and selfish wrongdoing. Small wonder that confidence languishes, for it thrives only on honesty, on honor, on the sacredness of obligations, on faithful protection, on unselfish performance; without them it cannot live. Restoration calls, however, not for changes in ethics alone. This Nation asks for action, and action now.

Our greatest primary task is to put people to work. This is no unsolvable problem if we face it wisely and courageously. It can be accomplished in part by direct recruiting by the Government itself, treating the task as we would treat the emergency of a war, but at the same time, through this employment, accomplishing greatly needed projects to stimulate and reorganize the use of our natural resources.

Hand in hand with this we must frankly recognize the overbalance of population in our industrial centers and, by engaging on a national scale in a redistribution, endeavor to provide a better use of the land for those best fitted for the land. The task can be helped by definite efforts to raise the values of agricultural products and with this the power to purchase the output of our cities. It can be helped by pre-

JOHN GUTMANN, Demonstration, San Francisco, 1934.

venting realistically the tragedy of the growing loss through foreclosure of our small homes and our farms. It can be helped by insistence that the Federal, State, and local governments act forthwith on the demand that their cost be drastically reduced. It can be helped by the unifying of relief activities which today are often scattered, uneconomical, and unequal. It can be helped by national planning for and supervision of all forms of transportation and of communications and other utilities which have a definitely public character. There are many ways in which it can be helped, but it can never be helped merely by talking about it. We must act and act quickly.

Finally, in our progress toward a resumption of work we require two safeguards against a return of the evils of the old order: there must be a strict supervision of all banking and credits and investments, so that there will be an end to speculation with other people's money; and there must be provision for an adequate but sound currency.

These are the lines of attack. I shall presently urge upon a new Congress, in special session, detailed measures for their fulfillment, and I shall seek the immediate assistance of the several States.

Through this program of action we address ourselves to putting our own national house in order and making income balance outgo. Our international trade relations, though vastly important, are in point of time and necessity secondary to the establishment of a sound national economy. I favor as a practical policy the putting of first things first. I shall spare no effort to restore world trade by international economic readjustment, but the emergency at home cannot wait on that accomplishment.

The basic thought that guides these specific means of national recovery is not narrowly nationalistic. It is the insistence, as a first consideration, upon the interdependence of the various elements in and parts of the United States—a recognition of the old and permanently important manifestation of the American spirit of the pioneer. It is the way to recovery. It is the immediate way. It is the strongest assurance that the recovery will endure.

In the field of world policy I would dedicate this Nation to the policy of the good neighbor—the neighbor who resolutely respects himself and, because he does so, respects the rights of others—the neighbor who respects his obligations and respects the sanctity of his agreements in and with a world of neighbors.

If I read the temper of our people correctly, we now realize as we have never realized before our interdependence on each other, that we cannot merely take but we must give as well; that if we are to go forward, we must move as a trained and loyal army willing to sacrifice for the good of a common discipline, because without such discipline no progress is made, no leadership becomes effective. We are, I know, ready and willing to submit our lives and property to such discipline, because it makes possible a leadership which aims at a larger good. This I propose to offer, pledging that the larger purposes will bind upon us all as a sacred obligation with a unity of duty hitherto evoked only in time of armed strife.

With this pledge taken, I assume unhesitatingly the leadership of this great army of our people dedicated to a disciplined attack upon our common problems.

Action in this image and to this end is feasible under the form of government which we have inherited from our ancestors. Our Constitution is so simple and practical that it is possible always to meet extraordinary needs by changes in emphasis and arrangement without loss of essential form. That is why our constitutional system has proved itself the most superbly enduring political mechanism the modern world has produced. It has met every stress of vast expansion of territory, of foreign wars, of bitter internal strife, of world relations.

It is to be hoped that the normal balance of Executive and legislative authority may be wholly adequate to meet the unprecedented task before us. But it may be that an unprecedented demand and need for undelayed action may call for temporary departure from that normal balance of public procedure.

I am prepared under my constitutional duty to recommend the measures that a stricken Nation in the midst of a stricken world may require. These measures, or such other measures as the Congress may build out of its experience and wisdom, I shall seek, within my constitutional authority, to bring to speedy adoption.

But in the event that the Congress shall fail to take one of these two courses, and in the event that the national emergency is still critical, I shall not evade the clear course of duty that will then confront me. I shall ask the Congress for the one remaining instrument to meet the crisis—broad Executive power to wage a war against the emergency, as great as the power that would be given to me if we were in fact invaded by a foreign foe. . . .

We do not distrust the future of essential democracy. The people of the United States have not failed. In their need they have registered a mandate that they want direct, vigorous action. They have asked for discipline and direction under leadership. They have made me the present instrument of their wishes. In the spirit of the gift I take it.

In this dedication of a Nation we humbly ask the blessing of God. May He protect each and every one of us. May He guide me in the days to come.

West Coast Hotel Co. v. Parrish, 300 U.S. 379

1937

In the years before this case was decided, the Supreme Court had repeatedly struck down legislation aimed at ameliorating the harsh working conditions of the time. The Court reasoned that minimum wage, maximum hour, and even child labor legislation interfered with the employer's "freedom of contract." After much criticism, and the announcement by President Roosevelt of his plan to pack the Supreme Court with additional justices who supported New Deal economic and social welfare legislation, in 1937, by a majority of 5 to 4, the U.S. Supreme Court held constitutional a twenty-four-year-old Washington State statute that provided for a minimum wage for women. The suit had originally been brought by Elsie Parrish, a part-time hotel maid, who had been denied her full wages in violation of the law. The opinion was written by Chief Justice Charles Evans Hughes (1862–1948), who served as governor of New York and associate justice of the Supreme Court before stepping down to run for president, serve as secretary of state, and be renominated as chief justice in 1930.

. . . This case presents the question of the constitutional validity of the minimum wage law of the State of Washington. . . .

The appellant conducts a hotel. The appellee Elsie Parrish was employed as a chambermaid and (with her husband) brought this suit to recover the difference between the wages paid and the minimum wage fixed pursuant to the state law. The minimum wage was $14.50 per week of 48 hours. The appellant challenged the act as repugnant to the due process clause of the Fourteenth Amendment of the Constitution of the United States. . . .

The principle which must control our decision is not in doubt. The constitutional provision invoked is the due process clause of the Fourteenth Amendment governing the States. . . . The violation alleged by those attacking minimum wage regulation for women is deprivation of freedom of contract. What is this freedom? The Constitution does not speak of freedom of contract. It speaks of liberty and prohibits the deprivation of liberty without due process of law. In prohibiting that deprivation the Constitution does not recognize an absolute and uncontrollable liberty. Liberty in each of its phases has its history and connotation. But the liberty safeguarded is liberty in a social organization which requires the protection of law against the evils which menace the health, safety, morals and welfare of the people. Liberty under the Constitution is thus necessarily subject to the restraints of due process, and regulation which is reasonable in relation to its subject and is adopted in the interests of the community is due process. . . .

What can be closer to the public interest than the health of women and their protection from unscrupulous and overreaching employers? And if the protection of women is a legitimate end of the exercise of state power, how can it be said that the requirement of the payment of a minimum wage fairly fixed in order to meet the very necessities of existence is not an admissible means to that end? The legislature of the State was clearly entitled to consider the situation of women in employment, the fact that they are in the class receiving the least pay, that their bargaining power is relatively weak, and that they are the ready victims of those who would take advantage of their necessitous circumstances. The legislature was entitled to adopt measures to reduce the evils of the "sweating system," the exploiting of workers at wages so low as to be insufficient to meet the bare cost of living, thus making their very helplessness the occasion of a most injurious competition. The legislature had the right to consider that its minimum wage requirements would be an important aid in carrying out its policy of protection. The adoption of similar requirements by many States evidences a deepseated conviction both as to the presence of the evil and as to the means adapted to check it. Legislative response to that conviction cannot be regarded as arbitrary or capricious, and that is all we have to decide. Even if the wisdom of the policy be regarded as debatable and its effects uncertain, still the legislature is entitled to its judgment. . . .

There is an additional and compelling consideration which recent economic experience has brought into a strong light. The exploitation of a class of workers who are in an unequal position with respect to bargaining power and are thus relatively defenceless against the denial of a living wage is not only detrimental to their health and well being but casts a direct burden for their support upon the community. What these workers lose in wages the taxpayers are called upon to pay. The bare cost of living must be met. We may take judicial notice of the unparalleled demands for relief which arose during the recent period of depression and still continue to an alarming extent despite the degree of economic recovery which has been achieved. It is unnecessary to cite official statistics to establish what is of common knowledge through the length and breadth of the land.

THE GRAPES OF WRATH

1939

After dropping out of Stanford University in 1925, California-born John Steinbeck (1902–1968) wandered from job to job, working as a ranch hand, road worker, and laborer in a sugar-beet plant. From 1929 to 1937, he wrote a series of novels, including *Tortilla Flat* and *Of Mice and Men*. Then, in 1939, he published his masterpiece, *The Grapes of Wrath*, which chronicles the hardships endured by the Joad family as they make their way from the depths of the Depression dust bowl in Oklahoma to California. The novel won the Pulitzer Prize in 1940, and in 1962 Steinbeck won the Nobel Prize for literature.

The cars of the migrant people crawled out of the side roads onto the great cross-country highway, and then took the migrant way to the West. In the daylight they scuttled like bugs to the westward; and as the dark caught them, they clustered like bugs near to shelter and to water. And because they were lonely and perplexed, because they had all come from a place of sadness and worry and defeat, and because they were all going to a new mysterious place, they huddled together; they talked together; they shared their lives, their food, and the things they hoped for in the new country. Thus it might be that one family camped near a spring, and another camped for the spring and for company, and a third because two families had pioneered the place and found it good. And when the sun went down, perhaps twenty families and twenty cars were there.

In the evening a strange thing happened: the twenty families became one family, the children were the children of all. The loss of home became one loss, and the golden time in the West was one dream. And it might be that a sick child threw despair into the hearts of twenty families, of a hundred people; that a birth there in a tent kept a hundred people quiet and awestruck through the night and filled a hundred people with the birth-joy in the morning. A family which the night before had been lost and fearful might search its goods to find a present for a new baby. In the evening, sitting about the fires, the twenty were one. They grew to be units of the camps, units of the evenings and the nights. A guitar unwrapped from a blanket and tuned—and the songs, which were all of the people, were sung in the nights. Men sang the words, and women hummed the tunes.

Every night a world created, complete with furniture—friends made and enemies established; a world complete with braggarts and with cowards, with quiet men, with humble men, with kindly men. Every night relationships that make a world, established; and every morning the world torn down like a circus.

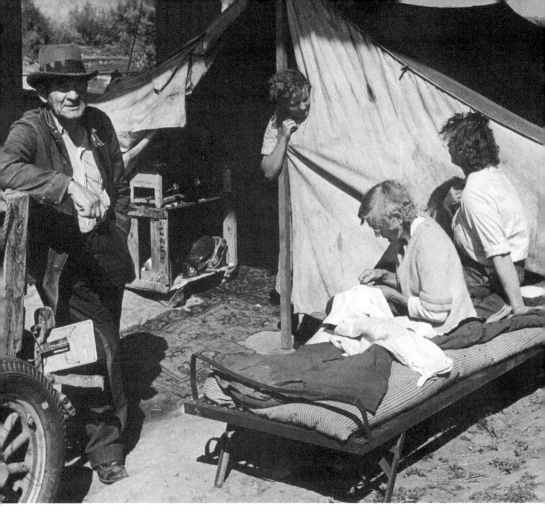

HORACE BRISTOL, Labor camp, Tulare County, California, 1938.

At first the families were timid in the building and tumbling worlds, but gradually the technique of building worlds became their technique. Then leaders emerged, then laws were made, then codes came into being. And as the worlds moved westward they were more complete and better furnished, for their builders were more experienced in building them.

The families learned what rights must be observed—the right of privacy in the tent; the right to keep the past black hidden in the heart; the right to talk and to listen; the right to refuse help or to accept, to offer help or to decline it; the right of son to court and daughter to be courted; the right of the hungry to be fed; the rights of the pregnant and the sick to transcend all other rights.

And the families learned, although no one told them, what rights are monstrous and must be destroyed: the right to intrude upon privacy, the right to be noisy while the camp slept, the right of seduction or rape, the right of adultery and theft and murder. These rights were crushed, because the little worlds could not exist for even a night with such rights alive.

And as the worlds moved westward, rules became laws, although no one told the families. It is unlawful to foul near the camp; it is unlawful in any way to foul the drinking water; it is unlawful to eat good rich food near one who is hungry, unless he is asked to share.

And with the laws, the punishments—and there were only two—a quick and murderous fight or ostracism; and ostracism was the worst. For if one broke the laws his name and face went with him, and he had no place in any world, no matter where created.

In the worlds, social conduct became fixed and rigid, so that a man must say "Good morning" when asked for it, so that a man might have a willing girl if he stayed with her, if he fathered her children and protected them. But a man might not have one girl one night and another the next, for this would endanger the worlds.

The families moved westward, and the technique of building the worlds improved so that the people could be safe in their worlds; and the form was so fixed that a family acting in the rules knew it was safe in the rules.

There grew up governments in the worlds, with leaders, with elders. A man who was wise found that his wisdom was needed in every camp; a man who was a fool could not change his folly with his world. And a kind of insurance developed in these nights. A man with food fed a hungry man, and thus insured himself against hunger. And when a baby died a pile of silver coins grew at the door flap, for a baby must be well buried, since it has had nothing else of life. An old man may be left in a potter's field, but not a baby.

A certain physical pattern is needed for the building of a world—water, a river bank, a stream, a spring, or even a faucet unguarded. And there is needed enough flat land to pitch the tents, a little brush or wood to build the fires. If there is a garbage dump not too far off, all the better; for there can be found equipment— stove tops, a curved fender to shelter the fire, and cans to cook in and to eat from.

And the worlds were built in the evening. The people, moving in from the highways, made them with their tents and their hearts and their brains.

In the morning the tents came down, the canvas was folded, the tent poles tied along the running board, the beds put in place on the cars, the pots in their places. And as the families moved westward, the technique of building up a home in the evening and tearing it down with the morning light became fixed; so that the folded tent was packed in one place, the cooking pots counted in their box. And as the cars moved westward, each member of the family grew into his proper place, grew into his duties; so that each member, old and young, had his place in the car; so that in the weary, hot evenings, when the cars pulled into the camping places, each member had his duty and went to it without instruction: children to gather wood, to carry water; men to pitch the tents and bring down the beds; women to cook the supper and to watch while the family fed. And this was done without command. The families, which had been units of which the boundaries were a house at night, a farm by day, changed their boundaries. In the long hot light, they were silent in the cars moving slowly westward; but at night they integrated with any group they found.

Thus they changed their social life—changed as in the whole universe only man can change. They were not farm men any more, but migrant men. And the thought, the planning, the long staring silence that had gone out to the fields, went now to the roads, to the distance, to the West. That man whose mind had been bound with acres lived with narrow concrete miles. And his thought and his worry were not any more with rainfall, with wind and dust, with the thrust of the crops. Eyes watched the tires, ears listened to the clattering motors, and minds struggled with oil, with gasoline, with the thinning rubber between air and road. Then a broken gear was tragedy. Then water in the evening was the yearning, and food over the fire. Then health to go on was the need and strength to go on, and spirit to go on. The wills thrust westward ahead of them, and fears that had once apprehended drought or flood now lingered with anything that might stop the westward crawling.

The camps became fixed—each a short day's journey from the last.

And on the road the panic overcame some of the families, so that they drove night and day, stopped to sleep in the cars, and drove on to the West, flying from the road, flying from movement. And these lusted so greatly to be settled that they set their faces into the West and drove toward it, forcing the clashing engines over the roads.

But most of the families changed and grew quickly into the new life. And when the sun went down——

Time to look out for a place to stop.

ARTHUR MILLER

DEATH OF A SALESMAN

1949

Although it took him only six weeks to write, *Death of a Salesman* is considered the greatest work of playwright Arthur Miller (1915–), earning him the Pulitzer Prize in 1949, two Tony Awards, and the New York Drama Critics Circle Award. The play is the final chapter in the life of Willy Loman, a battered man facing the truth of his failure as a traveling salesman and as a father. Miller's other award-winning plays include *All My Sons* (1947), *The Crucible* (1953), and *A View from the Bridge* (1955). Miller has written numerous essays, novels, and screenplays and published his autobiography, *Timebends: A Life*, in 1987.

BIFF: People are worse off than Willy Loman. Believe me, I've seen them!

LINDA: Then make Charley your father, Biff. You can't do that, can you? I don't say he's a great man. Willy Loman never made a lot of money. His name was never in the paper. He's not the finest character that ever lived. But he's a human being, and a terrible thing is happening to him. So attention must be paid. He's not to be allowed to fall into his grave like an old dog. Attention, attention must be finally paid to such a person. You called him crazy—

BIFF: I didn't mean—

LINDA: No, a lot of people think he's lost his—balance. But you don't have to be very smart to know what his trouble is. The man is exhausted.

HAPPY: Sure!

LINDA: A small man can be just as exhausted as a great man. He works for a company thirty-six years this March, opens up unheard-of territories to their trademark, and now in his old age they take his salary away.

HAPPY, *indignantly:* I didn't know that, Mom.

LINDA: You never asked, my dear! Now that you get your spending money someplace else you don't trouble your mind with him.

HAPPY: But I gave you money last—

LINDA: Christmas time, fifty dollars! To fix the hot water it cost ninety-seven fifty! For five weeks he's been on straight commission, like a beginner, an unknown!

BIFF: Those ungrateful bastards!

LINDA: Are they any worse than his sons? When he brought them business, when he was young, they were glad to see him. But now his old friends, the old buyers that loved him so and always found some order to hand him in a pinch—they're all dead, retired. He used to be able to make six, seven calls a day in Boston. Now he takes his valises out of the car and puts them back and takes them out again and he's exhausted. Instead of walking he talks now. He drives seven hundred miles, and when he gets there no one knows him any more, no one welcomes him. And what goes through a man's mind, driving seven hundred miles home without having earned a cent? Why shouldn't he talk to himself? Why? When he has to go to Charley and borrow fifty dollars a week and pretend to me that it's his pay? How long can that go on? How long? You see what I'm sitting here and waiting for? And you tell me he has no character? The man who never worked a day but for your benefit? When does he get the medal for that? Is this his reward—to turn around at the age of sixty-three and find his sons, who he loved better than his life, one a philandering bum—

HAPPY: Mom!

LINDA: That's all you are, my baby! *To Biff:* And you! What happened to the love you had for him? You were such pals! How you used to talk to him on the phone every night! How lonely he was till he could come home to you!

BIFF: All right, Mom. I'll live here in my room, and I'll get a job. I'll keep away from him, that's all.

LINDA: No, Biff. You can't stay here and fight all the time.

BIFF: He threw me out of this house, remember that.

LINDA: Why did he do that? I never knew why.

BIFF: Because I know he's a fake and he doesn't like anybody around who knows!

LINDA: Why a fake? In what way? What do you mean?

BIFF: Just don't lay it all at my feet. It's between me and him—that's all I have to say. I'll chip in from now on. He'll settle for half my pay check. He'll be all right. I'm going to bed. *He starts for the stairs.*

LINDA: He won't be all right.

BIFF, *turning on the stairs, furiously:* I hate this city and I'll stay here. Now what do you want?

LINDA: He's dying, Biff.

RICHARD NIXON AND NIKITA KHRUSHCHEV

THE KITCHEN DEBATE, MOSCOW

1959

A replica of a six-room American ranch house on display at an American National Exhibition in Moscow was an unlikely setting in 1959 for a debate between Soviet Premier Nikita Khrushchev (1894–1971) and Vice President Richard Nixon (1913–1994) on the merits of capitalism versus communism. Khrushchev, emboldened by a string of successes in the Communist world (the launching of Sputnik in 1957 and the fall of Cuba to Castro in early 1959), sneered with disdain when Nixon touted the good fortunes of the American worker during a stop in the model kitchen. But Nixon, the prospective Republican nominee for president in 1960, stood his ground in this celebrated cold war confrontation.

[Both men enter kitchen in the American exhibit.]

NIXON: I want to show you this kitchen. It is like those of our houses in California. [Nixon points to dishwasher.]

KHRUSHCHEV: We have such things.

NIXON: This is our newest model. This is the kind which is built in thousands of units for direct installations in the houses. In America, we like to make life easier for women . . .

KHRUSHCHEV: Your capitalistic attitude toward women does not occur under Communism.

NIXON: I think that this attitude towards women is universal. What we want to do, is make life more easy for our housewives. . . . This house can be bought for $14,000, and most American [veterans from World War II] can buy a home in the bracket of $10,000 to $15,000. Let me give you an example that you can appreciate. Our steel workers as you know, are now on strike. But any steel worker could buy this house. They earn $3 an hour. This house costs about $100 a month to buy on a contract running 25 to 30 years.

KHRUSHCHEV: We have steel workers and peasants who can afford to spend $14,000 for a house. Your American houses are built to last only 20 years so builders could sell new houses at the end. We build firmly. We build for our children and grandchildren.

NIXON: American houses last for more than 20 years, but, even so, after 20 years, many Americans want a new house or a new kitchen. Their kitchen is obsolete by that time. . . . The American system is designed to take advantage of new inventions and new techniques.

KHRUSHCHEV: This theory does not hold water. Some things never get out of date—houses, for instance, and furniture, furnishings—perhaps—but not houses. I have read much about America and American houses, and I do not think that this exhibit and what you say is strictly accurate.

NIXON: Well, um . . .

KHRUSHCHEV: I hope I have not insulted you.

NIXON: I have been insulted by experts. Everything we say [on the other hand] is in good humor. Always speak frankly.

KHRUSHCHEV: The Americans have created their own image of the Soviet man. But he is not as you think. You think the Russian people will be dumbfounded to see these things, but the fact is that newly built Russian houses have all this equipment right now.

NIXON: Yes, but . . .

KHRUSHCHEV: In Russia, all you have to do to get a house is to be born in the Soviet Union. You are entitled to housing . . . In America, if you don't have a dollar you have a right to choose between sleeping in a house or on the pavement. Yet you say we are the slave to Communism.

NIXON: I appreciate that you are very articulate and energetic . . .

KHRUSHCHEV: Energetic is not the same thing as wise.

NIXON: If you were in the Senate, we would call you a filibuster! You—[Khrushchev interrupts]—do all the talking and don't let anyone else talk.

This exhibit was not designed to astound but to interest.

Diversity, the right to choose, the fact that we have 1,000 builders building 1,000 different houses is the most important thing. We don't have one decision made at the top by one government official. This is the difference.

KHRUSHCHEV: On politics, we will never agree with you. For instance, Mikoyan likes very peppery soup. I do not. But this does not mean that we do not get along.

NIXON: You can learn from us, and we can learn from you. There must be a free exchange. Let the people choose the kind of house, the kind of soup, the kind of ideas that they want.

[Translation lost as both men enter the television recording studio.]

KHRUSHCHEV: [in jest] You look very angry, as if you want to fight me. Are you still angry?

NIXON: [in jest] That's right!

KHRUSHCHEV: . . . and Nixon was once a lawyer? Now he's nervous.

NIXON: Oh yes, [Nixon chuckling] he still is [a lawyer].

OTHER RUSSIAN SPEAKER: Tell us, please, what are your general impressions of the exhibit?

KHRUSHCHEV: It's clear to me that the construction workers didn't manage to finish their work and the exhibit still is not put in order . . . This is what America is capable of, and how long has she existed? 300 years? 150 years of independence and this is her level.

We haven't quite reached 42 years, and in another 7 years, we'll be at the level of America, and after that we'll go farther. As we pass you by, we'll wave "hi" to you, and then if you want, we'll stop and say, "please come along behind us."

. . . If you want to live under capitalism, go ahead, that's your question, an internal matter, it doesn't concern us. We can feel sorry for you, but really, you wouldn't understand. We've already seen how you understand things. . . .

NIXON: As far as Mr. Khrushchev's comments just now, they are in the tradition we learned to expect from him of speaking extemporaneously and frankly whenever he has an opportunity.

I can only say that if this competition which you have described so effectively, in which you plan to outstrip us, particularly in the production of consumer goods . . . If this competition is to do the best for both of our peoples and for people everywhere, there must be a free exchange of ideas.

There are some instances where you may be ahead of us—for example in the development of the thrust of your rockets for the investigation of outer space. There may be some instances, for example, color television, where we're ahead of you. But in order for both of us [to] benefit . . .

KHRUSHCHEV: [interrupting] No, in rockets we've passed you by, and in the technology . . .

NIXON: [continuing to talk] You see, you never concede anything.

KHRUSHCHEV: We always knew that Americans were smart people. Stupid people could not have risen to the economic level that they've reached. But as you know, "we don't beat flies with our nostrils!" In 42 years we've made progress.

NIXON: You must not be afraid of ideas.

KHRUSHCHEV: We're saying it is you who must not be afraid of ideas. We're not afraid of anything. . . .

NIXON: Well, then, let's have more exchange of them. We all agree on that, right?

KHRUSHCHEV: Good. [Khrushchev turns to translator and asks:] Now, what did I agree on?

ELLIS ISLAND INTERVIEW

MARCH 22, 1991

In 1924, Congress enacted the Johnson-Reed Act, which set yearly limits, by nationality, on the number of immigrants who could enter America. Despite those newly imposed restrictions, the following year a hopeful and excited nineteen-year-old Manny Steen was one of the fortunate Irish immigrants allowed to pass through Ellis Island. This interview was conducted over sixty years later during the reconstruction of Ellis Island.

His first day in America: . . . I go to the corner and . . . the trolley car stopped and I got on . . . and the conductor came over. And the conductors were all Irish . . . He says, "What are you doing, young fellow?" And I said, "Just taking a ride downtown." He says, "Is it Irish you are?" I said, "Aye." He said, "When did you get here?" I said, "Yesterday. I just got off the boat." . . . So he sat down beside me and he's pointing out the buildings. I was fascinated. Hey, America is a great place. I'm only here one day and I'm getting a royal reception . . . Finally I got off . . . and I'm feeling very adventurous . . . It's a beautiful day and I left my jacket off . . . and I'm beginning to feel comfortable now . . . I walk across the park and there's a street . . . and I look up and there's a street sign. It says, "Broadway." . . . That was one of the most exciting moments of my life. Broadway. I'm only one day in America and I'm on Broadway! . . . I start walking down Broadway . . . and I see Battery Park, where the day before I had come across from Ellis Island. I said, "One day in America and I'm right back where I started from." . . . I walked across Battery Park and I sit down on a bench and no one is bothering me. No one could identify me as a foreigner. Everybody's acting like I'm a full blooded American. And there was a guy with a pushcart . . . selling hot dogs. Now I had known about hot dogs from watching American movies in Dublin . . . They don't have hot dogs in Ireland . . . It was only five cents, so I figured I would speculate . . . He gave me one, I ate it and it tasted nice. And I was there eating my hot dog and taking the world in with my eyes and I said, "One day in America and I got it made." . . . I really had a ball. I had a hot dog . . . and I sat down . . . and I was seeing all the foreigners coming in from Ellis Island. It was a great feeling.

GROUCHO MARX

KING LEER

1950

The mustachioed, wisecracking ringleader of the zany comedy team of brothers, Groucho Marx (c. 1895–1977), whose real name was Julius, was born in New York City like his brothers Arthur (Harpo), Leonard (Chico), Milton (Gummo), and Herbert (Zeppo). They appeared on stage as a vaudeville act before launching their film career with comedies including *Animal Crackers* (1930), *Monkey Business* (1931), *A Night at the Opera* (1935), and *A Day at the Races* (1937). Groucho's 1950s hit quiz show *You Bet Your Life* made him one of the very few entertainers whose careers spanned the century from vaudeville to television.

I must say I find television very educational. The minute somebody turns it on, I go into the library and read a good book.

That's a pretty cynical attitude for "the leer"—that's me, Groucho—and now that I'm a part of television, or "TV" as we say out here on the Coast, I don't mean a word of it.

TV presents a completely new set of problems to me. In my thirty-five years in show business, I've learned the intricacies of the stage, then the movies, then radio. Now comes television. I can't even learn how to turn it on!

At first, I thought it would be simple to put our show on TV. Just me and a few contestants gabbing. That's all.

Little did I know there would be four cameras staring at me, a makeup man frowning from the wings if I raise my eyebrows, the light crew glaring from the rafters if I cast a shadow in the wrong place, my director making frantic motions if I step out of camera range, the studio audience whispering if I step out of mike range, the sponsor screaming if I forget the commercial.

I suppose I'll get used to all this. After all, television is progressing rapidly. I notice the home sets are improving all the time. For instance, the old sets used to have about thirty-five tubes, but now the sets are down to eighteen tubes. Now if they just eliminate the picture tube, they'll reach perfection.

I also notice that the television screens are getting bigger. Thank goodness for those screens. They're the only thing that keeps the stuff from crawling into the living room.

I think the ideal television sets should be equipped with two screens. Then you could use the second screen to hide the television sets.

In a nutshell, I'm happy to be plunging into television. Although frankly, I'd rather be plunging into a nutshell.

Sure, we've got a lot of problems to lick, since we're doing our show for radio and TV simultaneously. This means everything we do for television must be plain to the listener who can't see it, the old-fashioned fellow with the radio receiver. It will limit our plans for the time being, but I'm sure everything will work out for the best. I wish I could say the same for Harpo, who isn't working out at all.

As for me, I'm going to keep my cigar, my leer, and any old ad-lib wisecracks I find kicking around. My mustache is my own now. I bought it from the upstairs maid. But the frock coat and the old Groucho who chases blondes will be missing. Even the new Groucho will be missing, but that's only until I can get my spark plugs cleaned.

All I can say is this: Walk, don't run, to your nearest television set in October, tune to KNBH, and join us for our first TV session of *You Bet Your Life*. I think you'll like it.

TV dinners, 1950s.

COAL MINER'S DAUGHTER

1970

Loretta Lynn (1935–) grew up poor in the hills of Kentucky, listening to country music on the radio. Married at fourteen, a grandmother at twenty-eight, Lynn had six children and struggled for years to make it as a singer. In 1970, she released her number one country hit "Coal Miner's Daughter" and eventually became the first woman in country music history to become a millionaire. In 1981, actress Sissy Spacek won an Oscar for a film portrayal of Lynn's life.

Well, I was born a coal miner's daughter
In a cabin on a hill in Butcher Holler
We were poor but we had love
That's the one thing my Daddy made sure of
He shoveled coal to make a poor man's dollar

My daddy worked all night in the Vanlear coal mine
All day long in the field hoein' corn
Mama rocked the babies at night
Read the Bible by a coal oil light
And everthin' would start all over come break of morn'

Daddy loved and raised eight kids on a coal miner's pay
Mama scrubbed our clothes on a washboard ever day
I'd seen her fingers bleed
To complain there was no need
She'd smile in Mama's understanding way

In the summertime we didn't have shoes to wear
But in the wintertime we'd all get a brand new pair
From a mail order catalog, money made by sellin' hogs
Daddy always got the money somewhere

I'm proud to be a coal miner's daughter
I remember well, the well where I drew water
The work we done was hard

At night we'd sleep 'cause we were tired
I never thought to leave Butcher Holler

Well a lot of things have changed since way back when
And it's so good to be back home again
Not much left but the floor
Nothing lives here anymore
Only a memory of a coal miner's daughter

CHOOSING A DREAM: ITALIANS IN HELL'S KITCHEN

1971

Born to illiterate Italian immigrant parents, Mario Puzo (1920–1999) spent his youth in Hell's Kitchen avoiding the street gangs of New York and devouring books—like the works of Dostoevsky—in the public library. Feeling "hopelessly trapped by my family, by society, by my lack of skills and education," by the mid-1960s Puzo, in debt with a family to support, had written two books that had netted him only $6,500. In 1969 he published *The Godfather*, which sold over 21 million copies. He later won two Oscars for his film screenplays of *The Godfather* trilogy.

As a child and in my adolescence, living in the heart of New York's Neapolitan ghetto, I never heard an Italian singing. None of the grown-ups I knew were charming or loving or understanding. Rather they seemed coarse, vulgar, and insulting. And so later in my life when I was exposed to all the clichés of lovable Italians, singing Italians, happy-go-lucky Italians, I wondered where the hell the moviemakers and storywriters got all their ideas from.

At a very early age I decided to escape these uncongenial folk by becoming an artist, a writer. It seemed then an impossible dream. My father and mother were illiterate, as were their parents before them. But, practicing my art, I tried to view the adults with a more charitable eye and so came to the conclusion that their only fault lay in their being foreigners: I was an American. This didn't really help because I was only half right. I was the foreigner. They were already more "American" than I could ever become.

But it did seem then that the Italian immigrants, all the fathers and mothers that I knew, were a grim lot; always shouting, always angry, quicker to quarrel than embrace. I did not understand that their lives were a long labor to earn their daily bread and that physical fatigue does not sweeten human natures. . . .

My family and I grew up together on Tenth Avenue, between Thirtieth and Thirty-first Streets, part of the area called Hell's Kitchen. The particular neighborhood could have been a movie set for one of the Dead End Kid flicks or for the social drama of the East Side in which John Garfield played the hero. Our tenements were the western wall of the city. Beneath our windows were the vast black iron gardens of the New York Central Railroad, absolutely blooming with stinking boxcars freshly unloaded of cattle and pigs for the city slaughterhouse. Steers sometimes

BURT GLINN, Alien registration, New York, 1951.

escaped and loped through the heart of the neighborhood followed by astonished young boys who had never seen a live cow.

The railroad yards stretched down to the Hudson River, beyond whose garbagey waters rose the rocky Palisades of New Jersey. There were railroad tracks running downtown on Tenth Avenue itself to another freight station called St. Johns Park. Because of this, because these trains cut off one side of the street from the other, there was a wooden bridge over Tenth Avenue, a romantic-looking bridge despite the fact that no sparkling water, no silver flying fish darted beneath it; only heavy dray carts drawn by tired horses, some flat-boarded trucks, tin lizzie automobiles and, of course, long strings of freight cars drawn by black, ugly engines.

What was really great, truly magical, was sitting on the bridge, feet dangling down, and letting the engine under you blow up clouds of steam that made you disappear, then reappear all damp and smelling of fresh ironing. When I was seven years old, I fell in love for the first time with the tough little girl who held my hand and disappeared with me in that magical cloud of steam. . . .

My father supported his wife and seven children by working as a trackman laborer for the New York Central Railroad. My oldest brother worked for the railroad as a brakeman; another brother was a railroad shipping clerk in the freight office. Eventually I spent some of the worst months of my life as the railroad's worst messenger boy.

My oldest sister was just as unhappy as a dressmaker in the garment industry. She wanted to be a schoolteacher. At one time or another my other two brothers also worked for the railroad—it got all six males in the family. The two girls and my mother escaped, though my mother felt it her duty to send all our bosses a gallon of homemade wine on Christmas. But everybody hated their jobs except my oldest brother, who had a night shift and spent most of his working hours sleeping in freight cars. My father finally got fired because the foreman told him to get a bucket of water for the crew and not to take all day. My father took the bucket and disappeared forever.

Nearly all the Italian men living on Tenth Avenue supported their large families by working on the railroad. Their children also earned pocket money by stealing ice from the refrigerator cars in summer and coal from the open stoking cars in the winter. Sometimes an older lad would break the seal of a freight car and take a look inside. But this usually brought down the "Bulls," the special railroad police. And usually the freight was "heavy" stuff, too much work to cart away and sell, something like fresh produce or boxes of cheap candy that nobody would buy.

The older boys, the ones just approaching voting age, made their easy money by hijacking silk trucks that loaded up at the garment factory on Thirty-first Street. They would then sell the expensive dresses door to door, at bargain prices no discount house could match. From this some graduated into organized crime, whose talent scouts alertly tapped young boys versed in strong arm. Yet despite all this, most of the kids grew up honest, content with fifty bucks a week as truck drivers, deliverymen, and white-collar clerks in the Civil Service.

I had every desire to go wrong but I never had a chance. The Italian family structure was too formidable.

I never came home to an empty house; there was always the smell of supper cooking. My mother was always there to greet me, sometimes with a policeman's club in her hand (nobody ever knew how she acquired it). But she was always there, or her authorized deputy, my older sister, who preferred throwing empty milk bottles at the heads of her little brothers when they got bad marks on their report cards. During the great Depression of the 1930s, though we were the poorest of the poor, I never remember not dining well. Many years later as a guest of a millionaire's club, I realized that our poor family on home relief ate better than some of the richest people in America. . . .

When I came to my "autobiographical novel," the one every writer does about himself, I planned to make myself the sensitive, misunderstood hero, much put upon by his mother and family. To my astonishment my mother took over the book and instead of my revenge I got another comeuppance. But it is, I think, my best book.

And all those old-style grim conservative Italians whom I hated, then pitied so patronizingly, they also turned out to be heroes. Through no desire of mine, I was surprised. The thing that amazed me most was their courage. Where were their Congressional Medals of Honor? Their Distinguished Service Crosses? How did they ever have the balls to get married, have kids, go out to earn a living in a strange land, with no skills, not even knowing the language? They made it without tranquilizers, without sleeping pills, without psychiatrists, without even a dream. Heroes. Heroes all around me. I never saw them.

But how could I? They wore lumpy work clothes and handlebar mustaches, they blew their noses on their fingers, and they were so short that their high school children towered over them. They spoke a laughable broken English and the furthest limit of their horizon was their daily bread. Brave men, brave women, they fought to live their lives without dreams. Bent on survival, they narrowed their minds to the thinnest line of existence.

It is no wonder that in my youth I found them contemptible. And yet they had left Italy and sailed the ocean to come to a new land and leave their sweated bones in America. Illiterate Colombos, they dared to seek the promised land. And so they, too, dreamed a dream.

LEWIS W. HINE, Immigrant family, Ellis Island, New York, 1908.

RECAPTURING AMERICA'S MORAL VISION, UNIVERSITY OF KANSAS

MARCH 18, 1968

One month after he announced his candidacy for the presidency, Robert Kennedy delivered this powerful speech challenging America's reliance on material wealth as a measure of success. In February the Kerner Commission, appointed by President Johnson to analyze the urban riots of 1967, had concluded that America was "moving toward two societies—one white, the other black—separate and unequal." During his campaign, Robert Kennedy traveled to the Mississippi Delta, Native American reservations, Appalachian coal mining communities, and inner cities across America, highlighting the conditions of the poor and dispossessed, and confronting Americans with a moral dilemma.

I have seen these other Americans—I have seen children in Mississippi starving, their bodies so crippled by hunger; and their minds have been so destroyed for their whole life that they will have no future. I have seen children in Mississippi—here in the United States, with a gross national product of eight hundred billion dollars—I have seen children in the Delta area of Mississippi with distended stomachs, whose faces are covered with sores from starvation, and we haven't developed a policy so that we can get enough food so that they can live, so that their lives are not destroyed. I don't think that's acceptable in the United States of America and I think we need a change.

I have seen Indians living on their bare and meager reservations, with no jobs, with an unemployment rate of 80 percent, and with so little hope for the future that for young men and women in their teens, the greatest cause of death is suicide. That they end their lives by killing themselves—I don't think that we have to accept that, for the first Americans, for the minority here in the United States. If young boys and girls are so filled with despair when they are going to high school and feel that their lives are so hopeless and that nobody's going to care for them, nobody's going to be involved with them, nobody's going to bother with them, that they either hang themselves, shoot themselves, or kill themselves—I don't think that's acceptable and I think the United States of America—I think the American people know we can do much, much better. And I run for the presidency because of that. I run for the presidency because I've seen proud men in the hills of Appalachia, who wish only to work in dignity, but they cannot, for the mines have closed and their jobs are gone and no one—neither industry, labor, nor government—has cared enough to help.

I think we here in this country, with the unselfish state that exists in the United States of America, I think we can do better here also.

Robert F. Kennedy visiting Greenville, Mississippi, 1967.

I have seen the people of the black ghetto, listening to ever-greater promises of equality and justice, as they sit in the same decaying schools and huddle in the same filthy rooms, without heat, warding off the cold and warding off the rats.

If we believe that we, as Americans, are bound together by a common concern for each other, then an urgent national priority is upon us. We must begin to end the disgrace of this other America.

And this is one of the great tasks of leadership for us, as individuals and citizens this year. But even if we act to erase material poverty, there is another great task. It is to confront the poverty of satisfaction—a lack of purpose and dignity—that inflicts us all. Too much and too long, we seem to have surrendered community excellence and community values in the mere accumulation of material things. Our gross national product, now, is over eight hundred billion dollars a year, but that GNP—if we should judge America by that—counts air pollution and cigarette advertising, and ambulances to clear our highways of carnage. It counts special locks for our doors and the jails for those who break them. It counts the destruction of our redwoods and the loss of our natural wonder in chaotic sprawl. It counts napalm and the cost of a nuclear warhead, and armored cars for police who fight riots in our streets. It counts Whitman's rifle and Speck's knife, and the television programs which glorify violence in order to sell toys to our children.

Yet the gross national product does not allow for the health of our children, the quality of their education, or the joy of their play. It does not include the beauty of our poetry or the strength of our marriages; the intelligence of our public debate or the integrity of our public officials. It measures neither our wit nor our courage; neither our wisdom nor our learning; neither our compassion nor our devotion to our country; it measures everything, in short, except that which makes life worthwhile. And it can tell us everything about America except why we are proud that we are Americans. . . .

If this is true here at home, so it is true elsewhere in the world. From the beginning, our proudest boast was that we, here in this country, would be the best hope for all of mankind. And now, as we look at the war in Vietnam, we wonder if we still hold a decent respect for the opinions of mankind, and whether they have maintained a decent respect for us, or whether like Athens of old, we will forfeit sympathy and support, and ultimately security, in a single-minded pursuit of our own goals and our own objectives.

CESAR CHAVEZ

ADDRESS TO THE COMMONWEALTH CLUB OF SAN FRANCISCO

NOVEMBER 9, 1984

Relying upon the nonviolent tactics of Gandhi and his own magnetic personality, Cesar Chavez (1927–1993) spent his life battling powerful agricultural producers on behalf of millions of migrant farmworkers. As founder of the United Farm Workers of America, the first successful farm union in the nation, Chavez is credited with improving the lives of agricultural workers and offering inspiration to generations of Hispanic Americans.

Twenty-one years ago last September, on a lonely stretch of railroad track paralleling U.S. Highway 101 near Salinas, 32 Bracero farm workers lost their lives in a tragic accident.

The Braceros had been imported from Mexico to work on California farms. They died when their bus, which was converted from a flatbed truck, drove in front of a freight train.

Conversion of the bus had not been approved by any government agency. The driver had "tunnel" vision.

Most of the bodies lay unidentified for days. *No one, including the grower who employed the workers, even knew their names.*

Today, thousands of farm workers live under savage conditions—beneath trees and amid garbage and human excrement—near tomato fields in San Diego County. . . .

. . . tomato fields which use the most modern farm technology.

Vicious rats gnaw on them as they sleep. . . . They walk miles to buy food at inflated prices . . . and they carry in water from irrigation pumps.

Child labor is still common in many farm areas.

As much as 30 percent of Northern California's garlic harvesters are under-aged children. Kids as young as six years old have voted in state-conducted union elections since they qualified as workers.

Some 800,000 under-aged children work with their families harvesting crops across America.

Babies born to migrant workers suffer 25 percent higher infant mortality than the rest of the population.

Malnutrition among migrant worker children is 10 times higher than the national rate.

PIRKLE JONES, Grape harvest, Berryessa Valley, California, 1956.

Farm workers' average life expectancy is still 49 years . . . compared to 73 years for the average American.

All my life, I have been driven by one dream, one goal, one vision: To overthrow a farm labor system in this nation which treats farm workers as if they were not important human beings. . . .

I'm not very different from anyone else who has ever tried to accomplish something with his life. My motivation comes from my personal life. . . .

. . . from watching what my mother and father went through when I was growing up—from what we experienced as migrant farm workers in California.

That dream, that vision grew from my own experience with racism . . . with hope . . . with the desire to be treated fairly and to see my people treated as human beings and not as chattel.

It grew from anger and rage—emotions I felt 40 years ago when people of my color were denied the right to see a movie or eat at a restaurant in many parts of California.

It grew from the frustration and humiliation I felt as a boy who couldn't understand how the growers could abuse and exploit workers when there were *so many* of us and *so few* of them.

Later, in the '50s, I experienced a different kind of exploitation. In San Jose, in Los Angeles and in other *urban* communities, we—the Mexican American people—were dominated by a majority that was Anglo.

I began to realize what other minority people had discovered: That the only answer—the only hope—was in organizing.

More of us had to become citizens. We had to register to vote. And people like me had to develop the skills it would take to organize, to educate, to help empower the Chicano people.

I spent many years—before we founded the union—learning how to work with people.

We experienced some successes in voter registration . . . in politics . . . in battling racial discrimination . . .

. . . successes in an era when Black Americans were just beginning to assert their civil rights . . . and when political awareness among Hispanics was almost non-existent.

But deep in my heart, I knew I could never be happy unless I tried organizing the farm workers. I didn't know if I would succeed. But I had to try.

All Hispanics—urban and rural, young and old—are connected to the farm workers' experience. We had all lived through the fields . . . or our parents had. We shared that common humiliation.

How could we progress as a people, even if we lived in the cities, while the farm workers—men and women of our color—were condemned to a life without pride?

How could we progress as a people while the farm workers—who symbolized our history in this land—were denied self-respect?

How could our people believe that *their* children could become lawyers and doctors and judges and business people while *this* shame, *this* injustice was permitted to continue? . . .

And you cannot do away with an entire people; you cannot stamp out a *people's* cause.

Regardless of what the future holds for the union . . .

Regardless of what the future holds for farm workers . . . our accomplishments cannot be undone!

"La Causa"—our cause—doesn't have to be experienced twice.

The consciousness and pride that were raised by our union are alive and thriving inside *millions* of young Hispanics who will *never* work on a farm!

Like the other immigrant groups, *the day will come* when we win the economic and political rewards which are in keeping with our numbers in society.

The day will come when the politicians do the right thing by our people *out of political necessity* and *not* out of charity or idealism.

That day may not come *this year*. . . .

That day may not come *during this decade*. . . .

But it will come, *someday!*

And when that day comes, we shall see the fulfillment of that passage from the Book of Matthew in the New Testament, "That the last shall be first and the first shall be last."

And on that day, our nation shall fulfill its creed . . . and that fulfillment shall enrich us all.

Thank you very much.

MY HOMETOWN

1984

Bruce Springsteen grew up near a filling station in Freehold, New Jersey, the son of a bus driver and a secretary. In his powerful and poetic songs, Springsteen elevated the experiences of small-town life. "Rock 'n' roll reached down into all those homes where there was no music or books or any kind of creative sense, and it infiltrated the whole thing. That's what happened in my house." This song appeared on the 1984 album *Born in the U.S.A.*

I was eight years old and running with a dime in my hand
Into the bus stop to pick up a paper for my old man
I'd sit on his lap in that big old Buick and steer as we drove through town
He'd tousle my hair and say son take a good look around this is your hometown
This is your hometown
This is your hometown
This is your hometown

In '65 tension was running high at my high school
There was a lot of fights between the black and white
There was nothing you could do
Two cars at a light on a Saturday night in the back seat there was a gun
Words were passed in a shotgun blast
Troubled times had come to my hometown
My hometown
My hometown
My hometown

Now Main Street's whitewashed windows and vacant stores
Seems like there ain't nobody wants to come down here no more
They're closing down the textile mill across the railroad tracks
Foreman says these jobs are going boys and they ain't coming back to your
  hometown
Your hometown
Your hometown
Your hometown

Last night me and Kate we laid in bed
talking about getting out
Packing up our bags maybe heading south
I'm thirty-five we got a boy of our own now
Last night I sat him up behind the wheel and said son take a good look around
This is your hometown

ANDY WARHOL

POPISM

1975

The son of a steelworker from Pittsburgh, Pennsylvania, Andy Warhol (1928–1987) moved to New York, where he worked briefly as a department store window designer. He burst onto the art scene in the early 1960s with works like his Campbell Soup can that transformed advertising and Hollywood imagery into "pop art." Known for snapping pictures of his every encounter and founding *Interview* magazine, he became a chronicler of late-twentieth-century American society.

What's great about this country is that America started the tradition where the richest consumers buy essentially the same things as the poorest. You can be watching TV and see Coca-Cola, and you can know that the President drinks Coke, Liz Taylor drinks Coke, and just think, you can drink Coke, too. A Coke is a Coke and no amount of money can get you a better Coke than the one the bum on the corner is drinking. All the Cokes are the same and all the Cokes are good. Liz Taylor knows it, the President knows it, the bum knows it, and you know it.

In Europe the royalty and the aristocracy used to eat a lot better than the peasants—they weren't eating the same things at all. It was either partridge or porridge, and each class stuck to its own food. But when Queen Elizabeth came here and President Eisenhower bought her a hot dog, I'm sure he felt confident that she couldn't have had delivered to Buckingham Palace a better hot dog than that one he bought her for maybe twenty cents at the ballpark. Because there *is* no better hot dog than a ballpark hot dog. Not for a dollar, not for ten dollars, not for a hundred thousand dollars could she get a better hot dog. She could get one for twenty cents and so could anybody else.

Sometimes you fantasize that people who are really up-there and rich and living it up have something you don't have, that their things must be better than your things because they have more money than you. But they drink the same Cokes and eat the same hot dogs and wear the same ILGWU clothes and see the same TV shows and the same movies. Rich people can't see a sillier version of *Truth or Consequences* or a scarier version of *The Exorcist*. You can get just as revolted as they can—you can have the same nightmares. All of this is really American.

SPEECH TO THE DEMOCRATIC CONVENTION

AUGUST 12, 1980

Marking the end of his candidacy for president in 1980, Senator Edward Kennedy rocked the Democratic Convention, calling on traditional Democrats to "keep the faith." Kennedy returned to the Senate as one of our nation's longest-serving senators. He is the ranking Democrat on the Health, Education, Labor and Pensions Committee, and is a member of the Armed Services and Judiciary Committees.

. . . My fellow Democrats and my fellow Americans, I have come here tonight not to argue for a candidacy but to affirm a cause.

I am asking you to renew the commitment of the Democratic party to economic justice. I am asking you to renew our commitment to a fair and lasting prosperity that can put America back to work. . . .

The economic plank of this platform on its face concern only material things; but is also a moral issue that I raise tonight. It has taken many forms over many years. In this campaign, and in this country that we seek to lead, the challenge in 1980 is to give our voice and our vote for these fundamental Democratic principles:

Let us pledge that we will never misuse unemployment, high interest rates, and human misery as false weapons against inflation.

Let us pledge that employment will be the first priority of our economic policy.

Let us pledge that there will be security for all who are now at work. Let us pledge that there will be jobs for all who are out of work—and we will not compromise on the issue of jobs.

These are not simplistic pledges. Simply put, they are the heart of our tradition; they have been the soul of our party across the generations. It is the glory and the greatness of our tradition to speak for those who have no voice, to remember those who are forgotten, to respond to the frustrations and fulfill the aspirations of all Americans seeking a better life in a better land. . . .

The commitment I seek is not to outworn views but to old values that will never wear out. Programs may sometimes become obsolete, but the ideal of fairness always endures. Circumstances may change, but the work of compassion must continue. It is surely correct that we cannot solve problems by throwing money at them; but it is also correct that we dare not throw our national problems onto a scrap heap of inattention and indifference. The poor may be out of political fashion, but they are not without human needs. The middle class may be angry, but they have not lost the dream that all Americans can advance together. . . .

We are the party of the New Freedom, the New Deal, and the New Frontier. We have always been the party of hope. So this year, let us offer new hope—new hope to an America uncertain about the present but unsurpassed in its potential for the future.

To all those who are idle in the cities and industries of America, let us provide new hope for the dignity of useful work. Democrats have always believed that a basic civil right of all Americans is the right to earn their own way. The party of the people must always be the party of full employment. . . .

There were some who said we should be silent about our differences on issues during this convention. But the heritage of the Democratic party has been a history of democracy. We fight hard because we care deeply about our principles and purposes. We did not flee this struggle. And we welcome this contrast with the empty and expedient spectacle last month in Detroit, where no nomination was contested, no question was debated, and no one dared to raise any doubt or dissent.

Democrats can be proud that we chose a different course—and a different platform.

We can be proud that our party stands for investment in safe energy instead of a nuclear future that may threaten the future itself. We must not permit the neighborhoods of America to be permanently shadowed by the fear of another Three Mile Island.

We can be proud that our party stands for a fair housing law to unlock the doors of discrimination once and for all. The American house will be divided against itself so long as there is prejudice against any American family buying or renting a home.

And we can be proud that our party stands plainly, publicly, and persistently for the ratification of the Equal Rights Amendment. Women hold their rightful place at our convention; and women must have their rightful place in the Constitution of the United States. On this issue, we will not yield, we will not equivocate, we will not rationalize, explain, or excuse. We will stand for ERA and for the recognition at long last that our nation had not only founding fathers but founding mothers as well.

A fair prosperity and a just society are within our vision and our grasp. We do not have every answer. There are questions not yet asked, waiting for us in the recesses of the future.

But of this much we can be certain, because it is the lesson of all our history:

Together, a president and the people can make a difference. I have found that faith still alive wherever I have traveled across the land. So let us reject the counsel of retreat and the call to reaction. Let us go forward in the knowledge that history only helps those who help themselves.

There will be setbacks and sacrifices in the years ahead. But I am convinced that we as a people are ready to give something back to our country in return for all it has given us. Let this be our commitment: whatever sacrifices must be made will be shared—and shared fairly. And let this be our confidence at the end of our journey and always before us shines that ideal of liberty and justice for all.

In closing, let me say a few words to all those I have met and all those who have supported me at this convention and across the country.

There were hard hours on our journey. Often we sailed against the wind, but always we kept our rudder true. There were so many of you who stayed the course and shared our hope. You gave your help; but even more, you gave your hearts. . . .

And someday, long after this convention, long after the signs come down and the crowds stop cheering, and the bands stop playing, may it be said of our campaign that we kept the faith. May it be said of our party in 1980 that we found our faith again.

May it be said of us, both in dark passages and in bright days, in the words of Tennyson that my brothers quoted and loved—and that have special meaning for me now:

> I am a part of all that I have met. . . .
> Though much is taken, much abides. . . .
> That which we are, we are—
> One equal temper of heroic hearts,
> > . . . strong in will
> To strive, to seek, to find, and not to yield.

For me, a few hours ago, this campaign came to an end. For all those whose cares have been our concern, the work goes on, the cause endures, the hope still lives, and the dream shall never die.

DAVID BRIGHT

HOMELESS CHILDREN SPEAK

1986

In January 1986, the U.S. Conference of Mayors issued a report showing that the number of homeless children in twenty-five of America's largest cities had risen by 85 percent. The report also concluded that 27 percent of the nation's homeless were families with children. In March of that year, ten-year-old David Bright, then sheltered with his mother, brother, and two sisters in a New York City "welfare hotel" (along with 1,400 other homeless children), testified before the House Select Committee on Hunger.

My name is David Bright. I am ten years old. I am homeless. I am often hungry. Right now I live in the Martinique Hotel. The Martinique is a mad house. The hallways are dangerous. Many things could happen to you while you're in the hallways. Like you could be shot or raped. The roaches and rats are a big problem too. But being raped is worse. There are people who rape little boys in the hallways.

I am often hungry because I don't get enough to eat. Homeless kids are taken to schools far away. When the bus comes late I can't even get breakfast at school. When I arrive the bell rings, then breakfast just stops. I just can't think in school when I'm hungry. My mind just stops thinking and this can't go on forever. That's because I want to learn. I want to get a good education. Learning is fun for me.

There are too many little kids in the hotel who never go to school. There just is not enough room in the schools for them. Just like there's not enough homes for poor children and not enough food.

When I grow up I will be the President of the United States. When I am the President every American will have a home. Every American will have something to eat every day. Everyone in America will have a little money in his pocket. When I am President no ten year old boy like me will have to put his head down on the desk at school because it hurts to be hungry.

SPEECH AT THE REPUBLICAN CONVENTION

AUGUST 18, 1988

In his speech accepting the Republican presidential nomination in 1988, Vice President George Bush (1924–) celebrated voluntarism in America and concluded by leading the convention in a recitation of the Pledge of Allegiance. Bush began his public service career as a decorated World War II naval flying ace and also served as Republican congressman from Texas (1967–1971), chairman of the Republican National Committee (1973–1974), director of the CIA (1976–1977), and vice president under Ronald Reagan (1981–1989), before his election as president in 1988. As president, Bush led the United States into Operation Desert Storm, which repelled the Iraqi invasion of Kuwait.

. . . I seek the presidency for a single purpose, a purpose that has motivated millions of Americans across the years and the ocean voyages. I seek the presidency to build a better America. It's that simple, and that big.

I'm a man who sees life in terms of missions—missions defined and missions completed. And when I was a torpedo bomber pilot they defined the mission for us. And before we took off we all understood that no matter what, you try to reach the target. And there've been other missions for me—Congress and China, the CIA. But I am here tonight, and I am your candidate, because the most important work of my life is to complete the mission that we started in 1980. . . .

An election that's about ideas and values is also about philosophy. And I have one.

At the bright center is the individual. And radiating out from him or her is the family, the essential unit of closeness and of love. For it's the family that communicates to our children—to the twenty-first century—our culture, our religious faith, our traditions and history.

From the individual to the family to the community, and then on out to the town, to the church and the school, and, still echoing out, to the country, the state, and the nation—each doing only what it does well, and no more. And I believe that power must always be kept close to the individual, close to the hands that raise the family and run the home.

I am guided by certain traditions. One is that there's a God and he is good, and his love, while free, has a self-imposed cost; we must be good to one another.

I believe in another tradition that is, by now, imbedded in the national soul. It's that learning is good in and of itself. You know, the mothers of the Jewish ghettos of the East would pour honey on a book so the children would know that learning is sweet. And the parents who settled hungry Kansas would take their children in from the fields when a teacher came. That is our history. . . .

For we are a nation of communities, of thousands and tens of thousands of ethnic, religious, social, business, labor union, neighborhood, regional, and other organizations, all of them varied, voluntary, and unique.

This is America: the Knights of Columbus, the Grange, Hadassah, the Disabled American Veterans, the Order of Ahepa, the Business and Professional Women of America, the union hall, the Bible study group, LULAC, Holy Name—a brilliant diversity spread like stars, like a thousand points of light in a broad and peaceful sky. . . .

For seven and a half years I've worked with a president—I've seen what crosses that big desk. I've seen the unexpected crisis that arrives in a cable in a young aide's hand. And I've seen the problems that simmer on for decades and suddenly demand resolution. And I've seen modest decisions made with anguish, and crucial decisions made with dispatch.

And so know that what it all comes down to, this election—what it all comes down to, after all the shouting and the cheers—is the man at the desk. And who should sit at that desk.

My friends, I am that man.

I say it—I say it without boast or bravado. I've fought for my country, I've served, I've built—and I'll go from the hills to the hollows, from the cities to the suburbs to the loneliest town on the quietest street, to take our message of hope and growth for every American to every American.

I will keep America moving forward, always forward—for a better America, for an endless, enduring dream and a thousand points of light.

This is my mission. And I will complete it.

Thank you. You know, it is customary to end an address with a pledge, or saying, that holds a special meaning. And I've chosen one that we all know by heart, one that we all learned in school. And I ask everyone in this great hall to stand and join me in this. We all know it.

"I pledge allegiance to the flag of the United States of America and to the Republic for which it stands, one nation, under God, indivisible, with liberty and justice for all."

Thank you. God bless you.

AMY TAN

The Joy Luck Club

1989

California-born Amy Tan (1952–) wrote the multigenerational family saga of her Chinese immigrant family in her first novel, *The Joy Luck Club* (1989), which was a National Book Award Finalist, was translated into over twenty languages, and was made into a movie. It tells the powerful story of a Chinese American woman struggling to integrate her Chinese heritage and her family's traumatic history with contemporary American life.

The old woman remembered a swan she had bought many years ago in Shanghai for a foolish sum. This bird, boasted the market vendor, was once a duck that stretched its neck in hopes of becoming a goose, and now look!—it is too beautiful to eat.

Then the woman and the swan sailed across an ocean many thousands of li wide, stretching their necks toward America. On her journey she cooed to the swan: "In America I will have a daughter just like me. But over there nobody will say her worth is measured by the loudness of her husband's belch. Over there nobody will look down on her, because I will make her speak only perfect American English. And over there she will always be too full to swallow any sorrow! She will know my meaning, because I will give her this swan—a creature that became more than what was hoped for."

But when she arrived in the new country, the immigration officials pulled her swan away from her, leaving the woman fluttering her arms and with only one swan feather for a memory. And then she had to fill out so many forms she forgot why she had come and what she had left behind.

Now the woman was old. And she had a daughter who grew up speaking only English and swallowing more Coca-Cola than sorrow. For a long time now the woman had wanted to give her daughter the single swan feather and tell her, "This feather may look worthless, but it comes from afar and carries with it all my good intentions." And she waited, year after year, for the day she could tell her daughter this in perfect American English.

JING-MEI WOO: THE JOY LUCK CLUB

My father has asked me to be the fourth corner at the Joy Luck Club. I am to replace my mother, whose seat at the mah jong table has been empty since she died two months ago. My father thinks she was killed by her own thoughts.

"She had a new idea inside her head," said my father. "But before it could come out of her mouth, the thought grew too big and burst. It must have been a very bad idea."

The doctor said she died of a cerebral aneuryism. And her friends at the Joy Luck Club said she died just like a rabbit: quickly and with unfinished business left behind. My mother was supposed to host the next meeting of the Joy Luck Club.

The week before she died, she called me, full of pride, full of life: "Auntie Lin cooked red bean soup for Joy Luck. I'm going to cook black sesame-seed soup."

"Don't show off," I said.

"It's not showoff." She said the two soups were almost the same, *chabudwo*. Or maybe she said *butong*, not the same thing at all. It was one of those Chinese expressions that means the better half of mixed intentions. I can never remember things I didn't understand in the first place.

My mother started the San Francisco version of the Joy Luck Club in 1949, two years before I was born. This was the year my mother and father left China with one stiff leather trunk filled only with fancy silk dresses. There was no time to pack anything else, my mother had explained to my father after they boarded the boat. Still his hands swam frantically between the slippery silks, looking for his cotton shirts and wool pants.

When they arrived in San Francisco, my father made her hide those shiny clothes. She wore the same brown-checked Chinese dress until the Refugee Welcome Society gave her two hand-me-down dresses, all too large in sizes for American women. The society was composed of a group of white-haired American missionary ladies from the First Chinese Baptist Church. And because of their gifts, my parents could not refuse their invitation to join the church. Nor could they ignore the old ladies' practical advice to improve their English through Bible study class on Wednesday nights and, later, through choir practice on Saturday mornings. This was how my parents met the Hsus, the Jongs, and the St. Clairs. My mother could sense that the women of these families also had unspeakable tragedies they had left behind in China and hopes they couldn't begin to express in their fragile English. Or at least, my mother recognized the numbness in these women's faces. And she saw how quickly their eyes moved when she told them her idea for the Joy Luck Club.

Joy Luck was an idea my mother remembered from the days of her first marriage in Kweilin, before the Japanese came. That's why I think of Joy Luck as her Kweilin story. It was the story she would always tell me when she was bored, when there was nothing to do, when every bowl had been washed and the Formica table had been wiped down twice, when my father sat reading the newspaper and smoking one Pall Mall cigarette after another, a warning not to disturb him. This is when my mother would take out a box of old ski sweaters sent to us by unseen relatives from Vancouver. She would snip the bottom of a sweater and pull out a kinky thread of yarn, anchoring it to a piece of cardboard. And as she began to roll with one sweeping rhythm, she would start her story. Over the years, she told me the same story, except for the ending, which grew darker, casting long shadows into her life, and eventually into mine.

ARNOLD SCHWARZENEGGER

THE EDUCATION OF AN AMERICAN

SEPTEMBER 21, 2001

Actor, bodybuilder, and former Mr. Universe, Arnold Schwarzenegger (1947–) came from modest beginnings in his native Austria. The house he lived in had no phone, refrigerator, or indoor plumbing until he was a teenager. At age eleven, after seeing his first film, he became fascinated with America. "What I wanted was to be part of the big cause, the big dreamers, the big skyscrapers, the big money, the big action." In the late 1960s, he won the Mr. Universe contest and then starred in the documentary film, *Pumping Iron* (1977), followed by box office hits *Conan the Barbarian* (1982), *Terminator* (1984), and *Terminator 2: Judgment Day* (1991). He became a naturalized U.S. citizen in 1983.

. . . Actually for me, going out into the "real world" meant "coming to America." And it wasn't really the "things" I wish I'd known before I came—because I always thought I knew everything already. That's part of my charm!

But you know, the truth is, some of the things I knew when I came here were right on the money—and served me well. But some of the things I thought were true turned out to be terribly wrong. . . .

The first thing I was dead right about was this: where you're from is not as important as where you're going. Take it from me: if you're too focused on where you started, you'll never get where you're headed.

Where I started was a little farm community outside the Austrian town of Graz. Now, that may make you think of sunny hillsides with buttercups dancing in the breeze, and happy children with rosy cheeks, eating strudel.

But that's not what I think of.

First of all, strudel was a luxury. It was right after World War II, and the country was absolutely devastated and destroyed. We had no flushing toilet in the house. No refrigerator. No television. What we did have was food rations—and we did have British tanks around to give us kids an occasional lift to the elementary school.

But you know what? My background has never held me back. Instead, I've used it to my advantage—to fuel the intense desire to get the hell out of there! It's that desire that powered a very strong will in me.

I always say, "If you starve someone, you only make them more hungry." And I definitely was hungry to break out and do something very special. . . .

So we move on to another principle I was dead right about: No one's ever been successful without having a goal—and a plan for how to achieve it. . . .

And finally: the American Dream.

Perhaps the thing I was most dead right about was this country—America.

Ever since childhood, I fantasized over the pictures of America I saw in the magazines, the movies, the newsreels. I loved the skyscrapers and the beaches—the huge cars with fins, zooming down five-lane highways. I said to myself, "I want to be there! I want to be part of it!"

Well, I came here in 1968 with $20 in my pocket. And I have to tell you that within a week, I had an apartment and dishes and silverware and a television—all from people I had just met that week in the gym.

And within six months, I was asked to star in a movie. All right, granted they didn't use my real name—I was billed as "Arnold Strong." And they didn't use my real voice. They dubbed it in. But I was in a movie! It's called *Hercules in New York*. And I know every one of you has seen it. And you can rent it at Blockbuster!

But I have to say, I called all my friends back in Europe and said: "It's true! You can do anything in this country! Come over here! It's everything you imagine—and more!"

I decided right then—very early on—that I wanted to weave myself right into the fabric of America. I wanted to become a citizen. I wanted to work hard. I wanted to go to college and study politics, economics, and culture.

Today I stand before you—an immigrant success story.

I am the living, breathing incarnation of The American Dream.

I became the leading bodybuilder in the world. I've made millions as a businessman many times over. My movies have hit more than $2 billion at the box office.

I was dead right about it: If you have the desire and the determination—and you are willing to be a part of this country and embrace it—it will embrace you. There is nowhere like it on Earth. . . .

Which brings me to the biggest thing I was dead wrong about: whose dream is it, anyway?

It was a great day for me in 1989, when I was called to Washington. President Bush named me Chairman of the President's Council on Physical Fitness. I traveled to all 50 states, promoting fitness and sports programs in schools.

I thought I could inspire kids with a powerful message—especially in the inner cities: "If a poor kid like me from a farm town in Europe can make it, then anyone can make it in this great country!"

This was where I got my biggest and rudest awakening.

Because as I went around from inner city to inner city, I saw first-hand that this is not the land of opportunity for those kids. Most of them don't get any of the tools that I got.

Look at everything I had in my childhood: two parents, a well-equipped school with terrific sports facilities, the same education and books for every kid in the country. After school, there was a parent to help with homework—and safe places to do sports like soccer, sledding and skating.

I was accountable to someone all the time: parents, teachers, mentors, and coaches. Around the clock, I had people taking care of me, encouraging, and nurturing me. All this gave me a strong foundation, which gave me the confidence, which gave me the inner strength to believe in myself and know I could make it.

And it worked.

You know, I used to go around saying: "Everybody should pull himself up by his own bootstraps—just like I did!"

What I learned about this country is this: Not everybody has boots.

I saw it firsthand, when I met the children in the inner cities. We think we're motivating them by beaming the American Dream in to them—on TV and in movies.

Wrong!

Most of them don't get the motivation. Instead, they hear: "You're a loser. You'll never make it out of the barrio or the ghetto. You'll never get out."

The more I saw, the more I realized I'd been wrong when I thought the American Dream was available to everyone. Because even though it is the Land of Opportunity for me, and the majority of Americans, millions are left behind. It's not a level playing field for them. . . .

So really, it's not just the bodybuilding and the business and the box office for me anymore. Helping the kids who need help is the most important goal I have.

This is what it means for me to be an American. Maybe that's what it could mean for you, too! No matter how much success you have, you can be more successful by reaching out to someone who needs you.

A proton–anti-proton collider detector, Fermilab, Batavia, Illinois, 1999.

Capitalizing on the "Cognitive Niche"

1999

College dropout and computer whiz kid, corporate executive, and philanthropist, William H. Gates (1955–) was born and raised in Seattle, Washington. His interest in computers, which began at the age of thirteen, led Gates to realize the potential of a standard operating platform for the computer era, and through the success of his company Microsoft, he became one of the world's richest men. Criticized for its monopolistic practices, Microsoft was sued by the U.S. government in the 1990s. In 2000, Gates established the Bill and Melinda Gates Foundation, which has become the world's largest philanthropy dedicated to improving health and education worldwide.

Human beings are not the biggest animals. We're not the strongest or fastest. We're not the sharpest in sight or smell. It's amazing how we survived against the many fierce creatures of nature. We survived and prospered because of our brains. We evolved to fill the cognitive niche. We learned how to use tools, to build shelter, to invent agriculture, to domesticate livestock, to develop civilization and culture, to cure and prevent disease. Our tools and technologies have helped us to shape the environment around us.

I'm an optimist. I believe in progress. I'd much rather be alive today than at any time in history—and not just because in an earlier age my skill set wouldn't have been as valuable and I'd have been a prime candidate for some beast's dinner. The tools of the Industrial Age extended the capabilities of our muscles. The tools of the digital age extend the capabilities of our minds. I'm even happier for my children, who will come of age in this new world.

By embracing the digital age, we can accelerate the positive effects and mitigate the challenges such as privacy and have-vs.-have-not. If we sit back and wait for the digital age to come to us on terms defined by others, we won't be able to do either. The Web lifestyle can increase citizen involvement in government. Many of the decisions to be made are political and social, not technical. These include how we ensure access for everyone and how we protect children. Citizens in every culture must engage on the social and political impact of digital technology to ensure that the new digital age reflects the society they want to create.

If we are reactive and let change overwhelm us or pass us by, we will perceive change negatively. If we are proactive, seek to understand the future now, and embrace change, the idea of the unexpected can be positive and uplifting. Astronomer Carl Sagan in his last book, *Billions and Billions*, said: "The prediction I can make with the highest confidence is that the most amazing discoveries will be the ones we are not today wise enough to foresee."

As tough and uncertain as the digital world makes it for business—it's evolve rapidly or die—we will all benefit. We're going to get improved products and services, more responsiveness to complaints, lower costs, and more choices. We're going to get better government and social services at substantially less expense.

This world is coming. A big part of it comes through businesses using a digital nervous system to radically improve their processes.

A digital nervous system can help business redefine itself and its role in the future, but energy or paralysis, success or failure, depends on business leaders. Only you can prepare your organization and make the investments necessary to capitalize on the rapidly dawning digital age.

Digital tools magnify the abilities that make us unique in the world: the ability to think, the ability to articulate our thoughts, the ability to work together to act on those thoughts. I strongly believe that if companies empower their employees to solve problems and give them potent tools to do this with, they will always be amazed at how much creativity and initiative will blossom forth.

MARIO TAMA, A DNA plate used for sequencing and mapping the human genome, Rockville, Maryland, 2000.

OUR LAND

BRETT WESTON, Carmel Valley, California, 1949.

FOR THOUSANDS OF years, the American landscape has nurtured and sustained her people like no other. Native Americans celebrated their relationship with the land, and they have been joined by all those who followed. For the past four hundred years, America has fed, clothed, and sheltered the millions who settled here, and in modern times, has sent food to much of the world as well. This abundance has made possible a way of life unequaled by any society in history. We have returned the gift, in part, through a rich legacy of song and story. The myths and legends of the Native Americans; tall tales of frontier childhood; the poetry of Walt Whitman and Robert Frost; the songs of the great American musicals; and the folk ballads of Huddie Ledbetter and Woody Guthrie all celebrate the land we love. The contrasts between New England woods and whaling towns, the rich soil of the rural South, and majestic Western vistas give continued energy to American landscape writing and a constant sense of discovery and wonder as we travel across this continent.

Early American society was tied to the land, and America's wealth was based on an agrarian way of life. Larger plantations depended on slave labor, but the ideal of the rugged individualist, the yeoman farmer hacking a life out of a hostile wilderness, took hold of the American imagination. The values of hard work, self-sufficiency, and community participation were tied to farm and frontier life. The sense of manifest destiny and limitless resources shaped our mythology, and later, when more Americans lived in cities, poets, writers, and musicians celebrated the dynamic energy of our urban centers. Today our concern is to protect the wilderness without merely romanticizing it, to preserve the quiet places, the rushing water and the still pools, the wildflowers and the prairie, the seashore and the forests so that future generations of Americans will be able to call them home.

IRVING BERLIN

GOD BLESS AMERICA

1938

Irving Berlin (1888–1989), who passed through Ellis Island as a five-year-old Russian immigrant, grew up to become one of America's greatest composers. In addition to "God Bless America," Berlin wrote such classics as "White Christmas," "Anything You Can Do," and "Blue Skies." His Broadway shows include *Annie Get Your Gun* (1946) and *Call Me Madam* (1950). His songs were featured in films such as *The Jazz Singer* (1927), *Top Hat* (1935), and *Holiday Inn* (1942). In 1938, as the possibility of a new world war loomed over Europe and civil war still raged in Spain, Berlin felt obliged to write a "great peace song." Turning to an old composition he had tinkered with some twenty years earlier, he started to rework its lyrics. The result was "God Bless America," sung for the first time on radio by Kate Smith during her Armistice Day broadcast in 1938. In a gesture of thanks to his adopted country, Berlin donated his royalties from the song to the Boy Scouts and Girl Scouts of America, a practice that continues to this day.

While the storm clouds gather
Far across the sea,
Let us swear allegiance
To a land that's free;
Let us all be grateful
For a land so fair,
As we raise our voices
In a solemn prayer.

God bless America,
Land that I love.
Stand beside her and guide her
Through the night with a light from above.
From the mountains, to the prairies,
To the oceans white with foam,
God bless America,
My home sweet home.

THE THANKSGIVINGS

1891

The Iroquois, a confederacy of six Native American nations—the Mohawk, Oneida, Onondaga, Tuscarora, Cayuga, and Seneca—inhabited New York State in palisaded villages containing long houses. Their complex political structure and military strength was weakened when they supported the British in the American Revolution.

"The Thanksgivings" was originally translated by Harriet Maxwell Converse (1835–1903), who had devoted her life to the cause and culture of the Six Nations Tribe in the state of New York. Because of her efforts to defeat an 1891 law that would have pushed the New York Indians off their reservation, she was made a chief of the Six Nations—the only time such an honor was ever bestowed on a white woman.

We who are here present thank the Great Spirit that we are here to praise Him.

We thank Him that He has created men and women, and ordered that these beings shall always be living to multiply the earth.

We thank Him for making the earth and giving these beings its products to live on.

We thank Him for the water that comes out of the earth and runs for our lands.

We thank Him for all the animals on the earth.

We thank Him for certain timbers that grow and have fluids coming from them for us all.

We thank Him for the branches of the trees that grow shadows for our shelter.

We thank Him for the beings that come from the west, the thunder and lightning that water the earth.

We thank Him for the light which we call our oldest brother, the sun that works for our good.

We thank Him for all the fruits that grow on the trees and vines.

We thank Him for his goodness in making the forests, and thank all its trees.

We thank Him for the darkness that gives us rest, and for the kind Being of the darkness that gives us light, the moon.

We thank Him for the bright spots in the skies that give us signs, the stars.

We give Him thanks for our supporters, who have charge of our harvests.

We give thanks that the voice of the Great Spirit can still be heard through the words of Ga-ne-o-di-o.

We thank the Great Spirit that we have the privilege of this pleasant occasion.

We give thanks for the persons who can sing the Great Spirit's music, and hope they will be privileged to continue in his faith.

We thank the Great Spirit for all the persons who perform the ceremonies on this occasion.

Twelfth Song of the Thunder

1887

"Twelfth Song of the Thunder" is part of the ancient Navajo Mountain Chant, a nine-day ceremony of ritual, song, and dance intended to cure ailing members of the tribe while also calling forth a general blessing of healing for the whole tribe. The song was originally translated by Washington Matthews (1843–1905), an Irish immigrant who had first come into contact with Native Americans during service as a surgeon in Missouri during the Civil War. Later, Matthews was stationed in the American Southwest, where he encountered the Navajo and began to study their life and culture. In 1884, prior to returning to Washington, D.C., he was permitted to observe an entire Mountain Chant ceremony, which he chronicled in his 1887 publication *The Mountain Chant: A Navajo Ceremony*. It was the first time the ceremony had ever been brought to the attention of the public at large.

The voice that beautifies the land!
The voice above,
The voice of the thunder
Within the dark cloud
Again and again it sounds,
The voice that beautifies the land.

The voice that beautifies the land!
The voice below,
The voice of the grasshopper
Among the plants
Again and again it sounds,
The voice that beautifies the land.

STEPHEN FOSTER

OH! SUSANNA

1848

Born on the Fourth of July in Pittsburgh, Pennsylvania, Stephen Foster (1826–1864) composed some of America's most beloved songs. Influenced by black folk songs and minstrel shows, Foster wrote "Oh! Susanna" in 1846 while working as a bookkeeper in Cincinnati, Ohio, and the song became a favorite of the pioneers heading west during the Gold Rush of 1849. A terrible businessman, Foster never made any money from his music and died in poverty. His best known songs include "My Old Kentucky Home," "Jeanie with the Light Brown Hair," "Beautiful Dreamer," and "Camptown Races."

I come from Alabama with a banjo on my knee;
I'm gone to Lou'siana
My true love for to see.
It rained all night the day I left,
The weather it was dry.
The sun so hot I froze to death,
Susanna, don't you cry.

CHORUS:
Oh! Susanna, don't you cry for me;
I come from Alabama with a banjo on my knee.

I had a dream the other night,
When everything was still;
I thought I saw Susanna dear,
a'coming down the hill.
The buckwheat cake was in her mouth,
The tear was in her eye.
Says I, I'm coming from the South,
Susanna, don't you cry.

I soon will be in New Orleans,
And then I'll look all 'round,
And when I find Susanna,
I'll fall upon the ground.

But if I do not find her,
This darkey'll surely die,
And when I'm dead and buried,
Susanna, don't you cry.

OLD COTTON FIELDS AT HOME

1936

Born on a plantation in Louisiana, Huddie Ledbetter (1885–1949), later known as "Leadbelly," spent much of his early life traveling through Louisiana and Texas, picking cotton and working on railroad lines. During the early 1930s, while Ledbetter was in a Louisiana state prison for attempted murder, his music was discovered by John and Alan Lomax, the pioneering musicologists who recognized indigenous music as an American art form and preserved it for the Library of Congress. After his release from prison in 1934, Ledbetter headed north with his guitar and found national and international acclaim. His other well-known songs include "Goodnight, Irene," "Rock Island Line," and "Bring Me a Little Water, Silvy."

1.

When I was a little bitty baby
My mother would rock me in the cradle
In them old, old cotton fields at home.
When I was a little bitty baby
My mother would rock me in the cradle
In them old cotton fields at home.

Chorus:
Oh, when them cotton balls get rotten
You couldn't pick very much cotton,
In them old cotton fields at home.
It was down in Lou'siana,
Just about a mile from Texarkana,
In them old cotton fields at home.

2.

It may sound a little bit funny,
But you didn't make very much money
In them old cotton fields at home.
It may sound a little bit funny,
But you didn't make very much money
In them old cotton fields at home. (*Chorus*)

3.

I was over in Arkansas,
People ask me, what you come here for
In them old cotton fields at home.
I was over in Arkansas,
People ask me, what you come here for
In them old cotton fields at home. (*Chorus*)

DOROTHEA LANGE, Sharecroppers, Georgia, 1937.

LIGHT IN AUGUST

1932

Published in 1932, *Light in August* is the seventh in the series of Faulkner's novels set in the fictional Yoknapatawpha County, Mississippi. The book tells the story of Joe Christmas, an orphan whose mixed racial heritage dooms him to a life of social isolation and violence. In this opening passage, Faulkner interweaves lyrical external description with rich internal monologue as he introduces Lena Grove, a young woman who leaves home seeking the father of her unborn child.

Sitting beside the road, watching the wagon mount the hill toward her, Lena thinks, 'I have come from Alabama: a fur piece. All the way from Alabama a-walking. A fur piece.' Thinking *although I have not been quite a month on the road I am already in Mississippi, further from home than I have ever been before. I am now further from Doane's Mill than I have been since I was twelve years old.*

She had never even been to Doane's Mill until after her father and mother died, though six or eight times a year she went to town on Saturday, in the wagon, in a mailorder dress and her bare feet flat in the wagon bed and her shoes wrapped in a piece of paper beside her on the seat. She would put on the shoes just before the wagon reached town. After she got to be a big girl she would ask her father to stop the wagon at the edge of town and she would get down and walk. She would not tell her father why she wanted to walk in instead of riding. He thought that it was because of the smooth streets, the sidewalks. But it was because she believed that the people who saw her and whom she passed on foot would believe that she lived in the town too.

When she was twelve years old her father and mother died in the same summer, in a log house of three rooms and a hall, without screens, in a room lighted by a bugswirled kerosene lamp, the naked floor worn smooth as old silver by naked feet. She was the youngest living child. Her mother died first. She said, "Take care of paw." Lena did so. Then one day her father said, "You go to Doane's Mill with McKinley. You get ready to go, be ready when he comes." Then he died. McKinley, the brother, arrived in a wagon. They buried the father in a grove behind a country church one afternoon, with a pine headstone. The next morning she departed forever, though it is possible that she did not know this at the time, in the wagon with McKinley, for Doane's Mill. The wagon was borrowed and the brother had promised to return it by nightfall.

The brother worked in the mill. All the men in the village worked in the mill or for it. It was cutting pine. It had been there seven years and in seven years more it would destroy all the timber within its reach. Then some of the machinery and most of the men who ran it and existed because of and for it would be loaded onto freight cars and moved away. But some of the machinery would be left, since new pieces could always be bought on the installment plan—gaunt, staring, motionless wheels rising from mounds of brick rubble and ragged weeds with a quality profoundly astonishing, and gutted boilers lifting their rusting and unsmoking stacks with an air stubborn, baffled and bemused upon a stumppocked scene of profound and peaceful desolation, unplowed, untilled, gutting slowly into red and choked ravines beneath the long quiet rains of autumn and the galloping fury of vernal equinoxes. Then the hamlet which at its best day had borne no name listed on Postoffice Department annals would not now even be remembered by the hookwormridden heirs at large who pulled the buildings down and burned them in cookstoves and winter grates.

LET US NOW PRAISE FAMOUS MEN

1941

James Agee (1909–1955) was born in Knoxville, Tennessee, and attended Harvard University. In 1936, while working for *Fortune* magazine, Agee and photographer Walker Evans were sent to do an article about sharecroppers in Alabama. Out of that journey, Agee composed his journalistic masterpiece, *Let Us Now Praise Famous Men*. Agee later became a film critic for *Time* magazine and wrote several screenplays, including *The African Queen*, which won Humphrey Bogart his sole Oscar in 1951. His novel *A Death in the Family* was published after his death in 1957 and won the Pulitzer Prize the following year.

(On the Porch: 1

The house and all that was in it had now descended deep beneath the gradual spiral it had sunk through; it lay formal under the order of entire silence. In the square pine room at the back the bodies of the man of thirty and of his wife and of their children lay on shallow mattresses on their iron beds and on the rigid floor, and they were sleeping, and the dog lay asleep in the hallway. Most human beings, most animals and birds who live in the sheltering ring of human influence, and a great portion of all the branched tribes of living in earth and air and water upon a half of the world, were stunned with sleep. That region of the earth on which we were at this time transient was some hours fallen beneath the fascination of the stone, steady shadow of the planet, and lay now listing toward the last depth; and now by a blockade of the sun were clearly disclosed those discharges of light which teach us what little we can learn of the stars and of the true nature of our surroundings. There was no longer any sound of the settling or ticking of any part of the structure of the house; the bone pine hung on its nails like an abandoned Christ. There was no longer any sound of the sinking and settling, like gently foundering, fatal boats, of the bodies and brains of this human family through the late stages of fatigue unharnessed or the early phases of sleep; not was there any longer the sense of any of these sounds, nor was there, even, the sound or the sense of breathing. Bone and bone, blood and blood, life and life disjointed and abandoned they lay graven in so final depth, that dreams attend them seemed not plausible. Fish halted on the middle and serene of blind sea water sleeping lidless lensed; their breathing, their sleeping subsistence, the effortless nursing of ignorant plants; entirely silenced, sleepers, delicate planets, insects, cherished in amber, mured in night, autumn of action, sorrow's short winter, waterhole where gather the weak wild beasts; night; night: sleep; sleep. . . .

(We lay on the front porch:. . .

All over Alabama, the lamps are out. Every leaf drenches the touch; the spider's net is heavy. The roads lie there, with nothing to use them. The fields lie there, with nothing at work in them, neither man nor beast. The plow handles are wet, and the rails and the frogplates and the weeds between the ties: and not even the hurryings and hoarse sorrows of a distant train, on other roads, is heard. The little towns, the county seats, house by house white-painted and elaborately sawn among their heavy and dark-lighted leaves, in the spaced protections of their mineral light they stand so prim, so voided, so undefended upon starlight, that it is inconceivable to despise or to scorn a white man, an owner of land; even in Birmingham, mile on mile, save for the sudden frightful streaming, almost instantly diminished and silent, of a closed black car, and save stone lonesome sinister heelbeats, that show never a face and enter, soon, a frame door flush with the pavement, and ascend the immediate light-less staircase, mile on mile, stone, stone, smooth charted streams of stone, the streets under their lifted lamps lie void before eternity. New Orleans is stirring, rattling, and sliding faintly in its fragrance and in the enormous richness of its lust; taxis are still parked along Dauphine Street and the breastlike, floral air is itchy with the stilettos and embroiderings above black blood drumthroes of an eloquent cracked indiscoverable cornet, which exists only in the imagination and somewhere in the past, in the broken heart of Louis Armstrong; yet even in that small portion which is the infested genitals of that city, never free, neither of desire not of waking pain, there are the qualities of the tender desolations of profoundest night. Beneath, the gulf lies dreaming, and beneath, dreaming, that woman, that id, the lower American continent, lies spread before heaven in her wealth. The parks of her cities are iron, loam, silent, and sweet fountains shut, and the pure façades, embroiled, limelike in street light are sharp, are still.

ELIZABETH BISHOP

FLORIDA

1946

Elizabeth Bishop's early life was marked by her mother's mental illness and her father's death. Raised by her Canadian grandparents, Bishop (1911–1979) attended Vassar College, where she met her mentor, poet Marianne Moore. She traveled extensively through Europe and North Africa, settled in Key West, and lived in Brazil for sixteen years before teaching at Harvard, NYU, and MIT. In 1956, Bishop was awarded the Pulitzer Prize for *Poems: North and South—A Cold Spring*. *Questions of Travel* (1965) won the National Book Award. In addition to writing poetry, Bishop translated works from Brazilian authors and contributed often to *The New Yorker*. Bishop's precise yet subtle imagery is often concerned with the natural world.

The state with the prettiest name,
the state that floats in brackish water,
held together by mangrove roots
that bear while living oysters in clusters,
and when dead strew white swamps with skeletons,
dotted as if bombarded, with green hummocks
like ancient cannon-balls sprouting grass.
The state full of long S-shaped birds, blue and white,
and unseen hysterical birds who rush up the scale
every time in a tantrum.
Tanagers embarrassed by their flashiness,
and pelicans whose delight it is to clown;
who coast for fun on the strong tidal currents
in and out among the mangrove islands
and stand on the sand-bars drying their damp gold wings
on sun-lit evenings.
Enormous turtles, helpless and mild,
die and leave their barnacled shells on the beaches,
and their large white skulls with round eye-sockets
twice the size of a man's.
The palm trees clatter in the stiff breeze
like the bills of the pelicans. The tropical rain comes down
to freshen the tide-looped strings of fading shells:
Job's Tear, the Chinese Alphabet, the scarce Junonia,
parti-colored pectins and Ladies' Ears,

arranged as on a gray rag of rotted calico,
the buried Indian Princess's skirt;
with these the monotonous, endless, sagging coast-line
is delicately ornamented.

Thirty or more buzzards are drifting down, down, down,
over something they have spotted in the swamp,
in circles like stirred-up flakes of sediment
sinking through water.
Smoke from woods-fires filters fine blue solvents.
On stumps and dead trees the charring is like black velvet.
The mosquitoes
go hunting to the tune of their ferocious obbligatos.
After dark, the fireflies map the heavens in the marsh
until the moon rises.
Cold white, not bright, the moonlight is coarse-meshed,
and the careless, corrupt state is all black specks
too far apart, and ugly whites; the poorest
post-card of itself.
After dark, the pools seem to have slipped away.
The alligator, who has five distinct calls:
friendliness, love, mating, war, and a warning—
whimpers and speaks in the throat
of the Indian Princess.

MARK TWAIN

THE ADVENTURES OF HUCKLEBERRY FINN

1884

Raised in Hannibal, Missouri, Samuel Langhorne Clemens spent his early life along the Mississippi River, which was the source of his greatest inspiration. He worked as a journalist and riverboat pilot before beginning his lifelong career. The name "Mark Twain" is the riverboat term for water that is two fathoms deep. His classic tales *The Adventures of Tom Sawyer* (1876) and *Life on the Mississippi* (1883), and his masterpiece, *The Adventures of Huckleberry Finn* (1884), earned him an unrivaled position in the world of American writers. Nobel Laureate Ernest Hemingway once observed that "all modern American literature comes from one book by Mark Twain called *Huckleberry Finn.*"

Two or three days and nights went by; I reckon I might say they swum by, they slid along so quiet and smooth and lovely. Here is the way we put in the time. It was a monstrous big river down there—sometimes a mile and a half wide; we run nights, and laid up and hid daytimes; soon as night was most gone, we stopped navigating and tied up—nearly always in the dead water under a tow-head; and then cut young cotton-woods and willows and hid the raft with them. Then we set out the lines. Next we slid into the river and had a swim, so as to freshen up and cool off; then we set down on the sandy bottom where the water was about knee deep, and watched the daylight come. Not a sound, anywheres—perfectly still—just like the whole world was asleep, only sometimes the bull-frogs a-cluttering, maybe. The first thing to see, looking away over the water, was a kind of dull line—that was the woods on t'other side—you couldn't make nothing else out; then a pale place in the sky; then more paleness, spreading around; then the river softened up, away off, and warn't black any more, but gray; you could see little dark spots drifting along, ever so far away—trading scows, and such things; and long black streaks—rafts; sometimes you could hear a sweep screaking; or jumbled up voices, it was so still, and sounds come so far; and by-and-by you could see a streak on the water which you know by the look of the streak that there's a snag there in a swift current which breaks on it and makes that streak look that way; and you see the mist curl up off of the water, and the east reddens up, and the river, and you make out a log cabin in the edge of the woods, away on the bank on t'other side of the river, being a wood-yard, likely, and piled by them cheats so you can throw a dog through it anywheres; then the nice breeze springs up, and comes fanning you from over there, so cool and fresh, and sweet to smell, on account of the woods and the flowers; but sometimes not that way, because they've left dead fish laying around, gars, and such, and they do get pretty rank; and next you've got the full day, and everything smiling in the sun, and the song-birds just going it!

A little smoke couldn't be noticed, now, so we would take some fish off the lines, and cook up a hot breakfast. And afterwards we would watch the lonesomeness of the river, and kind of lazy along, and by-and-by lazy off to sleep. Wake up, by-and-by, and look to see what done it, and maybe see a steamboat, coughing along up stream, so far off towards the other side you couldn't tell nothing about her only whether she was stern-wheel or side-wheel; then for about an hour there wouldn't be nothing to hear nor nothing to see—just solid lonesomeness. Next you'd see a raft sliding by, away off yonder, and maybe a galoot on it chopping, because they're most always doing it on a raft; you'd see the ax flash, and come down—you don't hear nothing; you see that ax go up again, and by the time it's above the man's head, then you hear the *k'chunk*!—it had took all that time to come over the water. So we would put in the day, lazying around, listening to the stillness. Once there was a thick fog, and the rafts and things that went by was beating tin pans so the steamboats wouldn't run over them. A scow or a raft went by so close we could hear them talking and cussing and laughing—heard them plain; but we couldn't see no sign of them; it made you feel crawly, it was like spirits carrying on that way in the air. Jim said he believed it was spirits; but I says:

"No, spirits wouldn't say, 'dern the dern fog.'" . . .

Sometimes we'd have that whole river all to ourselves for the longest time. Yonder was the banks and the islands, across the water; and maybe a spark—which was a candle in a cabin window—and sometimes on the water you could see a spark or two—on a raft or a scow, you know; and maybe you could hear a fiddle or a song coming over from one of them crafts. It's lovely to live on a raft. We had the sky, up there, all speckled with stars, and we used to lay on our backs and look up at them, and discuss about whether they was made, or only just happened—Jim he allowed they was made, but I allowed they happened; I judged it would have took too long to *make* so many. Jim said the moon could a *laid* them; well, that looked kind of reasonable, so I didn't say nothing against it, because I've seen a frog lay most as many, so of course it could be done. We used to watch the stars that fell, too, and see them streak down. Jim allowed they'd got spoiled and was hove out of the nest.

Once or twice of a night we would see a steamboat slipping along in the dark, and now and then she would belch a whole world of sparks up out of her chimbleys, and they would rain down in the river and look awful pretty; then she would turn a corner and her lights would wink out and her pow-wow shut off and leave the river still again; and by-and-by her waves would get to us, a long time after she was gone, and joggle the raft a bit, and after that you wouldn't hear nothing for you couldn't tell how long, except maybe frogs or something.

After midnight the people on shore went to bed, and then for two or three hours the shores was black—no more sparks in the cabin windows. These sparks was our clock—the first one that showed again meant morning was coming, so we hunted a place to hide and tie up, right away.

ROBERT FROST

STOPPING BY WOODS ON A SNOWY EVENING

1923

Poet Robert Frost once told a friend that this poem was his "best bid for remembrance." Published as part of a collection of poems titled *New Hampshire* (which won him the first of four Pulitzer Prizes), the poem derives its power in part from its multiple interpretations. Images of natural beauty contrast with themes of faith and, some say, a foreshadowing of death.

Whose woods these are I think I know.
His house is in the village though;
He will not see me stopping here
To watch his woods fill up with snow.

My little horse must think it queer
To stop without a farmhouse near
Between the woods and frozen lake
The darkest evening of the year.

He gives his harness bells a shake
To ask if there is some mistake.
The only other sound's the sweep
Of easy wind and downy flake.

The woods are lovely, dark and deep,
But I have promises to keep,
And miles to go before I sleep,
And miles to go before I sleep.

MOBY-DICK

Moby-Dick, or the Whale, the epic story by Herman Melville of Captain Ahab's obsession with the white whale who had taken his leg, is universally acclaimed as one of the greatest novels ever written. A gripping adventure, rich allegory, and technical tour de force, the novel draws on Melville's own seafaring experience as a cabin boy bound for Europe, then on a whaler in the South Pacific, where he jumped ship and was captured by cannibals. He spent another year in the South Pacific, returning home in 1844. He later settled in Pittsfield, Massachusetts, and wrote several novels based on his seafaring adventures, such as *Typee: A Peep at Polynesian Life* (1846) and *Omoo, a Narrative of Adventures in the South Seas* (1847), which brought him financial and literary success. However, the failure of *Moby-Dick* left him in debt and poor health, and though he continued to publish such stories as "Bartleby the Scrivener" (1853) and "Benito Cereno" (1855), he had to sell his farm and work as a customs inspector in New York City. Melville died in poverty; *Moby-Dick* was not recognized as a literary masterpiece until the 1920s.

Nantucket! Take out your map and look at it. See what a real corner of the world it occupies; how it stands there, away off shore, more lonely than the Eddystone lighthouse. Look at it—a mere hillock, and elbow of sand; all beach, without a background. There is more sand there than you would use in twenty years as a substitute for blotting paper. Some gamesome wights will tell you that they have to plant weeds there, they don't grow naturally; that they import Canada thistles; that they have to send beyond seas for a spile to stop a leak in an oil cask; that pieces of wood in Nantucket are carried about like bits of the true cross in Rome; that people there plant toadstools before their houses, to get under the shade in summer time; that one blade of grass makes an oasis, three blades in a day's walk a prairie; that they wear quicksand shoes, something like Laplander snow-shoes; that they are so shut up, belted about, every way inclosed, surrounded, and made an utter island of by the ocean, that to their very chairs and tables small clams will sometimes be found adhering, as to the backs of sea turtles. But these extravaganzas only show that Nantucket is no Illinois.

Look now at the wondrous traditional story of how this island was settled by the red-men. Thus goes the legend. In olden times an eagle swooped down upon the New England coast, and carried off an infant Indian in his talons. With loud lament the parents saw their child borne out of sight over the wide waters. They resolved to follow in the same direction. Setting out in their canoes, after a perilous passage they discovered the island, and there they found an empty ivory casket,—the poor little Indian's skeleton.

What wonder, then, that these Nantucketers, born on a beach, should take to the sea for a livelihood! They first caught crabs and quahogs in the sand; grown bolder, they waded out with nets for mackerel; more experienced, they pushed off in boats and captured cod; and at last, launching a navy of great ships on the sea, explored this watery world; put an incessant belt of circumnavigations round it; peeped in at Behring's Straits; and in all seasons and all oceans declared everlasting war with the mightiest animated mass that has survived the flood; most monstrous and most mountainous! That Himmalehan, salt-sea Mastodon, clothed with such portentousness of unconscious power, that his very panics are more to be dreaded than his most fearless and malicious assaults! . . .

The Nantucketer, he alone resides and riots on the sea; he alone, in Bible language, goes down to it in ships; to and fro ploughing it as his own special plantation. *There* is his home; *there* lies his business, which a Noah's flood would not interrupt, though it overwhelmed all the millions in China. He lives on the sea, as prairie cocks in the prairie; he hides among the waves, he climbs them as chamois hunters climb the Alps. For years he knows not the land; so that when he comes to it at last, it smells like another world, more strangely than the moon would to an Earthsman. With the landless gull, that at sunset folds her wings and is rocked to sleep between billows; so at nightfall, the Nantucketer, out of sight of land, furls his sails, and lays him to his rest, while under his very pillow rush herds of walruses and whales.

JAMES W. BLAKE AND CHARLES B. LAWLOR

THE SIDEWALKS OF NEW YORK

1894

One day in 1894, New York vaudeville performer Charles B. Lawlor (1852–1925) whistled a tune to his friend James W. Blake (1862–1935), a hat salesman and part-time lyricist. The result, as the story goes, was the song "Sidewalks of New York." First performed at the Bowery's Old London Theater in New York by singer Lottie Gilson, it became Governor Al Smith's theme song during his 1924 presidential campaign.

Down in front of Casey's old brown wooden stoop
On a Summer's evening we formed a merry group;
Boys and girls together, we would sing and waltz
While the "Ginnie" played the organ
On the sidewalks of New York.

That's where Johnny Casey and little Jimmie Crowe,
With Jakey Krause, the baker, who always had the dough,
Pretty Nellie Shannon, with a dude as light as cork,
First picked up the waltz-step
On the sidewalks of New York.

Things have changed since those times,
Some are up in "G,"
Others they are wand'rers, but they all feel just like me.
They'd part with all they've got could they but once more walk
With their best girl and have a twirl
On the sidewalks of New York.

East side, west side, all around the town,
The tots sang "Ring-a-rosie," "London Bridge is falling down";
Boys and girls together, me and Mamie Rorke
Tripped the light fantastic
On the sidewalks of New York.

LESTER TALKINGTON, Jumping rope, New York, 1950.

FRED EBB AND JOHN KANDER

NEW YORK, NEW YORK

1977

The title song for the 1977 Martin Scorsese movie, *New York, New York*, was written by the team of composer John Kander (1927–) and lyricist Fred Ebb (1932–). Kander and Ebb also wrote the smash hits *Cabaret* (1966) and *Chicago* (1975). Frank Sinatra recorded his own version of the song in 1980, which quickly became a New York City favorite.

Start spreading the news, I'm leaving today
I want to be a part of it—New York, New York
These vagabond shoes, are longing to stray
Right through the very heart of it—New York, New York

I want to wake up in a city, that doesn't sleep
And find I'm king of the hill—top of the heap

These little town blues, are melting away
I'm gonna make a brand new start of it—in old New York
If I can make it there, I'll make it anywhere
It's up to you—New York, New York

New York, New York
I want to wake up in a city, that never sleeps
To find I'm A Number one, head of the list,
Cream of the crop at the top of the heap.

These little town blues, are melting away
I'm gonna make a brand new start of it—in old New York
If I can make it there, I'm gonna make it anywhere
It's up to you—New York, New York.

TONI MORRISON

JAZZ

1992

Toni Morrison (1931–) was born in Lorain, Ohio, and taught at Texas Southern and Howard Universities before working at Random House as an editor. She published her first novel, *The Bluest Eye*, in 1970. Her other novels include *Sula* (1973), *Song of Solomon* (1977), *Tar Baby* (1981), and *Jazz* (1992), from which this selection is taken. She received the Pulitzer Prize in 1988 for *Beloved*, a profound exploration of slavery and its aftermath through the tragic story of a young mother who escapes with her children to Ohio. In 1993, she became the first African American to win the Nobel Prize for literature. Morrison has continued teaching at Princeton University and published the novel *Paradise* in 1998.

Sweetheart. That's what that weather was called. Sweetheart weather, the prettiest day of the year. And that's when it started. On a day so pure and steady trees preened. Standing in the middle of a concrete slab, scared for their lives, they preened. Silly, yes, but it was that kind of day. I could see Lenox widening itself, and men coming out of their shops to look at it, to stand with their hands under their aprons or stuck in their back pockets and just look around at a street that spread itself wider to hold the day. Disabled veterans in half uniform and half civilian stopped looking gloomy at workingmen; they went to Father Divine's wagon and after they'd eaten they rolled cigarettes and settled down on the curb as though it were a Duncan Phyfe. And the women tip-tapping their heels on the pavement tripped sometimes on the sidewalk cracks because they were glancing at the trees to see where that pure, soft but steady light was coming from. The rumbling of the M11 and M2 was distant, far away and the Packards too. Even those loud Fords quieted down, and no felt like blowing his horn or leaning out the driver's side to try and embarrass somebody taking too long to cross the street. The sweetness of the day tickled them, made them holler "I give you everything I got! you come home with me!" to a woman tripping in shiny black heels over the cracks.

Young men on the rooftops changed their tune; spit and fiddled with the mouthpiece for a while and when they put it back in and blew out their cheeks it was just like the light of that day, pure and steady and kind of kind. You would have thought everything had been forgiven the way they played. The clarinets had trouble because the brass was cut so fine, not lowdown the way they love to do it, but high and fine like a young girl singing by the side of a creek, passing the time, her ankles cold in the water. The young men with brass probably never saw such a girl, or such a creek, but they made her up that day. On the rooftops. Some on 254 where there is no protective railing; another at 131, the one with the apple-green water tank, and somebody right next to it, 133, where lard cans of tomato plants are kept, and a pallet for sleeping at night. To find coolness and a way to avoid mosquitoes unable to fly that high up or unwilling to leave the tender neck meat near the street lamps. So from Lenox to St. Nicholas and across 135th Street, Lexington, from Convent to Eighth I could hear the men playing out their maple-sugar hearts, tapping it from four-hundred-year-old trees and letting it run down the trunk, wasting it because they didn't have a bucket to hold it and didn't want one either. They just wanted to let it run that day, slow if it wished, or fast, but a free run down trees bursting to give it up.

That's the way the young men on brass sounded that day. Sure of themselves, sure they were holy, standing up there on the rooftops, facing each other at first, but when it was clear that they had beat the clarinets out, they turned their backs on them, lifted those horns straight up and joined the light just as pure and steady and kind of kind.

PAUL HOSEFROS, Trumpet player, Harlem, New York, 1976.

CARL SANDBURG

CHICAGO

1916

Known as the "poet of the people," Carl Sandburg (1878–1967) was born in Galesburg, Illinois. He worked as bricklayer, shoe shiner, prairie field hand, and journalist, traveled west in boxcars as a vagabond, served in the Spanish-American War, and belonged to the Social Democratic Party. In 1913, he moved to Chicago, wrote for the *Chicago Daily News*, and in 1916 published his first book, *Chicago Poems*, to national acclaim. The second part of Sandburg's six-volume biography of Abraham Lincoln won the Pulitzer Prize in history in 1940. He won another Pulitzer in 1951 for his *Complete Poems*. In 1962, Sandburg became the poet laureate of Illinois.

Hog Butcher for the World,
Tool maker, Stacker of Wheat,
Player with Railroads and the Nation's Freight Handler;
Stormy, husky, brawling,
City of the Big Shoulders:

They tell me you are wicked and I believe them, for I have seen your painted
    women under the gas lamps luring the farm boys.
And they tell me you are crooked and I answer: Yes, it is true I have seen the
    gunman kill and go free to kill again.
And they tell me you are brutal and my reply is: On the faces of women and
    children I have seen the marks of wanton hunger.
And having answered so I turn once more to those who sneer at this my city, and I
    give them back the sneer and say to them:
Come and show me another city with lifted head singing so proud to be alive and
    coarse and strong and cunning.
Flinging magnetic curses amid the toil of piling job on job, here is a tall bold
    slugger set vivid against the little soft cities;
Fierce as a dog with tongue lapping for action, cunning as a savage pitted against
    the wilderness,

    Bareheaded,
    Shoveling,
    Wrecking,

Planning,
    Building, breaking, rebuilding,

Under the smoke, dust all over his mouth,
   laughing with white teeth,
Under the terrible burden of destiny laughing as a young man laughs,
Laughing even as an ignorant fighter laughs who has never lost a battle,
Bragging and laughing that under his wrist is the pulse, and under his ribs the
   heart of the people,
    Laughing!
Laughing the stormy, husky, brawling laughter of Youth, half-naked, sweating,
   proud to be Hog Butcher, Tool Maker, Stacker of Wheat, Player with Railroads
   and Freight Handler to the Nation.

THE SIGNIFICANCE OF THE FRONTIER IN AMERICAN HISTORY

1893

A professor at the University of Wisconsin and at Harvard, Frederick Jackson Turner (1861–1932) was the first to offer a course on the American West. In a speech delivered at the 1893 World's Columbian Exposition in Chicago (celebrating the four hundredth anniversary of Columbus's voyage), Turner advanced the theory that the frontier and the challenges of Western settlement played a formative role in shaping the American character. Turner won the Pulitzer Prize posthumously in 1933 for his book *The Significance of Sections in American History*.

In a recent bulletin of the Superintendent of the Census for 1890 appear these significant words: "Up to and including 1880 the country had a frontier of settlement, but at present the unsettled area has been so broken into by isolated bodies of settlement that there can hardly be said to be a frontier line. . . . This brief official statement marks the closing of a great historic movement. . . .

All peoples show development. . . . In the case of most nations, however, the development has occurred in a limited area; and if the nation has expanded it has met other growing peoples whom it has conquered. But in the case of the United States we have a different phenomenon. . . . [In the United States] we have the familiar phenomenon of the evolution of institutions in a limited area . . . the progress from primitive society . . . up to manufacturing civilization. But we have in addition to this a recurrence of the process of evolution in each western area reached in the process of expansion. Thus American development has exhibited not merely advance along a single line, but a return to primitive conditions on a continually advancing frontier line, and a new development for that area. American social development has been continually beginning over again on the frontier. This perennial rebirth, this fluidity of American life, this expansion westward with its new opportunities, its continuous touch with the simplicity of primitive society, furnish the forces dominating American character. The true point of view in the history of this nation is not the Atlantic coast, it is the Great West. Even the slavery struggle . . . occupies its important place in American history because of its relationship to westward expansion.

In this advance, the frontier is the outer edge of the wave. . . .

From the conditions of frontier life came intellectual traits of profound importance.
. . . The result is that to the frontier the American intellect owes its striking charac-
teristics. That coarseness and strength combined with acuteness and inquisitiveness;
that practical, inventive turn of mind, quick to find expedients; that masterful grasp
of material things, lacking in the artistic but powerful to effect great ends; that rest-
less, nervous energy; that dominant individualism, working for good and for evil, and
withal that buoyancy and exuberance which comes with freedom—these are traits of
the frontier. Since the days when the fleet of Columbus sailed into the waters of the
New World, America has been another name for opportunity, and the people of the
United States have taken their tone from the incessant expansion which has not only
been open but has even been forced upon them. . . . Movement has been its dominant
fact, and, unless this training has no effect upon a people, the American energy will
continually demand a wider field for its existence. But never again will such gifts of

P. A. MILLER & THOMAS CROFT, Land run, upon opening of the Cherokee Outlet, Oklahoma Territory, September 16, 1893.

free land offer themselves. For a moment, [with the closing of the frontier] . . . the bonds of custom are broken. . . . [And yet,] the stubborn American environment is there with its imperious summons to accept its conditions; the inherited ways of doing things are also there. . . . [Throughout American history] in spite of environment, and in spite of custom, each frontier did indeed furnish a new field of opportunity, a gate of escape from the bondage of the past; and freshness, and confidence, and scorn of older society, impatience of its restraints and its ideas, and indifference to its lessons, have accompanied the frontier. What the Mediterranean Sea was to the Greeks, breaking the bonds of custom, offering new experiences, calling out new institutions and activities, that, and more, the ever retreating frontier has been to the United States. . . . And now, four centuries from the discovery of America, at the end of a hundred years of life under the Constitution, the frontier has gone, and with its going has closed the first period of American history.

THE BALLAD OF DAVY CROCKETT

1954

Tennessee frontiersman and politician Davy Crockett (1786–1836) was one of America's great folk heroes. His legendary exploits in the backwoods of the west and in the halls of Congress provided colorful and romantic tales for a young American republic in the early years of the nineteenth century. He served under Andrew Jackson in the War of 1812, then as a state legislator in Tennessee, before becoming a three-term congressman in the House of Representatives. After his defeat in 1835, Crockett went to Texas, where he was killed at the Alamo fighting for Texan independence from Mexico. In 1955, Walt Disney released the film *Davy Crockett, King of the Wild Frontier.* Coonskin caps became the rage and the hit song "The Ballad of Davy Crockett," performed by singer Bill Hayes, sold millions and went to the top of the record charts.

Born on a mountain top in Tennessee
Greenest state in the land of the free
Raised in the woods so he knew ev'ry tree
Kilt him a b'ar when he was only three
Davy, Davy Crockett, king of the wild frontier!

. . .

Fought single-handed through the Injun War
till the Creeks was whipped an' peace was in store
An' while he was handlin' this risky chore
Made hisself a legend for evermore
Davy, Davy Crockett, king of the wild frontier!

He give his word an' he give his hand
that his Injun friends could keep their land
An' the rest of his life he took the stand
that justice was due every redskin band
Davy, Davy Crockett, holdin' his promise dear!

. . .

He went off to Congress an' served a spell
Fixin' up the Govern'ments an' laws as well

Took over Washin'ton so we heered tell
An' patched up the crack in the Liberty Bell
Davy, Davy Crockett, seein' his duty clear!

. . .

When he come home his politickin' done
The western march had just begun
So he packed his gear an' his trusty gun
An' lit out grinnin' to follow the sun
Davy, Davy Crockett, leadin' the pioneer!

He heard of Houston an' Austin so
To the Texas plains he jest had to go
Where freedom was fightin' another foe
An' they needed him at the Alamo
Davy, Davy Crockett, the man who don't know fear!

His land is biggest an' his land is best
From grassy plains to the mountain crest
He's ahead of us all meetin' the test
Followin' his legend into the West
Davy, Davy Crockett, king of the wild frontier!

WILLA CATHER

O PIONEERS!

1913

Willa Cather (c. 1876–1947), novelist, teacher, magazine editor, and master of the short story, was born in rural Virginia on a farm called Willowshade, where she spent her early days wandering the outdoors and reading the classics, like *Pilgrim's Progress*. When she was nine, her father uprooted the family and moved to the frontier town of Red Cloud, Nebraska, on the Great Plains. The harsh struggles of frontier life provided Cather with abundant material for her novels, including *O Pioneers!*, *My Ántonia* (1918), and *One of Ours*, which won the Pulitzer Prize in 1923.

The farm people were making preparations to start for home. The women were checking over their groceries and pinning their big red shawls about their heads. The men were buying tobacco and candy with what money they had left, were showing each other new boots and gloves and blue flannel shirts. Three big Bohemians were drinking raw alcohol, tinctured with oil of cinnamon. This was said to fortify one effectually against the cold, and they smacked their lips after each pull at the flask. Their volubility drowned every other noise in the place, and the overheated store sounded of their spirited language as it reeked of pipe smoke, damp woolens, and kerosene.

Carl came in, wearing his overcoat and carrying a wooden box with a brass candle. "Come," he said, "I've fed and watered your team, and the wagon is ready." He carried Emil out and tucked him down in the straw in the wagon-box. The heat had made the little boy sleepy, but he still clung to his kitten.

"You were awful good to climb so high and get my kitten, Carl. When I get big I'll climb and get little boys' kittens for them," he murmured drowsily. Before the horses were over the first hill, Emil and his cat were both fast asleep.

Although it was only four o'clock, the winter day was fading. The road led southwest, toward the streak of pale, watery light that glimmered in the leaden sky. The light fell upon the two sad young faces that were turned mutely toward it: upon the eyes of the girl, who seemed to be looking with such anguished perplexity into the future; upon the sombre eyes of the boy, who seemed already to be looking into the past. The little town behind them had vanished as if it had never been, had fallen behind the swell of the prairie, and the stern frozen country received them into its bosom. The homesteads were few and far apart; here and there a windmill gaunt against the sky, a sod house crouching in a hollow. But the great fact was the land itself, which seemed to overwhelm the little beginnings of human society that struggled in its sombre wastes. It was from facing this vast hardness that the boy's mouth had become so bitter; because he felt that men were too weak to make any mark here, that the land wanted to be let alone, to preserve its own fierce strength, its peculiar, savage kind of beauty, its uninterrupted mournfulness.

The wagon jolted along over the frozen road. The two friends had less to say to each other than usual, as if the cold had somehow penetrated to their hearts.

"Did Lou and Oscar go to the Blue to cut wood to-day?" Carl asked.

"Yes. I'm almost sorry I let them go, it's turned so cold. But mother frets if the wood gets low." She stopped and put her hand to her forehead, brushing back her hair. "I don't know what is to become of us, Carl, if father has to die. I don't dare to think about it. I wish we could all go with him and let the grass grow back over everything."

THEODORE C. TEEPLE, Jacob Rohr
Barnraising, Massillon, Ohio, c. 1888.

RESPONSE TO THE BREAKUP OF THEIR RESERVATION

1903

In 1887, the U.S. Congress passed the Dawes General Allotment Act. At the time, Native Americans possessed some 138 million acres. In 1934, when the act expired, 90 million of those acres were owned by whites. According to Commissioner of Indian Affairs Thomas Jefferson Morgan, in 1889, "The Indians must conform to the 'white man's ways.' Peaceably if they will, forcibly if they must . . . The tribal relations should be broken up, socialism destroyed, and the family and the autonomy of the individual substituted." The following dialogue is from a meeting between a representative of the federal government and members of the Northern Ute tribe of Utah as their reservation is about to be dismantled.

. . . *Inspector McLaughlin:* . . . Now my friends, Tim Johnson has raised a question that I am very glad to have brought up. He says there was a large tract of country set apart for your people, that you were to have for yourselves for all time. . . . The reservations were made large in days gone by when you could make a living by hunting and large reservations were then necessary and possible, but with the tide of immigration coming into the country, game has become scarce and you can no longer live by hunting: and therefore you must take to agriculture to make a living for yourselves and families. . . . Now, Congress has enacted a law affecting you people. It says you are to have lands allotted to you and I have been sent out here to explain the Act and obtain your consent to accept your allotments. . . . If the consent of you people cannot be obtained by June 1st, that is in eleven days from now, the secretary must proceed to allot the lands to you under the Act. . . . The policy of the Government in regard to Indian reservations has changed during the past year. There will be no more treaties made with Indians. The surplus lands will be opened to settlement but the Indians will be protected in their homes. . . .

Appah: You are my friend. What have you been telling these Indians? I do not like that. When the Indians were given this land and when they pulled the chain over and surveyed it, they told us that this land would be ours always and that it would never be opened. That is the reason we do not know anything about opening our reservation. The Indians have lots of horses, and when you tell us that we must take farms, we do not like that on account of our horses. I have a father in Washington. It is on account of this reservation that I have that father. That is the reason the Indians think of their father in Washington upon whom they depend for these things. We do not listen to any White Man out here. We do not listen to the Mormons here. That is the reason I do not like what you tell us.

WILLIAM STINSON SOULE, An Arapaho encampment, Oklahoma Territory, 1868.

Sowsonocutt: They did not put us here on this reservation for nothing. They put us here a long time ago. That is how we came on this reservation. That's the reason we like this land here and we are holding it tight. All this land belongs to us and this reservation here belongs to the little children growing up. We do not like what you tell us when you talk about giving us little pieces of land. It is not good. The Indians have lots of cattle and horses. When we take the Government's little pieces of land, how are we to run our horses inside on little pieces of land? . . .

DAVID GUION

HOME ON THE RANGE

1930

Texas-born composer and music teacher David Guion (1892–1981) began playing piano at the age of six and later studied at the Royal Conservatory in Vienna under the tutelage of Leopold Godowsky. Despite his classical training, he retained a lifelong passion for the western folk music he had heard as a boy in Texas, all of which contributed material for his songs. Other compositions and arrangements by Guion include "Turkey in the Straw," "What Shall We Do with a Drunken Sailor," "Ride Cowboy Ride," "Arkansas Traveler," and "The Yellow Rose of Texas."

Oh, give me a home where the buffalo roam,
Where the deer and the antelope play;
Where seldom is heard a discouraging word
And the skies are not cloudy all day.

    Refrain:
Home, home on the range,
Where the deer and the antelope play;
Where seldom is heard a discouraging word
And the skies are not cloudy all day.

Where the air is so pure and the Zephyrs so free,
The breezes so balmy and light,
That I would not exchange my home on the range
For all of the cities so bright.

The red man was pressed from this part of the West,
He's likely no more to return
To the banks of Red River where seldom if ever
Their flickering campfires burn.

How often at night when the heavens are bright
With the light of the glittering stars,
Have I stood here amazed and asked as I gazed
If their glory exceeds that of ours.

Oh, I love these wild flowers in this dear land of ours;
The curlew I love to hear scream;
And I love the white rocks and the antelope flocks
That graze on the mountain-tops green.

Oh, give me a land where the bright diamond sand
Flows leisurely down the stream;
Where the graceful white swan goes gliding along
Like a maid in a heavenly dream.

Then I would not exchange my home on the range,
Where the deer and the antelope play;
Where seldom is heard a discouraging word
And the skies are not cloudy all day.

Home, home on the range,
Where the deer and the antelope play;
Where seldom is heard a discouraging word
And the skies are not cloudy all day.

ANSEL ADAMS, Parker Ranch, Waimea, Hawaii, 1957.

THE OLD CHISHOLM TRAIL

C. 1880

The Chisholm Trail, which ranged through Native American territory from San Antonio, Texas, to Abilene, Kansas, became the passageway west for massive herds of cattle, some 600,000 in 1871 alone. Originally named for Indian trader Jesse Chisholm, who had carved out the path with a wagon in 1866, the trail was hard and dangerous for the young cowboys it attracted, but full of excitement and romance. In 1942, a popular film starring Johnny Mack Brown and Tex Ritter romanticized the cowboy way of life for a national audience.

Come along, boys, and listen to my tale,
I'll tell you of my troubles on the old Chisholm trail.

> Coma ti yi youpy, youpy yea, youpy yea,
> Coma ti yi youpy, youpy yea.

I started up the trail October twenty-third,
I started up the trail with the 2-U herd.

Oh, a ten-dollar hoss and a forty-dollar saddle,
And I'm goin' to punchin' Texas cattle.

I woke up one morning on the old Chisholm trail,
Rope in my hand and a cow by the tail.

I'm up in the mornin' afore daylight
And afore I sleep the moon shines bright.

. . .

My hoss throwed me off at the creek called Mud,
My hoss throwed me off round the 2-U herd.

Last time I saw him he was going 'cross the level
A-kicking up his heels and a-running like the devil.

It's cloudy in the west, a-looking like rain,
And my damned old slicker's in the wagon again.

No chaps and no slicker, and it's pouring down rain,
And I swear, by God, that I'll never night-herd again.

. . .

Last night I was on guard and the leader broke the ranks,
I hit my horse down the shoulders and I spurred him in the flanks.

The wind commenced to blow, and the rain began to fall,
Hit looked, by garb, like we was goin' to lose 'em all.

My slicker's in the wagon and I'm gittin' mighty cold,
And these longhorn sons-o'-guns are gittin' hard to hold.

Saddle up, boys, and saddle up well,
For I think these cattle have scattered to hell.

. . .

I hit my pony and he gave a little rack,
And damned big luck if we ever git back.

With my blanket and my gun and my rawhide rope,
I'm a-slidin' down the trail in a long, keen lope.
I popped my foot in the stirrup and gave a little yell,
The tail cattle broke and the leaders went to hell.

I don't give a damn if they never do stop;
I'll ride as long as an eight-day clock.

Foot in the stirrup and hand on the horn,
Best damned cowboy ever was born.

. . .

We rounded 'em up and put 'em on the cars,
And that was the last of the old Two Bars.

Oh, it's bacon and beans most every day—
I'd as soon be a-eatin' prairie hay.

I'm on my best horse and I'm goin' at a run,
I'm the quickest-shootin' cowboy that ever pulled a gun.

I went to the wagon to get my roll,
To come back to Texas, dad-burn my soul.

Well, I met a little gal and I offered her a quarter,
She says, "Young man, I'm a gentleman's daughter."

I went to the boss to draw my roll,
He had it figgered out I was nine dollars in the hole.

I'll sell my outfit just as soon as I can,
I won't punch cattle for no damned man.

I'll sell my horse and I'll sell my saddle;
You can go to hell with your longhorn cattle.

Goin' back to town to draw my money,
Goin' back to town to see my honey.

With my knees in the saddle and my seat in the sky,
I'll quit punching cows in the sweet by-and-by.

Fare you well, old trail-boss, I don't wish you any harm,
I'm quittin' this business to go on the farm.

No more cow-puncher to sleep at my ease,
'Mid the crawlin' of the lice and the bitin' of the fleas.

Coma ti yi youpy, youpy yea, youpy yea,
Coma ti yi youpy, youpy yea.

ANNIE PROULX

THE MUD BELOW

1999

The Pulitzer Prize–winning novelist Annie Proulx (1935–) is one of America's most exacting chroniclers of our contemporary landscape. After raising her three sons in rural Vermont, during which time she worked as a freelance journalist, in 1993, Proulx became the first woman to win the PEN/Faulkner Award for her debut novel, *Postcards*. The following year, *The Shipping News* was awarded the Pulitzer Prize and the National Book Award. More recently, Proulx moved to Wyoming and published *Close Range: Wyoming Stories*, from which this excerpt is taken.

Rodeo night in a hot little Okie town and Diamond Felts was inside a metal chute, a long way from the scratch on Wyoming dirt he named as home, sitting on the back of bull 82N, a loose-skinned brindle Brahma-cross identified in the program as Little Kisses. There was a sultry feeling of weather. He kept his butt cocked to one side, his feet up on the chute rails so the bull couldn't grind his leg, brad him up, so that if it thrashed he could get over the top in a hurry. The time came closer and he slapped his face forcefully, bringing the adrenaline roses up on his cheeks, glanced down at his pullers and said, "I guess." Rito, neck gleaming with sweat, caught the free end of the bull-rope with a metal hook, brought it delicately to his hand from under the bull's belly, climbed up the rails and pulled it taut.

"Aw, this's a sumbuck," he said. "Give you the sample card."

Diamond took the end, made his wrap, brought the rope around the back of his hand and over the palm a second time, wove it between his third and fourth fingers, pounded the rosined glove fingers down over it and into his palm. He laid the tail of the rope across the bull's back and looped the excess, but it wasn't right—everything had gone a little slack. He undid the wrap and started over, making the loop smaller, waiting while they pulled again and in the arena a clown fired a pink cannon, the fizzing discharge diminished by a deep stir of thunder from the south, Texas T-storm on the roll.

Night perfs had their own hot charge, the glare, the stiff-legged parade of cowboy dolls in sparkle-fringed chaps into the arena, the spotlight that bucked over the squinting contestants and the half-roostered crowd. They were at the end of the night now, into the bullriding, with one in front of him. The bull beneath him breathed, shifted roughly. A hand, fingers outstretched, came across his right shoulder and against his chest, steadying him. He did not know why a bracing hand eased his chronic anxiety. But, in the way these things go, that was when he needed twist, to auger him through the ride.

In the first go-round he'd drawn a bull he knew and got a good scald on him. He'd been in a slump for weeks, wire stretched tight, but things were turning back his way. He'd come off that animal in a flying dismount, sparked a little clapping that quickly died; the watchers knew as well as he that if he burst into flames and sang an operatic aria after the whistle it would make no damn difference.

He drew o.k. bulls and rode them in the next rounds, scores in the high seventies, fixed his eyes on the outside shoulder of the welly bull that tried to drop him, then at the short-go draw he pulled Kisses, rank and salty, big as a boxcar of coal. On that one all you could do was your best and hope for a little sweet luck; if you got the luck he was money.

The announcer's galvanized voice rattled in the speakers above the enclosed arena. "Now folks, it ain't the Constitution or the Bill a Rights that made this a great country. It was *God* who created the mountains and plains and the evenin sunset and put us here and let us look at them. Amen and God bless the Markin flag. And right now we got a bullrider from Redsled, Wyomin, twenty-three-year-old Diamond Felts, who might be wonderin if he'll ever see that beautiful scenery again. Folks, Diamond Felts weighs one hundred and thirty pounds. Little Kisses weighs two thousand ten pounds, he is a big, big bull and he is thirty-eight and one, last year's Dodge City Bullriders' choice. Only one man has stayed on this big bad bull's back for eight seconds and that was Marty Casebolt at Reno, and you better believe that man got all the money. *Will* he be rode tonight? Folks, we're goin a find out in just a minute, soon as our cowboy's ready. And listen at that rain, folks, let's give thanks we're in a enclosed arena or it would be deep mud below."

Diamond glanced back at the flank man, moved up on his rope, nodded, jerking his head up and down rapidly. "Let's go, let's go."

The chute door swung open and the bull squatted, leaped into the waiting silence and a paroxysm of twists, belly-rolls and spins, skipping, bucking and whirling, powerful drop, gave him the whole menu.

RICHARD RODGERS AND OSCAR HAMMERSTEIN II

OKLAHOMA

1943

In 1943, first-time collaborators composer Richard Rodgers (1902–1979) and lyricist Oscar Hammerstein (1895–1960) created the score for the musical *Oklahoma!* The production was an overnight sensation, transforming the Broadway musical; it won a Special Pulitzer Prize and ran for 2,212 performances. Rodgers and Hammerstein's collaboration was the most successful in American musical theater. Collectively, their musicals have earned thirty-five Tony Awards, fifteen Academy Awards, and two Pulitzer Prizes, and they defined the Broadway musical at mid-century, with classics like *Carousel* (1945), *South Pacific* (1949), *The King and I* (1951), and *The Sound of Music* (1959).

Oklahoma,
Where the wind comes sweepin' down the plain
(And the wavin' wheat
Can sure smell sweet
When the wind comes right behind the rain)

Oklahoma!
Every night my honey lamb and I
Sit alone and talk
And watch a hawk
Makin' lazy circles in the sky.
We know we belong to the land,
And the land we belong to is grand.
And when we say:
EE-ee-ow! A-yip-i-o-ee-ay!
We're only sayin',
You're doin' fine, Oklahoma!
Oklahoma, O.K.!

BRETT WESTON, Parker Ranch, Waimea, Hawaii, 1989.

GEORGE C. CORY JR. AND DOUGLASS CROSS

I Left My Heart in San Francisco

1954

Written in 1954 by composers Douglass Cross (1920–) and George Cory (1920–), this tune became the signature song of popular singer Tony Bennett in 1962. Founded by Spanish explorers in 1776, who created the mission of San Francisco of Assisi, San Francisco was established as an American city in 1850 with John Geary as its first mayor. The song was designated the city's official song in 1969.

The loveliness of Paris
Seems somehow sadly gay
The glory that was Rome
Is of another day
I've been terribly alone and forgotten in Manhattan
And I'm coming home to my city by the bay

I left my heart in San Francisco
High on a hill, it calls to me
To be where little cable cars
Climb halfway to the stars!
And the morning fog will chill the air

My love waits there (my love waits there) in San Francisco
Above the blue and windy sea
When I come home to you, San Francisco,
Your golden sun will shine for me!

I left my heart in San Francisco
High on a hill, it calls to me
To be where little cable cars
Climb halfway to the stars!
And the morning fog will chill the air

I don't care

My love waits there in San Francisco
Above the blue and windy sea
When I come

When I come home to you, San Francisco
Your golden sun will shine for me! Yeah.

MINOR WHITE, Golden Gate Bridge, San Francisco, California, 1959.

SUNSET

1960

Jack Kerouac (1922–1969) had dreamed of becoming a writer since he was in high school. After serving in the navy in World War II, Kerouac returned home and began traveling around the United States. His experiences formed the basis for his classic Beat Generation novel *On the Road*, which was published in 1957. In the 1960s, Kerouac turned to Buddhism and died in Florida at the age of forty-seven. This selection is taken from *A Lonesome Traveler*.

No man should go through life without once experiencing healthy, even bored solitude in the wilderness, finding himself depending solely on himself and thereby learning his true and hidden strength.—Learning, for instance, to eat when he's hungry and sleep when he's sleepy.

Also around bedtime was my singing time. I'd pace up and down the well-worn path in the dust of my rock singing all the show tunes I could remember, at the top of my voice too, with nobody to hear except the deer and the bear.

In the red dusk, the mountains were symphonies in pink snow—Jack Mountain, Three Fools Peak, Freezeout Peak, Golden Horn, Mt. Terror, Mt. Fury, Mt. Despair, Crooked Thumb Peak, Mt. Challenger and the incomparable Mt. Baker bigger than the world in the distance—and my own little Jackass Ridge that completed the Ridge of Desolation. Pink snow and the clouds all distant and frilly like ancient remote cities of Buddhaland splendor, and the wind working incessantly—whish, whish—booming, at times rattling my shack.

For supper I made chop suey and baked some biscuits and put the leftovers in a pan for deer that came in the moonlit night and nibbled like big strange cows of peace—long-antlered buck and does and babies too—as I meditated in the alpine grass facing the magic moon-laned lake. And I could see firs reflected in the moonlit lake five thousand feet below, upside down, pointing to infinity.

And all the insects ceased in honor of the moon.

Sixty-three sunsets I saw revolve on that perpendicular hill—mad raging sunsets pouring in sea foams of cloud through unimaginable crags like the crags you grayly drew in pencil as a child, with every rose-tint of hope beyond, making you feel just like them, brilliant and bleak beyond words.

Cold mornings with clouds billowing out of Lightning Gorge like smoke from a giant fire but the lake cerulean as ever.

August comes in with a blast that shakes your house and augurs little August-ticity—then that snowy-air and woodsmoke feeling—then the snow comes sweeping your way from Canada, and the wind rises and dark low clouds rush up as out of a forge. Suddenly a green-rose rainbow appears right on your ridge with steamy clouds all around and an orange sun turmoiling . . .

> *What is a rainbow,*
> *Lord?—a hoop*
> *For the lowly*

. . . and you go out and suddenly your shadow is ringed by the rainbow as you walk on the hilltop, a lovely-haloed mystery making you want to pray.

A blade of grass jiggling in the winds of infinity, anchored to a rock, and for your own poor gentle flesh no answer.

Your oil lamp burning in infinity.

SURFIN' U.S.A.

1963

In 1961, Bob Dylan was playing in Greenwich Village coffeehouses, the Supremes signed a contract with Motown Records, and three brothers, Brian, Carl, and Dennis Wilson, formed a band in Hawthorne, California. Over the next two years, the Beach Boys released ten American top-selling songs and four albums, including their 1963 hit "Surfin' U.S.A.," and catapulted the California lifestyle to national attention.

If everybody had an ocean
Across the U.S.A.
Then everybody'd be surfin'
Like Californi-a
You'd see 'em wearing their baggies
Huarachi sandals too
A bushy bushy blonde hairdo
Surfin' U.S.A.

You'd catch 'em surfin' at Del Mar
Ventura County line
Santa Cruz and Trestle
Australia's Narrabeen
All over Manhattan
And down Doheny Way

Everybody's gone surfin'
Surfin' U.S.A.

We'll all be planning that route
We're gonna take real soon
We're waxing down our surfboards
We can't wait for June
We'll all be gone for the summer
We're on surfari to stay
Tell the teacher we're surfin'
Surfin' U.S.A.

Haggerties and Swamies
Pacific Palisades
San Onofre and Sunset
Redondo Beach L.A.
All over La Jolla
At Wa'imea Bay.

Everybody's gone surfin'
Surfin' U.S.A.

Everybody's gone surfin'
Surfin' U.S.A.

Everybody's gone surfin'
Surfin' U.S.A.

JOAN DIDION

LOS ANGELES NOTEBOOK

1966

California native Joan Didion (1934–) was born in Sacramento and began her writing career at *Vogue* magazine in New York. Her early novels, including *Play It As It Lays* (1970), and her screenplay *Panic in Needle Park* (1971) were written in the same period as the collections of essays that have made her one of America's masters of that form. *Slouching Towards Bethlehem* (1968) and *The White Album* (1979) explore the dreams and disillusion of California life in the 1960s and '70s.

There is something uneasy in the Los Angeles air this afternoon, some unnatural stillness, some tension. What it means is that tonight a Santa Ana will begin to blow, a hot wind from the northeast whining down through the Cajon and San Gorgonio Passes, blowing up sandstorms out along Route 66, drying the hills and the nerves to the flash point. For a few days now we will see smoke back in the canyons, and hear sirens in the night. I have neither heard nor read that a Santa Ana is due, but I know it, and almost everyone I have seen today knows it too. We know it because we feel it. The baby frets. The maid sulks. I rekindle a waning argument with the telephone company, then cut my losses and lie down, given over to whatever it is in the air. To live with the Santa Ana is to accept, consciously or unconsciously, a deeply mechanistic view of human behavior.

I recall being told, when I first moved to Los Angeles and was living on an isolated beach, that the Indians would throw themselves into the sea when the bad wind blew. I could see why. The Pacific turned ominously glossy during a Santa Ana period, and one woke in the night troubled not only by the peacocks screaming in the olive trees but by the eerie absence of surf. The heat was surreal. The sky had a yellow cast, the kind of light sometimes called "earthquake weather." My only neighbor would not come out of her house for days, and there were no lights at night, and her husband roamed the place with a machete. One day he wuld tell me that he had heard a trespasser, the next a rattlesnake.

"On nights like that," Raymond Chandler once wrote about the Santa Ana, "every booze party ends in a fight. Meek little wives feel the edge of the carving knife and study their husbands' necks. Anything can happen." That was the kind of wind it was. I did not know then that there was any basis for the effect it had on all of us, but it turns out to be another of those cases in which science bears out folk wisdom. The Santa Ana, which is named for one of the canyons it rushes through, is a *foehn* wind, like the *foehn* of Austria and Switzerland and the *hamsin* of Israel. There are a number of persistent malevolent winds, perhaps the best known of which are the mistral of France and the Mediterranean sirocco, but a *foehn* wind has distinct characteristics: it occurs on the leeward slope of a mountain range and, although the air begins as a cold mass, it is warmed as it comes down the mountain and appears finally as a hot dry wind. Whenever and wherever a *foehn* blows, doctors hear about headaches and nausea and allergies, about "nervousness," about "depression." In Los Angeles some teachers do not attempt to conduct formal classes during a Santa Ana, because the children become unmanageable. In Switzerland the suicide rate goes up during the *foehn*, and in the courts of some Swiss cantons the wind is considered a mitigating circumstance for crime. Surgeons are said to watch the wind, because blood does not clot normally during a *foehn*. A few years ago an Israeli physicist discovered that not only during such winds, but for the ten or twelve hours which precede them, the air carries an unusually high ratio of positive to negative ions. No one seems to know exactly why that should be; some talk about friction and others suggest solar disturbances. In any case the positive ions are there, and what an excess of positive ions does, in the simplest terms, is make people unhappy. One cannot get much more mechanistic than that.

Easterners commonly complain that there is no "weather" at all in Southern California, that the days and the seasons slip by relentlessly, numbingly bland. That is quite misleading. In fact the climate is characterized by infrequent but violent extremes: two periods of torrential subtropical rains which continue for weeks and wash out the hills and send subdivisions sliding toward the sea; about twenty scattered days a year of the Santa Ana, which, with its incendiary dryness, invariably means fire. At the first prediction of a Santa Ana, the Forest Services flies men and equipment from northern California into the southern forests, and the Los Angeles Fire Department cancels its ordinary non-firefighting routines. The Santa Ana caused Malibu to burn the way it did in 1956, and Bel Air in 1961, and Santa Barbara in 1964. In the winter of 1966–67 eleven men were killed fighting a Santa Ana fire that spread through the San Gabriel Mountains.

Just to watch the front-page news out of Los Angeles during a Santa Ana is to get very close to what it is about the place. The longest single Santa Ana period in recent years was in 1957, and it lasted not the usual three or four days but fourteen days, from November 21 until December 4. On the first day 25,000 acres of the San Gabriel Mountains were burning, with gusts reaching 100 miles an hour. In town, the wind reached Force 12, or hurricane force, on the Beaufort Scale; oil derricks were toppled and people ordered off the downtown streets to avoid injury from flying objects. On November 22 the fire in the San Gabriels was out of control. On

November 24 six people were killed in automobile accidents, and by the end of the week the Los Angeles *Times* was keeping a box score of traffic deaths. On November 26 a prominent Pasadena attorney, depressed about money, shot and killed his wife, their two sons, and himself. On November 27 a South Gate divorceé, twenty-two, was murdered and thrown from a moving car. On November 30 the San Gabriel fire was still out of control, and the wind in town was blowing eighty miles an hour. On the first day of December four peole died violently, and on the third the wind began to break.

It is hard for people who have not lived in Los Angeles to realize how radically the Santa Ana figures in the local imagination. The city burning is Los Angeles's deepest image of itself: Nathanael West perceived that, in *The Day of the Locust*; and at the time of the 1965 Watts riots what struck the imagination most indelibly were the fires. For days one could drive the Harbor Freeway and see the city on fire, just as we had always known it would be in the end. Los Angeles weather is the weather of catastrophe, of apocalypse, and, just as the reliably long and bitter winters of New England determine the way life is lived there, so the violence and the unpredictability of the Santa Ana affect the entire quality of life in Los Angeles, accentuate its impermanence, its unreliability. The wind shows us how close to the edge we are.

ELLIOTT ERWITT, Detroit, Michigan, 1961.

JONI MITCHELL

BIG YELLOW TAXI

1970

Canadian-born singer/songwriter Joni Mitchell (1943–) released this ode to the disappearing natural landscape in 1970, the year of the first Earth Day celebration and the publication of *The Greening of America*. One of the most influential women songwriters of the 1960s and '70s, Mitchell is best known for the albums *Blue* (1971) and *Court and Spark* (1974). She was inducted into the Rock and Roll Hall of Fame in 1997.

They paved paradise
And put up a parking lot
With a pink hotel, a boutique
And a swinging hot spot
Don't it always seem to go
That you don't know what you've got
Till it's gone
They paved paradise
And put up a parking lot.

They took all the trees
And put them in a tree museum
And they charged all the people
A dollar and a half just to see 'em
Don't it always seem to go
That you don't know what you've got
Till it's gone
They paved paradise
And put up a parking lot.

Hey farmer farmer
Put away that D.D.T. now
Give me spots on my apples
But leave me the birds and the bees
Please!
Don't it always seem to go
That you don't know what you've got

Till it's gone
They paved paradise
And put up a parking lot.

Late last night
I heard the screen door slam
And a big yellow taxi
Took away my old man
Don't it always seem to go
That you don't know what you've got
Till it's gone
They paved paradise
And put up a parking lot.

WALLACE STEGNER

THE WILDERNESS LETTER

1960

Throughout his career, Pulitzer Prize–winning author, novelist, and educator Wallace Stegner (1909–1993) cherished the ideal of the American West, "not simply as a scientific reserve, or a landbank, or a playground, but as a spiritual resource, leftover from our frontier origins that could reassure us of our identity as a nation and a people." In December 1960, he wrote a letter to David E. Pesonen of the Wildland Research Center setting out his thoughts on the "wilderness idea," which was included in a collection of his writings titled *The Sound of Mountain Water*.

. . . What I want to speak of is . . . the wilderness idea, which is a resource in itself. Being an intangible and spiritual resource, it will seem mystical to the practical-minded—but then anything that cannot be moved by a bulldozer is likely to seem mystical to them.

I want to speak for the wilderness idea as something that has helped form our character and that has certainly shaped our history as a people. . . .

Something will have gone out of us as a people if we ever let the remaining wilderness be destroyed; if we permit the last virgin forests to be turned into comic books and plastic cigarette cases; if we drive the few remaining members of the wild species into zoos or to extinction; if we pollute the last clear air and dirty the last clean streams and push our paved roads through the last of the silence, so that never again will Americans be free in their own country from the noise, the exhausts, the stink of human and automotive waste. And so that never again can we have the chance to see ourselves single, separate, vertical and individual in the world, part of the environment of trees and rocks and soil, brother to the other animals, part of the natural world and competent to belong in it. Without any remaining wilderness we are committed wholly, without chance for even momentary reflection and rest, to a headlong drive into our technological termite-life, the Brave New World of a completely man-controlled environment. We need wilderness preserved—as much of it as is still left, and as many kinds—because it was the challenge against which our character as a people was formed. The reminder and the reassurance that it is still there is good for our spiritual health even if we never once in ten years set foot in it. It is good for us when we are young, because of the incomparable sanity it can bring briefly, as vacation and rest, into our insane lives. It is important to us when we are old simply because it is there—important, that is, simply as idea.

EADWEARD MUYBRIDGE,
Yosemite Falls, California, 1872.

PAUL SIMON

AMERICA

1968

Paul Simon (1941–) and Art Garfunkel (1941–), who began singing together in high school in Queens, New York, leaped to fame in the mid-1960s with the number one hit "The Sounds of Silence," followed by the album of the same name. This ballad of the American road, which features their uniquely poetic lyrics and melodic harmony, appeared on their fifth album, *Bookends*, released the same year as their soundtrack album for the film *The Graduate*. The duo split after their 1970 Grammy Album of the Year, *Bridge Over Troubled Water*. Paul Simon has continued as a dominant figure in American music with the release of Grammy-winning solo albums, including two Albums of the Year, *Still Crazy After All These Years* (1975) and his masterpiece, *Graceland* (1986). Simon was recognized for his lifelong commitment to the arts with a Kennedy Center Honors Award in 2002.

"Let us be lovers we'll marry our fortunes together
I've got some real estate here in my bag"
So we bought a pack of cigarettes and Mrs. Wagner's pies
And walked off to look for America
"Kathy," I said as we boarded a Greyhound in Pittsburgh
"Michigan seems like a dream to me now
It took me four days to hitchhike from Saginaw
I've gone to look for America."

Laughing on the bus
Playing games with the faces
She said the man in the gabardine suit was a spy
I said, "Be careful, his bow tie is really a camera,"

"Toss me a cigarette, I think there's one in my raincoat."
"We smoked the last one an hour ago."
So I looked at the scenery, she read her magazine;
And the moon rose over an open field.

"Kathy, I'm lost," I said, though I knew she was sleeping
"I'm empty and aching and I don't know why."

Counting the cars on the New Jersey Turnpike

They've all come to look for America

All come to look for America

All come to look for America

BURTON BERINSKY, Robert F. Kennedy, Oregon, 1968.

KATHARINE LEE BATES

AMERICA, THE BEAUTIFUL

1893

Katherine Lee Bates (1859–1929), the daughter of a Congregationalist minister, was born in Falmouth, Massachusetts. While a professor of English at Wellesley College she journeyed out west, a trip that provided inspiration for "America, the Beautiful": "One day some of the other teachers and I decided to go on a trip to 14,000-foot Pikes Peak," she later wrote. "We hired a prairie wagon. Near the top we had to leave the wagon and go the rest of the way on mules. I was very tired. But when I saw the view, I felt great joy. All the wonder of America seemed displayed there, with the sea-like expanse." The poem, written in 1893, was first published in the weekly journal *The Congregationalist* in 1895, and set to music by Samuel A. Ward in 1926.

1.

O beautiful for spacious skies,

For amber waves of grain,

For purple mountain majesties

Above the fruited plain.

America! America! God shed His grace on thee,

And crown thy good with brotherhood

From sea to shining sea.

2.

O beautiful for pilgrim feet

Whose stern impassion'd stress

A thoroughfare for freedom beat

Across the wilderness.

America! America! God mend thine ev'ry flaw,

Confirm thy soul in self-control,

Thy liberty in law.

3.

O beautiful for heroes prov'd

In liberating strife,

Who more than self their country lov'd

And mercy more than life.

America! America! May God thy gold refine

Till all success be nobleness,

And ev'ry gain divine.

4.

O beautiful for patriot dream,
That sees beyond the years
Thine alabaster cities gleam
Undimmed by human tears.
America! America! God shed His grace on thee,
And crown thy good with brotherhood
From sea to shining sea.

WOODY GUTHRIE

THIS LAND IS YOUR LAND

1940

The life of Woodrow Wilson Guthrie (1912–1967) reads like the folk songs he wrote. One of the greatest American musicians, Guthrie was born in Okemah, Oklahoma, into a pioneer family, quit high school at sixteen, and hit the road with his harmonica, playing and singing in pool halls and on street corners. He learned guitar and wrote over 1,000 songs, including the classics "This Train Is Bound for Glory," "Roll on Columbia," "Reuben James," and "So Long It's Been Good to Know You," in addition to "This Land Is Your Land." Guthrie was active in the socialist labor movement on behalf of migrant workers, and his guitar bore a sign reading "this machine kills fascists." He served in the merchant marine and in the U.S. Army during World War II. Guthrie collaborated with Leadbelly, Pete Seeger, and the Weavers, and influenced the young Bob Dylan. He died after a long battle with Huntington's chorea.

This land is your land, this land is my land
From California, to the New York island;
From the redwood forest, to the Gulf Stream waters
This land was made for you and me.

As I was walking that ribbon of highway
I saw above me that endless skyway.
I saw below me that golden valley:
This land was made for you and me.

This land is your land, . . .

I've roamed and rambled and I followed my footsteps
To the sparkling sands of her diamond deserts;
And all around me a voice was sounding:
This land was made for you and me.

This land is your land, . . .

. . .

When the sun came shining and I was strolling,
And the wheat fields waving and the dust clouds rolling,

646

As the fog was lifting, a voice was chanting:
This land was made for you and me.

This land is your land, . . .

As I was walking, I saw a sign there,
And on the sign it said "No Trespassing"
But on the other side it didn't say nothing:
That side was made for you and me.

This land is your land, . . .

In the shadow of the steeple I saw my people,
By the relief office I seen my people;
As they stood there hungry, I stood there asking,
Is this land made for you and me?

This land is your land, . . .

. . .

MINOR WHITE, The Grand Tetons, Wyoming, 1959.

PERMISSIONS AND PHOTO CREDITS

PERMISSIONS

James Agee and Walker Evans, excerpt from "All Over Alabama" from *Let Us Now Praise Famous Men: Three Tenant Families*. Copyright © 1960 by James Agee and Walker Evans. Reprinted with the permission of Houghton Mifflin Company. All rights reserved.

"Happy Days Are Here Again" Words by Jack Yellen, Music by Milton Ager. Copyright 1929 by Warner Bros, Inc. (Renewed) All rights reserved. Reprinted with the permission of Warner/Chappell Music, Inc.

Gloria Anzaldúa, excerpt from "How to Tame a Wild Tongue" from *Borderlands/La Frontera: The New Mestiza*. Copyright © 1987 by Gloria Anzaldúa. Reprinted with the permission of Aunt Lute Books.

W. H. Auden, "September 1, 1939" from *Collected Poems*. Copyright 1933, 1941 by W. H. Auden. Reprinted with the permission of Random House, Inc.

Stephen Vincent Benét, "American Names" from *Selected Works*. Copyright 1927 by Stephen Vincent Benét, renewed © 1955 by Rosemary Carr Benét. Reprinted with the permission of Brandt & Hochman Literary Agents, Inc.

"God Bless America" by Irving Berlin. © Copyright 1938, 1939 by Irving Berlin. © Copyright Renewed 1965, 1966 by Irving Berlin. © Copyright Assigned to the Trustees of the God Bless America Fund. International Copyright Secured. All Rights Reserved. Used by Permission.

Chuck Berry (words & music), "Surfin' USA" (Arc Music Corp.) Copyright © 1963 (Renewed) by Arc Music Corp and Isalee Music. International Copyright Secured. All Rights Reserved. Used by permission.

Elizabeth Bishop, "Florida" from *The Complete Poems 1926-1979*. Copyright © 1979, 1983 by Alice Helen Methfessel. Reprinted with the permission of Farrar, Straus & Giroux, LLC.

Gwendolyn Brooks, "Flags" from *A Street in Bronzeville* (New York: Harper & Row, 1945). Copyright 1944, 1945 by Gwendolyn Brooks. "The Chicago *Defender* Sends a Man to Little Rock, Fall 1957" from *Blacks*. Copyright © 1960 by Gwendolyn Brooks. Both reprinted by permission of Brooks Permissions.

"The Ballad of Davy Crockett." Words by Tom Blackburn. Music by George Bruns. © 1954 Wonderland Music Company, Inc.

George Bush, excerpts from "Speech at the Republican Convention (August 18, 1988). Reprinted with the permission of The Honorable George Bush.

Truman Capote, excerpt from "Hollywood" from *Local Color*. Copyright 1950 by Truman Capote. Reprinted with the permission of Random House, Inc.

Jimmy Carter, excerpts from Nobel Lecture (December 10, 2002). Reprinted with the permission of President Carter and The Carter Center.

Cesar Chavez, "Address to the Commonwealth Club" (San Francisco, November 9, 1984). TM/© 2002 the Cesar E. Chavez Foundation by CMG Worldwide www.cmgww.com.

Hillary Rodham Clinton, "Address to the Fourth UN World Conference on Women, Beijing, China" (September 5, 1993). Reprinted with the permission of The Honorable Hillary Rodham Clinton.

Stephen Crane, excerpt from "War Is Kind" from *The Works of Stephen Crane, Volume X: Poems and Literary Remains*, edited by Fredson Bowers. Reprinted with the permission of The University Press of Virginia.

"I Left My Heart in San Francisco" Words by Douglass Cross. Music by George Cory. Copyright © 1954 (renewed 1982) by Colgems-EMI Music Inc. All rights reserved.

Countee Cullen, "Incident" from *Color* (New York: Harper & Brothers, 1925). Copyrights held by Amistad Research Center. Administered by Thompson and Thompson, New York, NY.

E. E. Cummings, "as freedom is a breakfastfood" from *Complete Poems 1904-1962*. Copyright 1940 © 1968, 1991 by the Trustees for the E. E. Cummings Trust. Reprinted with the permission of Liveright Publishing Corporation.

Joan Didion, "Los Angeles Notebook" from *Slouching Towards Bethlehem*. Copyright © 1966, 1968 and renewed 1996 by Joan Didion. Reprinted with the permission of Farrar, Straus & Giroux, LLC.

John Dos Passos, "U.S.A." from *The 42nd Parallel*. Copyright 1930, renewed © 1958 by John Dos Passos. Reprinted with the permission of Lucy Dos Passos Coggin.

W. E. B. Du Bois, excerpt from "The Sorrow Songs" from *The Souls of Black Folk* (New York: A. C. McClurg, 1903). Reprinted with the permission of David G. Du Bois and Penguin Books, Ltd.

Bob Dylan, "Blowin' in the Wind." Copyright © 1962 by Warner Bros. Inc. Copyright renewed 1990 by Special Rider Music. "The Times They Are A-Changin'." Copyright © 1963, 1964 by Warner Bros. Inc. Copyright renewed 1991 by Special Rider Music. All rights reserved. International copyright secured. Both reprinted by permission.

"New York, New York" (Fred Ebb/John Kander). Copyright © 1977 by EMI Unart Catalog. Used by permission. All rights reserved.

Sherman Edwards, "But, Mister Adams" from *1776*. Copyright © 1964 (renewed), 1968, 1969 by Sherman Edwards. All rights reserved.

Thomas Edison, "They Won't Think" from *The Diary and Sundry Observations of Thomas Alva Edison*, edited by Dagobert D. Runes. Copyright 1948 by The Philosophical Library, Inc. Reprinted with the permission of The Philosophical Library, New York.

Albert Einstein, "The Fateful Decision" (1948). Reprinted with the permission of The Albert Einstein Archives, Hebrew University in Israel.

Ralph Ellison, excerpts from "Epilogue" from *Invisible Man*. Copyright 1947, 1948, 1952 by Ralph Ellison. Reprinted with the permission of Random House, Inc.

William Faulkner, "Upon Receiving the Nobel Prize for Literature" (December 10, 1950) from *Essays, Speeches, and Public Letters by William Faulkner*, edited by James B. Meriwether. Copyright 1950 by William Faulkner. Excerpt from *Light in August*. Copyright 1932 and renewed © 1960 by William Faulkner. Both reprinted with the permission of Random House, Inc.

F. Scott Fitzgerald, excerpt from *The Great Gatsby*. Copyright 1925 by Charles Scribner's Sons. Copyright renewed 1953 by Frances Scott Fitzgerald Lanahan. Reprinted with the permission of Scribner, a division of Simon & Schuster Adult Publishing, Inc.

Betty Friedan, excerpt from *The Feminine Mystique*. Copyright © 1963 by Betty Friedan. Reprinted with the permission of W. W. Norton & Company, Inc.

Robert Frost, "The Road Not Taken," "Stopping by Woods on a Snowy Evening," and "The Gift Outright" from *Complete Poems of Robert Frost*. Copyright 1916, 1923, 1928,

1930, 1934, 1939, 1943, 1945, 1947, 1949, © 1967 by Henry Holt and Co., copyright 1936, 1942, 1944, 1945, 1947, 1948, 1951, 1956, 1958, 1962 by Robert Frost, and copyright © 1964, 1967 by Leslie Frost Ballantine. Reprinted with the permission of Henry Holt and Company, LLC.

Ernesto Galarza, excerpt from *Barrio Boy*. Copyright © 1971 by Ernesto Galarza. Copyright © 1973 by the University of Notre Dame Press. Reprinted with the permission of the University of Notre Dame Press.

Bill Gates, "Capitalizing on the 'Cognitive Niche'" from *Business @ the Speed of Thought*. Copyright © 1999 by William H. Gates, III. Reprinted with the permission of Warner Books, Inc.

Grateful Dead, "U.S. Blues" (Jerome J. Garcia/Robert C. Hunter). Copyright Ice Nine Publishing Company. Used with permission.

"God Bless the U.S.A." Words and Music by Lee Greenwood. Copyright © 1984 by Songs of Universal, Inc. and Universal—Songs of Polygram International Inc. All rights reserved.

Woody Guthrie, "This Land Is Your Land." Copyright © 1956 (renewed 1984), 1958 (renewed 1986), and 1970 (renewed) by Ludlow Music, Inc., New York, NY. Reprinted with the permission of Ludlow Music, Inc.

"Oklahoma" by Richard Rodgers and Oscar Hammerstein II. Copyright © 1943 by Williamson Music. Copyright Renewed. International Copyright Secured. All Rights Reserved. Used by Permission.

Learned Hand, "The Spirit of Liberty" (Address at "I Am an American Day," New York City, May 21, 1944) from *The Spirit of Liberty: Papers and Addresses of Learned Hand*, edited by Irving Dilliard. Copyright 1952, 1953, © 1959, 1960 by Alfred A. Knopf, Inc. Reprinted with the permission of Alfred A. Knopf, a division of Random House, Inc.

E. Y. Harburg and Jay Gorney, "Brother, Can You Spare a Dime?" (1932). Copyright 1932, renewed © 1955 by Harms, Inc. Reprinted with the permission of Harms, Inc.

Lillian Hellman, excerpts from *Scoundrel Time*. Copyright © 1976 by Lillian Hellman. Reprinted with the permission of Little, Brown and Company, (Inc.).

Huang Zunxian, "Expulsion of the Immigrants" from *Land Without Ghosts: Chinese Impressions of America from the Mid-Nineteenth Century to the Present*, edited and translated by R. David Arkush and Leo O. Lee. Copyright © 1989 by The Regents of the University of California. Reprinted with the permission of the University of California Press.

Langston Hughes, "Let America Be America Again" and "Merry-Go-Round" from *The Collected Poems of Langston Hughes*, edited by Arnold Rampersad and David Roessel. Copyright © 1994 by the Estate of Langston Hughes. Reprinted with the permission of Alfred A. Knopf, a division of Random House, Inc.

Senator Edward M. Kennedy, "Speech to the Democratic Convention" (August 12, 1980) and "Statement on Americans with Disabilities Act" (May 9, 1989). Both reprinted with the permission of The Honorable Edward M. Kennedy.

Jack Kerouac, excerpt from "Alone on a Mountaintop" from *Lonesome Traveller* (New York: Granada Publishing Ltd, 1972). Copyright © 1960 by Jack Kerouac, renewed 1988 by Jan Kerouac. Reprinted with the permission of Sterling Lord Literistic, Inc.

Senator John Kerry, "Vietnam Veterans Against the War" (statement to the Senate Committee on Foreign Relations, April 22, 1971). Reprinted with the permission of The Honorable Senator John Kerry.

Martin Luther King, Jr., excerpts from "Address at the March on Washington," "Letter from Birmingham City Jail," and "The Drum Major Instinct" from *A Testament of Hope: The Essential Writings of Martin Luther King, Jr.*, edited by James Melvin Washington. Copyright

© 1963, 1968 by Dr. Martin Luther King, Jr., copyright renewed 1991, 1996 by Coretta Scott King. Reprinted with the permission of the Estate of Martin Luther King, Jr., c/o Writer's House as agent for the proprietor.

Huddie Ledbetter, "Old Cotton Fields at Home" (The Cotton Song). Words and music by Huddie Ledbetter. TRO- © copyright 1962 (Renewed) by Folkways Music Publishers, Inc., New York, NY. Reprinted with the permission of The Richmond Organization.

Harper Lee, excerpt from *To Kill a Mockingbird*. Copyright © 1960 and renewed 1988 by Harper Lee. Reprinted with the permission of HarperCollins Publishers, Inc.

Loretta Lynn, "Coal Miner's Daughter." Copyright © 1969 by Sure-Fire Music Company. Reprinted by permission. All rights reserved.

Groucho Marx, "King Leer" from *The Essential Groucho: Writings by, for, and about Groucho Marx*, edited by Stefan Kanfer. Copyright © 2000 by Stefan Kanfer. Reprinted with the permission of the Estate of Groucho Marx.

Senator John McCain, The Mike Christian Story from http://www.senate.gov/~mccain/mikechristian.htm. Reprinted with the permission of The Honorable John McCain.

H. L. Mencken, excerpt from "On Being an American" from *Prejudices: A Selection*. Copyright © 1958 by Alfred A. Knopf, Inc. Reprinted with the permission of Alfred A. Knopf, a division of Random House, Inc.

Nancy Boyd (Edna St. Vincent Millay), "I Like Americans" from *Distressing Dialogues* (New York: Harper & Brothers, 1924). Copyright 1924, 1951 by Edna St. Vincent Millay and Norma Millay Ellis. All rights reserved. Reprinted with the permission of Elizabeth Barnett, literary executor.

Arthur Miller, excerpt from *Death of a Salesman*. Copyright 1949 and renewed © 1977 by Arthur Miller. Reprinted with the permission of Viking Penguin, a division of Penguin Putnam Inc.

Joni Mitchell, "Big Yellow Taxi." Copyright 1970 (Renewed). Reprinted by permission. All rights reserved.

Toni Morrison, excerpt from *Jazz* (New York: Alfred A. Knopf, 1992). Copyright © 1992 by Toni Morrison. Reprinted with the permission of International Creative Management, Inc.

Tim O'Brien, excerpt from "On the Rainy River" from *The Things They Carried*. Copyright © 1990 by Tim O'Brien. Reprinted with the permission of Houghton Mifflin Company. All rights reserved.

Walker Percy, excerpt from *The Last Gentleman*. Copyright © 1966 by Walker Percy. Reprinted with the permission of Farrar, Straus & Giroux, LLC.

Cole Porter, words and music, "You're the Top." Copyright 1934 by Warner Bros, Inc. (Renewed) All rights reserved. Reprinted with the permission of Warner/Chappell Music, Inc.

Annie Proulx, excerpt from "The Mud Below" from *Close Range: Wyoming Stories*. Copyright © 1999 by Dead Line, Inc. Reprinted with the permission of Simon & Schuster, Inc.

Mario Puzo, excerpt from "Choosing a Dream: Italians in Hell's Kitchen" from *The Immigrant Experience*, edited by Thomas C. Wheeler. Copyright © 1971 by Doubleday, a division of Bantam, Doubleday Dell Publishing Group, Inc. Used by permission of Doubleday, a division of Random House, Inc.

Anna Quindlen, "A Country and a Conundrum." Reprinted with the permission of the author.

Eleanor Roosevelt, "Can a Woman Ever Be President of the United States?" from *Cosmopolitan* (1935). Reprinted with the permission of Nancy Roosevelt Ireland, Trustee, Anna E. Roosevelt Trust.

652

Carl Sandburg, "Chicago" from *Chicago Poems*. Copyright 1916 by Holt, Rinehart & Winston, Inc. and renewed 1944 by Carl Sandburg. Reprinted with the permission of Harcourt, Inc.

Arnold Schwarzenegger, excerpt from "The Education of an American" (September 21, 2001). Reprinted with the permission of the author.

Paul Simon, "America." Copyright © 1968 by Paul Simon. Used by permission of the Publisher, Paul Simon Music.

Bruce Springsteen, "Born in the U.S.A." Copyright © by Bruce Springsteen, ASCAP. "My Hometown." Copyright © 1984 by Bruce Springsteen, ASCAP. Reprinted by permission.

Manny Steen, excerpt from an interview with Paul Silgrist (March 22, 1991, Statue of Liberty-Ellis Island Foundation, Inc.). From the Ellis Island Oral History Program. Reprinted by permission.

Wallace Stegner, "The Wilderness Idea" from *The Sound of Mountain Water*. Copyright © 1969 by Wallace Stegner. Reprinted with the permission of Doubleday, a division of Random House, Inc.

John Steinbeck, excerpt from *The Grapes of Wrath*. Copyright 1939 by John Steinbeck. Reprinted with the permission of Viking Penguin, a division of Penguin Putnam Inc.

Wallace Stevens, "Martial Cadenza" from *Collected Poems*. Copyright 1954 by Wallace Stevens and renewed © 1982 by Holly Stevens. Reprinted with the permission of Alfred A. Knopf, a division of Random House, Inc.

Amy Tan, excerpt from *The Joy Luck Club*. Copyright © 1989 by Amy Tan. Reprinted with the permission of G. P. Putnam's Sons, a division of Penguin Putnam Inc.

Alexis de Tocqueville, excerpts from *Democracy in America, Volume I*, revised by Francis Bowen, further corrected and edited by Phillips Bradley. Copyright 1945 by Alfred A. Knopf, Inc. Reprinted with the permission of Alfred A. Knopf, a division of Random House, Inc.

Mark Twain, "As Regards Patriotism" from *Europe and Elsewhere*. Copyright 1923 and renewed 1951 by the Mark Twain Company. Reprinted with the permission of HarperCollins Publishers, Inc.

Alice Walker, excerpt from "In Search of Our Mothers' Gardens" from *In Search of Our Mothers' Gardens: Womanist Prose*. Copyright © 1974 by Alice Walker. Reprinted with the permission of Harcourt, Inc.

Andy Warhol, "POPism" from *The Philosophy of Andy Warhol (From A to B and Back Again)*. Copyright © 1975 by Andy Warhol. Reprinted with the permission of Harcourt, Inc.

E. B. White, "Freedom" from *One Man's Meat*. Copyright 1940 by E. B. White. Copyright renewed. Reprinted with the permission of Tilbury House, Publishers, Gardiner, Maine.

Thomas Wolfe, excerpt from *The Story of a Novel*. Copyright 1936 by Charles Scribner's Sons. Renewal copyright © 1964 by Paul Gitlin. Reprinted with the permission of Scribner, a division of Simon & Schuster Adult Publishing, Inc.

PHOTO CREDITS

ENDPAPERS—Library of Congress; PAGE 1—INP/Corbis; PAGE 7—Library of Congress; PAGE 10—New York State Historical Association; PAGES 24–25—Manchester Historic Association; PAGE 27—New York Times; PAGE 51—Brown Brothers; PAGE 57—Architect of the Capitol/Library of Congress; PAGE 67—NASA/Corbis; PAGE 73—Courtesy of the Photographer; PAGE 87—FSA/Library of Congress; PAGE 89—Bettmann/Corbis; PAGE 97—New York Times Photo Archives; PAGE 104—Black Star; PAGE 119—Photoresearchers; PAGE 121—New York Times; PAGE 148—UPI/Corbis; PAGE 151—New York Times; PAGE 155—Meserve-

Kunhardt Collection; PAGE 164—New York Times; PAGE 166—Corbis; PAGE 171—UPI/Corbis; PAGE 187—Courtesy of the Photographer; PAGE 193 (William Hutchings, upper left)—Andrew Cahan Books; PAGE 193 (all but Hutchings)—George Eastman House; PAGE 201—New York Times; PAGE 212—Courtesy of the Photographer; PAGE 221—New York Times; PAGE 227—Brown Brothers; PAGE 233—Bettman/Corbis; PAGE 249—New York Times; PAGES 252–253—FSA/Library of Congress; PAGE 263—New York Times; PAGE 267—Getty Images; PAGE 283—Bain News Service/Library of Congress; PAGE 300—NAACP/Library of Congress; PAGE 307—Time-Life; PAGE 309—AP/Wide World; PAGE 313—New York Times; PAGE 318—Abbie Rowe, National Park Service/JFK Library, Boston; PAGES 326–327—New York Times; PAGE 332—Courtesy of the Photographer; PAGE 334—Time-Life; PAGE 351—Woodfin Camp & Associates; PAGE 357—FSA/University of Louisville; PAGES 358–359—FSA/Library of Congress; PAGE 365—Library of Congress; PAGE 368—Magnum Photos; PAGE 372—Magnum Photos; PAGE 380—John F. Kennedy Library; PAGE 393—Argus Leader; PAGES 416–417—Library of Congress; PAGE 437—Time-Life; PAGE 439—Time-Life; PAGE 443—U.S. Army Signal Corps/J. Paul Getty Museum; PAGES 444–445—U.S. Coast Guard/National Archives; PAGE 451—U.S. Army Signal Corps/Associated Press; PAGE 460—U.S. Signal Corps/John F. Kennedy Library; PAGE 467—Magnum Photos; PAGE 471—Magnum Photos; PAGE 489—Magnum Photos; PAGE 495—New York Times; PAGE 504—Union Pacific Historical Collection; PAGE 506—Library of Congress; PAGE 508—George Eastman House; PAGE 513—Bettmann/Corbis; PAGE 525—Center for Creative Photography, University of Arizona; PAGE 531—Corbis; PAGE 541—New York Times Photo Archives; PAGE 545—Magnum Photos; PAGE 547—George Eastman House; PAGE 549—John F. Kennedy Library; PAGE 552—Courtesy of the Photographer; PAGE 569—Fermilab, U.S. Department of Energy; PAGE 571—Agence France-Presse; PAGE 573—Brett Weston Archive; PAGE 583—FSA/Library of Congress; PAGE 597—Courtesy of the Photographer; PAGE 600—New York Times; PAGES 604–605—Oklahoma Historical Society; PAGES 610–611—Massillon Museum; PAGE 613—Seaver Center, Los Angeles County Museum of Natural History; PAGES 616–617—Ansel Adams Trust/Center for Creative Photography, University of Arizona; PAGES 624–625—Brett Weston Archive; PAGES 626–627—Minor White Archive, Princeton University; PAGE 635—Magnum Photos; PAGE 639—Charles E. Young Research Library, UCLA; PAGES 642–643—Courtesy of the Photographer/John F. Kennedy Library; PAGE 648—Minor White Archive, Princeton University

INDEX